D1154599

Mutual Aid Groups,
Vulnerable and Resilient Populations,
and the Life Cycle

Mutual Aid Groups, Vulnerable and Resilient Populations, and the Life Cycle

THIRD EDITION

Edited by

Alex Gitterman
Lawrence Shulman

COLUMBIA UNIVERSITY PRESS

New York

COLUMBIA UNIVERSITY PRESS
Publishers Since 1893
New York   Chichester, West Sussex

Copyright © 2005 Columbia University Press
All rights reserved

Library of Congress-Cataloging-in-Publication Data
Mutual aid groups, vulnerable and resilient populations, and the life cycle / edited by
    Alex Gitterman, Lawrence Shulman.—3rd ed.
        p. cm.
    Rev. ed. of: Mutual aid groups, vulnerable populations, and the life cycle. 2nd ed. c1994.
    Includes bibliographical references and index.
    ISBN 0-231-12884-3 (cloth : alk. paper) — ISBN 0-231-12885-1 (pbk. : alk. paper)
        1. Social group work—United States. 2. Self-help groups—United States. 3. life cycle,
    Human. I. Gitterman, Alex, 1938– II. Shulman, Lawrence. III. Mutual aid groups,
    vulnerable populations, and the life cycle.

HV45.M88 2005
361.4—dc22   2005056035

∞
Columbia University Press books are printed on permanent and durable acid-free paper.
Printed in the United States of America
c 10 9 8 7 6 5 4 3 2 1
p 10 9 8 7 6 5 4 3 2 1

In memory of William Schwartz

This book is a tribute to William Schwartz—a valued friend, colleague, and mentor, who died August 1, 1982. While neither of us was a student of Bill's, we are both influenced by his unique and distinct ideas about social work practice in general and group work in particular. Bill's former students and colleagues who are eager to share in the endeavor contribute some chapters in this book. This is an opportunity to pay tribute to his influence in the way that he would have appreciated—by demonstrating in detail what their practice looks like in the real world. Other chapters are written by practitioners and academics who, while not specifically rooted in Bill's practice framework, nevertheless incorporate his concepts of mutual aid in their practice and teaching.

Thus the book represents a personal and professional statement of thanks to Bill for laying the groundwork that piqued our curiousity about methods and gave direction to our ongoing inquiry into the subject of practice.

Contents

Yetta H. Appel Retired professor, Rutgers University School of Social Work

Toby Berman-Rossi Professor, Barry University School of Social Work

Judith Bloch Founder/CEO, Variety Child Learning Center

George S. Getzel Professor Emeritus, Hunter College School of Social Work

Alex Gitterman Professor, University of Connecticut School of Social Work

Carol Irizarry Senior lecturer, Flinders University

Timothy B. Kelly Senior research fellow, Glasgow Caledonian University

Carolyn Knight Associate professor, University of Maryland, Baltimore County

Judith A. B. Lee Professor Emerita, University of Connecticut School of Social Work

Lois Levinsky Clinical associate professor, Boston University School of Social Work and private practitioner

Maxine Lynn Assistant dean, Adelphi University School of Social Work

Kathleen McAleer Bereavement social worker, CURA VNA Cranberry Hospice

Alice Schaeffer Nadelman Private practitioner

Danielle Nisivoccia Adjunct associate professor, Fordham University Graduate School of Social Service

Alberta L. Orr Director, National Aging Program, American Foundation for the Blind

Varsha Pandya Assistant professor, Ohio University, Department of Social Work

Beatrice R. Plasse Adjunct assistant professor, Columbia University School of Social Work

Linda Yael Schiller   Adjunct assistant professor, Boston University School of Social Work and private practitoner

Martin Seitz   Consultant, Variety Child Learning Center

Lawrence Shulman   Professor, School of Social Work University at Buffalo State University of New York

Carol R. Swenson   Professor, Simmons College School of Social Work

Dale Trimble   Private practitioner

Joan Weinstein   Social work supervisor, Variety Child Learning Center

Bonnie Zimmer   Private practitioner

S OCIAL WORKERS in practice today deal with profoundly vulnerable and disempowered populations. People with such life conditions and circumstances
as dealing with the impact of AIDS, homelessness, sexual abuse, community
and family violence, etc., are overwhelmed by oppressive lives, circumstances,
and events they are powerless to control. Their life stressors often appear intractable because they are chronic and persistent or acute and unexpected. Their
overwhelming stressors often overwhelm them. When they lack community and
family supports, they are often at risk of physical, psychological, and social deterioration. Moreover, when their internal resources are impaired as well, they become extremely vulnerable to social and emotional isolation. Yet, in spite of
numerous risk factors and overwhelming odds, a surprisingly large number of
people somehow—miraculously at times—manage their adversities. They adapt,
cope, overcome, meet the challenges of physical and mental conditions, severe
losses and traumas, chronic discrimination and oppression.

In preparing the third edition of this volume, we have focused on mutual aid
with vulnerable and resilient populations over the life cycle. With the help of our
talented contributors, we conceptualize, describe, and illustrate how the group
modality offers a powerful counter-force to vulnerability and risk by providing
protective forces that help people become more resilient in dealing with life's
challenges.

When people can support, help, and influence each other in a reciprocal manner, the inherent potential exists to provide group members with a sense of
greater personal, interpersonal, and environmental control over their lives and to
negotiate high-risk situations. Mutual engagement and mutual aid provide essential ingredients for effective protection and coping, including a sense of physical and emotional well-being and personal as well as collective identity.

In this edition we have rewritten the three introductory conceptual chapters
and the historical chapter. We have updated ten and eliminated seven of the

original practice chapters and added six practice chapters. The new chapters illustrate the power of mutual aid processes with a number of different populations dealing with a wide range of issues. For example, work with children grieving the loss of a loved one and children dealing with the trauma of 9/11 are illustrated. Mutual aid processes are also poignantly described with adult survivors of sexual abuse, parents with developmentally challenged children, addictive mothers, persons with AIDS in substance recovery and mentally ill older adults. We have also added a new chapter on major issues confronting contemporary group work practice. We hope that social work students and professionals will become excited by the healing power of group practice and will increasingly incorporate the group modality into their agencies' and their own practice.

Part 1 of this book contains three chapters that set out the theoretical model guiding the practice. In chapter 1 Gitterman and Shulman introduce five major sets of ideas: the life model as an approach to understanding and helping people, an oppression psychology, vulnerability and risk factors and resilience protective factors, a mutual aid approach to working with groups, and a theory of practice that views the role of the worker as mediating the individual-group-environment engagement. In chapter 2 Shulman elaborates on the practice theory by describing and illustrating the specific core skills used by the social worker as she or he puts the social worker's function into action. The dynamics and skills involved are illustrated with detailed excerpts of practice drawn from the chapters that follow. In chapter 3 Gitterman examines the tasks, methods, and skills involved in the critical group formation process. The steps between a worker's conceptualization of the need for a group and a successful first meeting require careful consideration if the group is to be effectively launched.

The focus in part 2 is on vulnerable and resilient children. Chapter 4 by Knight describes a group of children who have lost a parent or close relative. The author's sensitive practice excerpts and discussion demonstrate some of the unique ways in which children express their ambivalence about discussing painful feelings and her skillful efforts to normalize their experiences and reactions. In chapter 5 Lynn and Nisivoccia examine the profound traumatic impact 9/11 had on the lives of New York City's children. Through the support of the leader and their peers, and creative uses of program, the children express their fears and feelings of powerlessness and helplessness. One youngster's statement about his drawing captures the depth of their despair, "Just thinking about the explosion and body parts freaked me out and I can't quit drawing it."

Part 3 of the book examines mutual aid groups with vulnerable and resilient adolescents. In chapter 6 Irizzari and Appel illustrate creative and skillful practice with a community-based preadolescent group. They provide a sensitive description of the normative tasks facing this population with special attention to ethnic/racial and class factors. Since these youngsters are poor and members of minority groups (black and Puerto Rican), they experience a "double marginality."

In chapter 7 Levinsky and McAlear describe the stress experienced by young adolescents of color in inner-city schools. They illuminate, in a moving account of mutual aid, these youngsters' capacity to help each other with such complex problems as coping with racism and racial diversity, sexuality, and family, community and school violence. In chapter 8 Nadelman shares her practice with adolescents placed in a residential setting. These youngsters, who have lost contact with meaningful adults in their lives, must learn how to have peers meet their needs for support and intimacy. Nadelman demonstrates how apparently tough and hardened teens can be helped to discover their ability to help each other.

Part 4 includes nine chapters, poignantly demonstrating skillful practice with vulnerable and resilient adult populations. In chapter 9 Getzel's discussion and illustration of the suffering of gay men who have contacted the Acquired Immunodeficiency Syndrome (AIDS) is both heart wrenching and inspiring. These adults confront continuous crisis situations, prompted by health reverses and social rejection and isolation. Getzel dramatically depicts the way in which the mutual aid group provides a lifeline to adults affected by the pandemic. In chapter 10 Shulman describes how people suffering from AIDS and struggling to recover from substance abuse movingly help each other. Members uncover the trauma of childhood and adolescent physical, emotional, and sexual abuse, its impact on their interpersonal relationships and recovery efforts. One member captures the magic of mutual aid, "I didn't realize when I started this group there were people who have lived lives just like me, who had feelings just like me, who had struggles just like me . . . you've helped me see that I'm just not the only one going through this."

In chapter 11 Schiller and Zimmer bring us the powerful adult voices of survivors of child sexual abuse. As children these adults were oppressively exploited for the sexual satisfaction of an adult. For many years they internalized the oppression and the oppressor and turned the rage against themselves. Schiller and Zimmer poignantly help group members to bear witness and to lend each other unforgettable support (as a member stated, "Both hearing and telling knocked me out"). Through the workers' love and skill, group members help each other to work through the experience, come to terms with it, and begin the process of healing. In Chapter 12 Knight breaks new ground by leading a group of men and women survivors of sexual abuse. She vividly illustrates men and women listening to each other's pain, lending care and support, helping healing, and mobilizing coping efforts. Members help each other to confront the past in order to move forward and deal with the present and future. In chapter 13 Trimble focuses on work with men who batter their wives or women with whom they live. If there is any hope of reaching past the deviant behavior and beginning to help the offender as a client, Trimble insightfully discusses the worker's need to be in touch with his or her own anger. Groups such as this have often failed because of the inability of the group leader to understand the artificial dichotomy between being supportive and confrontation. Trimble demonstrates the necessity of using authority and confronting the group members to assume personal responsibility for their abusive behavior, while simultaneously synthesizing the demand with caring.

In chapter 14 Lee tackles a chronic and pressing social issue: the problem of homeless women with "no place to go." In an exciting mixture of direct practice skills with clients and social action activity around the problem, we see the social worker's dual function of helping group members to cope with the realities of today while simultaneously trying to organize to change those realities. Her work also richly illustrates some of the beginning-stage problems in engaging a difficult, often mistrusting population. In chapter 15 Bloch, Weinstein, and Seitz examine the painful issues confronted by parents of children with developmental disability. The parents sorrowfully share the devastation, despair, terror, shame, and family turbulence caused by the birth of a developmentally disabled child. In sharing their pain ("Friends don't understand . . . they want to reassure me that everything is OK," "I will go to the next park to avoid my neighbors," "I can't stand the accusatory eyes of others or to hear others talking about him"), members grieve together and subsequently feel less alone and less distressed. From mutual support and problem solving they gain new perspectives and coping strategies.

In Chapter 16 Plasse describes a parenting skills group that attempts to break the intergenerational cycle of child neglect and substance abuse. Before members could work on improving their parenting skills, they had to work on their own deprivations. One member captured the importance of personalizing a skills curriculum: "How can you ask me to give them all this praise and encouragement when that is something that I never got myself? . . . I remember waiting for her . . . to tell me she loved me. My mother died last year and I'm still waiting for those hugs and kisses." Finally, in this part of the book on practice with adults, in chapter 17, Shulman examines a short-term group experience for single parents. The group life lasted one evening and the following full day, and yet the depth of the concerns discussed raises interesting issues about the impact of time on group process. The discussion also highlights the capacity of group members to respond to a group leader's "demand for work" much more rapidly than many of us would have expected.

In part 5 of the book, work with vulnerable and resilient elderly completes the journey through the life cycle. In chapter 18 Orr describes her work with the visually impaired elderly living in the community. For these group members the mutual aid group is an important substitute for other support systems (such as friends and relatives) that are not always available to them. In a dramatic meeting the worker presses the group members to deal with the death of a valued and loved group member. The internal dialogue of each member, in which part of them wants to face the hurt and part of them wants to deny it, is acted out in the group discussion as different members voice the two sides of the ambivalence. With the gentle, caring, yet firm support of the leader, the members enter the taboo area of discussion about death and face the loss of this member, their sense of loss of others close to them, and their own impending deaths.

In chapter 19 Berman-Rossi examines the plight of the institutionalized aged who must fight against feelings of hopelessness and despair. In a powerful illustration of the social worker's mediating, or third force, function, Berman-Rossi demonstrate how support combined with demand can help group members to experience strength in numbers as they tackle the institution's dietary practices. As Berman-Rossi helps group members find strength to tackle the institution, an effort that really symbolizes the choice of life over resignation, she also reaches for their life transitional concerns such as the grief associated with physical and personal loss. In chapter 20 Kelly describes the simultaneous challenges of coping with mental illness and issues of aging. For the group members social isolation and limited control over one's life are major life stressors. The power of mutual aid is most evident in an exchange between members about taking their medication: Ella—"Amelia, did you stop taking your medication again? You remember what happened to me when I quit taking my medicine . . . I ended up in the hospital." Amelia—"(*Crying*) I hate those damn pills." Martha—"Oh, honey, I hate mine too, but I do crazy things when I don't take them." The combination of peer support and peer demand has a profound impact on members' lives.

In part 6 we examine important historical and contemporary group work themes. In chapter 21 Lee and Swenson reach back into our history for a scholarly examination of the mutual aid theory, reminding us of the roots of group work and social work practice. We think this historical view of mutual aid will have more meaning to the reader after vivid illustrations of its modern-day implementation. In Chapter 22 Pandya explores contemporary group work issues and trends. In examining vulnerable and resilient populations, she reviews current group work practice with persons with HIV/AIDS, persons with alternative sexual orientation, the older elderly population, caregivers, and persons affected by war, terror, and ethnic strife. The author provides an informative discussion of mutual aid groups with a social change and community-rebuilding focus. The author also examines the uses of technology to facilitate mutual aid through telephone groups and computer-aided groups as well as the future of small group research.

Mutual Aid Groups, Vulnerable and Resilient Populations, and the Life Cycle

Part 1

Mutual Aid: An Introduction

The Life Model, Oppression, Vulnerability, Resilience, Mutual Aid, and the Mediating Function

Alex Gitterman and Lawrence Shulman

THE PERSPECTIVE on practice presented in this book emerges from the convergence of five major sets of ideas: a life model for understanding and helping people, oppression psychology, vulnerability, resilience, a mutual aid approach to group work, and a theory of practice that views the role of the worker as mediating the individual-group-environment engagement.

Perhaps the easiest way to introduce these sets of ideas is by illustrating them with examples. In chapter 11 Schiller and Zimmer describe their work with a group of young women who are survivors of sexual abuse. Employing elements of the life model, each of the group members can be viewed as facing the normative life transitions for their age (entering young adulthood) while simultaneously having to cope with issues from earlier transitions that were not resolved because of the impact of their abuse (Germain and Gitterman 1996; Gitterman 2001a; Gitterman 1996). In chapter 9 Getzel describes group work with persons with AIDS who face both age-related transitions and the powerful, earthquake-like status change from being healthy to being ill with a terminal illness. Other status changes include the transition from being employed to unemployed and being independent to dependent. Age-related issues will interact with the status change issues since the impact of any serious illness varies depending upon the individual's stage of life.

For sexual abuse survivors and persons with AIDS, as well as for members of vulnerable population (e.g., the mentally ill, physically challenged), constructs from an oppression psychology, such as the one suggested by Fanon, can provide useful insights (Bulham 1985). Both survivors of sexual abuse and persons with AIDS can be understood as having experienced periods of oppression. Fanon describes a number of maladaptive means of coping with the "psycho-affective" injuries that result from long-term oppression. One is the process through which the oppressed person internalizes the negative self-image imposed by the "oppressor without," which results in the creation of a powerful and self-destructive "oppressor within." The commonly expressed self-description voiced by survivors of sexual abuse as feeling like "damaged goods" is one such illustration. The use of "fight or flight" behavior, for example alcohol and drug use or violence, is another maladaptive means for coping with the ongoing pain of oppression. Depression, apathy, and immobilization can be seen in the behavior of some persons with AIDS who have internalized the social stigma our society has put on people who contract this disease.

Oppression psychology, in addition to helping us to understand our clients' maladaptive responses to oppression, offers suggestions for healing responses. For example, survivors of sexual abuse need to be more in touch with their rage, which is often covered by their surface depression. This healthy anger can then be harnessed in their own self-interest instead of being turned inward. Persons with AIDS need to be strengthened to challenge the social and health systems so that they can take some control over their lives even if their illness is currently incurable. Active, assertive, and affirming steps on their own behalf help in the process of purging the oppressor within.

In spite of oppression, risk factors, and vulnerabilities, a surprisingly large number of people mature into normal, happy adults. Somehow they remain relatively unscathed by life's traumas and adversities. Some do not simply survive but rebound and thrive in the face of life's inhumanities and tragedies. The process of regaining functioning following on the footsteps of adversity does not suggest that one is incapable of being wounded or injured. Rather, a person can bend, lose some of his or her power and capability, yet recover and return to a previous level of adaptation. Resilience represents the power of recovery and sustained adaptive functioning (Gitterman 2001b; Gittterman 2001c).

Mutual aid support groups may provide the vehicle for these transformations through such commonly observed phenomena as strength in numbers and mutual support. In Schiller and Zimmer, and in Getzel's chapters, we see clients brought together in a mutual aid group so that the energies of group members can be mobilized to help each other. The concept of mutual aid in groups, one of Schwartz's major contributions to the literature, shifts the source of helping from the group leader to the members themselves (Gitterman 2004; Schwartz 1961; Shulman 1999). For example, as members in this group discover that they are not alone in their feelings, a powerful healing force is released. With the help of the group leader, members can support each other, confront each other, and provide suggestions and ideas from their own fund of experiences, concomitantly helping and supporting themselves as they help each other. The fifth set of ideas, the mediating function of the worker, which was also proposed by Schwartz (1977), provides a role statement for the group leader. While the potential for mutual aid is present in the group, members will need the help of the worker to activate its power and overcome the many obstacles that can frustrate its effectiveness. For the worker to carry out his or her tasks in the group, a clear and precise statement of function is necessary. Schwartz (1977) proposed a general functional statement for the social work profession as that of mediating the individual/social engagement. If one views the small group as a microcosm of our larger society, then the worker's role can be described as mediating the individual/group encounter. Thus, in our groups for survivors and persons with AIDS, we see the workers assisting each member to reach out to the group for help while simultaneously helping the group members to respond. Even if a group member presents a pattern of denial and refuses to face the impact of the illness, the worker's mediating function may involve providing support to that member, using the worker's capacity for empathy while also confronting the member's denial and reaching for the underlying fears and apprehensions. And if the other group members appear to turn away from a member's direct and emotional appeal for help (for example, changing the subject or looking uninterested), possibly because the issue raised their own level of anxiety, the mediating function would call for the worker to confront the group members on their evasion and denial.

These five sets of ideas, the Life Model, oppression, resilience, mutual aid, and the mediating function, are discussed in more detail in the balance of this chapter.

The Life Model

The Life Model is an application and specification of the ecological perspective and offers a view of human beings in constant interchanges with their environment (Germain 1973; Germain and Gitterman 1996; Gitterman 2001a). Their physical and social environments change people and they, in turn, change them through processes of continuous reciprocal adaptation. In these complex interchanges disturbances often emerge in the adaptive balance (e.g., in the "level-of-fit") between perceived individual needs and capacities and environmental qualities. People feel stress when they experience an imbalance between a perceived demand and the perceived capability to meet the demand through the use of available internal and external resources. These disturbances challenge and disrupt customary coping mechanisms and create life stress. The Life Model proposes a useful and viable approach to professionals for understanding and helping clients to deal with life stresses and their consequences. Clients' needs and "troubles" are identified as arising from three interrelated stressors in living: l. life transitions and traumatic events, 2. environmental pressures, and 3. dysfunctional interpersonal processes.

LIFE TRANSITIONS AND TRAUMATIC EVENTS

There is a well-developed literature describing the process by which we all proceed through biologically induced "life cycle" changes. Though biologically induced, psychological, socioeconomic, and cultural forces shape these processes.

This shaping creates unique pathways of development for each individual—from birth to death—rather than fixed, linear, predictable stages. Each person's "life course" is somewhat different: influenced by historical, societal, and cultural contexts (Germain 1994).

In order to capture the uniqueness of each person's life course, life cycle stage models must be used only as broad and general guideposts rather than normative conceptualizations. Erikson (1959), for example, conceptualizes epigenetic stages of development. Each stage requires changes and redefinitions in relationships with significant others, negotiations with the external environment, and struggles with one's self-definitions and self-identity. Successful mastery of the tasks in one stage sets the foundation for successful mastery of the tasks associated with the next stage. Personal, familial, and environmental resources support or frustrate an individual's ability to develop a sense of mastery and competence. Unsuccessful task resolutions create troubles and confusions that often pose problems at later phases.[1]

During the early years of a child's life, according to Erikson, we learn and achieve the acquired qualities of "trust," "autonomy," and "initiative." In the first years of life, the child is totally dependent upon parental figures. For trust to be developed, they have to be trustworthy and dependable. For autonomy and initiative to be accomplished, they have to encourage and support such behaviors. Using the ideas of "cog wheeling" between generations, Erikson identifies a potential "goodness-of-fit" between, for example, child's need to be nourished and parents' own stage-specific needs for intimacy and caring.

The social and physical environment profoundly influences this potential for reciprocal fulfillment of intergenerational needs. For parents to nurture children (and meet their own needs as well), they need the support of relatives, friends, and neighbors (in other words, social networks) as well as responsive economic, educational, and health structures. When such supports are available, the opportunities for personal growth, family integration, and social benefits are increased. When, however, a child is unable to respond to parents, or parents are unable to nourish the child, or social institutions are unable to provide required supports, they become potent sources for continuous stress and interfere with successful adaptation. And, consequently, in this and subsequent phases the individual as well as the family and environmental systems have to deal with the psychological and behavioral residue of "distrust," "shame," and "guilt."

We are becoming more aware of the complex developmental tasks confronting single parents. Over the last three decades a dramatic change has taken place in family structure and living arrangements. Between the period of 1980 and 1997 the number of single mothers has increased by more than 50 percent—from 6.2 million to 9.9 million (U.S. Bureau of Census 1997). Families headed by women are characterized by poverty. Solo fathers often suffer from role ambiguity and being out of sync with cultural expectations. The solo parent must double for other the parent and often experience additional financial, household management, and recreational stressors.

When children enter school (they do so at earlier ages than earlier generations), they confront two new developmentally linked relationship challenges: teachers and peers. A child who develops comfort in and acceptance from these new relationships and masters required learning tasks and social skills may incorporate a sense of "industriousness" into a concept of self. However, a child who is unable to trust, to separate, to initiate may become frightened and overwhelmed by the demands for new relationships with adult authorities as well as for intimacy with peers. A handicapped child (cognitive, emotional, or physical) may experience more intense challenges, as might the child of a parent who "holds on" and experiences difficulties with separation. If any of these more vulnerable children also confront an unresponsive school or peer system, their self-concepts may interject feelings of self-doubt and "inferiority." Same-sex families experience unique challenges. They often deal with many complications when children attend school, mostly emerging from discrimination and ignorance.

"Who am I?" "Who am I becoming?" are the questions adolescents ask in search of "identity."[2] The adolescent often experiences major biological changes (such as physical growth and sexual characteristics) and an emerging awareness of sexuality. These physiological and self-image changes elicit direct responses from parents, siblings, relatives, and institutional representatives. Turmoil and crises often characterize family interaction patterns as the adolescent demands greater autonomy and simultaneously struggles with dependency needs. To cope with the ambivalence of independence/dependence and a developing sexuality, in the United States the adolescent turns to the "teenage culture" for comfort and acceptance. In exchange for a sense of belonging, the teenager must meet peer expectations and pressures about dress, demeanor, behavior, and other matters. Since peer and family norms often conflict, the adolescent experiences heightened stress in the search for a clearer sense of self.

Most adolescents (and their families) somehow survive this painful life period and grow out of this stage and its perpetual crises with a more intact and integrating sense of individual and collective identity. Others, however, do not. Adolescents whose families are unable to tolerate testing behavior or to provide the essential structure may experience profound confusion. Adolescents who were abandoned, institutionalized, or abused by their families may develop a sense of helplessness, learning to believe that they are unworthy and incapable of influencing life events (Hooker 1976; Seligman and Elder Jr. 1986). Similarly, physically and cognitively challenged adolescents (such as orthopedic, learning disabled) or adolescents who deviate from peer norms (such as being obese or painfully shy) may experience peer group rejection and be denied a powerful source of support. Adolescents growing up in an unjust and hostile environment may interject negative stereotypes and prejudices into their self-identities. These adolescents are vulnerable to "identity confusion" and "role diffusion," which may carry over to adulthood.

To the request for criteria for the mature adults, Freud has been reported to respond: "Lieben und Arbeiten" (love and work). The young adult faces these two developmental transitions: the development of an "intimate" relationship (marriage or partnership) and the accomplishment of work (employment and career). The young adult, for example, has to form an initial dyadic relationship characterized by the task of establishing interpersonal intimacy (caring and giving to another person) without losing his or her own identity. If a partner has not mastered prior developmental phases and tasks, is withdrawn or abusive, or experiences such unforeseen events as unemployment or illness, disillusionment and conflict may block the establishment of interpersonal intimacy. A child born into such situations may intensify parental stress, as new accommodations are necessary to care for the needs of the dependent infant. Still other life transitions such as children entering school or leaving for college, the loss of social support associated with a geographical move, the pain of a separation and divorce, or the struggle related to reconstituting two families may create crises and generate feelings of isolation and alienation.

As children mature and leave home or leave and return home (psychologically and/or physically), adults have to restructure their life space and change patterns of relating to the children, partner, and others. The partner dyad rediscovers each other and forges a new level of caring and giving. The single parent develops other intimate relationships. Work provides career and financial advancement and meets creativity and self-esteem needs. The adult becomes concerned about other and future generations. When these tasks are achieved, the adult experiences a period of "generativity" and excitement with life. When, however, the adult is unable to separate from children or to forge new relationships, or work provides limited opportunities to demonstrate creativity and competence, the adult may experience a period of "stagnation" or depression with life.

In later adulthood one attempts to integrate life experiences within the reality of declining physical and mental functions. Added to these biological changes, older adults face numerous other sources of stress. They may have to relinquish the status of worker (and its associated roles) and assume the status of retiree. Older adults may lose their spouses, relatives, or close friends. At some point, they may be institutionalized. These life transitions and crises are extremely stressful and may create bitterness, despair, and even depression. Children, grandchildren, relatives, close friends, and community and organizational ties, however, can buffer these insults. And with these essential supports, older adults are better able to come to terms with the meaning of their lives and achieve a sense of emotional integrity.

The reader is reminded that the developmental cycle from birth to old age is not fixed or uniform. A developmental phase takes place within the context of historical and societal realities (Germain 1990). People born at a similar time experience common historical events. These common events affect the ways a particular generation experiences its developmental tasks. For example, the periods of war and peace, prosperity or depression, assimilation or acculturation profoundly affect the opportunities and worldviews of different generations. People's social context transacts with their historical context.

Currently, our economy is undergoing dramatic changes. The transformation from manufacturing to a service economy has contributed to a shrinking job market. The gap between the poor and the wealthy, the unskilled and the skilled is increasingly widening. Larder (1998) reported, "Since the 1970's, virtually all our income gains have gone to the highest-earning 20 percent of our households, producing inequality greater than at any time since the 1930's, and greater than in any of the world's other rich nations." In helping young adults, for example, to meet their simultaneous developmental tasks of developing career and intimate interpersonal relationships, families with financial means may provide for their young children to pursue graduate studies until the economy recovers. These young adults may postpone marriage and having children until they complete their studies and establish their careers. In contrast, our country's long history of oppression of communities of color through racial discrimination has a growing number of young adult males of color hopelessly locked into lives of unemployment. Lack of employment opportunities institutionalizes their poverty. A devastating cycle of physical, psychological, and social consequences follows. Without hope and opportunities, some of these youngsters may turn to self- and socially destructive activities such as selling drugs, fathering unwanted children, substance abuse, withdrawal, and violent behavior. Even though both the advantaged white young adults and the disadvantaged minority young adults encounter a common historical context, their experiences are dramatically different.

Within respective developmental phases people confront stressful life transitions and traumatic events. Some life transitions come too early in life or too late. A young adolescent who becomes a parent is caught between adolescent needs and adult demands. A person living with AIDS who is struggling to deal with death at a young age should be, according to "normal" life cycle tasks, wrestling with issues related to career and interpersonal intimacy. The traumatic event of a child being sexually exploited by an older person for her or his own sexual satisfaction while disregarding the child's own developmental immaturity may leave lifelong feelings of betrayal, shame, powerlessness, and rage. These types of experiences have a profound effect on the unfolding of a person's life course.

A social status in our society may be devalued and/or stigmatized. Prisoners, probationers, persons with AIDS, alcoholics, children of alcoholics, the mentally ill, and homeless persons carry with them heavy adaptive burdens. Beyond the social/environmental realities, they also have to deal with the psychological stigma associated with the status. To escape from a stigmatized status is extremely difficult, particularly when it has been internalized resulting in emotional scars. The status, for example, of being an "ex-con" has an intense staying power. Thus social status can have a powerful adverse effect on developmental opportunities and the mastery of life course tasks.

Finally, traumatic life events represent losses of the severest kind, e.g., the death of a child, sexual assault, the diagnosis of a terminal illness or disease, or a national disaster such as an earthquake or September 11. An increasing number of inner-city children, for another example, suffer from a similar posttraumatic stress syndrome seen in the Vietnam veterans (Lee 1989). These children have been exposed to violent attacks on and murders of their parents, friends, relatives, and neighbors. They are further traumatized by domestic violence and child abuse. These experiences have long-lasting physical, psychological, and social effects.

ENVIRONMENTAL PRESSURES

While the environment can support or interfere with life transitions, it can itself be a significant generator of stress. For lower-income people the environment is a harsh reality. By nature of their economic position, they are often unable to command needed goods and services. Similarly environmental opportunities for jobs, promotions, housing, neighborhood, and geographic and social mobility are extremely limited. As a consequence, lower-income families are less likely to remain intact and life expectancy is lower. For lower-income black families, the rate of physical illness is higher, life expectancy is shorter, and loss of employment greater. Thus the environment is a powerful source of trouble and distress, and often its intransigence overwhelms us. By specifying assessment and intervention methods, the Life Model attempts to broaden the profession's practice repertoire.

The social environment primarily comprises organizations and social networks. Health, education, and social service organizations are established with social sanctions and financial support to provide services. Once they are established, there develop external and internal structures, policies, and procedures that inevitably impede effective provision of the very services they are set up to provide. The organization proliferates, taking on a life of its own, and its maintenance assumes precedence over client needs. Latent goals and functions displace manifest goals and functions. An agency, for example, may create complex sets of intake procedures that screen out prospective clients whose problems are immediate and urgent and do not lend themselves to the delays and postponements congenial to agency style.

Low-income families are unable to compete for social resources; their leverage on social organizations is relatively weak. Similarly, hospitalized or institutionalized clients may be overwhelmed by their own vulnerability and relative powerlessness. With limited power, ignorance about their rights, and little skill in negotiation, such service users often become resigned to the unresponsiveness of various organizations' services. Because of cultural expectations and perceptions, physical or emotional impairments of lack of role skills, others may be unwilling or unable to use organizational resources that are actually available and responsive.

Social networks are increasingly recognized as important elements of the social environment. People's social networks can be supportive environmental resources in that they provide a mutual aid system for the exchanges of instrumental assistance (such as money, child care, housing) and affective (emotional) supports (Auslander and Levin 1987; Thoits 1986). When an adaptive level of fit exists between an individual's concrete, social, and emotional needs and available resources, intrapsychic, interpersonal, and environmental pressures are buffered. Some networks have available resources, but the individual does not want or is unable to use them. Others, however, encourage maladaptive patterns; for example, drug-oriented networks reinforce and support deviant behavior. Some exploit and scapegoat a more vulnerable member, taking unfair advantage of vulnerability. Still other social networks are loosely knit and unavailable for support. Finally, there are individuals without any usable social networks, extremely vulnerable to social and emotional isolation. For these individuals the network (or lack of one) is a significant factor in adding to distress.

The exchanges between people and their environments take place within the built and natural world. Each of us within the physical environment carries an invisible spatial boundary as a buffer against unwanted physical and social contact and a protection of privacy. Since this boundary is invisible people must negotiate a mutually comfortable distance. People experience crowding, intrusion, and stress when the boundary is crossed. In contrast, when the distance feels too great, people experience disengagement. In groups these spatial negations are often quite subtle, and, since the amount of desired space is influenced by many individual and social factors, it carries the potential for misperception, misunderstanding, and interpersonal stress.

These spatial negations are influenced by semifixed and fixed space. Semifixed space refers to movable objects and their arrangement in space. Tables, chairs, lighting, curtains, paint, and paintings provide spatial meanings and boundaries. These environmental props affect group member interaction and spatial negotiations. For example, one of the authors worked with a group of adolescent girls. Chairs were set up in tight circle formation. This spatial arrangement required much greater immediate intimacy than the members as well as the worker desired. Fortunately, semifixed space is movable or otherwise adaptable. In this particular group members preferred setting up the room in rectangular table arrangements. Six weeks later the tables were replaced by a circular chair arrangement. In contrast, fixed space such as a high-rise apartment house or a column in the middle of a group meeting room is not movable. The fixed structure limits or facilitates life processes. In a group setting, while the column in the middle of the room can not be removed, members can be engaged in work on what to do to limit its negative impact on group interaction.

The natural world of climate and landscape, water sources, quality of air, and animals and plants provides the resources essential to the survival of all life. Beyond supplying resources essential to survival, the natural world also endows special meaning to everyday life. Historically, social group work emphasized a sense of kinship with nature and encouraged the uses of the gifts of the natural world through trips to parks, swims in the ocean and lakes, hikes and walks and camping in the mountains, and the enjoyment of plants and animals. These resources are as essential to contemporary group practice.

Maladaptive Interpersonal Processes

In dealing with life transitional and environmental issues, families and groups are powerful mediating forces. They may, however, encounter obstacles caused by their own patterns of communication and relationships. When this occurs, dysfunctional family and group interpersonal patterns generate tensions in the system and attenuate the mutual aid processes. These maladaptive patterns are often expressed in withdrawal, factionalism, scapegoating, interlocking hostilities, monopolism, and ambiguous messages.

While these patterns are dysfunctional for most members, they often serve latent functions of maintaining a family's or group's equilibrium. When factions characterize a family or group, the subcliques provide its members greater affirmation and security than does the larger system. Similarly, the scapegoating of a member declared deviant enables the other members to contrast themselves favorably and thereby enhance their sense of self. The status of scapegoat offers such secondary gains as attention and martyrdom (Antsey 1982; Shulman 1967). After a while these relationship patterns become fixed, and potential change becomes exiguous. At the same time, however, the status quo makes all members vulnerable and thwarts the nurturing character of mutual aid.

Interpersonal obstacles are generated by various sources. Group composition is an important factor. A group of athletic preadolescents that includes a single very unathletic member has a built-in potential for a scapegoat (chapter 3 examines formation issues). Group structures can be another source for interpersonal difficulties. Some groups lack structure and boundaries. Members come and go as they please. The individual member enjoys a high degree of autonomy and privacy but sacrifices a requisite sense of group belonging and security. When the boundaries are unclear and unstable, members lack a sense of reciprocity, coordination, and integration. Group members pursue individual interests and become unavailable to and for each other. On the other hand, when group boundaries are too rigid and enmeshed, members have limited freedom. To be

sure, the individual member enjoys a strong sense of collective belonging and security, but it is costly to autonomy and privacy. The group demands unequivocal
loyalty, as individual interests threaten the collective enterprise.

Group members may also become overwhelmed by environmental expectations
and limitations. In a school system, for example, children may scapegoat a slow
learner because the institution makes them all feel "dumb." In response to a non-
nurturing or oppressive environment, some groups turn inward, displace, and act
out their frustrations, while others withdraw and become functionally apathetic.

Transitional phases of development also contribute to maladaptive communication patterns (Berman-Rossi 1993; Schiller 1997). Entrances, such as addition
of a new group member, and exits, such as the loss of a group member or leader,
may create interpersonal distress and problematic responses. When a group becomes stuck in a collective phase of development, they may turn away from or
turn on each other. And the potential resources for mutual aid become dissipated.

Oppression Psychology and Social Work Practice

Frantz Fanon, an early exponent of the psychology of oppression, was a black
West Indian revolutionary psychiatrist who was born on the French colonized island of Martinique in 1925. His experiences with racial and economic oppression
in Martinique, France, and Algeria shaped his views of psychology, which challenged many of the constructs of the widely held European American, white,
male-dominated psychology of the day. While Fanon's work emerged from his
observations of white-black oppression, many of his insights and constructs can
be generalized to other groups. In the remainder of this section a number of
Fanon's central ideas of oppression psychology are reviewed.

While the complete exposition of Fanon's psychology is more complex than
presented here, the central idea of the oppressor gaining an enhanced sense of
self by the exploitation of others can be seen in many different oppressive relationships. The abusing parent and the abused child, the battering husband and
his wife, societal male/female sexism, the scapegoating of religious groups (e.g.,
the Jews) and ethnic and racial groups (e.g., Southeast Asian immigrants, His-
panics, African Americans, Native Indians), the abled population and the differently abled (physically or mentally), the "normal" population and the "mentally
ill," and the straight society's repression of gays and lesbians are all examples in
which one group (usually the majority) exploits another group to enhance a
sense of self.

Repeated exposure to oppression, subtle or direct, may lead vulnerable members of the oppressed group to internalize the negative self-images projected by
the external oppressor—the "oppressor without." The external oppressor may be
an individual (e.g., the sexual abuser of a child) or societal (e.g., the racial stereotypes perpetuated against people of color). Internalization of this image and

repression of the rage associated with oppression may lead to destructive behaviors toward self and others as oppressed people become "autopressors," participating in their own oppression. Thus the oppressor without becomes the oppressor within. Evidence of this process can be found in the maladaptive use of addictive substances and the internal violence in communities of oppressed people, such as city ghettos populated by persons of color.

Oppressed people may develop a "victim complex, viewing all actions and communications as further assaults or simply other indications of their victim status. This is one expression of the 'adaptive paranoia' seen among the oppressed" (Bulham 1985:126). The paranoia is adaptive since oppression is so omnipresent that it would be maladaptive not to be constantly alert to its presence. For the white worker with a client of color, the male worker with a female client, the straight worker with a gay or lesbian client, the abled worker with a differently abled client, etc., this notion raises important implications for the establishment of an effective and trusting working relationship.

Indicators of the Degree of Oppression

Bulham (1985) identifies several key indicators for objectively assessing the degree of oppression. He suggests, "All situations of oppression violate one's space, time, energy, mobility, bonding, and identity" (165). He illustrates these indicators using the example of the slave. The model of a slave is an extreme example of these violations. One does not have to go as far as South Africa (apartheid) to find current examples of these restrictions. Institutionalized racism in North America toward persons of color (e.g., African Americans, Native Indians) currently offers examples of restrictions on all six indicators (Gutierrez and Lewis 1999; Wilson 1973; Solomon 1976).

While the slavery experience of African Americans in North America must be considered a unique and special example of oppression, the indicators may be used to assess degrees of oppression for other populations as well. In this way a universal psychological model may help us to understand the common element that exists in any oppressive relationship. Consider these six indicators while you read the following excerpt of a discussion by battered women in a shelter as they describe their lives.

One woman, Tina, said that when she called the police for help they thought it was a big joke. She said when she had to fill out a report at the police station, the officer laughed about the incident. The women in the group talked about their own experiences with the police, which were not very good. One woman had to wait thirty-five minutes for the police to respond to her call after her husband had thrown a brick through her bedroom window. I said, "Dealing with the police must have been a humiliating situation for all of you. Here you are in need of help and they laugh at you. It's just not right."

Joyce said that she wanted to kill her husband. An abused woman had expressed this desire in a previous group session. Other women in the group said it wouldn't be worth it for her. "All he does is yell at me all the time. He makes me go down to where he works every day at lunchtime. The kids and I have to sit and watch him eat. He never buys us anything to eat.... Plus, he wants to know where I am every minute of the day. He implies that I sit around the house all day long doing nothing."

Marie said her ex-husband used to say that to her all the time. She said, "But now I'm collecting back pay from my divorce settlement for all the work I never did around the house."

Candy said she watched while her father beat her mother. She said she used to ask her mother why she put up with it. She said now she sees that it's easier to say you want to get out of a relationship than it is to actually do it.... Candy said that leaving was better in the long run. By staying, the children will see their father abusing their mother. "What kind of example is that going to set for the children?" She felt her children would be happier by their leaving.

Joyce said her children were happy to leave their father. She said, "They're tired of listening to him yell all the time." She said her son was more upset about leaving the dog behind than he was about leaving his father.

Linda said another good reason for leaving is self-love. She said, "It comes to a point where you know he's going to kill you if you stay around."

Careful reading of the preceding excerpts provides examples of the violation for these women of their space, time, energy, mobility, bonding, and identity—the six identified indicators of oppression. Other examples with differing numbers of indicators violated, and different degrees of violation, could include an inpatient in a rigidly structured psychiatric setting, a wheelchair-bound person constantly facing buildings (e.g., work, school, social club) that are not accessible, an African American woman who is the only person of her race in an organization, held back from advancement by the "glass ceiling" and excluded from the "old boys network," an unemployed, fifty-five-year-old man who can't get a job interview because of his age, an elderly person in a home for the aged who is tied to a chair or tranquilized all day because of staff shortages, a large, poor family, forced to live in inadequate housing, a homeless shelter, or on the street. To one degree or another, space, time, energy, mobility, bonding, and identity may be violated for each of these clients.

ALIENATION AND PSYCHOPATHOLOGY

Bulham (1985) believes that Fanon's complete work suggests five aspects of alienation, associated with the development of "psychopathology." *Alienation* is a commonly used term in psychology and sociology to describe a withdrawal or estrangement. Fanon's five aspects of alienation included: "(a) alienation from the self, (b) alienation from the significant other, (c) alienation from the general other, (d) alienation from one's culture, and (e) alienation from creative social praxis" (188). An example illustrating wide-scale oppression and these five aspects of alienation can be found in the experience of the Native groups in the United States and Canada. These "first peoples" were displaced by the immigration of European, white settlers, eventually forced off their traditional lands, resettled on reservations, and cut off from their traditional forms of activity, such as hunting and fishing. Efforts on the part of Native people to fight back were met with brutal repression. Their children, during one period in our history, were removed from their families and sent to white boarding schools. Native children in many of these boarding schools report being told to "speak white" and punished for using their Native language.

In working with clients who are members of groups that have experienced long-term oppression, it would be important to understand the potential impact of alienation as an underlying cause of and contributor to the current problems. Cultural awareness on the part of the social worker can make a major difference in developing interventive approaches that uses the strengths of the culture to decrease the alienation (Bullis 1996; Chau, 1992; Congress 1994; D'Augelli, Hershberger, and Pilkington 1998; Delgado 1998; Devore and Schlesinger 1991; Dore and Dumois 1990; Hurd, Moore, and Rogers 1995; Orti, Bibb, and Mahboubi 1996; Paulino 1995; Rosenbloom 1995; Swigonski 1996; Williams and Ellison 1996). Examples of this approach to practice can be found in the chapters that follow.

A final element of the oppression psychology theory concerns methods of defense used by oppressed people. Bulham (1985:193) summarizes these as follows: In brief, under conditions of prolonged oppression, there are three major modes of psychological defense and identity development among the oppressed. The first involves a pattern of compromise, the second flight, and the third fight. Each mode has profound implications for the development of identity, experience of psychopathology, reconstituting of the self, and relationship to other people. Each represents a mode of existence and of action in a world in which a hostile other elicits organic reactions and responses. Each also entails its own distinct risks of alienation and social rewards under conditions of oppression.

This overly brief summary of some central ideas in oppression psychology theory sets the stage for the use of these constructs in later chapters. It is not the only theory that can inform our practice—since there are many models that can help us to understand our clients and to develop effective intervention strategies. It is, however, a very useful model in thinking about our work with oppressed and vulnerable populations that makes up a large part of the social worker's practice.

Vulnerability and Resilience; Risk and Protective Factors and Processes

Vulnerability and resilience are ecological phenomena, reflecting moment-to-moment consequences and outcomes of complex person and environment transactions and not simply attributes of a person. Anthony (1987) analogizes *vulnerability* and *risk* to three dolls made of glass, plastic, and steel. The blow of a hammer exposes each doll to a common risk. The glass doll completely shatters, the plastic doll carries a permanent dent, and the steel doll gives out a fine metallic sound. A person's internal armor and coping skills combined with the availability of family, extended networks, and agency resources determine the impact of the hammer's blow. *Webster's Dictionary* defines vulnerability as "capable of being wounded; open to attack or damage." Risk is a biological, psychological, and environmental factor that contributes to the development of a stressor, or makes it worse, or makes it last longer. Prolonged and cumulative stress, two risk factors, are associated with physical and emotional "wounding" (i.e., physical and emotional deterioration). And chronic poverty is responsible for both prolonged and cumulative stress. As a construct, risk indicates the probability of future difficulties and not an explanation for why difficulties occur.

In schooling, for example, two broad categories of risk factors, demographic and academic, have been empirically documented (Croninger and Lee 2001). Certain demographic factors have been correlated with higher chances of school difficulties: poverty, race, language-minority status, single-parent families, and parents not graduating high school. Academic risk factors (i.e., the actual manifestation of school-related problems) include absenteeism and skipping of classes, disengagement from school activities, low grades, early-grade retention, and discipline problems. The greater the accumulations of these social and academic risk factors, the greater the presumed risk of school failure.

In spite of these and other risk factors and vulnerabilities, a surprisingly large number of young people mature into normal, happy adults. Why do they remain relatively unscathed from poverty, racism, and other forms of oppression? What accounts for the surprisingly large number of children who somehow, at times miraculously, manage their adversities? Why do some thrive and not simply survive in the face of life's inhumanities and tragedies?

What accounts for their resilience? *Webster's* defines *resilience* as "the tendency to rebound or recoil, to return to prior state, to spring back." The process of rebounding from adversity does not suggest that one is incapable of being wounded or injured. Rather, a person may bend, lose some of his or her power and capability yet recover and return to prior level of adaptation. Thus the central element in resiliency lies in the power of recovery and sustained adaptive functioning.

Research into children living in highly stressed, trauma-inducing environments inform us about the *protective factors* that help them negotiate high-risk situations. By protective factor, we mean a biological, psychological, and/or environmental component that contributes to preventing a stressor, or lessens its impact, or ameliorates it more quickly. Protective factors include a person's 1. temperament, 2. family patterns, 3. external supports, and 4. environmental resources (Basic Behavioral Task Force 1996).

A person's *temperament* consists of such factors as her or his level of activity, coping skills, self-esteem, and attributions. In relation to activity level, for example, unfriendly and hyperactive children are more likely to encounter rejection than friendly and less hyperactive children. In chapters 4–8 social workers help children and adolescents to help each other develop greater social and communication skills. Similarly, the social workers in these chapters as well as in the other practice chapters help members to help each other enhance their coping skills by learning to more effectively problem solve and manage their feelings. Enhancing group members' coping capacities and skills is illustrated in every chapter in this book.

How people feel about themselves has a profound affect on day-to-day functioning. Self-esteem is not set in early or even late childhood; it is developed throughout the life cycle and is modified by life experiences. Self-esteem is a dynamic, complex concept as "individuals have not one but several views of themselves encompassing many domains of life, such as scholastic ability, physical appearance and romantic appeal, job competence, and adequacy as provider" (Basic Behavioral Task Force 1996:26). Being close to another person and successfully completing life-tasks have a profound affect on feelings of self-worth (Gitterman 2001b). The practice chapters in this book illustrate members learning to trust each other, developing greater intimacy, and completing essential life tasks such as unresolved grief and mourning for a lost relative, a group member, a worker, one's innocence, or for a world that no longer feels safe.

In traumatic experiences, attributions play an important role in recovery. When people blame themselves rather than blame the perpetrator, recovery is much slower. Generally, self-condemning attribution styles have strong negative impact on mental health. For example, when women survivors of sexual abuse blame themselves for the abuse, they tend to have more problems in recovery than those who blame the perpetrator (Feinauer and Stuart 1996; Liem et al. 1997; Valentine and Feinauer 1993). Helping members to develop adaptive attributions and to help each other transition from the status of a victim to that of a survivor is movingly illustrated in chapters 11 and 12.

Family relationship and communication patterns can serve as both risk as well as protective factors. For example, children dealing with parental alcoholism or persistent marital conflicts suffer from the daily pressures and hassles. They must find ways to disengage and develop psychological distance from their families. Adaptive distancing requires the ability to disengage internally while pursuing and sustaining external connections. The combination of internal distancing and external reaching out represent significant protective factors and processes. In contrast, a flight into social as well as emotional isolation symbolizes risk factors and processes (Berlin and Davis 1989). In family illness studies the presence of one good parent-child relationship served to reduce the psychiatric risk associated with family discord. The relationship serves as a protective factor in both cushioning the discord and in increasing the child's self-esteem (see chapters 15–17 for group practice with parents). Similar outcomes were evident with the presence of some caring adult such as a grandparent who assumes responsibility in the presence of partner discord or in the absence of responsive parents (Basic Behavioral Task Force 1996).

External support from a neighbor, parents of peers, teacher, social workers, and clergy also can serve as significant cushioning and protective factors. The importance of social support has been widely documented. In a longitudinal study of students in high schools, for example, Croninger and Lee (2001) found that teachers' support reduced the probability by half of students dropping out. Socially and economically disadvantaged students with academic difficulties were especially responsive to teacher assistance and guidance. Cushioning and protecting an individual in harm's way is achieved through the provision of four types of support: concrete goods or services (*instrumental*); nurturance, empathy, encouragement (*emotional*); advice, feedback (*informational*); and information relevant to self-evaluation (*appraisal*) (Auslander and Levin 1987). The practice chapters in this book poignantly demonstrate the exchange of instrumental, emotional, informational, and appraisal supports and their impact in providing group members with powerful cushions and incentives to deal with life stressors. Gitterman (1989) has metaphorically compared these supportive exchanges as providing the function to a group that energy provides to machinery. Without these types of supports (like machines without energy), groups are likely to lose their drive and momentum. For group members in the practice chapters, mutual aid provides protection and social and emotional cushions though the processes of giving and receiving essential instrumental and emotional resources, increasing of problem-solving skills and more effective management of emotions, and acquiring an improved sense of physical and emotional well-being. (Heller, Swindel, and Dusenbury 1986; Thoits 1986).

Finally, the *society* and its *institutions* provide the essential social context for vulnerability and risk and resiliency and protective factors and processes. When societal resources and supports are insufficient or unavailable, some people are apt to feel helpless and hopeless and lack self-confidence and skill in interpersonal an environmental coping (see chapters 7–20). In contrast, when societal resources and supports are sufficient or available, they act as critical buffers, helping people cope with life transitions, environments, and interpersonal stressors. These supportive social structures fortify people against physiological, psychological, and social harm and positively influence their worldviews and self-concepts.

Many risk or protective processes often concern key turning points in people's lives rather than long-standing attributes. What happens at a critical point determines the direction of the trajectory for years to follow (Rutter 1987). For example, the decision to stay in school represents one of those critical turning points often leading to more positive trajectories than dropping out from school. The consequences of not competing school are serious for young people. They include higher unemployment rates, lower lifelong earnings, higher rates of involvement in committing crimes, and higher rates of health problems than students who complete high school (Croninger and Lee 2001).

In making turning point decisions, planning skills in making choices emerges as a critical factor. The ability to exercise foresight and to take active steps to deal with environmental challenges is essential. In a follow-up study of girls reared in institutional care, for example, the extent to which they exercised planning in their choice of a partner, meaning that they did not marry for a negative reason, such as to escape from an intolerable situation or because of unwanted pregnancy, they were less likely to marry a man who was a criminal or had a mental disorder (Rutter 1987). Many of the practice chapters focus on improving group members' planning and problem-solving skills whether in relating to parents, partners, friends, or organizational representatives.

An additional protective factor to planning and problems-solving skills is humor and laughter. Humor and laughter creates a bond between group members and helps them to cope with painful realities. Gitterman (2003) identifies the social function of humor:

> Shared laughter serves as a social bridge and facilitates engagement and rapport. Laughing together softens the power differential, reduces social distance, normalizes the helping process, and advances the therapeutic relationship. Socially, laughter provides people with a common experience, akin to breaking bread together.

Moreover, laughter affirms that the injustices group members have suffered are "undeniably wrong" (Bowles 1994:3). Laughter in the face of adversity releases tensions and provides hope.

Finally, in *Man's Search for Meaning*, Frankl (1959) eloquently argues that meaning in life is found primarily through the processes of helping and giving to others rather than through the pursuit of self-gratification. In each practice chapter in this book we witness the special qualities of mutual aid—how group members help themselves by helping others. How group members, by helping others to heal, heal themselves. Essentially, when we lend our strength to others, we strengthen ourselves (Gitterman 2004; Shulman 1985/86; Shulman 1999).

The Mutual Aid Group

The idea of a group as system for mutual aid is rooted in a broader conception of the nature of the relationship between people and society. Schwartz (1977), drawing upon the ideas of Dewey (1916), Mead (1934), Kropotkin (1925), and others, postulated a view of reciprocity between individuals and their social surround. In chapter 21 Lee and Swenson explore the historical roots of mutual aid in more detail. For our immediate purposes, the crucial idea as proposed by Schwartz (1977:15) is that of a "symbiotic" relationship between the individual and societal needs, "each needs the other for its own life and growth and reaches out to the other with all possible strength at a given moment." Schwartz perceived the individual to have a natural impetus toward health and growth and belonging, with a similar impetus on the part of society to integrate its parts into a productive and dynamic whole.

If one then considers the small group to be a special case of this larger individual-social engagement and one carries this notion of symbiosis into the small group encounter, then Schwartz's (1977:19) definition of a social work group logically follows:

> The group is an enterprise in mutual aid, an alliance of individuals who need each other, in varying degrees, to work on certain common problems. The important fact is that this is a helping system in which the clients need each other as well as the worker. This need to use each other, to create not one but many helping relationships, is a vital ingredient of the group process and constitutes a common need over and above the specific tasks for which the group was formed.

THE MUTUAL AID PROCESS

There are a number of mutual aid processes that can be identified when one watches an effective small group in action. These have been described in some detail elsewhere and are illustrated through process recording excerpts in the chapters that follow (Shulman 1999). The nine processes briefly described in this section include the following: sharing data, the dialectical process, entering taboo areas, the "all-in-the-same-boat" phenomenon, mutual support, mutual demand, individual problem solving, rehearsal, and the strength in numbers phenomenon.

In *sharing data* group members can provide each other with ideas, facts, beliefs, and resources that they have found helpful in coping with similar problems. For example, in a welfare mothers' group, members offered suggestions about how to use the rules of the system to make maximum use of available benefits as well as what places to shop for the best buys. In a married couples group the older couples could often share their experiences from earlier in their marriages, some of which were similar to current crises experienced by the younger couples. The universality of the issues and members' suggestions for how to deal with them were often most helpful. While the content of the data varies according to the group type, the essential idea is that people facing similar problems can often be a resource for each other.

The dialectical process consists of one or more members advancing a thesis, other members countering with an antithesis, and the group members attempting to develop their own synthesis. This form of disputation process can be very helpful as one tries to develop insights into difficult problems. A group member can put forth a tentative idea (often only after the worker has helped the group to develop a culture of trust and respect) and have other members respond as soundingboards to the views. Other members may change their minds and be open to new ideas as they listen to a view being challenged. One extremely interesting process to observe in a group is the way in which the group may encourage debate between two members, or two subgroups, in which each side appears to take an opposing view to the other. For example, in a group for parents of teenagers one side argued impressively for the need to be "tough" and to set limits. The other argued just as passionately for the importance of providing support and of being able to communicate. The apparent dichotomy is of course a false one, with the skillful parent learning early of the need to integrate both support and limits at precisely the same time. In fact, each parent carries out the same dialogue internally, trying to find a way of resolving the split. In the group one part of each parent's ambivalence may be assigned to an individual group member or subgroup, and the dialectical process becomes a public airing of each individual's private confusion.

Of course, the assignments are not consciously made. A premeeting was not held for the purpose of deciding which group member would articulate what view. This group process emerges from the group's need to articulate and resolve an apparent schism, while simultaneously maintaining the split to avoid having to face it. Bion (1961), in his pioneering work on group processes, observed the way in which immature groups often go into "flight" (changing the subject) or "fight" (strenuous debates and personal attacks) when faced with difficult or frightening issues. Bion's "fight-flight" construct parallels Fanon's description of the defensive responses to oppression described earlier. Bion described the group leaders' job as pointing out the process and educating the group on its way of working to aid it in becoming a more mature group. In the model suggested here, the worker could identify the common ground, even at the point of conflict, by articulating the part of each group member that really agreed with the "other side." For example: "You're all arguing your points so strenuously; yet, I can't believe that some part of each of you isn't struggling to find a way to put together your love for your child with your sense of the importance of setting some limits and providing some structure."

A third area of mutual aid involves the help members can give each other in discussing a *taboo subject*. For example, while all group members in the married couples group may have some issues related to their sexual relationships, they may also see discussing this subject as taboo. An unstated norm of behavior exists in our society that forbids honest discussion of our fears and concerns in this area. We can joke about such subjects, but real talk is forbidden. Since the sense of urgency about dealing with the subject may be stronger for some couples than others, or the fear of discussion may be less powerful, one couple may take the initiative and lead the group into the formerly forbidden area. As group members listen to the discussion and see the courageous members supported and credited (often by the leader but just as often by other members), they find their own courage to participate.

In another example of this process in action, some group members may not be in touch with their own feelings if they believe these feelings to be inappropriate (for example, a nonoffending parent of an incest survivor who feels anger at the child). As these members hear others speak the unspeakable, it may cause them to experience openly the same emotions. The mutual experiencing of ideas and emotions leads to yet another powerful mutual aid process: the "all-in-the-same-boat phenomenon." This is the healing process that occurs when one realizes that one is not alone and that others share the problem, the feeling, the doubts, and all the rest. Students learning to practice social work are greatly relieved to find that other beginning students also wonder if they are right for the field. Parents who experience "improper" thoughts and feelings judge themselves less harshly when they find they are not alone.

A fifth mutual aid process can be observed in the way in which group members provide *mutual support* for each other. When a group member is in difficulty or has experienced a trauma (such as a death in the family) or is revealing painful feelings that have long been repressed, one can see direct and indirect efforts on the part of individual group members and the group as a whole to provide empathic support. Carrying a burden is often easier if others express their understanding. Having peers try to share in your painful feelings can be experienced as a form of a "gift," much more meaningful than artificial efforts to cheer you up. In a single parents group, one member began to cry with deep, heartfelt sobs as she described her tremendous sense of rejection by her ex-spouse. The leader could see the member next to the one in distress fidgeting and turning, apparently wanting to reach out. When the leader commented on this and asked if she wanted to hold the woman next to her, she replied that she did and then took her hand. This was a physical comforting, which was followed by words of support by the other group members. As they were supporting this member in her feelings of rejection, they were also helping themselves with their own similar feelings. Thus the giving of empathic support is often as helpful to the one who gives as to the one who receives. In the small group the support of peers can be even more powerful in its healing potential than the support of the worker.

While support is a crucial ingredient for mutual aid to take place, it is not enough by itself. The change process requires *mutual demand* as well. The artificial split between support and demand can be commonly observed in group practice. For example, Trimble (chapter 13) describes his early efforts in working with male batterers in which he felt that creating an accepting, empathic atmosphere was the key element in bringing about changes in behavior. Experience demonstrated that caring was not enough and that he had to integrate it with confrontation and demand, in which he needed to dig and push to get these men to accept responsibility for their actions and the change process. The key to the success of his work is the integration of the two essential elements in simultaneous action rather than structuring his groups to be all confrontation and no support. It is exactly at the moment that group members are confronted that they will need all the support they can receive.

Group members may be more ready than the worker to confront each other. The worker may hesitate, concerned about the member's possible fragility, and then sit back in wonder as the "fragile" member responds with strength to the peer group's demands. Somehow accepting a confrontation is easier from one who really knows what it is like than from an "outsider," however caring and empathic. Group members who share the problem may also be more astute in picking up the defenses, the denials, the many ways in which we all "con" ourselves out of facing the truth when it is painful. They are astute observers of these methods of avoidance because they can see them in their own behaviors.

Another simple yet powerful manner in which mutual demand operates in a group can be the expectation felt by the member that he or she take some difficult action. For example, a men's group discusses a member's difficulty communicating with his boss at work, and, after support, discussion, even role-play of how he should handle the conversation on the job, the group members expect to hear what happened when they return the next week. Group members have said they would rather face the boss than have to return the following week and reveal to their peers that they had "chickened out."

While group members can help each other through general discussion of common themes of concern, such as the feelings of loneliness of a single parent coupled with the fear of risking being hurt again in a new relationship, they must also offer help on a member-by-member, specific-example-by-specific-example basis. In fact, effective mutual aid groups are constantly moving back and forth between the specific case and the general issue. Individual problem solving is one of the important ways a mutual aid group works. As the group members help the individual with a specific problem, they are actually also helping themselves with their own variations on a theme. Workers who are unclear about this specific-general interaction often make the mistake of keeping the discussion on an overly general level. They express fears of "doing casework in the group." If one is clear that a mutual aid group involves members helping each other and that there is usually a connection between the individual's specific problems and the group's general purpose, then this issue of the individual need versus the group's need is revealed as yet another artificial dichotomy.

Take the example of a parents' group discussion about the difficulty in raising teenage children. One member raises it at the start of a group meeting as follows: "I have been thinking recently about how hard it is to raise teenage girls these days, what with the changes taking place in ideas about morality. It just isn't as clear as it was when I was a kid." The group leader who fears "casework in the group" might turn to the other members and ask for their comments on the issue. The resultant general discussion can become an "illusion of work" and, meanwhile, the initiator of the conversation may be sitting there still churning away over the fight she had the night before with her fifteen year old when she didn't return home until 3:30 in the morning.

If the leader is clear about the individual problem-solving process in mutual aid groups, he or she might ask the mother if she had a specific incident in mind. As the mother describes the fight, the worker would help the mothers share the incident with the other group members, invest the presentation with feelings, describe the actual conversation with the daughter, and mobilize the group members to offer feedback and advice. As they discuss this particular parent trying to cope with changing morals and parental responsibility, they will move back and forth between the specific problem and the general issues. As the group members offer help to this mother, they will be formulating new ideas on how they can handle similar issues with their children.

Discussion of the interaction with the daughter might reveal the mother to have been so distraught and worried about her daughter's safety that she may have translated her concern into an outburst of anger when the daughter returned. While the anger may have been appropriate, it often conceals the fear, anxiety, and caring from which it springs. If the group members and the leader help the mother to see how she needs to share these feelings as well, then rehearsal, a form of role-play in the group, can help the mother find the words and feelings for a follow-up discussion with her daughter. Sometimes just practicing a difficult task, with support and advice from the group members, can give the member enough confidence to attempt it. In addition, as the member struggles through the role-play, she or he often reveals ambivalent feelings about the issue that were not present during the discussion. For example, does some part of the mother not want to have such a discussion with the daughter because she is afraid of what she might hear? It is better if the ambivalence emerges in the group, where it can be explored, rather than in the conversation at home.

Finally, there is the *strength in numbers* phenomenon. Individual members often feel powerless to deal with large institutions and agencies, helping professionals (even the group leader), and apparently overwhelming tasks. In unity, however, one often finds strength. Take, for example, a group of welfare mothers living in a public housing development in which the management is insensitive to their needs, exploitative (for example, levying excessive charges for repairs), and authoritarian (threatening to evict them if they "make trouble"). For such a group the idea of confronting the management, dealing with city hall if they meet resistance, in other words, standing up for their rights, can be frightening and risky. In one such group they faced the additional problem of fear of reprisals from youth gangs in the project if they complained about the drug use in the halls, the welfare checks stolen from their mailboxes, and their general sense of lack of security (Shulman 1999). It was only through patient work by the group leader and a willingness to recognize the fears lurking beneath the surface that these group members were able to find the strength in numbers that allowed them to take a small first step. In another example, a group of survivors of sexual abuse participated in a "take back the night" march of women protesting violence in the street. None of the women felt comfortable joining the march on their own, but all were ready to go if the whole group participated.

This section has described a number of mutual aid processes that can be observed in a group. Of course, these will not necessarily happen by themselves. In fact, it is the difficulty for most groups in learning how to release these powerful forces for change and growth that creates the need for the group worker. In the next section we describe a number of obstacles that can block the mutual aid process, followed by a section describing how a group leader can assist the group in overcoming these problems.

OBSTACLES TO THE MUTUAL AID PROCESS

While the potential for mutual aid is present in the group, hard work by the group leader and all of its members is required if it is to emerge. In the next chapter on group work skills and in the illustrative chapters that follow you will see example after example of the delicate moments in which the ability of the group member to take help and the ability of the group to provide help seem to lie in balance. For example, group members will be struggling with feelings and ideas about which they may feel ashamed. "I am that handicapped child's mother! How can I feel such strong feelings of anger toward my own child?" Strong social taboos, which declare some areas of discussion or some feelings out of bounds (for example, sexual issues), operate to prevent us from honest discussion. These taboos will be brought from the broader society and enacted in the microcosm of the small group. As the small group gingerly approaches the taboo area, employing indirect communications such as "hints," the worker will have to call the group members' attention to the barrier and assist them in dealing with it, through a combination of support and demand. The members, for their part, will have to find the courage to enter the formerly forbidden areas, in response to the worker's gentle pushing, and begin to discover they are all in the same boat. The feelings for which they judged themselves so harshly are normal for their situations. The subjects they felt were not for open discussion, the feelings they experienced as possibly too painful to be faced, all take on a manageable status as the healing power of mutual aid begins its work.

A group culture (norms, taboos, rules of behavior, and so on) is just one example of the many obstacles that may frustrate the emergence of mutual aid in the group. Another common problem is the inability, in the early phases of the life of a group, for members to see the connection between their own sense of urgency and that of the other members. "What can these other people know of my problems and worries; their lives must be so different?" The connection between the agency service and the individual member's felt needs may also be unclear at the beginning.

Particularly in a mandated service, where involuntary participation is common, the group member may begin with strong expressions of denial, resistance, and anger to the offer of a group service. Skill will be required on the part of the group worker to help the members overcome their initial reactions to authority and their initial inability to see their stake in the agency service or in the other group members. The contracting process, described in the next chapter, can be the start of this change. Sensitivity to these issues is demonstrated in many of the group examples in the book as workers attempt to reassure members that they still maintain control of their inner lives. Trimble, in chapter 13, illustrates this beautifully in his opening statement to a group of men forced to come to a group for men who batter their wives. After recognizing that they may have been forced to attend (for example, by a judge's order), he speaks directly to the issue of control as he states: "But no one can reach into your mind and heart and order a change. That's where you have complete control."

These obstacles as well as others can serve to frustrate the emergence of the mutual aid potential. One way to view the role of the group leader is by seeing her or his job as that of helping the group to learn how to be a better mutual aid system. For example, the group leader can model effective helping behavior in the way she or he intervenes in the group. Another way of helping would be to call the group members' attention to the obstacles blocking their path. ("Every time someone raises an issue dealing with your difficulties in the sexual area, someone else changes the subject.") The group leader would need to provide support as the group members enter the previously taboo area ("Is it too scary or painful to deal with such a sensitive subject in this group?"), while, at the same time, making a demand for work by asking the group to explore and conquer the obstacle ("What is it that makes it hard to talk to each other about sex? Perhaps if we understand that, it might make it easier to risk.") As the group members discuss the obstacle, they are simultaneously overcoming its power to frustrate their efforts at mutual aid. Obstacles revealed are usually much less powerful than those that remain hidden from view and discussion.

Some obstacles, as Gitterman describes in chapter 3, may be avoided by skill-ful group composition and formation. All groups, however, experience some ob-stacles, problems, conflicts, and a process that often seems to go two steps forward and three steps back. These are not signs of the lack of mutual aid po-tential in the small group; rather, they are indicators to the worker of normative group issues that need to be handled with skill and sensitivity. The effective mu-tual aid group is not one without problems, but, rather, one in which the leader and members become more sophisticated about how to cope with the inherent problems. When they are dealt with, a number of important benefits can be ob-served in a mutual aid group. In the next section we propose a statement of func-tion that may help the group leader in her or his efforts to help the group.

The Mediating Function of the Group Worker

A worker must be clear about his or her function in the group. Function is de-fined here as a description of the specific role of the worker, that is, his or her part in the proceedings. All the interpersonal skill in the world will be of no use to a group worker without a clear sense of the job description. Group process can become very complex, and a worker without a clear, internalized sense of how one helps in the group will inevitably become as lost as the group members.

For example, when a group of teenage boys begins to scapegoat a smaller, weaker member, and that member exhibits a pattern of inviting the abuse, what will the worker say and do? When an individual raises a deeply felt issue and group seems to turn away from the member, changing the subject or downplay-ing the significance of the issue, how will the worker intervene? When a group splits into two opposing camps, seemingly unable to come to a decision or ap-pearing unwilling to listen and to understand each other, how will the worker help? When a group of foster adolescents begins to discuss their use of drugs or their involvement in some illegal activity, what is the group leader's responsibil-ity? When group members espouse positions opposed to the strongly held values of the worker, should he or she challenge them? The list of questions could go on for pages. What is common to each of these examples is that they describe moments when the worker will feel on the spot and unsure how to intervene.

No matter how well armed with interpersonal skills the worker may be, the question remains, to what immediate function will he or she harness those skills? If the worker is not clear about the question of role and is suffering from a form of functional diffusion (taking on many different roles, thus diffusing the clarity of the job description), then the intervention will often flow from the worker's past experiences, current sense of panic, personal value systems, and other sources. For example, the worker might start to protect the scapegoat, or exhort the group members who have turned away from the member in pain, or preach to the adolescents about the evils of drugs. In each case, as they protect, exhort, or preach, they will cut themselves off from the group members and lose their ability to help effectively.

Fortunately, functional diffusion is not a terminal illness. It can be treated with a dose of functional clarity. Schwartz (1961), building on the assumption of the symbiotic relationship between the individual and the group, proposed the role for the worker of mediating the individual/group engagement. This worker function within the group was an extension of his statement of the general function of social work in society as implemented in the small group modality.

If we return to some of those critical moments in the life of a group we have described earlier, then we can illustrate how functional clarity and, in particular, this mediating role, might help the worker intervene effectively. In the teenage scapegoating example, instead of taking the scapegoat's side and alienating the group, the worker would realize that she or he has two "clients" at this critical moment—the individual scapegoat and the group as a whole. One of the central tasks of the mediating function, as described by Schwartz (1961:25) involves the worker's effort to "search out the common ground between the individual and the group." Thus the worker needs to understand the purpose of scapegoating in the group, which is often displacing the feelings of the members on the individual who represents the worst example of their own "sins."

Scapegoating was part of the ancient Hebrew tradition, which is the source of the word itself. The Hebrews invested the skin (scape) of a goat with the sins of the people and placed it upon another goat's back, driving the goat into the wilderness. Thus, for another year, the community was absolved of its sins. With this understanding of the meaning of the scapegoating pattern in mind and with the mediating function as a guide, the worker can implement Schwartz's (1961:25) second set of tasks, that of challenging the obstacles that obscure the common ground between the individual and the group. Rather than siding with one versus the other, the worker must emotionally be with both at the same time. The worker is only able to implement this role if she or he has a clear understanding of the "two client" idea.

As the worker points out the way in which the group members and the scapegoat have chosen to avoid their own feelings, she or he must provide support to both clients. In chapter 3 the specific skills for implementing this functional role are described and illustrated. For now the important point is that clarity of function provides the worker with a clear direction for intervention.

In the second example provided earlier, rather than getting mad at the group for apparently rejecting the member in need, the worker mediates the engagement by helping the member articulate the pain of the issue while simultaneously acknowledging the group members' pain, which causes them to withdraw. For example: "Are Frank's feelings hitting you all so hard that you're finding it difficult to stay with him? Do you have so much pain yourself that it's hard to find any room left in your heart for his pain?" The worker has two "clients" in the mediating framework and must help both to reach out to each other. If the worker is busy trying exhortation to shame the group, he or she cannot be tuned in to the group members' pain, which is expressed indirectly through their behavior. The worker is in the ironic situation of demanding that the group members feel for the individual, while lacking empathy for them.

In the third example mentioned earlier, what will the worker do when the group polarizes around an issue with each side taking apparently opposite points of view and holding firm, not even listening to the other half of the group? If the worker's sense of function is diffused and the worker tries to play the role of expert, throwing support to the "right" side in the debate, once again a chance to help may be lost. In the mediating role, the worker would try to look deeply into the connections between the apparent dualism instead of getting lost in what may well be a phony dichotomy. The worker has a point of view about life and needs to share it in the course of the work of the group—what Schwartz (1961:27) described as another task—sharing data. However, whatever the worker's opinions, she or he still has the general function of mediation in the group, and sharing data is only one task.

An example from a parent-teen discussion group may help. At one point the teenagers articulated their need for more freedom from their parents and less structure. They wanted some recognition of their new status. The parents countered with their need to have a say in the lives of their children. The specific examples dealt with curfew times, supervision of schoolwork, the use of alcohol and/or drugs, and sexual freedom. A worker who is unclear about her or his role might get caught up in the details of the debate: for example, siding with the parents if the teens suggested curfew times that were too late or with the teens if the parents seemed overly protective. As the worker listened to the group, energy would be directed into making "expert" judgments on who was "right." Group members might even ask the worker to play the role of judge.

As the worker becomes caught up in these roles, she or he would fail to play the crucial role of mediating the engagement. Thus the worker might not listen to the argument unfolding, attempting to tune in to the stake that parents have in seeing their teenage children make a responsible transition to young adulthood. The parents have an investment in their children's learning to take responsibility for themselves, which is essentially what the teens are looking for. At the same time, what is the stake the teens have in having parents who still care enough to want to provide some structure? Would they really want their parents not to care about them any longer? A simple debate on the issue of curfew may change, with the intervention of the worker, into a more basic discussion of a life transition for both the parents and the teens, one that is never easy, one that has no clear and simple answers, and one that must involve some struggle. The worker's investment must not be in a specific curfew time but rather in bringing these mixed feelings into the open, in identifying the transitional questions, in helping the parents and teens truly understand what the other is saying and feeling as they experience a normative crisis. With this kind of help both parents and teens may develop the skills of dealing with the many specific structure/freedom issues they must face and master if they are to keep the family relationship sound through the transition work ahead of them. Functional clarity can help a worker implement this task.

In the final example, dealing with ideas, values, or beliefs expressed by the group members that trouble the worker, a clear sense of function is important. We suggested in the previous illustration that the worker should share her or his view of life, a process Schwartz (1961:28) described as "lending a vision." However, the view of life that the worker lends (implying members are free to take it or leave it), must be relevant to the current work of the group and not immediately available to the members. This means that the worker shares from her or his fund of life experience when the group members need access to it, not when the worker decides they need to be "educated." If the worker has a "hidden agenda" that guides the worker's activity, then the members will have to start to invest their energy into guessing what the worker has up her or his sleeve. They have probably already experienced professionals who are doing things to them in indirect ways. In fact, that is usually the reason for their early wariness about the worker's motives. If one believes the only way to help people is by doing with instead of doing to them, then the crucial questions are as follows: What are the group members working on at this moment in the group? Do I have information, beliefs, values, and so on that may be helpful to them? How can I share these in such a way that group members treat them as just one more source of data—not the final word from the final authority?

An example might help at this point. It comes from work with middle-class, white children in a suburban community center in a neighborhood undergoing a change from an all-white to a racially mixed community. In the course of one group meeting a disparaging comment was made about some of the new black children who had entered the local school. The worker in this example, feeling a great sense of responsibility for "teaching" the right attitudes, intervened and chastised the group member for having expressed a racist comment. The conversation changed immediately, and the worker felt the lesson had been learned. During the week before the next meeting, the worker tuned in (developed some empathy) for what these children might be experiencing at home, in school, and in the community during a tense transition period.

He began the next session by reopening the discussion, explaining that he had reacted quickly because of his own strong feelings on the matter and wondered if this kind of discussion was taking place in their homes and at the school. If they wished, he would try to help them talk about it, if it troubled them. The result was an outpouring of feeling about what they were hearing and experiencing, the pressures they were feeling from parents (in some cases) and peer group to act in certain ways toward the new members of the community. For many of them there was a real dilemma, as they felt torn between what they felt was right to do and what they felt they were being forced to do. Because of the worker's skillful catch of his mistake, his clarifying in his own mind what his functional role was, he was able to help the group members create a place where they could really talk about the issues. In an adult illustration of the same issue, staff at a transition house for battered women felt so strongly about the oppression experienced by their clients that they found it hard to accept the views expressed by women who were still coping with the "internal oppressor." When these women expressed views such as "Sometimes I asked for the beating," "My man really loves me and can be nice to live with most of the time," and "Living with him is really better than being alone," staff members found it hard to understand a view so different from their own. Lectures and admonishments designed to change the group members' attitudes often only drove them underground. The group members learned to participate in an "illusion of work," where they said what they thought the workers wanted to hear. The tragedy was that often, at the end of their time in the shelter, the women returned to the abusing spouse.

It was not that the ideology was wrong. In fact, it is in helping clients to deepen their understanding of gender issues that affect their lives, helping them to see how role stereotypes have been oppressive to them, helping them to understand how they have internalized these stereotypes and have lost touch with their sense of their own value as individuals and as women—it is these steps and others that will help them grow, change, and develop the strength to reject a life of abuse. The problem rested with the group leaders' sense of their function in the group, which was to "preach" these ideas. With functional clarity, the leaders might express their genuine understanding of the dilemmas expressed by group members and then help them to help each other in learning how to cope when you feel two ways at the same time. For example: "That's the struggle for you, isn't it? You know you can't live with him when he is this way. You know he can be dangerous to you and your kids. And yet, a part of you still feels you love him and need him and you're afraid to be without him. How about others in the group? Have you felt the same way as June? What can she do about this?" Often, the group members can offer support and advice, since June's struggle may be theirs as well. The workers can and must share their ideas about how and why women find themselves in this position. However, these must be shared when appropriate to the immediate work of the group members. That is the only time they can be heard, understood, and remembered. No matter how sound or important the ideas, values, and beliefs may be, the worker cannot substitute her or his experience for the work the group member must do.

In addition to thinking about the worker's function in relation to the group and its processes, one also has to consider the worker's function in relation to the life issues and needs being explored (the content of the discussions). The Life Model (Germain and Gitterman 1996) proposes a schema for understanding and helping group members to deal with life stresses and their consequences. As previously described, clients' needs and troubles are identified as arising from three interrelated problems of living: 1. life transitions, 2. environmental pressures, and 3. dysfunctional interpersonal processes. With life changes, the social work function is to help the group and its members to meet the particular task associated with developmental phases and the accompanying status and role demands and crisis events. Helping a group and its members move through life transitions so that their adaptive functions and problem-solving skills are supported and strengthened is a valuable and important professional activity. The social work function with environmental concerns is to help the group and its members to use available organizational and network resources and influence these environmental forces to be responsive. Mobilizing and strengthening the goodness-of-fit between natural and formed groups and their social environments provides social work with a core mediating function. With dysfunctional interpersonal group processes, the social work function is to help group members to recognize the obstacles and to learn to communicate more openly and directly and attain greater mutuality in their relationships.

The Life Model offers a normative perspective on the troubles people experience. Whatever a client's diagnosis, he or she still has to manage life stressors. The stressors-in-living schema (life transitions, environmental pressures, and dysfunctional interpersonal processes) accounts for the troubles of most clients. It enables the worker to design preventive services (see chapter 3) as well as to develop practice strategies in an orderly and focused way. To illustrate, a worker was assigned to a group of recent widows. In the fifth session members were agitated and complained about their sense of loneliness and isolation. At this particular moment were the members asking for help with the life transition—that is, with exploring their grief and helping them through their mourning stages? Or were they at this particular moment asking for help with environmental isolation—that is, with getting connected to new networks to do things to combat their loneliness? Or were they at this particular moment indirectly complaining that the worker and group experience were being unhelpful and requesting attention to their interpersonal concerns—that is, in dealing with their struggles about the worker's competence or the members' ability to help? At each moment the worker has to consider whether the members are asking for help with life transitional, environmental, or interpersonal issues and to be responsive to their primary concerns. Too often our interventions are not based upon an examination of members' latent messages but rather upon our own (or our agency's) preoccupations. A worker committed to "advocacy" practice might direct the group to environmental issues, the worker committed to "sensitivity work" might direct the members to interpersonal issues, and the worker committed to "psychological practice" may direct the members to life transitional issues. Group members are not responsible for confirming and conforming to our interests; our professional responsibility is to join their natural life processes, to follow their leads and be responsive to their cues.

We have given a number of examples of how functional clarity can come to the aid of a group worker when the going gets tough. While the mediating function was suggested as a helpful one in understanding this complex task, it is certainly not the only way to describe the group worker's part in the proceedings. This statement of function has been shared as one that has proved helpful to the authors of this chapter as they struggle to find ways of deepening their understanding of practice. In the next chapter the specific skills required to put this function into action in the various phases in the life of the group (preliminary, beginning, work, and transition/ending) will be described and illustrated. The ideas drawn from the Life Model, oppression, vulnerability, resilience, and mutual aid, will also be elaborated and illustrated in the group examples that follow.

Notes

1. In real life these life phases ebb and flow and overlap. People rarely neatly complete one stage and move on to a new one. Historical, individual, social, and cultural differences create unique experiences and issues.
2. It is important to note that puberty is biological but adolescence is a social and cultural phenomenon. Adolescence is not recognized in all societies.

References

Anthony, J. E. 1987. Risk, vulnerability, and resilience: An overview. In E. J. Anthony and B. Cohler, eds., *The invulnerable child*, pp. 3–48. New York: Guilford.

Antsey, M. 1982. Scapegoating in groups: Some theoretical perspectives and a case record of intervention. *Social Work with Groups* 5(3): 51–63.

Auslander, G. and H. Levin. 1987. The parameters of network intervention: A social work application. *Social Service Review* 61(June): 305–18.

Basic Behavioral Task Force of the National Advisory Mental Health Council. 1996. Basic behavioral science research for mental health: Vulnerability and resilience. *American Psychologist.* 51(1): 22–28.

Berman-Rossi, T. 1993. The tasks and skills of the social worker across stages of group development. *Social Work with Groups* 16(1/2): 69–92.

Berlin, R. and R. Davis. 1989. Children from alcoholic families: Vulnerability and resilience. In *The child in our times: Studies in the development of resiliency*, pp. 81–105. New York: Brunner/Mazel.

Bion, W. 1961. *Experiences in groups*. New York: Basic.

Bowles, D. D. 1994. Black humor as self-affirmation. *Journal of Multiculutral Social Work* 3(2): 1–10.

Bulham, H. A. 1985. *Frantz Fanon and the psychology of oppression*. New York: Plenum.

Bullis, R., ed. 1996. *Spirituality in social work practice*. Pennsylvania: Taylor and Francis.

Chau, K. L. 1992. Needs assessment for group work with people of color: A conceptual formulation. *Social work with Groups* 15(2/3): 53–66.

Congress, E. P. 1994. The use of Culturgrams to assess and empower culturally diverse families. *Families in Society* 75(9): 531–40.

Croninger, R. G. and V. E. Lee. 2001. Social capital and dropping out of high school: Benefits to at-risk students of teachers' support and guidance. *Teachers College Record*. 103(4): 548–81.

D'Augelli, A. R., S. L. Hershberger, and N. W. Pilkington. 1998. Lesbian, gay, and bisexual youth and their families: Disclosure of sexual orientation and its consequences. *American Journal of Orthopsychiatry* 68(3): 361–71.

Delgado, M., ed. 1998. *Latino elders and twenty-first century: Issues and challenges for culturally competent research and practice*. New York: Haworth.

Dewey, J. 1916. *Democracy and education*. New York: Macmillan.

Devore, W. and E. Schlesinger. 1991. *Culturally sensitive social work practice*. New York: Merrill.

Dore, M. and A. Dumois. 1990. Cultural differences in the meaning of adolescent pregnancy. *Families in Society* 71(2): 93–101.

Erikson, E. H. 1959. Growth and crises of the healthy personality. In E. H. Erikson, ed.. *Identity and the life cycle: Psychological issues*, pp. 50–100. Monograph 1. New York: International.

Feinauer, L. and D. Stuart. 1996. Blame and resilience in women sexually abused as children. *American Journal of Family Therapy* 24(1): 31–40.

Frankl, V. 1959. *Man's search for meaning: An introduction to logotherapy*. Boston: Beacon.

Germain, C. B. 1973. An ecological perspective in casework practice. *Social Casework* 54(July): 323–30.

———— 1990. Life forces and the anatomy of practice. *Smith College Studies in Social Work*. 60(March): 138–52.

———— 1994. Emerging conceptions of family development over the life course. *Families and Society* 75(5): 259–68.

Germain, C. B. and A. Gitterman, A. 1995. Ecological perspective. In R. L. Edwards, ed., *The encyclopedia of social work*, pp. 816–24. 19th ed. Silver Spring, Md.: National Association of Social Workers.

———— 1996. *The life model of social work practice: Advances in knowledge and practice*. 2d ed. New York: Columbia University Press.

Gitterman, A. 1989. Building support in groups. *Social Work with Groups* 12(2): 5–22.

———— 1996. Advances in the life model of social work practice." In F. Turner, ed., *Social work treatment: Interlocking theoretical perspectives*, pp. 389–408. New York: Free Press.

———— 2001a. The life model of social work practice. In A. Roberts and G. Greene, eds., *Social Worker's Desk Reference*, pp.105–8. New York: Oxford University Press.

———— 2001b. Vulnerability, resilience, and social work with groups. In T. Berman-Rossi, T. Kelly, and S. Palombo, eds.. *Strengthening Resiliency Through Group Work*, pp. 19–34. Binghamton, NY: Haworth.

———— 2001c. Social work practice with resilient and vulnerable populations. In A. Gitterman, ed., *Social Work Practice with Resilient and Vulnerable Populations*, pp. 1–38. New York: Columbia University Press.

——— 2003. The uses of humor in social work practice. *Reflections: Narratives of Professional Helping* 9(4): 79–84.

——— 2004. The mutual aid model. In C. Garvin, M. Galinsky, and L. Gutierez , eds., *Handbook of social work with groups.* New York: Oxford University Press.

Gutiérrez, L. and E. Lewis. 1999. *Empowering women of color.* New York: Columbia University Press.

Heller, K., R. Swindel, and L. Dusenbury. 1986. Component social support processes: Comments and integration. *Journal of Consulting and Clinical Psychology* 54(4): 466–70.

Hooker, C. 1976. Learned helplessness. *Social Casework* 21(May): 194–98.

Hurd, E. P, C. Moore, and R. Rogers, R. 1995. Quiet success: Parenting strengths among African Americans. *Families in Society* 76(7): 434–43.

Kropotkin, P. 1925. Mutual aid: A factor of evolution. New York: Knopf.

Larder, J. 1998. Deadly disparities: American's widening gap in incomes may be narrowing over our lifespan. *Washington Post*, August 16, p. C1.

Lee, F. 1989. Doctors see gap in blacks' health having a link to low self-esteem. *New York Times*, July 17, p. A 11.

Liem, J. H., J. B. James, J. G. O'Toole, and A. C. Boudewyn. 1997. Assessing resilience in adults with histories of childhood sexual abuse. *Amercian Journal of Orthopsychiatry* 67:594–606.

Mead, G. H. 1934. Mind, self, and society. Chicago: University of Chicago Press.

Orti, B., A. Bibb, and J. Mahboubi. 1996. Family-centered practice with racially/ethnically mixed families. *Families in Society* 77(9): 573–82.

Paulino, A. 1995. Spiritism, Santería, Brujería, and Voodism: A comparative view of indigenous healing systems. *Journal of Teaching and Social Work* 12(1/2): 105–24.

Rosenbloom, M. 1995. Implications of the Holocaust for social work. *Families in Society* 76(9): 567–76.

Rutter. M. 1987. Psychosocial resilience and protective mechanisms. *American Journal of Orthopsychiatry* 57:316–31.

Schiele, J. H. 1996. Afrocentricity: An emerging paradigm in social work practice. *Social Work*. 41(3): 284–94.

Schiller, L. 1997. Rethinking stages of development in women's groups. *Social Work with Groups*. 20(3): 3–19.

Schwartz, W. 1961. The social worker in the group. *The social welfare forum*, pp. 146–77. New York: Columbia University Press.

——— 1977. Social group work: The interactionist approach. In J. Turner, ed., *Encyclopedia of social work*, 2:1328–38. New York: National Association of Social Workers.

Seligman, M and G. Elder Jr. 1986. Learned helplessness and life-span development. In A. B. Sorenson and F. E. Weiner, eds., *Human development and the life course: Multidisciplinary perspectives*, pp. 377–428. Hillsdale, N. J.: Erlbaum

Shulman, L. 1967. Scapegoats, group workers, and pre-emptive interventions. *Social Work* 12(2): 37–43.

——— 1985/86. The dynamics of mutual aid. *Social Work with Groups* 8(4): 51–60.

——— 1999. *The skills of helping individuals families, groups, and communities.* 4th ed. Itasca. Ill: Peacock.

Solomon, B. 1976. *Black empowerment.* New York: Columbia University Press, 1976.

Swigonski, M. E. 1996. Challenging privilege through Afrocentric social work practice. *Social Work* 41(2): 153–61.

Thoits, V. 1986. Social support as coping assistance. *Journal of Consulting and Clinical Psychology* 54(4): 416–23.

U.S. Bureau of Census. 1997. Press release. U.S. Department of Commerce Economic and Statistics Administration.

Valentine, L. and L. Feinauer. 1993. Resilience factors associated with female survivors of childhood sexual abuse. *American Journal of Family Therapy* 21:216–24.

Williams, E. E. and F. Ellison. 1996. Culturally informed social work practice with American Indian clients: Guidelines for non-Indian social workers. *Social Work* 41(2): 147–51.

Wilson, W. J. 1973. *Power, racism and privilege: Race relations in theoretical and sociohistorical perspectives.* New York: Free Press.

Chapter 2

Group Work Method

Lawrence Shulman

THIS CHAPTER focuses on skill: what the group leader does when he or she tries to help group members help each other. Most of the skills used by the group leader are core communications, relationship, and problem-solving skills, which are important in all helping modalities (such as individual or family work). Some skills are unique to work with more than one client at a time. Since so many of the skills are generic in nature, readers who have worked with people in other modalities will soon discover that they already know more about group work than they had imagined.

In order to provide illustrations of the skills in action, process recording excerpts have been drawn from the articles found in this book. Thus the skill will be named, described, and illustrated with examples of real workers responding to real group members on a moment by moment basis.

This attention to the details of method was central to Schwartz's work (1961, 1976, 1977). He stressed that the worker's knowledge and values were made known to the client through the worker's actions. He pointed to a need to describe method in a way that was specific but not overly prescriptive, thereby developing a structure for practice that provided freedom for spontaneous and artistic responses. For example, although a number of specific empathic skills will be described in this chapter, the way in which each group leader demonstrates her or his capacity to empathize with clients might differ depending upon highly personal factors. One worker's facial expressions might convey as much meaning to the client as another's hand on a shoulder or another's tears. The injunction against an overly prescriptive approach cautioned against mechanical descriptions of process in which each client behavior called forth a specific worker response. Attention to method had to be at a level that provided answers to the worker's legitimate need to know how to practice while still leaving room for individual artistry.

In order to simplify the complex task of describing the helping process in groups, Schwartz borrowed ideas about time and its impact on process from Taft

(1949). He then built upon these to develop his four phases of work: the preliminary, beginning, work, and ending/transition phases. The preliminary phase involves the worker's activity before the first group meeting. Gitterman describes the worker's tasks in setting up a group in chapter 3. The beginning phase refers to the first sessions in which important contracting work takes place. The work phase is the ongoing or middle period, and the ending/transition phase comes into play as the group completes its work. An open-ended group, in which new members join and others leave at different points in time, represents a special variation on this theme. Any one session, for some members, may be a beginning, middle, or ending phase. A number of articles in this book address this open-ended variation on the phases of work concept (see, for example, Trimble, chapter 13).

These phases are useful when thinking about group work, since each one contains its own interesting dynamics and calls for specific worker activity. This framework is used to organize the balance of this chapter. In addition to being useful in understanding the life process of a group over time, the phases of work concept is also helpful in understanding each individual group session, which has its own preliminary, beginning, middle, and ending phase. Thus the framework is used to understand the life of the group over time as well as the dynamics of each individual session.

The Preliminary Phase of Work

A major skill in the preliminary phase of work is the development of the worker's preparatory empathy. This technique can be used before the first meeting. Schwartz (1977) termed this process "tuning in." It involves the worker's efforts to get in touch with potential feelings and concerns group members may bring to the encounter. The four major areas for tuning in include issues related to the authority of the group leader (for example, "What kind of person will this leader be?"), concerns related to the group ("Who are these other people and how will they react to me?"), concerns related to the purpose of the group (for example, the guilt often experienced by parents of sexually abused young children who may feel they should have been able to protect them from the abuse, and the indirect ways in which the group members may use group process to communicate (such as scapegoating).

The rationale for employing tuning-in skills relates to the indirect nature of communications used by group members, particularly in the early sessions before a climate of trust can be developed. Group members will often only hint at their real feelings in relation to taboo subjects (such as authority, dependency, death, sexuality). By tuning in, the group leader can be more sensitive to the group members' indirect cues. This increased sensitivity compliments a second skill, responding directly to indirect communications and, when used together, can significantly speed up the work of the group, allowing the leader and the members to deal more quickly with significant issues. The responding skill involves anticipating and putting into words the thoughts and feelings of the group members. Elsewhere I have referred to this skill as "articulating the client's feelings" (Shulman 1999). In addition to speeding up the work of the group, the use of this skill reveals to the group members early in the life of the group the worker's capacity to be empathic, honest, and direct. Each of these qualities is important in the building of the working relationship.

For example, when a member of a group for parents inquires in the first session if the worker is married, a direct response might be as follows: "No, I'm not married, and I don't have children. Are you wondering if I'm going to be able to understand what it's like for you?" Such a response, if said with genuine feeling and not merely as an intellectual inquiry, will often help to open up the working relationship. The alternative response of defensively describing the worker's credentials (such as, "At my school of social work I took a course in child development theory" or "We are here to talk about you, not me!") will often serve to distance worker and group members further.

Of course, if the worker is to respond directly and without defensiveness, he or she must have tuned in to his or her own normal feelings of insecurity, which may arise during the preparation for such a first meeting. Being sensitive to one's own feelings and fears lessens the likelihood of responding inappropriately; however, the group leader should anticipate that she or he will make mistakes. In fact, effective practice is described in this chapter as shortening the time between making and catching a mistake. Perfect work is a myth. Group leaders who are viewed as paragons of virtue—always tuned in and always correct in their responses—are a part of this fiction. This image tends to immobilize new leaders. A more forgiving and reasonable view would expect a new group leader to miss the first cues of concern about her or his understanding of the group members and the problems. Acknowledging a mistake can be helpful to the group work. For example, the group leader questioned about his or her marital status could begin the next session by saying: "When you asked if I had children last week, I felt on the spot and told you about my training. I thought about it during the week, and I think you may have really been wondering if I could understand what it was like for you to raise children. If I'm going to help, I'm going to have to understand what it feels like for each of you. Can you let me know?" Not only has the group inquiry been answered, the worker has also begun to demonstrate a desire to understand.

Tuning in also includes sensitizing oneself to potential client concerns about the work of the group and anticipating some of the indirect ways in which these concerns may be communicated. For example, in married couples groups I have led, issues of a sexual nature were difficult to discuss both between the partners in the marriage and within the mutual aid groups. Tuning in to sources of stress may make it easier to pick up the call for help, which is often raised through con-flicts over other issues. Tuning in can help to clarify the common pattern in which sexual dysfunctioning leads to a vicious cycle of mutual blaming stem-ming from each partner's own feelings of inadequacy. A worker who has tuned in effectively can more easily pick up the cues, reach for the hidden agenda, and then help members deal with the difficult feelings—the ones that, when revealed, often offer the possibility of reestablishing a caring and supportive relationship.

Finally, in the group situation, one needs to learn to tune in to the language of the group as a whole. This is one of the skills unique to group and to family work that helps to differentiate group work practice from individual work. In ad-dition to the individual indirect communications of group members, the group itself may communicate through its process of interaction. Often operating on an unconscious basis, the group acts as a dynamic organism where the movements of each member are affecting and being affected by the interaction. Thus a group of teenage boys, struggling with issues of male identity, may scapegoat a mem-ber who embodies the ambivalence they fear in themselves as their way of "speaking" to the group leader. Preliminary-phase work, both before the first ses-sion and from week to week, can help a group leader to identify patterns of in-teraction and to understand the particular function played by these individual members. Of course, experience over time helps the group leader to better un-derstand this subtle language of the group.

The Beginning Phase of Work

First meetings in all helping relationships are important. If handled well, they can lay a foundation for productive work, begin the process of strengthening the working relationship between group leader and members as well as initiating the process of helping the group members develop a productive culture for work (such as mutual trust). If handled badly, they can turn the group members away from the services. The skills involved in making a positive start can be grouped together under the rubric of contracting. The general goals of this contracting process include clarifying to group members the agency's purpose in offering the group (agency service) and identifying the common ground between these purposes and the group members' sense of immediate urgency (client needs). The overlapping area between services and needs, as pictured by Schwartz (1961, 1976, 1977), provides the core of the working contract.

The contracting process also involves specifying for the group members the role that the worker will play, the mutual need members have for each other, and the mutual expectations and obligations of group leader and group members. The argument is made that group members desperately need some clear struc-ture in order to free them to work. They begin a new situation with some anxiety about what will happen to them, or perhaps be done to them, and their defenses will be understandably raised until the contracting process eases their minds. In addition, unless group members can perceive a clear and immediate stake in the work of the group, they will not invest themselves in a meaningful way. This connection is often subtle, partial, and changeable over time; however, some clear stake must exist for effective work to proceed. If group members suspect that the agency, through its agent, the group leader, has a "hidden agenda" aimed at changing them or indirectly influencing them, then their participation will be at best an "illusion of work."

In addition to a clear idea about group purpose, group members also need some reassurance about the way in which the group leader will help. They may initially fear the power of this authority figure, a fear arising from previous experiences with symbols of authority (such as teachers, other helping professionals, and so on). By understanding that the worker's job lies in helping them to help each other, group members become increasingly able to make effective use of the worker's assistance.

Group members must also appreciate how the other members of the group relate to their own concerns. They often feel that they are alone with their feelings and are reassured when they discover that the group members are often experiencing similar feelings. Finally, group members need to know the rules of the game, such as what the leader and other group members will expect of them and what they can expect in return. Confidentiality is another important area to address in a first meeting.

While the contracting agenda is an imposing one, it does not have to be completed in the first session. In fact, first sessions should be seen as the beginning of this process. The leader may need a number of sessions to work it through. As the group begins to work, its purpose becomes clearer to members as specific issues are raised and discussed. As group members watch the worker in action, she or he gives meaning to the description of the group leader's role articulated in the first session. As group members listen to the concerns and feelings of others, they discover their common ground in deeply meaningful ways. Working contracts thus may evolve and change over time.

In order to accomplish the task of contracting, the following skills are needed: clarifying purpose, clarifying role, reaching for member feedback, defining mutual expectations and obligations, and encouraging intermember interaction. The skills of clarifying purpose and role can be encompassed in the worker's efforts to make an "opening statement" to the group members, one that clearly states the worker's agenda (for offering the group) and the way in which the worker wishes to help. It is crucial in this statement to avoid the use of typical professional jargon (such as *facilitate*, *enhance*, and *enable*) and to find ways of verbalizing purpose in words that can have direct meaning to the group members. It is often useful to prepare such a statement and to try it out with colleagues or clients in order to develop an effective opening. The statement of role should be simple and may be similar to the following: "My job will be to help you talk to and listen to each other, to share your problems, and to help you help each other. Whenever useful, I'll throw my own ideas in along the way."

Reaching for feedback can be done through a simple exercise in which members are asked to share, with each other, the concerns and issues they feel should be part of the agenda. The sharing with each other, a form of "problem swapping," is also the way in which the worker begins the process of encouraging intermember communications. Group members are used to talking to the leader, the symbol of authority; therefore, they require help to see that their work is really with each other. Mutual expectations and obligations, which can be discussed at the start or the end of the first session, provide an open statement of the group's structure as it has been negotiated with the group members. Issues of confidentiality, attendance, expectations of participation of all members, and the like can be discussed at this time.

Some examples of this process, drawn from the following chapters, illustrate the skills and the variations in the contracting process introduced by setting, client population, issues of mandatory versus voluntary involvement, and so on. In the first excerpt, drawn from Shulman's work with a "semivoluntary" group for persons with AIDS in recovery from substance abuse (chapter 10), purpose is described in the opening statement, partialized into potential themes of concern, and offered to group members as "handles" with which they begin their work.

> There are groups for persons with AIDS and there are groups for people in early recovery from substance abuse. This is a support group for persons who are dealing with both. The focus will be on how your recovery issues and your AIDS issues affect each other. We know a number of you attend AA or NA, as well as other groups to support your recovery, and we encourage you to continue to attend these groups if you find them helpful. The difference in this group is that you will be able to discuss your AIDS issues as well, something you may not feel confortable doing in your other groups. We think that as you help each other in this group, you will be helping yourselves.

The group members accept the invitation and start the problem-swapping process. The role of the leader is to express empathy and to identify the potential themes of concern. In working with substance abusers, as with other areas where denial may be high in the initial stage, it was important for the leaders to accept member's perceptions of their problems. Prochaska and DiClimente (1982) have identified stages in the change process that can be seen in the members' reponses. At least one, Kerry, appears to be in the "precomtemplation stage" while others in the group are either in the "contemplation" or "action" stages.

Jake jumped in and said he wanted to tell a story about what had happened over the weekend. He had gone home to visit his family in another town in the state. He said, "I couldn't stay. They started to make me crazy right away. Everyone there was drinking and drugging, and I knew, if I stayed, they would pull me in, and I can't let them pull me in. I have to fight that. I know I can't control this. If I take one drink or use drugs once, I'm going to be back to going into the bar at eight in the morning and staying right through until 2 A.M. drinking myself to death."

I said that it sounded like, in addition to giving up the drinking and drugging, he was also having to give up his family. He agreed. Kerry said that he had been in a bar in the last week and had two drinks. He said, "I can handle that. Just because I have two drinks doesn't mean I am going to go back to where I was a year ago. I know you people are going to say I am in denial, but it's not true. I know I can handle this." John, my co-leader, said that we had to understand recovery was different for each person and we had to make room in the group for people to feel safe and not defensive as they described their own ways of handling their recovery. I nodded in agreement. The rest of the group did as well.

Theresa jumped in at that point and said that she was not living at this residence. She was living in a single room occupancy building two blocks away. She said that most of the people in that building were active users and, for her, it was a fight every day to make sure that she didn't get pulled in. She said that she knew that she didn't want to go back to all the drinking and drugging she was doing. She told us that she had gotten out of the penitentiary after a five-year sentence, and that in the penitentiary she had dried out and learned not to use. She said that she didn't want to go back to when she hated herself and she would spend her time on street corners "sucking old men's dicks" in order to get enough money for a shot of crack. Tania agreed and said that, when she thought of some of the things she did for the ten-year period that she was drinking and drugging all the time, she couldn't believe she actually let herself do those things. Theresa said, "I still have to deal with the housing, even though I am not in this residence; but I know the real question is how we deal with ourselves. For me, religion has been the answer."

In addition to clarifying purpose and role and reaching for client feedback, it is important to address the group members' concern about the leaders—what has been called the authority theme and the related issue of confidentiality. In the excerpt that follows from the same group, the group leader uses his tuning in to respond directly to an indirect communication related to the question "Who is this group leader and what kind of person is he/she going to be?" The issue is raised indirectly by Tania at the end of the session.

Tania went on about all the holiday parties that were going on, and how difficult it was for her to party. She said, "I don't know how to party without first drinking and drugging. As I looked at the people at this party I attended last week, through clean and sober eyes, I said, My God, was this me? Was this the way I lived my life? I left the party when they started passing around the cocaine, because, if I had stayed, I might have given in." (Tania was only one month into her recovery and still obviously very shaky.) She commented, "I know you all know what I'm talking about, since you're in recovery as well, although I don't know about them" (pointing toward us).

I decided to use this as an opportunity to address the authority theme and to review the limits of confidentiality. I pointed out that Tania had mentioned a couple of times her concern about confidentiality and had alsoindirectly raised the question whether we were in recovery. I said that I would have to speak for myself.

"I'm not in recovery, so I am an outsider." I went on to say that I thought the issue of trust with myself and John was a major one for them today, and they were worried about whether an "outsider" like myself could understand and were concerned about what we might share outside of the group. I pointed out that, for three of them, they were concerned that we might divulge information that would affect their ability to continue in a clean and sober residence. They agreed that they wanted to hold onto their apartments, which were the best of this type available to people with AIDS in the city.

I told them that I was a social worker and that I taught social work at the university. I told them I had asked John and AIDS Action if it were possible for me to co-lead this group because I thought it was important that as a teacher I continued to work directly with people. Tania exploded and said, "I thought you were a narc." I laughed and said, "A narc? You mean I look like a narcotics detective?" She continued: "I thought you were just going to sit there, take notes, and, right after this session, you were going to march me off to the police station and that I'd be arrested." I laughed again and said, "Look (holding my sweater up), no wire and no badge." They all laughed. I said, "I'm not a narc, but it's going to take a while for you to really believe and trust that we will keep what you raise here confidential, except for those conditions we mentioned earlier . . . if you are involved in illegal activity in the house, such as selling dope, or if you are danger to yourself or to others. I'm hoping we can earn your trust." Their heads were nodding in agreement.

My co-leader John asked the members of the group if they were ready to sign an agreement we had discussed about such issues as attendance and confidentiality. They said they were ready, and I said, "Maybe we should sign as well."

The issue of the role of the social worker in dealing with the "second client," the agency or institution that provides a setting for the group, is illustrated in a second example. Berman-Rossi, in her work with a group of institutionalized aged (chapter 19), tries to explain how she will play the mediating role between the residents and the staff:

In the midst of a heated discussion of their relationship with some nursing staff members, Mrs. Mann said she thought I should go and tell them off for them. Mrs. Rosen said she didn't agree, because, if I did, the staff would never listen to me again. They would think I was on the residents' side. There was a hush, and Mrs. Mann looked at me and said, "Aren't you on our side? Don't you agree with us?" I said that I thought she was asking an important question. I said that, actually, I thought I was on neither side, but rather on the side of working out the troubles between them and nursing. To do that, I had to have a special relationship with each, where each knew I was listening to them while not siding with the other. Mrs. Mann thought and said, "That's pretty tricky." I said I agreed. I thought she had put her finger on what was the hardest part of being a social worker—listening hard to both sides in a conflict, siding with neither, while working in the middle to help with the conflict between them. Mrs. Mann winked at me, smiled, and said, "But you really know we are right." We all laughed. I let the comment go as I recalled staff making a similar bid for my allegiance. We moved on to thinking through the next steps in their work with nursing staff.

In the third and final example, the issue of authority and the mandatory nature of a group is dealt with directly by Trimble as part of his opening statement to a group of male batterers (chapter 13), most of whom have been forced to come to the group by a judge or through the threat of losing their marriages. While not evading his authority or soft-pedaling the demands he will place on the men, he still demonstrates sensitivity to the underlying issue of control in their lives:

Leader (after explaining attendance rules and expectations of participation of members, as well as the mandatory reporting role of the group leader): I'm sure it is possible to follow all these rules and not change, not open up to facing yourself or the other men here. You can probably get through this group and not really change. That's up to you. The judge may order you to be here or your wife may be saying that she won't come back unless you get help. As I said, we require your participation and regular attendance in order for you to stay here, but no one can reach into your mind and heart and order a change. That's where you have complete control.

The Work Phase

Describing the skills of the group worker using the phases of work to organize the discussion can be misleading. In many ways these skills cross boundaries and are important in every phase of work. Even phase-related skills, such as the contracting skills, become important again at crucial points in the life of the group. For example, contracts are renegotiated to reflect the changing nature of the group process. The use of time as a backdrop to the discussion is a somewhat artificial device; however, it can be helpful in partializing a complex process.

In the work phase, sometimes referred to as the middle or ongoing phase, the general goal of the worker is to help the group develop an effective mutual aid system. The worker recognizes that effective contracting is crucial for laying the foundations of a good working group. However, it is only the beginning. The worker's task is not completed with contracting. He or she must be an active participant in the process of helping the group members and the group as a whole overcome the barriers to effective work that are inherent in any small group system.

The idea of expecting things to go wrong in the group is a crucial one, especially for those new to group work who tend to take total responsibility for the process. If the group could work effectively on its own, the group leader would not be needed. While groups vary from those that are immature (where members are unable to see their connections, much less work on them), to those that are more mature working groups (where members can freely share more difficult and taboo feelings, to reach out and offer direct support and help), most groups need the worker's help to become more efficient mutual aid systems. When there is a problem in the group, the work seems to stop, members turn away from each other, and the group regresses; the group leader is not failing,rather the group is giving signals to the leader that it needs intervention. Assistance is required to help the group cope with the many different ways in which the mutual aid process can and will be sidetracked during the life of the group. As group leaders increase their sense of competency, the obstacles become less threatening. The worker's energy is then free to invest in his or her tasks designed to help the group members take increasing responsibility for their work.

This chapter is too short to allow for a full discussion of the dynamics and skills of this phase of work. In an oversimplified summary, however, the major goals of the leader in the work phase are to help the individual group members reach out for help from the group as a whole, to help the group members provide mutual aid to others (thus helping themselves), and to help the group as a whole pay attention to its own developmental tasks, such as developing a consensus on the directions of work and the development of a climate of trust.

For the reasons cited in the discussion of the preliminary phase, group members will reach out for help with some ambivalence. They may raise their concerns and then deny they have them. They may hint at serious problems by sharing problems that are safer to discuss. They will share their anger, often directing it at group members or the leader, while trying simultaneously to hide and reveal the deep hurts just below the surface. Since they cannot get help unless the group understands their true feelings, a third force, the group leader, must concentrate on helping the individual reach out to the group even at those times when she or he appears to be turning away.

The group worker in the mutual aid model has a unique responsibility in that he or she always has "two clients." The first is the individual member and the second is the group as a whole. Thus, at precisely the same time that the leader is emotionally with the individual, she or he must also be able to identify with the second client, the group.

This function is illustrated when an individual raises painful feelings that are shared by group members. It is not uncommon for the group to seem to turn away from the member, ignore the offering, change the subject, rush in to provide premature and artificial reassurances (such as, "Don't worry, you'll get over it") or even attack the member. If the group leader identifies with the member, for example by siding with or protecting him, then the leader will miss communications from group members on their feelings related to the issue. In this specific example, the mediating function calls for the leader to search out the common ground between the two clients. For example, "You all seem to be angry at Frank right now for feeling helpless and hopeless, and yet isn't that what you have all felt yourselves from time to time? It must be hard for you to hear it from Frank."

In the third general area of work the group leader needs to educate the group as a whole as to how it will operate and must help it to develop the structures it requires to work more effectively. For example, in my married couples groups the first direct issue in the sexual area often comes at the "doorknob" as members are ready to leave. This, of course, makes it hard to deal with the subject and serves to protect the member raising it. A discussion of why it is difficult to talk about sex and raised so often at the end of the session may help the group to develop a more open culture for work in this area, with more accepting norms of behavior and a greater ability to deal with taboo subjects. Members who are made aware of their tendency to raise issues at the end may become members who have the courage to raise them more directly at the start. A group that acknowledges its dependency on trust, honesty, and a willingness to risk will work on creating conditions that support and even demand such behavior on the part of members.

Important skills for group leaders as they carry out this mediating function and work on these three major tasks include the following: sessional tuning in, sessional contracting, elaborating, empathic, sharing worker's feelings, demand for work, pointing out obstacles; sharing data, and sessional ending. These skill groupings will be discussed and illustrated in the balance of this section.

SESSIONAL TUNING IN

Sessional tuning in is similar to the general tuning in described earlier. In this case it is the preparatory empathy the worker endeavors to develop before each group meeting. In some cases the events of the group session itself can be used to deepen one's feelings for the work, as illustrated in this excerpt from Berman-Rossi's work with the institutionalized aged (chapter 19).

Many years ago, at the end of my first group meeting with older persons (average age eighty-four), I said to the members that I would see them next week. Mrs. Gross rose slowly, turned, looked at me, and said, "God willing." She slowly continued walking. I was stunned. Could it mean that she did not know from week to week whether she would be alive? What was it like to live with the reality that life might end at any instant? I was only twenty-nine years old and had just given birth to my first daughter. I could hardly grasp the meaning of what had just occurred between us. It would be a while before I understood how this incident would affect our work together, individually, and in the group.

At other times it may be the worker's awareness of events that take place in the life of group members between meetings that activates the tuning in process. For example, Orr, writing about her work with the elderly in a community setting (chapter 18), describes her attempts to put herself in her group members' shoes after hearing about the death of a member.

Worker (*putting herself in her group members' place and carrying on a form of internal dialogue*): It really hits hard when a member of the group dies; it hits so close to home. I could be next. So Maddie died; I'll hear about two more people soon; you know they always happen in threes. It's not just Maddie. Maddie's death reminds me of when my closest friend died, not so long ago. It makes me go back to when I lost a husband. That was so terribly difficult for me. Whenever someone else dies, I remember how long it took me to get over it. You never get over a death of someone that close to you. Maddie's husband will certainly have a hard time. He was devoted to her. That's how it was with my husband. It makes you feel so empty, like the world's caving in . . . like there is no way of knowing when your time is up.

As Orr skillfully demonstrates in her description of the meeting that followed this tuning-in exercise, her preparation helped her to hear the indirect cues of many of these concerns and, in turn, made it possible for her to help her elderly members deal with them.

Sessional Contracting

It was earlier suggested that the phases of work could be used to understand each individual group session. Thus each meeting has a beginning phase in which the central task is to identify what the individual members, or the group as a whole, will work on in that session. Because of the many indirect ways in which individuals and the group itself may raise issues, the worker must be tentative in the first part of each session, listening carefully to pick up the often difficult to perceive thread of the current theme of concern. Therefore it is important for the worker not to latch onto a concern too quickly until he or she really knows what the group is working on. Even if the group members had all agreed on an agenda at the previous meeting, events between sessions can often change their current sense of urgency.

The assumption underlying sessional contracting is that the agenda for work emerges from the sense of urgency felt by the members and that the group leader's task is not to select the agenda but rather to help the members identify the issues they need and want to work on. That does not mean that the worker never raises an issue for discussion. Some items may be raised because the agency structure requires the group to pay some attention to them (for example, a change in agency policy). In other cases the worker may be aware of an important event in the lives of the members and, rather than waiting for the group to deal with it, the worker may tackle it directly.

Elaborating Skills

The elaboration skills are those used by the worker to help the client tell her or his story. These same skills are important in individual counseling, with the difference in the group context that the member is helped to talk to the other members. Thus, as the worker helps the individual to elaborate, he or she simultaneously encourages intermember communications.

In order to implement these elaborating skills, the worker must first demonstrate the skill of containment. Simply put, the worker keeps quiet as the member speaks and contains the impulse to jump in with solutions, interpretations, a change of subject, and so on. This skill appears to be a passive one; however, in reality, the temptation to take over the session and to "help" can be so powerful that I view containment as an active skill.

As the worker contains her or himself, the skill of focused listening is important. Focused listening involves listening while keeping in mind both the purpose of the group and the tuning-in exercises. All conversation, even the premeeting chatter that often precedes the official start of the meeting, can be understood as potential indirect communications to the worker and the group. Not only is conversation important, but action (such as a nervous new member spilling a cup of coffee) and nonverbal cues (depressed expressions, arms folded with face flushed—apparently signaling resistance) can be significant cues to the underlying communications. In one example, used later in this section, an empty chair in the circle signals the group members' need to talk about a member who died during the week. While focused listening is important in all counseling, once again, the group variation emerges from the "two client" idea; the worker must listen to the individual members and to the group as a whole.

Another skill useful in helping the client tell the story is the skill of questioning. The worker seeks to help the member elaborate on the question, statement, problem, conflict, or incident. For example, take the following seemingly simple question asked in an adoption group: "How do you tell your child he was adopted?" The worker who does not use containment and instead uses the question as an opening for a prepared lecture on the "right" way to handle this difficult question may miss the real issue. Instead, by asking the member to speak some more, to explain why he or she is raising the question right now or to explain why the question is troubling the worker may yield a number of difficult (themes of) concerns that go beyond the simple phrasing of an answer to an adopted child. Often, it is not the adoptive child's feelings about the adoption that are at issue but rather those of the adopting parents: "Will I be able to handle the stresses of raising such a child?" "Can we love this child as one of our own?" "Will this child still love us or want to find his or her real parents?" In effect, the worker and the group need to know much more about the question before they can provide meaningful answers.

Often, indirect communications are most evident when the subject is taboo. In those cases, a strategy that helps the members discuss taboo subjects is needed. The taboo subject of the following example is the anger felt by young adult women survivors of sexual abuse. In this excerpt from the start of the second session, the anger against the perpetrators emerges first, followed by the more difficult feelings of anger against the nonoffending parent, and finally the fears shared by all that they have already or may yet "annihilate" or "lose" their families. Many of the skills cited in this section thus far are illustrated in the process recording as the group leaders, Schiller and Zimmer (chapter 11), identify the "sessional contract," encourage elaboration of these feelings, provide empathic responses, and then confront the members to convert their anger as "victims" to the anger of "survivors."

> ANDREA: I've been really angry ever since last week's group. I'm so sick of being in therapy and having to talk endlessly about this abuse. What if it doesn't help? I swear, I'm going to sue my therapists if I'm not better by the end of therapy.
> BECKY: I can really relate to that. I've been in a rage. It feels like some entity inside me. As I named my perpetrators here in this group, I heard myself for the first time. And I thought, "Oh my god, those animals."
> CARMEN: Well, this may sound strange, but I've been really happy since last week. I felt so "given to" by each of you and so good about myself that I was finally "giving myself" the group I've wanted. But this group is so great and my individual therapist isn't measuring up anymore. Actually I've been really angry at her for not being an expert on this like Bonnie and Linda. I feel safe here, but I'm furious with her for not having what I need now.
> WORKER: It's clear that group is already having a powerful impact for many of you and that hearing and talking about your abuse is eliciting a flood of powerful feelings. (*Notices Sally in silent distress.*) Sally, I want to check in with you and see how you are.

SALLY (*bursts into tears*): I'm so jealous of all of you. I've never gotten angry. I need to get angry but I can't! What if I never get angry?

WORKER: Can you name what it is that keeps you from getting angry?

SALLY: If I get angry at him, I'll lose my whole family (*more tears*).

CARMEN: Boy, I understand that one! I feel responsible for annihilating my family.

JO: I'm afraid of losing my family, too. I really relate to your fears around that.

SALLY: Yeah, thanks. That's good to know. As I'm sitting here I realize I can get angry at one person. I'm really mad at my mother for just standing by. She should have protected me. I call her the "psycho bitch from hell" (*murmurs and head nodding all around*).

WORKER: We believe all your anger is justified and powerful and righteous. You had your rights taken away and you were left unprotected. You are entitled to feel angry about both those feelings. There are lots of different forms of anger. Some make us feel helpless and some make us feel powerful. As we move along in this group, we hope you will each discover a way to move out of the kind of anger that feels helpless and impotent (the anger of the victim) into a powerful, righteous anger (the anger of the survivor). This is something we will undoubtedly come back to again and again. You have lots to give one another from your varied yet similar experiences.

The first "offering" of the (theme of) concern was raised by Andrea as she challenged the value of therapists. In some ways she is also challenging the value of this group and indirectly raising her (and the group's) anger against adult women who do not help them. The second offering comes from Sally, through her silence and her nonverbal signals. As the worker skillfully reached for Sally's feelings, she reveals the depth of pain under the anger and the fears that make it difficult for her to experience her feelings.

The silence on Sally's part, in response to the members' expression of anger, raises another important set of elaborating skills: the skills of exploring silences. Silences in group meetings can be stressful for workers. They often feel something may have gone wrong and have a difficult time containing themselves. Actually, as in this preceding example, the silence meant that the work had been going well. In one of my early studies of practice skill (Shulman, 1978b, 1981), we analyzed 120 hours of videotaped social work practice, half with individuals and half with groups. Employing a categorized observation system developed in the project, we were able to identify and code interactions at three-second intervals and then analyze these numeric patterns by computer. Most often, when faced with three seconds or more of silence, the worker changed the subject. Silences were clearly uncomfortable for the workers. Helpful skills in exploring silences include remaining silent in the fact of silence and reaching inside the silence.

Remaining silent in the face of silence simply means respecting the quiet in the group. If emotions are being felt, the worker allows the members time to feel them while trying to connect to her or his own feelings. If it's a thoughtful silence, time to think can help. It is important that the silence not go on too long, since it could easily turn into a battle of wills as worker and group members each wait for the other to speak. At those moments exploring the silence might be attempted by saying, "You're quiet now. What are you thinking?" or "Are your feelings hitting you hard right now?" or "You are all so quiet right now. What's going on?" If the worker can sense the feeling under the silence, it can be helpful simply to articulate it.

The final elaborating skill, a crucial one in all counseling situations, involves reaching from the general to the specific. Group members often raise specific concerns through overly general questions or comments. For example, "Men are harder to deal with these days" may really be "My husband and I had a terrible fight last night, and I think he is ready to walk out." The skilled worker will encourage the group member to be specific in response to general comments, to the point of asking for the specific conversation of the fight: "What did he say to you?" "What did you say back?" "How did you feel when he said that?" It is only in the particulars of the situation that the group members can be helpful to the individual raising the example and at the same time be helpful to themselves.

Empathic Skills

The empathic skills are those through which the worker communicates to the group members her or his capacity to experience their feelings. These include reaching for feelings, acknowledging feelings, and articulating feelings. In reaching for a group member's (or the group's) feelings, the worker is asking for the affect associated with the information. For example, "How did it make you feel when your son said that to you?" Acknowledging feelings requires the worker to communicate her or his understanding of feelings already expressed by the members. The skill of articulating feelings involves expressing the unstated affect about one half a step ahead of the client. For example:

> GROUP MEMBER: I was furious at my daughter when she responded that way to me.
> WORKER: You must have felt really hurt and unappreciated.

Before illustrating these skills, it is important to deal with a number of issues associated with the use of the empathic skills. First, it is crucial that the expression by the group leader be genuine. That is, the leader must really be feeling something when he or she expresses empathy. The emergence of prescriptive training programs that appear to encourage artificial responses to clients without the worker genuinely experiencing the affect is a serious problem for the profession. Clients see workers who mechanically echo them as artificial. For example:

CLIENT: I am really angry at that kid.
WORKER: You are really angry at that kid.

Commonly used expressions, such as "I hear you saying," when used by the worker ritualistically without affect, will also come across to group members as phony. The major problem with these more mechanical approaches is not the words themselves. I have heard very skillful workers use the phrase "I hear you saying," and, because they are really feeling the emotions, they came through to the group members as genuinely caring. The problem is evident when the words or expressions become a substitute for the much more difficult task of really feeling with our clients.

For beginning workers who are leading their first groups, it is very understandable that the only thing they may feel in their first meetings is their knees knocking. That is why it is so important to incorporate into the idea of skillful work catching one's mistakes as soon as possible. As workers become more comfortable with affect, their own and that of their group members, each group meeting will teach the worker more about the group members' lives. The workers' capacity for genuine empathy will grow not only in the professional context but in their personal lives as well.

The second major issue relates to the reasons for dealing with affect. Why inquire about feelings in the first place? It is not uncommon for workers who involve themselves in the feelings of the group and who empathize with their clients to be stuck for words when I ask them why they are interested. One responded: "Because I'm a social worker." That answer is not good enough.

There are three major reasons why affect is important in our work. First, the worker's capacity to empathize with the group members contributes to the development of a positive working relationship. Group members who perceive that a worker is trying to be "with them" will have a greater degree of trust in the worker and will be more likely to risk difficult feelings. They will not experience the worker as judging them harshly. Nonjudgmental acceptance by the worker creates the conditions that help group members to lower their defenses. By articulating even the most taboo feelings, the worker sets the stage so that group members know that when they are ready to deal with these feelings the worker will also be ready.

This fund of positive feelings between the group members and the worker then allows the worker to make a demand for work on the group, a form of confrontation in which the worker insists the group invest work with meaning and not tolerate its illusion. These concepts, the illusion of work and the demand for work, are discussed in the next section. For now the important point is that a worker must express caring through empathy before he or she can confront and demand.

The second major reason that affect is important has to do with the way in which the group leader models her or his beliefs about how one relates to other people. Schwartz (1961) described this as part of the task of "lending a vision." When group members observe the worker as a caring, supportive, and yet at times demanding person, they are free to experiment and adopt some of these qualities in their relationship to each other and to others who are important in their lives. This "vision" is shared by example, not subtly or directly imposed upon the members by the worker. They are free to use the worker as a model if they wish.

Finally, feelings must be dealt with in pursuit of purpose. There is a connection between how we feel and how we act, what I call the "feeling-doing" connection. Group leaders are always looking for the often subtle connections between the clients' emotions and their actions in order to help the clients understand and deal with the feelings. For example, a foster adolescent who has been rejected by his own parents and has been through a number of group homes and foster parents could well begin to feel he has no value as a person. This lack of self-esteem easily translates into activities that confirm the judgment (such as drug use, criminal activities, prostitution). The deepening sense of depression and low self-judgment can lead to self-destructive behavior. Understanding this vicious cycle can be the start of breaking it, and, as the group member begins to cope more effectively with his feelings and takes some small steps to change his life, positive responses to these steps strengthen self-esteem, allowing further positive action. The foster adolescent's feelings of low self-esteem are dealt with in pursuit of the purpose of the group—to help foster adolescents cope with their problems of living.

In another less dramatic but very common example, we have the foster child who has been rejected often. She or he begins each new alternative care placement assuming the rejection is coming. The inevitable acting out fulfills the prophecy. As one teenager put it, speaking of his relationship with a child care counselor he really liked, "I didn't build it [the relationship] too high because I knew it wasn't a forever place."

The following is an example of the empathic skills drawn from my work with single parents (chapter 17). In this excerpt I reached for the pain under their anger at their former partners, which is experienced by many parents in this situation. Just hearing these feelings expressed by others is a healing process as group members discover they are "all in the same boat" and that their feelings are quite understandable.

As members listen to others describe strong feelings, they may be put in touch with similar feelings within themselves that they have long denied. We can often easily see in other people those things that we have the most difficulty seeing and facing in ourselves. In the following example one member described her frustration at trying to get her ex-spouse to be "more of a dad" for their five-year-old boy. He appeared to reject this boy while at the same time showing his love for the youngest child. I put her feelings into words by articulating how hard it must be on her when the child questions the father's rejection. I also connect feelings to purpose when I inquire as to how she deals with it.

> I told Ginette I thought this must have put her in an awful bind with the child when, for example, he asked her, "When is Daddy going to visit me?" I wondered how she dealt with it. Ginette described her conversation, which indicated she tried to cover up the problem, told "white lies," and did what she could to avoid dealing with the child's feelings. I acknowledged to her, and the group, that I could appreciate the bind she felt.
>
> June, a new member who had been listening quietly all morning, began to speak. She spoke with a low, soft voice, and began to cry before she could complete her comments: "I have been sitting here listening to Ginette thinking that what she is describing is my problem exactly. And now, I think I realize that I'm going to have to face my own rejection by my husband, who walked out on me, before the healing can start . . . and I can help my kids face their rejection."

With deep emotions triggered by Ginette's comment, June moved the whole group into the underlying theme of rejection, beautifully stating the connection between their own need to resolve their feelings and their ability to help their children do the same. As is often the case, group members are moved and concerned by such a strong display of emotion. In my mediating role I tried to help group members release the part of them that wanted to reach out to June but might be embarrassed to do so. Note also how much help is available from members in the group. This is a relief for the worker, who does not have to provide all the help but can concentrate instead on releasing the group's inherent potential for mutual aid.

> We all felt very moved by June's words. I could see the group members were upset. Marie was sitting next to June, and I could tell she was very agitated—looking around the room, looking at June, and literally moving in her seat. I said, "I think June's feelings have hit all of us very hard. I have a feeling you would like to reach out to June, wouldn't you, Marie?" Marie said she really would. When I asked her: "Why don't you?" she said: "Well, I'm afraid to." After a slight pause, she reached over and took June's hand, holding it tightly. June responded warmly to the gesture. I reassured Marie that it was O.K. to share her feelings with us and that her tears were an important part of how she felt. I told her that I felt she spoke for all the group members, and they quickly assured her that I was correct.
>
> We then returned to Ginette and her difficulty in being honest with her children and allowing them to express their feelings. She said, "I want my son to share his feelings within certain guidelines." I responded, "You mean, you want him to share the feelings that are not too tough for you." The group members, including Ginette, laughed in recognition of the point. Ginette admitted she

realized she had to be honest with him. The group members, at my suggestion, agreed to help her role-play the conversation so she could find a supportive way of being honest.

It is important to note how the group, in response to the leader's demand, did not get lost in the feelings of rejection and instead began specific work of how to deal with their children effectively. This is what is meant by the concept already introduced: dealing with feelings in pursuit of purpose. As these parents help their children with their sense of rejection, they will be helping themselves cope with identical feelings. This is another example of the feeling-doing connection.

Sharing Worker's Feeling Skills

Many models of professional practice have suggested the importance of separating the personal self from the professional self. The skillful worker is described as one who is in control at all times. There is an element of truth to this construct. As workers develop, they learn the importance of not judging people against their own personal standards, of not stereotyping people, of not acting out and expressing inappropriate feelings, of not turning the group meeting into a discussion of their own personal problems. However, this is not the same as a process in which workers monitor their feelings and never openly express them. A group leader's spontaneous reactions, including the moments when he or she is angry with group members, can be important contributions to the development of group process.

For the new worker, this appears to pose a paradox that might be expressed as follows: "First he [Shulman] tells me to be honest and spontaneous and then he tells me not to do all the things I probably will do if I follow his advice." The apparent paradox can be resolved by recalling my advice about allowing oneself to make mistakes, to learn from them, and then to make more sophisticated mistakes. I would argue that honesty and spontaneity are central elements to professional practice. The real paradox arises when we tell our group members that they should be open, honest, nondefensive, and ready to risk their most deeply held feelings while at the same time modeling a role as group leader in which we do just the opposite. As helping professionals, we need to learn to trust our feelings and to use them to implement our helping function.

If workers wait until they are certain they are going to say exactly the right thing, they will never say anything at the right time. Thus they have to be willing to risk making mistakes and be prepared to apologize to their clients if they are wrong. The image workers will then project is not one of the all-knowing group leaders who have life's problems worked out, who are always in control and never make mistakes, but rather that of real human beings who more closely resemble their clients. It is a great relief to group members to see that the worker is not a paragon of virtue. Also, workers can model for clients the very skills they are helping them to develop in their interpersonal relationships (the "lending a vision" task).

If group leaders sit on their feelings and churn away inside while pretending to be calm, the energy they need to invest in the lives of the group members, to feel their feelings, will simply not be available. Thus the task workers need to work on all during their work lives is how to synthesize personal and professional selves, not how to split them into two artificially separate entities. For example, I often have participants in workshops describe a problem with a group or group members, which is a common middle or work phase issue. The group has begun well, developed a clear working contract, but now seems to be doing a "dance," an illusion of work. The group leader has been supportive for weeks, has genuinely expressed empathy for the group members' dilemmas; however, she or he gets a very strong feeling that the group is resisting taking the next step, perhaps not taking responsibility for their own part in their problems. When I ask what the worker is feeling, it is often frustration and anger at the group members, feelings generated because the worker really does care for these clients. When I ask if she or he has let the group know these feelings, the worker often looks shocked and says: "But that wouldn't be professional."

I would argue that it would be very professional indeed and, as will be discussed in the next section, that this kind of confrontation (a form of demand for work) may be just what the group members need at the moment. Close analysis of the worker's feelings often reveals that the worker is simply afraid to take the risk. When group leaders say, "But is the group ready for that?" they often really mean, "Am I ready for that?"

In a study of social work practice skill (Shulman 1978b, 1981), I found that the capacity to share thoughts and feelings honestly was one of the highest correlating skills with developing a good working relationship and with helping effectively (as judged by clients). These findings were replicated in my studies of supervision and medical practice.

It is not only the angry feelings that need to be shared openly. Often group leaders can be as moved as the members by the work of the group. In my own groups I have found myself in tears in response to strong emotions expressed by group members. Group members did not see this as weakness. They interpreted my strong emotions as a gift to them of my willingness to experience their feelings. Other group leaders communicate this gift differently, through respectful silence, an arm on the shoulder, facial expressions; there is much room for individual difference and style. The important point is that the group leader's feelings are shared when appropriate to the work of the group, to implement the leader's professional function.

Workers often fear they may be immobilized by their feelings. For example, they fear they will feel as hopeless as a client about a problem and therefore not be able to help. In one example a group member described the experience of learning that her young husband had a terminal illness. As she spoke she cried, and the worker as well as the group members cried with her. There would be time later for the "demand for work" that would help this woman address the many issues she needed to deal with (such as telling the children, supporting her husband, obtaining support for herself). At the moment, however, the gift of sharing in the feelings was what was needed and what was helpful.

In the following example Orr helps a group of blind senior citizens face the death of one of their group members (chapter 18). At one point, they talk about all the losses they have experienced, and one of the members suggests that they stand for a moment of silence.

> (*Silence.*) WORKER (*speaking of the dead member*): I guess what's always most difficult for me is when I feel there was no closure, that I didn't have a chance to say goodbye, and a feeling that I've been deprived of having that person with me longer.
>
> TESSIE: That's what hurts so much about Maddie, that I tried and tried to call and couldn't get through. They didn't know I was calling. That's what I feel deprived of, making sure that she knew I cared.
>
> ALLEN: But you've called so many times while she was sick. She knew you cared.

THE DEMAND FOR WORK (FACILITATIVE CONFRONTATION)

Reviewing the helping skills discussed thus far, we see a premium placed upon preparation (tuning in), on clarifying a working contract to provide a structure for work, on skillful sessional contracting and elaboration skills designed to help the clients tell their story, and on the empathic skills and sharing of one's own feelings designed to invest the work with affective substance and strengthen the worker-member and member-member relationships. While all these skills and processes are necessary in setting the stage for work, another essential dynamic must be introduced, the dynamic embodied in what Schwartz (1961) termed the demand for work.

This process becomes clearer if one considers ambivalence to be central to all human change processes. A part of us wishes to move ahead, to grow, challenge life, confront difficult tasks, be responsible, and so on. Another part of each of us fears such changes, does not want to take risks, is hesitant to experience painful emotions, feels deeply responsible for our own problems, and thus sets up elaborate defenses to deny responsibility and blame others. For some, depending upon many personal, historical, and socioeconomic factors, the forces for change may be stronger or the forces of resistance may dominate. As helping professionals, our work involves engaging these forces in our clients. We must understand and have compassion for the forces that block change, synthesizing this support with a continuous expression of our belief in the client's strength for change, however faint it may be. The many skills contained in making a demand for work are found in the way in which the group leader puts this basic assumption of client strength into action.

For example, consider an employment group leader working with middle-aged women whose children have grown up. The women have expressed a desire to find a job and become financially independent. The group focuses on job-finding skills (résumé writing, interview skills, and so on), and a number of possible positions are identified. Suddenly the worker perceives resistance to the idea of applying for a new job. Upset that the group members are not taking up the opportunity with gusto and in fact seem to be finding superficial reasons to avoid it, the worker pressures them and then is disappointed when they miss or "blow" the arranged interviews. After all, jobs are difficult to find in this economy, and the worker is rated on how many of these women she can place.

In her eagerness to accomplish her task, the worker loses sight of the process. She is so anxious to do something for the women that, when she perceives the resistance, she is upset by it and tries to override it using exhortation as a major tool. If, instead of being upset by the resistance, she could have been guided by the understanding that resistance is part of the work, she could have tuned in to the part of the group members' natural fears and concern that led to the ambivalence and then offered them support. The resistance was a signal to the worker not that the group was going badly but that the group was going well.

She was at a crucial point in her work, when these women had to face what could be termed the second decision about changing their life status from home-maker to employed person. The first decision, coming to the group, was the easier one to make. Now that the real crisis was imminent, the group members would need all the help they could get from the worker and each other.

The skill of exploring the resistance would be one way in which the worker could make a demand for work. The general and superficial discussion about going to an interview and getting a job was an example of the illusion of work in which the real fears, anxieties, and questions are left for the bus ride home: "Am I still competent after so many years at home?" "Can I compete with younger women who have all these new skills I know nothing about?" "Are my kids really old enough for me to work? Ever since I started this program Jane is regressing—having trouble at school—is it too soon for her?" "Everyone else in the group seems so confident, so competent. The worker keeps telling us we can do it, but in my heart, I'm scared stiff." "Before we split up, my husband told me for years that all I was good for was housework and raising kids. Maybe he was right."

Workers often sense the "lurking negatives" and ambivalences under the surface in their groups. However, they fear their power and try to override the negatives with the thought "If I can just push them through, they will be all right." Actually, the negatives that remain below the surface have all the power. When brought to light in a mutual aid group, they often lose their ability to block growth and change. The all-in-the-same-boat phenomenon helps people put their feelings into better perspective. In addition, hearing how others have overcome a similar problem, having group members challenge others' own low estimation (for example, "It's funny to hear you say you were afraid you couldn't make it in the work world. I've been sitting here for weeks thinking how strong you seem.") These and other supportive forces can be brought into play if the group leader understands and works with resistance rather than avoiding it. In fact, if the resistance is not evident (for example, of everyone agrees it will be a piece of cake to go to the interviews), the smart leader would be wise to look for trouble when everything is going his or her way. In this example, it might sound like this:

> WORKER: You know it's great to hear your enthusiasm about the job interviews. However, you have been out of the work field for a long time. I wonder if, in addition to your enthusiasm, there aren't also some doubts and concerns. You know, for example, "Do I still have it to compete out there after fifteen years of diapers and car pools?"

Ambivalence and resistance are very much a part of the life of the group as well as its individual members. Thus the illusion of work in a group may be a signal of the collective hesitation about entering a difficult or taboo subject area. Once again, the skillful leader must provide a subtle blend of support and demand as he or she helps this second client, the group, to identify the obstacles blocking effective work and to deal with them. In many ways a group can be seen as more or less sophisticated in its ability to work effectively. Part of the group leader's responsibility is to help the group's individual members and the group as a whole to mature. In an example from Knight's work with male and female survivors of sexual abuse (chapter 12), we see a member in an individual session raising his difficulty in sharing particularly painful and embarrassing information about his maladaptive way of dealing with his abuse. With the group leader's help, he brings the disclosure to the group and, by doing so, changes the group culture for the other members.

> George was a fairly silent member of the group. He was the youngest member, had less experience with therapy, and was socially quite awkward. Although his abuse experiences were similar to others in the group, he often said he felt uncomfortable and different from them. After one session George asked me if he could talk with me. With great hesitancy and embarrassment, he said he was worried about himself, found himself doing "weird shit" to himself. When pressed, he told me he had been getting angrier and angrier over the last several weeks and that the only thing that was helping him to release the anger was to watch pornography that featured anal sex while sodomizing himself with the handle of

a large hairbrush. George began crying as he shared this with me, saying he was embarrassed by this but couldn't stop it. I credited George for being able to tell me, acknowledging that it might have been particularly hard because I was a woman. I also reminded him that I saw my job as one of helping him tell the group what he had shared with me, and, while he was understandably reluctant to do this, saying, "They'll think I'm really fucked up," he also admitted that he wanted to be able to talk about it, because he didn't like the feeling that somehow he "deserved to be fucked." We then talked about how I could be helpful to him in disclosing his "secret" to the group.

George agreed to come the following week, and I called him before the next session to make sure that he wasn't going to "chicken out." I began the group as I always did, by summarizing my sense of the previous session. I then said that George had talked with me after the last session and had something he really needed to talk with the members about. As George and I had agreed, I began the conversation by saying that I sensed the group was bringing up a lot of anger for members and that anger was a really difficult emotion for survivors to manage, that survivors often turned it inward against themselves. I also said that my sense was that what George needed to talk about was related to this as well as to the confusion that he and others in the group felt about sex and their sexuality. At that point George began to talk about his behavior. Members listened intently, nodding their heads in agreement. The first to respond was Sally, who said, "I can only get off if the guy is hurting me, like biting me or something." Another man reported, "Things are so bad between me and my girlfriend now that I can't even get it up anymore. My girlfriend wants to have sex and I just can't. But when I go to an S/M bar and get picked up and fucked up the ass I get all excited. I must be sick or something." Another woman revealed that as an adolescent she had posed for a variety of hardcore pornographic photos and still had the photos and "got off" by looking at herself.

Once again the synthesis of content (the substance of the work) and process (the way of working) is clear. As the worker explores the resistance expressed through Goerge's reluctance to disclose, she helps the whole group move into a formerly taboo area of discussion. By helping the group understand the barriers to disclosure and their resistance (the process), she is able to help them deepen the work on particularly disturbing content. In addition, the other artificial dichotomy, that between the individual and the group, also dissolves as we search out the connection between the one (George) and the many (the group). By addressing George's concern, she is also addressing the concerns of other group members.

In some situations the worker must deal with the group members' apathy about influencing their systems (even the agency employing the worker). For example, in chapter 19 Berman-Rossi tries to help a ward group of senior citizens take responsibility for influencing the dietary department of their long-term care facility. She can make this demand for work, in part, because she has not given up her belief in the ward group's ability to influence the system. For workers such a demand is awkward to continue to press because of their own ambivalent feelings about the systems they work in. It is important for the worker to keep alive a belief in the ability of systems to change through negotiation, mediation, advocacy with social pressure, or whatever means can be helpful.

POINTING OUT OBSTACLES

This skill is a collection of activities in which the worker brings the members' attention to the various obstacles blocking the group's ability to work effectively. Many of the earlier examples illustrated these skills in action. Two themes emerge here that require special attention—the "authority" and the "intimacy" themes in group dynamics. These ideas are drawn from the group dynamics literature, particularly the work of Bennis and Sheppard (1948). Their theories were based on the interactions they observed in T-groups (training groups). While some of their views are probably unique to that type of group, the two central constructs have meaning for all groups. The first is that the group members have to deal, early in the life of the group, with their relationship to the leader— the authority theme.

Many of the central issues have to do with dependency; that is, how dependent will the group members be on the leader? In the model presented here the mutual aid group is seen as having to take responsibility for its own process, with the help of a leader. Since most people bring to the group an image of an all-powerful leader, one who takes responsibility for the work of the group, the leader must teach the group members a new way of thinking about the division of labor between leader and members.

For example, in one of my married couples groups, during a middle-phase session, a couple carried out a prolonged conversation on an issue without ever getting to the point. I noticed the group looking bored, and I asked what was going on. Fran responded by saying it was getting boring and she was waiting for me to do something. Since this was well into the middle phase, I found myself angry that everyone was waiting for me, and I said, "How come you are all waiting for me to do something? This is your group, you know, and I think you can take some responsibility."

The resulting discussion indicated that they felt it was risky to say things like that to each other, so they left it to me. I asked them to talk about what made it risky for them. They discussed their reluctance to embarrass people, their reticence about being critical, their fear of angry reactions, and other similar feelings. We continued to discuss how we could set ground rules about honesty in the group in which they also would take responsibility for helping the group work effectively.

This discussion dealt simultaneously with both the authority theme and the second major driving theme in a group, that of intimacy. The intimacy theme has to do with the way in which the group members deal with each other. Since all group members bring into the group some clearly established norms of "polite" behavior, many of which lead to the obstacles that result in the illusion of work, the leader must help the group members examine these assumptions and develop new and more honest ways of working. Bennis and Sheppard describe the struggle in terms of how "personal" members wish to be with each other. One example would be deciding whether to risk intimate personal details with people who are still strangers. This was illustrated in the previous example with George's hesitation about bringing his concerns to the group. That members learn to trust each other is as important as, and often more difficult than, their learning to trust the worker.

Another way of conceptualizing these ideas is to consider that at any one time the group might be working on their contract (issues of content that bring them together) or on their way of working (the process or interaction). The way of working will break down into two major subthemes: the group member–leader relationship (authority) and the member-member relationship (intimacy). As illustrated earlier, even this division between content and process is artificial, since examination of process issues, for example, the resistance of George and the other group members to talking about taboo areas, often leads us more deeply into the content, in this case the difficulty of coping with the pain and embarrassment of self-abusive behavior.

It is not possible in this section to discuss adequately the major issues of authority and dependency in group process. However, one issue requires some discussion. As the group works, strong feelings toward the group leader, both positive and negative, will be generated. This process is sometimes referred to in individual counseling as "transference." These feelings may be an important source of energy that can help to power the activity of the group. This affect must be discussed at appropriate times. For example, when the group leader makes his or her demands for work, some anger will be generated. This anger is healthy and a normal part of the process. It can be brought out in the open, discussed, understood, and accepted. In fact, if a group is never angry at the leader, there is a good chance that the leader has not pressed hard enough. It's important to acknowledge here the issue of timing and readiness. In the group for sexually abused men and women it would be inappropriate for the leader to push for disclosures when the members are not ready. Survivors who did not have control over what was done to them must feel in control of the process of disclosure.

Alternatively, there will be times when the group members may feel positive affection for the leader, whom they perceive as a caring and nurturing person. In my married couples group, members raise this aspect of the authority theme. One of the members, who had come into the group alone, sat next to me and shared a frightening problem she was facing. She cried during the presentation. The other group members and I tried to comfort her.

Fran said, "I knew this was Jan's night to get help the minute she walked in the door." When I inquired as to how she knew, she said, "Because she sat in the crying chair." She went on to point out that all of the people who had cried in sessions, four of the ten group members, had sat in that chair at the beginning of the session. Other members nodded in recognition. I inquired if they had any thought about why that was so. Rose said, "Because that's the chair next to you, and we sit there to get some support when the going gets rough." I encouraged them to elaborate on what they felt they got from me, since that was also what they probably wanted from each other.

Louise said, "It's because we can feel free to say anything to you, and you won't judge us. We can tell you our feelings." Rose continued, "And we know you really feel our hurt; it's not phony—you really care." Lou said, "It's safe next to you. We can share our innermost feelings and know that you won't let us get hurt." As I listened to the members, I felt myself deeply moved by the affect in their voices, and I shared that with them. "You know, it means a great deal to me to have you feel that way—that you can sense my feelings for you. I have grown to care about you quite a bit. It's surprising to me, sometimes, just how hard things in this group hit me—just how important you have really become."

It is important to recognize that the group members will also generate feelings in the worker. These feelings must also be understood and accepted.

SHARING DATA

Sharing data involves the worker communicating to the group members his or her ideas, facts, beliefs, view of life, biases, and so on. There is much misunderstanding about the use of this skill in group work. At the one extreme there are those who argue that the worker should be neutral, never sharing an opinion that might influence the group members. Self-determination is raised as the sacred value. At one extreme, it is argued that the group leader should clearly establish herself or himself as the "expert" so that the group members are more likely to accept the "right" views. Group leaders who try to be impartial often fall victim to the pressure to influence their clients indirectly. That is, they ask questions designed to lead their group members to the "right" ideas, or they encourage members to provide their ideas, then immediately question the offered viewpoint when it does not conform to the accepted doctrine. Group members quickly suspect that this impartial worker really does have a hidden agenda and redirect their energy to determining what the worker wants them to think or do.

At the other extreme, the worker who tries to use "expert power" to convince group members of the right view makes the mistake of confusing his or her view of life with reality. In the last analysis the worker, no matter how "correct" his or her ideas may be, is only one resource among many. The group members must work to develop their own view of the real world. Assuming the task of making judgments for the group members is futile and, in fact, dangerous, since it is the group members who must live with the result. In fact, as a group leader I would begin to worry when group members appeared to be too dependent upon me for their answers.

The argument made at this point might be that we are always attempting to influence people. That is what effective practice is all about. However, it must be done openly and honestly. The group member should be encouraged to weight the worker's contributions as they weight those made by other group members and by other significant people in their lives. The worker's ideas must be open to challenge and accepted only if they have merit, not because the worker is the expert on life. The other requirement when a worker shares data is that the information be relevant to the work of the group members. Information we think is important for them but is not related to the group members' current sense of urgency will be experienced as a hidden agenda.

I remember my social work student days as a group leader in a community center working with middle-class, white adolescents in a neighborhood undergoing racial tensions between whites and blacks. I would not miss an opportunity to slip in comments encouraging positive racial attitudes, even when such ideas were irrelevant to the group's immediate work. My hidden agenda soon became obvious to the group, and they avoided such comments in my presence. In retrospect I realize, if I had not been so busy trying to preach to the youngsters, that I would have been able to hear the real struggles they were experiencing in relation to this conflict. Coping with parents, a peer group, and others in relation to the race issue was at times of deep concern to them. They needed to discuss these concerns with an adult who could listen and understand their struggles and who would not immediately judge them and lecture them. In my eagerness to teach them my values I lost many opportunities to help them with the complex process of developing values of their own.

Finally, not only does a group leader allow the members to have access to his or her views of the world but the mutual aid concept also calls for the worker to help members tap each other's fund of experience. Each group member is an expert in their own areas of concern. A fundamental form of mutual aid involves freeing the group members to give and take help in this way. In the illustration that follows, drawn from my single parents group (chapter 17), we see members providing specific ideas to a woman who has just discovered that she lost her positive credit rating of twenty-five years when her husband left her. While much may have changed in the area of credit maintenance for women since the time of this group, gender (and race) discrimination still exists. The group members encourage her not to accept this form of gender oppression and, instead, to assert her rights.

Carrie told her [Rose] she had given up too soon. She said that Rose was going to have to assert herself if she wanted to obtain her rights. I asked Carrie how she thought Rose could do this, and she suggested the following plan. She advised Rose to visit the credit bureau and discuss her desire to establish a credit rating. She pointed out that Rose was making monthly payments on a number of bills, for example, rent, telephone, and utilities, and that she could use this to impress the credit bureau with her credit worthiness. She should also speak to the bank manager directly and point out that she had been part of the family that had given his bank all of her business up to that point and that she would like his cooperation in developing a plan to establish a credit rating on her own.

The group members agreed this might be a first step. They also felt that, if she ran into difficulty with this approach, she consider bringing this to the attention of the bank's head office by writing to the president. Another member suggested that she contact the Provincial (British Columbia, Canada) Human Rights Commission, since this actually constituted a form of discrimination. It was obvious that everyone was angry at her situation. Rose agreed she could do more than she had thus far. She said, "I guess I began to believe that they were right about me not having earned a credit rating. It never occurred to me to refuse to accept the decision." Carrie said, "The hard part is understanding that you're going to have to fight for your own rights, because nobody else is going to do it for you."

Sessional Endings and Transitions

The skills required in this subphase are those that help bring a session to a close and make the transition to future events. Future events may be activities of the group member that flow either from the session or from an activity of the group such as moving into a new area of discussion, continuing a theme, or inviting a speaker. An example would be a member trying to open up communications with a boss or a family member after having discussed the problem at the group meeting. Summarizing the discussion is one of these skills. This may or may not involve a formal, point-by-point review of the issues, observations, or decisions. In a community action group, such as a tenants' association, a formal review may be appropriate. In my married couples group a few words at the end to help to articulate the major themes or observations may serve the same purpose (for example, "It seems that all the couples here have put their fingers on how hard it is to talk to each other about sexual matters without becoming defensive").

Another skill that is often useful in the ending subphase of a group meeting is moving from the specific to the general. This is the reverse of the skill discussed earlier—that of moving from the general to the specific. The worker in this instance points out the connections between the particular work of the session and the concerns, issues, or observations that emerged in earlier sessions. For example, continuing with the practice excerpt after I summarized the problem of communicating about sexual issues, I said, "You know, this sounds very similar to the issues we have been discussing thus far. Everytime you describe

how you deal with a sensitive issue such as sexual functioning, sharing responsibilities in the home, or conflicts with the kids, it seems you have all admitted
feeling defensive and guilty, and the conversation with your spouse breaks down
into mutual blaming. It seems to be a common pattern." Thus looking back over
the sessions allows the group members to gain insight and perspective into their
patterns of behavior or responses in particular situations.

Another connected skill would be that of identifying next steps. It is important to articulate what next steps are needed for the individual member or the
group. It is not unusual for this apparently simple step to be overlooked. Most
readers have probably experienced sitting through a committee or staff meeting
during which decisions were made and later discovering that nothing happened
because no one was identified to take responsibility for implementing the action.
Actually, avoiding being specific about the next step can be a subtle form of resistance. It is one thing to decide to confront a difficult problem, perhaps even
role-playing how to handle it, and then quite another actually to do it. When specific next steps are identified, an additional demand is placed on the members to
implement them. In the example of the married couples group, after generalizing
about the communication problem, I said, "Since this issue seems important to
all of you, do you want to begin with it next week? If so, maybe we could look at
some of the things you have discovered thus far about dealing with touchy areas
and then examine how they would apply in this particularly difficult one."

Another useful skill in ending group sessions is one I call the skill of rehearsal.
This involves using the group for a form of role-play in which the member tries
out what she or he will say in an actual conversation outside the group (such as
handling an employment interview). Role-play is a useful group learning device;
however, it is often used in such a formal way that it increases the pressure on the
members. Even the use of the words *role-play* can establish a mindset that increases tension. Setting up special chairs in the middle of the group places the
group members too much "onstage." Compare these formal approaches with the
following excerpt from an employment counseling group for ex-convicts.

> WORKER: It sounds like the job interview has you really worried. No wonder it's
> scary. It's been a while since you've had to face this. You're probably also won-
> dering how you're going to explain the three-year gap in your work record.
> LOU: That's it exactly! What do I say when he asks me where I've been?
> WORKER: Why don't we try it out in advance right here? I'll be the interviewer, and
> I'll ask you questions, and the rest of the group can give you some ideas about
> how you handle the answers. How about it? Is that O.K. with you, Lou, and with
> the rest of you?
> LOU: Well . . . I'll give it a try. (Group members nod.)
> WORKER: Welcome, Mr. Franklin. Why don't you have a seat here and we can talk
> about the job. . . .

The Ending and Transition Phase

The fourth and final phase in the life of the group involves endings and transitions. The endings and transitions of the previous section were sessional in that they applied to each group meeting. In this section I refer to the phase of work in which worker and group members bring to a close their experience together. This phase has its own unique dynamics and skills. First, one often observes a form of denial as a first stage in the process. Members seem to forget the impending ending of the group. To make sure the process begins early enough to have time to discuss the ending and to ensure that the ending is not experienced as abrupt or as a form of rejection, the worker should use the strategy of pointing out the endings early. For example, simply commenting on the number of weeks remaining may set the process in motion. The timing of this strategy depends on how long the group has been meeting. In a short-term, three-session group the worker might comment on the last session at the end of the second meeting. In my married couples group, which lasted nineteen weeks, I reminded the group of the ending the third meeting from the last. Sometimes a signal from the group may trigger the worker's beginning discussion. For example, a comment after a break in the flow of meetings or a session canceled by the worker because of illness may mark the first signs of concern.

A second stage in the ending process often involves the emergence of anger toward the group leader, sometimes expressed indirectly in the form of missed sessions or acting-out behavior in a children's group. The reader may have already noted the parallel between these stages of endings and those described by Kubler-Ross (1969) in her classic work on death and dying. This anger is followed by a period of mourning. This sadness may be expressed through apathy and listlessness at group meetings or through other verbal and nonverbal means. For example, in my married couples group I entered the meeting room at the start of the third from the last session to find the lights still off and the normal premeeting conversation missing. I commented that the room reminded me of a wake, and one of the members responded: "Yes, and it's for this group." As the group moves through the ending phases, the worker can help the members to take control of the process, rather than just letting it happen to them, by using the strategy of identifying the stages.

This approach seeks to avoid the possibility that the group will be so overwhelmed by the ending that it will close down prematurely by withdrawing from meaningful work. Since the ending phase has the possibility of being the most significant time in the work of the group because of the increased urgency brought on by the lack of time, the worker wants to ensure that the ending process does not become an obstacle to what could be the most powerful period of work. For example, in the group of older foster teens who were preparing to leave the care of the child welfare agency, a discussion of the ending process in the group can be directly related to the many endings they have faced both from their families and from foster homes, and of how these experiences make it difficult for them to risk themselves in new relationships.

The next noticeable stage is the one in which the group appears to be trying the ending on for size. In the situation where the group worker is leaving, there may be discussion about the new worker. The worker may notice members trying to cope with problems and demonstrate their abilities to handle things on their own. During the ending of my groups, I found the group members almost ignoring me, eager to work on their own without my intervention and help. The final stage in the process has been described by Schwartz as the "farewell party syndrome." This is the tendency for the group members to avoid the painful feelings of endings by planning a party for the last session or by padding the experience by remembering only the positive aspects of the group, not the problems. Worker's skills I have already identified are important in this phase and include the following: sharing his or her own feelings about the endings (for example, "I wanted you all to know that I'm going to miss you and think about you a great deal"), reaching for the ending feelings of the group members ("You all seem down this week. Are you starting to think about missing the group?"), and reaching for the negative feelings as well as the positive ("It can't always have been the best group you have ever been in. Let's also talk about the meetings that weren't so great").

Just as structure is important in the beginning, it can also be helpful in the ending phase. I usually ask members to prepare for the last session by identifying ideas in the group that have been important to them, areas they still feel they need to work on, the strengths of the group and my leadership as well as the problems with both. Even if the group has gone badly and both the members and the worker are glad to see it end, an honest evaluation may be helpful to both in any future efforts to lead or participate in a mutual aid group.

The last session can be used to summarize the work as the members share their understandings and feelings with each other, completing a process that began in the first session when they shared their concerns in the problem swapping. The sense I hope to convey is not that they have solved all their problems but rather that they have learned something about how to deal with them and how to get help along the way. Transition issues can include the question of where they can get help in the future and how they can use their learning in the group to cope more effectively with the issues that first brought them together. Although the last session may have a more formal ending structure, this process should be viewed as taking place over time.

In the following, Knight working with a group of children dealing with loss (chapter 4), describes how she structures the ending phase of work, and illustrates once again the importance of adapting the work to the particularly population, in this case children.

I use several ending activities to assist members with this transition. I ask members to identify things that they like about themselves and things that they like to do. This activity sends a message that is important for members to hear, which is that it is okay to have fun to feel good about themselves.

Another important activity I use has members think about and describe happy memories associated with their loved one. To facilitate this discussion, in the session before, I suggest that members bring in a photo or other memento of their loved one that makes them smile. It would have been premature to use this activity earlier in the group, since it easily could have blocked members' expressions of grief. Members can only remember the good times if they'd had the opportunity to talk about their pain and sadness.

As in any group members should have the opportunity to provide feedback to the worker about their experience as well as to say goodbye to each other. The leader should expect, however, that members' ability to do this may be limited because of their ages and immaturity. I have found that it often is easier for members to say their goodbyes during our final snack time, which I portray as a farewell party. Typically members are excited about this final time together and with just a little help from me, they are able to discuss the group and what it meant to them. While there is some sadness about ending, the more prevalent mood is one of excitement about and anticipation of the future.

To reinforce the idea that it is OK for members to have fun and move on with their lives, I ask them to pose for two photos, one a "normal" group shot, the other a group shot of them acting and looking "silly." I inform the members that I will send each of them copies of each photo as a way for them to remember their time together and what they learned from one another. When I send the photos I also include a brief note in which I thank each child for coming, identify something unique about her or his participation, and remind her or him of what we talked about.

This chapter has been used to set out a framework for viewing group work practice through the preliminary, beginning, work, and ending and transition phases and to identify some of the core dynamics as well as core worker skills useful in leading groups. It is an effort to describe a methodology for putting the ideas of chapter 1 into action. In the chapters that follow, which are organized according to the stages of the life cycle, these skills will be evident as workers try to help their clients make use of the powerful healing force of mutual aid.

Before we proceed to examples of these skills in action, the crucial issue of group formation needs to be addressed. In the next chapter Gitterman examines some of the pitfalls and strategies central to the process of forming a group.

Note

This chapter is an expanded and updated version of a paper presented at the Jane Addams School of Social Work, Chicago, Illinois, at a 1983 school memorial service for William Schwartz, a former faculty member. For a more complete discussion and a video tape presentation of this group work model see Shulman (1978, 1999). See also Germain and Gitterman (1996).

References

Bennis, W. G. and H. A. Sheppard. 1948. A theory of group development. *Human Relations* 9:415–37.

Germain, C. B. and A. Gitterman 1996. *The life model of social work practice: Advances in theory and practice.* 2d ed. New York: Columbia University Press.

Kubler-Ross, E. 1969. *On death and dying* New York: Macmillan.

Prochaska, J. O. and C. C. DiClimente. 1982. "Transtheoretical therapy": Toward a more integrative model of change. *Psychotherapy: Theory, Research, and Practice* 19:276–88.

Schwartz, W. 1961. The social worker in the group. In *New perspectives on services to groups: Theory, organization, and practice,* pp. 7–34. New York: National Association of Social Workers.

———— 1976. Between client and system: The mediating function. In R. W. Roberts and H. Northen, eds., *Theories of social work with groups,* pp. 44–66. New York: Columbia University Press.

———— 1977. Social group work: The interactionist approach. In *The encyclopedia of social work,* vol. 2. New York: National Association of Social Workers.

Shulman, L. 1978a. *The skills of helping* (a series of three video tape programs) Available from the Instructional Communications Centre, McGill University, Montreal, Quebec and Insight Media, 2162 Broadway, New York, NY 10024-0621 (800 233-9910).

———— 1978b. A study of practice skills. *Social Work* 23:274–81.

———— 1981. *Identifying, measuring and teaching the helping skills.* New York: Council on Social Work Education and the Canadian Association of Schools of Social Work.

———— 1999. *The skills of helping individuals, families, groups, and communities.* 4th ed. Monterey: Brooks/Cole.

Taft, J. 1949. Time as the medium of the helping process. *Jewish Social Service Quarterly* 26:230–43.

Chapter 3

Group Formation
Tasks, Methods, and Skills

Alex Gitterman

WHY DEVELOP group services? Why bring people together in a group? Mutual aid, the subject of this book, is a primary rationale for the development of group services (Gitterman 2003). By its very nature, the group mutual aid system has the potential to universalize individual problems, reduce isolation, and mitigate stigma. This potential evolves from powerful, yet quite subtle, interpersonal processes.

As members develop a sense of purpose and commonality, they begin to share common experiences and concerns. Initially, members present safer and less threatening issues in order to test the worker's and each other's trustworthiness and competence. The interplay of two factors, the worker's authority and members' interpersonal relationships, "provides much of the driving force of the group experience" (Schwartz 1971:9). In most instances the preoccupation with the worker's authority either precedes or occurs simultaneously with group members learning to trust and become intimate with each other. Although in some women's and elderly groups the preoccupation with intimacy appears to precede concerns about the worker's authority (Berman-Rossi 1992; Berman-Rossi 1993; Kelly and Berman-Rossi 1999; Schiller 1995; Schiller 1997). However, in many groups the worker's authority—its function and limits—receives immediate attention (Garland, Jones, and Kolodny 1968; Kurland and Salmon 1993). And, through a testing process, group members begin to develop and reinforce mutual bonds and alliances as they figure out where the worker belongs in the interpersonal system. A number of years ago the author worked with a group of high school girls. They were uncomfortable with a male adult stranger (as was the writer with a group of adolescent girls). At our third meeting a member, with the support of others, confronted the awkwardness by asking the worker to share a happy and a painful life experience. At that moment the group coalesced to test the worker's willingness to "belong" to the group. Upon sharing a happy experience as well as a painful loss, members responded by sharing their own experiences, and the work began, focused and intense. A social work student, for another example, was assigned to a group of recently released mental patients who had been meeting for a year:

> After a short pause, I stated that I understood that this patient group has been meeting for about a year. Ms. B interrupted by saying, "I don't like being called a patient." I asked her why, and Ms. B suggested in effect that "patient" connoted sickness. I asked the group how they felt about it. Ms. C agreed that she did not like to be classified as a patient either. Mr. A asked her what she wanted to be called. Ms. C paused thoughtfully for a moment and said she would like to be called a "client." I asked the rest of the group how they felt about that. Ms. B said that was all right, and she would just like to be called a "member." The group responded positively to this, nodding, with a few members saying that they like that better. I said that since I was new to the group and they had been members for some time, could they bring me up to date on how the group began, what they talked about, dealt with, and so on.

The group members challenge the worker. Her openness encourages members to become involved with the new intern. In contrast, if she had turned their concerns into manifestations of psychological problems or had treated the content with lack of seriousness and respect, members might have become withdrawn or engaged in exploitative behavior such as scapegoating the dissonant participants.

From this type of experience and collective support, group members develop increased comfort and a willingness to risk personal and sometimes taboo concerns (Gitterman 1989). This process alone helps members to experience their difficulties and problems as being less unique and deviant. And, as members share and reach out to each other, they experience a "multiplicity of helping relationships" with all members invested and participating in the helping process rather than only the worker assuming that function and role (Schwartz 1961:18). Members may receive support for their perceptions and behaviors or they may be challenged to examine them further. Since their experiences have been similar (in other words, they are "in the same boat"), they are often receptive to each other's views and suggestions. Moreover, the group experience itself is a microcosm of members' interpersonal self-presentation and therefore serves as a rich arena for members to examine their respective adaptive as well as maladaptive perceptions and behaviors. From these exchanges members develop and practice new interpersonal and environmental strategies and receive feedback on such efforts.

Finally, the mutual aid group also has the potential to be a force for people to act and to gain greater control and mastery over their environments. Collective action has greater visibility and is more likely to gain organizational or community attention, mitigating individual isolation and reprisals, diminishing potential risks, and increasing chances for success. To be passive, to retreat from one's environment, inevitably leads to a sense of incompetence and impotence. In contrast, to be active in a group, to influence one's environment provide opportunities to experience a sense of competence and efficacy.

These powerful mutual aid processes and potentials are marvelously illustrated in the practice chapters that follow. However, despite growing interest and efforts in the field to develop group services, the actual outcomes are quite uneven and sometimes discouraging (Galinsky and. Schopler 1977, 1994; Gitterman 1979; Schopler and Galinsky 1981). After much effort, some groups never begin, others begin and then disintegrate, and still others seem to reinforce deviant and maladaptive behaviors (Bostwick 1987; Harpaz 1994).

Practitioners often attribute these problems to the clients' lack of motivation and resistance. Administrators may question the motivation and competence of the staff. Though these factors may contribute to the problem, they do not explain the persistent false starts, the attendance problems, the scapegoating, the factionalism, and other internal group difficulties. Other factors, such as clarity of group purpose, compositional balance, and structural and organizational supports, may be more relevant and salient (Garland 1992).

Formulating the Group's Purpose

Lack of clarity about group purpose is a common problem.[1] A group has to evolve from a common need/concern/ interest around which prospective members are brought together. Schwartz (1971:7) defines a group as "a collection of people who need each other in order to work on certain common tasks in an agency that is hospitable to those tasks." The commonality provides the foundation for and is essential to the development of a mutual aid system. In contrast, if members' needs are too divergent, or an agency's agenda is discrepant with group interest, or a worker's conception of group purpose is ambiguous, then members may withdraw, test incessantly, or act out. Mutual aid is more likely to evolve in a group where members need each other to deal with common needs/concerns/interests. Thus it is essential for the worker to develop a clear conception about potential group purpose, translating commonality into specific operational tasks (Croxton 1985; Germain and Gitterman 1996; Kurland and Salmon 1998; Shulman 1999; Wright 1999). Groups can be formed around natural life stressors that people experience. Germain and Gitterman (1996) conceptualize stressors as emerging from three interrelated areas: life transitions, environmental pressures, and interpersonal processes.

Life Transitional Stressors

Life transitions are stressful. Group services help people with developmental changes over the life cycle, such as adolescents dealing with issues of sexuality, ethnic identity, and independence/ dependence (Jagendorf and Malekoff 2000; Malekoff 1994, 1999; Steinberg 1990). Physiological, cognitive, and emotional impairments exacerbate developmental stress (Lynn and Nisivoccia 1995; Solomon and Zinke 1991). A group experience for learning, emotionally, developmentally and/or physically disabled adolescents and adults can be effective in helping members to deal with their common and distinctive struggles for competence, mastery, and a sense of identity (Dowds 1996; Fraher and McNally 1979; Garvin 1992; N. Gitterman 1979; Goelitz 2001; Harper and Shillito 1991; Lee 1977; Miller and Mason 2001; Raines 1991; Waite 1993). Similarly, groups can be helpful for people coping with stigmatized life statutes, such as developmentally challenged, foster child, substance abuser, mentally ill; homeless, sexually abused child, person with AIDS, and so on (Albert 1994; Berman-Rossi and Cohen 1988; Brown and Dickey 1992; Efron and Moir 1996; Hardman 1997; Levin 1992; Mellor and Storer 1995; Miller 1997; Plasse 2000; Walsh and Hewitt 1996). Adults with HIV/AIDS have been particularly vulnerable to social and emotional isolation and need the social support provided by groups (Amelio 1993; Anderson and Shaw 1994; Child and Getzel 1989; Getzel and Mahony 1993; Mancoske and Lindhorst 1991; Mayers and Spiegel 1992; Subramanian, Hernandez and. Martinez 1995). Moreover, some people carry the burden of dually stigmatized social statutes such as homosexuality and HIV/AIDS and drug abuse and mental illness (Ball 1994; Brown 1998; Foster, Stevens, and Hall 1994; Groves and Schondel 1996; Helfand 1994; Kelly 1999; Millan and Elia 1998; Neisen 1998; Sandstrom 1996; Saulmier 1997). These stressful life statutes and events carry heavy adaptive burdens and complex interpersonal and environmental demands (Dean 1998).

Life changes are equally stressful (Cardarella 1975; Cummings 1996; Oygard and Hardeng 2001). Natural school transitions require children and parents to deal with the status changes associated with beginning elementary, junior high and high schools, and college. Also, marriage and parenthood are both exciting and complex life transitions (Webb 1985). Recent retirees or parents confronting the "empty nest" phenomenon or divorcing couples encounter acute status losses and may experience depression (Charping, Bell, and Strecker 1992; Farmer and Galaris 1993; Greif and Kristall 1993). Immigrating into a new country creates a host of transitional stressors (Lopez 1991). Leaving a battered relationship requires dealing with potential violence and confronting uncertainty from the unknown (Browne, Saunders, and Staecker 1997; Caplan and Thomas 1995; Chauncey 1994; Evans and Shaw 1993; Fatout 1993; Joyce 1995; Pressman and Sheps 1994; Sakal 1991; Wood and Middleman 1992; Wood and Roche 2001). Recovering from the loss of a loved one requires a great deal of support (Adolph 1996; Rothenberg 1994; Zambelli and Derosa 1992). Organizational transitions such as agency admissions require coping with the new status of patient, client, or resident; agency discharge requires coping with new demands and expectations. (Armstrong 1990; Hanson 1998; Hanson et al.1994; Nightengale 1990). Some status changes may come too early in life such as adolescent pregnancy. Others may come too late in life such as elderly people carrying primary respon- sibility for child rearing (Vardi and Buchholz 1994). Since most status changes are stressful, they represent viable points of entry for group services (Brennan, Downes, and Nadler 1996; Brown, Krieg, and Belluck 1995; Butler and Beltran 1993; Daste 1990; McCallion and Toseland 1995).

Traumatic events also represent complex life transitions (Regehr and Hill 2000). People may confront various traumas: pre- or post-surgery (cardiac, mas- tectomy); physical assaults (amputation, sexual abuse, rape, homicide); the sud- den and unexpected loss of a loved one (child, spouse, parent). When a sudden, unexpected, overwhelming loss occurs (or is about to occur), the victim/survivor and relatives urgently need emotional and instrumental support from significant others. Group services can provide those "significant others" to help cope with the overwhelming stress (Barth, Yeatin, and Winterfelt 1994; Bauman and James 1989; Brown and Kerslake 1990; Duhatschek-Krause 1989; Hack, Osachuk, and De Luca 1994; Knight 1990; 1993; Lyon, Moore, and Lexius 1992; Reid, Mathews, and Liss 1995; Sparks and Goldberg 1994; Stokes and Gillis 1995; Subramanian and Ell 1989).

ENVIRONMENTAL STRESSORS

Social and physical environments are a major source of stress (Goodman 1997; Pollio 1994). A group formed to help with life transitional issues may also need to deal with external organizational concerns (Cohen and Mullender 1999). Par- ents of developmentally challenged children, for example, can be helpful to each other in dealing with child-rearing concerns. But they may also need to work on the lack of community resources and deal with the unresponsiveness of organi- zational representatives. Similarly, a group formed for life transitional issues may also need to deal with intraorganizational obstacles including the agency's structure (for example, lack of evening hours) or the quality of services (such as institutional food).

Group services may be also formed explicitly to deal with internal and/or ex- ternal organizational issues. Thus groups may be formed to involve consumers more fully within the agency's planning and decision-making structures. A plan- ning committee, an advisory group, or a leadership council fulfill important functions for both members and agencies (Abramson 1989; Ephross and Vassil 1988). Workers also organize groups with a social action focus to help con- sumers negotiate organizational structures and services (such as welfare rights, tenants' associations). These services enable people to act to gain greater control and mastery over their environments (Lipton 1971; Weiner 1964).

In contemporary environments many people are vulnerable to social and emotional isolation. Social network and self-help groups provide social and emotional linkages and establish "life lines," such as groups for new tenants in public housing, new immigrants, elderly residents of a building or neighborhood, recently released mental patients, patients with a chronic physical condition, groups for widows and widowers. Social network and self-help groups provide concrete day-to-day assistance in which interpersonal belonging, caring, and hope replace despair, isolation, and alienation (Auslander and Auslander 1988; Black and Drachman 1985; Borkman 1991; Kurtz 1990; Kurtz, Mann, and Chambon 1987). Unfortunately, some agencies and practitioners seem unsure about the therapeutic value of attention to environmental concerns and do not offer such services. However, for people to act upon their environment and to develop social and emotional connections is, in fact, most therapeutic. These processes engage cognition and perception, improve emotional and physical well-being, and provide social identity and a sense of belonging, competence, and human relatedness (Getzel 1982; Swenson 1979).

Interpersonal Stressors

Natural units such as families, patients on wards, students in classrooms, roommates in hospitals or dormitories may experience relational and communication problems (Miller and Donner 2000; Norman 1991). These units may develop maladaptive patterns that promote scapegoating or reinforce mutual withdrawal. In a residential cottage, for example, child care staff and children may experience difficulties in living, working, and communicating together (Birnbach 1971). Or in a classroom teacher and children may find themselves at cross-purposes. A social worker can intervene within the natural unit (the cottage, the classroom, the hospital ward) and identify and challenge the maladaptive patterns and facilitate communication (Abrams 2000; Lee 1977). Beyond intervening in natural units, workers form groups with an explicit interpersonal focus. Couples and multi-family groups, for example, provide a natural modality to examine and work on relational and communication patterns.

The life stressor conceptualization emphasizes life stressors and natural life processes around which people at risk or in need or with common interests may be clustered. And clarity of commonality increases the likelihood of engaging members' motivation and strengths in the mutual aid and problem-solving processes as well as of eliciting organizational sanctions and supports.

Selecting the Type of Group

Life transitional, environmental, and interpersonal life stressors offer a conceptualization for the provision of a variety of group services. At the same time the worker considers the group's potential purposes she or he also considers what type of group to offer. Five different types of groups allow for mutual aid (Gitterman and Knight 2000; Toseland and Rivas 2001; Wayne and Cohen 2001).

Workers form groups with an *educational* focus through which participants acquire relevant information and unlearn misinformation. These types of groups include sex education, parent education, new statuses such as preparation for parenthood, dialysis, diabetic, cancer patient, foster or adoptive parent, HIV/AIDS, pre-/postsurgery, and health education (Barth, Yeatin, and Winterfelt 1994; Butler and Beltran 1993; Cummings 1996; Drews and Bradley 1989; Kuechler 1997; Magura et al. 1989; Neisen 1998; Sternbach 1990; Subramanian, Hernandez,and Martinez 1995; Walsh-Burke and Scanlon 2000). In these groups the worker must find a balance between presentation and discussion in which members have an opportunity to process and help each other use the information. Within the current emphases on prescribed curricula and protocols, the potential for mutual aid is too often unrealized.

Workers form other groups in which members help each other with *common life* issues and stressors. In these groups members help each other deal with life's common transitional, environmental, and interpersonal challenges and stressors, examine personal behavior in its situational context, and develop new perceptions and skills. These include groups for bereaved children, siblings of handicapped children, developmental tasks, school issues, probationers, parolees, and prisoners, health and mental health issues, sexual abuse survivors, batterers, homeless, divorced and single parents, retirees, and so on. (Berman-Rossi 2003; Block, Margolis,and Seitz 1994; Brown 1994; Drisko 1992; Gitterman 1971; Irizarry and Appel 2003; Jones 1994; Kelly 1999; Levinsky and McAleer 2003; Orr 2003; Nadelman 2003; Poynter-Berg 1994; Schiller and Zimmer 2003; Stephenson and Boler 1981; Trimble 2003; Vastola, Nierenberg and Graham 1994). In these groups the worker must pay equal and simultaneous attention to the group as a group, helping it develop a mutual aid system, and to the needs of each individual member. To focus only on one or the other limits the capacity of members to help each other and to obtain help for themselves.

Other groups may be formed with a *behavioral change* focus through which the group serves as a context for individual treatment and change, such as anger management, smoking-cessation, phobia, and eating-disorder groups (Albert 1994; Fisher 1995; Greene and McVinney 1998; Laube 1990; Rose 1977; Schames 1990; Solomon and Zinke 1991; Straussner 1998; Sultenfuss and Geczy 1996; Vardi and Buchholz 1994). In this type of group the worker faces the challenge of helping with individual problems without turning the experience into doing casework in a group (Kurland and Salmon 1992). Adolescents often resist these types of groups because the problem is lodged within them.

Workers form still other groups with a *social developmental* focus through which members learn skills, make friends, and build emotional and social connections, such as an after school group, regressed schizophrenics' coffee club, a widow/ widowers' group, a men's cardiac club, Parents Without Partners, isolated homebound adults, a senile elderly music reminiscence group, and so on

(Gardella 1985; Getzel 1983; Hartford and Lawton 1997; Lynn and Nisivoccia 1995; Schopler, Galinsky, and Abell 1997; Stein, Rothman, and. Nakanishi 1993). The worker's task is to integrate having fun, doing activities, and helping with developmental life tasks and issues.

Finally, workers form groups with a *task* focus through which participants use their talents to complete prescribed objectives, such as planning committees, advisory and social action groups, ad hoc task forces, and the like (Abramson 1989; Ephross and Vassil 1988; Garvin 1992; Gummer 1995). While the focus is on accomplishing specific tasks, the process of contributing to a collective activity, of committing oneself to a cause also has great psychological benefit. In these groups the worker must pay equal attention to the identified tasks as well as the interpersonal group processes. To focus on task accomplishment over process or process over task limits the full potential of the group experience.

The worker should attempt to select the type of group that most fits the prospective members' expectations and comfort. For example, the author formed a group for parents of developmentally challenged children to develop community resources for their children. Although members enthusiastically agreed to the offer of service, they did not invest energy into the work or follow through on agreed upon tasks. After a few weeks the worker reached for the obstacle and learned that the members wanted to share their concerns about having a developmentally challenged child; they wanted an opportunity to ventilate their frustration about the child and lack of social supports and to help each other with child rearing. While the author had proposed a task group, members desired a group that focused on common life issues and stressors. The reverse just as easily could have happened. The suggested principle is that, whatever group type is selected, the social worker has to be flexible and responsive to renegotiations.

Composing the Group

The composition of the group affects its development and direction and dictates whether the group will move toward mutual aid, disintegration, or parasitism (Toseland and Siporin 1986). Group purpose and type provide the context for its composition. Within this context groups composed of members with common backgrounds (age, sex, ethnic and social class), and common personality capacities and behaviors (ego functioning, role skills, authority/intimacy orientations) tend to be stable and supportive, more quickly developing a group identity and esprit de corps. Similar life experiences, concerns, interests, and adaptive styles provide members with a sense of commonality and a collective stability (Chau 1992; Glasgow and Gouse-Sheese 1995; Simoni and Perez 1995). While these commonalities create a sense of immediate closeness and support, they also reflect a lack of diversity and vitality. Members may be too alike, and their "likeness" may reinforce dysfunctional patterns. This is sometimes seen in a gang that supports antisocial and delinquent behavior, in a depressed patients' group that exacerbates hopelessness and despair, or in court mandated, involuntary groups of substance abusers or batterers that reinforce minimization and avoidance (Behroozi 1992; Milgram and Rubin 1992; Thomas and Caplan 1999). Excessively homogeneous groups limit the diversity essential to challenge the status quo, to create the necessary tension for change, and to provide models for alternative attitudes and behaviors.

Groups composed of members with diverse backgrounds (age, sex, ethnic, social class) and diverse personality capacities and behaviors (that is, in ego functioning, role skills, authority/intimacy orientation) tend to be less stable and less predictable (Bilides 1990; Brown and Mistry 1994; Burke et al. 1994; Martin and Shanahan 1983; Sowers-Hoad and Hoag 1987; Tsui and Schultz 1988). They may have trouble in developing a sense of group identity and cohesion. Differing life experiences, concerns, interests, or adaptive styles create internal obstacles to achieving a common agenda and open communication. Members are too different, and their differences become the central issue rather than the group purpose and tasks. The author, for example, formed a racially balanced group of youngsters with school difficulties. The racial heterogeneity, however, led to factionalism and scapegoating. These internal barriers inhibited the group from working on its purpose. On the other hand, if such a group can overcome its internal problems, it has the potential for dramatic impact. The inner diversity provides vital and rich resources for members to draw upon (Davis 1980; Schutz 1958, 1961; Shalinsky 1964; Slavson 1955, 1964; Wax 1960).

Ideally, groups require both stability (homogeneity) and diversity (heterogeneity). Redl (1951) defines this balance as the "law of optimum distance." At the very least, prospective members need to have common concerns and interests—a commonality of purpose. Once these have been identified, then key background and personality factors may be specified. For each such factor, the desired range of commonness or difference must be determined. As an example, in developing a group service for pregnant adolescents, the worker considers the following factors: their common concerns about delivery, available services and resources, relationships with parents, boyfriends, school representatives, and future plans for their babies. These will bind members together and provide collective stability. The worker then needs to think through the relative advantages of commonality or difference for such other factors as age, first pregnancy, religion, ethnicity, parental and boyfriend relationships, health, stage of pregnancy, geographic location, and others.

As a rule of thumb, members usually tolerate and use greater diversity when common interests and concerns are experienced intensively. Thus, for example, the author organized a group of women with limited life expectancy due to advanced breast cancer. Their profound commonality made differences in age, class, and ethnicity seem inconsequential. In contrast, the youngsters in the racially balanced school group were identified by school personnel as problem students. They did not feel they had behavior problems and, therefore, experienced the need for the group service less intensely. Thus the less the members perceive common concerns and interests, the more homogeneous the group composition must be (Bond and De Graaf-Kaser 1990).

In composing a group, a worker must be particularly careful not to isolate and potentially scapegoat a member because he or she is different and alone on important background or personality factors such as a "butterfly chaser" would be in a group of athletic youngsters. The worker must assume responsibility for group composition. To relinquish this responsibility to someone else, e.g., to a teacher in a secondary setting, may result in a group of only acting out children, or, if to a nurse, a group composed of diabetics with severely mixed symptomatology (i.e., early and amputation stages). Such combinations do not encourage mutual support and end in either conflict or despair or both. A client poignantly describes the experience and consequence of being different:

> My previous social worker referred me to a group at a mental health clinic. She told me it would give me something to do and people other than my children to talk to. Then I found out it was a group for recently released hospital patients, many of whom were still psychotic. They talked to themselves and sometimes lost sight of reality for moments. I was frightened by them, and upset that I was placed in a group with them. Look, I know I'm nuts, but I'm not that nuts. Maybe someday I will be, but let me get there in my own time. When I have a nervous breakdown, I want it to be my very own and not taught to me by members of my therapy group.[2]

To avoid potential isolation and alienation, each member should have at least one other member on factors assessed to be important. Yalom (1995) refers to this compositional guideline as the "Noah's Ark Principle." Beyond these compositional guidelines, more elaborate and precisely designed scales are available and particularly useful for residential settings (Bertcher and Maple 1985).

Considering Group Time, Size, and Setting

The worker relates the group's temporal arrangement to the need being met, the type of group, and its purpose. Most groups are *planned short term*. Research has demonstrated that for a wide range of life issues and client populations planned short-term services are more effective, or as effective, as long-term services (Epstein 1970; Koss and Bucher 1986). The time boundary helps members focus quickly and maintain purpose, direction, and a sense of urgency. The time-limited commitment results in fewer unplanned terminations. Thus a one-session orientation group, a two-session postsurgical group, a four-session adoptive parents group, an eight-session couples group, or a twelve-session group of foster care adolescents may be more productive than an ongoing, long-term service (Block 1985; Bloom and Lynch 1979; Caspar 1981; Finzi and Stange 1997; Gladstone and Reynolds 1997; Holmes-Garrett 1989; MacKenzie 1996; Rotholz 1985; Waldron, Whittinton, and Jensen 1985; Weisberg 1987). For certain populations a time limit is imperative. The group of cancer patients previously mentioned with a limited life expectancy, for example, would have been devastated by a gradual loss of membership, even if new members had been substituted. As a group nears completion of its tasks and evaluates its progress, members and worker may decide to recontract for another cycle or a specific number of additional sessions. Similarly, the group and worker may decide to meet a few additional sessions after a certain time set aside for experimentation and integration has passed.

Time-limited (six to twelve months) group services utilize all the principles of planned short term services. The worker, for example, clearly identifies the ending date in the first session. Certain settings such as schools have a natural time calendar in the academic year. Therefore, the worker can time group services with the calendar's natural time boundaries. For example, Christmas/Chanuka, Easter/Passover, winter/spring breaks, end of school are natural time breaks to either end the group service or as benchmarks to evaluate progress and determine if additional time is needed. If additional time is needed, the worker continues the service until the next benchmark (Gemain and Gitterman 1996; Rittner and Smyth 1999).

Long-term and open-ended group services in which departing members are replaced by new members best serves members with chronic, intractable personal and environmental stressors. For example, chronic mentally and developmentally challenged members benefit from the continuous instrumental and emotional support provided by long-term groups. These group members need much more help than short-term services can provide. In these groups "members tend to invest more in their relationships with each other and with the worker as well as in the group's traditions and norms" (Northen and Kurland 2001:138). These groups, however, do have two chronic problems: 1. the ongoing, long-term nature may lead worker and members to lose their original sense of purpose and vitality and 2. the shifts in membership may require ongoing contracting and recontracting and result in the group's inability to move beyond an early stage of group development (Galinsky and Schopler 1985, 1989; Schopler and Galinsky 1984). To minimize disruptive membership shifts, the worker, to the extent possible, attempts to control group entrances and exits. If only one new member joins a group, the group is able to incorporate the new member into its current phase of development. In contrast, the arrival and departure of a few members require the group to slow its processes and return to beginning group issues. In long-term groups periodic evaluation of group progress and a recontracting of issues are also beneficial.

Other time considerations are the *frequency* and *duration* of sessions. Many agencies offer group services on the traditional weekly hour rather than structuring and arranging time in ways that are responsive to the special needs of the population being served. In providing group services for young children having difficulty with school, for example, the author discovered that weekly sessions for an hour were insufficient. During the interval between sessions the youngsters confronted various school crises, and the group was unavailable for assistance. Consequently, the worker restructured meetings for greater frequency (twice or three times weekly) and for shorter duration (thirty or forty minutes). This time change made dramatic impact upon both the substance and intensity of our work. Generally, children and mentally impaired adults are responsive to more frequent and shorter sessions, while well-functioning adolescents and adults are responsive to weekly and longer sessions (one and a half to two hours). However, adolescents and adults in states of crisis, such as presurgery groups or discharge groups, especially those facing difficult consequences, require more frequent sessions. In medical settings physical discomfort and pain make necessary sessions of shorter duration. Essentially, the worker must creatively structure time by taking into account group members' developmental stages and special population attributes and their effect on attention span and capacity for session-to-session carryover.

The worker also has to consider the potential consequences of the *scheduled time* for the meetings (Steinberg 1999). Some members may only be able to attend meetings in the day time because their children are in school or because of safety concerns. Others, due to employment or other reasons, may be able only to attend evening hours. To the extent possible, involving potential group members in identifying the most and least preferable times for scheduling group meetings increases the likelihood of their participation. Temporal accessibility is essential.

The worker relates group *size* to group objectives, primary interventive methods, and client needs. Generally, large groups become more formalized through establishing rules, procedures, and possibly electing officers. Communication tends to be channeled through the formal or indigenous leader with limited opportunity for individual attention, accessibility to the worker, and intimate, spontaneous participation. For some mental patients or the frail elderly, the size of community meetings may be overstimulating and confusing, leading to inappropriate behavior or withdrawal. To shy, anxious, or less adequate members, however, the large group may provide a sense of identification and belonging without a loss of autonomy and the desired degree of interpersonal anonymity. A large group also obtains community and organizational visibility and can be an effective resource for self-help and influence. Thus purposes and objectives influence the selection of appropriate group size.

Group purposes and objectives also affect the selection of appropriate interventive methods. The worker may primarily use a didactic method in a one-session orientation group to introduce new members to an agency's or community's available resources and requisites. In this instance a large group (fifteen or more members) can be effective in achieving the purpose and objectives. A one-session presurgery preparation group may use didactic methods to present factual data while also reaching for underlying concerns and inviting ventilation of feelings. In this instance purpose and objectives can best be achieved in a small group (approximately three to five members).

Appropriate group size is also related to members' needs and communication styles. Small groups offer greater opportunity for individualization, providing each member with sufficient time and accessibility to peers and the worker. Members in crises, for example, often need the attention afforded by small groups. Similarly, emotionally deprived children need the continued and special attention more likely in a small group. Small groups, however, do make greater demands for participation, involvement, and intimacy. For shy, anxious, or less adequate members, the pressures may be too great. The level of demand may exceed their level of tolerance. A moderate-size group (approximately seven to nine) can provide regressed schizophrenics, for example, the necessary interpersonal space that may be unavailable in a smaller group. Moreover, a small group may have insufficient resources for diversity and vitality or for linking up with a "buddy." Finally, absences leave a small group extremely vulnerable to disintegration.[3]

The *physical setting* also has a significant impact on a group's activities and interactions. Light, ventilation, room size, and furniture arrangement facilitate or inhibit the development of a mutual aid system. Within the limits imposed by space and design, the worker must consider the usefulness of structuring space and defining expectations and boundaries. Children meeting in a large room need spatial boundaries to structure their activities and interactions. Prearranged tables and chairs symbolize spatial limits. As members (and the worker) develop comfort and security, the worker uses available space more flexibly.

The worker, in arranging space, assesses members' comfort and interactional style. A circular sitting arrangement facilitates member-to-member communication and is usually the preferred sitting arrangement. However, in certain situations the circular arrangement may create self-consciousness and unease. When the author met with the group of adolescent girls, for example, he discovered they were initially uncomfortable with chairs arranged in a small, intimate circle. They were self-conscious about what to do with their miniskirts, hands, feet, and so on. The small circle can also be threatening to members who do not seek or are not ready for the degree of physical and emotional intimacy such a structure demands. Tables provide, in these situations, the necessary spatial boundary and distance members require. If, however, members need physical movement, then tables are restrictive. Since predicting members' spatial needs is difficult, the worker should involve members in assessing and planning for their own spatial needs, including changes during a session and over time (Germain 1978, 1983).

Staffing the Group

Staffing the group is still another important factor in the development of group services. The usual and most effective model for the staffing of groups is one worker who possesses substantive knowledge and practice skills. Modifications may sometimes be considered. When roles are clearly delineated, as in some interdisciplinary settings, co-leadership may be an effective arrangement. A nurse or doctor for medical expertise and a social worker for interpersonal and environmental expertise can jointly provide a more integrated service that is responsive to patients' total needs than either one can do alone. For the arrangement to be effective, the co-leaders must reach an explicit agreement on their respective roles and the tasks, particularly in beginning, ending, and focusing sessions. Contracting respective co-leadership roles with group members is also helpful (Galinsky and Schopler 1980; Nosko and Wallace 1997; Roller and Nelson 1991; Schlenoff and Busa 1981; Starak 1981).

As previously mentioned, the worker may also use co-leadership to gain sanctions for group services by providing two disciplines and mutual accountability and by acquiring interdisciplinary involvement and support. Finally, the worker can use co-leadership to institutionalize group services. In developing group services at an adoption agency, for example, the author developed a structure in which a primary and secondary leader offered a particular group service. Having gained experience and a sense of competence, the secondary leader assumed primary responsibility for the next group. In the subsequent group the new primary leader would break in a new secondary leader. Through this staffing structure, numerous staff developed on-the-job training and comfort in working with the group modality. Toseland and Rivas (2001:129) summarize the most cited benefits of co-leadership: additional source of support, opportunity for feedback and professional development, greater objectivity achieved with two sets of eyes and ears, inexperienced leaders gain skills and comfort, role model open communication and dealing with differences, and support in setting limits and structuring activities.

While these benefits do exist, co-leadership should only be used purposively and discriminately. While numerous rationales are offered, co-leadership too often reflects workers' discomfort and anxiety about working with groups; "Their are so many of them and only one of me." Besides being an uneconomical arrangement, co-leadership adds a complex dynamic to group process, namely, the workers' struggles to synchronize their interventions and to cope with role ambiguities, competitiveness, and discrepant interventions (Dies 1983; Galinsky and Schopler 1980; Herzog 1980; Kolodny 1980; Middleman 1980; Toseland and Rivas 2001). Unwittingly, this arrangement, therefore, may inhibit the group's mutual aid processes by encouraging withdrawal, testing, or identification with one worker at the expense of the others.

Creating a Responsive Organizational Climate

Too often, the group service is an anomaly added to workers' existing workloads. Within the context of managed care (Mechanic 1999), agencies may construe the group modality to be more economical and to provide more profitable reimbursement fees than the individual modality. Group services are too often an exception to the primary service and inadequately conceptualized and supported by agency structures and procedures. Repeatedly, an agency and worker develop an idea for a group, but somehow it never gets off the drawing board or becomes unsatisfactorily implemented and therefore never institutionalized. Too often agencies, workers, and clients experience these failures and become reluctant to be involved with a group again. Inattention to formal and informal organizational structures and processes accounts for many of these difficulties (Bilides 1992; Congress and Lynn 1994; Sultenfuss and Geczy 1996).

Organizational sanctions are essential to the development and institutionalization of group services (Holloway 1987). Without vertical, administrative approval, the worker "walks on egg shells." In response to any perceived problem, such as "uncooperative patients" in a hospital or "noisy children" in a school or social agency, the medical or psychiatric chief, the school principal, or the agency director may precipitously terminate the group (Dane and Simon 1991; Gitterman and Miller 1989). Similarly, without horizontal, interdisciplinary, and peer staff involvement, the service is easily undermined or sabotaged. It may be time for the group to begin, yet co-workers have not referred appropriate clients, or nurses suddenly have to take the patients' temperatures, or teachers decide to punish children for class behavior by disallowing group participation.

Along with organizational sanctions, structural supports are also essential to the development and institutionalization of group services. Without them, group services are doomed to fail. If children are to participate freely, a worker's office or an auditorium may inhibit activity or encourage destructive behavior, and therefore more suitable space is required. To engage working parents, the agency has to be open in the evening or on weekends. If young single mothers are to participate, child care assistance is essential. If the agency is located in a large catchment area or if special populations are to be recruited, transportation may be necessary. To welcome group members, the worker needs petty cash to buy refreshments. If workers do not have confidence and skill in providing group services, the agency should provide supervision, consultation, or in-service training. If workers are to maintain investment, time for preparation and follow-up, the agency must provide statistical credit for the service. When these supports are not negotiated beforehand, the result is administrative, worker, and client frustration.

To acquire institutional sanctions and supports, the worker must be an active participant in her or his organization (Arches 1991; Packard 1989; Sunley 1997).

The worker begins by analyzing which environmental, organizational, and interpersonal forces are apt to support or to restrain the development of group services. Lewin's (1952) "force-field analysis" helps the worker visualize the salient forces promoting and resisting change. The worker *analyzes* the organization to determine whether and what types of group services are feasible (Berger 1990; Brager and Holloway 1978, 1992; Germain and Gitterman 1996). Since environmental forces affect all organizational processes, the worker must evaluate features in the environment that may affect the desired outcome. With the current demands for accountability, federal, state, and local reimbursement mechanisms increasingly circumscribe time and services. Thus, for example, in developing outpatient hospital group services for Medicaid patients, a worker had to become an "expert" in reimbursement policies and procedures. This expertise can make a group service feasible. Similarly, many agencies have increased their reliance upon computer technology. Unfortunately, agencies often use this technology against clients to determine ineligibility, to decrease entitlements, and to violate confidentiality. Computers (as well as telephones), however, may also be used on behalf of clients' interests and needs (Finn 1995; Galinsky, Schopler, and Abell 1997; Kaslyn 1999; Meier, Galinsky, and Rounds 1995; Rittner and Hammons 1992; Schopler, Galinsky, and Abell 1997; Stein, Rothman, and Nakanishi 1993; Weiner et al. 1993). As previously mentioned, in a child welfare agency with a large catchment area, the author used computer technology to locate clusters of children and adolescents in diverse geographic areas and to provide outreach group services. Because of insurmountable transportation barriers, all prior efforts to offer group services at the agency had failed.

Internal organizational structures also affect the feasibility for group services. In agencies characterized by a high degree of formal structure, a proposed new service that challenges established routine will likely confront resistance. Thus, for a worker to gain acceptance of a group service in a hospital or school setting, it has to be responsive to the nurses' and teachers' daily schedules (Dane and Simon 1991; Gilbert 1989). The worker has to adapt the service to existing structures rather than disrupt them.

Complex agencies, characterized by a large number of professional disciplines, have been found to be more responsive to programmatic innovation (Haige and Aikens 1970; Holloway 1987). The diversity and advanced training create a greater openness to new ideas, methods, and technologies and therefore offer the worker a certain degree of organizational maneuverability. At the same time, the actual program implementation requires complex coordination with numerous turf-conscious disciplines, because a division of labor is required to allocate and specify work roles and tasks. And the differential role assignments are conducive to the development of a preoccupation with one's own role and function. One's own turf takes on increasing personal importance, and protecting that turf becomes the driving concern. A latent consequence of a "protectionism" culture is that client needs may be held "hostage" to turf-interests. Consequent-ly, the worker should anticipate that departments and staff may resist sharing and referring their clients to a newly formed group service (behaving as if the clients "belonged" to them). On the basis of an assessment of this organization-al characteristic, the worker develops a strategy to involve the staff and to address their self-interests. The group has to be "owned" by the setting and its staff. To achieve this institutional ownership, the author, for example, encouraged hospi-tal social workers to collaborate with nurses and doctors in developing and co-leading groups. This arrangement is more productive than staff and departments competing for clients. In one setting the author observed the same patients simultaneously invited to four newly formed groups conducted respec-tively by an occupational therapist, a nurse, a rehabilitation counselor, and a so-cial worker.

Since the work group develops a system with its own culture of values, norms, and expectations as well as its own system for distributing rewards and punish-ments, the worker must take into account the informal organizational structures. Just as the formal structures socialize each organizational participant to the agency culture, the informal system socializes the participants to its own culture. And since the informal system significantly influences participants' perceptions and behaviors, it affects the development of group services. A new worker, for ex-ample, attempted without success to develop a group in a mental health clinic. She confronted a long-standing psychodynamic orientation that channeled all clients into long-term individual psychotherapy. In requesting referrals for "her" group, she received none, and colleagues ignored subsequent requests. More-over, the worker experienced interpersonal ostracism as she violated, without re-alizing it, a powerful peer norm.

In addition to analyzing the potential effect of environmental forces and or-ganizational characteristics, the worker identifies the key participants who will affect and be affected by the proposed group service and attempts to estimate their likely response. To gauge their potential reactions, the worker evaluates the impact of the group service on the participants' job performance and satisfaction. If the group service increases the participants' self-esteem, visibility, praise, or in-fluence, then the worker can anticipate their support. Conversely, if the group service threatens the participants' self-interests, then the worker can anticipate resistance.

The worker assesses where he or she is located in the organization's formal and informal structures. The worker's structural location may or may not provide opportunities to interact with and therefore influence key participants. Some workers can not isolate themselves in their organizations as though they were engaged in private practice; they do their work and leave. These social workers limit their conception of professional function to client contact; consequently, they limit their potential to develop group services. If workers have limited access to influential organizational participants, they have to improve their positions in order to acquire sanctions and supports.

Moreover, the worker also has to take stock and assess how he or she is viewed by significant others in the organization. In developing this specialized self-awareness, the worker must differentiate between how he or she would like to be perceived and how he or she is actually perceived. The worker might consider such questions as: Am I considered competent? Am I viewed as a valuable colleague? Am I thought of as being fair? Am I someone colleagues seek out for advice, for informal socializing, or for favors? A newly employed social worker illustrates this process:

> After six months my position in the agency (child welfare) is somewhat mixed. I am fairly sure I am perceived as smart, competent, and enthusiastic about the work at the agency. I have a solid, constructive relationship with my supervisor. With the most senior worker I have the beginning of a personal friendship. With another prestigious worker I collaborated extensively on a family case and thus also have a strong working relationship.
>
> I have recently become aware of a problem in my agency participation. I tend to be somewhat oppositional and critical of agency procedures. While I do see many problems with the extremely loose way in which agency operations have evolved, I have been insensitive to the fact that both my supervisor and senior worker have been with the agency since its inception. Despite their general respect for me and my ideas, I have become aware that at times I offend them with an adversarial and caustic stance in some of my comments. I realize, to change the written policies and loose decision making, I will have to alter my stance.

Self-awareness in an organizational context provides guidelines for professionally effective behaviors.

Through the analysis of environmental, structural, and interpersonal forces, the worker evaluates feasibility—that is, the potential to develop a group service. Where forces strongly promote the valued outcome, a group service has an excellent potential for success. Where forces strongly restrain a group service, the worker must reevaluate, and most likely change, the service objectives and means for implementation. Where forces neither promote nor restrain a group service, the worker must court and mobilize the supports before she or he can implement the group service. And, finally, where forces strongly promote as well as strongly oppose a group service, the resulting unpredictability and potential conflict requires a low-key approach to test the waters before selecting appropriate strategies.

After assessing feasibility, the worker attempts to develop a *receptive organizational climate* (Brager and Holloway 1978; Dalton 1970; Frey 1990; Germain and

Gitterman 1996; Mechanic 1964). Since practitioners usually have limited formally ascribed authority, they have to achieve organizational influence. Visible professional competence is a major pathway to being influential. A social work student describes her efforts to make her competence more visible in a hospital in order to gain staff confidence and receptiveness for developing a group service on a neurology ward:

I have made a conscientious effort to show my competence to staff in ways that would encourage their support for the group. For example, during discharge planning meetings, I have contributed knowledge about community resources as well as helped nurses deal with certain difficult patients. Four of the patients who were management problems became more cooperative with nursing staff in caring for their own needs and going for tests because of my helping efforts. My own enthusiasm and willingness to take on "difficult" placement cases and work with their families allowed staff to view another area of my competence as I discussed my work with them. I conscientiously adhere to the hospital's value system, i.e., planning for discharge and getting the job done, and gained respect for adhering to the dominant value system.

Recognized knowledge and expertise gains prestige, respect, and, in effect, informal influence.

Another pathway is involvement in the agency's interpersonal network. The worker who is an "insider," attentive to colleagues' interests and concerns, acquires support systems and allies. Since an organization's informal system represents the "grease" that makes the machinery run, an effective presence in the informal system is essential to the development of group services.

I gave myself a pep talk and decided to change my quiet, shy image. In the lunch room I began to talk to my new colleagues so that they would get to know me and vice versa. I began to relax a little—rather than avoid coffee machines, elevator, main office—I began to be more sociable. At Christmas time I joined the party planning committee. This enabled me to get to know other staff members on a more personal level. They began to invite me into their offices for coffee breaks. Recently, at a staff meeting, the senior case supervisor was too critical of my handling of a case assignment. To my surprise, several colleagues supported me and enabled me to assert my position.

Involvement in the informal system provides the worker with potential support and alliances in the sanction-building process.

Similarly, in the formal system, active and skillful involvement in committees, teams, consultations, conferences, and staff meetings provide still another significant arena for appropriately positioning oneself. And, finally, clients themselves represent a critical resource. Their informal opinions and feedback or more formal need's assessment provides essential data.

Before the worker presents the idea for a group service to the appropriate formal organizational structure and representatives, she decides upon an overall strategy from among demonstration, collaboration, and persuasion (Brager and Holloway 1978; Germain and Gitterman 1996; Morris and Binstock 1966). When there is some recognition of the need for group services and the worker's competence has been recognized, *demonstration* is a particularly effective strategy. By skillfully showing the value of group services, the worker may solidify organizational support before restraining forces have had the opportunity to mobilize resistance. In appropriate situations, action speaks louder than words.

In relatively open and fluid organizations where goal consensus and close interpersonal ties exist, *collaboration* is an effective strategy (Gentry 1987). The worker openly discusses the problems associated with the lack of group services with key participants invited to explore and develop programmatic ideas. In this process the worker has to be careful about "overselling" rather than inviting genuine feedback. A worker, relatively new to the hospital, illustrates the problems when she approaches an established head nurse and attempts to sell a group (Shulman 1999).[4]

> I said to Miss Ford that I had been doing some thinking which I would like to share with her. I told her that I had been on the ward quite a bit and felt quite at home on it. I said to her that I, as everyone else on the ward, am here to try to service the patients to the best of my ability. I then asked her what she thought of a group having any value on the ward. She said that it has been suggested before, so that it was nothing new. She said that the room full of ladies could do with something of that sort but that that's the only ladies' room there is. I asked if she thought that only ladies could benefit from a group experience and she said "no," but that she was thinking in terms of room number 1403. She asked what the group would be about and for. I said that I'm open to suggestions but that perhaps the basic purpose could be for the patients to discuss their hospitalization, frustrations, etc. It would be open to all patients.

The nurse quickly senses the worker's agenda when she left unexplored the suggestions about the patients in room 1403. In being preoccupied with selling, the worker does not listen and is not open to a collaborative exploration. In response, the nurse became agitated.

> Miss Ford asked how the patients would know or how I would tell them. I told her that, in order to make it a voluntary thing, perhaps written invitations to each patient would be a good idea. She asked when and where it would be held. I told her that I hoped she could help make the decision, especially the time, because I

realize they are busy. As far as the room goes, perhaps an empty bedroom or the sunroom. She said that by October 16th all rooms should be filled up. I suggested we could decide on that at a later date. I asked if she could, however, talk to the doctors and staff about this, get some ideas, and we could discuss it again next week at rounds. She said that would be fine.

Miss Ford did not seem too enthusiastic and was quite resistant (mentioning no rooms, how would patients know, etc.). However, I feel she can see some value in a ward group. Next week I plan to give her some examples of why I can see a need for the group.

In collaboration, premature agreement and superficial closure often become unraveled at a later date. Unexpressed negatives fester and often lead potential allies to sabotage the group service. The nurse attitude changes when the worker addresses her concerns:

I told Miss Ford that I felt I may have been too pushy about the ward group. I said that I had asked for her participation and interest, yet I hadn't given her a chance to express herself, and I wasn't really listening to her. I then apologized and suggested that we might go back to the beginning. I said I was interested in knowing her true feelings regarding the group. She said she thought the group would be very good for most patients, but she was worried about the nurses. She said it was difficult enough to get all the nurses to attend her ward conference without having them attend a patients' group. I asked if she was thinking in terms of all the nurses going to the group at once. She said she didn't know and wondered what I thought. I said that the decision of nurses was up to her. I suggested that it might be just as effective to have one nurse drop in on the group or have the nurses rotate. . . .

I suggested that one important gap existed between patients and doctors or patients and nurses. I explained further that I believed that if a patient could release some of his anxieties or fears about his medical problems or share his hostilities in the group, he might be an easier patient to cope with. Rather than expressing his feelings in an undesirable way, he might be happier on the ward and easier to deal with. Miss Ford agreed with this and then asked about the resident on the ward. How could we keep him involved? We discussed this for a while.

As the discussion continues, the nurse becomes more involved, active, and collaborative.

Miss Ford asked how the patients would know about the group, who would go, etc. I suggested that the nurses see all the patients, and they could tell who could benefit from a group experience, who was ready to go. She asked how patients

would find out about the group. I suggested we stick notices to their bedside tables. She said it would not be a good idea because the tables must be washed. She
suggested we put them in the bathrooms where the beauty salon advertises. I
said it was a good idea, and we went to the bathroom to select the best spot. I
then brought up the subject of confidentiality. I asked how Miss Ford felt it should
be handled. For example, if one patient or more complained about a certain nurse
or herself, would she like to know or not? Rather than directly answering, she told
me about a patient on the ward who would complain of different shifts of staff
and play one against the other. I asked her if the gist of her story was that it was
better to know the complaints so that they can be investigated and dealt with.
She said "yes." I told her I felt the same way and that I would like to know when
patients made complaints about me.

   We then talked about where the group could be held. I again suggested the
sunporch. This time Miss Ford said that it would be all right because patients
used it anyway. We then discussed further clearances in the hospital and set up
a meeting with the nursing staff to clarify the group purpose and to select
members.

Through the collaborative process, a critical organizational participant develops
a stake in the group service. A worker has to engage colleagues in collaborative
problem solving through a shared search for data, resources, and exploration of
potential problems.

   In situations characterized by goal dissent and disparity in power, *persuasion*
(a process of argumentation and bargaining) may be the appropriate strategy. Because the status quo represents the established way of thinking and practicing,
any effort to persuade others to change requires careful preparation. How one
defines the need for a group service determines to a large extent the parameters
of continued discussion and potential resistance. Thus the worker has to make
an effective case for an unmet need using relevant data to support this definition.
Case excerpts or anecdotal experiences make the need more clearly understandable and more readily recognizable. After the worker establishes that a need is
not being met, she or he can anticipate that those opposed may turn their attention to dismissing or negating the proposed solution—a group service. The
worker must present the proposal for a group service in language that is in accord with the values of the key participants' addresses their major concerns (Frey
1990). Opponents usually attack a proposed solution in two areas: its feasibility
and its desirability. The worker prepares to deal with these oppositional arguments, building a case for feasibility and desirability. If the worker anticipates
significant resistance, persuasion research suggests the two-sided argument
(statement of one's own commitment to group services and the potential oppositional counterargument) is more effective in disarming resistance and influencing more neutral participants (Karlins and Abelson 1970). Throughout the

process, the give and take, the worker's posture needs to reflect respect for others' opinions and a pressing of one's own position out of professional concern and organizational identity and loyalty.

After sanction for a group service has been obtained, the worker still has to put a program into action. For the practitioner much work and frustration may still lie ahead. Organizational machinery may move too slowly to sustain key participants' interest. Some organizational structures may be incompatible with group services. Staff assigned to lead groups may lack the knowledge and skill or may be overwhelmed by the additional demands and suffer from competing pressures. Thus, even after an agency adopts the idea for a group service, the worker must maintain structural and interpersonal supports. Therefore, the worker makes needed modifications in existing structures (such as agency hours, intake procedures) to increase the chances for success before *implementing* the group service. The worker concerns him or herself with the organizational participants who will be assigned responsibility for the group service, providing a clear conception about group purpose and role requirements (Holloway 1987; Pressman and Wildavsky 1973).

Recruiting Group Members

After the worker enlists organizational sanctions and supports, formulates the purpose and type of group, selects appropriate temporal and other structures, identifies compositional factors, and resolves staffing issues, she or he begins to recruit potential members for the group. The worker uses various sources to recruit potential group members, such as the worker's own organization, other organizations, the local community, and the broader community. Within one's own organization the worker may develop a group from her or his own *assigned services* and *caseloads*. In hospitals, for example, natural group clusters exist in particular medical services or wards. In these situations, as well as in developing a group from a worker's caseload, the worker and client know each other. Their relationship may lead to a quick service involvement and often propels the group past the typical "feeling out" and testing phase characteristic of group beginnings. At the same time, members have greater difficulty in refusing the service and, certainly, in sharing the worker with others. In fact, sharing the same worker in itself does not necessarily provide commonality and a shared purpose.

Referral is a frequent method of recruitment. To obtain referrals within one's own agency, the worker has to have an organizational presence. By cultivating interpersonal relationships and by demonstrating day-to-day professional competence, the worker establishes a reservoir of goodwill. To receive appropriate referrals of potential group candidates, the worker clearly identifies and communicates group purpose and membership criteria. As the worker receives the referrals, he examines available data and may conduct individual or even small group intake sessions to interpret service, assess need and interest, answer questions, and determine appropriateness. Examinations of agency *waiting lists, central files*, and *recording systems* are other internal recruitment sources.

In certain situations the worker's agency may have an insufficient pool of potential group members. Reaching out to other *community agencies*, such as schools for a children's group, is yet another recruitment strategy. Previously cultivated interpersonal relationships serves the worker well in gaining referrals or, at least, in acquiring leads from other staff. Community leaders also are a significant recruitment resource.

The worker can also use *census* data to locate a cluster of potential members with in a geographic area (Toseland 1981; Toseland and Rivas 2001). In developing group services for a large urban foster care agency, for example, the author used agency census data to offer group services within children's neighborhoods. Eliminating travel removed a significant barrier to implementing group services.

Still another method of recruiting members for the group is *random invitation*: putting up signs; inserting notices in a union newsletter; an advertisement in a local paper and community publicity. Computer and internet technology are yet another resource for recruitment. In all these sources, wording must be clear and should capture the attention and interest of the reader. Random open invitations invite voluntary participation, place least pressure for involvement, and may even recruit new "customers" for the agency. At the same time, the worker has only limited control over composition. This "pot luck" quality will characterize groups recruited by random methods. These methods also tend to be quite impersonal and rarely reach nonjoiners and nonreaders. Follow-up telephone calls, home visits, and group intakes can personalize the offer of service to some degree and simultaneously clear up misconceptions and screen out inappropriate candidates.

Whichever recruitment method the worker uses, the he or she must maintain professional responsibility for group composition. This is a specialized area of our professional expertise. Groups composed inappropriately of either highly homogeneous or heterogeneous members end in great frustration or even hopelessness, decreasing the probability that worker and client will invest themselves in a future group.

Preparing for the First Meeting

After group members are recruited for the group, the worker has two additional tasks to undertake; Namely, to prepare her or himself as well as the group members for the first meeting. Through processes of anticipatory empathy or "tuning in," the worker anticipates what members might be thinking or feeling as they arrive for the first meeting. Germain and Gitterman (1996) recommend four steps for developing an empathic understanding:

(1) identification, through which the social worker experiences what the client is feeling and thinking; (2) incorporation, through which the worker feels the experiences as if they were personal; (3) reverberation, through which the worker tries to call up personal life experiences that may facilitate understanding those of the client; and (4) detachment, through which the worker engages in logical, objective analysis.   (64)

A worker might find it difficult to identify with certain devastating life circumstances such as homelessness, AIDS, grave injury, drug addiction, and incarceration. To develop anticipatory empathy, the worker searches for parallel experiences that led to feelings of powerlessness, profound loss, and despair. The processes of incorporation and reverberation move the worker closer to group members' experiences. As a caution, workers must be careful not to project their own reactions onto the group members. They need to detach from the experience in order to separate what is the worker's "stuff" and what belongs to group members.

The worker uses anticipatory empathy to prepare for group members' potential concerns about the offer of service, the worker, and the other members. Since group members often indirectly express their reactions, the worker prepares to model the skill of putting the group members' feelings into words (Shulman 1999). The worker prepares to invite doubts or hesitations about the group's focus, the proposed type of group, temporal and spatial arrangements, the worker's background and competence, the degree of commonality with other members, issues related to confidentiality, and so on (Vichnis 1999). By inviting concerns and speaking the unspoken, the worker demonstrates professional competence and engenders greater confidence of members.

Whenever possible, preparing members for the group experience is also beneficial (Manor 1986; Meadow 1988). In a school setting, for example, the author initiated discussions with prospective group members about the differences between classrooms led by teachers and social work groups led by social workers. These conversations were extremely helpful in clarifying role expectations and mitigating ambiguity and confusion. The focus of these conversations was on notions of mutual aid and clarifying misconceptions and not on the establishment of rules of conduct. Hannah (2000:55) identifies six expectations that require discussion with prospective group members. They include 1. commitment to the group and its work, 2. belief in the democratic/collective process, 3. the value of here-and-now experiences and honest interaction among members, 4. the importance of mutual support and acceptance, 5. clarification of the worker's role, 6. the value of taking risks in order to achieve goals. The author recommends these preparatory conversations be conducted within small sunbgroups rather than within individual intakes. Members are extremely curious and concerned about other members. Presubgroup conversations create the context for the future group and demonstrate the process and the worker in action.

AT THE TURN of the century our profession's pioneers grappled with enormous problems associated with industrialization and urbanization. A few leaders believed a special institution was needed to help people cope and survive mass dislocation and poverty. The settlement house was born to stand against the forces of isolation, alienation, and anonymity. And, within the settlements, the group modality served as the primary mechanism to focus on people's fundamental needs to belong and to express themselves socially and intellectually. In contemporary society pervasive social and emotional isolation continues to call forth the extraordinary potentials inherent in the offering of group services. And so we discover the same themes exist today as in the past, altered only by the growth and changes in our society. Groups serve and continue to serve as a powerful healing force for people who share common needs and aspirations.

Notes

1. Discussions about formulation of group purpose; group composition factors; time, size, and space factors; and group recruitment factors are elaborated from the author's earlier publication (Gitterman 1982).
2. Edited excerpt from Gitterman and Schaeffer 1972; Gitterman and Nadelman 1999.
3. For a classic review of research related to the impact of group size, see Bales and Borgatta 1965.
4. This practice illustration is reprinted with the permission of Lawrence Shulman (1999:321–25).

References

Abrams, B. 2000. Finding common ground in a conflict resolution group. *Social Work with Groups* 23(1): 55–69.
Abramson, J. 1989. Making team work. *Social Work with Groups* 12(4): 45–64.
Adolph, M. R. 1996. No longer an outsider: A social group worker as a client in a bereavement group for older women. *Social Work with Groups* 19(2): 17–34.
Albert, J. 1994. Rethinking difference: A cognitive therapy group for chronic mental patients. *Social Work with Groups* 17(1/2): 105–22.
Amelio, R. 1993. An AIDS bereavement support group: One model of intervention in a time of crisis. *Social Work with Groups* 16(1/2): 55–72.
Anderson, D. B. and L. S. Shaw. 1994. Starting a support group for families and partners of people with HIV/AIDS in a rural setting. *Social Work* 39(1): 135–38.
Arches, J. 1991. Social structure, burnout, and job satisfaction. *Social Work* 36(3): 202–206.
Armstrong, K. 1990. The discharge issues group: A model for acute psychiatric inpatient units. *Social Work with Groups* 13(1): 93–101.
Auslander, B. and G. Auslander. 1988. Self-help groups and the family service agency. *Social Casework* 69:7–80.
Bales, R. F. and E. F. Borgatta. 1965. Size of group as a factor in the interaction profile. In E. F. Borgatta and R. F. Bales, eds., *Small Groups*, pp. 495–512. New York: Knopf.

Ball, S. 1994. A group model for gay and lesbian clients with chronic mental illness. *Social Work.* 39(1): 109–15.

Barth, R. P., J. Yeatin, and N. Winterfelt. 1994. Psychoeducational groups with foster parents of sexually abused children. *Child and Adolescent Social Work Journal* 11(5): 405–24.

Bauman, J. A. and G. L. James. 1989. A support group for burn victims and their families. *Social Work with Groups* 12(4): 159–69.

Behroozi, C. 1992. A model for social work with involuntary applicants in groups. *Social Work with Groups* 15(2/3): 223–28.

Berger, C. S. 1990. Enhancing social work influence in the hospital: Identifying sources of power. *Social Work in Health Care* 5(2): 77–93.

Berman-Rossi, T. 1992. Empowering groups through understanding stages of group development. *Social Work with Groups* 15(2/3): 239–55.

—— 1993. The tasks and skills of the social worker across stages of group development. *Social Work with Groups* 16(1/2): 69–92.

—— 2003. The group as a source of hope: Institutionalized older persons. In A. Gitterman and L. Shulman, eds., *Mutual aid groups, vulnerable and resilient populations, and the life cycle,* this volume. New York: Columbia University Press.

Berman-Rossi, T. and M. Cohen. 1988. Group development and shared decision making: Working with homeless mentally ill women. *Social Work with Groups* 11(4): 63–78.

Bertcher, H. and F. Maple. 1985. Elements and issues in group composition. In M. Sundel, P. Glasser, R. Sarri, and R. Vinter, eds., *Individual change through small groups,* pp. 180–203. 2d ed. New York: Free Press.

Bilides, D. 1990. Race, color, ethnicity, and class: Issues of biculturalism in school-based adolescent counseling groups. *Social Work with Groups* 13(4): 43–58.

—— 1992. Reaching inner-city children: A group work program model for a public middle school. *Social Work with Groups* 15(2/3): 129–44.

Birnbach, D. 1971. The skills of child care. In W. Schwartz and S. Zelba, eds., *The practice of group work,* pp. 176–98. New York: Columbia University Press.

Black, R. and D. Drachman. 1985. Hospital social workers and self-help groups. *Health and Social Work* 10(1): 95–103.

Block, L. R. 1985. On the potentiality and limits of time: The single-session group and the cancer patient. *Social Work with Groups* 8(2): 81–98.

Bloch, J. S., J. Margolis, and M. Seitz. 1994. Feelings of shame: Siblings of handicapped children. In A. Gitterman and L. Shulman, eds., *Mutual aid groups, vulnerable and resilient populations, and the life cycle,* pp. 97–118. 2d ed. New York: Columbia University Press.

Bloom, N. D. and J. G. Lynch. 1979. Group work in a hospital waiting room. *Health and Social Work* 4(3): 48–63.

Bond, G. R. and R. De Graaf-Kaser. 1990. Group approaches for persons with severe mental illness: A typology. *Social Work with Groups* 13(1): 21–36.

Borkman, T. J., ed. 1991. Self-help groups. *American Journal of Community Psychology* 19(5).

Bostwick, G. 1987. Where's Mary? A review of the group treatment dropout literature. *Social Work with Groups* 10(3): 117–32.

Brager, G. and S. Holloway. 1978. Changing human service organizations: Politics and practice. New York: Free Press.

———— 1992. Assessing prospects for organizational change. *Administration in Social Work* 16(3/4): 15–28.

Brennan, F., D. Downes, and S. Nadler. 1996. A support group for spouses of nursing home residents. *Social Work with Groups* 19(3/4): 71–81.

Brown, A. and A. Kerslake, eds. 1990. Child sexual abuse: The group work response. *Groupwork* 3(2).

Brown, A. and T. Mistry. 1994. Group work with "mixed membership" groups: Issues of race and gender. *Social Work with Groups* 17(3): 5–22.

Brown, C. 1998. A hospital-based early recovery group program for HIV-infected inner-city clients: Engagement strategies. *Journal of Chemical Dependency Treatment* 7(1/2): 53–66.

Brown, D. G., K. Krieg, and F. Belluck. 1995. A model for group intervention with the chronically ill: Cystic fibrosis and the family. *Social Work in Health Care* 21(1): 81–94.

Brown, J. 1994. Agents of change: A group of women in a shelter. In A. Gitterman and L. Shulman, eds., *Mutual aid groups, vulnerable and resilient populations, and the life cycle*, pp. 273–96. 2d ed. New York: Columbia University Press.

Brown, P. A., and C. Dickey. 1992. Critical reflection in groups with abused women. *Affilia: Journal of Women and Social Work* 7(3): 57–61.

Browne, K., D. Saunders, and K. Staecker. 1997. Process-psychodynamic groups for men who batter: A brief treatment model. *Families in Society* 78(3): 265–71.

Burke, J., D. Coddington, R. Bakeman, and P. Clance. 1994. Inclusion and exclusion in HIV support groups. *Journal of Gay and Lesbian Psychotherapy* 2(2): 121–30.

Butler, D. G. and L. R. Beltran. 1993. Functions of an adult sickle cell group: Education, task orientation, and support. *Health and Social Work* 18(1): 49–56.

Caplan, T. and H. Thomas. 1995. Safety and comfort, content and process: facilitating open group work with men who batter. *Social Work with Groups* 18(2/3): 33–52.

Cardarella, J. A. 1975. A group for children with deceased parents. *Social Work* 20(3): 328–29.

Caspar, M. 1981. The short-term group. In M. Goroff, ed., *Reaping from the Field—from practice to principles: proceedings three*, pp. 733–56. Hebron, Ct.: Practitioner.

Charping, J. W., W. J. Bell, and J. B. Strecker. 1992. Issues related to the use of short-term groups for adjustment to divorce: A comparison of programs. *Social Work with Groups* 15(4): 15–42.

Chau, K. 1992. Needs assessment for group work with people of color: A conceptual formulation. *Social Work with Groups* 15(2/3): 53–66.

Chauncey, S. 1994. Emotional concerns and treatment of male partners of female sexual abuse survivors. *Social Work* 39(6): 669–76.

Child, R. and G. Getzel. 1989. Group work with inner city persons with AIDS. *Social Work with Groups* 12(4): 65–79.

Cohen, M. B. and A. Mullender. 1999. The personal in the political: Exploring the group work continuum from individual to social chnage goals. *Social Work with Groups.* 22(1): 13–31.

Congress, E. P. and M. Lynn. 1994. Group work programs in public schools: Ethical dilemmas and cultural diversity. *Social Work in Education* 16(2): 107–14.

Croxton, T. 1985. The therapeutic contract. In M. Sundel, P. Glasser, R. Sarri, and R. Vinter, eds., *Individual change through small groups*, pp. 159–79. 2d ed. New York: Free Press.

Cummings, S. 1996. Spousal caregivers of early stage Alzheimer's patients: A psychoeducational support group model. *Journal of Gerentological Social Work.* 26(3/4): 83–98.

Dalton, G. 1970.Influence and organizational change. In G. Dalton, P. Lawrence, and L. Greiner, eds., *Organizational change and development*, pp. 234–37. Homewood, Ill.: Irwin-Dorsey International.

Dane, B. and B. Simon. 1991. Resident guests: Social workers in host settings. *Social Work* 36(3): 208–13.

Daste, B. 1990. Important considerations in group work with cancer patients. *Social Work with Groups* 13(2): 69–82.

Davis, L. E. 1980. Racial balance—a psychological issue. *Social Work with Groups* 3(2): 75–85.

Dean, R. 1998. A narrative approach in groups. *Clinical Social Work Journal* 26(1): 23–37.

Dies, R. R. 1983. Clinical implications on research on leadership in short-term group psychotherapy. In R. R. Dies and K. R. MacKenzie, eds., *Advances in group psychotherapy*, pp. 27–78. New York: International Universities Press.

Dowds, M. 1996. Paranoia and ethnically diverse population: The role of group work. *Social Work with Groups* 19(1): 67–77.

Drews, J. R. and T. T. Bradley. 1989. Group treatment for adults molested as children: An educational and therapeutic approach. *Social Work with Groups* 12(3): 57–75.

Drisko, J. W. 1992. Intimidation and projective identification in group therapy of physically abused early adolescent boys. *Journal of Child and Adolescent Group Therapy* 2 (1): 17–30.

Duhatschek-Krause, A. 1989. A support group for patients and families facing life-threatening illness. *Social Work with Groups* 12(1): 55–70.

Efron, D. and R. Moir. 1996. Short term co-led intensive group work with adult children of alcoholics. *Social Work with Groups* 19(3/4): 117–29.

Ephross, P. and T. Vassil. 1988. *Groups that work.* New York: Columbia University Press.

Epstein, N. 1970. Brief group therapy in child guidance clinic. *Social Work* 15(4): 33–38.

Evans, D. and W. Shaw. 1993. A social group work model for latency-aged children from violent homes. *Social Work with Groups* 16(1/2): 97–116.

Farmer, S. and D. Galaris. 1993. Support groups for children of divorce. *American Journal of Family Therapy* 21(1): 40–50.

Fatout, M. 1993. Physically abused children: Activity as a therapeutic medium. *Social Work with Groups* 16(3): 83–96.

Fatout, M. and S. Rose. 1995. *Task groups in the social services.* Thousand Oaks, Cal.: Sage.

Finn, J. 1995. Computer-based self-help groups: A new resource to supplement support groups. *Social Work with Groups* 18(1): 109–17.

Finzi, R. and D. Stange. 1997. Short-term group intervention as a means of improving the adjustment of children of mentally ill parents. *Social Work with Groups* 20(4): 69–80.

Fisher, M. 1995. Group therapy protocols for persons with personality disorders who abuse substance: Effective treatment alternatives. *Social Work with Groups* 18(4): 71–89.

Foster, S. B., P. E. Stevens, and J. M. Hall. 1994. Offering support services for lesbians living with HIV. *Women in Therapy* 15(2): 69–83.

Fraher, J. and M. McNally. 1979. Group work with physically disabled adolescents. *Social Work with Groups* 2(4): 321–30.

Frey, G. 1990. A framework for promoting organizational change. *Families in Society* 71(3): 142–47.

Galinsky, M. J. and J. Schopler. 1977. Warning groups may be dangerous. *Social Work* 22(2): 89–94.

—— 1980. Structuring co-leadership. *Social Work with Groups* 3(4): 51–63.

—— 1985. Patterns of entry and exit in open-ended groups. *Social Work with Groups* 8(2): 67–80.

—— 1989. Developmental patterns in open-ended groups. *Social Work with Groups* 12(2): 99–114.

—— 1994. Negative experiences in support groups. *Social Work in Health Care* 20(1): 77–95.

Galinsky. M., J. Schopler, and M. Abell. 1997. Connecting group members through telephone and computer groups. *Health and Social Work* 22(3): 181–88.

Gardella, L. G. 1985. The neighborhood group: A reminiscence group for the disoriented old. *Social Work with Groups* 8(2): 43–52.

Garland, J. 1992. Developing and sustaining group work services: A systemic and systematic view. *Social Work with Groups* 15(4): 89–98.

Garland, J., H. Jones, and R. Kolodny. 1968. A Model of stages of development in social work groups. In S. Bernstein, ed., *Explorations in group work*, pp. 12–53. Boston: Boston University School of Social Work.

Garvin, C. 1992. A task-centered group approach to work with the chronically mentally ill. *Social Work with Groups.* 15(2/3): 67–80.

Gentry, M. E. 1987. Coalition formation and processes. *Social Work with Groups.* 10(3): 19–54.

Germain, C. B. 1978. Space: An ecological variable in social work practice. *Social Casework* 59:515–22.

—— 1983. Using social and physical environments. In A. Rosenblatt and D. Waldfogel, ed., *Handbook of clinical social work*, pp. 110–33. San Francisco: Jossey-Bass.

Germain, C. B. and A. Gitterman. 1996. *The life model of social work practice: Advances in knowledge and practice*, pp. 241–78. 2d ed. New York: Columbia University Press.

Getzel, G. S. 1982. Group work with kin and friends caring for the elderly. *Social Work with Groups* 5(2): 91–102.

—— 1983. Poetry writing groups and the elderly. *Social Work with Groups.* 6(1): 65–76.

—— 2004. No one is alone: Groups during the AIDS pandemic. In A. Gitterman and L. Shulman, eds., *Mutual aid groups, vulnerable and resilient populations, and the life cycle*, this volume. New York: Columbia University Press.

Getzel, G. S. and K. Mahony. 1993. Confronting human finitude: Group work with people with AIDS. *Social Work with Groups* 16(1/2): 27–42.

Gilbert, M. 1989. Developing a group program in a health care setting. *Social Work with Groups* 12(4): 27–44.

Gitterman, A. 1971. Group work in the public schools. In W. Schwartz and S. Zalba, eds., *The practice of group work*, pp. 45–72. New York: Columbia University Press.

—— 1977. Social work in the public schools. *Social Casework* 58:111–18.

—— 1979. Survey of group services in maternal and child health. In *Social work with groups in maternal and child health: Conference proceedings*, pp. 8–14. New York: Columbia University School of Social Work.

—— 1982. The use of groups in health setting. In A. Lurie, G. Rosenberg, and S. Pinsky, eds., *Social work with groups in health settings*, pp. 6–21. New York: Prodist.

—— 1989. Building support in groups. *Social Work with Groups* 12(2): 5–22.

—— 2003. The mutual aid model. In C. Garvin, M. Galinsky, and Gutierrez, eds., *Handbook of social work with groups.* New York: Guilford.

Gitterman, A. and C. Knight. 2000. The power of group work. *New Social Worker* 7(2): 15–20.

Gitterman, A. and I. Miller. 1989. The influence of the organization on clinical practice. *Clinical Social Work Journal* 17(2): 151–64.

Gitterman, A. and A. S. Nadelman. 1999. The white professional and the black client revisited. *Reflections: Narrative of Professional Helping* 5(2): 67–79.

Gitterman, A. and A. Schaeffer. 1972. The white professional and the black client. *Social Casework* 53:280–91.

Gitterman, N. 1979. Group services for learning disabled children and their parents. *Social Casework* 60:217–26.

Gladstone, J. and T. Reynolds. 1997. Single-session group work intervention in response to employee stress during workforce transformation. *Social Work with Groups* 20(1): 33–50.

Glasgow, G. F. and J. Gouse-Sheese. 1995. Themes of rejection and abandonment in group work with Caribbean adolescents. *Social Work with Groups* 17(4): 3–27.

Goelitz, A. 2001. Dreaming their way into life: A group experience with oncology patients. *Social Work with Groups.* 24(1): 53–67.

Goodman, H. 1997. Social group work in community corrections. *Social Work with Groups* 20(1): 51–64.

Greene, D. and L. McVinney. 1998. Outpatient group psychotherapy with chemically dependent and cluster-b personality disordered male clients. *Journal of Chemical Dependency Treatment* 7(1/2): 81–96.

Greif, G. L. and J. Kristall. 1993. Common themes in a group for noncustodial parents. *Families in Society* 74(4): 240–45.

Groves, P. and C. Schondel. 1996. Lesbian couples who are survivors of incest: Group work utilizing a feminist approach. *Social Work with Groups* 19(3/4): 93–102.

Gummer, B. 1995. Go team go! The growing importance of teamwork in organizational life. *Administration in Social Work* 19(4): 85–100.

Hack, T. F., T. A. G. Osachuk, and R. V. De Luca. 1994. Group treatment for sexually abused preadolescent boys. *Families in Society* 75(4): 217–28.

Haige, J. and M. Aikens. 1970. *Social change in complex organizations.* New York: Random House.

Hannah, P. J. 2000. Preparing members for the expectations of social work with groups: An approach to the preparatory interview. *Social Work with Groups* 22(4): 51–66.

Hanson, M. 1998. The transition group: Linking clients with alcohol problems in outpatient care. *Journal of Chemical Dependency Treatment* 7(1/2): 21–36

Hanson, M., L. Formena, W. Tomlin, and Y. Bright. 1994. Facilitating problem drinking clients' transition from inpatient to outpatient care. *Health and Social Work* 19(1): 23–28.

Hardman, K. 1997. A social work group for prostituted women with children. *Social Work with Groups* 20(1): 19–32.

Harpaz, N. 1994. Failures in group psychotherapy: The therapist variable. *International Journal of Group Psychotherapy* 44(1): 3–19.

Harper, K. V. and L. S. Shillito. 1991. Group work with bulimic adolescent females in suburbia. *Social Work with Groups* 14(1): 43–56.

Hartford, M. E. and S. Lawton. 1997. Groups for the socialization to old age. In J. K. Parry, ed., *From prevention to wellness through group work*, pp. 33–45. Bingampton, N.Y.: Haworth.

Helfand, K. L. 1994. Therapeutic considerations in structuring a support group for the mentally ill gay/lesbian population. *Journal of Gay and Lesbian Psychotherapy* 2(1): 65–76.

Herzog, J. 1980. Communication between co-leaders: fact or myth? A student's perspective. *Social Work with Groups* 3(4): 19–29.

Holloway, S. 1987. Staff initiated organizational change. *Encyclopedia of social work*, pp. 729–36. 18th ed. Silver Spring: National Association of Social Work.

Holmes-Garrett, C. 1989. The crisis of the forgotten family: A single session group in the ICU waiting room. *Social Work with Groups* 12(4): 141–58.

Irizarry, C. and Y. H. Appel. 2004. Preteens in double jeopardy: Supporting developmental growth through a natural friendship group. In A. Gitterman and L. Shulman, eds., *Mutual aid groups, vulnerable and resilient populations, and the life cycle*, this volume. New York: Columbia University Press.

Jagendorf, J. and A. Malekoff. 2000. Groups-on-the-go: Spontaneously formed mutual aid groups for adolescents in distress. *Social Work with Groups* 22(4): 15–32.

Jones, M. J. 1994. Speaking the unspoken: Parents of sexually victimized children. In A. Gitterman and L. Shulman, eds., *Mutual aid groups, vulnerable and resilient populations, and the life cycle*, pp. 239–56. 2d ed. New York: Columbia University Press.

Joyce, P. A. 1995. Group work with mothers of sexually abused children. In R. Kurland and R. Salmon, eds., *Group work practice in a troubled society*, pp. 165–76. New York: Haworth.

Karlins, M. and H. I. Abelson. 1970. *Persuasion: How opinions and attitudes are changed.* New York: Springer.

Kaslyn, M. 1999. Telephone group work: Challenges for practice. *Social Work with Groups* 22(1): 63–77.

Kelly, T. 1999. Mutual aid groups with mentally ill older adults. *Social Work with Groups* 21(4): 63–80.

Kelly, T. and T. Berman-Rossi. 1999. Advancing stages of group development theory: The case of institutionalized older persons. *Social Work with Groups* 22(2/3): 119–38.

Knight, C. 1990. Use of support groups with adult female survivors of sexual abuse. *Social Work* 35(3): 202–6.

—— 1993. The use of therapy group for adult men and women sexually abused in childhood. *Social Work with Groups* 16(4): 81–94.

Kolodny, R. 1980. The dilemma of co-leadership. *Social Work with Groups* 3(4): 31–34.

Koss, M. and J. Butcher. 1986. Research on brief psychotherapy. In S. Gardfield and A. Bergin, eds., *Handbook of psychotherapy and behavior change*, pp. 627–70. New York: Wiley.

Kuechler, C. F. 1997. Psychoeducational groups: A model for recovery and celebration of the self. In J. K. Parry, ed., *From prevention to wellness through group work*, pp. 47–59. Binghampton, N.Y.: Haworth.

Kurland, R and R. Salmon. 1992. Group work vs. casework in a group: Principles and implications for teaching and practice. *Social Work with Groups* 15 (4): 3–14.

———— 1993. Not just one of the gang: Group workers and their role as an authority. *Social Work with Groups* 16(1/2): 153–69.

———— 1998. Purpose: A misunderstood and misused keystone of group work practice. *Social Work with Groups* 21(3): 5–17.

Kurtz, L. 1990. The self-help movement: Review of the past decade of research. *Social Work with Groups* 13(3): 101–16.

Kurtz, L., K. Mann, and A. Chambon. 1987. Linking between social workers and mental health mutual-aid groups. *Social Work in Health Care* 13(1): 69–78.

Laube, J. J. 1990. Why group therapy for Bulimia? *International Journal of Group Psychotherapy* 40(2): 169–87.

Lee, J. A. B. 1977. Group work with mentally retarded foster adolescents. *Social Casework* 58(2):164–73.

Levin, A. E. 1992. Group work with parents in the family foster care system: A powerful method of engagement. *Child Welfare* 71(5): 457–73.

Levinsky, L. and K. McAleer. 2004. Listen to us! Young adolescents in urban schools. In A. Gitterman and L. Shulman, eds., *Mutual aid groups, vulnerable and resilient populations and the life cycle,* this volume. New York: Columbia University Press.

Lipton, H. 1971. The social worker as mediator on a hospital ward. In W. Schwartz and S. Zelba, eds., *The practice of group work,* pp. 106–20. New York: Columbia University Press.

Lewin, K. 1952. Group decisions and social change. In E. Maccoby, T. Newcomb, and E. Hartley, eds., *Readings in social psychology,* pp. 207–11. New York: Holt, Rinehart and-Winston.

Lopez, J. 1991. Group work as a protective factor for immigrant youth. *Social Work with Groups* 14(1): 29–42.

Lynn, M. and D. Nisivoccia. 1995. Activity-oriented group work with the mentally ill: Enhancing socialization. *Social Work with Groups* 18(2/3): 33–52.

Lyon, E., N. Moore, and C. Lexius. 1992. Group work with families of homicide victims. *Social Work with Groups* 15(1): 19–34.

McCallion, P. and R. Toseland, R. 1995. Supportive group interventions with caregivers of frail older adults. *Social Work with Groups* 18(1): 11–25.

MacKenzie, K. 1996. Time-limited group psychotherapy. *International Journal of Group Psychotherapy* 46(1): 41–60.

Magura, S., J. Shapiro, J. Grossman, and D. Lipton. 1989. Education/support groups with AIDS prevention with at-risk clients. *Social Casework* 70:10–20.

Malekoff, A. 1994. A guideline for group work with adolescents. *Social Work with Groups* 17(1/2): 5–19.

———— 1999. *Group work with adolescents: Principles and practice.* New York: Guilford.

Mancoske, R. G. and T. Lindhorst. 1991. Mutual assistance groups in a shelter for persons with AIDS. *Social Work with Groups* 14(2): 75–86.

Manor, O. 1986. The preliminary interview in social group work: Finding the spiral steps. *Social Work with Groups* 9(2): 21–40.

Martin, P. Y. and K. A. Shanahan. 1983. Transcending the effects of sex composition in small groups. *Social Work with Groups* 6(3/4): 19–32.

Mayers, A. and L. Spiegel. 1992. A parental support group in pediatric AIDS clinic: Its usefulness and limitations. *Health and Social Work* 17(3): 183–91.

Meadow, D. 1988. Preparation of individuals for participation in a treatment group: Development and empirical testing of a model. *International Journal of Group Psychotherapy* 38(3): 367–85.

Mechanic, D. 1964. Sources of power of lower participants in complex organizations. In W. Cooper, H. Leavitt, and M. Shelly II, eds., *New perspectives in organizational research.* New York: Wiley.

——— 1999. Mental health and social policy: The emergence of managed care. Boston: Allyn and Bacon.

Meier, A., M. Galinsky, and K. Rounds. 1995. Telephone groups for caregivers of persons with AIDS. *Social Work with Groups* 18(1): 99–108.

Mellor, D. and S. Storer. 1995. Support groups for children in alternate care: A largely untapped therapeutic resource. *Child Welfare* 74(4): 905–18.

Middleman, R. 1980. Co-leadership and solo-leadership in education for social work with groups. *Social Work with Groups* 3(4): 39–50.

Milgram, D. and J. Rubin. 1992. Resisting resistance: Involuntary substance abuse group therapy. *Social Work with Groups* 15(1): 95–110.

Millan, F. and N. Elia. 1998. The model of multiple oppression in group psychotherapy with HIV-infected injecting drug users. *Journal of Chemical Dependency Treatment* 7(1/2): 97–116.

Miller, D. 1997. Parenting against the odds: African American parents in the child welfare system—a group work approach. *Social Work with Groups* 20(1): 5–18.

Miller, J. and J. Donner. 2000. More than just talk: The use of racial dialogue. *Social Work with Groups* 23(1): 31–53.

Miller, R. and S. Mason. 2001. Using group therapy to enhance treatment compliance in first episode schizophrenia. *Social Work with Groups* 24(1): 37–51.

Morris, R. and R. Binstock. 1966. *Feasible planning for social change.* New York: Columbia University Press.

Nadelman, A. 2004. Sharing the hurt: Adolescents in a residential setting. In A. Gitterman and L. Shulman, eds., *Mutual aid groups, vulnerable and resilient populations, and the life cycle*, this volume. New York: Columbia University Press.

Neisen, J. 1998. An inpatient psychoeducational group model for gay men and lesbians with alcohol and drug abuse problems. *Journal of Chemical Dependency Treatment* 7(1/2): 37–52.

Nightengale, J. 1990. Discharge planning promoting patient involvement through group process. *Social Work with Groups* 13(2): 83–95.

Norman, A. J. 1991. The use of the group and group work techniques in resolving interethnic conflict. *Social Work with Groups* 14(3/4): 175–86.

Northern, H. and R. Kurland. 2001. *Social work with groups.* 3d ed. New York: Columbia University Press.

Nosko, A. and R. Wallace. 1997. Female/male co-leadership in groups. *Social Work with Groups* 20(2): 3–16.

Orr, A. L. 2003. Dealing with the death of a group member: Visually impaired elderly in the community. In A. Gitterman and L. Shulman, eds., *Mutual aid groups, vulnerable and resilient populations, and the life cycle*, this volume. New York: Columbia University Press.

Oygard, L. and S. Hardeng. 2001. Divorce support groups: How do group characteristics influence adjustment to divorce? *Social Work with Groups* 24(1): 69–87.

Packard, T. 1989. Participation in decision-making, performance, and job satisfaction in a social work bureaucracy. *Administration in Social Work* 13(1): 59–73.

Plasse, B. R. 2000. Components of engagement: Women in psychoeducational parenting skills groups in substance abuse treatment. *Social Work with Groups* 22(4): 33–50.

Pollio, D. E. 1994. Wintering at the earle: Group structure in the street community. *Social Work with Groups* 17(1/2): 47–70.

Poynter-Berg, D. 1994. Getting connected: Institutionalized schizophrenic women." In A. Gitterman and L. Shulman, eds., *Mutual aid groups, vulnerable and resilient populations, and the life cycle*, pp. 315–34. 2d ed. New York: Columbia University Press.

Pressman, B. and A. Sheps. 1994. Treating wife abuse: An integrated model. *International Journal of Group Psychotherapy* 44(4): 477–98.

Pressman, J. and A. Wildavsky. 1973. *Implementation*. Berkeley: University of California Press, 1973.

Raines, J. C. 1991. Social skills groups with learning disabled students. *School Social Work Journal* 16(1): 9–23.

Redl, F. 1951. Art of group composition. In S. Schulz, ed., *Creative Group Living in Children's Institutions*, pp. 76–96. New York: Association.

Regehr, C. and J. Hill. 2000. Evaluating the efficacy of crisis debriefing groups. *Social Work with Groups* 23(3): 69–79.

Reid, K., G. Mathews, and P. Liss. 1995. My partner is hurting: Group work with male partners of adult survivors of sexual abuse. *Social Work with Groups* 18(1): 81–87.

Rittner, B. and K. Hammons. 1992. Telephone group work with people with end stage AIDS. *Social Work with Groups* 15(4): 59–72.

Rittner, B. and N. J. Smyth. 1999. Time-limited cognitve-behavioral group interventions with suicidal adolescents. *Social Work with Groups*, 22(2/3): 55–75.

Roller, B. and V. Nelson, eds. 1991. *The art of co-therapy: How therapists work together*. London: Guilford.

Rose, S. 1977. *Group therapy: A behavioral approach*. Englewood Cliffs, N.J.: Prentice-Hall.

Rothenberg, E. 1994. Bereavement intervention with vulnerable populations: A case report on group work with the developmentally disabled. *Social Work with Groups* 17(3): 61–76.

Rotholz, T. 1985. The single session group: An innovative approach to the waiting room. *Social Work with Groups* 8(2): 143–46.

Sakal, C. E. 1991. Group intervention strategies with domestic abusers. *Families in Society* 72(9): 536–42.

Sandstrom, K. 1996. Searching for information, understanding, and self-value: The utilization of peer support groups by gay men with HIV/AIDS. *Social Work in Health Care* 23(4): 51–74.

Saulmier, C. 1997. Alcohol problems and marginalization: Social group work with lesbians. *Social Work with Groups* 20(3): 37–59.

Schames, G. 1990. New directions in children's group therapy. *Social Work with Groups* 13(1): 67–92.

Schiller, L. Y. 1995. Stages of development in women's groups: A relational model. In R. Kurland and R. Salmon, eds., *Group work practice in a troubled society*, pp. 117–38. New York: Haworth.

——— 1997. Rethinking stages of development in women's groups. *Social Work with Groups* 20(3): 3–19.

Schiller, L. Yael and B. Zimmer. 2004. Sharing the secrets: women's groups for sexual abuse survivors. In A. Gitterman and L. Shulman, eds., *Mutual aid groups, vulnerable and resilient populations, and the life cycle,* this volume. New York: Columbia University Press.

Schlenoff, M. and S. Busa. 1981. Student and field instructor as group co-therapists: Equalizing an unequal relationship. *Journal of Education for Social Work* 17(1): 29–35.

Schopler, J. H. and M. Galinsky. 1981. When groups go wrong. *Social Work* 26(5): 424–29.

—— 1984. Meeting practice needs: conceptualizing the open-ended group. *Social Work with Groups* 7(2): 3–21.

Schopler, J., M. Galinsky, and M. Abell. 1997. Creating community through telephone and computer groups: Theoretical and practice perspectives. *Social Work with Groups* 20(4): 19–34.

Schutz, W. C. 1958. *F.I.P.O.: A three dimensional theory of interpersonal orientation.* New York: Holt, Rinehart and Winston.

—— 1961. On group composition. *Journal of Abnormal Social Psychology* 62:275–81.

Schwartz, W. 1961. The social worker in the group. *The social welfare forum,* pp. 146–77. New York: Columbia University Press.

—— 1971. On the uses of groups in social work practice. In W. Schwartz and S. Zelba, eds., *The practice of group work,* pp. 3–24. New York: Columbia University Press.

Shalinsky, W. 1964. Group composition as an element of social group work practice. *Social Service Review* 43 (March): 42–49.

Shulman, L. 1999. *The skills of helping: Individuals, families, and groups, and communities.* 4th ed. Itasca, Ill: Peacock.

Simoni, J. M. and L. Perez. 1995. Latinos and mutual support: A case for considering culture. *American Journal of Orthopsychiatry* 65(3): 440–45.

Slavson, S. R. 1955. Criteria for selection and rejection of patients for various kinds of group therapy. *International Journal of Psychotherapy* 5:3–30.

—— 1964. *A textbook in analytic group psychotherapy,* pp. 178–232. New York: International Universities Press.

Solomon, K., and M. R. Zinke. 1991. Group psychotherapy with the depressed elderly. *Journal of Gerontological Social Work* 17(1/2): 47–57.

Sowers-Hoad, K. M. and J. A. Hoag. 1987. Effects of sex composition on behavior in groups. *Affilia: Journal of Women and Social Work* 2(1): 18–23.

Sparks, A. and J. Goldberg. 1994. A current perspective on short-term groups for incest survivors. *Women and Therapy* 15(2): 135–49.

Starak, Y. 1981. Co-leadership: A new look at sharing group work. *Social Work with Groups* 4(3/4): 145–57.

Stein, L., B. Rothman, and M. Nakanishi 1993. The telephone group: Accessing group service to the homebound. *Social Work with Groups* 16(1/2): 204–43.

Steinberg, D. M. 1990. A model for adolescent pregnancy prevention through the use of small groups. *Social Work with Groups* 13(2): 57–68.

—— 1999. The impact of time and place on mutual-aid practice with short-term groups. *Social Work with Groups* 22(2/3): 101–18.

Stephenson, S. J. and M. F. Boler. 1981. Group treatment for divorcing parents. *Social Work with Groups* 4(3/4): 67–78.

Sternbach, J. 1990. The men's seminar: An educational and support group for men. *Social Work with Groups* 13(2): 23–40.

Stokes, N. and J. Gillis. 1995. Effective treatment strategies with adult incest survivors: Utilizing therapeutic group work methods within the context of an immediate family. In R. Kurland and R. Salmon, eds., *Group work practice in a troubled society*, pp. 189–201. New York: Haworth.

Straussner, S. 1998. Group treatment with substance abusing clients: A model of treatment during the early phases of outpatient group therapy. *Journal of Chemical Dependency Treatment* 7(1/2): 67–80.

Subramanian, K. and K. Ell. 1989. Coping with a first heart attack: A group treatment model for low-income Anglo, Black, and Hispanic patients. *Social Work with Groups* 12(4): 99–118.

Subramanian, K., S. Hernandez, and A. Martinez. 1995. Psychoeducational group work for low-income latina mothers with HIV infection. *Social Work with Groups* 18(2/3): 53–64.

Sultenfuss, J. and B. Geczy Jr. 1996. Group therapy on state hospital chronic wards: Some guidelines. *International Journal of Group Psychotherapy* 46(2): 163–76.

Sunley, R. 1997. Advocacy in the new world of managed care. *Families in Society* 78(1): 84–94.

Swenson, C. 1979. *Social networks, mutual aid, and the life model of practice.* In C. Germain, ed., *Social work practice: People and environments*, pp. 215–38. New York: Columbia University Press.

Thomas, H. and T. Caplan. 1999. Spinning the group process wheel: Effective facilitation techniques for motivating involuntary client groups. *Social Work with Groups.* 21(4): 3–21.

Toseland, R. 1981. Increasing access: Outreach methods in social work practice. *Social Casework* 62:227–34.

Toseland, R. W. and R. F. Rivas. 2001. *An introduction to group work practice.* 4th ed. Boston: Allen and Bacon.

Toseland, R. W. and M. Siporin. 1986. When to recommend group treatment: A review of the clinical and research literature. *International Journal of Group Psychotherapy* 36(2): 171–202.

Trimble, D. 2004. Uncovering kindness and respect: Men who have practiced violence in intimate relationships. In A. Gitterman and L. Shulman, eds., *Mutual aid groups, vulnerable and resilient populations, and the life cycle*, this volume. New York: Columbia University Press.

Tsui, P. and Schultz, G. 1988. Ethnic factors in group process: Cultural dynamics in multiethnic therapy groups. *American Journal of Orthopsychiatry* 58(1): 136–42.

Tutty, L. and Wagar, S. 1994. The evolution of a group for young children who have witnessed family violence. *Social Work with Groups* 17(1/2): 89–104.

Vardi, D. J. and E. S. Buchholz. 1994. Group psychotherapy with inner-city grandmothers raising their grandchildren. *International Journal of Group Psychotherapy* 44(1): 101–22.

Vastola, J., A. Nierenberg, and E. H. Graham. 1994. The lost and found group: group work and bereaved children. In A Gitterman and L. Shulman, eds., *Mutual aid groups, vulnerable and resilient populations, and the life cycle*, pp. 81–96. 2d ed. New York: Columbia University Press.

Vichnis, R. 1999. Passing the baton: Principles and implications for transferring the leadership of a group. *Social Work with Groups* 22(2/3): 139–57.

Waite, L. M. 1993. Drama therapy in small groups with the developmentally disabled. *Social Work with Groups* 16(4): 95–108.

Waldron, J. A., R. Whittinton, and S. Jensen. 1985. Children's single session briefings: Group work with military families experiencing parents' deployment. *Social Work with Groups* 9(2): 101–9.

Walsh, J. and H. Hewitt. 1996. Facilitating an effective process in treatment groups with persons having serious mental illness. *Social Work with Groups* 19(1): 5–18.

Walsh-Burke, K. and P. Scanlon. 2000. Beyond reviving Ophelia: Groups for girls twelve to fourteen and women who care about them. *Social Work with Groups* 23(1): 71–81.

Wax, J. 1960. Criteria for grouping hospitalized mental patients. *Uses of groups in psychiatric settings*, pp. 91–100. New York: National Association of Social Workers.

Wayne, J. and C. S. Cohen. 2001. *Group work education in the field*. Alexandria, Va.: Council on Social Work Education.

Webb, N. B. 1985. Transition to parenthood: A time-limited mutual-aid group to facilitate a major role change. *Social Work with Groups* 8(2): 29–42.

Weiner, H. 1964. Social change and group work. *Social Work* 9:106–20.

Weiner, L., E. Spencer, R. Davidson, and C. Fair. 1993. National telephone support groups: A new avenue toward psychosocial support for HIV-infected children and their families. *Social Work with Groups* 16(3): 55–72.

Weisberg, A. 1987. Single session group practice in a hospital. In J. Lassner, K. Powell, and E. Finnegan, eds., *Social group work competence and values in practice*, pp. 99–112. Binghampton, N.Y.: Haworth.

Wood, G. G. and R. Middleman. 1992. Re-casting the die: A small group approach to giving batterers a chance to change. *Social Work with Groups* 15(1): 5–18.

Wood, G. G. and S. E. Roche. 2001. Representing selves, reconstructing lives: Feminist group work with women survivors of male violence. *Social Work with Groups* 23(4): 5–23.

Wright, W. 1999. The use of purpose in on-going activity groups: A framework for maximizing the therapeutic impact. *Social Work with Groups* 22(2/3): 31–54.

Yalom, I. 1995. *The theory and practice of group psychotherapy*. 4th ed.. New York: Basic.

Zambelli, G. C. and A. P. Derosa. 1992. Bereavement support groups for school-age children: Theory, intervention, and case example. *American Journal of Orthopsychiatry* 62(4): 484–93.

Part 2

Mutual Aid and
Vulnerable and Resilient
Children

Chapter 4

Healing Hearts
A Bereavement Group for Children

Carolyn Knight

D EATH IS a part of living. This statement is a fundamental truth that is all too often avoided, denied, and resisted. Children will take their cues from adults in their environment. When faced with the loss of a loved one, they will look to those closest to them for support, guidance, and comfort. Since the adults themselves may be struggling to cope with the loss, their ability to effectively respond to the child's needs may be compromised. For adults and children alike, grieving the loss of a loved one may be a solitary and lonely journey, occurring as it does within a broader social context that treats death as a taboo subject.

A bereavement group for children provides members with an opportunity to acknowledge, express, and understand their feelings and reactions. The purpose is not to take the pain away or to provide answers to questions that are, ultimately, unanswerable. Rather, a grief group for children normalizes their experience and their reactions to it. The group is based upon three basic assumptions. First, death and grieving are normal, inevitable aspects of life. Second, children *can* understand and cope with their loss, to varying degrees based upon their age and developmental maturity, and can learn and grow from the experience. Finally, the social worker's own views about and experiences with the loss of a loved one will inevitably influence her or his leadership. Depending upon the worker's own comfort with death and dying, her or his actions may either hinder or facilitate members' ability to do the difficult work they have come to do.

Developmental Tasks and Issues

Children's understanding of death varies by their age and emotional and cognitive maturity. This chapter focuses on groups for children ages five through twelve. Long-standing debate has centered on how very young children understand and respond to death (Bowlby 1960; Hurd 1999; Lonetto 1980; McCown and Davies 1995; Norris-Shortle, Young, Williams 1993; Wass 1984). The social worker should assume that children younger than age five typically are less able to benefit from the type of group described in this chapter since their ability to understand death and to express feelings about it are more limited. On the other hand, while a group would be a very appropriate intervention for children older than twelve, it would have a different emphasis and focus, given members' more sophisticated cognitive capacities.

Having said this, however, I've facilitated groups that have included children as young as five and as old as thirteen *in the same group*. In a perfect world younger children would be grouped with other young children, and older, latency-age children would participate in a groups together. However, the world in which I practice, and in which many other social workers practice, is far from perfect. Thus, out of necessity and a desire to respond to families' and the agency's sense of urgency, I've included in the same group children of various ages and at various developmental stages. Rather than this resulting in a barrier to mutual aid, I have found that it can enhance it in significant and powerful ways.

Children at different ages do conceptualize death differently and have varied capacities for expressing their feelings about losing someone close to them. Yet there are important underlying similarities, including sadness at the loss of a loved one, fears for the safety of self and others, and questions about what happens to a loved one after death. As group members tackle these very important and difficult issues together, they learn and grow from one another. As the following example reveals, younger children may be able to give voice to certain concerns that may be embarrassing for older children to express. Older children's ability to put their feelings into words may assist younger members to understand their emotional reactions.

Tommy, age five and a kindergartner, was referred to the group by his parents. Four months before, his older brother, Mike, age eight, died of complications that resulted from a bone marrow transplant he received after being diagnosed with leukemia. Tommy was the donor, and his parents were particularly concerned because he blamed himself for his brother's death, believing, as he said, "my blood made my brother sick, and he died." The other children in the group ranged in age from seven to thirteen, the oldest being Megan, an eighth grader whose mother had died five months before from breast cancer.

In the second session of the group Tommy spontaneously remarked, "Mikey played with me yesterday. He made my helicopter move." He matter-of-factly added that he knew his brother was with him because toys moved and he talked with Mike in his dreams. Initially, group members reacted to Tommy's comments with thoughtful, though not anxious, silence. Members continued to draw or scribble (as discussed below, the bereavement groups for children are activity based). I commented on the silence, asking members what they thought about what Tommy had said, about his believing that his brother was still with him. Megan was first to respond.

"I get these feelings sometimes that my mom is with me too. I like it. It doesn't scare me or anything. But I don't really say anything to anyone, because they probably would think I was crazy or something." Others in the group related similar experiences, expressing some confusion and concern about what others, particularly their friends, would think about them.

Because of his age, Tommy had no difficulty sharing his belief that he had encountered his brother. Unlike the older children in the group, Tommy didn't experience any embarrassment about this, nor did he question the reality of his experience. As a young teenager, however, Megan was acutely aware of how others might perceive her experiences in this regard. It was only when the issue was raised by Tommy that she, and others in the group, could acknowledge and talk about the possibility that their loved one was still with them.

As the discussion of this issue continued, some of the older members were able to speculate on what their experiences might mean. Were their loved ones, in fact, really with them? Were their experiences a way for them to cope with their loss? Questions such as these reflected their more sophisticated ability to understand death and their own reactions to it. While Tommy and the other young member of this group, Sarah, age seven, were less directly involved in this discussion, at a point later in the same session, Sarah remarked, "I think my daddy [who had died six months before of a massive heart attack] comes to me when I sleep because I need him to." This powerful comment suggested that while Sarah may have been less able to participate verbally in the conversation that had taken place, she nonetheless was attending to and able to benefit from it.

Whether the bereavement group includes children of approximately the same age and developmental stage or children at different stages, it is important for the social worker to understand the ways in which children understand death and dying and express their feelings about it. The work of Piaget and others studying the cognitive development of children is particularly useful (Bowlby 1960; Furman 1974; LeShan 1988; Lonetto 1980; Piaget 1950; Speece and Brent 1984). Younger children, ages two and a half to six, are characterized by preoperational thinking. Children at this stage will typically have a difficult time understanding the finality of death and may assume that the dead continue to possess qualities of the living, such as the ability to eat, sleep, play, and work. Thus, concerns about how a loved one will breathe or eat after being buried in a coffin are common, as is the fear that the deceased, whose body has been cremated, felt pain. Children at this stage also are described as being egocentric in their thinking, assuming that events that occur in their world result from something they did or did not do. A noteworthy consequence of this is the child's belief that they somehow caused the death of the loved one.

In the example mentioneded earlier, Tommy believed that his blood caused his brother's death. While the bone marrow transplant he donated to his brother did lead to a deadly infection, his belief that he was somehow the cause of his brother's death is typical and linked to his egocentric view of the world and his place in it. While it was important for Tommy to have correct information about how and why his brother died, his ability to fully appreciate and understand this also depended upon his developing more mature cognitive abilities.

Finally, children in the preoperational stage typically will have limited ability to express their emotional reactions to the death of a loved one. In many instances their emotional responses may be more analogous to separation anxiety. Young children's grief reactions may be more likely to be acted out rather than talked about (McCown and Davies 1995). For example, Tommy was able to say his blood caused his brother death, but was far less able to articulate the sense of responsibility that his comment reflected.

Older children, ages seven to eleven, move into the stage of concrete operations. They become increasingly able to view death as final and to express their feelings about losing a loved one. For children in the early part of this stage, fears about dying, as well as losing others close to them, are common. These fears may manifest themselves through nightmares, belief in a "bogeyman," and the like. For example, in the same group described above, during a discussion of members' fears, the older children had expressed concern for the health of a surviving loved one. Sarah, the second grader, said, "I think there's a monster in my room, under my bed." She further disclosed that she worried the monster would take her mother and brother away.

Elementary and early middle school age children also display heightened interest in the details of death and dying. Rather than reflecting morbid curiosity, this reflects a more general inquisitiveness about how the world works that is characteristic of this stage. Thus, questions about how a loved one "caught" cancer, what happens to a loved one's body after she or he is pronounced dead, and an interest in the rituals associated with funerals and burials are common.

In a group comprised primarily of eight, nine, and ten year olds, I introduced the topic of the causes of death, suggesting that members might have some questions about how their loved ones had died. The children had lost loved ones to heart attack, lung and breast cancer, pneumonia, drowning, and a car accident, and their questions were, as a result, quite varied. The children had an intense need to know more about what had led to their loved one's demise. Yet their comments also suggested that they felt that their questions were "taboo." Courtney, age nine, lost her grandmother to lung cancer, and her questions were typical of others in the group, "I try to ask my mom what happened to MeMe. But she cries and gets upset and tells me that she's with God and that's all that matters. I know my grandma smoked a lot and she had cancer in her lungs, but what is cancer? Did she get it just from smoking? Does everyone who smokes get cancer? My dad smokes cigarettes. Does that mean he will get cancer too?"

I answered her and other members' questions as best I could. But I'm neither a doctor nor a fortune-teller. Courtney and the other members of this group did need more factual information about how their loved ones died. But they also asked questions to which there are no clear answers: "My dad died in a car accident, how do I know my mom won't die, too?" "My granddad was really healthy and then he caught cold and he died. Why did this happen? They say he got pneumonia, but lots of people get pneumonia and they don't die. Why did he?"

I commented, "It seems like you guys really want to know more about what caused your loved ones to die. And you can get answers to those questions. But it also sounds like you are asking why did it have to happen to *your* loved one, and could someone else that you love die, too. And the problem with these questions is that I can't answer them, no one really can. That's one of the things that makes losing a loved one so hard." Angela, ten, began crying, and said, "Billy [her three year-old brother who accidentally drowned in a swimming pool] was just a baby. Why did he have to die? I miss him. He was so sweet and cute." Several other children also became teary-eyed, and the members began to talk, really for the first time, about their feelings of loss, sadness, and anger.

This exchange is typical and reveals both the concrete thinking that is characteristic of children at this stage as well as their developing ability to think more abstractly. As children's questions about the causes of death are asked and answered, they begin to confront the sorts of questions and affective reactions more typical of the formal operational thinking of adolescents and adults.

Vulnerabilities and Risk Factors and Resilience and Protective Factors

Much of the earliest research and theory dealing with children's reactions to the loss of a loved one focused on negative consequences. It was long assumed that the death of a loved one placed a child at greater risk for a host of serious problems ranging from childhood and adult depression to serious mental illness, though research to support this assumption is scant and has produced inconsistent, contradictory findings (Gersten, Beals, and Kallgren 1991; Pfohl, Stangl, and Tsuang 1983; Rutter 1971; Rutter, Izard, and Read 1986; Siegel, Mesagno, and Christ 1990).

More recently, attention has shifted to ascertaining the ways in which children typically cope with the loss of a loved one. It is assumed that, like adults, children progress through stages of grieving. Different conceptualizations exist, but the common theme is one of moving from recognition of the separateness of the loved one and the finality of death to mourning and accepting the loss and moving on with life (Baker and Sedney 1992; Cox 2000; Furman 1974; Glass 1991; LeShan 1988). Short- and long-term difficulties are presumed to result when children are unable to move through these stages. This inability may stem from a variety of sources, the most common of which appear to be misunderstanding about and/or inattentiveness to his or her need to grieve on the part of significant others, and a lack of support and nurturance from surviving caretakers.

Consideration also has been given to identifying the more common difficulties children may experience as well as why some children appear able to cope with their grief and others aren't. Not surprisingly, loss of a parent is particularly traumatic and places the child at greater risk for later difficulties, as do situations in which the child has witnessed the death of the loved one (Burman and Allen-Meares 1994; Costa and Holliday 1994; Schilling et al. 1992).

While guilt over the loss of the loved one may be explained developmentally, for some children this guilt is intense, and, if not addressed, may lead to diminished feelings of self-efficacy that may carry over into adulthood (Costa and Holliday 1994; McGoldrick and Walsh 1991). When children feel stigmatized and unable to talk about their loved one or their feelings of loss, this contributes to low self-esteem (Schilling et al. 1992; Vianello and Lucamante 1988). Feelings of abandonment also are common and may be manifested as a difficulty in forming significant attachments. While scant, there is some evidence to suggest that these difficulties are much more likely to occur when the child's parent or parents are, themselves, grieving (Rando 1985; Schwab 1997; Weber and Fournier 1985).

Matt, eleven, and Paul, nine, were referred to the group by their guardian, their maternal aunt. She was concerned about their behaviors following the death of their mother six months earlier. Paul was withdrawn and sullen, refusing to talk about his mother's death. His teacher reported that he had had angry outbursts in class and was having difficulty getting along with classmates. Matt, on the other hand, appeared sad, crying frequently at home and in school.

Both boys had recently come to live with their aunt, following the death of their thirty-two-year-old mother from a heart attack, brought on by years of drug abuse and alcohol addiction. Prior to their mother's death, the boys had lived out of state. Their aunt was the only relative willing to take them, so they were forced to move only days after their mother died. The boys came to live with their aunt during the middle of the school year. Because of differences in the school curricula, both boys ended up in a grade lower than they had been in at their previous school. Matt and Paul had not seen their aunt for several years, since she was estranged from their mother. On several occasions prior to their mother's death, Matt and Paul had found her unconscious from drug overdoses and had to call 911. It was Paul who found his mother already dead when he returned home from school.

The circumstances of their mother's death, coupled with her history of over-dosing, placed both Matt and Paul at risk of experiencing complicated and in-tense grief reactions. In fact, the boys were dealing with multiple losses, not just their mother's death. Her death necessitated a move out of state, the conse-quence of which was the loss of all things familiar. In addition, they were forced to start over in a new school in a lower grade, and they were living with a relative whom they hardly knew. It is no wonder that these boys were having difficulties. While they had experienced the same losses, with the exception that Paul actual-ly found his mother dead, the brothers reacted quite differently.

Both boys did join the group, but they participated in contrasting ways. Though younger by two years, Paul was much better able to articulate his feel-ings of loss, responsibility, and anger. Matt, on the other hand, often acted out in group, making silly jokes, teasing other members, and declining to participate in the activities. It was important for me to point out to the boys and the group as a whole that each member had his or her own way of dealing with and manag-ing feelings about the loss. It was also important to help the group understand Matt's behavior, because members were often were put off and angered by his ac-tions, and at the same time help Matt connect in some way with them. Both Paul and, particularly, Matt needed much more than this six-week group. Yet, it did provide both of them with a place to begin to understand and acknowledge their feelings.

It has only been in the last several years that efforts have been undertaken to identify factors that enhance children's ability to cope with loss. Not surprisingly, most of this attention has focused on family support (Ellis and Stump 2000; Hurd 1999; Weber and Fournier 1985). Allowing children to participate in age-appropriate ways in death-related rituals and to discuss their concerns within their families appears to mitigate feelings of loss and promote healing, as does maintaining positive, loving relationships with surviving family members. It also appears that affording the child the opportunity to discuss her or his fears and reactions to the loss and understand the death and dying process outside of the immediate family also facilitates healing (Christ et al. 1991; Haasl and Marnocha 1990; Schilling et al. 1992; Siegel, Mesagno, Christ 1990).

Agency and Group Context

For the last six years I have facilitated the bereavement group for children for my county's hospice program. I do this as a volunteer and am not a member of the agency staff. The agency employs healthcare professionals and paraprofessionals with a great deal of experience working with terminally ill adults and their fami-lies, but far less experience working with children and with the use of mutual aid groups. A children's group had been offered in the past and was essentially open to any child who was referred. The agency staff wanted to reach as many children as possible, so little consideration was given to screening members to determine their readiness or appropriateness for the group or to limiting the group's size. The group format relied upon a curriculum and activity book designed for children's grief groups. While it was a very good curriculum and I still use it as a guide (Heegard 1991; Heegard 1992), the group's emphasis was on the activities themselves rather than using them to promote mutual aid among members.

Consistent with Gitterman's discussion in an earlier chapter, I felt it was critical to have a conversation with the agency's social worker and bereavement coordinator to make sure we were all on the same page about the group, since what I wanted to do and felt would be helpful was different in some significant ways from what had been done before. I took the position that we all wanted the same thing for the children and that was a place where they could begin to understand their grief and feel connected to other children who were going through the same thing. I credited the staff members for having initiated the group in the first place in response to an unmet need in the community. I then described the kind of group that I envisioned as well as the reasons for the changes I wanted to make. Fortunately, the first priority of both women was to the clients they served, so they were very receptive to my suggestions.

While my situation with this agency is somewhat unique, I would suggest that it is always important for the social worker to develop a clear contract with the agency regarding a bereavement group for children. There is some evidence to suggest that adults, even those in childcare and educational settings, don't appreciate how, or even that, children grieve (Ellis and Stump 2000; Glass 1991; Schilling et al. 1992). Therefore, the social worker may need to specifically advocate for a group that reflects and is responsive to the unique needs of children. For example, attention must be paid to composition issues, given the varying developmental needs of children. To maximize the benefits of mutual aid, size is also an important consideration, as is the timing and length of the group. Activity is likely to be used to facilitate the group's work, so it is important that agency staff understand the role that it plays and make the necessary space available.

Composition

Though I have been able to make some changes in how the children's group is run, I have had to work within some agency constraints and mandates that other social workers will no doubt face. One of the most challenging relates to composition issues.

In preparation for the group, ads are placed in the local newspaper announcing its formation, and parents or caregivers are encouraged to call the agency directly. In addition, hospice personnel refer children they think might need the group, based upon their work with their terminally ill patients. Finally, children who have participated in a summer bereavement camp sponsored by the agency and their parents or caregivers are told about the group and advised to contact the agency if they are interested. On those rare occasions when these efforts have not produced a sufficient pool of potential group members, announcements have been circulated at local elementary and middle schools about the group's formation.

The agency intentionally doesn't include age limitations in its announcements, beyond stating that the group is for children five and older. No restrictions are placed on the nature of the child's loss. So, in addition to contending with referrals for children who may be as young as five or as old as thirteen, I also have to make decisions based upon diverse experiences. For example, in the first group I facilitated, most of the children were dealing with the loss of a parent or grandparent due to natural causes. However, Amanda, age eight, was referred by her mother after her father had fatally shot himself in the head. In an ideal world I would not have placed Amanda in this group, since her father's suicide represented a very different kind of loss. Yet it was her mother's and my view that Amanda really needed and would benefit from this group. Though only in third grade, Amanda herself was able to say that she wanted the chance to talk with other children.

The reality was there was no other group experience available to Amanda, so if she didn't participate in this group, she wouldn't participate at all. To me that was unacceptable. Amanda did join, and, she connected easily with the other members. In fact, the acceptance and understanding she received were particularly helpful in countering the stigma associated with her father's suicide.

When I facilitated this first group, I admit to feeling as if I had "settled" for something that was less than ideal. I had children of various ages and at different stages of development with varying capacities to articulate their feelings. I had a "mixed bag" in terms of the loss the members had experienced. Yet, somehow the group worked, and I now believe that it was helpful not in spite of the differences in experience and maturity but *because* of them. I am not arguing that the worker should deliberately construct a group that is this heterogeneous. What I am suggesting is that many workers will find themselves in a situation similar to mine, where they are unable to exert much control over who joins and who doesn't. When this is the case, the worker can use the variety of experiences to enhance mutual aid and the group's work. Whether this happens or not, however, depends upon the worker's sensitivity to the individual needs of each child and a recognition of how these relate to those of the group as a whole, as the following example reveals.

Sarah, thirteen, and Sam, eleven were referred to the group by their mother. Their father died of a self-inflicted gunshot wound. The parents had been divorced for several years, but had remained on friendly terms. The siblings lived with their mother and had been visiting their father two weekends a month.

Both children expressed interest in talking with other children about their loss, but Sarah said she was embarrassed that her father killed himself. I said I understood this and acknowledged that she and her brother would be the only children in the group who lost someone to suicide. I reassured Sarah and Sam that they would not have to say anything that made them uncomfortable, that it was up to them—not me—to share with the others in the group the nature of their loss. I observed, however, that the feelings they had—anger, sadness, confusion, guilt—were feelings the others in the group would have as well.

Sarah and Sam decided to attend, and during the opening activity, when the children introduced themselves and described the nature of their loss, neither revealed their dad's suicide. Later in the same session, when members were talking in detail about what had led to the death of their loved one, both remained largely silent, occasionally asking a question of one of the other children. Neither appeared to be uncomfortable, and none of the other members inquired of them what had caused their dad's death.

In the second session I suggested to the group that they might have questions and concerns about where their loved one was. Melissa, ten, whose mother had died of breast cancer, was the first to respond, "I think my mom must be in heaven. I think she's like an angel and she watches over me." Peter, twelve, whose father died of a massive heart attack while jogging, said, "I don't know where my dad is. I'm afraid he's not anywhere. We didn't go to church, so I don't know about heaven. If there's a heaven, maybe my dad can't go there because he didn't believe in God or anything."

During this exchange I noticed Sam fidgeting and looking anxious. He and Sarah exchanged looks and began whispering to each other. I commented on this, saying, "It looks like you two might have some thoughts about what we're talking about. Maybe you have some questions about where your dad is?" Sarah replied, "I think my dad may be in purgatory or something. I worry about that, that he's in a bad place because of what he did."

I noticed puzzled looks on the faces of some of the other children, so I asked Sarah if she could explain what purgatory was and why she was worried about her dad being in a "bad place." Sarah hesitated, so it was Sam who replied, "Purgatory is the place between heaven and hell. It's where people who aren't good go, who don't deserve to go to heaven." Sarah continued, "Our dad killed himself. He shot himself in the head. We don't know why. He just did it. I'm afraid that because he committed suicide he won't get to heaven."

The other members in the group were matter-of-fact in their reactions. Stacey, eight, whose grandmother had died of brain cancer, asked, "Was your daddy sad? Is that why he hurt himself?" Melissa said, "Why would God punish your dad just because he took his own life? That wouldn't be fair." Peter added, "Yeah, who says there even *is* a heaven and hell? I think it's whatever *you* want to believe. Just because your dad killed himself doesn't mean he was a bad guy."

Sarah's question about where her father was and concern that he was in purgatory was her indirect way of reaching out to the group, signaling that she was ready to let them know her dad committed suicide. Sam and Sarah's disclosure not only brought them closer to the group, it also lessened for them the taboo nature of their father's death since the group members reacted with support and understanding. Their disclosure also led to an important discussion of members' questions and concerns about what happened to a loved one after death. In the session that followed this one, it was Sarah's expression of anger at her father for committing suicide that prompted a powerful discussion of some of the more confusing feelings members had about the loss of their loved one—anger at him or her for dying, relief that his or her suffering had ended, and guilt over these feelings.

Preparation of Members

While I am unable to do much screening, I do have a conversation with each prospective member in advance of her or his coming to the first group session. Ideally, I would have an individual session with each child, explain the group's purpose, elicit relevant social history information, and ascertain her or his readiness to participate. This is not possible for a variety of reasons. Instead, I follow up with each parent that referred a child to the agency and, after determining that the child is able to attend the group on the scheduled day and time, I talk with her or him by phone. I use this brief telephone conversation to introduce myself, explain the purpose of the group, and prepare prospective members for the first session. I also ask them for their thoughts about the group and invite them to ask any questions they may have.

I do most of the talking, but I believe this gesture sends the child an important message. In most instances the children do not have a choice about whether they will participate in the group. That decision is made by a parent or caregiver. Taking the time to talk to prospective members, even by telephone, conveys interest and reinforces the idea that they are individuals, with their own unique perspective on their loss. This phone conversation also provides me with some idea of the child's ability to relate and connect to others in the group. In those few instances when I made a decision that a child was not appropriate for the group, it was based upon his or her demeanor on the phone coupled with the nature of the loss.

During this brief phone contact I also review with parents or caregivers the group's purpose and obtain their assessment of the child. I alert them to the possibility that, as the group progresses, their child may display more signs of distress and explain the reasons this might occur. I want them to understand that such behavior doesn't mean the group isn't helpful. In fact, it may mean the group is providing just the sort of assistance their child needs. I provide suggestions for what parents or caregivers should do if they see this behavior and let them know they can contact me if needed.

GROUP STRUCTURE

There is some evidence to suggest that when children are given the opportunity to talk about their loss, particularly in a group format, they are better able to cope with it and less likely to experience long-term difficulties (Christ et al. 1991; Schilling et al. 1992; Zambelli et al. 1988). It is most appropriate to characterize this bereavement group for children as psychoeducational. Its purpose is twofold. The group provides children with information on the grieving process and a forum for them to ask questions about the loss of their loved one. Members also have the opportunity to interact with others experiencing the same thing, thus lessening their sense of isolation and universalizing and normalizing their feelings and experience, what Shulman has called the "all-in-the-same-boat" phenomenon (1999).

Given its focus, the group is short-term, six sessions, and is offered one evening a week for one and a half hours. Membership is closed and limited to eight children. For the first hour the group engages in its formal work. The last half hour is reserved for snack time, with different members volunteering to bring a treat each week. Members also take turns bringing in their favorite music, which is played as they eat and talk informally.

The work these children are there to do is very difficult. Their loss has, in some ways, forced them to grow up much too quickly. Therefore, it is important for members to have the opportunity to be simply children, so the snacks tend to be unhealthy, the music loud, and the conversation focused on school, sports, boyfriends and girlfriends, and the like. Snack time builds on children's natural resilience. They can, *and are encouraged to*, act their age, but they do so with other children who are grieving the loss of a loved one. This weekly ending activity reinforces an important lesson I want members to take with them when they leave, which is that it is OK for them to be happy and go on living. An added advantage is that members have a more informal and natural means of processing what we have talked about earlier in the session.

USE OF ACTIVITY

The group is centered around art-based activity. Each week I present two or three different but related topics, beginning with causes of death and what happens after death, moving on to what grief is and what to do with the feelings associated with it, and ending with getting on with life. I introduce the topic for discussion, allow the children time to draw or write out their thoughts about it, and then encourage them to share what they've done with the group. The activities serve as a way of "getting things going," of helping members understand the issue that has been introduced and providing them with a nonthreatening way of sharing their thoughts and feelings with others.

In the third session I raised one of the more important topics that we deal with in the group—feelings. I began by reminding the children of some the feelings that had already surfaced in the group, like sadness, anger, and fear, and introduced an activity that required members to draw "feelings faces"—one that reflected how they really felt and one that depicted the "mask" they wore to cover it up. I commented to members that I suspected that sometimes it was hard to talk about what they were feeling and that maybe that caused them to wear a "mask." As Marianne, age eight, said, "Yeah, you mean that you wear one face to hide how you really feel."

After allowing the children some time to work on the activity, I invited them to share what they had done. All were eager to participate, because, as Tim, eleven, said, "We got to keep our feelings inside a lot." In response to his comment, I asked him if he would like to start. Tim held up his drawing and said, "I drew a happy face. I have to be happy. If I get upset, my mom gets upset and starts to cry [Tim's father died in a car accident]. I know she's sad because she and my dad were really close to one another. I think she's scared because he's not around anymore and she has to do a whole lot more than she's used to. I don't want to make her more upset than she already is."

I noticed other children nodding their heads, so I asked if others felt the same way that Tim did—that they had to keep in their real feelings to protect others they cared about. Joseph, also eleven, said, "I don't want my dad to worry about me [Joe's mother died of breast cancer]. He's got enough on his mind. Plus, you can't just go and talk about how you feel about losing your mom or dad, or whoever. Your friends just don't understand. And they think you're weird or something. It kind of makes me mad, that I have to keep stuff in."

The discussion that was prompted by the mask activity was such an important one for members of this group to have. They not only struggled with their grief, they also felt responsible for protecting their loved ones from their feelings. As members shared their response to the activity, the extent to which they hid their feelings became even clearer. Another child in the group, Lucas, ten, observed, for example, that as a boy he felt he had to act "strong," otherwise his friends would make fun of him for crying about the death of his grandmother. Heather, twelve, commented, "People tell me that my dad's been dead for almost a year now, so I shouldn't be getting so upset. So I just pretend everything's OK because that's what everyone wants."

It is important to use activity flexibly. Older children may be quite capable of articulating their thoughts and feelings without the use of activity, particularly as they develop greater comfort with one another. For this reason, I let members know from the beginning that, if they prefer, they can write out or talk about their thoughts and feelings instead of drawing them. On the other hand, younger children may be able to participate only if they can continue to draw and stay active, even as members are sharing and talking with one another. Consequently, I always have scribble paper available to any child who wants it, explaining to members that "sometimes it's easier to talk to one another about this stuff if you have something to do with your hands."

It is also important to hold the group in a space that is conducive to the way in which children work and express their feelings. Obviously, if art activities are going to be used, members must have a hard surface on which to work and must have available to them pens, pencils, markers, crayons, etc. The space must allow for members to get up and move around as well as provide a sense of privacy.

GROUP RULES

I have found it necessary to begin the conversation with members about group rules by talking about what the group and I *aren't*—I'm not their teacher, the group is not a class, and there aren't any right or wrong answers. Therefore, unlike what the children might have expected, they will not have to raise their hands, though they must be considerate of and not interrupt each other. They don't have to always stay in their seats, but they must be respectful of the agency's furniture, since we use the boardroom for our sessions. Members may draw whatever they want and use the crayons, markers, and pencils any way they want, but they can't draw on the furniture or the table. They may talk about whatever they want and ask any question that they have, but they must keep what we talk about in the group *in* the group. I assure them that this expectation applies to me as well. Unless there's a compelling reason to do so, I don't talk with the members' caregivers or parents.

I also rely upon several other rules, which reflect the group's purpose and the fact that the members are children. First, members are entitled to their feelings, whatever these may be, about their loss. Everyone grieves in her or his own way. This is a particularly important rule when siblings participate in the same group, since they may, and probably will, grieve in different ways. This rule is also important when the group includes children of varying ages and at different stages, since members' ability to articulate their feelings and describe their experiences may vary widely. Second, I inform the children and their caregivers that they need to attend each session, if at all possible. This expectation is particularly important for the adults to understand. While the children come to look forward to the group, their caregivers often do not seem to appreciate its significance or the importance of consistent attendance. Finally, I reassure members that, while they should feel free to bring up anything that is on their minds, they also should feel free to *not* share with others, if they don't want or aren't ready to. I also let them know that part of my job will be to help them disclose their thoughts and feelings to the rest of the group.

Work and Group Themes

Bereaved children are "all-in-the-same-boat" not just because they have experienced the loss of a loved one but also because they often have not had the opportunity or even been given permission to talk about their thoughts and feelings. Therefore, members' shared sense of urgency facilitates their coming together quickly and easily. I want to capitalize on this by sending a message from the very beginning that the group will be a safe place where members *can* talk about their loss. During the first session I clarify the role and purpose of the group, as well as my role, and briefly share with members my own experience of losing a loved one. When members hear that, even for adults, it is hard to lose a loved one, they are learning that their grief is normal and also observing what it is they will be doing in the six sessions—talking about *their* loss and their feelings about it.

WORKER'S VIEWS OF AND EXPERIENCES WITH DEATH AND DYING

It's not necessary or even advisable for the leader to reveal a great deal about his or her personal losses. In fact, depending upon the worker's personal style and preferences, he or she may choose to avoid disclosing anything at all. What or whether the worker discloses or doesn't disclose is far less important than her or his comfort in talking about death and dying. The worker's ability to engage in this sort of honest discussion is related to her or his own experiences with the loss of a loved one as well as a willingness to examine more basic views about life and death.

As I prepared to lead my first children's group, I understood intellectually the need to be aware of my own feelings about death and dying. However, it wasn't until I led that first group that I realized just how important this was and how much work of my own I needed to do. I wanted to provide the children with answers to their questions and take away their pain. But I knew that I didn't have those answers, and I couldn't make their grief go away. So I had to learn, as the members themselves were learning, to sit with their sadness and live with the uncertainty that is so much a part of living and dying. As ten-year-old Jimmy, whose father was accidentally killed in a construction accident, asked, "How do I know that something also won't happen to my mom?" and eight-year-old Caitlin, whose grandmother had died after suffering a stroke wanted to know, "Where is my grandma now? Is she in heaven? What *is* heaven?" I was forced to confront my own questions and fears about losing individuals who were close to me.

During that first group, I consciously had to resist the temptation to rush in too quickly with meaningless reassurances. Since that time it has gotten easier, though there are still occasions when I am challenged to reexamine my own beliefs and assumptions. For example, earlier I described five-year-old Tommy's statement to the group that his deceased brother had played with him and made his helicopter move. This prompted other children to disclose what they believed to be their own encounters with their loved ones. While I had no doubt that the children believed what they were saying, I wasn't sure about my own views. I was skeptical, but knew that my job wasn't to convince them that what they thought had happened wasn't real. What *was* important was to help members make some sense of their experiences in a way that was helpful to them and assisted them in coming to terms with their loss.

During the first several years that I facilitated these groups, I was fortunate to have experienced very few losses of my own. It was relatively easy for me to begin a group by showing members a photo of my grandmother (who died at age ninety-two) and telling them that, even though I was an adult when she died and she had been dead for quite some time, I still missed her and mourned her passing.

My circumstances changed dramatically two years ago when, within the span of three months, I lost a close friend and my father, both to cancer. For some time after their passing I didn't even consider facilitating the group. When I finally felt ready, I thought long and hard about how I was going to get things going. I wanted to use my father's passing in my opening activity, but I wasn't sure how I would react. While I wasn't concerned about the children seeing how profoundly I was affected by his death, I didn't want to burden them with my own grief.

After talking with colleagues, however, I became convinced that it was best to begin this group as I always had, and that was to be genuine. As Shulman discusses here and elsewhere (1999), I wanted to use my own recent experience with grieving to assist members in connecting with one another. In this particular group the majority of the children had lost their loved one to cancer, and, in most of these cases, their loved one's passing was prolonged. Therefore, I decided to bring in two photos of my father, one taken when he was healthy and one taken shortly before his death when he was frail, weak, and clearly dying. As I passed these around, I told members my father had died of cancer and that his passing had been difficult for me not only because I loved him but also because I had to watch him die. I told them that there was a part of me that missed him terribly, but another part that was relieved that he wasn't suffering any longer. I then commented that I suspected some of the members might have similar feelings, since they too had watched their parent, grandparent, or sibling slowly die, and that this might have left them with many confusing feelings.

I was very deliberate in revealing this much information about my own loss. I wanted to convey to the members, right from the beginning, that this really was a place where they could talk about anything—even feeling relief that their loved one had died.

Members were quick to respond to my comments. With little or no prompting from me, for example, Melanie, eleven, whose mother had died of leukemia, held up a photo that showed her mother without any hair, a result of chemotherapy. "My mom lived for about a year after she was diagnosed with cancer. We thought she was going to make it, but then she got bad again. She lost all her hair and got real weak and started to slobber. I didn't like seeing her like that, it made me afraid." Jason, twelve, said, "I brought a picture of my dad when he was healthy, before he got sick, that I wanted to share. I don't like to think about how he was after he got the liver cancer. He got so thin and weak and turned a funny color. I was sort of glad when he died, even though I cried."

Beginning Phase

Like many adults, children will approach a group experience with a mixture of apprehension, confusion, and ambivalence. Therefore, it's important to address members' anxieties and concerns directly and early. I begin the group by reviewing with members why they are there and what we will be doing, go over group rules, and ask for their thoughts and feedback. Members typically think they are going to be in a class and that I will be their teacher. Some children assume the discussion will be religious, while others have no idea why they are there. As I noted earlier, few members are there voluntarily, so it's particularly important to address any resentment they may have about having to attend. While most members will not be able or even need to talk about their feelings directly, this nonetheless sends a valuable message that it is OK to talk openly and honestly about feelings.

In our phone conversation I let the child know that in the first session I'll ask members to introduce themselves, including where they go to school, what grade they're in, and what they like to do, and who their loved one was and how she or he died. I also suggest that members bring in one or two mementos of their loved one, including a photo that can be shared with others. Children, therefore, have something concrete they can share with others about their loss. Further, as they introduce themselves and talk about school, sports, music, and the like, members have a chance to connect with each other in a way that is less threatening and more natural.

Many of the questions and emotional reactions that are troubling members will become apparent through their introductions, as earlier case examples reveal. However, at this early stage in the group's development, their ability to directly acknowledge and discuss these will be limited. This is attributable both to where they are developmentally and also to their anxiety and lack of familiarity with one another. An advantage of the opening activity mentioned above is that it provides the leader with a way of pointing out connections between members related not only to their loss but also to their interests and common experiences as children. The worker also can use the members' introductions as a way of identifying for the group the topics they will focus on during the time they are together.

The themes that emerge in the beginning stage of the group tend to revolve around members' questions about how their loved one died and the existence of an afterlife, as earlier case examples demonstrated. Members have a need to know what led to the passing of their loved one, but their questions go beyond just the cause of death. Fundamentally, members are trying to figure out, "Why did this happen to *my* loved one?" and, just as important, "Why did this have to happen to *me*?"

An effective and simple activity requires members to draw or write out their response to the statement, "My loved one died because . . . " In the first session of one group, Peter, twelve, whose father died of an apparent heart attack while jogging, held up his drawing, showing a very large red heart that was divided into two parts and said, "My dad died of a heart attack. He was only forty-one. He didn't smoke, he hardly ever drank. He ran all the time and stayed in shape. We lifted weights together. But he died of a heart attack. I don't get it!"

In another group Angela, ten, and Stephanie, nine, whose three-year-old brother drowned in the family swimming pool, shared their responses to the same activity. Stephanie's drawing depicted a child with a sad face beneath the water. Other people were shown standing above the water. She said, "My brother fell into the pool and nobody saw him. We were all there having hamburgers and stuff, and he sneaked away or something. My mom said it couldn't have been for more than a couple of minutes, but he drowned anyway." Angela wrote out her thoughts in three words, "I don't know!" When I asked her what she meant by this, she said, "I know my brother drowned, but I don't know why! We were all there. He had his water wings. My whole family was there, but nobody saw him go in the pool." In the same group Allison, eight, held up her drawing of a heart, and said, "My pap-pap died of a heart attack. His heart just stopped beating, my mommy said. But why? What made it happen? Katy's [her friend] grandpa had a heart attack but he didn't die. Why did my pap-pap die?"

These questions are typical of those voiced by children early in the group. The leader's challenge is to encourage their expression, even while recognizing that there are no satisfactory answers. There *is* no good reason why Peter's seemingly healthy father dropped dead of a heart attack or why, in an instant, Angela's and Stephanie's little brother was able to slip unnoticed into the pool or why Allison's grandfather died and her friend's grandfather survived. While the leader may be tempted to protect members from this reality, it is much more helpful to assist them in facing it, to the extent that they are able. In response to members' questions in this particular group, I observed, "While many of you seem to know something about what led to the death of your loved one, you seem to really be asking something else, and that's '*Why?*' Why you? Why your loved one? And, you know what, I don't have a really good answer for you. I wish I did, but I don't."

The discussion that followed was a powerful one, prompted by Allison's comment that "Mommy said that Pap-Pap died because God wanted him in heaven with him. But why *my* pap-pap?" Several other children also said they had been told that their loved one had been "called" to heaven by God, yet it was clear that they were having a hard time accepting or even understanding this. Still others had no explanation at all for their loved one's passing, religious or otherwise.

What the group was struggling with at this point was the desire to make sense of their loss. Religious beliefs may be helpful to some children, but may have little meaning or relevance to others. The worker, therefore, has to achieve the delicate balance of validating such beliefs for those members for whom they are helpful while also acknowledging that no one—not her or him, the members, or other adults in their lives—knows all there is to know about death and dying.

This theme is closely linked to a second one that is apparent early in the group, and that is what happens to a loved one after death. Members' exposure to and involvement in death rituals, coupled with their developmental levels, may have resulted in a variety of misconceptions and unwarranted fears. Children may worry that their loved one felt pain when the body was cremated or fear that their loved one won't be able to breathe in a casket buried in the ground. Still others, upon seeing the body of their loved one in an open casket, may assume the loved one is sleeping and thus worry that other loved ones may die in their sleep.

In contrast to the worker's interventions regarding members' "why" questions, he or she can and *should* provide members with concrete, accurate information about cremation, funerals, and burials. Members don't need or want detailed information. What they must begin to understand is that their loved one, as they knew her or him, no longer exists. Inevitably, this discussion leads to a final theme that is characteristic in the beginning phase of the bereavement group, and that is members' questions about the afterlife best expressed as "Where *is* my loved one?"

Once again, it is more what the worker *doesn't* say than what he or she says that will be helpful to members. I use two activities to assist children in articulating their thoughts about afterlife. One activity requires members to draw or write down what made their loved one special to them. The second activity calls for members to draw or write about where they think their loved one is.

The concepts suggested by these activities are, admittedly, fairly abstract. The intent is not to involve members in an extended philosophical discussion of life after death. Rather, it is to provide a forum for them, in a beginning way, to consider what it is about their loved one that will live on and to answer for themselves their questions about the afterlife. As earlier examples reveal, children *do* have questions, thoughts, and opinions about where their loved one went after death. In some instances they have voiced these questions to parents, caregivers, and others, but were provided with answers that have little or no meaning to them. In still others, members have not disclosed their questions to anyone. In group, children are able to see that they are not alone, that they have similar questions. The worker, however, must help members recognize that they will arrive at different answers, answers that must make sense to them and assist them in coming to terms with the death of their loved one and moving on with their life.

MIDDLE PHASE

It is not until members' initial questions are addressed that they can move into what will be their most difficult work together, and that is dealing with their feelings about the loss they have experienced. In a six-session group, it is in the third, fourth, and fifth sessions that work around feelings generally takes place. In earlier sections of this chapter, I identified the range of emotional responses that are typical of bereaved children. The worker can expect that, to a greater or lesser extent depending upon the nature of the losses experienced by members and where they are developmentally, each of these reactions will surface in the group.

The leader also can expect that, without her or his guidance and assistance, members may be overwhelmed with their feelings since, as one seven year old put it, they are "all jumbled up inside." Children's grief reactions are clearly interdependent. Yet, I have found it useful and, in some cases, necessary to have members focus on only one feeling at a time, starting with those that are easier for them to acknowledge and talk about, and moving into the more taboo areas like anger at the loved one or at self.

Children rarely have difficulty getting in touch with or acknowledging their sadness over their loss, so I begin the formal discussion of feelings with an activity that simply requires members to draw or write out what makes them sad. As they share feelings of loss with one another, members are once again reminded that they are not alone. Equally important, however, they have the opportunity to console and reassure one another, which can be very validating.

It was the week before Thanksgiving, and, as members began sharing their drawing or writing about sadness, I observed that I sensed a great deal of unhappiness, perhaps due to the approaching holiday. Members readily acknowledged that they were not looking forward to the holiday. Angela said, "My mom and dad are trying to act happy and all, but I know they're not. My family is all coming over for Thanksgiving like always, but it's not going to be the same because my little brother won't be there. I wish we didn't have to celebrate at all." Her sister, Stephanie, began to cry and added, "I feel sad that Billy won't be there. I miss him so much." Courtney, nine, said, "I love my grandmother so much and I miss her. We always went to her house for Thanksgiving and now we can't. It will not be fun going somewhere else." Courtney, too, began to cry, as did several other children. Susie, ten, whose fifteen-year-old brother unexpectedly died of pneumonia and who was sitting next to Courtney, reached over and patted Courtney on the arm, saying, "It's OK. You'll be OK. We're here for you."

As Stephanie and Courtney and then others began to cry, I wanted to provide reassurances of my own. However, I resisted the urge to do this, believing that it was better to give the members themselves the opportunity to reach out to one another. Susie was struggling with her own loss, a struggle that was made even more difficult because of the intensity of her parents' anguish. However, Susie's willingness to reach out to Courtney was beneficial not only to Courtney but also to her, since it provided her with a way of feeling helpful and as if she was making a difference.

As this conversation progressed, a range of other reactions and feelings became apparent. For example, when Susie said, "I miss my brother a lot. But my mother just cries all the time. She says she doesn't want to do anything for the holidays even though my dad and I want to have turkey and all that," I observed that Susie seemed angry and I suspected that others in the group probably felt angry, too, at their loved one, at their parents and caregivers, at friends, at the world. Brian, eleven, lost his mother to cirrhosis of the liver and was the first to respond. "I loved my mom a lot, but she drank too much. And everybody tried to tell her that, but she didn't listen. I know I shouldn't be, but I get angry at her for drinking and for dying."

As I suggested earlier, the leader needs to make flexible use of activity. In this particular group, members' own disclosures led naturally to their being able to acknowledge and talk about their anger. Therefore, an activity to get at this feeling simply wasn't necessary. In fact, introducing an activity for this purpose would have been counterproductive and could have stifled a valuable conversation among members. This particular session ended before we were able to explore in detail members' thoughts and feelings about anger. However, in the next session I was able to use their own words and experiences to help them resume the discussion, reminding members of Susie's, Brian's, and others' comments. As the children resumed the discussion about anger, yet another emotional reaction surfaced, and that was members' feelings of guilt about being angry at their loved ones or at others. This feeling, too, surfaced naturally and evolved out of the discussion that was taking place between members. So, again, a planned activity was unnecessary.

Even though members become more comfortable with one another and are able to express themselves more freely as the group progresses, their ability to directly articulate and process their feelings may be limited because of their emotional immaturity and the sensitive and taboo nature of their reactions. Thus the worker must be sensitive to the indirect way that members may express their feelings about their loss. In addition, in groups that include children at different stages, she or he must be prepared to help members understand and accept that everyone has his or her own way of expressing, dealing with, and managing grief.

In the fourth session members began to talk about their feelings, in response to an activity I introduced, which required them to identify things that made them angry. Megan, thirteen, said, "I get angry at my friends because they have both of their parents and I only have my dad, now that my mom is dead. I mean I don't want them to lose a parent like me, but I still get angry at them." Andrew, twelve, added, "Yeah, I get angry too sometimes at my friends. Like everything is fine for them and I don't have my dad anymore. It sucks!" As other members shared their own feelings of anger over their loss, Tommy, five, was humming quietly to himself, scribbling on a large piece of paper. Periodically he would describe what he was drawing, more to himself, than to anyone in particular: "I'm drawing a dinosaur"; "This is my superhero. He can kill anyone with his sword," and the like. John, ten, whose father died of a heart attack, was spinning around in his chair and drumming his fingers on the table, and appeared to be uninterested in the conversation.

I noticed Megan and Andrew exchange glances with one another, rolling their eyes. Jill, ten, who was sitting next to Tommy, told him several times to be quiet and appeared to be exasperated with him. I observed, "We've been talking about anger, and my guess is that all of you have some feelings of anger about what happened, but that for some it may be easier to talk about it than it is for others. Remember something I said to you all when we first started, and that is that each of us has our own way of dealing with our loss. Sometimes people can talk about their feelings and sometimes they can't. It's not that they don't have the feelings, they just can't talk about them. I think, for example, that John probably feels angry just like some of the rest of you. His dad was alive one day and dead the next. And Tommy might be angry, not only that he doesn't have his brother around any more but that his parents seem so sad all the time. But maybe John and Tommy just might have a harder time talking about it." While neither John or Tommy responded to my comment, Megan said, "Yeah, I know it is really hard to talk about how I feel. I don't do it except when I'm here." Others nodded in agreement.

For the remainder of this group, John continued to display behaviors that were mildly disruptive, and on two other occasions I had to intervene with similar comments. However, group members became more tolerant, even encouraging and specifically inviting John to share his feelings. While John never was able to talk openly about his grief, the fact that he ultimately was accepted in the group no doubt was helpful to him and allowed him to process his grief in his own way and at his own pace. Tommy also was not able to talk directly about his feelings and continued to scribble and talk to himself. The other members, however, displayed increasing patience with his behavior, and were often gently amused by it, perhaps in recognition of his young age.

As members become aware that there are different emotional responses to grief and different ways of expressing these feelings, they begin to address a final important theme of the middle phase and that is what to do with their feelings. In a previous case example I described the use of the mask activity, and I have found that this is a good way to help members think and talk about managing feelings. I want the children to understand that no feeling is a bad feeling. What *is* bad is if they don't feel they have a place to talk about it.

Other activities also may need to be used to assist children in identifying sources of support and ways of venting feelings that are not harmful to self and others. The leader can explore with members what they, themselves, have found works for them. I have noticed that members often identify pets, stuffed animals, and the like as sources of comfort and support. In addition, they will identify thoughts of or conversations with their loved one as helpful. While these coping strategies are readily accepted by the group members, themselves, some, particularly older children, admit to feeling embarrassed about relying upon such strategies. The validation and understanding they receive from others in the group is invaluable in dispelling this awkwardness.

ENDING PHASE

As I noted at the outset, the purpose of a bereavement group is not to take away members' pain. Rather it is to help them understand it better and assist them with getting on with their lives. Perhaps because of its short-term nature and members' natural resilience, I have found that endings have not been difficult for members. In contrast to dynamics like regression that are typical in many groups, the children have been forward looking. That is, their focus easily turns to the future and their interests as children.

I use several ending activities to assist members with this transition. I ask members to identify things they like about themselves and things they like to do. This activity sends a message that is important for members to hear, which is that it is OK to have fun to feel good about themselves.

Another important activity I use has members think about and describe happy memories associated with their loved one. To facilitate this discussion, in the session before I suggest that members bring in a photo or other memento of their loved one that makes them smile. It would have been premature to use this activity earlier in the group, since it easily could have blocked members' expressions of grief. Members can only remember the good times if they'd had the opportunity to talk about their pain and sadness.

As in any group, members should have the opportunity to provide feedback to the worker about their experience as well as to say goodbye to each other. The leader should expect, however, that members' ability to do this may be limited due to their ages and immaturity. I have found that it often is easier for members to say their goodbyes during our final snack time, which I portray as a farewell party. Typically members are excited about this final time together and, with just a little help from me, they are able to discuss the group and what it meant to them. While there is some sadness about ending, the more prevalent mood is one of excitement about and anticipation of the future.

To reinforce the idea that it is OK for members to have fun and move on with their lives, I ask them to pose for two photos, one a "normal" group shot, the other a group shot of them acting and looking "silly." I inform the members that I will send each of them copies of the two photos, as a way for them to remember their time together and what they learned from one another. When I send the photos, I also include a brief note in which I thank each child for coming, identify something unique about his or her participation, and remind her or him of what we talked about.

The agency has developed two informal feedback forms, one to be completed by the members and the other by their parent or caregiver. At the close of the last session, the children, with the assistance of their parent, if needed, complete their form. Consistent with the group activities, the questions are simple, and children can draw or write out their answers. Parents or caregivers receive their questionnaire in the mail and are asked to return it to the agency. Questions focus on how well they felt their child did in the group and whether or not they felt he or she benefited from it.

Feedback from both groups has been uniformly positive. Members' feedback suggests that they are reassured by being in the presence of others who have experienced a loss. Members also report feeling less afraid of and confused by their feelings and more willing to ask others for help when they need it. Generally, parents or caregivers indicate that their child seems happier and less distressed. In those few instances where either the child or the parent or caregiver believes further assistance is necessary, I provide appropriate referrals.

WORKING with children in a bereavement group is challenging but extraordinarily rewarding. To be sure, these groups deal with death and dying, a subject that few people, adult and children alike, want to talk about. Yet, children are resilient and, over the years that I have worked with them, I have learned as much from them as they have learned from the group and me. Their natural curiosity, honesty, laughter, and resilience have been sources of inspiration and hope to me. As I did, any worker contemplating facilitating such a group will have to confront her or his own views about death. In doing so, however, the worker will no doubt find that her or his perspective about life will be enriched and enhanced immeasurably.

References

Baker, J. and M. Sedney. 1992. Psychological tasks for bereaved children. *American Journal of Orthopsychiatry* 62:105–16.
Bowlby, J. 1960. Grief and mourning in infancy. *Psychoanalytic Study of the Child* 15:9–52.
Burman, S. and P. Allen-Meares. 1994. Neglected victims of murder: Children's witness to parental homicide. *Social Work* 39:28–34.

Christ, G., K. Siegel, F. Mesagno, and D. Langosh. 1991. A preventive intervention program for bereaved children: Problems of implementation. *American Journal of Orthopsychiatry* 61:168–78.

Costa, L. and D. Holliday. 1994. Helping children cope with the death of a parent. *Elementary School Guidance and Counseling* 28:206–13.

Cox, G. 2000. Children, spirituality, and loss. *Illness, Crisis, and Loss* 8:60–70.

Ellis, J. and J. Stump. 2000. Parents' perceptions of their children's death concept. *Death Studies* 24:65–70.

Furman, E. 1974. *A child's parent dies: Studies in childhood bereavement.* New Haven: Yale University Press.

Gersten, J., C. Beals, and C. Kallgren. 1991. Epidemiology and preventive interventions: Parental death in childhood as a case example. *American Journal of Community Psychology* 19:481–500.

Glass, J. C. 1991. Death, loss, and grief in middle school children: Implications for the school counselor. *Elementary School Guidance and Counseling* 26:139–48.

Haasl, B. and J. Marnocha. 1990. *Bereavement support group program for children.* Muncie: Accelerated Development.

Heegard, M. 1991. When someone very special dies: Children can learn to cope with grief. Minneapolis: Woodland.

——— 1992. Facilitator guide for drawing out feelings series. Minneapolis: Woodland.

Hoffman, S. and S. Strauss. 1985. The development of children's concepts of death. *Death Studies* 9:469–82.

Hurd, R. 1999. Adults view their childhood bereavement experiences. *Death Studies* 23:17–41.

LeShan, E. 1988. *Learning to say goodbye.* New York: Avon.

Lonetto, R. 1980. *Children's conception of death.* New York: Springer.

McCown, D. and B. Davies. 1995. Patterns of grief in young children following the death of a sibling. *Death Studies* 19:41–52.

McGoldrick, M. and F. Walsh. 1991. A time to mourn: Death and the family life cycle. In F. Walsh and M. McGoldrick, eds., *Living beyond loss: Death in the family,* pp. 30–49. New York: Norton.

Norris-Shortle, C., P. Young, and M. A. Williams. 1993. Understanding death and grief for children three and younger. *Social Work* 38:736–42.

Pfohl, B., D. Stangl, and M. Tsuang. 1983. The association between early parental loss and diagnosis in the Iowa 500. *Archives of General Psychiatry* 40:965–70.

Piaget, J. 1950. *The psychology of intelligence.* London: Routledge and Kegan Paul.

Rando, T. 1985. Bereaved parents: Particular difficulties, unique factors, and treatment issues. *Social Work* 330:19–23.

Rutter, M. 1971. Parent-child separation: Psychological effects on children. *Journal of Child Psychology and Psychiatry* 12:233—60.

Rutter, M., C. Izard, and P. Read. 1986. *Depression in young people: Developmental and clinical perspectives.* New York: Guilford.

Schilling, R., N. Koh, R. Abramovitz, L. Gilbert. 1992. Bereavement groups for inner-city children. *Research on Social Work Practice* 2:405–19.

Schwab, R. 1997. Parental mourning and children's development. *Journal of Counseling and Development* 75:258–65.

Shulman, L. 1999. *The skills of helping individuals, families, groups, and communities.* 4th ed. Itasca, Ill: Peacock.

Siegel, K., F. Mesagno, and G. Christ. 1990. A prevention program for bereaved children. *American Journal of Orthopsychiatry* 60:168–75.

Speece, M. and S. Brent. 1984. Children's understanding of death: A review of three components of a death concept. *Child Development* 55:1671–86.

Vianello, R. and M. Lucamante. 1988. Children's understanding of death according to parents and pediatricians. *Journal of Genetic Psychology* 149:305–16.

Wass, H. 1984. Concepts of death: A developmental perspective. In H. Wass and C. Colt, eds., *Childhood and death,* pp. 3–24. Washington, D.C.: Hemisphere.

Weber, J. and D. Fournier. 1985. Family support and a child's adjustment to death. *Family Relations: Journal of Applied Family and Child Studies* 34:43–49.

Zambelli, G., E. Clark, L. Barile, and A. DeJong. 1988. An interdisciplinary approach to clinical intervention for childhood bereavement. *Death Studies* 12:41–50.

Chapter 5

When the World No Longer Feels Safe
Helping Children Through Mutual Aid

Maxine Lynn and Danielle Nisivoccia

IT IS 8:45 A.M. on September 11, 2001. The school buses are pulling up and discharging their noisy and excited young passengers. Children are thinking about their homework assignments done or not done, how to seek revenge for a child who teased them, how to get the attention of a cute girl, hoping their teacher is absent, and hoping lunch period is soon. Teachers are organizing their desks and lesson plans. A secretary has the radio on and hears an announcement that one of the World Trade Center towers has had an explosion and they are evacuating the building. Children and teachers enter their classrooms and begin their morning rituals. The administrative office becomes aware of the horror of 9/11. A few teachers also know from turning on a radio or watching CNN in the media room. One teacher becomes hysterical, since her husband works in the World Trade Center. Suddenly the bells ring and there are emergency assemblies in the auditorium and lunchrooms. The children have picked up the vibes of their teachers and recognize that something is very wrong. Considering the sheer numbers of children in the public school, there remains a sense of quiet and organization.

The principal gives a short statement saying that, because of planes crashing into the World Trade Center towers, the city is on special alert and children will be dismissed if a parent or recognized caretaker picks them up or is reached and gives permission for the child to go home. Meanwhile, movies and videos will be shown. Some teachers join support staff in reaching families.

Children went home caught in a web of feelings totally foreign to them. Parents, caretakers, teachers could not make them feel safe since they were struggling with their own feelings. This was the beginning of continued fears from witnessing multiple losses exacerbated by media coverage and anthrax scares. Individuals are either asking them strange questions or ignoring their pleas to listen.

Mild or severe, the disaster of 9/11 has deeply affected children in the New York City area as well as other parts of the nation. Even when a child has not experienced a direct loss or demonstrated obvious symptoms the trauma can have an impact (Pfefferbaum et al. 2000). This frightening experience has left children traumatized with feelings of terror and helplessness. Their immature defenses, limited coping abilities, and feelings of not being protected have left many children living with emotional pain and confusion. Generally, children react to trauma and show some stress within days of the traumatic event. Although parents, the school, and community have attempted to get life back to "normal," the lingering thoughts, feelings, and visual images often remain. Symptom-free children will often develop reactions over time or at the anniversary of the event. Memories and feelings of 9/11 can be triggered at any time, thus intruding into and disrupting a child's life. They fear that a similar disaster will happen again and do not feel safe (Monahon 1993).

While bombarded with reports on the short-term psychological and behavioral symptoms manifested by children traumatized by the disaster of 9/11, we are just beginning to assess the impact of the long-term effects. As seen in children after World War Two and most recently in reactions to the Oklahoma City bombing, children cannot grasp the entire reality (Pfefferbaum et al. 2000; Phillips 2001). Non-normative life events create disequilibrium and the ability to deal with negative feelings and anxieties is challenged (Germain 1991). At a time where the need for a supportive parent is most important, many adults are unable to provide this because of their reaction to the event.

Six months after 9/11, according to a New York City Board of Education survey, 87 percent of the city's public school students reported feeling terrorized. It reported that 26.5 percent of the aforementioned youth from the fourth grade through high school have serious mental health problems that are interfering with their normal functioning (Applied Research and Consulting et al. 2002). The Board of Education survey highlighted that children were suffering from agoraphobia, separation disorder, generalized anxiety, conduct disorders, major depression and posttraumatic stress symptoms (Applied Research and Consulting et al. 2002). There is a sense that business is back to normal and a denial of increased absences, acting out, and poorer grades if one talks with local school officials. Children and families who had personal physical exposure to the events of 9/11 were most at risk for difficulties. However the survey showed that children in the fourth and fifth grades, and children with previous traumatic events in their lives, had more serious symptoms and were at higher risk for posttraumatic stress disorder (Applied Research and Consulting et al. 2002). Based on the above report, discussions with school personnel, and the children's reported reactions and behaviors, these authors saw a need for groups to be utilized in the public schools where children could begin to feel safe to explore their concerns and feelings.

Developmental Tasks and Issues

Latency spans from ages seven to twelve. It is the time that a child's major developmental tasks are to gain an increasing sense of competence, self-mastery, and autonomy. These domains include physical, cognitive/intellectual, and emotional/psychological, social, and moral development. The tasks are achieved through school activities, play and social interaction with peers, family, and friends (Germain 1991). Latency-age children who have experienced traumatic stress from the 9/11 disaster often lose interest in those activities that help them achieve age appropriate developmental tasks. Physically they may be lethargic or agitated. Stomach distress and headaches are also common symptoms (Shelby 2000).

Latency is the time to master concrete operational understanding and begin to think abstractly and problem solve. These processes are often impaired when extreme stress occurs, resulting in poor problem solving and decision making. By mid-latency children have a command of expressive language and understand that death is inevitable and irreversible. Older latency children begin to make logical inferences beyond what can be seen as well as deal with hypothetical situations. Normatively, children less than eleven years old are unlikely to talk freely or at any length about their uncomfortable and painful feelings. The 9/11 disaster falls within this realm, and even more avoidance is to be expected. Latency-age children understand right and wrong, good and bad and can evaluate their own actions and experience guilt. Children traumatized by the 9/11 disaster and subsequent events such as the anthrax scare are often preoccupied with the aforementioned and usually blame others. Latency-age children have very detailed, long-term, factually accurate memories for the traumatic event, but they usually contains gross distortions or embellishments. The ability to concentrate and reason is also effected. Normatively, they can step back from, reflect on, and attend to their thoughts and take in additional information and experiences. They empathize and view events from more than one perspective and generate multiple alternatives to a problem and order and relate various parts to a coherent whole. These functions become impaired as thoughts become confused, and information and problems become overwhelming. Issues of rules, fairness, loyalty, and justice are often central, but as it relates to 9/11 these also become clouded by the impact of the trauma and external influences. Their cognitive abilities combined with their immaturity and limited coping abilities may put mid-and late-latency age children at risk for experiencing trauma (Shelby 2000). Thus they feel inadequate and inferior.

The latency age child's social world is expanding beyond the family to school, church, neighborhood, clubs, and other nonparental adult role models, all of whom are potential influences and supports in their striving to cope and bounce back from the traumatic experience. Many children will pull back from socializing.

Usual ways of coping with stressful situations are no longer successful (Germain 1991). This creates feelings of confusion, fear, and anxiety that usually manifest in avoidance (Shelby 2000).

Peer group explorations and support, usually same-sex, becomes increasingly important in dealing with issues of conflict, norms, and values (Lieberman 1979). Using problem-solving skills to deal with the stress of the 9/11 disaster enhances feelings of mastery. Being industrious and feeling competent enhances a child's feelings of self-worth and self-esteem and motivates him or her to continue to take on new challenges.

Vulnerabilities and Risk Factors and Resiliencies and Protective Factors

The children who became members of this group have various vulnerabilities and risk factors from numerous stressors in their young lives. The brief descriptions that follow highlight these risk factors.

Three of the boys have had to struggle with the transition of leaving their country of origin and begin a new life in a foreign country. Three members are living in single-parent homes and have low incomes. One youth has a stepfather in the home. Todd has recently lost both parents and is being raised by grandparents. Steve continues to struggle with his biracial background. All the boys' parents are struggling with working hard and trying to make it, which prevents them from giving a great deal of time and attention to their children. Many of the parents themselves are suffering from the effects of 9/11. These inconsistencies in family background and the contextual effects of environment are risk factors, which contribute to their current concerns. The community is not impoverished, but aspects of impoverishment have certainly touched many of their young lives.

The children also demonstrate many protective factors, which contribute to their resiliency. Until 9/11 all the members were on grade level or above in their schoolwork. The location of the school is in a neighborhood with many community supports and resources. These include a powerful community school board that makes sure the children are getting their educational needs met. There are many youth programs and organized sports teams led by various religious and community groups. The families are committed to providing for the children. Parents, guidance counselors, teachers, and youth workers provide excellent adult role models. The environment has a great deal of diversity and until 9/11 was very accepting of ethnic differences. The boys, especially Roger, Alan, and Todd, are coping by displacing their anger toward youth who are different from them. Several of the boys have increased sensitivity because of prior losses, but seem to have overcome them.

The 9/11 tragedies resurfaced some of the stressors and increased vulnerability. The members suddenly found supportive adults confused, frightened, and helpless. They vividly viewed the multiple losses through the media. Roger's parents are constantly dealing with WTC issues. Several of the boys were forced to confront prejudices and profiling. One of the boy's cousin's was lost in the tragedy. The anxieties and fears of the adults increased their concerns. Things that seemed important are no longer viewed in the same way. The boys suddenly feel adults are against them and are making unfair demands about their poor grades and misbehavior. The children had many expectations for achievement, so that the present-day difficulties create a sense of confusion and frustration. They feel isolated, angry, and unable to figure out what is happening. If they discuss this, they find the adults become even more upset.

This group provided opportunities for the boys to explore their concerns, find social support, and problem solve around issues that are affecting their ability to control their situations. Social support is a major protective factor with both direct and indirect effects on behavior (Kirby and Fraser 1997; Smith and Carlson 1997). The group experience becomes a protective factor. An important protective factor in lessening the effects of traumatic experiences is a caring, supportive adult (Kirby and Fraser 1997; Smith and Carlson 1997). One of the themes of this chapter is the ever present diversity issue since two of the members have been profiled and already experienced the results of prejudice. These children have been exposed to community rejection and anger.

Agency and Group Context

The group takes place in an urban public school in a neighborhood that is bordered by public housing and expensive coops and condominiums. Between the borders are subsidized middle-class housing and rent controlled and stabilized apartments. The location is five miles from the World Trade Center site. The school is overcrowded and there are some classes in a prefab building in the yard. The community has a diverse population. However, the wealthiest and many of the middle-class children attend several local private and parochial schools. Middle-class, working-class children, and impoverished children attend the school.

The school administration has education as a primary goal and does not see mental health services as necessary to achieving the goal. The administration did not truly feel the children were experiencing any long-term effects after 9/11, although teachers and guidance counselors have noticed changes in the children. They reported more absences, less attention to learning, and more incidents of acting out. The school allowed the group as long as it did not interfere with major education and was short-term. A ten-session group was agreed upon. Fourth and fifth grade boys were chosen as the target population, since there seemed to be most concern with this population. Their teachers referred them to the guidance counselor, the time selected to coincide with when this grade level splits up for music and art periods. Twenty-five children were referred and ten children emerged for the group. Permission was obtained from the parent. The group met in a small conference room used to teach ESL (English as a Second Language) classes. The room was quiet and separate from classrooms but very small and could not contain a great deal of physical activity, a large table dominating the center of the room.

Use of school facilities gives the worker a captive audience but also sets the stage for the group having to fit within the rules of the school, i.e., no noise. Children who are not doing well in school and children who have negative feelings about school transfer their feelings to the group, which affects confidentiality since teachers and guidance counselors want to know what is happening to the children. This is a major issue in all school-based groups (Lynn and Nisivoccia 2001). The children in the group see each other throughout the school day, and those children who are not members of the group know who is in the group. The concerns and anxieties generated by 9/11 have affected school personnel and family members, which contributes to the boys' reactions and not feeling safe to deal with it. The issue of self-determination, which is a fundamental principle of social work practice, is a concern, since the boys did not volunteer to become members. The above-mentioned factors contribute to the awkward beginnings and create challenges in the engagement phase.

Julio, from a Dominican background, is ten and a half years old and in the fifth grade. He is in little league and has quit going to practice and games. He seems sad and at times withdrawn. The guidance counselor reported that he goes home and stares at his grandmother. His parents are legal immigrants from the Dominican Republic who are working at low wage jobs.

Edward, from a West Indian background, is nine years and in the fourth grade. He has been going to the nurse with headaches. His mother is a single parent who is a registered nurse.

Roger, African American, is eleven years old and in the fifth grade. The teacher reported that he is daydreaming and not paying attention in class. From a two-parent home, his father is a police officer and his mother works as a legal secretary in area of the World Trade Center.

Alan, Caucasian, is ten and a half years old and in the fifth grade. Guidance counselor reported that he gets into fights in school, is a bully and verbally aggressive. He recently told a teacher to "go to hell." His single-parent mother is a receptionist

Ari, from Lebanon, is nine years old and in the fourth grade. He is absent a great deal. The lunchroom teacher reported that he has been teased. His parents are immigrants and the father owns a newspaper and candy store.

Todd, Caucasian, is ten years old and in the fifth grade. His teacher reported that he misses school a great deal and when he does attend has been clinging and demanding. He is living with his maternal grandparents since his mother's death from a drug overdose; his father's whereabouts are unknown

Sam, Caucasian, is nine and a half years old and in the fourth grade. The guidance counselor reported that his grades have dropped dramatically. His father is a schoolteacher and his mother is a social worker.

Satish, from India, is ten years old and in the fifth grade. The guidance counselor reported that his grades have dropped. His father works for the railroad and his mother is a homemaker.

Steve, Eurasian, is ten and a half years old and in the fifth grade. He is reported absent a great deal, and the art teacher saw disturbing pictures of body parts in his notebook. He lives with his single-parent mom who is an artist.

Juan, Latino, is nine and a half years old and in the fourth grade. His teacher reported that he has been increasingly verbally aggressive. He moved to New York City three years ago. He lives with his stepfather, a computer analyst, and his mother, a beautician.

Work and Group Themes

Activity groups have always been a source of healing for latency-age children and provide opportunities to master traumatic experience (Lynn and Nisivoccia 2001; Gitterman and Shulman 1994). Children who have been traumatized have a range of behavioral reactions including abandonment of play, avoidance of closeness, lack of trust, fear of adults, etc. (Shelby 2000). Group becomes an ideal modality because it breaks isolation, can become a benign mother, raises self-esteem, helps children recognize effective limits, and enhances relatedness (Nisivoccia and Lynn 1999).

Group work skills and activity programming help children receive nurturance and provide a place for the children to have corrective emotional experiences and increase interpersonal skills. The use of group will build on the strengths and resiliency of the children so that they move beyond traumatic experiences. Interventions will include learning mutual aid and increasing social networks. The goals of the group include learning to trust, learning to share, making friends, recognizing and talking about self and feelings, and handling conflicts. This chapter will demonstrate, with examples from this latency-age boys' group, the way in which activity is used following the stages of group development, the group member's age, gender, and type of experience.

INITIAL ENGAGEMENT AND PURPOSE

The initial stage is always a time of approach and avoidance. In this group feelings of avoidance to becoming a member are high because the boys were not able to self-determine their membership. They are not sure why they have been asked to come, feel labeled and have a negative association about what social workers do. Negative feelings about the purpose of the group exist, and the boys make it clear they do not want to talk about the reason for the group. Some of the members are anxious, and this comes out in testing the worker. The worker must clarify her role, be empathetic to their struggles, and acknowledge their resistance. The following example illustrates the initial engagement of worker and group members.

> The worker arrives and sets up the room, putting eleven chairs in a circle. Alan arrives first and angrily states, "I do not know why I am here, and this is a place for kids who don't speak English." Juan and Ari enter the room while Alan is speaking, and Juan says that the teacher sent him. Julio and Roger arrive and Roger asks, "Are you the teacher?" The rest of the group arrives, with the exception of Sam and Satish, who are absent. There is whispering and general feelings of uneasiness about being in the room. The worker is unsure what the boys have been told and begins by saying her name and that she is a social worker. She invites them to sit down and asks; "Do you know what a social worker does?" Roger states that a social worker works with dummies. Julio counters with, "Oh, no, they work with the crazies." Todd chimes in, "Yeah, and they also take you away from your mom and put you in foster care." The worker, Rachel, explains that social workers do lots of things, including help people work on their concerns about stuff that is bothering them: "Recently I have been helping kids with stuff that happened with the World Trade Center tragedy." Roger blurts out, "Not that shit again." Juan remarked, "I don't care about it." Several of the boys give the worker a "what are you going to do about it" look. Edward pushes his chair out of the circle, and Juan announces he has got to go to the bathroom. After giving Juan permission, the worker responds that she knows life might be different for each of the boys since 9/11 and she has heard that they do not want to be here and deal with these issues right now. "Actually your teachers and guidance counselor asked your parents if you could attend this group because they felt it could be helpful."

The group engages in an introductory exercise of what they might like to do in the group and what they do not want to happen. During introductions the members distribute snacks. A major group theme is that the boys do not want to discuss anything about the World Trade Center. Rachel needs to contract and be clear about the purpose. She also needs to reflect on their feelings of being labeled and issues of confidentiality.

> RACHEL: I hear you guys loud and clear that you do not want to talk about anything related to WTC. However I know that since it happened things have been different for you and for me. We can spend some time talking about why you do not want to talk about it and also play some games and do activities. The school did ask me to have this group deal with concerns related to what happened on September 11. You are not alone in this and you are not crazy or a dummy to be here. It is a chance to learn from each other, share, and have fun.

This is a special time and place, and anything that happens in here will stay in here. This means that I will not be reporting back to your teachers and parents what you say in here unless you tell me it is OK or you are going to hurt yourself or someone else. What do you think about what I just said?

JUAN: (*Shouts*) I want some more chips now.

ARI: Do we have to come?

JULIO: Maybe they will fail us? Can they fail us?

RACHEL: No, you will not fail. It is not a class and I am not a teacher. Your parents did give permission for you to be here. However, if you decide that you truly do not want to be in the group, I could talk to the school and your families.

ALAN: I guess we got to stay.

EDWARD: But we don't have to talk.

ROGER: You got it, man. Silence.

STEVE: Maybe I got here because my grades went down.

ROGER: I guess I got here because I got in a big fight in the lunch room a couple of weeks ago.

By the end of the first session there begins an understanding about issues in membership, the purpose, contracting, and confidentiality. The boys are starting to demonstrate signs of mutual aid through the distribution of snacks. The worker has acknowledged that she hears and respects they do not want to participate in the group. She also discloses, in an attempt to normalize their reactions to an abnormal event, that things have been different for her since 9/11. The work themes include the diversity issue (Ari is being left out), the resistances to being there, and the connections of various individual behaviors and group purpose.

POWER AND CONTROL

The second session will need to focus on integrating the meeting's agenda and purpose with the member's ideas. The activity planned is a variation of charades. It has been chosen because it is focused on task rather than relationships.

The boys slowly enter the room whispering among themselves about an exam and other school-related activities. They grab the bag of snacks. There are two new members. The worker is concerned that the boys have separated themselves from Ari. She begins by asking the group to tell the new members, Sam and Satish, what happened in the first meeting.

Todd responds, "We ate lots of chips and talked about not wanting to come here." Edward interrupts, "There are only four cookies left." Alan responds that they should be for him because he found them. Sam, who is new to the group, suggested that they cut them in half so there would be more, but Roger, in an angry voice, says, "There still won't be enough for everyone." In the midst of the argument Juan takes a cookie, eats it, and announces; "Now there are only three!" Alan grabs the bag with the three remaining cookies, and Roger jumps up and yells, "That's not fair." Alan tosses him a cookie. Rachel states strongly, "I think we need to talk about group rules, and you need to finish telling Sam and Satish what the group is about." Roger points to Rachel and says, "The teacher wants us to talk about 9/11, but we don't want to. We think this is a waste of time." Edward adds "We can play the whole time and get out of boring art class." Several of the boys are having side conversations in loud whispers.

Rachel is aware that the group members are interacting and there is a great deal of testing. This behavior is not unusual in early stages of power and control. She needs to reiterate the purpose and get the group working because it is a short-term group. She also needs to set some controls while addressing authority issues.

RACHEL: 9/11 was a different kind of day for most of you and things have been different since then. You were asked to join this group because people who care about you have noticed that things have not been the same.

ROGER: (*Shouts out*) what do you mean "different"?

RACHEL: There has been more fighting, your grades have gone down, you have been absent more, and some of you have quit the fun things that you like to do. I am hoping that this group will give you opportunity to talk as well as play. How does that sound? Do you want to give it a try?

EDWARD: (*Shouts*) you need to bring more cookies, and I am all for the playing.

TODD: There are there too many of us in here to talk.

ALAN: Yeah, two too many.

SAM: Who? (*Several side conversations and whispers.*)

RACHEL: For this group to work there needs to be a couple of ground rules.

JUAN: Is this going to be like a classroom?

RACHEL: No, we are going to make the rules together.

THE USES OF ACTIVITIES

The members go about setting rules and putting them on newsprint. There is concern about being thrown out if rules are broken, and Rachel states that the group has ten members and no one is going to be dropped out of the group. She tells the group that it is time to play and introduces the game of charades. At first the boys are ambivalent and say that it is a girl's game. Rachel asks them to choose their favorite TV show or movie and write it down. She explains how points will be given and demonstrates certain signals, i.e., how many words, first word, second word, etc. Juan wants to go first and picks *Spiderman*. He whispers his question to Rachel—whether it is one or two words. He does a comedic rendition of a "macho man." The group struggles with Spider until he decides to draw a web on the blackboard. Todd guesses and then he chooses *Men in Black*. Roger acts out the movie *Black Hawk Down* and this leads to the following discussion:

ALAN: I saw this movie. It was awesome.

TODD: I can't wait until I am old enough to join the air force. I am going to fly one of those birds and kill all the terrorists.

ROGER: My uncle is in the National Guard and on high alert.

EDWARD: What does that mean?

ROGER: He is on call and can kill all those Arabs that don't belong here.

SAM: I don't think so.

EDWARD: My mom, she's a nurse, and she hates being on call. She curses whenever the phone rings.

SATISH: I have a cousin in the National Guard and he has been working at the railroad station and he does not carry a gun.

ROGER: Well, do you expect them to give a gun to a foreigner?

SATISH: I am not a foreigner. I was born here and have a cousin who died in the WTC. (*Silence.*)

TODD: Let's go back to the game. (Several boys nodded in agreement. Others asked questions about Satish's relative.)

RACHEL: The game is important but I think we need to spend sometime looking at what is going on.

TODD: Do we have to?

STEVE: I want to know more about Satish's cousin. Did they find the body or just parts? Is he pulverized? (Several members comment that Steve is gross.)

SAM: My father says that when there has been a war the government makes you go fight even if you don't want to.

EDWARD: Sometimes I wake up and think my mom has been killed.

The other members are getting somewhat restless. Rachel asks which of the members saw *Black Hawk Down*. Several had, and a discussion ensued, first about gory war movies and then about horror movies.

The worker reviews the purpose of the group by asking the boys to tell new members what the group is about. Again, several members verbalize that they do not want to participate in discussions about the World Trade Center. There is testing and competition going on in the group. The worker points out the commonality among the group members and makes the unknown known by also identifying some of their behaviors. The taboo words have been said. She invites the members to mutually develop the rules so there is ownership of the limits. This is the beginning of group decision making. The norms of the group are also being developed and clarified. While the group is somewhat ambivalent about the activity, they become involved and this leads to a discussion of their experiences and feelings about 9/11 and subsequent developing opinions. There are conflicts around different ethnic backgrounds and power and control issues. The boys are also struggling with how to keep their internal controls while dealing with difficult issues. They are dependent on Rachel to help them with this issue; she thus decides to stop the work when the group becomes anxious and goes back to the activity using *Black Hawk Down* to initiate a discussion of the taboo areas. However, it is early in the group's development and the members need to feel safe to deal with their concerns. The group is becoming a safe place to deal with their concerns after the 9/11 tragedies.

Taboo Issues

The worker recognizes that the members have begun to disclose some of their feelings and experiences about the World Trade Center disaster. There is a beginning sense of cohesion, although she continues to be concern about Ari and Satish's role in the group. She prepares to introduce the activity of designing and decorating T-shirts. She wants the members to feel safe and nurtured. Rachel is tuned in to the fact that the group might be anxious today because of a recent explosion of a commercial paint manufacturing building in the neighborhood. An incident like this often reactivates memories and feelings of 9/11. The members exchange greetings with the worker but continue discussing the explosion among themselves. They go directly to the snacks. The worker states that she bought T-shirts for the group members to design and decorate. She continues by saying that she heard some of them talking about the recent explosion that happened the other day and that she was not at their school that day. She asked them to tell her what happened. Alan and Roger simultaneously begin talking about what class they were in, how their teachers acted, the sounds of the explosion, and how they felt the school shake. Ari quietly shared that his father had to close his store for three days because it was very close to the paint factory. Several of the members asked him for details of the explosion, while other members excitedly added their experiences. Rachel exclaimed how frightening the explosion must have been. Roger: "Shit, I thought it was the World Trade Center explosion all over again!" Roger told the group how scared the recent explosion made his mom because she worked near the World Trade Center on 9/11 and it reminded her of that.

RACHEL: I bet everyone was scared.
STEVE: The school didn't let us go home and that was a sign that it wasn't as serious as 9/11. We had to stay in school without lights and wait for them to come back on.
EDWARD: Nobody did any work, all the lunchroom periods were late, and some of the teachers were freaked out.
RACHEL: Most New Yorkers would connect the sounds of an explosion with the things that happened the day that the towers went down. Many people are jumpy now.

ROGER: Everything freaks my mother out now.

JUAN: My mother is the same way and she wasn't anywhere near the World Trade Center when it happened. She talks about moving back to Santo Domingo but won't take a plane.

RACHEL: It must be weird and kind of scary to see some of the adults in their life so nervous and upset.

STEVE: I heard that they kill lots of people in Santo Domingo.

SAM: My grandparents were supposed to visit over the Christmas holidays, but they didn't because my dad did not want them fly.

RACHEL: The World Trade Center has affected many people but particularly those of us living in New York City. We have concerns and feelings we never had before and some of us don't want do things we used to do. How about you guys? (*Silence.*)

Edward and Roger began throwing popcorn at the other members, some of whom used their pencils and rulers to bat the popcorn back. Rachel responded that she guessed that this was hard to talk about. They continued playing.

RACHEL: Some parents and teachers are feeling "freaked out," like Roger said. Then it's understandable that you guys might also have some heavy feelings about what has happened not only with the recent explosion but when the towers went down.

TODD: I didn't want to come to school.

JULIO: Boy this is fun! (Alan continues to throw popcorn at him to bat.)

JULIO: I love baseball! Could we play it in the group?

RACHEL: It looks like you are doing that already. This stuff must be hard for you to talk about.

JULIO: I miss little league.

RACHEL: What about it.

JULIO: (*He hangs his head slightly and says in a low voice*) since the attack I haven't felt like going. (Several of the members continue to play.)

RACHEL: Have any of the rest of you quit doing some of the activities that you used to enjoy? (*Silence.*)

ROGER: I'd like to get those Muslims!

ALAN: Me too. (*Silence.*)

JUAN: Not all Muslims are bad. (*Silence.*)

EDWARD: I went to visit Rasheen's house and it was really strange! His mother and all the girls had scarves on their heads and wore long dresses, there wasn't any soda, and there were all these rules.

ROGER: But they're black, right? My Dad's a cop and he said forget about arresting black guys, just get guys who look like Arabs.

RACHEL: Maybe we can talk about being different.

ToDD: Hey aren't we going make the T-shirts now? (The rest of the group yells, "Let's do it.")

The worker is where the members are at and recognized the opportunity for work by using the recent explosion to make connection to their experiences and feelings regarding 9/11, which is the group's purpose. Her questions, encouragement, and empathy encourages the members to tell their stories. Roger's connection to the World Trade Center incident gave her the entrée to focus the discussion on the group's purpose. Thus she continues to create a culture for work. Being concerned about Ari's place in the group, she did not, however, respond to his sharing about his father's store.

As Rachel puts their feelings into words they feel safe enough to elaborate and make connections between recent feelings that reminded them of the past World Trade Center incident. It is easier and safer for the members to talk about others reactions than their own. The identification of these highly emotional feelings has created anxiety. Steve attempts to change the subject. He may be making an association with people killed. The worker does not pick up on Steve's comment, as other members begin to describe how the 9/11 events have affected their families. They are beginning to do the work of the group. The worker normalizes their experiences and feelings by validating and generalizing. Others get anxious and try to stop the discussion by playing around. The leader continues to acknowledge and reflect on the difficulty of hearing the material and uses humor as she gently pushes them to do the work.

Some group members risk and disclose that they haven't felt like doing some of their usual activities such as sports or going to school. Some of the members are having trouble tolerating the process and the tension and anxiety in the group is mounting. There is also internal group conflict as some members continue to stop the work by turning their anxiety outward. The group is experiencing disequilibria. New norms are being created as members risk and self-disclose reactions of family members as well as some of their own feelings and responses to the 9/11 tragedy.

Racial and Ethnic Differences

The worker realizes that the members need to talk about ethnic and racial differences so as to dissipate the tension that is directed toward Ari and Satish. This will also help them lessen the conflict and increase cohesiveness. She attempts to take the group in that direction by using the themes and content presented while doing the activity. The members discuss what they want to put on their T-shirts. Roger says he wants to put NYPD (New York Police Department) on his, with a badge. Alan wants an American flag on his. Steve states, "Hey, that's going to be patriotic, maybe I'll put the World Trade Center on mine." Alan asks Steve if he would draw the flag for him. Roger sarcastically asks Ari what he was going to put on his.

ARI: I'm American just like you! I was born here! I'm Lebanese American and I'm a Muslim. (Ari begins to design a rainbow on his T-shirt that is red, white, and blue. Satish's head is half-bowed in an attempt not to be noticed.)

JULIO: Steve, are you going to make the towers standing up or exploding?

ALAN: Yeah, neat! Make them exploding like it was the day it happened.

JULIO: That's gross! Rachel, can we put anything we want on our T-shirts? (Rachel answered yes. Julio responded that he wanted to put the Dominican flag on his.)

ALAN: Why the hell would you do that?

JULIO: Because I'm proud to be Dominican. The best ball players are from there.

RACHEL: There seems to be a lot of conversation today about differences.

ROGER: We'd have a lot less problems if there were only Americans here!

ALAN: Yeah, and lets get rid of anyone who isn't American. (Several of the members nod in agreement.)

RACHEL: What does being American mean?

JUAN: It's making a lot of money!

ROGER: It means loving and protecting the USA.

TODD: Being born here.

JULIO: He's crazy. I'm born here and I'm American and a Dominican.

JUAN: Yeah, me too.

STEVE: I'm American, too, but I don't look it.

ALAN: Where are you from?

RACHEL: (*Asks pensively*) what does an American look like? In this room there are many different looks and shades of color, yet you all are Americans.

STEVE: My mother is Japanese American and my father is white. This makes me Eurasian. (Many members remark that they had never heard of this.)

JUAN: (*States proudly*) I'm a Nuyorican, that is a New York Puerto Rican!

RACHEL: It would be great if other members share their backgrounds.

ARI: (Holding his T-shirt with pride) My family came to the U.S. to get away from killing. America was our dream.

SATISH: I was born here, but my family came from India where there were always riots and killings. They came to get away from all that.

RACHEL: America, and New York City particularly, is a place of many ethnic groups.

ROGER: My father told me to be careful because black guys are always getting picked up just because they were black.

RACHEL: Roger, thanks for bringing this up, because it is a very important issue. Do you all know what stereotyping and racial profiling is? (The group continues to work on the T-shirts.)

RACHEL: While we all may be suspicious of people who look like the 9/11 hijackers, we have to be careful not to single people out by their appearance or color like Roger was talking about. Ari and Satish, have you been treated differently since 9/11?"

ARI: My parents came to the U.S. because of terrorists in Lebanon, and now they sometimes feel scared and tell me to be careful because people will think that, since my parents are Arab and Muslim, they must be terrorist.

ALAN: Satish, what are you?

SATISH: What do you mean?

ALAN: Are you Muslim?

SATISH: No. I'm Hindu.

The group uses the activity to move into ethnic and racial tensions and stereotypes. This is a highly charged area that continues to surface because of the two members singled out for their resemblances to the profiles of the 9/11 terrorists. The worker knows that this important topic needs to be addressed. Some of the tension also has to do with the members establishing their place (roles, rank, and relationships) in the group. The older boys, Alan and Roger, have formed a clique. Differences are threatening to them, as emphasized by Alan's cursing, which is also is way to pull rank and test. But sharing and mutual aid has also begun with Alan acknowledging Steve's artistic abilities.

Several members have chosen themes for their T-shirts that reflect the World Trade Center incident and patriotism. It is not until Juan states that he wants to put the Dominican flag on his T-shirt that Rachel points out the theme of differences. She is tuned in to the fact that tension is escalating and that Ari and Satish are being profiled. The group is becoming a microcosm of the community's intolerance of people with Middle Eastern backgrounds. She knows that she wants to protect them. She intervenes by asking, "What does an American look like" and pointing out that everyone in the group is ethnically different looking—they are all Americans. This gives permission and creates a more relaxed environment for members to ask questions about each other. Steve's self-disclosing deepens the sense of trust and sharing. Juan also feels safe enough to share his bicultural heritage. The worker continues to encourage them to learn about each other's background. Ari, who is less intimidated by the group than Satish, shares information. This gives Satish strength, and he talks about his background. The sharing of information creates the opportunity for Rachel to generalize about differences. The association triggers Roger to pick up on being black. The leader' intervention validates Roger's comment. She takes this as an opportunity to educate the group about stereotyping and racial profiling. The tension focused on Ari and Satish has begun to diminish. The worker feels comfortable enough to point out how Ari and Satish have been treated in the group. Exploring differences and connecting it to the group's behavior has helped deal with the tension and conflict. The members are now freer to be curious, ask questions, and learn more about one another.

Cohesion, Relatedness, and Mutual Aid

The group members straggle in and seem to have some difficulty assembling. In the previous meeting members have begun to touch the content and struggle with some of the issues that are surfacing. The activity needs to focus member's energies on the major content of the group and the interpersonal themes that emerged.

With borrowed equipment, Rachel introduces a make-believe radio station where members can become broadcasters, guests, interviewers, interviewees, and observers. She began the activity by stating that the group could make up a new program. The members grew excited, calling out news station initials with enthusiasm. They were curious about the equipment, with some members sharing what expertise they had. Roger, Steve, and Alan argued over who would be the director. The worker stated that in a few days it would be the six-month anniversary of the 9/11 tragedy. There were several moans and groans as well as a kind of excitement over who would interview whom and about what. The following excerpt reflects the members' involvement in the activity and the continued issue around diversity.

> SATISH: Let's focus on the war in Pakistan
> JULIO: They're fighting in Afghanistan.
> SAM: You are both wrong. They are fighting in both places.
> ROGER: We could talk about what is going to be done at Ground Zero. My dad took me down there. It was awesome. (Members were very curious and asked Roger numerous questions.)
> EDWARD: Let's talk about the terrorists around us.
> ALAN: We could talk about getting rid of foreigners, especially Arabs.
> JULIO: Not all foreigners. The bad ones.

The group started interviewing each other. Emerging from the process was the following excerpt of Alan interviewing Ari. Ari had entered the group with a bruised face and a black eye.

> ALAN: How did you get that bruiser?
> ARI: (*Hesitantly*) some guys jumped me on the way home from school.
> STEVE: Why? (The other boys are also looking with questioning looks.)
> ARI: It's over. I don't want to talk about it.
> ALAN: We are interviewing you.
> ARI: Rachel said that we didn't have to answer any questions if we didn't want to.
> ROGER: I bet I know the answer. It's because you are one of them.
> ARI: (*Shouting*) I am not. I told you, I am American now. I came from Lebanon because there was all this fighting and bombs.

STEVE: What are you talking about? (There was a moment of silence. Ari then describes hiding in a bunker while bombs were bursting all over.)

ARI: My dad told me that I was very lucky to be here. My uncle and his family were killed. It's like it is starting all over again.

SATISH: You mean like in a new country?

ARI: No, people being killed and fighting for no reason, or because they have a different religion.

ROGER: Well, there are reasons.

SATISH: I've been chased and yelled at and sometimes I am scared to go down certain streets. And my sister has had her headscarf snatched. (Roger is whistling and acting uninvolved.)

ALAN: Let's get back to Radio News.

JULIO: This is the news.

RACHEL: Yes, this is the news of the group. One of our members has been attacked.

ROGER: Wait a minute.

JULIO: Ari, did you get the guys who did this?

EDWARD: How many were there?

JUAN: Ari, we can help you get them good.

RACHEL: Is fighting the only way? (The members tell Rachel that for them it is.)

ROGER: Well, Ari, what can you expect?

ALAN: Why are you so pissed at Ari?

ROGER: I am pissed that everything is different now.

The group rallies around Ari, except for Roger and Todd. Ari shares that sometimes he wakes up and sees buildings burning. Edward shares that he closes his eyes but does not go to sleep until his mother comes home from work.

In this meeting the activity helps them to get into the work with the leader acting as facilitator. By interviewing Ari he is given the opportunity to tell more of his story. Mutual aid is emerging and there is more tolerance for hearing and discussing differences and painful issues.

SCARED, BRAVE AND SAVE

In session eight the worker introduces an activity using three different code words. They are *scared, brave,* and *safe.* They are emotionally charged. The members are struggling with their feelings of being scared, not feeling safe, and being brave in regard to the 9/11 tragedy. The purpose of this activity is to continue to bring out the content and the purpose of the group through the members sharing various feelings and experiences about the World Trade Center incident, increase cohesion and mutual aid, enhance mastery through problem solving and decision making, as well as support individual and collective strengths.

Before the group's scheduled meeting, the worker arranged three tables, with chairs for each subgroup. On them she placed blank index cards, colored markers, and glue. When group members arrived, the worker explained that the tables and material on them were for today' activity. She had them to count off. Each sub-group is asked to take a different table. One member, Sam, is absent. Some of the members remarked that they wanted to sit together. Rachel responded that by the counting off by numbers it would give them an opportunity to play and talk with someone they did not know very well. They are asked to go to their spe-cific table, each member being told to take one blank index card. Rachel then gives each subgroup an index card with a code word on it. They are told to look at the word on the card, pass it around, and then write another word that it re-minded them of or that they associated with the code word. Each table's card had one of the following code words: SCARED, BRAVE, and SAFE. Roger stated that if this was a test he didn't want to take it. Satish added that he was already in trou-ble because of his grades. Rachel explained that it wasn't a test, there would be no grades, and that the exercise was just a sort of word poster activity. The mem-bers slowly begin writing a word on their individual cards. As they finished writ-ing, several members began talking to one another and going to the other tables to see which word they had written. Rachel commented positively about their cu-riosity and asked them to go back to their table, since the activity was not fin-ished. She gave each subgroup's table a piece of poster board and asked them to place and then glue their three individual cards into some kind of group picture or design. In each subgroup she heard them exchanging the experiences and feelings that their code word evoked. There was conflicting opinions and negoti-ations as they made decisions about placing the cards and fought over who would glue. After gluing the cards on the poster board they were told to use the mark-ers to draw connections between the cards. Several of the boys became posses-sive of the markers and threw them at each other. They spoke loudly about how the connections were going to be made and by whom, as they continued to share feelings about the word associations. There were arguments about who would write what on the poster board. Each subgroup accomplished the tasks. The worker encouraged them throughout to be creative and have fun. She further di-rected them to write or draw anything they wanted to add to the poster. Again, there was more sharing of feelings amidst the arguments and compromises. They were able to complete the tasks with minimal interventions by the worker. Rachel then asked them to talk among themselves about their table's poster and pick a person to tell the rest of the group what their poster was about. The ten-sion mounted, with some of the boys horsing around and punching as they de-cided who would be the spokesperson for the group.

Rachel asked the group who had the word *scared* to explain their poster first. Steve presented for his group, which also included Roger and Julio. He told the group that they had the word *scared* and this reminded them of the words *freaked, dead,* and *nervous,* which they had written on their cards. He presented their designed poster. Roger announced proudly that Steve wanted to be an artist and he did most of the artwork. Steve explained that *dead* was Roger's word and he helped draw Bin Laden because "we hope that somebody gets him or that he's dead so that all the trouble will be over." Julio's word was *nervous* because he was nervous about playing ball again. He put a baseball, bat, and hat around his word. Steve added that he knew that Julio was really good and was supposed to go to the All Star Little League. He then explained *freaked,* which was his word and "just thinking about the explosion and body parts freaked me out and I can't quit drawing it." They decided that Steve should draw a man in a cloak who represented death with his sickle swinging around to frame all the words on the poster. Several of the other group members complimented Steve on his artistic skills.

The group that had the word *brave* was Alan, Satish, and Juan. Alan explained about the words and decoration of the poster. They had associated the words *tough, heroic,* and *courage.* He explained each member's reason for choosing their word. They drew a picture of the World Trade Center towers standing, which made the numeral eleven, with a number nine in front of it. It read 911. There were symbols of firemen, police, and civilians around it.

The next group included Edward, Ari, and Todd. Edward proudly interpreted the poster using the code word *safe* to which they had associated the words *protect, rescue,* and *hope.* They had drawn a bright yellow sun with bursts. He explained that they decided that "when all the terrorism stuff is over and people are not trying to kill us, we'll all feel happy and sunny again." Rachel thanked them for all their hard work and for sharing and said that she would save their posters until next week when they would continue working on them and make plans for the last meeting.

The Collective Experience

The worker explained the next step for them was to take the three posters and decide as a large group how to make one big group poster. The members deliberated about what the large poster should look like, the theme(s), and how to place the subgroups' designs. They shared ideas and feelings about the large poster, 9/11, and their life now. They argued as Roger and Alan wanted their poster to take center stage. There was some playful punching, with less dominant members actively participating. Again, Steve was encouraged to take the artistic lead. Members again revisited and shared their feelings of fear and confusion about the events of 9/11, such as how they got home, curiosity about death, and the lingering feelings of uncertainty. They decided to make a Road to Conquest map that displayed their journey using the *scared* code word poster first, then the *brave* poster, and, at the end of the map, the *safe* poster. They decided to make it like a subway map because it had various stops along the way. Each subgroup's poster would be the express stops, and they would put some of their experiences in between as the local stops. Some of the feelings shared, which were put at local stops, were Roger's fear for his father's life, Julio's desire to be near his family, Alan's need to protect his mother and siblings, Satish's learning to be strong and have courage, Ari's fighting to be happy and fit in, Edward's fear of subways, and Todd's wish to make sure that he could live with his grandparents forever. The boys laughed and teased as they encouraged Steve to make the big poster. Some of the other members who were also good in art were encouraged to draw while others colored and made names of subway stops that represented their experiences and feelings. When they were finished, Rachel asked them to explain the large poster to her. They did so with enthusiasm. She praised them not only making a great poster but for sharing, helping one another, and working together. Some members asked if the poster could be hung up in the hallway. Rachel said that she would look into it. Other members did not want to be identified with it.

The group has become more comfortable with each other and has developed enough intimacy and trust to risk and self-disclose. They are now doing the work of the group through the activity. Play, or the doing, makes it easier for them to share their experiences and feelings about the World Trade Center incident.

The forced grouping changed some of the cliques. It also expands relationships, creating the opportunities for differentiation of the members. Some of the members verbalize concern about being graded, and their poor grades as they question whether they can achieve what is being asked of them. Their sense of mastery and self-worth is low. The worker has chosen an activity that is more relational and less focused on tasks. She created a safe, accepting environment where they are praised, encouraged to have fun, and be curious and creative. She does not want the activity to be seen as another adult demand.

This activity has many aspects of problem solving and decision making. It forces the group to engage in a give-and-take process, deliberate, negotiate, compromise, and be productive. There is conflict as a result of the members' positioning for leadership, competition, and the anxiety the content elicits. The worker lets the group evolve and realizes that the conflict is constructive. She purposely holds back and allows the members to work out their differences and take ownership as much as possible before she intervenes.

As each subgroup shares with the larger group the individual word associations and their collective poster, a sense of "we" has developed. The members are beginning to share very profound feelings and information. They are not defensive or threatened, although the content has understandably raised their anxiety. Strengths are being verbalized and supported. A sense of safety and intimacy has made them comfortable enough to share their vulnerabilities, fears, and confusion. No one is made fun of.

Making a large group poster forges mutual aid as the members work together to conceptualize the subgroups poster into an overarching theme. This problem-solving, collaborative process done through the activity enhanced mutual aid, co-hesion, sharing, and reflection of the deeper struggles the members are experi-encing. It has also created a sense of mastery and control.

ENDINGS

The group will need to deal with endings. This group has developed a sense of cohesiveness. They have developed mutual aid and are more related. There is still a pull away from expressing strong emotions and this will be seen as they move toward the ending. During the second half of the meeting Rachel told the group that the next meeting was the last meeting. She asked the group what they wanted to do to end the group. Several members asked why it had to end and wanted to keep meeting. Other members wanted the to end.

Members talked about going out for pizza or going on a trip, which they have when school ends. Sam shared that he had read that some school groups are doing special things around 9/11 like sending cards to other guys who lost a rel-ative, visiting the local firehouses, or raising money to help. There were groans and moans. Near the end of the meeting an idea was presented to plant a tree in the schoolyard. A member of the group had read that another youth group did this. The members were excited about digging in the yard. There was a heated discussion about what kind of tree. Satish had a relative who was a gardener and became very involved in the discussion. Sam wanted to invite other guys who had lost relatives to help. Other members disagreed. The group wanted to have a party with special snacks. Steve said that he would ask his mother to design a wooden plaque. Ari raised the issue that the tree needs to be taken care of after the group ends. Rachel asked the group if they wanted to know where they could go if they needed to talk after the group. At the end of the meeting she asked then to think about what they might want to say to each other at the last meeting. Roger said, "Good bye and see you later." He reminded Rachel that they were not leaving, only she is.

The final meeting was filled with joking and mild physical playfulness. The tree was planted, with the help of the janitor. The ground was hard and there was some logistics to work out. Some members were late and three of the members were absent.

There was resistance to discussing the ending. A great deal of time was spent on who would care for the tree. Steve brought in his mother's contribution to the effort. Satish brought in Indian pastries, while Ari brought candy from his father's store.

The content of the last session highlighted the member's ambivalence about dealing with their emotions. Satish and Ari wanted to be accepted, but the group had mixed feelings until the end. The meeting demonstrated termination phenomena that were presented in the mild "acting out" and absenteeism. The members seemed happy with the planting of the tree because it again represented an accomplishment achieved through cooperation. At the end they quickly scattered to their classrooms.

THE TERROR-INDUCED violence of 9/11 continues to have far-reaching effects on children. This is seen in the remembrances and other actions taken by children in youth groups and schools. The terror is acknowledged in their dreams of monsters, planes exploding, buildings collapsing, and fears of being away from home and on subways and bridges. The children of New York City have had even more intense struggles in a world that is forever changed.

The contemporary world of advanced media has kept the WTC incident fresh in our collective memories. The constant threats of other events happening and an ongoing war are new experiences for young minds to process. Children with previous trauma in their young lives are at higher risk and even more vulnerable.

Groups provide protective factors in that they help children feel less isolated, give them needed support, and, through mutual aid, provide them with tools to problem solve and deal with some of the issues. Groups dealing with issues of terrorism and trauma are moving into uncharted territory. Leaders need to expect the unexpected. They must possess heightened sensitivity to their own feelings and an understanding of members wanting to forget and not deal with the material as well as wanting to express themselves without being judged. The group as a "benign mother," or caretaker, can give the members a place to feel safe again.

References

Applied Research and Consulting, LLC, Columbia University Mailman School of Public Health and New York State Psychiatric Hospital. 2002. *Effects of the world trade center attack on NYC public school students: Initial report to NYC board of education,* New York.

Drewes, A. 2001. Developmental considerations in play and play therapy with traumatized children. In A. Drewes, L. Carey, and C. Schaefer, ed., *School-based play therapy,* pp. 297–314. New York: Wiley.

Germain, C. 1991. *Human behavior and the social environment.* New York: Columbia University Press.

Germain, C. and A. Gitterman. 1996. *The life model of social work practice: Advances in theory and practice.* 2d ed. New York: Columbia University Press.

Gitterman, A. and L. Shulman. 1994. *Mutual aid groups, vulnerable populations, and the life cycle.* 2d ed. New York: Columbia University Press.

Kirby, M., and M. Fraser. 1997. Risk and resilience in childhood. In M. Fraser, ed., *Risk and resilience in childhood: An ecological perspective,* pp.10–32. Washington, D.C.: National Associate of Social Workers.

Lieberman, F. 1979. *Social work with children.* New York: Human Science.

Lynn, M. and D. Nisivoccia. 2001. Crisis intervention activity groups in the schools. In A. Drewes, L. Carey, and C. Schaefer, ed., *School-based play therapy*, pp. 77–193. New York: Wiley.

Monahon, C. 1993. *Children and trauma: a parent's guide for helping children heal.* New York: Lexington.

Nisivoccia, D. and M. Lynn. 1999. Helping forgotten victims: Using activity groups with children who witness violence, pp 74–103. In N. Webb, ed., *Play therapy with children in crisis.* 2d ed. New York: Guilford.

Pfefferbaum, B., R. Gurwich, N. McDonald, M. Leftwich, G. Sconzo, A. Messenbaugh, and R. Schultz. 2000. Posttraumatic stress among young children after the death of a friend or acquaintance in a terrorist bombing. *Psychiatric Services* 51 (3): 386–88.

Phillips, A. 2001. Bombs away. In A. Phillips, ed., *Promises, promises: Essays on psycho-analysis and literature*, pp. 350–58. New York: Basic.

Shelby, J. 2000. Brief therapy with traumatized children: A developmental perspective. In H. Kaduson and C. Schaefer, eds., *Short-term play therapy for children.* New York: Guilford.

Shulman, L. 1999. *The skills of helping individuals, families, groups, and communities.* 4th ed. Itasca, IL: Peacock.

Smith, C., and B. Carlson. 1997. Stress, coping, and resilience in children and youth. *Social Service Review* 71:231–56.

Part 3

Mutual Aid and
Vulnerable and Resilient
Adolescents

Chapter 6

Preteens in Double Jeopardy
Supporting Developmental Growth
Through a Natural Friendship Group

Carol Irizarry and Yetta H. Appel

S OCIAL WORK intervention with children has always had to pay attention to developmental issues and within that context to young people's strengths and life-affirming abilities under adverse conditions. The child's stage of development, cognitively and psychosocially, presents both opportunities and constraints for the social worker, and more often than not the issues that emerge have developmental components. Thus a lifespan perspective that focuses on the biopsychosocial transitions that need to be negotiated through the life cycle, but also recognizes the significance of strength and resilience in adaptation, becomes a framework within which social workers can understand and engage young clients at this potentially turbulent time of their lives. In fact, "Early adolescence has been characterized as a potentially chronic stressful experience, owing to the largely uncontrollable changes in every aspect of individual development and in every important social context" (Smith and Carlson 1997:233).

This chapter presents interventions by a social group worker with a naturally formed group of preteen girls aged ten to thirteen years who were struggling with the typical developmental tasks and stresses of this transitional stage. Environmentally they had to cope with being members of ethnic minority groups (African American and Hispanic) as well as being subject to the socioeconomic deprivations associated with low-income status in American society. These young people can be viewed as experiencing a "double marginality" within mainstream society while at the same time displaying a range of innovative survival skills in response to their situation.

Developmental Tasks and Issues

By virtue of being preadolescent they were at the cognitive stage where they could begin to grasp, very likely for the first time, their marginal position: passing from childhood with some sense of loss at being compelled to give up this stage, into the unknown stage that was looming, that of early adolescence, and to feel oneself as not belonging fully to either. As Weenolsen has described this stage, "Pubertal changes in themselves signify a loss of the old self and the emergence of a new one. Either way, there are losses that must be transcended in some way" (Weenolsen 1988:278).

When one views adult social functioning in American society from a life span perspective, the psychosocial importance of this preadolescent stage becomes clearer. Much adult behavior greatly depends on peer associations, peer interaction, and developing interpersonal competence with peers. This interpersonal competence requires learning to be comfortable with equals, a redefinition of one's relationship to authority, eventually becoming able to use authority, and essentially becoming able to establish close working relationships, including intimate relationships, with strangers.

Erikson's (1950) epigenetic formulation of the psychosocial stages of development has been widely incorporated within social work's knowledge base, but there has been a discernible tendency to emphasize the crucial nature of the early stages of childhood, such as establishing basic trust versus mistrust, achieving autonomy versus shame/doubt, initiative versus guilt, and then usually focusing on the identity crisis of adolescence. Less attention tends to be given to the in-between stage of industry versus inferiority, although some highly significant psychosocial development takes place. This is the stage, for example, where peers become as meaningful to the growing child as one's family, and even more so in adolescence.

Sullivan (1940) and Piaget (1970), more than Erikson (1950), have perceived this stage as needing to provide the child with critical social experiences with age mates, which, if absent, can have a detrimental impact on later social functioning. Because of the work of Sullivan and Piaget, social experiences with peers both in groups and in paired relationships are now accorded almost as much importance as the family with regard to the achievement of mature social functioning (Youniss 1980). Both Sullivan and Piaget agree that this development begins in the preadolescent period, between the ages of nine and twelve, and is further elaborated and consolidated in the stage of adolescence.

If one is to be able to make friends, one has to develop skill in expressing oneself verbally, in communicating one's needs, especially to strangers, and in establishing and maintaining relationships with others in a nonfamily environment. This becomes the child's "work" in the preadolescent stage, and it is enormously facilitating for children's social development to be able to begin to do this initially with peers. The beginning of interpersonal sensitivity probably dates to this stage. True relationships, which acknowledge the intrinsic value of another and in which one is gratified by the experience of providing satisfactions to another, "the satisfaction in giving satisfaction," as Sullivan (1940:42) has stated it, emerge at the end of this stage.

The developmental tasks that have been identified for this psychosocial stage tend to be largely instrumental in nature. It is the stage in which the growing child learns how to use one's body more skillfully as the child's gross and fine motor coordination continually progress. These years have been viewed as relatively stable and quiescent, as generally "untroubled," since there are no major biophysical changes occurring (as will all too soon become evident with puberty) and a modicum of self-regulation with regard to instinctual demands has been achieved by the child.

However, there is a significant gender difference. For girls aged ten to twelve the biological changes of puberty are imminent and will be experienced by the end of this stage, whereas for boys this stage is prolonged and the experience of puberty will occur later chronologically. For both boys and girls the pubertal changes become the means by which peers recognize one's developmental maturity, and those who are "early maturers" begin to differentiate themselves from those who are still untouched by this biological watershed. As puberty looms, both sexes tend to experience greater anxiety and to search for information in order to understand the bodily changes that are making their physical selves— so taken for granted—now unpredictable.

Because the organism is more quiescent biologically, the preteen can concentrate on developing technical and social skills, in particular how to "connect" with age mates and be able to function in a nonfamily environment. In Erikson's (1950) view the child is exploring "how things work," and "how to make things." This stage is one in which the developing young person needs to experience a growing sense of mastery. Thus school becomes a major, if not dominating, institution in the young person's expanding social environment, for it is the arena wherein one's level of mastery tends to be extended and continually tested.

In the process of relating to strange children and strange adults that attendance at school essentially initiates, which becomes extended through formal and informal group associations, the child begins to develop a repertoire of social skills and gain social knowledge that becomes the basis for later extensive social development in adolescence and young adulthood. "Knowledge and intelligence, and especially problem-solving skills, are also coping resources. Good social skills and contacts facilitate one's access to social supports," according to Smith and Carlson's research (1997:237). They further cite the research of Kolvin, Miller, Fleeting, and Kolvin, who agree that "late childhood and early adolescence in particular provide opportunities for new behaviors to emerge as adolescents increasingly have experiences beyond the family sphere, in school, with peers, and in social opportunities" (Smith and Carlson 1997:238).

Piaget's (1970) work has demonstrated also that the cognitive resources available to the preadolescent enable the child to move into more socially demanding situations. The young person, cognitively, is in Piaget's stage of concrete operations, which is characterized by a decreasing subjectivity, by the ability to decenter, that is, to begin to be able to view things from another's perspective. The child at this stage can begin to think about things and demonstrates comprehension in the physical sphere, that is, that the essential nature of an object does not change even if its appearance can be variously manipulated. Greater precision in the use of language becomes evident, and memory becomes a repository of experience that tends to be more orderly and subject to relevant recall. An example of this is one of the girls remarking to the worker that, when they had earlier refused to let her discuss "periods and babies," it was "because we were younger then."

Vulnerabilities and Risk Factors and Resiliencies and Protective Factors

As ethnic minority preadolescent girls living in a New York City lower-income neighborhood, this psychosocial stage presented certain risk factors. Smith and Carlson (1997:235) comment, "It is noteworthy that environmental and contextual risk factors are more highly concentrated in the lives of children from ethnic minority groups." They identify the cumulative effect of multiple stressors: "Evidence suggests that it is the *cumulative* (emphasis added) effect of risk factors rather than a single risk factor that tends to produce more consistently negative outcomes" (Smith and Carlson 1997:235).

Miranda has also identified this same vulnerability, which he has called a "double crisis" (1979). He notes that a developmental perspective sensitizes the professional to the increased vulnerability to both psychological and physical disorders that stage transitions can initiate. Miranda suggests that ethnic minority individuals have to cope with "the added stress created by society's reaction to their ascribed status [that] seriously increases the potential for breakdown. The developmental process thus becomes part of a double crisis at each stage of unfolding" (Miranda 1979:111).

At the same time that vulnerabilities and risk factors are identified it is essential to recognize that the young people in this group, while coping with developmental issues common to all preteens in our society, also had at their disposal a somewhat different array of strengths and adaptive responses when compared with their white, middle-income counterparts. "That many poor families of color survive extreme poverty, racism, and oppression is a tribute to their resilience in overcoming odds" (Gitterman 2001:22).

The preteens in this group showed the ability to interpret and adapt to changing circumstances and resolve complex interpersonal issues in imaginative and creative ways. These capacities, however, were often not identified, even by themselves, because unconventional social behavior, often defined as "acting out," masked their underlying strengths.

The relationships between the girls in this group were intense, intimate, confrontational and purposeful. They used each other to negotiate their neighborhood as well as their struggles with family and school. They were fiercely loyal and possessed uncanny insights into each other's motivations and intentions. Allowing an adult stranger—the worker—into this network was a significant change in behavior, one that reflected the characteristic of adaptability and resilience. They were able to accept change because of the perceived benefits to be gained through contact with this outsider.

When available on an acceptable basis to preteens, adult support contributes to development. This support involves modeling interaction with strangers, encouraging the young person to explore the physical and social environment, providing a range of experience and activities in which the child will be able to develop appropriate social skills and technical mastery, but also providing a "home base" where failures will be understood and accepted. To acquire a feeling of mastery, of "industry," in Erikson's terms, requires that the young person experience some degree of success, which, in turn, helps her or him to cope with the inevitable failures. If there is little or no experience of success, or no recognition of success in activities that are successfully carried out, or no value attributed to the skills of survival and coping, impaired self-esteem and a pervasive sense of inferiority can result and become entrenched.

As can be seen in the process recording selections that follow, the group provided an opportunity for the girls to demonstrate their ingenuity and openness and for them to receive recognition of their abilities to establish and maintain supportive friendships. The worker recognized and overtly identified their strengths while guiding them into age-appropriate social achievements. The relationship with the worker added another dimension to their ability to organize activities and carry out plans that resulted in these abilities contributing to increased self-esteem and feelings of success.

In our society as presently structured, children growing up in low-Income families in general, but especially ethnic minority children, may have few opportunities to experience success and mastery or to feel valued by the broader community. Sullivan (1940) was one of the first neo-Freudians to recognize that a child's emotional health in the juvenile and preadolescent stages can become impaired if the "school, neighborhood, and other social environments are blighted by poverty, economic injustice, intellectual stagnation, widespread vice, and ethnic prejudices" (Chapman 1976:179). This view of Sullivan's has received empirical support in the work of Jerome Kagan (1977).

Middle-income children, both within the dominant white majority and ethnic minorities, usually have more opportunities to experience some measure of success as they become involved with the wider social environment. They expect to be able to achieve, according to Kagan (1977), which becomes in part a self-fulfilling prophecy. Their families expect this as well because they can provide more material resources, and they do not feel as alienated from the majority culture to which they proceed to introduce their children. In contrast, socioeconomically marginalized parents cannot readily do this and may well reinforce a sense of isolation and alienation in their children.

That same perception of alienation was evident in this group of preteens, who demonstrated considerable fearfulness toward venturing "off their block" into surrounding areas, which could have provided access to desired recreational activities. These possibilities were literally at their doorstep. Psychologically, however, they felt hesitant to leave their "block" and, to some extent, were never "off their block," even when they gained new experiences through activities and group trips carried out with the worker. Their sense of exclusion, of not fully belonging, of being different and possibly performing inadequately seemed to induce anxiety and extreme self-consciousness, which affected their behavior on trips out of the neighborhood. As one of the girls indicated following their eviction from a subway train because of noisy and generally disruptive behavior, "I feel funny on the subway, people stare."

The bravado behaviors that brought them the positive result of respect in their neighborhood caused them to feel shame when exhibited to the wider community. When the worker responded to this shame aspect of the girls' behavior without labeling it as "bad," their resilience allowed them to consider more socially acceptable alternative behavior for public occasions. They certainly grasped the unwanted consequences of their disruptive actions and were astute enough to try to solve the problem by adopting new approaches.

These preteens were revealing, in part, the lack of opportunity to develop expected social behaviors and to acquire the social knowledge that helps middle-class preadolescents appear more socially competent in the wider social environment. Nowhere was this more evident than in these preteens' feelings about, and actual performance in, the neighborhood schools they attended. School was almost always an anxiety-provoking experience and perceived as an alien place. The girls viewed the schools as primarily rule-enforcing institutions. But the "rules" bore little relationship to the social context in which these preteens daily found themselves, a context that included their being poor and from diverse cultural backgrounds, specifically, African American and Hispanic. For a good many Spanish was their first language as well. The schools they attended appeared to largely ignore these contextual factors.

Thus school was not a place where they could expect to achieve even small successes. Instead of beginning to acquire the technical skills that engender a sense of instrumental mastery, of "how things work," their school experiences tended to instill feelings of failure, ineptness, and lowered self-esteem. Before joining the agency group, the alternative forms of expressive and/or recreational activities through which they might be helped to develop some sense of accomplishment and a more positive self-image were largely activities that were not seen as beneficial by the school or community, such as minding younger siblings or spending time with friends. The fact that assistance with childcare was given to single parents, that mutual protection was provided for the girls, and that social networks were established was overlooked.

In the school system their experience of authority was arbitrary and unpredictable. Coercive approaches tended to prevail; compliance was demanded and secured through bribes and/or punishment. The girls portrayed their teachers as insensitive when comparing them to the worker, but they also emphasized that the worker did not "fit" their normal conception of an adult authority figure. In time they verbalized to her that they only outwardly complied with the teachers' demands, but really didn't "respect" them. For, at this point in their development, they were distrustful, as they put it, of all "grown-up people." This feeling made it all the more remarkable that they were able to overcome such a conviction and develop trust with a new kind of adult, a social worker, who had entered their lives.

Living in poverty or occupying what has been labeled a lower-income status also exposes children to a quite different experience of authority relations. All families tend to be undemocratic. However, there is accumulating evidence that families continually confronting material deprivation and the associated interpersonal stresses stimulated by such privation are not as able as more affluent families to be "looser" and to encourage "participatory" processes in the rearing of their children (Eckstein 1984). All but one of the girls lived in mother-only families, and there was a pervasive lack of parental nurturing.

Most of the mothers wanted their daughters to "do better" and not just to follow their own life patterns. Yet the stress levels in these families and the mothers' own handicapping socialization experiences seemed to prevent them from involving their children in any kind of decision making or working out compromises by trying to view things from their daughter's perspective. Also, there was little support for the verbal expression of feelings and concerns, which tended to reinforce acting out behavior.

For example, these girls increasingly raised questions about sexual functioning as a consequence of the onset of puberty. In response, the mothers were highly prescriptive, emphasizing what the girls "shouldn't do," but were unwilling to discuss with their daughters the pubertal changes and their implications. (The worker had to be very cognizant of this maternal prescriptiveness when she attempted to respond to the developmentally appropriate needs of these preteens for accurate sexual information.) These preteens were still in need of adult caring and support related to their stage of development, but were receiving limited help with identifying and validating their own feelings. Alice Miller (1987:80) identifies the critical nature of developing strength within oneself during childhood and feels it can only be obtained through the child's having "access to his own real needs and feelings and the possibility of expressing them!" She feels this task is made "enormously more difficult through living in contact with various different value systems" (Miller 1987:80). It is a tribute to the girls' resilience that, given opportunities, understanding, and encouragement to express deeply personal feelings and vulnerabilities, they did so enthusiastically.

In the last few decades there has been increasing interest in the human capacity to transcend detrimental circumstances and to live out ordinary lives in the face of extraordinary hardships (Werner and Smith 1992; Higgins 1994; Lifton 1994; Meier 1995). This capacity has been defined as resilience and recognizes the ability of individuals to transform, change, and adapt in unexpected and creative ways. Researchers such as Werner and Smith (1992), who followed children born into extremely high-risk environments, found that at least 50 percent, and usually 70 percent, grew up to be confident, competent, caring persons. The resilience skills demonstrated by the children included being able to form relationships, solve problems, develop an identity, plan, and hope. Likewise the preteens' group members showed similar skills and resisted being defined solely by levels of academic achievement or social conventions.

In looking at factors that foster resilience in children, Bernard (1991) found that teachers and mentors could provide protective factors that contributed significantly to resilience. The social work role with this group of preteens was largely carried out through a mentor role in an informal setting. A critical question for researchers has been to identify the aspects of this teacher/mentor role (and, by inference, the social work role) that are most helpful in strengthening resilience in children (Bernard1991; Kohn 1993; Higgins 1994; Meier 1995; and Delpit 1996). Some of the significant attitudes and behaviors they found were: demonstrating positive beliefs about the children, refraining from judging their behavior along a good-bad continuum, not taking negative behavior personally, providing time for reflection and dialogue, recognizing strengths, allowing expression of opinions and imagination, and providing opportunities for choice and decision making.

The practice examples that follow attempt to illustrate how the social work role within the group context engaged the preteens in a manner that utilized the approaches that strengthen resilience in young people. Developmentally, these preteen girls were at a stage in their lives where the natural friendship group was an integral part of their social growth. The mutual aid approach used by the worker provided an opportunity to support and expand the positive aspects of the many strengths evident in these vibrant young women, thus helping them in their drive to burst into the fullness of life.

Agency and Group Context

A settlement house in New York City was the locus for this social work service. Traditionally, settlement houses have attempted to provide supplementary educational, recreational, and social services to the neighborhood's residents. These residents frequently have been disadvantaged populations, including many waves of immigrants. As is well known, the settlement has served in the past as a vehicle for immigrant groups in particular to achieve a sense of personal worth and some degree of upward mobility. "Historically, social group work via the settlement houses, community centres, camps, residential settings, school services, leadership training programs, and community clinics has helped generation after generation of group members to feel better about themselves" (Gitterman 2001:24).

As with all innovative approaches, institutionalization overtook the settlement house movement. A discernible tendency took hold, with the settlements becoming more restrictive regarding membership and setting standards for behavior on their premises and on the uses of their facilities. They appeared to gear their programs to the upper strata of the lower-income population, to working and lower middle-income groups. They also tended to have some difficulty involving the newer waves of immigrants, primarily Spanish speaking, who were arriving in large numbers in New York City in the 1950s.

A number of the settlements began to recognize the distancing that had occurred, and attempts to remedy this took the form of outreach programs of various kinds. A particular target group were young adolescents, usually very streetwise, who could not tolerate the degree of structure and some of the restrictiveness inherent in traditional settlement house programs.

The social work intervention described below was part of a settlement's outreach program in a densely populated area of New York City. The settlement contracted for the use of a neighborhood housing project's basement, which served as the physical base for this program. Contact was made with groups of preteens in the neighborhood that had gained reputations for getting into various kinds of trouble. Master's level social workers made these contacts and offered service to start a clublike group on a frequent and ongoing basis for some of the natural friendship "cliques" of girls ranging in age from nine to thirteen years. Typically, the groups formed averaged about ten preteens.

The only other condition was that the worker would be available to family members of the club group. The worker kept a daily log for as long as she was involved with the group.

The population designated for outreach in this project and discussed in this chapter was made up of ten- to thirteen-year-old preteen girls in a natural friendship group who lived in a poverty area of New York City. They had been identified by the school system as "troublemakers" and were often asked to leave the regular settlement house programs because of their antisocial behavior. The challenge of the project was to offer the social work service to this hard-to-reach population in a way that fit with the needs, interests, and strengths of girls at this particular stage of development, while clearly and honestly representing the professional role of the worker and her commitment to an agency base.

The worker and the project supervisor, an agency staff member who was well known and accepted in the community, initially visited the designated girls in their homes. The offer was made to form "a club" for the girls that would meet three times a week for the summer using a nearby housing project basement as headquarters. The statement was made to the girls and their parents that the worker, Carol, would be responsible for the club but that as part of her job she would also be available to help other family members if requested.

The group included three cultural strands: Hispanic/Puerto Rican, African American, and Caucasian. The girls were quite aware of their cultural differences and the social discrimination experienced by minorities of color. Those preteens in the group who were Puerto Rican and African American appeared more aware of their marginality, of their being pulled between two cultures. As a result, they seemed to be confronting emerging identity issues earlier. One of the black members of the group, very aware of society's prejudices toward her race, revealed her struggle with achieving some self-acceptance as a young woman of color when she shared with the worker her poignant observation that "black don't look good on nobody."

Because they had to live in and negotiate a culturally diverse, complex environment, they tended to be rather cautious with adults and to have learned quite early and accurately how to "read" people and their intentions. They used nonverbal cues, paid close attention to body language, and one of their most recognizable abilities was that they appeared to have a heightened interpersonal sensitivity that belied their years.

The individual members of this natural friendship group manifested a number of personal strengths that had not been initially anticipated. In addition to the accuracy of their perceptions of others' attitudes and intentions (their "reading" of people), they had a basic reality orientation, an ability to look at life realistically. Learning to survive in a sometimes violent, unpredictable, depriving environment, which they certainly were doing, required disillusionment, the giving up of childish naïveté. Because less was hidden from them in the homes in which they were growing up, they were not as confused about their feelings. They expressed directly their anger and frustration, their being "mad." They could express just as directly what and whom they liked. And they could abandon themselves to the existential moment, from which they derived sustenance. Also, one can recognize that they demonstrated mastery, but not as conventionally defined. Given their social context, the only available outlet for them was to be "good at being bad," which they demonstrated on many an occasion. This sense of "negative" mastery created a strong bond among the members of the group. With this strong group subculture, they developed a considerable ability to handle various crises by themselves, using the inherent impetus within the group toward mutual aid.

Work and Group Themes

Getting Started

The girls immediately responded with enthusiasm to the idea of any club that would enable them to take trips and hid any reservation they might have felt. The evolvement of a contract between the girls and the worker around how the group would function took many weeks and presented numerous struggles. Negotiation with this new adult in their lives became the first overt theme of work, a theme that reflected their ambivalences about striving for independence while experiencing the necessity for compromise and cooperation.

This contract acted as the vehicle around which the theme surfaced. The group provided the medium through which it could be expressed. The mutual aid process gave rise to the impetus for a successful resolution. In the excerpts that follow, the firsthand recorded accounts of the social worker are presented, followed by the authors' comments, abridgments, summaries, and interpretations around the work.

At the first formal meeting the girls identified their interest in having a club to "go places and have fun." They indicated that this was only possible with the assistance of the adult worker, conveying the attitude that due to this practical necessity she would be tolerated. The girls were slightly aloof in affect, listened but did not respond to her comments, excluded her from any intimate exchanges, and particularly avoided any suggestions regarding the worker's availability for family members.

The worker's task was to respond to their concrete presentation of need, to help them to "have fun" while continuously finding ways to present her broader role and function and seek out their feedback. Simultaneously, she needed to be attuned to developmental issues and needs, that is, to help with growth and change. Almost immediately (the second meeting) such an issue surfaced, that of having a party but "with boys, " which became the means for further specification of the worker's role.

Negotiating the Role of the Worker

The second meeting was a trip to the local swimming pool. As the girls were walking home, plans were discussed for next week and became the first interaction around the contract.

> Carmen asked if they would have a party, and Nilda added, "with the boys?" Margarita said that they could tell their mothers it was just a party-and then later sneak the boys in. I asked what the reaction would be if I brought up the idea of inviting boys at the first parents' meeting to be held the following week. The girls all responded that the mothers would never allow it. Nilda became quite angry

and said she didn't know why the mothers had to know everything. I said that I could see they were upset about my wanting to talk to their parents about it. Nilda asked why the mothers had to meet at all anyway. I said that this was part of my job—to work with families as well as with them. Margarita exclaimed, "Well, if that's what she's supposed to do, Nilda, then that's what she's supposed to do." Nilda replied maybe, but she didn't think any parents would come to the meeting anyway.

The group saved face by Nilda's comment that no one would come to the meeting, but an important step had been made in their recognition of the "job" classification of the worker's activities and the parameters this presented. Subsequent discussions with the girls led to agreement that the topic of boys could be introduced at the parents' meeting. When it was agreed that the party would be allowed, with the supervision of settlement house staff, the girls were ecstatic, and their attitude toward the worker shifted to one of sudden curiosity. She was temporarily seen as a miracle worker, one who really possessed the key to new and possibly forbidden "adult" experiences.

Trusting and Testing a Stranger

The first theme of adult negotiation continued, but the second theme of work also emerged this early: trusting and testing a stranger. This powerful theme took many forms and dominated all aspects of interaction between the worker and the girls. It appeared in its infancy linked to sorting out her role and function as the worker continuously tried to clarify the unique aspect of her involvement with the group.

During the first few weeks on a picnic to Central Park, the girls kept referring to me as a teacher. When I inquired into this, I was told it was because I looked like a teacher and because teachers also took them places. I said that this was probably why they did call me a teacher, but then maybe they would feel toward me what they felt toward teachers. Nilda replied, "Oh, no, we like you." Then followed a series of complaints about teachers who shout a lot, punish unfairly, and never listen.

The primary nonfamilial authority figure with whom the girls had constant interaction was, of course, a teacher, and the comparison was obvious. It was many months before the differences in roles were experienced and accepted as easily as the similarities. The worker did impose limits, but they were directly related to their personal safety or possible destruction of property. She did not censor verbal expressions or physical behavior that fell outside these parameters.

The worker used the term *social worker* frequently and informally in referring to herself and her purpose in spending time with the group. Since the actuality and visibility of an agency was minimal and the external manifestations of the professional stance were significantly limited while sitting on the steps of a tenement building, the importance of verbal repetition of purpose and function was great. Over the summer months, with the worker's help, the girls began to experience a sense that this new adult in their lives was different from others they had known in the family or school and that her responses were unique.

The testing of the few worker-imposed limits did occur, but it was almost always obvious to the girls and verbalized by the club president, Nilda, that they would not be allowed to continue going on trips if there were injuries. The club existed from the girls' point of view so that they could "go places and do things," a feat not easily accomplished by preadolescent girls living in a restricted, impoverished urban environment. The group members immediately identified with their stake in working together to enable the club to continue functioning, and as a consequence of their being a strong, natural friendship group they had their own well-oiled system of internal control. The worker on many occasions, such as in the following example, had only to use and strengthen this system by pointing it in the direction of self-interest.

> Mrs. Vilar spoke to me one day about Carmen (her daughter) being afraid of Tata beating her up in the club. For this reason she didn't like Carmen coming. I spoke with the president, Nilda, who at the time was the only one with influence over Tata. I explained that I felt responsible to their mothers if someone was hurt, although I knew Carmen also teased Tata a lot. Nilda, Tata, and I had a meeting, and Nilda told Tata to stop beating up Carmen because her mother was mad about it. Tata refused to discuss the matter at all with the worker, but responded to Nilda and stopped.

This type of intervention was frequent and smooth, easily recognized and accepted by the girls for what it was—a way to help them stay together as a group. This part of the social worker's role still closely resembled other authority figures in their lives—especially the teacher. The specific characteristics of the social worker's responses lay in the exploration of the girls' behavior rather than the censorship of it. This they had not experienced before, and it confused them. The testing in this area came first in the form of imitation and ridicule of the worker's gestures, manner of speech, and personal idiosyncrasies, in particular from Tata, the group member who often acted out the most extreme feelings in the group. The worker did not respond to this behavior.

Swearing, or "cursing" as the girls called such language, was a normal part of conversation when adults were not present, as was public unsocial behavior, such as rude gestures or insults, to pedestrians or subway riders. Very quickly the testing for worker reaction moved into the arena of expressing some type of unconventional behavior.

All such behavior was embarrassing and unpleasant, but it was also obvious that stringent demands from various authority agents in society, familial and nonfamilial, had not been successful in inhibiting its expression. A new process was begun with the presence of a nonjudgmental adult. The group members were left to feel and react to the impact of their behavior themselves. The worker was not passively accepting of all and any behavior. She watched for and used opportunities to help the girls examine together what they wanted for themselves.

Developing Group Norms

The girls hovered on the threshold of the first step toward autonomy, that is, of making decisions about themselves and their behavior that were not simply reactions to external demands to avoid punishment. This second theme of work was a painful struggle of hesitatingly testing new responses and retreating to safer, previously familiar patterns. Only by recognizing the impetus toward self-motivated decisions could the worker use intervention that mirrored their behavior back to the group for scrutiny and exploration.

Becoming Autonomous

In midsummer an extensive trip was planned to Coney Island, a distance of one and a half hours by subway. As usual on the subway, the restraint of space and apparent scrutiny by passengers led to noisy behavior by the girls. During the trip the antisocial quality and subsequent interaction with passengers increased. I was glanced at frequently but not spoken to directly and sat without comment in my seat. Eventually, the authorities evicted the girls from the train and I accompanied them. The event was treated as a great joke, even though the trip itself was aborted and the group returned home because of lack of funds. I was excluded from discussion about the event as the bravado attitude prevailed.

The next day, while we were eating cookies at the center, the whole episode was spontaneously reviewed. Judy remarked, quite somberly, that she imagined passengers thought they were girls on a trip from a "loony house." Nilda added, without laughter, "We all looked crazy—no wonder people stared." Comments ensued about various crazy people from the neighborhood and how they acted. I asked if they wanted people to think that about them. Carmen instantly replied no but that it was my fault because I hadn't screamed at them and made them stop.

I said I hadn't thought I was a policewoman to go around watching how they behave, and that they were always telling me how much they didn't like their teachers bossing them around so much. Nilda said I could be in some ways like a teacher. Judy agreed—to tell them to sit down. I said that I was willing to remind them to sit down if they wanted me to, but also asked them if they thought it would really stop them. Tata led the general response that no one could stop them when they got going "like that." I said that I thought one of the hardest things for anyone to learn in life was to act the way they really wanted. There was silence. Nilda said, "I feel funny on the subway, people stare!"

The group members immediately ended the discussion and rushed into other activities. But since the mirror had been held up before the girls, it had been looked into, and things would never be as simple again. The worker had introduced the idea of how hard it is to obtain desired personal outcome—the message was also a challenge to work rather than simply establishing blame.

Exploration of behavior with preteens girls living in stressful socioeconomic conditions often accompanying racial or cultural minority status could feel like a double exposure. Not only were they feeling the self-consciousness that accompanies the change from childhood to early adolescence but they also had to deal with the very powerful impact of being identified by society as "different." Interpreting and reacting to this difference seemed always a part of their attempts to define themselves and their relationship to this outsider, the worker, whom they saw as belonging to the mainstream of society.

The impetus of the girls toward growth and change was strong and strengthened by the bond of the group. What was fascinating was the way in which the themes of work merged together. Negotiating with the adult authority continued, taking on new dimensions as trust deepened. Self-exploration surfaced not only around increasingly threatening areas but subjects that were seldom talked about with this population as well.

One of the first things that came up was a discussion of cursing, raised at a Christmas party.

Judy said she wondered what their mothers thought of the worker when she let them curse in front of her. Everyone seemed in agreement that I should be "teaching" them good things and that teachers at school would never let them curse. I responded by saying that if everyone else, like teachers and so on, was teaching them all these things, they did not need me to do it. There was some engagement around what cursing meant to them, how "everyone always said that anyway" when they were angry. (The "everyone" referred to people on the block and in the area.) This particular meeting was ended by Margarita concluding that the worker really didn't want them to curse, and they should do it no more around the center.

The worker consistently continued clarifying her role and purpose. She gave legitimacy to subjects relating to discussion of behavior and feelings toward societal authority figures. She understood and accepted the girls' ambivalent feelings. By the end of the summer the girls were meeting twice a week in the center after school.

One day Tata and Kathy seemed upset because they did not have a certain kind of ball. They ran around awhile, then lay down on the table laughing and chanting, "We hate (substitute name)." Everyone's name in the center was mentioned except mine. I sat saying nothing, and gradually the "I hate" started to include gestures toward me. After fifteen minutes Tata looked at me and said, "Well?" I knew what Tata meant—What was I going to do?

I told her that I really didn't know what to say to them, since they seemed to be angry and mad, and that I wasn't sure if they wanted me to say anything about it. Kathy said they were mad, and Tata agreed. I said I could see this and asked them if they knew what it was they were so mad at. Kathy said yes, but that they weren't going to tell me. She went on, "Why should we always tell you everything? You never tell us your personal life." I responded, "No, I don't, and I guess that makes you feel bad." Kathy asserted that it did and then asked why I wanted to know anyway. I said that the reason I wanted to know was because their being so mad today seemed to have stopped them from doing anything. Tata said that they didn't want to play anyway, and I remarked that this was unusual since they usually liked to play.

I said that they really didn't have to find a thing to say that they were mad at— maybe it made them mad to feel both hate and liking for someone. This was too much, and again they began laughing and chanting that I knew who it was they really hated and that it was me. Margarita stayed in the clubroom and showed her disapproval of Tata and Kathy by saying, "You should respect Carol" (the worker) and by suggesting to me that I should make them respect me. I replied that I really was more interested in what they were feeling, even if those feelings were hard to talk about. Kathy shouted, "And don't think we respect our teachers just because we're polite to them cause we don't. We don't like any grown-up people."

The worker sought out the underlying ambivalence usually felt toward authority figures at this stage of development, which was intensified with a population who felt excluded from society in so many ways. The response from the girls in the group was an expression of this ambivalence. The worker's intervention was one of the strongest statements she would ever make to facilitate work on developmental issues: she was more interested in what they were feeling than in making them respect her. No matter how threatening or difficult it was to talk about something, she would try to help.

Establishing Group Trust

This intervention lent the group a specific tool for addressing their issues of concern: experience and support in talking about subjects that were usually not addressed verbally. This tool was particularly significant, since the girls' environment presented a dearth of socially acceptable opportunities to explore feelings and attitudes verbally. In the group context they felt less self-conscious about experimenting with verbal (group) discussions and in helping each other articulate confusing and threatening feelings. Drawing on the support of the worker and each other, more taboo subjects started to be approached.

Exploring Taboo Concerns

As the girls were returning from swimming, Carmen remarked that she was so tired she felt "old enough to be a mother."

> I inquired how old she thought this was, and Carmen replied that she didn't know, but that it had to be older than they were. Judy laughed, saying that wasn't true because since she had "started" a few months ago she had stopped "fooling around with boys." I said that any time after a girl started her period she was able to have a baby. Several girls exclaimed uncomfortably at this, and Tata told me that I shouldn't say it. "When I asked them if it was my talking about a girl's period that upset them, Tata started jumping around exclaiming, "What you said, what you said!" The others imitated her, and the conversation ended on that occasion.
>
> When they were back in the center, I asked them why they had been so upset before on the street. The president, addressing me in great seriousness, said that she had almost called a policeman. To the inquiry of why, she replied that people weren't allowed to talk about things like that, and he would have stopped it. Another girl added that they were too young to know about babies and that I shouldn't be "giving them advice on them." As if to make the final point, Tata added that if her mother knew they talked about things like that in the club she would take her out of it immediately. The others seemed to agree with this, and, when I asked if they had ever seen any movies on menstruation at school or talked about it in health class, I received the same negative answer and again the comment from someone that her mother would take her out of school if such a thing happened.

As a natural consequence of self-exploration, the girls had plunged headlong into a taboo area—sex. The fact that sexual identity and a need for information was of central developmental concern did not alter the fact that family and cultural restraints on the expression of sexual interest were firm. The worker could only allow the girls to set the pace for further discussion and give them sanction and support for entering taboo areas.

References to sex took the form of third-person jokes, fantasies, or spontaneous remarks for several months. The worker was asked nothing directly and not included in the interaction. She remarked occasionally that there seemed to be interest in the subject of sex. This was always denied.

> One afternoon the girls rushed into the center saying how upset they had been at school that day. Tata began shouting that they had been talking about "periods and that stuff" at school and added that they had called it "hygiene or something."

(This was said in a disgusted tone as if to indicate "hygiene" was a cover-up.) I replied that I had noticed they got upset when they talked about periods or sex.

Tata explained the health class further, saying the teacher had asked fresh things like who had their period. She had said the eggs turned to blood and came out of them, but not to look for them because they were too small to see. I said that I didn't think the egg exactly turned to blood, but that it came out of you and after that the blood came. Judy said that that's what the teacher had said and I suggested that it must be hard to understand just what the nurse was saying, especially if they felt upset about her even talking about it.

Kathy asked if it were true that we had eggs inside of us. I replied that they were inside of every girl, and that, when she got her period, this meant the egg came out of you, once a month, since it wasn't going to grow into a baby. Kathy said she (the teacher) had said it was where a baby came from, and I agreed with this, saying it was terribly small, like a little seed, but that the baby started from that. Tata said she had never known this, and Judy said that was why you had to stop fooling around with boys when you got your period. (I didn't reply.) Lydia declared emphatically that she knew the boys were listening at the door when the teacher asked those fresh questions. Margarita said that in her school they had the same kind of meeting with the girls, and the nurse had said not to be embarrassed about it, but that if they got their period, they should come and ask for "a—a—a—I think she said a sanitary napkin or something." (Seemed to be a lack of understanding of what this was.) Tata replied that their nurse had said not to be shy either, and I asked if this stopped anyone from being shy. Everyone laughed, saying they weren't going to talk about "those things." I asked if there had been a time when they could ask questions about sex. Judy replied, "Hell, yes, but who's going to open their big mouth?" Again laughter. I said that it must be very hard for them, since, probably like most girls, they had questions they wanted to ask but couldn't there.

Tata said, "Why can't you answer our questions?" Cautioned by their previous reactions, I replied that I remembered having brought up a discussion before with them in the summer about periods and babies, and they were so upset that they wanted to call a cop. This produced some smiles of recollection. Tata explained the situation by saying, "Well, it's because we were younger then." I replied, "Oh" and said I felt that they should know about it, if they wanted to, and that was her feeling. Margarita said she thought girls should know, too, especially after they had their periods.

Establishing Intimacy

The worker, at last, could be very active as the girls tackled the subject. She gave information, clarified misconceptions, and helped find comfortable words to use, acknowledged the anxiety around the subject, supported the girls around the risk of talking about a taboo subject, and always accepted the level and speed at which the work could progress.

Timing was crucial. Any response to the question "Why can't you answer our questions?" which shifted control from the girls' pace to the worker's preconceived idea of how the discussion should proceed might have stopped the action. The correct timing involved remembering and using everything she had experienced and learned about this group and how the mutual aid process operated with this population. The girls worked together to solve the problem of gaining sex-related information and expressing feelings related to the subject. The worker intervened in supplementary ways, with her responses attuned to the natural helping efforts that were reflected in such responses as the rationale that made it permissible now to discuss sex: "We were younger then." This rationale possessed wisdom far beyond the girls' years and yet was uniquely within their framework and culture. The work continued moving further into the even more threatening topics of babies and rape.

Working Through Sexual Issues

Tata again asked me if I was sure you couldn't have a baby before you had your period. I replied yes, I was sure. Tata said that, when she was a little girl, she had gone into the hall to get something and that some strange man had talked to her nicely, then he "took" her right there, and she didn't even know what it was all about. I said she must have been very scared, and she replied that she cried and cried, and her mother tried to arrest him, but he had run away. Margarita said that at least she couldn't have a baby, and Tata said, no, that she didn't have her period. In fact, she didn't know why she didn't even have it yet. Lydia shouted hadn't she even heard what the nurse had said—it comes anywhere between ten and sixteen or seventeen. There was some discussion of who started when, and so on.

Judy said I must remember when she started, in the summer, as she came to the center that day. I said that I did remember, and Judy added that if she "fooled around" after that time she would be able to have a baby. Judy said she still wanted to know how babies came, and before I could respond, everyone started screaming at her. Tata said she didn't know why Judy was always talking about those things—babies and periods. Everyone chimed in on this. Lydia didn't know why she had brought it up in the first place, and Kathy ridiculed her for thinking kissing made babies.

I had a feeling that this was the moment and, raising my voice in a louder scream than any of theirs, I shouted: "Maybe it's that everyone has this question and only Judy is brave enough to say it." My words created immediate silence, with everyone looking at each other. Kathy responded quietly, "Well, I brought it up anyway; I asked if we really had eggs." Margarita added, "There is no reason why girls shouldn't know." (She had said this before.) I said, "No, there isn't any reason why you shouldn't know, although I do remember your saying your mothers would take you out of the center if they knew you talked about it." Margarita smiled, "And who tells their mother everything?" Everyone laughed.

The worker reframed Judy's continued pressing for information about sex as bravery and acknowledged the appropriateness of their curiosity on the subject. The girls were deep into the discussion, but, checking that the pace was not moving faster than they could handle, the worker reminded the group of the parental censorship on the subject of sex. Margarita's response of "Who tells their mother everything?" was perfect, as once again the preteens chose their own age-appropriate explanations to help them keep working. The laughter broke the ice; it also told the worker she was a part of their more private and intimate thinking and that the discussion could continue.

Kathy, Lydia, and Margarita left the room (for a drink of water?), leaving Noemi, Tata, and Judy, who turned to me and said, "Well, Carol, I still want to know—if a guy starts messing around with me and does me wrong, I'll get a baby, won't I?" I said that it depended on what she meant by messing around, and Judy said it was F (pronouncing the letter). I said that people used F to mean different things and that maybe I should just tell her what happens between two people to make a baby. She said yes.

I said that they knew a man had a thing on his body and asked Judy what word she used for it. She said a *dick*, and I said that in books it was usually called a *penis*, but that I wanted to talk so they would understand me. Judy said she hadn't heard the other word—they called it *dick*—and they began laughing. I asked Tata if they were laughing because it was strange to hear about, and she said no—that some men were named Dick and that when they heard the name they thought of the other thing. I said "oh" and continued. I said that, when a man put his dick inside of a woman, he became very excited and that some white stuff comes out. When the white stuff meets the egg that they had been talking about before, it made the egg start to be a life and that from that moment it began growing into a baby.

Judy said, "That's all?" and I replied that this was the main thing that happened. Tata asked if anything else could make you pregnant, and I replied no, not kissing, hugging, grinding, or a boy touching or putting his fingers into you. Tata shouted, "What did you say? Fingers could do it?" Judy explained, "No, nothing but the dick, right, Carol?" I replied, "Right." Tata asked if the boy was going to the bathroom, and I replied that was why I said it was kind of white stuff because it wasn't like going to the bathroom, that this was special stuff which was the only thing that could join with an egg to make a baby. Kathy, Lydia, and Margarita returned—there hadn't been laughing until they arrived; then Tata and Judy started, "Oh, guess what Carol is telling us, she is telling us about babies," in a chanting fashion. Margarita closed the door, and I said that I had been telling them what happens to make a baby, and Judy said, "Fingers can't do it, either." Kathy said she wanted to know, and Judy said "Tell it again, Carol, like you did."

I repeated the explanation, as before; everyone was more relaxed and listened intently. Kathy asked why each contact didn't result in a baby, and Judy asked the purpose of the monthly bleeding. The questions were answered, and they continued.

> Lydia asked if the white stuff was scum," and I said it was called that sometimes too. Kathy asked why a guy's "dick" had a rubber thing on it sometimes. I replied that guys put them on sometimes in order to have less chance to have a baby, because then when the white stuff came out, it stayed inside of the rubber thing and didn't meet with the egg inside of the woman. Judy added that only when they met did a baby start, and I said yes. Tata asked why the rubber thing didn't work all the time, and I said that sometimes it broke and then the stuff came out. Lydia asked how she [Carol] knew all about it. Judy replied that Carol had a fiancé, and Tata said, "You haven't slept with him, or have you, Carol?" I replied: "I remember from last week that you felt mad when you couldn't know more about my personal life, but I don't think it really matters here whether I sleep with him or not. There are lots of ways to find things out about sex—the hard thing is to talk about it. As a matter of fact, you are always asking me what I have to learn to be a social worker and one of the things they try to teach us is how to help people talk about things "like sex, that are usually hard to talk about!"

The discussion had taken close to two hours and broke up with a game requiring physical activity and contact.

The worker had helped the girls to feel secure enough in a taboo area to gain information that was vital to their stage of development. Within the supportive context of the group, the worker performed an important educational function. The restraint of the taboo was broken through by legitimizing the desire for information and for labeling it as normal. This was only possible when trust had been established between the girls and the worker (a "stranger" representing broader societal sanctions). Timing, as always, was pivotal, because only at this point could the worker's support be accepted and the real questions arising out of the girls' curiosity be asked. It is only when real questions surface that they can be answered. The answer can only be heard when fear doesn't deafen the response.

The girls had always shared intimately with each other, fiercely reacting and responding to pent-up emotions and feelings. With the entrance of a nonjudgmental worker into their inner world they gained access to additional help besides each other in dealing with their feelings.

Confronting Racial Differences
Sexual interest was indeed a strong taboo, but it paled in light of the emerging recognition and struggle against the implications of racial minority status.

Developmentally the girls needed to experience success and accomplishments. Coinciding with this need was the increasing impact of racial and cultural stereotyping on their lives. The worker had no greater area of strain than was experienced in helping elicit real emotions and feelings around racial concerns, largely because it was inevitable that such tensions be expressed to her personally.

The pattern was similar to other emotionally stressful areas—tentative and superficial exploration of the subject expressed indirectly in front of the worker but not involving her. Worker response at this stage was important—it was a time for observation, restraint, and identification of patterns, as shown in the following three excerpts.

> On a summer trip to the swimming pool we were changing from our bathing suits into clothes when Noemi (a Puerto Rican group member) came running into the dressing room screaming and crying. She reported that she had been out in the hall looking for the front door when "a black man" had started following her and, frightened that he was going to grab her, she had come racing back to the rest of us. She ignored any questions I asked about the episode and in a few minutes was fooling round with the other girls as if nothing had happened.

For a brief period in the fall, the girls joined a YWCA out of their neighborhood, in a predominantly white area. There was frequent conversation among themselves about the other girls in attendance there.

> Margarita had mentioned how boring our club was compared to the "Y." There was general agreement on this, and Noemi started describing how many pretty girls she had seen, how many blondes with "eyes like in the books." Tata said she thought she was pretty "smart" to be going there, and again several voices indicated agreement. Judy, one of the black girls in the group, proudly described the ballet class, adding casually that she was the only "colored" girl there. Then glancing nervously at me, she left for a drink of water.
>
> I was walking unnoticed behind Kathy, the darkest girl in the club and Lydia, a light-skinned blonde girl, as they left the pool. Lydia asked Kathy if she could borrow her hair brush, and Kathy handed it to her. Lydia started combing her hair, then stopped to pull out the little pieces of black hair that were stuck in the brush. Kathy watched silently while Lydia struggled in vain to fix the brush to her liking, and then handed it back, saying, "Thanks anyway." Kathy looked at this brush and asked, "Was it dirty?" Lydia nodded yes and then ran to join the other girls, shouting at Kathy to "come on." Kathy continued walking alone, hitting her leg with her brush as she walked.

The most common form of interaction around ethnicity or race was in the form of insults hurled at each other, and any girl in anger would scream "dirty nigger," "spic," or "black bastard" to any other girl in the club. One afternoon, when Tata was particularly vexed with the worker, she thrust her arm in the worker's face and, pointing to her own skin, shouted, "I'm glad you're whiter than I am."

The worker had originally been an authority to be negotiated, a stranger representing adulthood and wider society. As the group members gained strength from successfully negotiating one small part of this outside world and in making sense out of some of their behavior and feelings, a deeper level of their original lack of trust emerged. The worker represented the white, middle-class world, the world of teachers, policemen, nurses, dentists, and "directors" of society. The girls clearly felt not only themselves but their families were excluded from an effective and active role in the community. The avenue of resentment was directed toward each other and eventually included the worker.

The intervention was a difficult one—it was not to respond to the girls' derogatory remarks or insults about race and not to interfere in their conversations with each other on the subject. Gradually, they began to be less self-conscious and stop glancing up nervously whenever a derogatory remark was made about "guineas," paddies," or "niggers." A deliberate choice was made not to use these opportunities to teach a preferred approach to racial differences but instead wait until an opening presented itself where the energy of group members was directed toward working on the issue.

One afternoon Judy and Tata came first to the center and into the clubroom, where I was sitting. They were laughing and, after a few minutes of fooling around, Tata started telling me about a lady who had "called down" Judy. She stopped and asked Judy if it was all right to tell me. Judy nodded consent. Tata continued about a "guinea" lady on the street who had passed them and called Judy something. They couldn't remember the name but it was "something like blackie." Judy said she didn't even know what name it was but that she had told her teacher, and he had tried to look serious but then laughed when he turned away. They were laughing loudly this whole time, and I remarked on their laughter, saying it sounded to me as if what the lady had said would make Judy feel bad—not like laughing. Judy responded that she didn't laugh at that old guinea, that she had called her down right back. She included some of the insults. I told Judy that I thought she probably felt mad and hurt by this lady. Judy replied that she had been told she had knots in her hair, adding that she didn't want straight old hair anyway. I said that I didn't think anyone liked being called names and I was sorry she had been hurt. Judy looked surprised and asked me if I thought her hair, which was always very neat, looked nice. I replied yes but that I doubted if that would help her feel better about the insults she had received.

The other girls had started to arrive and had been listening carefully. Tata rushed in at this point, again laughing and making jokes, and the subject was changed. But the ice had been broken, rawer feelings had been presented directly to the worker, allowing for her recognition of their impact and her sharing in their pain. It became more acceptable to say angry things about white people in general, but it was Kathy, a black girl who was very popular in the group, who first related this general anger specifically to the worker.

One day Kathy was continually hitting a little six-year-old girl (who was waiting in the center) on the head. I insisted that she stop, and she started calling me "white trouble," saying she wouldn't stop. Several of the others gasped at this and tried to hush Kathy. I replied that I was sure I did seem like "white trouble" to her right now but that I wanted her to stop hitting the little girl.

On another occasion several of the girls were talking about which pool they liked best, and Noemi asked me my preference. I gave my opinion, and Kathy jumped on the answer, saying of course I liked that one since "all the guineas went there." Again the others looked worried about her remark, and Noemi tried to reassure me that she liked that pool also. I replied that I didn't blame Kathy for saying what she had, since white people often did not like to swim with black people and likely they weren't sure about my reasons.

One afternoon six months after the club had started the girls became very upset when they could find only a golf ball to take to the park. When I did not agree to give them the money for a new ball, Kathy and Tata started shouting that I was "cheap," gradually changing this to "cheap white."

When I asked if they thought I didn't like them when I didn't give them something, they both replied that I "couldn't" like them. Both Tata and Kathy went through a whole hour of "hating" me following the above episode, but even in the anger of that moment they couldn't seem to relate their hatred directly to my color or their own but instead alluded to it through subtle remarks and insults.

As the intensity of feelings around the subject increased, the worker focused on the feelings behind the accusations rather than responding to or defending herself from attacks. This approach was carried out when the attacks were toward her or other group members. She was aware of the fact that all group members were deeply identified with the content of interactions on this subject, as evidenced by their intense concentration.

I'm not sure exactly how it started, but Kathy asked me for something I couldn't give her (potato chips, I believe) and then shouted I was "no good." Tata said the whole club was no good and that they were never given anything around here. I told Kathy that I was sorry, since I knew she always got upset when I couldn't give her something she wanted. She responded, "Shut up!" Judy remarked that you couldn't do anything with white people anyway and Kathy agreed, saying none of them were any good, they were cheap, and never gave you anything. I opened my mouth, and Kathy shouted, "Shut up, you white cracker." She looked surprised herself at the remark, and I mentioned this to her. Kathy just called me a "white cracker" and repeated this over and over.

During my talk with Kathy, Tata had begun laughing and continued doing so, pointing to Lydia. She motioned to Kathy, who apparently caught on immediately and joined her in the laughter. Lydia looked embarrassed and told them to stop. Tata continued laughing, Noemi and Rosa imitated her. Their laughter intensified as she told the story of "a girl" at school who had arrived in the morning with a dirty line around her neck. The point was that she had apparently washed only her face and not her neck. It was not mentioned who this girl was, although there was increased laughter and pointing at Lydia. Finally Lydia jumped up and shouted, "It wasn't me, you know. Immediately Tata and Kathy began shouting that it was her and that she knew it was and that she was "dirty" and didn't wash, etc. Lydia was becoming increasingly upset and exasperated and in desperation turned to me on the verge of tears, insisting, "It wasn't me, Carol, it was another girl. I never did such a thing." I said it didn't seem like such a big deal anyway whether someone forgot to wash their necks. Tata screamed, "Well, it left a line around her neck, that's why."

I sensed there was something much deeper behind this and, looking at Tata, replied, "Maybe what you're really saying is that because Lydia is a lighter color, the line showed more." Tata just stared, Kathy jumped up, shouting, "White bastard, that's a white bastard for you. Shut up, you white cracker box." I replied to Kathy that she should know by now that I was not very good at shutting up.

Yvette, one of the quieter group members, said she thought the others were mean to Lydia "for no reason." Tata became quite serious and explained she did have a reason, since Lydia had previously insulted her. Noemi, Judy, and Rosa said they hadn't meant to hurt Lydia. The girls started to talk, pulling their chairs spontaneously together in a circle. The discussion centered on asking each other about being black or Puerto Rican, which names were most insulting, and how much color differences were noticed and used against them. The conversation was serious; the girls deeply involved in it, and the circle drew closer and closer. The session ended with the conversation again reverting to me when Yvette reminded everyone how they had asked the bingo man at Coney Island to announce that I was a "cheap white." After general laughter Noemi quickly added, "But we were only kidding," to which they all strongly gave accord. Tata summed up the afternoon by emphatically proclaiming to the girls, "Well, Carol always said we could get mad at her!" Then, shifting her glance nervously, added, "Right, Carol?"

The subject of racial tensions and confusions began to move into the domain of things that could be talked about with the worker. The group's taboo against it turned to a group norm in support of sharing feelings. More dramatically than with other subject areas, the worker faced the dilemma of being perceived as too lenient in her responses for not establishing and enforcing codes of behavior and language that were more socially acceptable. Certainly the girls expected this role and continually tried to provoke a more familiar response.

The worker's decision not to respond to the girls' interactions, negative or positive, in relation to racial attitudes was based on an awareness that at this stage of development they were ready to examine attitudes that had been handed to them by various influences and were in the process of being accepted as their own. Younger children are more directly influenced by role modeling and respond to the security of tighter boundaries. Adolescents have moved even further from direct adult influence and carry out their struggle for autonomy in relation to the thoughts, ideas, and codes of their peers. The preteen stands in between, a child still wanting and reaching for adult involvement while simultaneously experiencing a strong pull to break away from earlier adult controls. Most typically, the adult feels and responds to the first part of this duality expressed by the preteens and treats them in a way that would be successful with a younger child. The effect is often the opposite of what is intended when in response the preteen gains impetus for turning away from adults and leans more exclusively on peers for help with the task of sorting through and selecting attitudes, values, and self-concepts.

The worker observed from the beginning that the girls were very verbal with each other. Her focus was to become a part of the conversations where threatening topics were discussed. In terms of racial and ethnic issues, there was no way to smooth the hurt. There was no way to avoid their real confusion—a rejection of and identification with the same attitudes. This was not necessarily a permanent state, for many future influences and experiences would undoubtedly shape and contribute to new identifications. But for the moment it was painful and confusing, and, as with anyone who deeply feels a hurt that cannot be removed, the worker's most important job was to stand close and help the client know that she had been understood.

> At Coney Island Judy and I were standing alone while the others were on a ride. Judy asked if we were going to the beach, and I said I thought so, if they all wanted to go. Judy said she couldn't understand why some people wanted to get tans. She looked up at me, pointing to her skin, "You know, most colored people would like to take their color away," and she laughed as if it were the funniest joke. I didn't laugh or say anything, and she added, "It really isn't so pretty." I replied, "On you it looks good, Judy." "No," she answered, "black don't look good on nobody." She didn't move away as I had expected but just stood beside me, now with a perfectly serious face. She seemed to have expressed so directly and with such feeling the essence of this whole issue and struggle. I felt very moved by her words and said, "I guess it is easy for me to say that just standing here looking at you. But the hard part is to know what you are really feeling like inside your skin." Everyone, rushing

back, screaming from the ride, interrupted us. I began gathering things up to move to another place. As we started walking along, Judy slipped her arm through mine.

Understanding and reflecting that understanding in a way that can be accepted by a preadolescent requires a constant interpretation of what is happening and what feelings are being expressed. In terms of racial attitudes, ambivalence can often cause great unrest and anxiety.

One afternoon, Tata, Noemi, and Elisa sat down to do homework, but Kathy started knocking things off the table. When I asked if she had something she wanted me to help her with, she shouted that she was leaving now. I said I thought she had seemed pretty restless all afternoon, and she replied that she was sick of this center. The other three were working at a table and ignoring her. Kathy put on her coat and started for the door, then returned and knocked over chairs by the door.

When she didn't stop in a few minutes, I went over and asked her to stop, since kids from our club and the other clubs were doing homework. She shouted, "Shut up, white cracker," and I suggested that, since she didn't feel like going, she at least come and sit down. She sat down at the table, saying something about white people and how they were no good and always making trouble and, without stopping, she just continued along in that vein. I said that I had a pretty good idea about some of the things she felt about white people, but that I didn't really think she felt just this way about me. She shouted that she did, started for the door, knocked over a few chairs, and returned, continuing along the same lines.

Noemi told her to shut up, and Kathy lowered her voice. She said she knew what had happened to me, anyway, that when I was being baptized they had dipped me into white paint by mistake, thinking it was water. We both started laughing at this, and Kathy added, "You're really black, just black painted white." She seemed to be afraid to stop talking and continued without ceasing about how this "accident" had happened to me, and how it was going to wash off in the rain or she was going to wash it off. I tried to answer her and said, "Maybe, Kathy, you would really like to think that I was black because you like me."

She stopped laughing and replied, "But my people don't like your people!" There was a silence, then, returning to her former tone, she started again about white bastards and how they couldn't be trusted, etc.I said that I thought she had a problem. She asked, "What problem do I have?" I said that I thought she liked me but was afraid, in case she wasn't supposed to or because she'd always thought white people were the same. She immediately shouted they were "all the same, all those crackers were bastards," then she stopped and looked at me. I said I still thought she was at least thinking it all over and that it was going to be pretty hard for her to figure it out.

She left for a drink of water and returned, asking quietly if she could have her two cookies, since she'd missed them before. I got her the cookies and said I'd see her Thursday. She calmly and casually replied, "Yeah, see you Thursday. Bye." As if nothing had happened, she went out the door.

Only after clear bonds of affection had developed could the worker risk this level of interpretation and confrontation. It had taken eight to ten months of contact in various degrees of intimacy to feel secure in a judgment of the girls' feelings. But the bond had been formed, the affection was strong, and the group had experienced using a worker, in addition to each other, to find their way through the maze of preteens emotions pertaining to racial attitudes.

Termination

No emotion catches one as unaware as the feelings associated with loss. The worker's resignation to marry and move away introduced all the realities of grief to this group of girls. It is evidence of their stage of development that they experienced the loss acutely—they had loved another outside themselves and realized the implications in that person's leaving. It is evidence of the strength of the mutual aid process, as fostered by the worker, that the group moved through the termination process with awareness and self-disclosure, eventually making the connection to a new worker.

Five months before her departure the worker introduced the fact that she would be leaving at the end of summer. The reaction was anger and disengagement, a message that the information had been heard but could not yet be accepted.

Facing the Feelings of Loss Together

Judy asked if I were going away when I was married. I replied yes, that I would be living in Puerto Rico. Tata insisted that she didn't see why I had to leave; after all, Shirley, the center's secretary, was married . . . lived in New York. Rosa said it was because Shirley's husband was here. Noemi asked why mine couldn't stay here too. I answered that he was in school, and there were questions about why he couldn't change and move here. Finally Noemi said brightly that she might go to Puerto Rico for a visit, and Tata shouted, "I don't ever want to go to Puerto Rico just to see you!"

I said that I couldn't blame her or any of them for being mad when I had helped them make a club, had taken them places, and had lots of fun with them. Maybe they were even getting to like me, and now I was getting married and moving away. I added I thought anyone would hurt at this. There was surprise and no one spoke for a few minutes. Then Carmen asked if I would be here for the summer, and I answered that I would be for most of it and it was still a long time away. This seemed to bring general relief and agreement, and the conversation ended with Noemi demanding they all be invited to the wedding.

The worker acknowledged the hurt that was embodied in Tata's anger, recognizing the loss that the girls instantly felt in relation to the "fun" they had shared together and with her. But she did not push them to talk about how they were feeling. The impact of the shock associated with the news meant that the girls needed time to retreat, to speak with each other, and to put space between the news and themselves. The worker knew that the news was heard and that the subject would be raised again.

> A few weeks later I was walking the girls home when Noemi and Tata started to complain that I "never" came to their houses any more. I remarked that they had been saying this a lot lately and asked if they were worried about something. Tata asked why the club couldn't meet on Saturdays and Sundays. I answered that maybe even if we met every day it wouldn't seem enough and that maybe they were really worried about my leaving in the summer. There was no response.

The worker expected that feelings about her leaving might be raised indirectly, and she related one concern of the girls to the possible deeper issue of termination. The fact that they didn't overtly agree with her is not as important as the message she had given them that she realized they must feel bad about the event and that she cared. For leaving is associated with not caring, and whether or not they were loved permeated the girls' concern over the next few months.

> The girls continued insisting that I loved my fiancé more than them. I said I wonder if what they were really asking was if I could love him and love them. Tata replied, "Don't tell me you do!" I said, "Yes, Tata. I do," and she responded, "Huh." Noemi questioned how I could know such a thing, indicating that I couldn't. I told her that I thought people got a feeling when they started to feel love for someone else and this feeling could tell them when they liked someone or someone liked them.
>
> Kathy commented on that time when they had said how much they "hated" me in the other room. I replied, "Oh, well, I don't mean that when you love a person—it doesn't mean you can't feel mad at them or hate them too." The discussion diverted at this point to talking about the paradox of loving and hating, particularly mothers. I ended by pointing out how hard it is, many times, to know what you really feel.

The intervention here was to lay the groundwork for the gradual unraveling of the complexities of saying good-bye. The worker did state that she loved them, for the first time using the word directly, but also acknowledged the anger of "hate" that someone can feel for the same person who is loved. The agony in termination is exactly that issue, the experiencing of affection and anger for someone at the same time. The girls are once again asked not what they are feeling but rather given the message that it is hard to sort out feelings of such intensity.

For several months the subject of "the leaving" was not mentioned, but as summer drew nearer it again surfaced in the form of behavior indicative of the beginning stage of the group's development.

> Walking back from the bus, I noticed again what had frequently been happening lately: the girls were very "busy" talking to themselves and teasing each other and, although it looked as if we were together, I was quite obviously apart. At one point they actually walked in front of me, laughing over some joke, while I walked behind alone.

This had essentially not happened for a year, and I felt much as I had then—isolated from them. It made me very sad, a feeling that must have reflected in my face, for suddenly Judy "noticed" I was walking alone and came and took my arm condescendingly.

> Tata's response was, "Shit on her," at which she, Judy, Carmen, and Kathy laughed hysterically. When we were eating in the center, I said that I thought they had seemed kind of unhappy with me lately and asked if they wanted to talk about it. Kathy said they weren't unhappy about anything. I asked, "Even about my leaving in the summer?" Tata jumped up and shouted, "Nobody gives a shit about your leaving. Go ahead and leave now if you want to!" There were tears in her eyes as she spoke. I replied I really didn't think she meant that. Kathy interrupted, jumping up, raising her hand and shouting with authority, "We are not talking about this anymore!

This time the worker was trying to reach for more direct involvement to interpret the actions via the feelings they represent. The girls were not ready, and when Kathy insisted that they were not talking about "this" anymore, the worker conformed to their wishes. Shortly after that afternoon, the anger surfaced again.

> We were playing tag until I ran into a table and hurt my leg. Tata immediately began remarking how stupid I was and how my "husband" would be so mad he wouldn't let me come to the center again. I said I thought I'd live without too much trouble, but she continued along this line. I replied that I thought maybe she was the one who was mad at him. She answered that she couldn't care less about him, that he could marry me tomorrow and take me away for all she cared. I answered that I thought it was very hard to have someone leave when you didn't want her to, and that I could really understand if she felt mad. She responded, "Hub," and walked away, mumbling, "I don't know why you always talk that way!"

The worker again indicated that anger was an understandable response to her leaving. She accepted the verbal and nonverbal expressions of anger as appropriate to the occasion. The girls had developed a joke about her over the year, telling her that she didn't "talk" like other people. They would, at times, imitate her with each other. They recognized her response as distinctively hers and as connected to her being a social worker. Tata's reference to not knowing why she talks "that way" was deeply affectionate. The group members continued indirect references to the worker's leaving and appeared uninterested in the new worker, Joanne.

Looking Back and Planning Ahead

Nilda asked me again why we were having club only three days a week. I replied that I knew it was hard for them, but that I had many things to finish before I left and needed two days a week to do them. As soon as I mentioned leaving, Nilda turned away and started looking at pictures on the bulletin board. She asked if it would be the same all fall, and I said she'd have to check again with Joanne when she came. She asked, "Who's Joanne?" and I answered that she was the social worker who was taking my place. Nilda turned from the board, insisting emphatically, "Carol, we don't talk about her!" I replied that I had noticed this and guessed that it must be pretty hard for them to talk about her. Nilda hurried from the room, saying it was her turn to give out the cookies.

Again, the worker identified how difficult these feelings were to discuss. She opened opportunities and waited for a response. A group discussion was too anxiety provoking, but individual group members cautiously approached the subject while others listened.

As Lydia and I were walking slightly apart from the others, she asked when the club would end. I said I didn't think it was ending as far as I knew and inquired if she was thinking about my leaving. She said she was wondering what would happen when I left. I told her another social worker was coming to take my place and that they could still have the club. Lydia responded, "But I may not like her." I nodded in agreement, and she went on to say that, if she didn't like her, she wasn't coming to the club. I said I thought most of the girls felt this way and they would have time to see what they thought of her. She felt this was a good thing, since she didn't know how it would be. I added that they weren't too sure of me in the beginning and asked if she remembered how they didn't like to talk to me much when I first came but mostly whispered together, Lydia roared with laughter.

By this time the others had joined us, and the laughter increased. Spontaneously the girls began telling stories about the early club days—how "weird" I had seemed. One after another led off with another "Do you remember?" They described in minute detail a trip, a conversation, a party, a fight, or an episode. Even at this stage, after so much time together, the girls surprised me with the total recall of so much of my words, actions, and expression. Never lacking a sense of drama, they acted out with great flair different gestures and comments I had made months before. I ended the sessions with the comment "A lot sure happened, and it's fun to remember." The smiles of satisfaction showed agreement.

The worker had initiated a looking back at past feelings and experience. She had linked Lydia's fear over a new "stranger" to the earlier fear of the worker. The tone of Lydia's comment was reflective and thus led naturally to remembering. This was an important influence in choosing an intervention aimed at reviewing the past, for both reflective moods and laughter are more conducive to reminiscing than emotions such as anger.

Having once gained the experience and pleasure of reviewing the past, the girls openly and frequently referred to events from the previous year. It was obvious that the girls did not want the club to end, that the impetus for planning for the future after the worker left was strong. Finally, only a few weeks before the new worker's arrival for introductions, the girls engaged in the first direct conversation with the worker around her leaving.

> We were eating on the Coney Island Beach when suddenly Tata blurted out, "When is that other girl coming anyway?" I answered that it would be in the middle of August, in about a month. She shouted, "We are going to kick her ass!" I said that didn't surprise me. She added, "Well, you better tell her about us!"
>
> Nilda asked me if I had seen her and talked to her. I replied that I'd seen her a few times. Tata asked if I'd told her about them. Kathy answered immediately, "Of course! What do you think they'd talk about?" I agreed with Kathy, saying Joanne had asked me about them and I'd said they might feel like kicking her ass at first but this didn't mean they wouldn't get to like her. Everyone laughed, and I said I was serious, that that was just what I'd told her. Judy asked me how tall she was, and I answered that she was a little taller than I am. Nilda exclaimed, "My God, another tall one," and asked if she was older than I. I replied, no, younger. Tata said she'd be too young to take care of them, and Judy asked how old she was. I said she was the same age as I was when we had started the club. She said, "Oh, that's all right."
>
> Laura, who hadn't spoken until that point, said she didn't see why they had to have another girl. Everyone was quiet, and by this time the air was pretty heavy with gloom. I said that I kept wanting to say something to them about leaving, but nothing I could find to say seemed to make any of us feel any better. Judy was the only one who spoke, "Well, you can write to us." I said of course I would.

Saying Good-bye

The worker had helped the girls to partialize their loss into pieces of emotion that could be faced in the singular. They had experienced and expressed the avoidance, denial, projection, and anger involved in grief and had these feelings accepted by the worker without judgment. Inevitably, the more poignant feelings of sadness began to emerge, and, left on their own, they were clearly an essential aspect of saying good-bye.

Thus followed the saddest and yet closest of moments. The intensity of feelings increased as the time shortened, and gingerly the worker began to share some of her own emotion. This was done with caution because the girls were overwhelmed enough by their own concerns. What helped them was seeing their sadness mirrored in the person who had witnessed so much of their inner world.

The weekend before a scheduled meeting with the new worker, Joanne, the girls went on an overnight camping trip with Carol. A wonderful, carefree time was experienced until, exhausted, everyone piled on the bus. Only then did the mood change.

> The girls related to Bill, the bus driver, everything that had happened, with special emphasis on the terror experienced when a raccoon had frightened them at night. Then they sat down sleepily. I was sitting with Judy and overheard Noemi telling the others how I had held her when she was crying in her sleep. Kathy said that I had done this with everyone when they cried, and Tata said she had only been able to go back to sleep because I held her. I told them I wanted them to feel good.
>
> Nilda asked, "Will you miss us a lot?" I answered, yes, that I would miss them and think of them a lot too. Kathy said, "We're going to miss you so much." Judy put her head in my lap and cried. I asked Kathy if she would write to me and she shrugged. Noemi said she would. I told her I was sure Joanne would help her mail the letter. Norma asked, "Who's Joanne?" Laura answered slowly, "The new girl." There was quiet. Tata said, "She's coming Monday, right?" I nodded and everyone insisted it couldn't be so soon. Nilda asked me if I was sure. I said I was and that I had wanted to be with them to help them meet her and look her over because I knew it would be hard at first. Noemi asked if she would really help them mail a letter to me. I answered that I was sure she would.

Moving On

Monday, the long-anticipated day, finally arrived. Joanne arrived at the center before the girls, and we had a few moments of apprehension and waiting.

> Tata came in, her first question being if "she had come." I replied yes and introduced them. Tata smiled (very politely) and stood close to me, holding my arm while looking Joanne over carefully. Joanne and I continued talking to give her a few minutes to do so quietly. She then interrupted us, asking if we were going to stand around talking all day or go over to pick up the other girls.

Walking over to their street, Tata walked between Joanne and me, talking mostly to Joanne. She began asking about her name, how to spell it and say it, and where she had picked up such a funny one. From this she continued asking questions and talking easily and warmly to Joanne. I never remembered seeing her as open or moving out so quickly to a stranger; her approach to volunteer teachers had always been a period of initial insulting and ignoring. None of this occurred that first day with Joanne. From the beginning Tata seemed to feel comfortable with her.

Tata's reaction and response to Joanne was unprecedented, as her initial relationship with the worker had been honed through hostility, aggression, and mistrust. The worker had allowed expression of these feelings and encouraged talking about them individually and among group members. She had not tried to change feelings but acknowledged them as appropriate within the context of the life stage and environmental experience of the girls. Tata had accepted the emotional support of an outsider to both her family and peer system. She feared this "new stranger" less and, along with the other girls, she possessed negotiation skills, built on her relationship to the current worker, as a beginning point for interacting with a new worker.

> Noemi, Nilda, and Judy were waiting on the street. They were a little shyer with Joanne than Tata had been and tended to avoid conversation, but I think Tata's attitude had an effect on all of them. She continued acting as if having Joanne there was the most natural thing in the world. We walked to the pool, picking Kathy up on the way. There were some whispered comments and giggling behind our backs, but during most of the walk the girls were really just looking Joanne up and down; a few remarked on her height. Joanne didn't say much but responded to their questions and occasionally asked a few about the neighborhood or the pool. By and large, she was very quiet, just giving them the time to study her.
>
> In the pool a series of comparisons started, when Noemi tried getting Joanne into the pool and Joanne hesitated because it was too cold. Tata shouted, "Just like Carol, doesn't like cold water," and they splashed her and coaxed her in, which set everyone into fits of laughter. Judy wanted to know if Joanne had long hair, too, and proceeded to take down Joanne's hair and examine it. It wasn't as long as mine, but it was fairly long, and Judy said that it would soon be really long.
>
> But the real excitement came when in a series of pointed and direct questions Tata asked Joanne if she could come on the rides with them at Coney Island. Joanne responded that she'd love to go with them to Coney Island, but not on the rides because they made her dizzy. "Just like Carol, just like Carol!" Tata started shouting in a mocking yet delighted tone. It was agreed by the rest that this was the ultimate and most striking coincidence, and Tata added, "But I suppose you won't mind the merry-go-round." Joanne agreed this would be just her speed. I was sure by this time that each of them was thoroughly convinced that at least

women social workers didn't have the guts for real thrills at Coney Island. The similarities were so striking that by this time both Joanne and I found ourselves
laughing as much as the girls. The example of the merry-go-round (the only ride I
had ever gone on with them) was preserved as the classical one, and in the next
week or so I would hear Tata and the others telling it to impress people with the
like qualities of Joanne and me. I told all the girls as we were standing in front of
Noemi's house that I was glad today had gone pretty well because I knew they
had been worried about it for a long time. Nilda said, "She's nice," with a big smile
at Joanne. The others sort of smiled. Tata said she didn't know why all their social
workers had to be tall.

The girls were looking for ways in which the workers were alike and had exag-
gerated external manifestations of similarities. The two workers also held similar beliefs about what they were there to help with and had spent considerable
time planning for the transition. With Carol, the term *social worker* had been a
word with little concrete meaning. In meeting Joanne the girls now had expectations related to professional function. They expected her to listen to them, to talk
"that way" about behavior and emotions, and to be more related to what they
were feeling than what they were doing. It was, of course, necessary to test
out some of their assumptions, and the worker helped through this transitional
phase.

Behavior in public had been fairly calm for most of the school year, but it was
inevitable that the classic subway scene would be repeated for Joanne's benefit. I
had a totally different response in this situation than previously, based on my relationship over time with the girls and my interpretation of the meaning of the
behavior. On a trip to the beach, the girls were noisy and provocative as they
walked to the subway.

Everyone got on the subway and the whole thing started again. This time with
cursing at a man in another train who answered them back in the same tones. The
train moved away, and the running up and down continued, much to annoyance
of the other passengers. This didn't stop the girls, who kept looking at Joanne and
me, mostly Joanne, to see our reactions. We both didn't react too much, although
it was obvious I wasn't pleased. Joanne's face was a little more noncommittal. I
kept waiting for the girls to sit down, but they didn't, although I noticed they kept
looking more and more frequently in my direction. After ten or fifteen minutes I
got up and very authoritatively told everyone to sit down, which they did with little resistance. I said that they probably wanted to see what Joanne was going to
do, and that she wasn't going to do anything, and that I didn't feel like having
them make so much noise, so they should sit still or we'd go back. They looked relieved and no one protested. Judy asked Joanne if she liked girls that acted like
that, and Joanne replied she didn't dislike them because of the running around,

etc. Nilda asked if she was mad. Joanne replied no, but that she could see how they might be worried about what she was thinking. That was just about the end of the noisy behavior—it broke out now and then, but in a very mild form.

The worker interpreted the girls' furtive glances as a request for an excuse to stop the behavior without losing face. She had learned (from them) how they felt about themselves in such situations, and, once they had seen Joanne's reaction, they felt they would want to end the demonstration. Timing and interpretation are again crucial to the intervention. The behavior was not felt to have been primarily generated by anxiety and, in addition, explorations of various behaviors by the girls among themselves and with the worker had given the worker tools for intervention that were not available earlier in the group's existence.

The worker's role continued right into the good-bye party, helping the girls to adjust to Joanne and fit her into their world.

Nilda came into the office while the others were getting the food ready, asking me to come and get some. As I got up she asked exactly when I was leaving. I explained the days to her. She said she hadn't realized it was so close. I said it did seem pretty close now, and I asked her how she liked Joanne. She repeated what she'd said Monday, "She's nice," but I noticed she was hesitating and asked, "What else?" She answered, "Well, you know what my mother and father say?" I replied that I didn't, and she explained that, although they liked Joanne, they didn't think she was "one of us, like you are." I asked her if she thought it was because I spoke Spanish to her parents, and she said yes and because I understood how they felt. She added that her mother felt good about this and let Nilda come with me. I told Nilda that I was glad her mother and father felt that way, because I did try to understand how they were feeling, but I asked her if she remembered the last summer when I started with the club. She answered, "Yes, why?" I answered that I didn't think her parents felt right from the beginning that I was one of them and understood them. She started to protest and then smiled as she started to remember her parents' negative attitudes to the club.

I said that it was too bad Joanne didn't know much Spanish yet, that I thought she did want to understand, and that maybe together they would find a way. Nilda said, "Maybe." I said I would never forget how much she (Nilda) had helped me in the beginning. Nilda grinned at this and remarked that I had needed a lot of help! Noemi and Judy came in to see what we were doing, and Nilda said we should go to eat.

The worker had tried to make the transition as easy as possible, and it had gone well. The girls were launched into a new helping relationship. The other part of leaving—the inevitable sense of loss—could not be removed. The sadness was open and real. "Termination" is the professional designation for the ending of the work between a group and a social worker. But who can completely define or understand what passes between human beings, who, under the most difficult of situations, break through barriers of fear, prejudice, and years of mistrust to reach some degree of communication and love? Truly, this is an intimate part of any explanation of the helping process.

The worker's final log entry, difficult as it was to experience and write, captures the remarkable capacity of the preteen for emotional growth and expression and the poignancy of a moment forever frozen in time.

> After a few minutes of playing with the others, Noemi came out of the pool and sat alone beside me "to get some sun." She was strangely quiet and avoided any conversation or questions I asked. I knew she was sad, and I was feeling the same way myself, but there didn't seem any way to put it into words. I was avoiding looking at her because of my feelings but suddenly I felt my hand getting wet. Noemi was playing with my fingers and crying. She tended to cry a lot, with big loud sobs that attracted attention and response. Just the way she was crying, without moving and without a word or sound, was heartbreaking.
>
> I said, "You are very sad, aren't you, Noemi?" She nodded her head and mumbled that she didn't see why I had to go. I replied, "You know I feel very, very sad, too. It's really hard to say good-bye." She looked up, "It is?" I added, "But I want you to remember that I love you very much and that I won't ever forget you." She started to cry and put her head in my arms and said quietly, "Promise you won't ever forget me." I answered that I wouldn't forget her, that I was sure I would think of her many, many times.

The others were busy playing in the water and Noemi stayed that way for a long time. It was one of the saddest moments I ever remember, and I'm sure both of us shared in the same despair.

Social work intervention with this group of preteens illustrates the interweaving of developmental issues with the work and group themes that emerged as a result of the initiation of a social work process. That there was growth and change is evident in the way the girls moved into the relationship with the new worker in the process of dealing with impending separation and loss. Their capacity to embrace life and their struggles to help each other survive was evident from the beginning, but as they gained successes in social encounters in a wider social context, experienced more positive interactions with mainstream society, and sustained a relationship with a consistent mentor their repertoire of socially acceptable behaviors expanded. Through group membership and participation they experienced increased success at achieving personal and group goals. As Smith and Carlson stated (1997:243), "Group methods used in school, agency, or health settings can be particularly useful in "normalizing" common stresses for children, as well as offering social support, an important protective factor and coping strategy."

References

Bernard, B. 1991. *Fostering resiliency in kids: Protective factors in the family, school, and community.* Portland: Northwest Regional Educational Laboratory. Abstract Retrieved from ERIC database.

Chapman, A. H. 1976. *Harry Stack Sullivan: His life and his work.* New York: Putnam.

Delprit, L. 1996. The politics of teaching literature discourse. In W. Ayers and P. Ford, eds., *City kids, city teachers: Reports from the front row.* New York: New Press.

Eckstein, H. 1984. Civic inclusion and its discontents. *Daedalus* 113:126–31.

Erikson, E. H. 1950. *Childhood and society.* New York: Norton.

Gitterman, A. 2001. Vulnerability, resilience, and social work with groups. In T. Kelly. T. Berman-Rossi and S. Palombo, eds., *Group work: strategies for strengthening resiliency,* New York: Hawthorn.

Higgins, G. 1994. *Resilient adults: Overcoming a cruel past.* San Francisco: Jossey-Bass.

Kagan, J. 1977. The child in the family. *Daedalus* 106:35.

Kohn, A. 1993. Choices for children: Why and how to let students decide. *Phi Delta Kappan* 75(1): 8–16.

Lifton, R. 1994. *The preteen self: Human resilience in an age of fragmentation.* New York: Basic.

Meier, D. 1995. *The power of their ideas: Lessons for America from a small school in Harlem.* Boston: Beacon.

Miller, A. 1987. *The drama of being a child.* London: Virago.

Miranda, M. R. 1979. The life cycle: An ethnic minority perspective. In *The Social Welfare Forum,* pp. 103–15. New York: Columbia University Press.

Piaget, J. 1970. Piaget's theory. In Paul Mussen, ed., *Carmichael's manual of child psychology,* pp. 703–32. New York: Wiley.

Smith, C. and B. E. Carlson. 1997. Stress, coping and resilience in children and youth. *Social Service Review* 71:231–56

Sullivan, H. S. 1940. *Conceptions of modern psychiatry.* New York: Norton.

Weenolsen, P. 1988. *Transcendence of loss over the life cycle.* New York: Hemisphere.

Werner, E. and R. Smith. 1992. *Overcoming the odds: High-risk children from birth to adulthood.* New York: Cornell University Press.

Youniss, J. 1980. *Parenty and peers in social development.* Chicago: University of Chicago Press.

Chapter 7

Listen to Us!
Young Adolescents in Urban Schools

Lois Levinsky and Kathleen McAleer

C HILDREN in our inner cities face many obstacles in their efforts to experience success in school. Their families, oppressed by chronic environmental
stressors such as poverty, racism, limited or nonexistent medical care, hunger
and malnutrition, violence, substance abuse, inadequate housing, and limited
access to employment or educational resources, are struggling to survive. Their
neighborhoods are often crowded, noisy, disintegrating, and dangerous. Their
schools, old and poorly funded, reveal overcrowded classrooms, facilities in dis-
repair, and limited support services.

The young adolescents of color discussed in this chapter, the majority of
whom identify themselves as Latino/a (mostly Puerto Rican, with some newer
immigrants from Central and South America) or Southeast Asian (primarily
Cambodian and Vietnamese), with a smaller but significant number of black
(African American and Caribbean) students, are facing tremendous stress in
their struggles to understand and cope with the academic, social, and behavioral
demands of school. Many of these teens are relatively new immigrants; some
cannot yet speak English well; most are poor; all have tremendous responsibilities to support and assist their families. All report experiencing distress and confusion around experiences of racism, sexism, disempowerment, and lack of
access to information and resources. Many report feeling neglected or unsafe in
their classrooms and schools, as well as in their homes and in their community.
For these young teenagers, their school and learning are in constant competition
with their survival and self-protection. They must feel safe, respected, and valued, by peers and by adults, in order to be able to learn and grow into healthy and
competent older teens.

This chapter describes social work practice in an urban middle school setting
with groups of young adolescent females of color whose well-being is often compromised and challenged by experiences of vulnerability and oppression in society, in families, in neighborhoods, and in peer groups. The groups presented are

time-limited, normative, developmental groups, offered to address concerns around increasing incidents of conflict and violence in the school and in the community. The group program provides structured activity, discussion and support for normative adolescent issues and concerns, as well as opportunities for mutual aid and empowerment around coping with stressful and unsupportive life experiences. Emphasizing appreciation for and reinforcement of the many and diverse strengths, competencies, and resources of this population, the group is homogeneous with regard to gender and age and heterogeneous around differences in race, culture, ethnicity, immigration experiences, and degrees of assimilation and biculturalism. Empowerment theory is prominent, focusing on helping group members develop, practice, and enhance the skills and confidence, individually and collectively, to influence and change their environment and life experiences.

Developmental Tasks and Issues

Adolescents face a daunting set of developmental tasks and challenges as they transition, during their second decade of life, from childhood through early, middle, and late adolescence, to young adulthood. Our group members, ages twelve to fourteen years and in the seventh grade, are in their early adolescence. In addition to managing the many implications of the rapidly changing size and shape of their bodies, these young teenaged girls must also begin to psychologically and socially mature as they consider multiple, competing priorities and choices, refine their capacity for critical thinking and self-reflection, and reassess and redefine relationships with adults and peers. A barrage of new challenges, demands, and expectations accompany this life stage, consuming much time, energy, thought and feeling.

Malekoff (1997) describes the developmental tasks of adolescence as follows:

- separating from family: includes testing and experimentation in relationships with adults and authority figures, in pursuit of emotional independence, increased autonomy, and more intimacy with peers;
- forging a healthy sexual identity: includes body image, self-esteem, capacity for making safe and healthy choices, developing social roles;
- preparing for the future: includes skill development, career exploration, relationship development and planning;
- developing a moral value system: includes forming and assessing values and ethical beliefs to guide socially responsible behaviors.

Mishne states that early adolescence is a time of great stress, when "diminished coping skills and high vulnerability" occur as "shifts of varying intensity are made towards separation and independence" (1986:12). During this period of major identity and role disorganization, young teens are faced simultaneously with increased academic work, pressures and expectations in school, and also with considerable biological and psychosocial changes. No longer children, but rather participants "in a teen culture with a need for a new set of reference persons, values and behaviors" (fifteen to sixteen), young adolescents, even under the best of circumstances, are truly in turmoil.

Vulnerabilities and Risk Factors and Resiliencies and Protective Factors

Given that early adolescence, as discussed previously, can be described as a chronically stressful experience, the additional pressures and strains of biculturalism, competing demands of family and peer group, and repeated experiences of alienation and oppression all threaten to overburden and overwhelm the young Latina or Southeast Asian adolescent girl in her efforts to develop a sense of her own identity and role in life. According to Parsons (1989:30), "Low income minority girls are members of at least three stigmatized groups: women, ethnic, and poor . . . they often lack knowledge, skill and confidence to access and manage resources in ways that enhance active problem-solving and role attainment on their own behalf" and are perceived as "disempowered in attitudes, real capacity and resources." Additional risk factors for some of these young women include family disruption, separation, neglectful or abusive parenting, family violence, mental or physical illness, and substance abuse. Chronic and cumulative social and environmental influences such as poverty, racism, sexism, unemployment, social isolation, unsupportive school systems, corrupt and disorganized city services, and dangerous neighborhoods further increase vulnerability and negatively influence well-being. As noted in statistics presented later in this chapter, these young women are at high risk for many unsafe and unhealthy social and behavioral problems: school dropout, risky sexual practices, early pregnancy and parenthood, dating violence, alcohol and substance abuse, eating disorders, depression, and self-harm (Azzarto 1997:299). During these most stressful and threatening times, academic, social, and emotional growth and development are delayed, arrested, or constricted, as these young teens muster all their energy and resources to defend and protect themselves from various psychic and physical assaults while still persevering in their efforts to succeed.

It is critical, in our opinion, to recognize and appreciate the capacities and strengths of this population. Often forced by life situations into premature adult roles as provider, caretaker, protector, translator, and family advocate, many of these young women have demonstrated remarkable competency and proficiency in negotiating complex systems of health, welfare, and social services, resiliency and adaptability in the face of obstacles and challenges, deep loyalty and commitment to family and culture, and strong motivation to achieve and succeed in school.

What protective factors exist in the lives of these young women, enabling them to cope with and manage multiple risk factors and vulnerabilities with courage, hope, and resiliency? Smith and Carlson (1997) and Gitterman (2001) identify areas of consideration: *individual capacity*—personality characteristics and traits, such as belief in one's ability to solve problems, positive self-esteem, intelligence, and social competency; *family attributes and resources*—parental and extended family members' ability to provide support and guidance and model resiliency and coping skills; *external supports*—healthy positive relationships with adults in the community, namely, neighbors, teachers, parents of peers, clergy and youth workers, as well as the supportive social networks of natural and formed groups; and *environmental support systems*—helpful, effective social service agencies and schools, churches and clubs, recreational and neighborhood enrichment programs, to name a few.

A most significant influence on the resiliency and well-being of children and youth of color, as presented by Vasquez (1991) is that of culture—"La culture cura." Recognizing that "it is not culture that puts youth at risk; it is lack of it," he notes that the positive power of culture can counteract and neutralize risk factors, as "enhancing one's sense of belonging to a rich culture will help to build pride, self-esteem and motivation, creating stronger family bonds, with healthy expectations and a more positive outlook from our children" (1991:3). Urging us to change and improve our social systems, he emphasizes the critical need to help schools support "one of the greatest protective factors for children of color—their culture and its norms and values" (2). Nearly all protective factors and resiliency-promoting influences suggest the enormous potential of the small group to encourage these young women to use their strengths "to help and support each other to see themselves differently and learn skills through the mutual aid process to negotiate . . . powerful systems" (Parsons 1989:31). Malekoff (1997:16) states that

> group work has been, for the past century, a significant protective factor for youth. It has helped to guide many young people through normative life transitions, supporting mastery of the developmental tasks that confront them. . . . For those young people at risk, group work has always been there to address specific needs and enable members to find ways to better mediate the various systems impacting on their lives, reducing the probability of a poor outcome in one's life.

For all these reasons, school-based mutual aid groups are designed to build upon the existing strengths of this population by addressing obstacles and supporting efforts to accomplish the normative developmental tasks of early adolescence. As might be predicted, group themes with this population reflect urgent and intense needs to be recognized and listened to, included and informed, valued and respected, and protected and supported by their peers and by the adults in their world.

Agency and Group Context

The city's infrastructure, suffering from chronically inadequate funding, is decaying, with crowded, dilapidated housing, limited green space, and uneven city services exacerbating the constant challenges of a mixture of different languages, cultures, religions, and needs. The community is a multiracial, multiethnic, poor, and distressed inner city near Boston, Massachusetts, home to many new immigrant and refugee families, with a diverse population substantially larger than the thirty-five thousand documented in the 2000 census, living in a densely populated area of about 1.8 square miles. Of the reported residents 48 percent are Latino, 58 percent are white, 5 percent Southeast Asian/Asian, 5 percent African American, and about 2 percent are of African/Afro-Caribbean descent. Approximately 30 percent of the population identify as multiracial, and residents speak over 22 distinct languages. The per capita income in this city is the lowest in the state ($13,633). In 1991 the city was bankrupt, and city management was taken over by the state. A subsequent FBI investigation into corruption resulted in the indictments of three former mayors.

Extended families often live in crowded apartments and neighborhoods where many adolescents and young adults, unemployed and undereducated, are involved in gangs and problems with crime, domestic violence, alcohol and substance abuse are present. Many immigrants have histories of trauma, having fled war-torn countries and lived in refugee camps; others are overwhelmed by the demands of daily living in a stressful and nonsupportive environment. Resources do exist, however, to address some of the many and diverse needs in the community; community organizing efforts have resulted in improved recreational and social services to children and youth. Efforts to increase representation, advocacy, and participation in local government and service systems have persevered, with some positive results. Many neighborhoods throughout the city enjoy vibrant and successful cultural and ethnic celebrations and events, and have special markets, social clubs, schools, and churches, all of which support and affirm strong ethnic and cultural identity and pride, create a sense of belonging and connection, and promote an experience of increased safety and well-being.

The public school system, on the verge of collapse in 1989 and placed under the management of a local urban university by the school committee, is being returned to city management. Suffering from chronically inadequate funding, the schools strive to serve a student population that is more than three-quarters children of color (61 percent are Latino), with a high school dropout rate that is three times the state average and the highest teen pregnancy rate in the state. Eleven percent of the students report gang involvement and 42 percent are living below poverty level (U.S. Census 2000). Challenges and obstacles to positive and successful teaching and learning experiences have historically included "unacceptable test scores in the basic subjects, drug abuse, teen pregnancy, high school drop-out rates, truancy, the challenges of a mixture of languages and cultures, racial tensions, and disabling attitudes toward education and toward schools" (Greenes and Greer 1989:14).

At the same time, school personnel and faculty are frustrated and overwhelmed with the demands of teaching and supporting an economically disadvantaged, multicultural student population with tremendous diversity of needs, abilities, and competencies. In older communities where recent immigration of people of color has created rapid and significant racial and ethnic population shifts, students and teachers face many obstacles in the path of their mutually shared goals of teaching and learning. Gitterman describes one such obstacle as follows:

> The teachers, by and large, are white, with middle-class value orientations. They have been socialized into a certain lifestyle, being taught from grade school through college, by teachers with similar experiences. They have developed curricula with certain established methods of learning and teaching. They have come also to fear and develop stereotypes of cultures that feel alien to them. . . . In essence, the different value and attitude orientations of predominantly white, middle-class teachers and administrative personnel and a curriculum that is typically discontinuous with lower-class life and culture represent serious sources of strain. (1971:46)

Even while recognizing these tremendous stresses affecting feelings of well-being and competency for everyone in inner city schools, it has been our experience that nearly all students wish to be able to trust and respect their teachers and strive to learn and succeed in school and that the vast majority of teachers seem genuinely concerned about their students, motivated to pursue opportunities for professional growth and development, and very willing to work with the various demands of the changing school climate.

To meet these challenges, schools are attempting to develop and implement comprehensive interventions and resources in response to current needs of children and families. An array of learning and social services and supports is necessary to enable, encourage, and enhance the focus on education and learning. The social work function, then, according to Gitterman, supports a reciprocal model for school social work or a "bring[ing] together the need of the child to use the school and the need of the school to serve the child . . . to help the child and the school rediscover their stake in each other" (Gitterman 1971:49).

Under the school system management plan discussed previously, the university's School of Social Work has been actively involved in the city's schools for several years. The groups described in this chapter were part of a comprehensive social work service plan implemented to improve the quality of educational and social experiences for students at school, at home, and in the community at large. There were several rationales for choosing group work as the modality: it is common knowledge that group work is the treatment of choice for adolescents whose psychosocial concerns are primarily normative and who share common struggles and life experiences. Additionally, mutual aid groups of peers can serve to combat feelings of differentness and isolation, support sharing of feelings and concerns, teach and model problem-solving and decision-making skills, and offer safe places to experience and practice new behaviors. Further, groups are the normative experience in schools, and many classroom groups were presenting acting out behaviors around issues of concern described above. Last, short-term group interventions can maximize the effectiveness of service delivery to the greatest number of students within a relatively brief time frame.

Before the groups began, the worker and her supervisor met with administrators and teachers to hear their ideas about how the groups might be of help to them and the students. Their major concerns were that interpersonal and intercultural conflicts were becoming more frequent and often resulted in physically assaultive behavior. They also expressed worries about the high number of students at risk for becoming pregnant or of contracting sexually transmitted diseases. The worker and her supervisor continued to meet from time to time throughout the year with administrators and teachers while the worker met with them more frequently to discuss issues raised by different groups and to solicit feedback about how things were going outside the groups. She was careful not to share confidential group material.

Members first learned about the groups early in the school year when the worker visited their classrooms to introduce herself. These visits included a description of her role and a discussion of what the groups might be like. She told students that their teachers and administrators had invited her to offer groups to seventh-grade students because they felt that it might help students to do better in school if they had a place to talk about things that were on their minds. She noted that sometimes if students are distracted by outside worries they have difficulty concentrating on their studies. In order to give a better idea about the types of things people their age often worried about that might be discussed in group she offered some common topic themes such as family issues, peer relationships, boyfriend or girlfriend troubles, and school problems. The worker concluded each classroom visit with an opportunity for students to raise other questions or concerns that they might have about the groups. Common concerns centered around issues of confidentiality, group structure and rules, as well as further questioning about how the group would be different from a class. These areas needed to be regularly revisited with members both during pregroup screenings and throughout the life cycles of the groups.

As a result of this extensive preparation, six groups, each consisting of approximately ten to twelve girls meeting for eight sessions, were organized and offered during the school year. Group members were all seventh-grade girls between the ages of twelve and fourteen. A typical twelve-member group might have one Haitian member, two Vietnamese and three Cambodian members, one Euro-Caucasian member, one Salvadoran, and four Puerto Rican members. Many members were first-generation immigrants, having arrived in the United States as long ago as infancy or as recently as within the past two years. All spoke English fluently, although individual comfort levels varied. Despite cultural differences, members' socioeconomic statuses were quite similar, with adults being underemployed or unemployed. Members were as likely to live with extended family members as with both parents. Some members lived in foster homes. In the classroom teachers reported that the girls as a whole were doing academically better than their male counterparts. However, Southeast Asians were perceived to be the best students. Excerpts from these groups illustrate work on the three major themes introduced earlier: racism and diversity, social relationships and sexuality, and danger and violence.

Work and Group Themes

It is both interesting and reassuring that work themes identified by school administrators, teachers, and group members themselves consistently focused on the same three areas of concern, although they were described by each group quite differently:

1. racism and diversity issues, including fear, ignorance, and misunderstandings around differences in culture, language, race, ethnicity, and class;
2. social relationships, dating, and sexuality, including urgent requests for specific information about "safe sex," appropriate behaviors and limit setting, responsible decision –making, and AIDS; and
3. violence, including home, neighborhood, community, and school experiences of various forms of conflict, abuses and threats to individual, family, and group safety.

Adults identified these three work areas in terms of risk factors for the future coping of group members while group members identified their concerns as immediate and critical sources of stress. Intense feelings of fear, anger, confusion, powerlessness, and despair were expressed among group members, who voiced repeated concerns that they were without significant and trustworthy adult support or attention, without reliable sources of accurate information or assistance, and without opportunities for safe and private discussion and sharing. Multiple risk factors and social stressors often presented, simultaneously increasing the important function of the group as a protective environment in which members could safely share concerns and develop coping strategies.

Each group developed its own unique expression of the three central work themes, which were frequently experienced and explored concurrently. As group members became more adept at identifying multiple ongoing problems in their environment, they also became more proficient at examining their interrelatedness. In one group the girls decided that it would be good to use the group as a place where they could strategize about how to protect themselves in the school as a whole and their classroom in particular. The girls were experiencing the classroom as an unsafe, male-dominated environment in which there was an almost constant state of turmoil. The white, middle-aged, female teacher was spending most of her instructional time attempting to manage the boys, who were vying with her and with one another for power and control in the classroom. Stealing, fighting, harassing, teasing, tantrumming, and scapegoating were normal classroom behaviors. Disciplinary intervention by the assistant principal was taking place on an almost daily basis.

Although most of the upheaval in the classroom was confined to interactions between the boys and the teacher, the girls were not exempt from involvement. They complained that the boys would alternately fight with and make sexual advances toward them. They were angry that the boys were so "immature" and expressed frustration when certain girls would betray the rest of the group by aligning themselves with the boys. Additionally, the girls had divided into cultural subgroups that were in competition with one another, serving to further fragment and disempower them as a group and as individuals within the classroom. Over time members were able to acknowledge that many of the conflicts that took place were the result of clashes between different cultural and ethnic groups. It also became apparent that the classroom experience was paralleled for many members in the broader social environments of home and community.

During the life cycle of each group, three common group themes emerged from the central work themes previously identified:

1. understanding and managing differences including establishing new ways of interpreting and responding to the culturally based actions and reactions of other group members;
2. addressing taboos and obstacles and developing a safe group culture for the exploration of members' concerns and questions about subjects not traditionally discussed in school, including racism, sexism, domestic violence, sexual behaviors, and HIV/AIDS; and
3. promoting individual and group empowerment, including strategizing ways in which members could individually and collectively draw on coping strengths and resources to better manage challenges in their classrooms, communities, and families.

UNDERSTANDING AND MANAGING DIFFERENCES

In the early stages of the groups' development, members tentatively acknowledged difference and sameness and appeared relatively free of the underlying mutual suspicion and mistrust that were later to be revealed. Direct confrontation was minimal and out-of-cultural-group questioning took place within the realm of normative adolescent concerns as well as common immigration and acculturation experiences. As is often the case with bicultural adolescents, many were struggling to find a balance between their desire to blend in with their peers and American teen culture while receiving pressure from home to conform to traditional roles. The following process excerpt is taken from the final minutes of one group's first meeting. Many members had been silent and looked uncomfortable throughout the session, which was spent discussing what the group would be like and developing the group's working contract. The excerpt shows how the group became a safer, less stressful place once the worker normalized members' concerns about difference.

As the final minutes approached, I said that I didn't know for sure, but I wondered if some people might still be feeling a little bit nervous. There were a few giggles, some nods of agreement, a couple of shrugs, and at least one blank stare. I said that sometimes part of what makes people feel nervous is the fact that members don't really know each other and don't know what to expect. Marilyn said that was part of how she was feeling. I told her that it was pretty normal to feel that way. I then said that as I looked around the room I was struck by the range of differences that was represented among members. I noted that I am white, many members are Latina, one member is African American, and three are Southeast Asian. I said, "Sometimes feeling different can make people feel nervous too." This seemed to ease the tension somewhat, and a discussion ensued about what countries people had been born in. The immigrant members agreed that it had been very hard to come to the United States and to learn English. Millie said that her mother hadn't learned English yet. Dang said that neither of her parents knew English and that they had been in this country for a very long time. Dang had been silent in the group up until this point. When she spoke, some of the more verbal members, most of whom were Latinas, turned as if observing her for the first time.

Millie then told Dang how much she admired her hair. She said that it was beautiful and that she loved the way it was kind of red and brown and shiny. Louisa reached over, lifted a long lock off of her shoulder and smoothed it behind her ear, saying how soft it felt. Dang beamed. Gloria added that she wished she could make her bangs curl around her forehead like Dang's did.

In the above excerpt the more verbal, though still nervous, Latina members were able to successfully join with a silent Southeast Asian member by admiring her hair. Many such connecting efforts took place throughout various group life cycles, enhancing development of the group as a whole and also helping to dissipate tensions created by member differences. As the level of intimacy and tension between members ebbed and flowed, each group became a more cohesive organism. This cleared the path for the worker to make demands for work that mandated members' collective change.

> It is important that the group worker adopt a posture that he/she is not asking the individual to the individual to change but expects the group to change. There is always a clear unequivocal expectation that change will occur. The paradox of being told to stay as you are (individually) while being expected to change (collectively) mirrors the contradictory nature of adolescent relationships. (The adolescent in defying the parents' attempt to change his/her behavior, enters a group which in reality exerts a much greater influence on his/her growth and development.) In a group an adolescent can change and resist change without contradiction. (Hurley 1984:78)

The following excerpt is taken from the middle phase of one group's third meeting. This group had chosen "culture" as the session's topic, although members were working as hard to avoid the subject as they were to explore it. The excerpt illustrates how the worker was able to respond to individual concerns about behavior and to promote members' understanding of how behavior may be influenced by culture. With this understanding, the culture of the group began to change as individual members utilized new patterns of communication to learn more about each other.

Members had been discussing the way they consistently chose to seat themselves, with the Latinas to my right, the Southeast Asians to my left, and Karen, who is German American, and Daphne, who is Haitian, bridging the two groups in the middle. Suddenly, Jasmine, who is Latina, pointed to the other side of the circle and asked how come "they" never answered. There was no response. I attempted to reach for the underlying meaning of this question and to tune into the cultural implications being raised. I asked her what it was like to be in a group where many of the members were so quiet. Jasmine offered that she felt like they were thinking bad things about her. I then wondered if other members felt the way Jasmine did. Anita offered an emphatic yes. The quiet members had begun to look very uncomfortable.

I said that it seemed like we were still talking about culture. Claudia loudly and defiantly said that she did not think that this discussion had anything to do with culture. I asked what other members thought we might be talking about. Sim said she thought we were talking about culture, as did Justina and Jenine. Justina continued that she thought we were talking about the way people acted, and they acted a certain way because of their culture. I pointed out that the members to my left were quiet and the members to my right were pretty outgoing and asked what influence, if any, culture played in this observation. Sim offered that in her culture it is a sign of respect to listen quietly to what others have to say and not interrupt them. Jasmine enthusiastically responded that in her culture she had learned that if she didn't speak loud and fast she never got to say anything. Claudia observed that lots of the Asian students in school were quiet, and she thought that they were acting like snobs, but maybe, she added, they were just acting the way they had been taught to act. Sim again responded, saying that sometimes at home she is punished for speaking back to her parents. Davan and Pheap nodded their agreement. Pheap added that it is hard for her because in school people think she is quiet and at home her family thinks she is noisy and rude. "Really," she said, "I am just trying to act like me."

The conversation continued with members discussing how they were expected to act at home with their families. At one point the group became very noisy. Jenine stood up and turned to the other Latina members and told them in Spanish to be quiet for just one second, which they did. She then translated what she'd said for the non-Spanish speaking members and invited them to join the discussion. One by one these previously silent members told the group what their homes and families were like.

With members' increased understanding of and respect for one another's cultures, new group values and behavior patterns emerged. In most of the groups the level of intimacy among members also increased. Although in some groups, as in the group described in the previous excerpt, intimacy between members often appeared only fleetingly or was very late in coming. For those groups where members were able to resolve intimacy issues, the group became a safe place within which to explore other concerns and proved a tremendous resource to members who felt consumed by the pressures they were beginning to experience in their evolving roles as young women.

Taboos and Obstacles

During the first session of each group, members chose topics they felt would be important to discuss during the group's life cycle. Without exception, every group's number one topic of choice was boys. More specifically, members wanted to know the truth about HIV/AIDS, STDs, and pregnancy; they wanted to discuss their feelings about boys and wished to obtain concrete information about how and when to say "yes" or "no." Additionally, members were eager to discuss these "womanly" concerns with the worker, who was obviously pregnant.

Because the groups were time limited, the worker developed a format for an integrated discussion of these issues over a period of two and sometimes three consecutive sessions. During the first week the worker provided members with information about AIDS transmission and pregnancy. She used plain language and encouraged members to share with the group any stories they had heard, no matter how far-fetched, about how one could be infected with the AIDS virus or become pregnant. This proved a crucial interventive strategy since so many members possessed dangerously inadequate information.

The first part of the next meeting was generally spent discussing and demonstrating condom use. The worker was able to obtain permission from the school's administration to give each member her own condom for educational purposes within the group. The city had recently been embroiled in a debate over condom distribution in the public schools and had decided against making them available to students. For this reason it was important to be clear with members that condoms could not be removed from the room. Remarkably, members were diligent about this, making sure that wrappers and condoms were always properly disposed of at the end of each meeting. The condom demonstration invariably provided the group with an opportunity to question the worker about her pregnancy. During these discussions the worker was able to use herself differentially to help members explore responsible decision-making processes. In some cases members posed very personal questions to which the worker needed to respond respectfully as well as in a manner in which she felt comfortable. The following excerpt occurred just after one group opened their condoms.

Rosie, who was squeamishly poking her opened condom package around the table, turned to me and asked if I had gotten pregnant because "the condom broke." Before I could respond, Dania told her that it was none of her business how I got pregnant. Patricia, giggling, said that everyone knew how I got pregnant but they couldn't be too sure that I wanted to. I said that in fact my husband and I had decided that we were ready to start a family, but the decision about whether or not to have a baby is an important one that other people have to decide for themselves. I added that equally important is the need for couples to decide whether or not it's OK to have unprotected sex. I then wondered if some individuals might be worried about how safe a condom really is. Rosie said that she didn't think it looked too safe. Besides, how could she tell her boyfriend to wear one?

Often these kinds of discussions ended with groups engaging in endless role plays about how they could determine if they and their partners were ready to have sex, acting out how they would get their partners to wear condoms, or practicing how to ask their partners to have an AIDS test. Invariably these role plays were performed "as if" they were much older. Even though there is evidence that this age group is likely to be sexually active, none of the members of any of these groups was willing to talk about it publicly. Clearly, there are limits to the level of safety that members experience within time-limited, in-school psychoeducational groups. What did help members to discuss their questions in this difficult area was when the worker would provide a more or less anonymous means of presenting their concerns. Members wrote their questions, comments, or real or fictitious scenarios on a slip of paper. These were then read to the group by the worker and discussed. Sometimes, when members found even this process too difficult, the worker simply made up possible dilemmas for group discussion.

The following is an excerpt from a fourth-group session. The worker offered a story about a seventh-grade girl who had accepted a date with an older boy. She really liked this boy, but knew that her parents probably wouldn't let her go, so she told them that she would be out with some of her girlfriends. She and her date had planned to go to a movie and then straight home. After the movie, however, the boy had suggested that they take a drive. The worker asked what the girl should do and what might be some possible consequences of her choices. Dania said that there was a boy in her neighborhood who was in high school who had asked her to go out on a date. She thought he was nice but knew that if she went out with him her older sister would find out and tell her parents, so she didn't go. Patricia joked that if he were "really fine" she'd go anywhere with him. Sue said that she would be afraid that he might try to pressure her into "doing something" and she wouldn't know what to say, especially if she really liked him. Rosie said that you could ask him if he wanted to drive or really wanted to park. If he wanted to park, then she thought it would be good to say that kissing was OK, but nothing more than that. Sue said that he might agree to that but then change his mind. She wanted to know how other members would then handle him.

This discussion concluded without members reaching a consensus on what the right choice would be. Few of these types of conversations ever did. However, they did provide a safe forum for the exploration of popular concerns without causing members to worry about disclosing personal information.

Individual and Group Empowerment

For many of the members of these groups, conflict and violence were part of their everyday lives. Often viable means of coping with the lack of safety and prevalence of danger were not readily available to them. The group provided a forum for the discussion of members' worries about violence, as evidenced in this excerpt from the first few minutes of a second-group session.

Sopham was the first member to enter the room and sat down next to me. As the rest of the group was sitting down she asked me if I had heard about the woman and baby who were killed by the woman's husband during the past weekend. I said that I had. She told me that they had been neighbors of hers. I said that it was a very sad and tragic thing to have happened and asked if she would like to suggest it as a possible topic for discussion today. She said that she would. After a few minutes, the group had all assembled and members agreed that this would be a good subject for the session.

Initially, conversation focused on a detailed retelling of the story for the less informed, with members noting their various sources of information (e.g., the TV news, newspapers, friends, etc.). Then members began to speculate about why these murders had occurred. Maya thought that the husband was on crack and didn't realize what he was doing. Remy said it could be that he had been abusing his wife for a long time and finally lost control, but she couldn't understand why he hurt the baby. Sopham said that she knew someone who left her husband and moved into a shelter because he wouldn't stop hitting her. She added that she wished she could have warned her neighbor to leave before this happened. I said that part of what makes it hard to live with something like this is that we always wonder if we could have helped if only we'd known something was wrong. I added that it is especially scary when someone who is from our same group is the victim, in this case a woman who also happened to be Vietnamese and her baby. Betty asked why it is that men are sometimes so violent toward women. Sopham said that she thought it was because they think they are so tough and can make women do anything they want. Maya said she wished that she could wave a magic wand and make the world forget about violence.

For the remainder of the session the group continued to discuss this incident and others like it as well as their sadness and frustration. Each member expressed fear and concern about the possibility of becoming a victim herself. The school, traditionally thought of as a safe haven, provided no relief from the tension and anxiety group members felt about being physically and emotionally at risk. Classroom disruptions were cited by most group members as the number one reason that they were unable to do well in their studies and disliked attending school. For some members the group was the only place during the school year where they felt safe and protected.

The following excerpt is taken from the middle phase of one group's fourth session. The group had been offering support to one member who had recently become the latest favorite scapegoat of the boys in the class. Their behavior toward her included name calling, stealing and hiding her papers and book bag, pinching her and pulling her hair, and kicking her desk when the teacher's back was turned.

I said that it seemed like what had happened to Phuong was troubling both to her and to the rest of the group. She was listening intently but did not look up. I attempted to move from this specific problem to the more universal problems that all the girls experienced in the classroom. I asked if members had similar stories about how the boys had mistreated them. Various members shared instances in which they had had conflicts with the boys. I offered that it is awfully hard to be teased and picked on. Christina said that you just have to ignore it when someone bothers you. India said that it was hard to do that. Others agreed. I reached for the underlying feelings and asked if it were really possible not to be bothered. Elena said that she thought you could only pretend not to be bothered. Jasmine observed that if you let the boys know that they got to you they would keep after you. I wanted to reinforce the commonality of their concerns and commented that it sounded as if the boys at one time or another had victimized everyone. I wondered what would help to make things feel safer in their classroom. After some consideration of this question, Lilly said that she thought it would be best if the boys were separated from the girls in the classroom. She described how boxes could be built for each girl to sit in, with a little window that would be too small for the boys to reach inside. There was much noisy agreement with this suggestion, as other members contributed their own suggestions on how this system might work. Patricia said that sooner or later the boys would still bother them and thought the best way to cope with the boy problem would be to just smack them. Many members also favorably received this idea. Lisa pointed out that she used to beat the boys up in fifth and sixth grade but now a lot of them were bigger than her. I said that it seemed like everyone felt a need to protect herself but that we hadn't really come up with any truly effective ways to make that happen. I continued that I was impressed by the ways members had been able to provide Phuong with support and wondered what would happen if they were able to do this for her as well as for each other outside the group.

After this session members returned to the classroom and confronted the boys about the way they had treated Phuong. They told the boys that if they did not leave her alone they would report their behavior to the vice principal. It was empowering for the girls to have addressed the problem as a cohesive group. Having done this, members had a concrete example of the collective and individual strength and benefits experienced together as a group of young women.

CHECKING IN with group members later in the school year, the worker learned how powerful the groups had been for all of them. The group had assisted them in becoming more aware of their individual cultures and helped them to realize some commonalities where they had previously only experienced difference, isolation, and mistrust. They had acquired concrete and useful information with which to make better-informed sexual and social choices and had had opportunities to practice new conversations and behaviors. They were also now better able to draw on innate resiliencies and coping strengths to further enhance protective factors when negotiating high-risk situations (Gitterman 2001).

The worker found leading these groups to be a challenging and rewarding experience. She observed the way in which her interventions had assisted the groups to make critical positive changes and had also served to enhance members' mastery of the tasks of early adolescence. Because of the many groups she was able to lead, she had an opportunity to fine-tune her group skills while also developing her ability to anticipate trouble spots. She learned to revisit oversights and mistakes in order to promote group process. By taking risks herself, she was able to make demands for work of the groups that mandated members' own risk taking. Most important, the groups taught her a tremendous amount about the overwhelming experiences these young women faced, and how members could mobilize their strengths to empower themselves and each other when provided with a safe, supportive environment to understand and reflect on their experiences. Open to relationships with providers who invest the time and energy to know, respect, and engage with them, these young women, while significantly at risk for unhealthy experiences and behaviors, remain still very accessible and available for intervention, support, advocacy, and guidance. They are survivors whose wit, humor, bravado, energy, and hopefulness remain as strengths and resources to them and as an inspiration to those of us who work with them.

We persist in our efforts to identify and evaluate risk and protective factors and to promote empowerment in our practice, consistently choosing the group work method "to identify, mobilize and build upon people's strengths and resilience" (Germain and Gitterman 1996:45–46).

References

Azzarto, J. 1997. A young women's support group: prevention of a different kind. *Health and Social Work* 22(4): 299–305.

Germain, C. B. and A. Gitterman. 1996. *The life model of social work practice: Advances in knowledge and practice.* 2d ed. New York: Columbia University Press.

Gitterman, A. 1971. Group work in the public schools. In W. Schwartz and S. Zalba, eds., *The practice of group work*, pp. 45–72. New York: Columbia University Press.

——— 2001. Vulnerability, resilience, and social work with groups. In T. Kelly, T. Berman-Rossi, and S. Palombo, eds., *Group work: strategies for strengthening resiliency*, pp. 19–33. New York: Haworth.

Greenes, C. and P. Greer. 1989. A private approach to public schools. *Philanthropy*, July-August, pp. 14–15.

Hurley, D. J. 1984. Resistance and work in adolescent groups. *Social Work with Groups* 7(4): 71–81.

Malekoff, A. 1997. *Group work with adolescents: principles and practice.* New York: Guilford.

Mishne, J. M. 1986. *Clinical work with adolescents.* New York: Free.

Parsons, R. J. 1989. Empowerment for role alternatives for low income minority girls: A group work approach. In J. A. B. Lee, ed., *Group work with the poor and oppressed*, pp. 27–45. New York: Haworth.

Smith, C. and B. E. Carlson. 1997. Stress, coping, and resilience in children and youth. *Social Service Review,* June 1997, pp. 231–56.

U.S. Census. 2000. Washington, D.C.: U.S. Government Printing Office.

Vasquez, H. J. 1991. La cultura cura: A protective factor. Oakland: Todos Institute.

Chapter 8

Sharing the Hurt
Adolescents in a Residential Setting

Alice Schaeffer Nadelman

"BUT YOU'RE not all alone. You have us. We'll help you, and sometimes you'll help us." With these simple words, a fourteen-year-old girl, living away from home in a residential treatment center (RTC), crystallized the meaning of her experience in a mutual aid group. Such groups may be better suited to adolescence than to any other developmental stage. One of the essential tasks of adolescence is to move away from primary family ties and to turn toward peers for norms, values, and support (Kimmel and Weiner 1995). A positive peer culture may provide a source of strength, confidence, and self esteem. Supportive relationships among adolescents may also serve as a protective factor in dealing with adverse family environments (Rutter 1987). This phenomenon is nowhere clearer than for institutionalized adolescents who have been placed in constant and intimate interaction with their peers because of their removal/ejection from their families.

This chapter will illustrate how a mutual aid group in a residential treatment setting, led by a trained social worker, can provide an opportunity to harness some of the tremendous power of adolescent peer influence for positive, resilience-promoting outcomes.

Developmental Tasks and Issues

Adolescence has been defined as a period of tremendous and rapid physiological, sexual, intellectual, emotional, and social changes (Kimmel and Weiner 1995). Manaster (1977) conceptualized the essential developmental tasks of adolescence as follows:

1. to establish a stable identity;
2. to develop rewarding, reciprocal relationships with peers;
3. to establish independence from family;
4. to accept one's sexuality and assume a mature sexual role;
5. to make educational/vocational/career choices.

Havighurst (1972:2) defined developmental task as "a task which arises at or about a certain period in the life of the individual, successful achievement of which leads to his happiness and to success with later tasks, while failure leads to unhappiness in the individual, disapproval by the society and difficulty with later tasks." The resolution of the developmental tasks of adolescence determines the resources with which the young adult will face the world. The already complex demands of adolescence are further complicated for those youngsters living in institutions, in which the environment is not always supportive of the struggles of adolescence. Maier (1965:33) defined three inherent features of institutional living as anonymity, standardization, and authoritarianism. These features present obstacles to institutionalized adolescents trying to negotiate their daily world. It is doubly hard to answer the question "Who am I?" in an anonymous, standardized, and authoritarian environment.

Institutionalized adolescents must also come to terms with the meaning of their ejection from their families. Regardless of the objective assignment of "blame" for their removal from their families, institutionalized adolescents frequently feel a profound sense of rejection, failure, and isolation. They have fewer supports and resources than adolescents living successfully with their own families. The concerns of adolescents in an institution become superimposed on the general tasks of adolescence. The overriding concern is day-to-day coping—how to negotiate the institutional system with its myriad and sometimes contradictory subsystems. There are at least two, and generally more, cultures within an institution—that of the staff (or subgroups within the staff) and that of the residents (or subgroups therein). Polsky (1962) documented this in his research. "The belief that . . . [RTC] is a unified therapeutic milieu is a cultural fiction and contributes to the disparity between the cottage peer group and staff values. The staff and cottage subcultures are, in fact, quite insulated from each other" (136).

Adolescents must make their way among the discrepant cultures in the institution, which may or may not be compatible with the cultures from which they come. They must struggle with all the usual tasks of adolescence as well as with a task unique to institutionalized adolescents. That is, to cope with the requirements of the new and different environment, in which they have been placed, generally without their approval. They must do this without the day-to-day support of family, friends, and established peer group, all of whom they have left behind.

The specific tasks of institutionalized adolescents may be experienced in the following manner.

1. *Identity*

"How do I begin to answer the questions 'Who am I ? What do I want? What do I believe?' when I'm all alone in a strange, impersonal place, being bossed around by strangers and living with kids I hardly know and may not like? How do I handle my pain, rage, and shame at having been 'put away' by my family? How can I trust my own feelings, ideas, and beliefs when I don't know or trust anyone enough to share them?"

2. *Peer Relationships*

"How do I fit in, get along, make friends with all these strangers? How do I keep from being embarrassed, bullied, or betrayed? How do I know whom I can and cannot trust? How do I deal with the pressure of a bunch of them telling me, 'this is how we do things?'"

3. *Independence from Family*

"How can I still be part of my family? Do I really want to stay connected? Was I ever really connected? Do they still want me? Will I become everything my family is not—or everything they don't want me to be? How can I manage without them? How can I manage with them?"

4. *Sexuality*

"What must I do, or say, or say I did to become popular? Will anyone want to be with me? Who do I want to be with? How do I begin to discover myself sexually when there's never any freedom or privacy? What if I'm no good at sex? What if I'm gay?"

5. *Educational/Vocational*

"What do I want to do with my life? How can I make something of myself living in this place, where everyone thinks we're weirdos or retards? What can I learn at this place? Am I good at anything? What will I be able to do when I finally get out of here?"

6. *Dealing with the Institution*

"How can I put up with this place, with the rules, restrictions, bossy adults? How can I get along here when I couldn't get along at home? How can I be myself and still get along with all these kids? How do I avoid being controlled by the staff or the kids? How can I make things work out for me?"

These concerns and tasks must be tackled within the institutional setting, which values compliance, conformity, and dependence and may view disagreement and independence as defiance. Fahlberg (1990) defined the residential treatment center as providing "all services in one facility, thereby maximizing the potential of milieu therapy, which is the heart of residential treatment. The milieu is the daily environment of structure and interactions. The child is immersed in his surroundings. He responds on a continual basis" (10). "Every interchange has the potential for providing the child with an opportunity to experience growth andchange. The kinds of demands the environment will make on a child in relation to his ability to respond adequately can be controlled in this setting" (141). Institutionalized adolescents face the challenge of fitting in and getting along in a closed and controlled setting while simultaneously figuring out who they are and where they want to go.

VULNERABILITIES AND RISK FACTORS AND RESILIENCIES AND PROTECTIVE FACTORS

Adolescents confront the challenges of living in a residential treatment center with their own unique personality, temperament, strengths, and weaknesses. Anthony (1987:4) stated, " As in much research, it took time and effort to establish the truism that people are different and react differently to seemingly similar events, and that the differences are located in the apperceptive mechanisms, the biological make-up and the psychosocial setting." These differences may be viewed as the individual resilience and vulnerability of each person.

Resilience has been described as the ability "to overcome developmental hazards and adversity without apparent negative outcome" (Smith and Carlson 1997:236). Resilience enables the individual to utilize protective factors to cope with and recover from stress and risk factors. (Masten, Best, and Garmezy 1991).

Vulnerability has been described as a heightened susceptibility to negative outcomes (Anthony 1987). That is, the individual appears predisposed to become easily damaged by stress and risk factors. Garmezy (1983) described risk factors as conditions that would increase the chances of a child developing an emotional or behavioral disorder.

Both resilience and vulnerability are impacted by internal and external conditions. Garmezy, Masten, and Tellegen (1984:97–100) identified three "domains" that influence resilience and vulnerability: individual attributes of the child or adolescent, the climate and resources within the family, the supports and resources of the wider environment. By definition, adolescents in residential treatment centers have not had enough resources in any of the three domains to enable them to function successfully while living at home. Often their lives were negatively affected by environmental stressors of poverty, deprivation, inadequate schools, and sparse community resources. Their family resources tended to be limited, with unresolved discord, dysfunction, and disengagement. They may have experienced domestic violence, physical abuse, sexual abuse, and/or neglect. While some of their siblings may have been able to cope with these stressors and minimize their negative impact, adolescents requiring residential treatment were unable to do so. Their protective factors were not sufficient to enable them to cope with the risk factors in their lives to remain with their families and communities. Common individual risk factors for youngsters in residential treatment include exposure to prenatal substance abuse, learning disabilities, irritability, impulsivity, low frustration tolerance, and poor emotional regulation (Fahlberg 1990).

Yet these youngsters survived. They functioned well enough to make it to a treatment center rather than to a criminal justice facility or the morgue. They had sufficient protective factors not to be destroyed by the stress they endured but to get them to a place where services and opportunities were available. Some of these protective factors may include intellectual abilities, street smarts, relationship skills, persistence, willingness to accept placement. Similarly, families and/or communities of youngsters in residential treatment centers had the resources to get them into these centers. In many situations parents realized the family could not adequately provide what their teenager required and sought and obtained help. School personnel may have alerted parents that their teen had special needs and provided psychoeducational services. Community agencies may have been enlisted to provide services to the teen and/or family. When these services did not produce desired results, the families did not give up but looked for further assistance. School and agency staff may have continued to provide services, including identifying and facilitating the application to residential treatment. Extended family and friends may have provided support and encouragement to enable the family and teen to accept out-of-home placement while maintaining their family connection. In general, residential treatment centers require participation in treatment by teen and family, in contrast to detention centers, which have an involuntary population. This is a clear indication that these were not simply "throwaway" youngsters, but those for whom some protective factors were in operation.

AGENCY AND GROUP CONTEXT

Fahlberg (1990) described quality residential treatment as providing a variety of coordinated services under one roof, with one consistent philosophy. "The milieu is carefully organized to meet each child's needs for relearning while simultaneously providing . . . therapy that is well coordinated and integrated with the daily living program" (36). The essential goals of residential treatment are virtually identical to the categories of intervention suggested by research to promote resilience and coping: 1. enhancing self-esteem, 2. improving academic achievement, 3. promoting social skills, and 4. strengthening families and social supports (Smith and Carlson 1997). To provide these goals-related interventions, residential treatment centers consist of a network of interrelated groups. Whether by choice or by assignment, adolescent residents find themselves in many groups. Schwartz's (1961:18) definition of a group as "an enterprise in mutual aid, an alliance of individuals who need each other, in varying degrees, to work on common problems" is particularly relevant. Since adolescents need and value peer experiences, and since they need each other to accomplish many of their life tasks successfully within the institution, the basic energy for work and growth is provided.

Into this arena steps the social worker, hoping to help harness that energy toward constructive ends. Birnbach (1971) described the professional task in residential treatment as being "to find the viable and operational connections between the institution's need for 'a tight ship' and the client's need to develop autonomy and to negotiate within and among the various systems with which he must come to terms" (177). The worker's task further involves helping the members of each group communicate with and use each other in solving problems of daily living and in working on common tasks.

The particular RTC discussed here was co-ed, housed two hundred youngsters from six to eighteen years of age, and was located in a major metropolitan suburb. The residents lived in cottages of fourteen to sixteen youngsters, supervised by three live-in cottage parents. They attended a specialized, on-grounds school that was geared toward their academic and social needs. The RTC was designed for two essential purposes: 1. To provide an alternate living and educational setting for youngsters who could not function successfully at home, at school, and in their communities; 2. to provide necessary therapeutic and remedial services to the youngsters and their families, so they could resolve their problems and return to the community.

The specific functions of the RTC entailed the following:

- to provide, food, shelter, and clothing for the children;
- to provide schooling for the children and to include remedial services for learning disabilities;
- to provide a complete recreational program;
- to provide individual psychotherapy for the children;
- to provide family therapy, whenever appropriate, to resolve family problems.

The RTC needed to maintain itself as an orderly and viable institution that could offer an array of services to its residents and their families. These services were designed to facilitate the children's cooperation with, and adjustment to, the routines of the institution and to develop their coping skills, which would facilitate their return to families and the community.

WORK AND GROUP THEMES

The decision to offer problem-solving groups came from the conviction that youngsters in residential treatment, especially adolescents, would benefit from an opportunity to share common concerns and work on them with their peers. The purpose of this particular adolescent girls group was to give five girls, who lived together in a cottage, a chance to talk about and try to help each other deal better with their common problems. These included general concerns of adolescent girls as well as specific issues related to living away from home in an RTC, among which were

1. getting along in the cottage and larger institution, living within rules while gaining personal satisfaction, getting along with adult authorities and feeling listened to and cared about, getting along with cottage mates and classmates, making and keeping friends;
2. addressing family problems that had necessitated placement;
3. dealing with emergent sexual development and relationships with boys;
4. coping with school, learning, achievement, aspirations, feelings of competence or incompetence.

All the girls in the group were white and were between thirteen to fifteen years of age. Each girl had at least one living parent who had been unable to provide inadequate care at home. Each girl had exhibited difficult behavior at home and/or in the community with which her parents were unable to cope. These included difficulty in getting along with family members, poor peer relationships, unsatisfactory academic and social functioning in school, minor delinquency such as lying, truanting, and running away.

Beth, age thirteen, came to the RTC because of her explosive temper at home and school and a hostile, often violent relationship with her mother.

Donna, age fourteen and a half, had been ping-ponged between her divorced parents since she was two and had been abused and rejected by both stepparents. When she came to the RTC, she was quite depressed and withdrawn, feeling that no one wanted her.

Gladys, age thirteen and a half, had been in various foster homes since birth because her unmarried mother could not take care of her but refused to surrender her for adoption. She had lived in one foster home for several years but was sent to the RTC because of increasing defiance, tantrums, and lying.

Jill, age fourteen, had been placed in foster care by her father when her mother deserted the family. She was sent to the RTC because of repeated runaways from her foster home.

Margie, age thirteen, had become increasingly depressed and uncommunicative. Her mother had died three years earlier, and her father was unable to provide a stable home. She was not responding to psychotherapy while living at home.

The worker, here called Miss D., was a twenty-five-year-old white woman who had worked at the RTC for two years before the formation of the group. She was the individual caseworker for each girl in the group as well as for all their cottage mates. She knew the girls and their families quite well and was also very familiar with cottage life. The worker had the following assumptions prior to beginning the group:

These girls live together in a cottage, away from home and family. They know each other well, share daily experiences, and affect each other's lives. They confront similar, as well as different, tasks and problems. Each girl, in her own way, is trying to grow up, get more satisfaction from her life, and make some kind of "peace" with other people—family, friends, and outside authorities. Within this framework, how can they be helped to help each other to recognize and tackle some of the problems they face individually and as a group? How can they use each other to learn more about themselves, to begin to meet more of their needs, to find new ways of dealing with difficult situations? How can they develop enough trust in each other so they can share honestly some of the pain and problems they experience? How can they become sources of protection and strength for each other? How can they develop an investment in helping each other and themselves?

Before talking to the girls about ideas for a group, the worker tried to tune in to some of the girls' feelings about groups, to put herself in their shoes, so that she could be more sensitive to their reactions and work *with* them rather than *on* them in establishing a meaningful group:

"I'd like to be in a group with *some* kids, the ones I like and get along with, they understand me, they want to help me. I can trust them with my real feelings and problems." "But, I'm not going to tell my personal secrets to *them*, it's none of their business, what'll they think of me, they'll use it against me." "I'm not crazy like the rest of them, I don't need them to help me—I just mind my own business until I get out of here." "How can we help each other when we can't help ourselves? We'll mess up and ruin things, we're just hopeless." "What's it all about? What do you really want from me?" "How do I play the game?" "Can I really expose myself in front of these girls? How will I stack up to them? What will they think of me?"

The worker also tried to tune in to possible feelings about her:

What will you do with the information you find out about us—whom will you tell? Will you use it to hurt us? Will you play favorites in the group? Will you like the others more than me? What will you think of me? Will you continue to like me if I don't perform, as you want? What if I say too much? What if I embarrass myself? Will you protect me, help me, and condemn me? Will I be good enough? Will I satisfy you, the others, myself?

Following this period of tuning in, the worker approached each girl individually to discuss possible groups, offering her own ideas and reaching for feedback. In general, the responses of the girls, with the exception of one, were hesitantly positive: "Let's give it a try. We got something out of it last year, you've never double-crossed us before, maybe it'll work for us." The worker selected the members for each group and set up the first meetings.

Getting Started

The main task of the beginning of the group was to answer the questions "Why are we here and what are we going to do together?" Schwartz (1971) defined this "contracting" phase as the time during which the worker helps the group members "to understand the connection between their needs, as they feel them, and the agency's reasons for offering help and hospitality" (15).

For these adolescent girls the contacting phase was particularly significant because it touched their need to run their own show. They began to tackle the question "Is this *our* group? Do we really have a say in what we're doing together and how we'll do it ?" This is an important issue for all adolescents, but even more so in an institution, where so many opportunities for autonomy and control have been limited.

It was essential that the worker make a clear statement about group purpose and then invite and welcome genuine feedback.

> I began the meeting by saying that I'd like to try to tell them my ideas about a group like this and how it could work and then get their reactions. I said that they were all living away from home and in the same cottage at the center. They were all girls, all around the same age. Although they were each different, unique, I'd say (there were giggles), they did have many things in common. Jill piped up, "Yeah, like getting out of here!" The girls cheered. Gladys added, "And keeping cottage parents off our back!" There were more cheers. I said, "That's it exactly. You're dealing with many of the same concerns and problems, and maybe you can help each other figure out how to handle them."
>
> Beth said, "I'd like to handle a few of the boys around here." There were giggles. I said, "We can talk about boys, too, and anything else that's important to you— like things going on at the center, or with friends, or at home, or with your families." Jill said, "I get it—we talk about whatever we want to, whatever is on our minds, and we help each other?" Gladys said, "Yeah, that's right, but we only want kids in the group who are friends." And they all began saying, "Yeah, we don't want Harriet. We don't want Harriet!" Gladys said, "And I don't want Beth either!" Jill picked up this idea and said, "Yeah, we want to have a *good* group—no creeps!" Beth hung her head. Margie said, "Hey, Beth is OK I want her—just not Harriet." Gladys said she wasn't sure.

The girls spent the major part of the first meeting discussing who should be in their group, what they would expect of each other, and how they would work together. Despite their differences and brief temper flare-ups, they did a good job of beginning to settle these issues. The worker credited their work as an actual demonstration of how their groups could function. She then helped them to reach out to each other to resolve the remaining obstacles in beginning.

After a while I said, "It looks to me like you kids really can begin to work with each other, even though you have a lot of differences, and you really are doing quite well." Margie smiled and said, "I knew that we could do it." Jill said, "Yeah, I think it's worth a try with this group." Once again Gladys tightened up and said, "No, I absolutely refuse. I won't have her in this group." I turned to the others and said to them, "How do you react?" They tried to persuade Gladys and reason with her, but she absolutely wasn't having any of this. I turned to her and said, "I have to intervene here and repeat that I can't leave it up to you whether or not Beth is in the group. It looks like the others feel that it is worth a try, and to me that means Beth is in the group, and I hope that you will be in it also, but you don't have the right to kick her out." Gladys then turned and said, "Well, then, I won't come." I turned to the others and said, "Is that what you want? Can you tell Gladys how you feel?" Once again the kids tried to reason with her and explain, but Gladys just sat there with her hands crossing, "No, no, no." At one point I interrupted and I turned to her and said, "Look, Gladys, can I ask you one thing? Are you in one of those moods when you're just being obstinate and unreachable, or is it still worthwhile to reason with you?" Gladys seemed to be taken by surprise and said to me, "What do you mean?" I said, "You know. We've talked about this before. There are times that you become impossible to reach and it really doesn't matter what kinds of arguments—you've made up your mind and you won't hear them, and the wisest thing to do is to come back and talk to you at another time. And, if you're not in that kind of mood now, why don't you tell us, because there's no point going on with this." Gladys kind of thought about it for a minute, and then she said, "No, I'm still reachable. You can reason with me." Once again, and this time I was in it also, everyone was really trying to persuade Gladys to give it a try. Finally, Gladys turned to us and said, "OK, I'm not happy about it, but I'll be willing to give it a try." Everybody heaved a sigh of relief.

The worker was able to reach for input from all the girls in the group, encouraging them to express their ideas, needs, and feelings, even when these were painful. While she encouraged them to work out their own disagreements, she made clear the limits of their control and those areas of her own and agency responsibility. Although these limits were tested and negotiated repeatedly over time, the beginning contracting set the stage for future work together. The girls seemed satisfied with their degree of freedom and control, while appearing relieved that the worker's authority could be a protection to them. This conflict between the need to feel in control and the need to feel protected is common to adolescence and was an important area of ongoing work. The girls needed to know that they would not have the "freedom" to mistreat each other and would, therefore, be protected from mistreatment. While there were times of painful confrontation, they were in the interest of the work of the group—problem solving, facing or clarifying an issue, giving up a self-defeating behavior—and not just for the sake of confrontation. The worker's limits actually gave the girls greater freedom, because it enabled them to risk becoming vulnerable to each other.

Doing the Work

During the twenty-five sessions of this group, the girls dealt with major concerns of adolescents living in residential treatment centers:

1. coping with daily life in the RTC—living with rules, getting along with staff and peers;
2. dealing with their emergent sexuality;
3. confronting family relationships and problems;
4. developing a positive sense of unique identity;
5. making use of educational, recreational, and vocational opportunities at the RTC.

However, they did not deal with these concerns equally, in terms of time, energy, or intensity of emotional involvement. The most important issues to these five girls clearly were the first three. Although the identity question, or "Who am I?" did seem to underlie many of the other issues, it was usually not dealt with explicitly. This is likely because the girls were still young adolescents and did not yet see themselves as needing to establish their own separate identities as distinguished from their peers and families. Regardless of the issue the girls were tackling, the process of developing and using their mutual aid system was similar. They needed to learn how to talk to each other in a real way, about real concerns, and with real feeling—revealing pain, doubt, fears, weaknesses, thereby leaving themselves vulnerable, yet more open to be helped by each other. The girls needed to learn to listen to each other, to try to put themselves into each others' place, accepting each other for who she was. They had to learn how to give real feedback—not intellectualized platitudes, sentimental reassurance, or diffusely angry attacks. They needed to ground their questions in curiosity and caring, and learn to express their own suggestions, opinions, supports, and criticism. They needed to learn to identify commonalities as well as differences—in background, needs, styles, and goals. Ultimately, each girl needed to learn to take what she could from the group and use it in her unique way. All this involved taking risks with the other and with the worker—putting their fragile self-esteem on the line. The girls needed to group—with each learning to confront her own vulnerabilities and the serious risks in her life in order to mobilize her strengths and protective factors, especially the mutual support of group members.

The worker functioned alongside the girls, using her skills to help them with their work of developing a mutual aid network in the group. She also guided them in how to give and receive help to develop their own strengths in dealing with their concerns. She was careful not to intrude into the girls' work but to focus on her own job of helping the girls do their work.

That attention is illustrated in the above excerpt in which the girls tried to include a silent group member. The worker was careful not to join the chorus demanding that the girl talk, but maintained a mediating position between the isolated member and the rest of the group. Worker skills include encouraging intermember interaction and clarifying mutual obligations and expectations.

> The girls were talking excitedly about drinking, when someone noticed that Gladys wasn't talking, but was making strange clucking noises. Jill yelled, "Hey, what's wrong with you, are you an animal?" Gladys didn't answer. Beth and Jill began yelling at her to talk. Gladys just hung her head. I said that Gladys seemed upset about something, and the others seemed angry about her silence. Margie said gently, "Can you tell us?" Gladys shook her head. The others again began yelling at Gladys, demanding she talk to them. I said they seemed so angry, as if they felt insulted by her silence. Was it possible to be too upset to talk, even with people you trusted? I looked towards Gladys, who remained silent. Margie began to say something, then stopped. I encouraged her, asking if she could reach out to Gladys without attacking her. Margie said, "Would you like us to leave you alone until you're ready or should we keep trying?" I touched Gladys's arm and said, "Can you respond?" Gladys nodded and whispered, "Give me a few more minutes, then I'll talk more."

The themes that occupied the major part of the girls' time and energy in the group involved coping with the daily demands of the RTC, especially relating to peers and adult authorities at the center, dealing with their emergent sexuality, and getting along with their families.

Coping with Residential Living

The ongoing concern about coping with the many daily demands in the RTC consumed the greatest amount of group time, although not necessarily with the greatest intensity. The girls did their share of griping, blaming others, and denying their own roles in whatever happened to them. However, there was a part of each girl that really wanted to make things work at the RTC, and the worker (and later the girls themselves) relentlessly reached for that part, to supply the energy to keep working.

The most frequent topic discussed was making and keeping friends, reflecting the crucial adolescent need for peer acceptance. This touched on the girls' needs for affiliation, affection, and genuine closeness as well as their fears of rejection and their defensive provocations. The worker tried to bring these complex factors to their attention so that they could confront them together.

> Then somebody picked up on the point that Beth had made about Donna not having any real friends. Gladys said, "Yeah, Donna, you let everybody use you and take advantage of you, and that's not real friends." Beth said, "Gladys, didn't you ever think that maybe Donna can't face the truth that she has no real friends? And, at least it's better to have make-believe friends than nobody at all, so she just tries not to think about it." Gladys said, "Well, she can't live like that. She's here to be helped, and part of her help means she has to face the truth!" Beth said to her, "But can't you understand how hard that is?" I said, "It sounds like you're talking from experience, like you really know how it feels." Beth said that she did, that many times she'd do anything to have a friend, and even though she knew that these kids weren't being true to her, she couldn't stand the thought of it so she just tried to fool herself, and she thought that that's what Donna was doing too. Donna hung her head. Gladys said, "But, don't you see that in order to change, you have to face it? You can't deny the truth—that's just running away." I said to all of them, "Maybe you can help Donna face it a little bit rather than only screaming at her." Beth smiled and said, "Well, I'm no adviser on personality." I said, "Sure, you are. Go ahead. You all are." Beth talked to Donna about trying to figure out if even one kid liked her just for being her and said she could get close to her. Then, if you had one real friend, it wasn't as hard to admit that maybe the others weren't such real friends. Gladys said, "I'd rather be all alone and the most unpopular kid in the world than have a false friend." I said, "I think they're realizing how terribly that would hurt—to have no one." Gladys said, "Well, I had to take it. I had to learn how that would feel, and there is a lot more that I have to learn, but that's the only way I'm going to get well."

Just as all the girls became "advisers on personality," they became advisers, challengers, and comforters on everything else. The worker encouraged them to open up to each other as they tried to tackle the problems together. Continually making a "demand for work," while being sensitive to the difficulties of this undertaking, the worker used skills of holding focus, reaching for feelings, and pointing out the members' responsibility to each other.

In the following excerpt, from the fourteenth meeting, the girls confronted their responsibility to each other at those times when they lost control.

> While they were discussing how to have friends, Beth kept running back and forth, looking out of the window, and was very wild. The kids were kind of laughing and encouraging her, and she just got wilder and more disruptive. At one point, I kind of blew up at them and I said that here, on the one hand, we were trying to talk about Beth's difficulty in getting along with Gladys, and they were

pretending to try and work it out, when right at that moment Beth was acting wild and out of control and they weren't reacting at all; if anything, they were encouraging her. They weren't even acting like they cared, they were just allowing her to get wilder and wilder, and, if they really meant it when they said that they cared about her and they wanted to help her, this was the opportunity to do it.

They all seemed kind of stunned for a moment, including Beth. Margie asked, "You mean you expect us to try and stop Beth when she acts crazy?" I said, "What do you expect from each other? Beth, what do you expect from them?' Beth said, "Well, I do expect them to help me if they're my friends." Jill said, "Well, we do try to help you." Margie said, "We try to keep you out of trouble." Gladys said, "When we try to stop you from acting crazy, sometimes you get mad at us and you turn on us." Beth said something like, "Yeah, I can't take it very much, but don't give up."

As they began to experience their real ability to help each other, the girls experienced satisfaction, pride, and greater closeness with each other.

I said to the girls, "You notice how different Gladys is now than from what she was at the beginning of the meeting—how much calmer, how much more at peace?" All the kids said that it was amazing—she was like a different person. Gladys said, "And I feel very different—I feel like I just got a million pounds off my back." I asked how did the others feel. Beth said that she felt good, too—that helping people make her feel good. I said to them, "You really did help Gladys." Beth said, "Gladys helped herself—she helped herself with our help." And Margie said, "Gladys helped herself by telling us, by opening up to us and trusting us." Donna said, "It would have hurt her to keep quiet—to hold things in. It was the best thing for her to get it out of her system." Gladys shook her head, and once again she began to cry. She said that was true. Again there was a moment of quiet in the room. I said, "This is exactly it—how you're helping each other right now." Beth said to Gladys, "People may say that they hate you, and even we say that once in a while—but no one likes you more than the people up here at school, and no one likes you more than the people in this room, and the more you let us get to know you, and the more we understand you, the more that we feel close to you and then we want help you and we want to like you." Gladys said to her, "Thanks. That means a lot to me." I said, "This closeness to each other, this helping each other—what does that feel like?" Gladys said, "It makes me feel great." Beth said it made her feel good too. Margie said that in a way it was half and half—she felt good that they had helped Gladys, and yet she felt depressed because Gladys had had such a hard life and because there was so much pain.

The girls' growing conviction that they could help each other despite each ones' "hard life" gave them strength to tackle many problems. The worker credited their accomplishments, pointing out when they really reached or came through for each other. The girls learned that pain could lead to growth and closeness, that out of vulnerability could come strength. They could see that even while Gladys cried she was feeling something positive, of which they were all a part. Margie's apt description of "feeling half and half" was a beginning identification of the ambivalence that characterized their feelings about so many things in their lives. It also represented their early recognition that life is not black and white but has many shades of grey.

Another major concern of the girls was their relationship with authority figures at the RTC, particularly cottage parents. The girls grappled with such issues as whether the staff really cared about them or just tolerated them in order to be paid; whether they could really trust the cottage parents; whether they would be hurt if they became too attached to or dependent on staff.

This was a difficult process, because the girls needed to get along with the cottage parents and feared that any negative comments would be reported back to them. They were sometimes unsure whether they could trust each other, or the worker, to keep their confidences.

The worker identified obstacles to their working effectively, even when she, herself, was one of the obstacles. She persisted in reaching for real feelings about herself and other staff members. She recognized and respected their feeling of powerlessness in the face of adult authority, but shared her belief that their opinions and desires did matter and that they could have an impact on the authority figures in their lives. In this manner the worker helped the girls to recognize and mobilize their own coping capacities, even in the face of frightening risks.

I said, "You're saying that the cottage parents are doing things you don't like." Beth said, "Aw, there isn't anything we can do about it anyway," I asked, "Is that how the rest of you feel?" And there was no answer. Then I said, "What's happening here? Are you all afraid to speak?" Margie said, "The cottage parents know that we talk about them with you, and they really hate it. They don't want us to do it." I said, "Is that what you're afraid of—that if you talk about them now I'll go back and tell them?' Margie said, "Well, we're supposed to be able to talk about them with you." I said, "Yeah, that's right. So what's getting in the way?" Again there was no response. I said, "Look, I feel as if I'm not helping you with this, and I want to. Can you tell me—is there something that I'm doing that's cutting you off?" There was no response to that, and then they began talking about other things, something that had happened in school. They would talk, and then they would stop talking. I asked once again, "Are you telling me that you want me to tell you that, whatever you raise in here about the cottage parents, I won't tell them?' The kids said, "Yeah, we don't want you to tell them." I said, "But you don't really believe me? You think that I will go back and tell them?" Donna said, "Yeah, you have in the past." But nobody picked up on that, and there was a tone of hopelessness. I said, "Wow, you seem to feel so helpless, like there's nothing you can do. Like it doesn't even do any good to talk about it, like there is nothing I can do to help you. Is that how you're feeling?" There was no response to that.

Then they talked about E., the cottage parent, who is supposed to come back from her vacation this week, and they said they were happy she was coming back because she cared about them. Gladys said no, that E. does not, E. only works for the money and that G. had told them that she was only here to get the experience until she could move on to something else. Then they said at least L. cared about them and really wanted to work with them. They felt like B. was going to leave the school and go to work someplace else and that they were on the verge of losing her. I said, "Wow, it sounds like you're feeling that the cottage parents really don't care about you that much, that they're only here to tell you what to do and boss you around, but somehow they really don't care." A couple of them said, "Well, they don't." I said, "Well, where does that leave you? How does that make you feel?" There were silent shrugs, and then someone changed the subject.

In dealing with their feelings about authority figures in their lives, the girls were encouraged to talk directly to the worker about their feelings toward her. This, too, was sometimes difficult and painful, especially when ambivalent feelings were involved. The worker tried to reach for honest feedback from the girls, even when it was critical or negative, to demonstrate that a relationship could continue, and even grow, despite, negative feelings.

We were discussing the coming staff meeting about Beth. She said that she was afraid that no one would stick up for her. Jill said, "Yeah, who sticks up for us at these meetings?" I said, "I would hope that everybody at that meeting will have as their purpose to stick up for you, but I know that, when I have a meeting on you, I like to think I'm sticking up for you, and I guess what you're telling me is that you don't really believe that, that you don't really trust me to act in your interest." I said, "Maybe I've hit on an important thing and also a hard thing to talk about, my doing things that you kids don't always like, and maybe you really don't trust me not to hurt you."

Nobody responded to that, and they continued to talk about how they can't trust the cottage parents, and the cottage parents don't tell them things, and they want to be at the meetings, and they have the right to be at the meeting. I tried to pull them back, and I said, "Come on, give it a try, talk to me directly about my role in these things in your lives and what power I have over you, what I'm going to do for you. I know it's hard, but I think that's what you're thinking about." Donna said, "Well, I don't feel like anybody sticks up for me when you have meetings. Everybody is trying to do what they want to, and nobody sticks up for me." Margie said, "Miss D. (worker) is the one who is going to stick up for you. That's what she's telling us." I said, "But you don't believe that for one minute. You think that's a lot of shit." Jill smiled and said, "That's true. I don't believe it. I don't think you stick up for us." I said, "I'm glad you could tell me that." Donna said, "Well, I don't think you stick up for me, either, because when I wanted go home you were making plans for me to go to another institution." They began remembering times when I had not "stuck up" for them and became quite critical of things I had done in the past. Suddenly, they became silent, as if they had gone too far in their criticism. I said, "Hey, it's OK; it's OK for you to tell me these things. I know I don't always do what you think I should. I'm glad you can tell me about it."

The above two excerpts reflect the worker's persistence in pursuing and validating the girls' right to have negative feelings about authority figures. She did not take herself or the girls off the hook easily by accepting evasion or glib superficialities. Rather, she hung in there, exposing herself to criticism, as she modeled the very behaviors she was asking of the girls—allowing herself to become vulnerable in order to gain the strength of genuine communication. She was sensitive to the girls' fears of retaliation and loss of love and approval if they criticized those in charge of them. She encouraged them and credited their efforts. The worker had to stay close to the girls' feelings, matching their intense mood and effort with her own. Her use of profanity and slang reflected her attempts to stay on the same wavelength, to use "real talk," which she demanded of them. As always, the worker needed the sensitivity to know when to back off, to stop pushing, to credit the work, and assuage some of their fears.

Dealing with Emergent Sexuality

The theme which generated the greatest excitement, not surprisingly, was sex. Like many mid-adolescents, the girls had difficulty in discussing sexual matters in any depth or detail. The seriousness of their interest and concern was somewhat masked by the silliness and wildness that accompanied their discussions about sex. However, they did make a beginning at putting their concerns openly on the table, to be shared with each other and their worker rather than just whispered and giggled about in secret. The worker encouraged this sharing of common concern and common embarrassment, reaching inside awkward silences, moving from general to specific issues, as she supported the exploration of this as well as other "taboo" material.

As the girls came into the room, it was apparent that they were talking about their boyfriends, whom they liked and were making out with. They were enthusiastic about it, and they continued talking about it even while in the room, and I said to them, "It sounds to me like you want to talk about boys," and they all said, "Yeah." Beth said, "Boys, boys, boys—that's what we live for," and all the girls began to laugh. They were talking about Beth's hickey, and they told Beth to come up and let me look at it. She did, and I looked at it, and Jill said she had one too. I said to Beth, "Wow, you wear that like a badge of honor—what does it mean?"

Then the kids began telling me that when a boy gives you a hickey it means that he really likes you and that you like him, and it *is* an honor to have it. They talked about making out. Their conversation was sprinkled with slang and profanity. Also, they talked about marriage, and they talked about loving these boys forever. At one point I picked that up and said that it was like they really, really like them and they wanted to feel like it would last forever. They began telling me about their individual boyfriends, whom they really did like and felt they'd marry, like it was true love and it was the real thing. The conversation was coming fast and furious—it was loud and it was very enthusiastic. There was a lot of talking all at once and interrupting each other. Then Beth began talking about how her boyfriend had tried to go too far last night and put his hand on her ass and she didn't like that. I asked if this had happened to a lot of them, with boys trying to go too far, and they said, "Yeah, the boys always try, but it was up to the girl to stop them and the girl had to keep control, because the boy always tried to get as much as he could." They said it was hard to say no, because the boys kept pushing them.

Relationship with Families

The girls' most compelling concern, and the one to which they returned repeatedly, involved their relationships with their families. Initially, the girls seemed to feel isolated from each other, each alone in her pain of family rejection, feeling that she was the only one who had "nobody who cares." While the concerns about coping with the daily hassles of the RTC were clearly shared by all, and the excitement and embarrassment about sex seemed to be universal, the pain of being rejected by one's own family seemed to be a private matter. Perhaps because it exposed not only their own vulnerability but the vulnerabilities and risk factors of their families, the girls were extremely reluctant to break the taboo of divulging "family secrets." However, as the girls were helped to begin to share family experiences and feelings, they not only recognized the commonality of their "private" pain but were also able to help each other deal with it.

This process of using the peer group to deal with family problems is a basic part of adolescence. Polsky (1962) stated, "The translation of personal insecurities into public issues, resolving them constructively in the group, and yet retaining individual responsibility, is a dilemma . . . that faces all adolescents" (136). It is developmentally appropriate for adolescents to look to each other for support and validation about family difficulties. This support can provide "protective relationships" for adolescents who have experienced adverse family environments (Smith and Carlson 1997).

Initially the worker was quite active in pointing out commonalities and helping the girls tell each other about difficult family experiences. But as the girls became absorbed in each other's stories, they were able to provide their own energy and momentum.

The girls were talking about their wish for a volunteer Big Sister. Jill and Donna said they really wanted and needed one. Donna said, "I really have no one—nobody in my family really cares for me." Gladys responded by saying, "Well, do you think I have? I have nobody either." Donna said, "At least you have a mother" Gladys said, "To hell with her. Having somebody like her is like having no one." Donna said, "Well, my mother is in Chicago. She doesn't even want to be near me." Jill said, "My mother is in Puerto Rico, and I'll probably never see her again." Donna said, "My stepmother treats me lousy, and it makes it worse."

The girls continued exchanging notes on how terrible it was not to have a mother who cared about you. I said, "What I hear coming from all of you is how rotten it really is to have been gypped, not having a mother who would care for you" Donna said, "You know how it makes me feel? It makes me feel so bad that I can't even cry. I just get numb, and I can't even feel sadness anymore." Gladys said, "Shit. My life's been like that since the day I was born." Jill said, "Eight years of my life have been ruined because I haven't had a family." Then she turned to Donna and said, "At least when you go home, you have stepbrothers and stepsisters. I have nobody. I used to have a stepbrother, but he died." As Jill said this, she began to cry a little bit. I said in a soft voice, "That's really rough for you." Donna said to Jill, "Gee, I didn't even know that your stepbrother died. I'm really sorry." Gladys said, "Yeah, I can imagine how bad it must make you feel. I wish there was something that I could say to make you feel better." Jill said it was really terrible to lose somebody who you loved. There was a moment of real closeness and real trying to reach out to each other in grief, and it was kind of quiet in the room.

As they continued to share with each other, they reached more deeply into themselves. Donna turned to the group and said, "I want to tell you all a thing that I've never told anybody before. When I was living in Texas with my real mother, she kicked me out of the house two times and told me she didn't want me anymore, and I felt so bad that I wanted to die." Jill said, "Oh, my God, that's terrible. You must have felt so bad. There were times I felt real bad in the foster home too—like I wanted to get out because they really didn't care for me." Gladys said, "Me too—same here." Donna said, "A lot of times I feel like I want to kill her because she treated me so bad, because she walked out on me." Jill said, "How about me? My mother walked out on six kids. She just walked out on us like she didn't even care for us." Then Jill switched and began knocking her foster mother and talking about times she didn't feel like the foster mother cared for her either. Then there was a quiet and a tension in the room, almost like the kids had become frightened of what they were talking about. I said, "Is it scaring you a little, talking like we are, about your real mothers and the terrible hurts you've had?" Gladys said, "It's OK. I want to talk about it even though it hurts. I remember getting all my hopes up about my real mother and hoping and working on it so that things could be ironed out between us, but after a while I realized that it was impossible and I just gave up. Then that happened in the foster home too, and I had to give up." Jill said, 'Yeah, that happened to me, too. I couldn't keep knocking my brains out. I knew it wouldn't work in the foster home, and I just gave up and stopped trying." Donna said that lots of time she had given up everywhere and didn't know where she would go from here.

Again there was quiet in the room. And I said, "This is very hard, and it's also very sad." The kids nodded and just kind of hung their heads. Then Gladys said, "But you don't really give up. You keep on looking for people to be close to" I nodded to her and asked, "Like when you reach out for a Big Sister?' She said, "Yeah, and I know because I love D. There are people in the world who can love me."

The worker's early interventions were to reach for and display understanding of the girls' feelings as well as to share her own. She encouraged them to really listen to each other and to respond to the feeling behind the words. Gradually, she began to help them to partialize and specify their needs and concerns. This enabled them to break down the overwhelming problems of family dysfunction and disruption into more manageable ones, such as looking for people who would care about them. Always, the worker tried to convey her own caring for the girls, her belief that they were capable of giving and receiving love and were deserving of that love.

The girls' remarkable ability to share painful memories and revelations with each other became an important protective factor in coping with their problem-filled family situations. As they developed trust in each other and came to believe that their disclosures would be received with respect and empathy, they grew able to probe more deeply into themselves. Their discovery that they were all "in the same boat" reduced their shame and guilt about family problems. Their growing ability to *give* support and help as well as to receive it empowered them and enabled them to feel less helpless. Their experience of themselves as capable help givers increased their feeling of self-worth. This, in turn, made it easier for them to risk revealing further problems and weaknesses, thus facilitating the process of sharing and giving and receiving help. They were able to use these growing protective factors as buffers against the ongoing risk factors in their families and communities.

The girls returned to the theme of family relationships at several sessions, deepening their probing, revealing more of their pain. As they faced their essential aloneness and need to make it without adequate family support, they experienced the gamut of painful emotions, from rage to bitterness to fear to despair. Out of their pain, and the sharing of that pain, and their growing sense that others really understood and cared, emerged those part of themselves that were hopeful and alive. They began to discuss what they could do to make things better for themselves. They began to look toward other sources of "family" within the RTC, within their cottage, and especially with each other. Rutter (1987) identified the opening of new opportunities and "avenues of escape" from stressful life situations as an important way to enhance protection for adolescents and encourage their coping abilities.

The worker helped the girls to listen and respond to each other, sticking with the pain, not rushing to "fast and easy" solutions. She helped them to partialize, to generalize, and to use each other for real problem solving. Whenever faint glimmerings of hope emerged, she tried to nurture them, without being pressuring. Thus she tried to help the girls to reach for growth out of pain, to see themselves as being able to gain something positive from even the most difficult experiences, again emphasizing their resilience, even in the face of risk and stress.

Beth asked Gladys about her real father. Gladys hung her head and said she never knew him. Beth said, "Gee, that's sad—maybe he ran away from your mom because he couldn't stand her either—just like you don't want to have anything to do with her." Gladys nodded her head and was on the verge of tears. Beth said, "It must really hurt you very much." Gladys nodded her head, and everybody was quiet. Beth said to Gladys, "I wonder if you ever think that, if he had really cared about you, he wouldn't have left, even if he couldn't get along with your mom." Gladys said that she tried not to think about it—that it hurt so much that she never really had a father, and she didn't even know if she had a father. Margie said to her, "Well, everybody has to have a father." Gladys said, "No, no, that's not what I mean." I said to her, "Can you tell us what you mean?" Gladys nodded, and with tears now streaming out of her eyes she said, "I mean, I don't know if my parents were ever really together. I don't know if I ever really had a family. Maybe my mom had me just for kicks. Like she had sex, got pregnant, and that was that." Then Gladys put her head down on the table and began to cry.

Everybody got very quiet. Beth said, "I didn't mean to hurt you. I'm sorry." I said to her, "No, that's OK. I think Gladys wants to talk about it, even though it hurts very much. And, I think she need to get it out of her system and be able to talk about it. It's OK to cry and to feel hurt." I turned to her. Gladys lifted up her head and nodded, and she said to them, "I have to talk about it." I turned to them and said, "And you're helping her to do that, even though it hurts very much." Beth said, "I don't like to see anybody this unhappy. It makes me feel very sad." I nodded and everybody else nodded. Margie said, "It makes me feel very bad for Gladys." Gladys said to her, "I don't want you to feel bad for me." Margie said, "No, no, I don't mean I feel pity. I mean I know a little what it feels like and what you're going through." Margie began talking about when her mom had passed away and how she had cried all the time for almost a year, and the terrible, terrible pain that had been in it for her. She said that now she could talk about it and it didn't bother her anymore. I said, "And, I think part of the reason that you are stronger about it now is because you were able to cry and able to feel all that hurt and all that pain and get it out of you. And that's why Gladys has to cry."

Margie said, "Yeah, in a way that's true. Because I remember how bad I felt and how lonely I felt. But then gradually I got over it." Then they all began talking about sad things that had happened to them and that the best way to handle it was to let yourself feel really bad, to cry and get it out of your system. Margie said, "But maybe in a way it's easier for us to talk, because even though we've all had hurts, none of us has been hurt as much as Gladys has, not even to know her father." Beth said that was true—that even though she had a hard time at home with her parents, at least she had parents and Gladys didn't even have that. Gladys said that was true and it made her very lonely and frightened. Beth then said to Gladys, "Maybe your father was a good guy. I bet that he did care about you, but he couldn't cope with your mom." Gladys said that maybe that was true—that she just didn't know, that she often wondered about it. I asked if this was on her mind a lot. She nodded. Then Margie asked if Gladys had ever talked about this with her mom. Gladys shook her head no and said, "Are you kidding? I can't talk with her about anything." Once again Gladys began to cry and put her head down on the table. Beth said to Gladys, "Come on, Gladys, get it out of your system, it'll help you." Donna reached over and patted her and gave her a tissue. Gladys wiped her eyes and lifted up her head. She then began to tell them of the incident where she was living in the foster home and her mom had come to visit her and had stolen some money, and her humiliation when the foster parents told her about it, and how angry she felt, and how she wanted to kill her mom and swore she never wanted to see her again.

All the girls were listening very intently. I turned to them and I said, "Can you imagine what that must have felt like for Gladys?" They all nodded and moved physically closer to her. Gladys continued talking as she was crying. They began asking her more of the details about it. And Gladys continued to tell them, and she talked about all these years of harboring this hatred toward her mom and feeling that all her mom could ever do was ruin things for her and that she had ruined her life from the moment she was born. Margie asked if she could talk about any of this with her mom. Gladys again shook her head and said her mother would either lie about things or blow up at her and have a fit. One of the other kids asked if Gladys had been able to talk about it with anybody. Gladys shook her head no. I said, "So there you were, all alone, holding it in, having all this anger, having all those fears of not being able to talk about it, not being able to have anybody to help you with it." Gladys nodded. Margie said, "Now I understand you more than I ever did!" The other girls said they understood more about Gladys, too, and it helped them to see her in a new way. Gladys said she was glad she finally let it out with them—she knew she could trust them.

Ending

The ending of this group was very difficult for these often abandoned and rejected girls. It not only meant the loss of their valuable group, but it revived memories of past losses. In addition, the planned ending of the group, at the close of the school year, coincided with the worker's leaving the RTC. So, the good-byes were more final, with no possibility of "see you in September." The issue of separation and moving away from the dependent ties, which is a crucial part of adolescent development, was especially poignant for these girls. For them separation had often meant desertion, leaving them with fewer resources to cope with life tasks. They had rarely been prepared for endings, frequently not even having a chance to say good-bye.

This group ending gave the girls an opportunity to come to terms with some of their feeling about endings and separation. They were able to take the time to experience the process fully, to examine their range of feelings and reactions. They were able to experience and help each other with issues and feelings common to endings—anger at being left and having something taken away, sadness about loss, fear of not being able to make it alone. But as the girls and their worker dealt with these painful feelings and confronted as well as comforted each other, the strength and richness of what they had done together began to emerge. Even as they were saying good-bye, and even through their rage and fear and tears, they were able to experience the power of their mutual aid and caring. They were able to remember the moving moments they had shared, the problems they had struggled to solve, and the closeness they had experienced. This is what they were able to take with them as an enduring protective factor—the skills of having worked together to help each other and to help themselves. This experience of accomplishment had become part of each of them, hopefully to be used, as needed, at other times and other places.

The skills of the worker during the ending phase of the group included many that she had used throughout the life of the group, but particularly emphasized the following: reaching for and sticking with the pain of saying good-bye, reaching behind the joviality and "farewell party" chatter to real feelings about separation and loss, identifying and crediting the work each girl had done, and summing up the work of the group as a whole.

It was essential that the worker share her own feelings honestly, not to detract from or change the girls' own reactions, but to contribute fully to the richness of what they had all shared. Only in this way could the group's ending affirm the value of the life of the group itself.

In the next to the last session of the group, Beth suddenly began to cry. "You can't leave. We need you. Don't leave." I said, "You mean you're afraid you won't be able to make it without me?" Margie said, "You're the best social worker I ever had. I won't be able to talk to anybody else." I said, "We have been real close, me and every one of you, and I guess the thought of starting with somebody else is scary . . . " There was a lot more talk that they didn't want anybody new. And I said, "You're angry at me. You have a right to be, and even though your anger hurts me, and a big piece of me wants to say "Don't be angry at me," I can understand that you are and I know the kind of pain that must be underneath and I feel some of that pain also. It's hard as hell for me to leave you." Beth said, "If it was hard for you to leave us, then you wouldn't leave us." Margie said, "No, Beth, that's just not the truth. It was hard for me to leave home . . ."

Beth got up and walked over to Gladys and put her arms around her and said to her, "You're scared because everybody's leaving, right?" Gladys nodded her head and said, "Everybody leaves me. I have no one." One of the other kids at the table said, "We're all in that situation too. Miss D.'s leaving us too. Not only you." Beth said. "But maybe it is different for Gladys." Gladys said, "You have a mother and a father. Every one of you has at least a mother or a father. Who do I have?" Beth said, "You have your foster parents." Gladys said, "Big deal. They don't want me." There was a hush in the room at the pain of those words, and I said, "Wow, you really know how that feels." Beth said, "I think I know how it feels. I think I know how bad it feels. And if you want to cry that's OK, but you gotta live. You got to pick yourself up. You gotta face it." Gladys shook her head. "No," she said, "I can't." I said, "It seems like she's feeling so miserable and so knocked down that she feels that she can't pick herself up." Donna said, "Even when you're alone, you have to trust yourself." Margie said, "That's pretty hard to do." Beth said, "But you're not all alone, Gladys. You have us. We'll help you, and sometimes you'll help us." Margie said. "You gotta have confidence in yourself." I said, "How do you do that Margie? Can you tell her?" Margie said, "You gotta think of the things that you do right, not only the bad things. Even when people leave you you gotta think of what you did have with them and all that was good. And then you gotta believe that you're going to have somebody else too." Beth said, "You gotta learn how to stand on your own feet. You gotta learn how to make friends." Jill said, "You gotta take responsibility for what you do, even when it's hard." I said, "It sounds like you feel that Gladys *can* do those things, even though now she doesn't think that she can." Beth said, "That's right. I even mean it coming from me. Lots of times I hate her, but other times I really like her, and I remember when she was nice to me, and when she helped me, and I do believe in her, and I believe she can pick herself up." Beth took Gladys' hand and brought her back to the table. Then Gladys said, "I feel real, real bad; Miss D.'s leaving hurts me more than anybody can know, but you've helped me and I want to thank you." There were tears in everybody's eyes. I said, "This is what it's about. This beautiful thing that you can do in helping each other, and you've got that now. You own that. And no matter who leaves, no matter how much it hurts, you can't lose that. Beth said, "I hate you for leaving, but I know what you mean. I know you're right."

As THESE compelling selections demonstrate, the small group experience, guided by a trained leader, can provide an invaluable opportunity for mutual aid, mutual problem solving, and the development of protective factors and resilience in adolescence. Since an essential characteristic of adolescence involves looking to peers for norms, values, and supports, such groups are particularly well suited to this age. The is especially true in residential treatment centers, where adolescents are in constant, close interaction with each other and influence each other in myriad ways.

The already complex demands of adolescence are further complicated for institutionalized teens because they generally have individual, family, and community risk factors not present for those growing up in their own families. By definition, adolescents in residential treatment centers have not had sufficient internal or external protective factors to enable them to overcome the stressors in their lives in order to function successfully while living at home. Their lives may have been impacted by poverty, deprivation, inadequate schools, and sparse community resources. Their families may have had limited resources, with unresolved discord, dysfunction, and disengagement. Their own biological, cognitive, psychological and psychosocial resources may have been weakened by adverse life events. In addition, the institutional environment is often not supportive of the developmental needs of adolescents, especially needs for autonomy and independence.

The mutual aid group provides a chance for institutionalized adolescents to "put their heads together" and, by pooling their resources, to deal better with their common concerns. The group literally produces a sum greater than its parts, which creates protective factors to strengthen each group member. Teens in mutual aid groups support, validate, and learn from each other, thereby experiencing themselves as competent and caring.

The major concerns of institutionalized adolescents have been identified as

1. negotiating the day-to-day demands of the institution;
2. developing a sense of personal identity;
3. making friends and gaining peer acceptance;
4. dealing with emergent sexuality;
5. coming to terms with family problems and rejections
6. making constructive educational/vocational choices.

The mutual aid group in a residential treatment setting can be an important vehicle for dealing with these concerns as well as for helping adolescents develop skills, mastery, confidence, and satisfaction. These resources become the foundation of more effective protective factors and coping skills and may serve as buffers against future stress.

The five girls in this group came away from their group experience with the beginnings of those resources and with emerging positive feelings of hope for the future. When their social worker summed up her own feelings at the end of the group by saying, "Wow, you kids are fantastic!" they simply replied, "Sure, maybe we'll become social workers too!!!"

References

Anthony, E. J. 1987. *Risk, vulnerability, and resilience: An overview.* In E. J. Anthony and B. J. Cohler, eds., *The Invulnerable Child.* New York: Guilford.

Birnbach, D. 1971. *Residential treatment: The skills of child care.* In W. Schwartz and S. Zalba, eds., *The Practice of Group Work.* New York: Columbia University Press.

Fahlberg, V. 1990. *Residential treatment: A tapestry of many therapies.* Indianapolis: Perspectives.

Garmezy, N. 1983. Stressors of childhood. In N. Garmezy, ed., *Stress, coping, and development,* pp. 43–84. New York: McGraw Hill.

Garmezy, N., A. Masten, and A. Tellegen. 1984. The study of stress and competence in children: A building block for developmental psychopathology. *Child Development* 55:97–111.

Gore, S. and J. Eckenrode.*Context and process in research on risk and resilience.* In R. Haggerty, L. Sherrod, N. Garmezy, and M. Rutter, eds., *Stress, risk, and resilience in children and adolescents.* Cambridge: University Press.

Havighurst, R. J. 1972. *Developmental tasks and education.* New York: McKay.

Kimmel, D. and I. Weiner. 1995. *Adolescence: A developmental transition.* New York: Wiley.

Maier, H. 1965. *The social group work method and residential treatment.* In H. Maier, ed., *Group Work as Part of Residential Treatment.* New York: National Association of Social Workers.

Manaster, G. 1977. *Adolescent development and the life tasks.* Boston: Allyn and Bacon.

Masten, A., K. Best, and N. Garmezy. 1991. Resilience and development: Contributions from the study of children who overcome adversity. *Development and Psychopathology* 2:425–44.

Polsky, H. 1962. *Cottage Six,* p. 136. New York: Wiley.

Rutter, M. 1987. Psychosocial resilience and protective mechanisms. *American Journal of Orthopsychiatry* 57:316–31.

Schwartz, W. 1961. The social worker in the group. In *New perspectives on services to groups.* New York: National Association of Social Workers.

——— 1971. On the use of groups in social work practice. In In W. Schwartz and S. Zalba, eds., *The practice of group work.* New York: Columbia University Press.

Smith, C. and B. Carlson. 1997. Stress, coping, and resilience in children and youth. *Social Service Review* 231—56.

Part 4

Mutual Aid and
Vulnerable and Resilient
Adults

Chapter 9

No One is Alone
Groups During the AIDS Pandemic

George S. Getzel

IN THE more quoted than read masterpiece *Mutual Aid: A Factor in Evolution*, Petr Kropotkin (1903) challenged Thomas Huxley's defense of Darwinism as an explanation of historical events and human development. Kropotkin argued that the thrust of human achievement rests on mutual aid within species rather than the less frequent competition among the species (survival of the fittest). The group, through cooperative activities, assures the survival of its members.

Recent biological research on human beings' social interactions gives corroborating evidence that cooperative activities are related to brain activity that creates pleasurable responses as seen on a Magnet Resonance Imaging (MRI) screen. In studies that control for gender, subjects freely chose cooperative behaviors over competitive ones (even if there was a monetary reward for the latter). Cooperation was a more intrinsically satisfying behavioral option in problem-solving situations. It may be that neurological wiring in human beings is programmed in favor of cooperation, suggesting an evolutionary, survival advantage (Angier 2002).

Small groups with a mutual aid focus have been an integral aspect of people's survival response to the Acquired Immunodeficiency Syndrome (AIDS) pandemic. For example, in New York City a small group of gay men, who felt overwhelmed because their friends and partners were dying of an "unknown" illness, came together to support each other and to urge reluctant government officials and health providers to respond to their concerns. These early efforts resulted in the founding of the Gay Men's Health Crisis, the first and largest voluntary AIDS organization in the world. In New York City, San Francisco, Los Angeles, and subsequently in hundreds of cities throughout the United States, the AIDS health emergency prompted mutual aid efforts—first, for gay men and then for all persons with AIDS (Kramer 1989).

More than twenty years after the discovery of the first AIDS cases, there can no longer be simple denial of the consequences of the pandemic that has reached more than 40 million cumulative cases worldwide by the year 2000 (Stine 2001). Given the current high mortality rates in many parts of the world, hundreds of thousands will not survive the disease for more than a few years after diagnosis (Smith 2001). In the competition for survival, the Human Immunodeficiency Virus (HIV) is spreading and leaving in its wake desperately ill and dying human beings who serve as biological hosts for the virus's replication. Through unprotected sexual contact (anal, oral, and vaginal), the sharing of drug paraphernalia, transfusing of HIV-infected blood, and fetal and/or uterine transmission, more people become infected each day.

Without any new significant technological breakthroughs and the availability of inexpensive antiviral medication, the chance of infected human beings living full and productive life spans is doubtful. It is my contention that short of a "magic bullet" that would make AIDS a faint memory, the mutual aid function in small groups continues to be the lifeline to so many persons affected by the pandemic.

This chapter will present a conceptual formulation and a rationale for mutual aid groups used by persons affects by AIDS and HIV. Special attention will be given to the existential issues that surround AIDS as a life-threatening disease process. The skill requirements in forming and working with such groups will be specified through the analysis of case illustrations. Implications for the future development of mutual aids groups will also be specified.

Developmental Tasks and Issues

The consequences of AIDS on the lives of people are specific in detail for each person who becomes diagnosed with a condition that has been pragmatically and politically defined by government and the public health establishment. AIDS is an uncertain, life-threatening condition that demands people confront their mortality.

At this time AIDS is a finite condition, because it follows a course leading to functional impairment and a possible premature death. As a condition of human finitude AIDS reminds all people affected of the underlying limitation of the body's immune system that profoundly affects their lives. To the extent that persons know they may become or know they are HIV-infected, they will experience periods of uncertainty and anxiety. For example, if they believe that they might die from the disease process, what is the point of forming groups of people with AIDS (PWAs) or kin and friends caring for them? Might the result be an exacerbation of the uncertainty, the fears, and the pain?—factors that probably keep people affected by HIV/AIDS away from small group experiences. Denial of HIV-AIDS and its consequences can be a gentle and necessary balm and coping strategy that allows PWAs and their care givers to survive the constant possibility of a health crisis.

The second characteristic of AIDS is crisis situations, prompted by health reverses and psychosocial responses to new symptoms and functional impairment. Crises, unlike the underlying finite condition, are self-limiting, although during lulls PWAs and their caregivers must contend with uncertainty about the next crisis mobilization. For example, Richard, a PWA who was recently diagnosed with AIDS because of two small skin lesions on his arm, told members of his support group that he was just waiting "for the beginning of the beginning." Richard had seen his lover and several close friends die of the complications of AIDS shortly after notification of their diagnoses. Richard was living with bouts of panic, persistent anxiety, and periods of depression. Other members nodded in agreement and provided words of support. One member, looking at Richard, said that if life is going to be short he should not squander whatever time he had left waiting for the worst to happen.

Self-worth is strongly challenged by the disease. One of the early biopsychosocial consequences is the sense of disarray in how affected persons now see themselves, particularly persons' expectations after discovering that they have an HIV infection or AIDS diagnosis. One group member in a PWA support group referred to his reconsideration of identity as crossing a border and not being followed by others; he felt alone and unloved. Other group members concurred: they believed their diagnosis was an intense transformative experience that they could not adequately communicate to others. They shared their recognition of having a stigmatized identity. In some cases these feelings were related to past issues of diminished self-worth.

A sense of urgency may develop that is heightened by PWAs seeing their time as limited. One PWA in a group said that he saw life as time measured by a lapsed clock, constantly reminding him of how little was left.

Knowing that you may die prematurely has both an immobilizing and an energizing potential for PWAs, in which developmental features must be explored and understood. Young adults in their twenties diagnosed with AIDS are apt to feel acute depressive responses followed by tremendous anger for being denied a future to develop personal goals and accomplish some of them. Very often, heightened aspirations take the form of questing for job accomplishments and stable intimate relationships.

Women with AIDS may, additionally, feel guilty about leaving children, particularly if their spouses are ill or have died of AIDS or when other caring relatives are not available. These women desperately try to make provision for the care of their children. The possibility of mobilizing oneself in the time available very often is expressed in projects to be accomplished for others, so that one will be remembered in the best possible light.

Older PWAs are apt to be more resigned to their life as ending and use their past accomplishments to justify the completion of their lives. PWAs in their forties, fifties, and sixties may take on what appears to be a more "philosophical" stance, which features moments where they review their lives in a more steady and measured manner. PWAs in their middle years are more likely to know other peers who may have died from AIDS or from other causes. While this circumstance by no means guarantees serenity or wisdom, it does give some useful perspectives that can be used in expanding ways to understand and to cope with troubling situations that arise from day to day.

Persons with histories of self-abusive behaviors, in some cases, are able to be mobilized to accept care from others, because they are now accepted in a different way as a PWA. For example, AIDS-specific services have become more readily available; and some highly marginalized PWAs, with long histories of substance abuse and poverty, are now treated in a more caring and comprehensive manner. As one PWA said in a sad tone with a smile on his face, "It took AIDS for me to finally be treated as a human being by the system."

Erikson (1964) wrote that all human beings must protect themselves through maintaining a "sense of wholeness, a sense of centrality in time and space, and sense of freedom of choice" (148–49) through what he describes as the secret delusions and collective illusion that are maintained by social relationships. Any life-threatening disease or chronic disease may seriously weaken the interpersonal resources that support personal identity. The support group becomes an adjunctive interpersonal resource or a literal substitute for absent kin, friends, and others.

> AIDS as a finite, life-threatening condition is an overwhelming challenge to modern medicine, with its array of sophisticated technologies. Medical advances have not been without serious medical and psycho-social consequences. As more persons are living longer after diagnosis, not succumbing as readily to respiratory illnesses as was the case when AIDS was first recognized, it has meant that PWAs may develop other opportunistic diseases and or chronic impairments that profoundly affect the quality of their lives and their caring kin and friends. Dementia and problems with gross motor skills may necessitate placements in skill nursing facilities. For example, cytomeglovirus is occurring more often in long-living PWAs who develop symptoms of chronic diarrhea and inflammation of the retina that results in partial or complete blindness. In addition, wasting syndrome and neurological impairments are being seen more often among PWAs. (Bartlett and Finkbeiner 2001)

If you do not have control over the course of the disease process, there is a natural wish to at least have control over the extent and the types of treatments that you may be receiving. Dependency on the curative and palliative attributes of modern medicine grows for PWAs, as they become sicker and require more complex and often technically sophisticated treatments, which involve difficult judgment calls by doctors and other health care providers. In addition to the high cost of such care, the treatments themselves may make PWAs less capable of managing self-care. The need for home attendants, housekeepers, and home health care providers represent additional indicators of dependency on others and a diminishment of some of the quality-of-life factors that most people judge to be necessary for the maintenance of self-esteem and competence.

Quality-of-life questions inevitably bring up the question of withdrawal of treatment, even if it means the foreshortening of longevity, especially when there is little or no likelihood of reversing the disease's course. It is not unusual for persons who are HIV positive or PWAs to discuss plans to commit suicide, so as not to repeat what they have seen as a painful and humiliating disease course. The need to disclose thoughts and feelings serves as a basis for deeper expressions of mutual aid among persons with HIV infections and AIDS.

Vulnerabilities and Risk Factors and Resiliencies and Protective Factors

AIDS can be wholly seen as crisis and a downward health trajectory without sufficient attention to the ample clinical evidence of the extraordinary resiliency of PWAs in the face of seemingly overwhelming challenges within their bodies and in their environments after discovering they have an HIV/AIDS diagnosis. Social workers are simultaneously struck with how some PWAs have exacerbations of psychiatric conditions and increased difficulties with psychosocial problems while others with comparable histories take on a proactive stance and appear to thrive with the daunting issues of HIV/AIDS. To professionals' chagrin, some PWAs have expressed the belief that AIDS is a gift, because of the positive changes they have made in their lives with a new priorities.

Although definitions of resiliency reflect differences of perspective (Smith and Carlson 1997; Gitterman 2001a; Gitterman 2001b), the concept itself sensitizes practitioners to dimensions for assessment that might otherwise be neglected. Very early in the HIV/AIDS pandemic, persons with AIDS diagnoses chose the formal description *people with AIDS*, emphasizing first and foremost that they were human beings and *not* the stigmatized medical condition; PWAs wished to be seen as proactive advocates for themselves.

Persons may positively rebound from a HIV/AIDS diagnosis by demonstrating a great deal of energy to make significant affirmative transformations in their lives, including recovery from substance abuse and the assumption of more healthful nutritional and exercise regimes. Some PWAs seek spiritual practices to address the challenges of a life-threatening prognosis. To more effectively manage changing vulnerabilities, PWAs frequently assume survival strategies, prompted by the vicissitudes of the disease process and and psychosocial responses in the environment.

Two extreme dysfunctional proclivities face PWAs: either becoming morbidly and fatally resigned to an inevitable horrific death or effecting a complete denial of HIV/AIDS through refusal to follow beneficial treatment protocols and engaging in substance abuse or unsafe sexual activities.

Getzel (1991) has identified four salutatory survival strategies in groups associated with the remarkable resiliency among members abetted by the group process. A member may assume a *heroic* stance by bravely battling each health crisis as a warrior so as to be remembered after his or her death. Others may assume a beneficent stance, caring generously for others while being helped themselves. It is not unusual for a member to occupy a *rational-instrumental* role in the group by becoming an expert on available treatments or new scientific breakthroughs. Members also may use *spiritual-artistic* expression as their way of making sense of illness and its varied consequences.

These survival strategies reflect the personality organization of group members and are the sources of resiliency. Group workers should be accepting and not judgmental about survival strategies and understand their importance in addressing overwhelming existential concerns. At their core these strategies represent human beings' efforts at mastery and transcendence in the face of the boundary questions of illness, death, and meaning.

Resiliency has been defined objectively and subjectively as the individual's successful responses (moving from immobilization to activation) to individual stressors and cumulative stresses from within or outside. The format of the group allows for group members' exploration of the variegated stressors caused by the disease process on bodily functions and the anticipated and the actual responses of significant persons in the environment whom PWAs need for instrumental and emotional support. As important as these predictable stressors may be for group members, the group interaction frees participants to express their subjective responses to stressors. Within the group over time, specific members can demonstrate by example their coping strategies and instill hope in other participants. Faltering members overwhelmed by stressors can identify with other peers' heroism and steadfastness. The group process can enhance so-called protective factors that contribute to the resiliency of participants. The acceptance of peers can enhance self-esteem when the group itself acts as an additional external support for all participants. Members learn new social skills that contribute to their repertoire of coping strategies.

Agency and Group Context

Schwartz (1961) described the mutual aid function embedded in all social relationships as symbiotic striving. Schwartz emphasizes the faith of the group worker in the small group as it explains overwhelmingly finite conditions, serial crises, and personal identity concerns. Groups allow their members to discover a sense of belonging to counter loneliness. Buffeted by changes from within and without, the group becomes the constant holding environment, which allows for confrontation with crises that overwhelm members' capacity to cope. Groups reinforce acceptance and forbearance of members who heroically struggle to maintain a sense of health or well-being despite the presence of pain, disfigurement, and dementia. Caring is made manifest, especially when all other sources of nurturing may be found wanting.

Beginning in the early 1980s with the development of community-based organizations that started in the gay community, a variety of local organizations have arisen to address the multidimensional nature of the AIDS pandemic. Typically, community-based organizations have simultaneously sought to serve PWAs and their loved ones with the provision of HIV prevention education and various advocacy activities. In recent years some community-based organizations have begun to specialize in advocacy, direct-service, or prevention strategies. Public agencies have assumed greater responsibility in providing basic social services, entitlements, and health care to impoverished PWAs. Public health agencies on the local and state level and, belatedly, on the federal level, have increased funding for the delivery of HIV prevention programs and HIV screening and testing.

So-called traditional social agencies have become more involved in the delivery of HIV prevention services and psychosocial services to specialized populations such as children, adolescents, the mentally ill, the disabled, people of different color, or those who would not otherwise be reached because of linguistic barriers.

Social workers in hospitals have played a significant role in the delivery of direct services to PWAs and their families, beginning with the discovery of the first cases in large epicenters of the pandemic in the United States (New York City and San Francisco). Hospitals have become crucial locations for doing case management, particularly for the very poor who are dependent on emergency care services, because of the absence of comprehensive outpatient care services in inner-city neighborhoods.

Social agencies, hospitals, residential settings, and other community programs have been hospitable environments for the establishment of a variety of groups of PWAs, family members, caregivers, and for AIDS volunteers and professional providers. Various support group models, run either by volunteer lay or professional leaders, are currently used. Preparation and training of group leaders vary widely. In addition, the recovery movement is increasingly having an HIV/AIDS emphasis in Alcoholics Anonymous and Narcotics Anonymous programs.

Groups are the most ubiquitous approach in the delivery of HIV prevention services in schools and other community settings. The use of support formats with cognitive-behavioral approached are the most commonly used.

Groups to assist persons with HIV infections, PWAs, and their caregivers are most effective if workers have sufficient opportunity to reach out to potential members and interpret the possible benefits of participation. A preliminary introduction to the group members affords a safe opportunity to communicate some of their more pressing concerns about being in a group and to check out the workers.

In groups for persons who are HIV positive, areas to be explored include the following: When were potential members diagnosed as positive for HIV and what were their reactions to the news? What might be the sources of HIV infection as they perceive it? What are their reactions to being in a group with other persons with HIV infections who may behave the same or who may have different sexual orientations, gender, and histories of drug use? Have they had other group experiences, including twelve-step programs? What sources of informal supports, including family, friends, and others, are currently available to them? Have they made use of formal help like psychotherapy and counseling? Histories of depression and the occurrence of suicidal ideation and gestures should be gently explored. Readiness to be in a group should be agreed upon by the person and the worker.

If a person is acutely anxious and confused, a support group with somewhat closed membership and a culture of commitment may not be suitable. If drop-in groups are available, they often provide safer, less confining structures for more acutely anxious persons who have been recently diagnosed or have preexisting emotional difficulties exacerbated during the crisis of diagnosis.

For PWA support groups, intake should focus on the extent to which opportunistic disease and HIV-related symptoms have functionally limited persons in their self-care, instrumental functioning, and mental acuity. The time and location of meetings may have significant importance, if the PWA continues to work full- or part-time. Concerns about confidentiality and maintaining anonymity should be explored directly. In this respect the extent to which a PWA has self-revealed her or his diagnosis to kin or friends and others is important information in assessing a potential member's readiness to be open to others. The group may be used by PWAs to explore their readiness to reveal their diagnoses to family member and others.

Sources of support in their lives now and in the future are continuing themes in support groups. The abandonment of kin and friends shortly after hearing about a PWA's diagnosis is not uncommon. Stresses in extant relationships, particularly with spouses, lovers, and others who assume significant caregiving responsibilities are to be expected and should be explored in a gentle manner.

Caregivers in support groups may wish to be in a group to discuss the stresses they experience in the day-to-day assistance given to PWAs. Frustration and lack of support or recognition from others should be explored in assessing the readiness of caregivers to discuss common concerns. Caregivers mirror some of the same issues of estrangement and loneliness that PWAs evince, which can make for much confusion and turmoil. Clearly, caregivers need their groups as much as PWAs do.

In pregroup planning, co-leadership should be considered for pragmatic and therapeutic reasons. Two group workers assure that even if one worker is ill or away on vacation, the group still goes on. Commitment becomes so strong to the group that members have been known to come from the hospital to groups, even on the coldest days and in the most inclement weather. Because of the emotional intensity of group meetings, the presence of two workers allows for the absorption of feeling and response. Co-leaders can and should give each other support in and outside the group. Co-leadership creates a familial tone in the group, which may activate latent issues related to members' kinship systems.

If a group is underway, it is important to involve the current members in the decision to add new members. This can be a very sensitive subject if new members are replacing members who have left the group because of illness or death. Yet the very difficulty provides an opportunity to address the underlying theme of all groups—separation, loss, and death. This demand creates situations that severely challenge the ego identities of affected people. The use of groups for PWAs, caring kin, and others is posited to created the conditions by which members can address the cognitive, emotional, and action requirements necessary to handle the multiplicity of challenges that may not be successfully addressed through casework and family treatment.

An early benefit that occurs in groups is a feeling of relief in experiencing others in a similar situation. As a woman in an HIV positive support group said, "Although intellectually I knew that I was not the only one, I felt I was. I was becoming insane."

Groups with a mutual aid focus create reciprocal demands that can support developmental enhancement. Since AIDS largely affects adults and their children, the mutual aid function of groups responds to developmental needs of these populations.

The sense of nurturing from a stable and constant holding environment is evidenced in many forms within the group, most poignantly when a member is absent with a serious health emergency. For example, when visiting a seriously ill and demented PWA in the hospital, the social worker found Robert to be confused about the hospital procedures and his treatment; nonetheless, he accurately reminded the social worker that the group was meeting that evening. Robert asked the worker to be sure to tell members that he would try to get to the next meeting. The PWA had internalized the group within himself as a caring and supportive environment.

A group worker must have faith in the group process and a vision of how a group can be of benefit to its membership. Persons with HIV, PWAs and caregivers face comparable issues.

Work and Group Themes

The following represents a synoptic view of the phases of group development with illustrations from groups of persons with HIV infection, PWAs , and caregivers. Phase-specific issues over the course of the "life" of the group metaphorically reflect concerns emanating from the biopsychosocial course of HIV/AIDS.

Beginning Phase

During the earliest phase of a group, members are orienting themselves to the worker's role and presenting themselves. Approach-avoidance behaviors reflect the natural ambivalence members have in revealing themselves too quickly or inappropriately; they simultaneously may have the urge to find emotional relief and peer recognition. To the extent the "secret" of HIV/AIDS has dominated their minds and deleteriously interfered with their interpersonal relations, some members may find the group to be very seductive and a frightening environment. The group worker's skills should encourage members to find ways of telling their personal narrative. For some members this means revealing their forays into an inhospitable interpersonal world that is rejecting and judgmental. These early exchanges invite trust and beginning efforts at problem solving that suggest themes the group might address.

The following illustration from an early session of an HIV-positive support group of men and women who have recently found out about the infection reflects the content and interactional issues that occur during the beginning phase. Group members reflect a mix of races, sexual orientations, and histories of substance abuse.

> Arnold talked in a soft-spoken, friendly, and somewhat distant manner about hearing from a friend that his ex-lover was just diagnosed with Kaposi's sarcoma. His friend did not realize what effect this news would have on him. Arnold quickly decided to get tested and discovered that he was HIV positive; he became obsessed with suicidal plans as a way of remedying his predicament. Although he cannot quite figure it out, Arnold now feels that he is glad that he is positive, because he now sees himself as different from other persons, and Arnold is always amazed at how persons can be so preoccupied with "small things."
>
> Ann then told the group about a woman in her Narcotics Anonymous meeting who became jealous of her and is flamboyantly disregarding her. Ann noted that this reminded her of her own family where the women criticized other women. Ann finds this rejection ironic, and she has the impulse to tell this rejecting woman about her HIV positive status. Ann says sadly to the group, "I wonder then if she still would be jealous of me?"
>
> Two women in the group started speaking about how their older daughters acted at first kindly to them, when they told them that they were HIV positive.

However, in short order their daughters were again very rejecting and cruel . . . later the women discussed having to place their children in foster care or with relatives, because they could not handle the demands of parenting. Linda said quietly that her children were reasons to want to live. I suggested that it sounded like you have found relationships with various important persons in your lives to be very stressful and that you might want to continue to discuss these concerns at this and future meetings.

Middle Phase

The group has, during the middle phase, developed sufficient norms and patterns of interaction to permit members to focus on specific personal crises and link them to problem-solving activities that address group-level themes. Sustained problem solving allows group members to explore and to understand areas of conflict between members and subgroups that become increasingly visible and difficult to evade. These group conflicts reflect immediate and historic issues with families of origins and current caregivers. Group workers' motivations and intents in the group may be subject to close scrutiny by members.

The mutual aid function is closely linked to the creation of group culture, which serves to normalize what by all accounts is the bodily dissolution of different members. They cannot take their health for granted any longer. As one PWA ruefully said, "Everyday brings new presents." PWAs will sometimes open their shirts to show the deepening purple color of cancer lesions that are "progressing." The need to come to terms with the palpable character of the disease through sharing its personal reality becomes an important aspect of the group's culture. A group worker must appreciate the significance of a group's symbols that are used to normalize the disease, freeing it of some stigma, at least in the context of group. The group culture allows the membership to go through difficult transitions by providing rites of passage that can be superimposed upon the disease and its consequences and gives important cognitive guidance and emotional support. An example of a rite of passage is how a group prepares members to accept frightening medical procedures like the implanting of a chest catheter needed by PWAs who must take large quantities of infused medication and nutrition. PWAs often see the implantation as a disfigurement and yet another sign of their bodily deterioration. New medication or infused nutrition presents many quality-of-life issues, as PWAs grow more dependent on others for their care. The instrumental and symbolic implications of the chest catheter can be carefully discussed in the group; members over time hear how others handle this significant benchmark in treatment. The concern and advice of other members are visible benefits gained through a group culture that encourages expressions of mutual aid; the group will be a constant presence through the vicissitudes of the disease process.

The following are themes that occur in the group over time:

1. exploring the ways in which family members, friends, and others are prepared to provide emotional and practical support during periods of crisis;
2. expressing otherwise difficult feelings of rage, depression, guilt, jealousy, and shame occasioned by the highly conflict-ridden consequences of the disease course;
3. finding ways of countering periods of acute anxiety about death and dying occasioned by the lifting of denial about the life-threatening aspects of HIV/AIDS;
4. finding practical ways to live hopefully and affirmatively day –by day;
5. finding ways to give and accept support and assistance from others despite feelings of helplessness and dependency;
6. exploring quality-of-life options (how people want to live and die) as they grow more dependent on health and social service providers for their care;
7. finding ways to affirm the meaning of lives that may be concluding and creating a legacy of positive memories;
8. constructing a personal belief system with peers that gives more positive meaning to the plight of dealing with HIV/AIDS.

There is a reciprocal mutual aid process between persons with HIV infection, PWAs, and caregivers that link them inextricably in symbolic and concrete ways to one another. Although each group needs its own space to address felt concerns, the progress of mutual aid within each group reverberates to other affected groups. Together these groups have the potential to create a more viable informal support system that enhances the quality of life of its extended membership.

The following illustration of the middle phase took place in a support group of African American men in a prison ward for PWAs of a public hospital:

Tom tells me that AIDS is a conspiracy of the white man to kill off the black man, when another member raised the question of taking a new treatment for the prevention of pneumonia. Tom indicates that anyone who gives into the disease will use the doctors' poisonous medicines. Ethan and Sam nod their heads in vigorous agreement with Tom's position. The group seems ominously still, but I wait out my own and the group's discomfort. Finally, I say that something seems to be going on in the group that I do not quite understand and am I alone in that impression. More silence.

Finally, I ask if I am not part of the white man's medicine. Tom becomes stone-faced as some other members seem to choke with muffled laughter. Ethan demands to know why I always think the group is talking about me. I remark that social workers are hospital employees, so there may be reasons to question whose side I am on; AIDS is really frightening and confusing for patients, particularly if they do not know if they will become sicker from a treatment or if a treatment will work.

After a little hesitation, Philip asks me if he could refuse treatment. Ethan quips, "And they'll kick your ass out!" An animated discussion begins with members telling each other about treatments that they have rejected or were thinking of starting.

After challenging the worker and each other, in the following practice excerpt from the middle phase of group development members are able to sustain problem solving in the group. The worker reinforces the natural appearance of mutual aid, which occurs with greater frequency as members experience more safety by accepting negative feelings and affirming positive feelings. This becomes no small accomplishment for them, because of their feelings of shame for being both prisoners and PWAs, coupled with the cumulative burdens of poverty and racism that they have experienced throughout their lives.

Ethan looked very somber, sticking closely to Tom, who took quick looks at Ethan as the session began. I had spoken to Ethan before the group, when I discovered that Ethan's common-law wife had just died from AIDS, and their two children would have to be placed in foster care if his mother-in-law would not continue to care for the children. This was a distinct possibility because she was currently suffering from uncontrollable high blood pressure and was subject to periodic blackouts.

There was a long, heaving silence in the group, which felt as if it would never end. Finally, in a loud pleading voice, Tom said, "If AIDS doesn't kill you, life fucks you over. Shit!" Ethan began to shake and the veins at his temples seemed to expand and pulsate. Tom held him closer, and Ethan's head leaned against Tom's shoulder.

Philip then asked me if I thought the judge would let Ethan go to the funeral. I said that instead of asking me, why doesn't he ask Ethan or the group. Suddenly, Ethan opened his eyes and said that he did not want to go to his wife's funeral, because he was "useless" and everyone there would know it. Philip responded that it was his life, but later he would regret not going, if not for himself then for his children. Ethan snapped back that his kids were nobody's business, and that Philip should shut up or expect to get beat up by someone. The group quickly and in unison told Ethan and Philip to "stop acting like sick fools."

In the brief silence that ensued, I asked what seemed to be happening in the group. Ethan said that he was a fool to have me tell the group of his wife's death, and that the members were fools or else why would they have AIDS and be in jail. Ryan said that it just goes to show you that Ethan is sick in his mind. A heavy silence fell over the group; I said that they were having trouble in the group today being there for each other. Philip said it just bothers him, how Ethan seemed to want the group to know his problem, and then he has to reject you and put you down; he acts as if he is the only person who is suffering from AIDS. Philip noted he had learned that you got to be careful who you show your cross or otherwise be prepared for people to attack you—that you can't trust people when you're down.

Philip then began a monologue about how both his brother and sister-in-law died of AIDS within six months of each other, last year. Although he knew that he should not blame himself because they were both heavy users before him, he gave them drugs when they both started to get sick. Tom told him that he had to be crazy to blame himself, and that his job was to get well himself and try to get released.

I said that group members seemed to be struggling with each other about how they should discuss AIDS, not only as it affected them but also their family members. I guessed it was hard for them to think about having AIDS and trying to recover, if family members, whom they cared about, died from the same disease. Philip said that he wished he could cry; when he has cried, he wondered whether it was for himself or for them.

I noted that even though it may be painful to talk about their loved ones dying of AIDS, I hope the group could be a safe place to talk about these sad feelings that just do not go away. Philip said that he did not want the group to bring him down—he has enough keeping him down. Then he mentioned how sick he was getting from the TB medicine, which he was required to take. I indicated that Philip seemed to be having a hard time sticking to the topic of losing loved ones. Ethan then said to group members, regardless of what anyone thought, he could not go to the funeral; that he would rather be dead now. I asked the other group members what they thought.

Wendell said that the group was not on his case but was concerned with how stressed out he looked; and they were worried he would get sicker. Agreement was expressed nonverbally to that comment.

I said that I imagined that Ethan might have been overwhelmed by the group members telling him that he had to go to the funeral, and the decision to go was clearly his to make. I then asked Ethan if he might tell the group a little about his wife. Without hesitation, Ethan described what a beautiful wife he had; when he was with her he could not feel bad. Having her love was something that he did not really deserve; he did not know how she put up with his using drugs. Ethan, in great detail, spoke about how both men and women liked his wife. He blamed his wife's mother for trying to keep them apart when he was arrested for armed robbery four years ago. Ethan never knew if it was because his wife was diagnosed as HIV positive that his mother-in-law "put things into her head" against him. He started to choke up.

Tom and Wendell put their arms around him. Wendell said to Ethan that even if he may have infected her, he did not know it, and there was no point in punishing himself because that would not bring her back. Ethan wept that he still loved his wife and that he only wanted to be with her soon.

The session was ending. I asked the group members how they felt about what happened in the group that day. Allan remarked that it was good that Ethan cried about his wife; where can you talk about your pain; who cares if you are suffering?

I asked if the group members cared. There were muted expressions of assent from members present. I noted that even though there was disagreement in the group today, I also saw some powerful expressions of shared pain about deaths of family members from AIDS, which seemed to make it hard to feel hopeful about yourself and whether you should continue to fight this disease. I said that I was very touched by members' concern for each other; they could continue to discuss this subject next week, if they wished.

Ending Phase

The underlying motif of the early life of the group is coping with that which can be understood. The group develops a stability of membership that is very comforting to members and group workers. Members experience the security that comes from having a "closed" membership group: the illusion fostered is that if members stay together AIDS and its mortal consequences will be averted. Sadly and realistically, this cannot be for the longer period of the group's existence. With mounting illnesses and deaths, closed membership connoted diminishing membership and a palpable indication that AIDS is a life-threatening and fatal disease. The succession of generations through deaths and births that occurs over decades in a kinship system occurs over months within the group context. Acceptance of new members must be reconciled with loss of old members— a powerful intimation of each group member's mortality.

All groups must deal with issues of separation and loss, which occur from a number of sources. The discontinuation of the group, the loss of members, or experiences related to loss and death engender aspects of the ending phase as members attempt to reconstitute themselves as a group or move on to other experiences (going through a transition in social attachments). Typical of this phase are interactive behaviors that are forms of denial, regression, recapitulation, and flight, all of which represent collective efforts to handle the emergence of separation anxiety about members. The very shift of membership in particular meetings, for example, is often representative of the toll of illness and, over time, the toll of HIV/AIDS-related deaths.

Getzel and Mahony (1990) wrote:

> Group workers need to help members focus on finding solutions that avoid the extremes of a morbid, fearful preoccupation with death and disengagement from life's demands, or a wishful magical scheme to deny the

realities of an AIDS diagnosis. Between these two poles lies the safe environment where one can focus on living with AIDS . . . the ego strengths of individual members buttressed by the mutual aid process provide a variety of practical, heroic, beneficent and artistic/spiritual solutions to the otherwise unacceptable insults of the disease and premature death. (119)

In the following excerpt, from a caregivers' support group, aspects of the ending phase arise as members face the effects of the cumulative toll that AIDS has taken on them and their group.

There was a palpable sense of sadness and heaviness in the atmosphere of the group as members slowly walked into the room. The week before Ann's son had died, and nearly all the members attended the funeral. Both Ira and Roger had to take their lovers to the hospital, where they remain. Ira's lover has become very demented and now weighs only 110 pounds.

After a long silence Tom asks me how Ann is doing after the funeral. I indicated that Ann is very tired and numb, at least that is how she sounds from a phone call I received; I then ask group members what were their impressions. Group members talk at length about how well Ann was able to plan her son's funeral, but maybe she did not have enough time to grieve and take care of herself. Mary indicates that she is worried about Ann and hopes she can come back to the group before too long.

Later in the meeting Ira speaks about a recurrent wish that his lover would die soon: Ira is not sure if he is fantasizing his lover's death as a compassionate thought or a selfish wish to be over the whole ordeal. After struggling to get these thoughts out, Ira convulsively cries. Tom and Mary embrace him.

Group work with PWAs and their caregivers represents one of the most demanding practice domains. While the personal and skill demands are great, the practice itself affirms the power and healing benefits of group experiences abetted by professional knowledge and values. Group workers must respond to the crisis proportions of the pandemic by providing leadership for such groups and training others to respond to profound needs in the inner city neighborhoods, rural areas, and elsewhere devastated by the cumulative toll of AIDS-related deaths of gay and drug recovering providers.

The AIDS pandemic has also taught us that professionals and volunteers need support groups to continue their efforts at HIV prevention and to provide psychosocial support to others.

The stark, painful repercussions of HIV/AIDS reveal the human truth of reciprocity and mutual aid. The human species stands alone as it ponders the ultimate consequences of the pandemic, but human beings stand together in their search for solace and solutions.

References

Angier, N. 2002. Why we are so nice: We're wired to cooperate. *New York Times*, July 23, pp. D1, D8.

Bartlett, J. G. and A. K. Finkbeiner. 2001. *The guide to living with HIV infection: Developed at the Johns Hopkins AIDS Clinic.* Baltimore: Johns Hopkins University Press.

Erikson. E. H. 1964. *Insight and responsibility.* New York: Norton.

Getzel, G. S. 1991. Survival modes for people with AIDS in groups. *Social Work* 36:7–11.

Getzel, G. S. and K. F. Mahony. 1990. Confronting human finitude: Group work with people with AIDS. *Journal of Gay and Lesbian Psychotherapy* 1:105–20.

Getzel, G. S. and S. Willroth. 2000. Acquired immune deficiency syndrome (AIDS). In A. Gitterman, ed., *Handbook of social work practice with vulnerable resilient populations,* pp. 39–63. 2d ed. New York: Columbia University Press.

Gitterman, A. 2001a. Social work practice with vulnerable and resilient populations. In A. Gitterman, ed., *Handbook of social work practice with vulnerable resilient populations,* pp. 1–38. 2d ed. New York: Columbia University Press.

———— 2001b. Vulnerability, resilience, and social work with groups. In T. Kelly, T. Berman-Rossi, and S. Palombo, eds., *Group work: Strategies for strengthening resiliency,* pp. 19–33. New York: Haworth.

Kramer, L. 1989. *Reports from the Holocaust: The making of an AIDS activist.* New York: St. Martin's.

Kropotkin, P. 1903. *Mutual aid: A factor of evolution.* New York: McClure Phillips.

Schwartz, W. 1961. The social worker in the group. In *New perspectives on services to groups: Theory, organization, and practice,* pp. 7–34. New York: National Association of Social Workers.

Smith, R. A. 2001. *Encyclopedia of AIDS: A social, political, cultural, and scientific record of the HIV epidemic.* New York: Penguin.

Smith, C. and B. K. Carlson. 1997. Stress, coping, and resilience in children and youth. *Social Service Review* 64:233–55.

Stine, G. J. 2001. *AIDS update.* Upper Saddle River, N.J.: Prentice Hall.

Chapter 10

Persons with AIDS in Substance-Abusing Recovery
Managing the Interaction Between the Two

Lawrence Shulman

THIS IS the story of five clients, all facing the dual struggle of coping with AIDS and early substance abuse recovery. For each client an additional and related issue was dealing with the impact of serious early physical, emotional, and sexual abuse in childhood and adolescence. Maladaptive efforts to cope during their teenage and early adult years, including serious susbstance abuse, also had a devastating impact on group members. For each client there were added layers of complexity caused by polysubstance abuse, criminal behavior, prostitution, homelessness, prison time, and destructive interpersonal relationships. The group members' ability to trust and to develop true intimacy after so many years of being exploited as well as having exploited others to meet their emotional and drug needswas severely diminished. In spite of these obstacles, this is also a story of magnificent courage in the face of adversity and the wonderful ability of mutual aid to uncover and nurture the essential impetus toward social connection and caring.

John, my co-leader, was a full-time, trained substance abuse counselor with the agency and was not a social worker. As an academic, I was primarily involved in teaching and research volunteering to co-lead the group as a form of "fieldwork." John was in recovery; I was not. He was experienced in twelve-step programs, such as Alcoholics Anonymous and Narcotics Anonymous, and employed the organization's philosophy and recovery strategies. Over the years I have helped to develop a social work, mutual aid support group model, an approach that was relatively new to my co-leader. He is African American, and I am white and Jewish. Thus as we worked together we were dealing with differences in professional disciplines, practice orientation, life experience, race, and ethnicity. Each of these differences would create obstacles while also providing the impetus for our own professional and personal growth. Working together, across these differences, profoundly affected our practice and thus our impact on our group members. This experience illustrates how much we can learn from other professionals and other models if we see collaborations such as this one as an opportunity to grow our own practice understanding and skills.

Developmental Issues and Tasks

The five members of the client group had areas of common ground as well as differences in where they were developmentally and in the life cycle. While all were adults, ranging in age from twenty-six to forty-four years old, they all had experienced some form of arrested emotional and social development usually related to the onset of their childhood victimization and the start of their addictions. Members included Kerry, a twenty-eight-year-old white gay male, Tania, a forty-four-year-old white transgendered woman, Theresa, a twenty-six-year old white heterosexual woman, Jake, a forty-two-year-old African American male, and Gerry, a thirty-three-year-old African American male who had to leave the group at one point for two weeks to enter a residential detox program. Their ability to cope with the normal life cycle issues associated with each age was severely impaired by their early and current experiences, their stage in the recovery process, and their status in terms of their AIDS.

For example, early recovery for these clients ranged from one day clean and sober (one member insisted he could handle a drink once and a while) to the beginning of the second year of sobriety, what one member described as "the year of the feelings." This was the year, she indicated, that "you start to face all of the feelings you have used addictive substances to avoid." Using a stage change model described by Prochaska and DiClemente (1986), their readiness to deal with their addictions ranged from the "contemplative stage," considering making changes in their addictive behavior, to the "action stage," taking significant steps to deal with their addiction. The group met in a special residence that provided independent living with support for persons with AIDS. Three of the five members lived in the residence.

Differences also existed in relation to members' struggle with the "virus," as they referred to AIDS. Jake and Gerry were included as subjects in a drug testing protocol and were receiving the new triple-drug AIDS therapy. They had evidenced significant drops in their viral loads (the amount of the HIV virus in their system) and significant increases in their T-cell counts, which measures the strength of the antibodies that would fight the opportunistic infections that eventually could kill them. For these two members the issues were living with AIDS and the deeply poignant question raised at one session, "Is it possible? Am I cured of the virus?"

Theresa, on the other hand, was waiting for her viral load and T-cell count to reach the levels required to enter the drug test subject group. She was battling weight loss and other physical symptoms but was hopeful that the therapy would eventually reverse her decline. Kerry was refusing to take the new drug therapy, even though one look at his physical condition suggested that he should qualify for inclusion. Kerry seemed to have a fatalistic attitude and never clearly explained his reluctance. Tania, our transgendered member, after years of drugging and the use of hormones, had too many physiological problems to be given the new treatment. For Tania it was, in her words, "waiting to die" and trying to stay drug free so that she could take some control over the part of her life that remained "and die with dignity."

Vulnerabilities and Risk Factors and Resiliencies and Protective Factors

The vulnerabilities and risk factors for all of these members related to significant social and emotional deficits, their difficulty in maintaining nonabusive and nonexploitive relationships, the obvious physical, social, and emotional vulnerability associated with AIDS, and the serious risk of their inability to maintain their sobriety.

The social and emotional deficits were associated with members' inability to find adaptive means of coping with their underlying emotional pain. Substance abuse for each of them was self-described as a form of "flight" from the effects of their early and later traumatization. There was always a concern on the leaders' part to keep disclosures in the group under the control of the member so that a balance could be maintained between their efforts to engage in an emotional healing process and protection of their fragile state of recovery. As trust developed and disclosures were shared with the group, the risk of these serving as "triggers" for relapse needed to be addressed. The members' willingness to share with others, perhaps for the first time, their painful experiences both as youths and adults was a sign of their resilience and their sense of urgency. A protective factor was the care taken by the group to always focus on how, after a particularly painful disclosure, a member could guard his or her sobriety. The willingness of other members to be available for a call or a contact also served to provide important support.

Members had chosen different routes for dealing with relationships. Many of their maladaptive strategies were a result of early patterns of defense associated with their abusive life experiences. They ranged from Jake, who practically kept himself locked in his room and avoided social relationships with friends and family members, to Kerry who engaged in a pattern of superficial liaisons, often with partners who replicated his early experencies of abuse and exploitation. These relationships or their absence were major risk factors for all members. Members described the risks involved in maintaining contacts in the community—contacts that often tempted them into relapse. A protective factor for Jake was his job and his earning "employee of the month" status, leading to a newfound sense of self-worth. For Theresa the promise of eventual reunification with her three-year-old daughter, living by court order with her mother, was a driving force in her recovery.

For all members the impact of the AIDS diagnosis on their recovery and, in turn, the potential impact of their fight for sobriety on their disease was commonly discussed. Protective factors included the availability of self-help groups such as Alcoholics Anonymous (AA) and Narcotics Anonymous (NA). While each of these groups may differ in some ways, common themes emerged, including a focus on achieving and maintaining sobriety and helping others to do so as well, the use of structure to help control anxiety, and the use of traditions and slogans to support recovery efforts.

Many of these self-help groups describe twelve-step models that identify the route to achieve and maintain sobriety. My co-leader and members of the group would often refer to these steps as guidelines for behavior when faced with difficult choices in their relationships with others. For example, steps 8 and 9 provide a means for members to deal with their guilt over their past behaviors by having "made a list of all persons we had harmed, and become willing to make amends to them all." and having "made direct amends to such people whenever possible, except when to do so would injure them or others." These principles were invoked one night when men in the group discussed their guilt over having had unprotected sex with women after they knew they were infected with AIDS.

While members more or less took advantage of the availability of these meetings, a common theme was their inability to talk about their AIDS at twelve-step meetings because of their sense of shame and feeling they would be rejected. In turn, the AIDS support groups offered by the agency seemed less available to them since their status as recovering alcohol and drug addicts was also perceived by them as embarrassing. Thus this group, in which they could freely deal with both interdependent themes, served as an important protective factor in their lives.

Agency and Group Context

The group was sponsored by the local AIDS Action Committee and was held in a special residence for persons with AIDS. The residence were coveted, assisted living accommodations that required residents who had relapsed to participate in some form of a group counseling program. This mutual aid support group met this requirement, and, in the beginning, at least two members joined solely to maintain their residence status. One member lived in a neareby single room occupancy hotel, where drugs were easily available, and she hoped that group participation would facilitate her move to this "clean and sober" residence. While the group was "voluntary," members experienced attendance as "necessary," particularly in cases where residence rules had been violated (i.e., using susbsances in the residence or fighting) and participants were "on notice" of possible eviction. Meetings with clinical and residence staff employed by AIDS Action prior to the start of the meetings helped to clarify issues of confidentiality, including safety limitations, as well as to engage the residence staff in support of the group. Periodic reports of group progress were shared with staff, however, confidentiality of individual group members was respected. Residence staff and group members understood that limits to confidentiality existed and that the group leaders would report to staff if members were a threat to themselves, or others, or were using or dealing drugs in the residence itself. Relapses involving using outside of the residence would not be reported to residence staff, although members were encouraged to share these incidences with staff and to seek their help.

The group met from 6 to 8 P.M. one night each week at the residence itself. Members gathered in the central recreation room before the group moved to a comfortable lounge. Refreshments were served. My early arrival each night lent itself to informal conversations with group members that often contained direct or indirect communications about issues for that evening. By listening to the "premeeting chatter" in the lounge, I could often obtain clues to issues that would emerge later in the meeting. The five members of the group were "selected" because they were the only ones available who met the requirements of both having AIDS and being in recovery.

Work and Group Themes

THE BEGINNING PHASE OF GROUP

Developing a Common Group Purpose
I have discussed elsewhere (Shulman 1999), and earlier in this book, the tasks of the group leader and group members in the beginning phase. I have suggested that members bring a series of questions to a first session: Who are these leaders and what kind of people will they be? What is the purpose of this group and do I feel any connection to my sense of urgency and my current needs? Who are these other group members and what kind of people will they be? Do I share anything in common with them? I have described the worker's tasks in the first session as clarifying the group's purpose and the role of the worker, addressing authority theme concerns such as confidentiality, inviting feedback from the members as they attempt to find connections to the group's purpose and the other members, and developing a positive and supportive culture for work. I will illustrate these dynamics and skills in the sections thatfollow.

Our first efforts at *contracting* were directed at clarifying the purpose of the group and identifying the potential connections each member had with the group service and each other. The purpose was explained to members in the recruitment interviews and in the first session as follows :

> There are groups for persons with AIDS and there are groups for people in early recovery from substance abuse. This is a support group for persons who are dealing with both. The focus will be on how your recovery issues and your AIDS issues affect each other. We know a number of you attend AA or NA, as well as other groups to support your recovery, and we encourage you to continue to attend

these groups if you find them helpful. The difference in this group is that you will be able to discuss your AIDS issues as well, something you may not feel confortable doing in your other groups. We think that as you help each other in this group, you will be helping yourselves.

As our group developed it became clear that issues of early victimization and trauma would emerge in the discussion. The group leaders were not aware of the specifics of the members' traumatic experiences at the start of the group. However, given how commonly these issue are reported, we were not surprised when they did surface. For example, Tania, our transgendered female member, described how when she discovered she was really a woman, at age seventeen, her working-class family reacted violently to her revelation. At first her parents had her admitted to a psychiatric hospital where electric shock therapy was used to try to "straighten her out." In another incident her older brother took a gun and held it to her head, threatening to kill her if she did not move away and stop "shaming the family." For Tania, as with all of the members, family issues and unresolved trauma related experiences have played a significant part in their addictions and in their lives.

To return to our first group session, after some discussion of confidentiality issues, the group members began to share some of their life issues that represented their feedback to our opening statement and our offer to work. Since we had purposely started the group just before the Thanksgiving holiday, it was not surprising that coping with holidays, families, loneliness, and sobriety were early issues. In these first excerpts you will note that I continually reach for the feelings associated with the member's comments, and John, my co-leader, clarifies issues related to recovery. Our collaboration began with each of us influencing the work of the group and each other. The excerpt continues with what I have called problem swapping (Shulman 1999): group members sharing their response to our offer.

Jake jumped in and said he wanted to tell a story about what had happened over the weekend. He had gone home to visit his family in another town in the state. He said, "I couldn't stay. They started to make me crazy right away. Everyone there was drinking and drugging, and I knew, if I stayed, they would pull me in, and I can't let them pull me in. I have to fight that. I know I can't control this. If I take one drink or use drugs once, I'm going to be back to going into the bar at eight in the morning and staying right through until two A.M. drinking myself to death."

I said that it sounded like, in addition to giving up the drinking and drugging, he also had to give up his family. He agreed. Kerry said that he had been in a bar in the last week and had two drinks. He said, "I can handle that. Just because I have two drinks doesn't mean I am going to go back to where I was a year ago. I know you people are going to say I am in denial, but it's not true. I know I can handle this." John, my co-leader, said that we had to understand that recovery was different for each person and that we had to make room in the group for people to feel safe and not defensive as they described their own ways of handling their recovery. I nodded in agreement. The rest of the group did, as well.

Theresa jumped in at that point and said that she was not living at this residence. She was living in a single room occupancy building two blocks away. She said that most of the people in that building were active users and, for her, it was a fight every day to make sure that she didn't get pulled in. She said that she knew that she didn't want to go back to all the drinking and drugging she was doing. She told us that she had gotten out of the penitentiary after a five-year sentence and that in the penitentiary she had dried out and learned not to use. She said that she didn't want to go back to when she hated herself and she would spend her time on street corners "sucking old men's dicks" in order to get enough money for a shot of crack. Tania agreed and said that, when she thought of some of the things she did for the ten-year period that she was drinking and drugging all the time, she couldn't believe she actually let herself do those things. Theresa said, "I still have to deal with the housing, even though I am not in this residence; but I know the real question is how we deal with ourselves. For me religion has been the answer."

The Authority Theme

In any first session, early issues for the group revolve around their relation to the group leaders, what I have referred to as the authority theme (Shulman 1999). This is the ongoing struggle of group members to come to grips with the group leaders as demanding and yet supportive symbols of authority. In this first session the authority theme emerged as group members needed to deal with me—the stranger—and the question of whether or not I had "walked the walk," been a substance abuser, and "talked the talk," participated in a twelve-step group. Some members already knew that my co-leader, who served as their individual substance abuse counselor, was in recovery, but my status was unknown. The question emerged, as it often does, in an indirect way:

Tania went on about all the holiday parties that were going on, and how difficult it was for her to party. She said, "I don't know how to party without first drinking and drugging. As I looked at the people at this party I attended last week, through clean and sober eyes, I said My God, was this me? Was this the way I lived my life? I left the party when they started passing around the cocaine, because if I had stayed, I might have given in." (Tania was only one month into her recovery and still obviously very shaky.) She commented, "I know you all know what I'm talking about, since you're in recovery as well, although I don't know about them" (pointing toward us).

I decided to use this as an opportunity to address the authority theme and to review the limits of confidentiality. I pointed out that Tania had mentioned a

couple of times her concern about confidentiality and also had raised the question indirectly about whether we were in recovery. I said that I would have to
speak for myself.

"I'm not in recovery, so I am an outsider." I went on to say that I thought the
issue of trust with myself and John was a major one for them today, and they were
worried about whether an "outsider" like myself could understand, and were concerned about what we might share outside of the group. I pointed out that, for
three of the members, there were concerns that we might divulge information
that would affect their ability to continue in a clean and sober residence. They
agreed that they wanted to hold onto their apartments, which were the best of
this type available to people with AIDS in the city.

I told them that I was a social worker and that I taught social work at the university. I told them I had asked John and AIDS Action if it were possible for me to
co-lead this group because I thought it was important that as a teacher I continued to work directly with people. Tania exploded and said, "I thought you were a
narc." I laughed and said, "A narc? You mean I look like a narcotics detective?" She
continued: "I thought you were just going to sit there, take notes, and, right after
this session, you were going to march me off to the police station and that I'd be
arrested." I laughed again and said, "Look (holding my sweater up), no wire and no
badge." They all laughed. I said, 'I'm not a narc, but it's going to take a while for you
to really believe and trust that we will keep what you raise here confidential, except
for those conditions we mentioned earlier . . . if you are involved in illegal activity in
the house, such as selling dope, or if you are danger to yourself or to others. I'm
hoping we can earn your trust." Their heads were nodding in agreement.

My co-leader John asked the members of the group if they were ready to sign
an agreement we had discussed about such issues as attendance and confidentiality. They said they were ready, and I said: "Maybe we should sign as well."

The authority theme would variously emerge often in the group during later sessions. Once members felt safer with my co-leader and me, and when we responded directly to indirect cues from group members, we would explore its
implications for our differences in gender, race, sexual orientation, class, and status. The authority theme remained a powerful source of energy for our work
right up until the last session I attended as we discussed our ending and what
the group had meant to my co-leader and me and to the members.

The Intimacy Theme
In addition to their relationship to the leader, group members must also work on
their relationship to each other; what I have described elsewhere (Shulman,
1999) as "the intimacy theme." Bennis and Sheppard (1956) refer to the conflict
to decide the level of intimacy members are willing to risk, with the group's ambivalence expressed by members who are "counterpersonal," resisting intimacy,

and those who are "overpersonal," wanting more intimacy. In the excerpts that follow Tania at first expresses the counterpersonal force while Theresa attempts to lead the group into a deeper level of intimacy.

The struggle was evident in the group members' willingness to address their AIDS. Although many powerful themes emerged in the first few meetings, the group members seemed to avoid discussion of AIDS. When it did emerge, it was briefly mentioned, with members quickly changing the subject. In Bion's terms (1961), the unsophisticated group would turn to "fight" or "flight" as a way of avoiding the underlying pain. In addition, a pattern developed of group members presenting problems while the others listened in a generally supportive manner, followed by the sharing of their own "story." The idea of the group staying with a particular member's concern and offering specific help was foreign to them. While members acknowledged and empathized with other members, they often quickly shared their own versions of the issue. They appeared to use a model they were comfortable with from their twelve-step experiences. During these sessions my co-leader focused on maintenance of recovery issues; I continued to reach, sometimes successfully, often unsuccessfully, for the mutual aid potential.

One member, Jake, started bringing in handouts, which he shared with members at the end of each meeting. These were used in twelve-step groups he attended and provided recovery advice and philosophy. It was not until the fifth session that he finally told me, in a gentle manner, that he was bringing the handouts to help me out since I "obviously didn't know how to lead a recovery group." I thanked him and told him I could use all the help I could get.

An important turning point in the group came during this fifth session. My co-leader and I had agreed at our last postgroup meeting to confront the group with the avoidance of AIDS discussion and to recontract on the purpose and structure of the group. By attending the group and accepting us as leaders, as well as accepting each other, our group members had made what I call the "first decision." We would now be asking them to make the "second decision"; they needed to make the transition from the beginning phase to the work phase. A deepening of the discussion and a clearer sense of mutual aid would characterize the work phase. Unfortunately, my co-leader was ill the night of the next meeting. We spoke by phone and he agreed I should proceed with our strategy. My record of the fifth session follows:

> Kerry, Jake, and Tania were in the lobby when I arrived. Tania was angry because John (my co-leader) was not going to be there that evening. She said she had business with him. I pointed out that he would be at the meeting the next week and I would be glad to pass along her concerns. She said, "I don't think I'm coming to the meeting." She was in a bathrobe and looked physically terrible. She said she wasn't feeling well, but said she would come for just the beginning. I spoke to Kerry, who was sulking as well, saying he could only come for the first half hour.

I discussed his holiday plans with him for a few minutes and, at one point, he complained about the group as being just "bitching sessions." And then he said, "Some people (and he secretively pointed toward Tania) talk too much." I told him I understood what he was raising and that I would be dealing with it today. Jake was talking to another resident during this time. He joined us when we went upstairs.

Theresa arrived. Tania said, "Maybe we should fill the people who weren't here in on what happened last week." Then she turned to me and said, "But, I'm doing your job, aren't I?" I encouraged her to continue. She filled in Jake and Theresa about the discussion they had around the residence and some of their issues about the group. At this point I felt it was important to make a "demand for work" and to recontract with the group members. I knew it would be hard for them to take the next step on their own and that they had to feel that I, the group leader, was ready to take the step with them.

I said I wanted to raise a question right at the beginning. I had spoken to John and we felt it was important to find out whether or not there was a real commitment to the group. I knew that some members had only come because they believed they had to come or risk losing their housing. (Tania and Kerry had recently relapsed and were mandated to enter some form of treatment, this group being one option). Tania said, "I suppose it helps to sit around and bitch each week. I guess that makes me feel a little bit better."

I told her that was not the purpose of the group, and that I wanted to restate the purpose and to see whether or not we had some agreement on it. I pointed out, once again, that it was a group for people who were dealing with both the virus and early recovery as well as how one affected the other. Tania said she didn't think that was the group's purpose. Theresa said, yes, that was exactly what she understood it to be, a place where she could deal with the impact of her having the virus.

I went on to tell them that, unless this group could become a place where they could be helpful to each other, where they could make connections and be supportive to each other, it would not succeed. I told them that the purpose of the group was to help each of them figure out how to deal with some of the difficult issues in their lives they were raising each week, not just to complain about them. I said I knew it was hard to set aside some of their own concerns and invest themselves in someone else's issues, but that's what the group was about. I said I thought all of them had problems in their lives trying to get close and make connections to people and that this group was a place for them to relearn how to do that. I went on to say that the group would not be valuable unless they could learn to really care for each other. I pointed out that most of them had described experiences where people exploited them or they exploited people, that trust in others was difficult. I said it seemed that their most serious connection in recent years was the one they had with drugs and booze and that making connections was what the group was all about.

Theresa enthusiastically said that that's why she wants help from the group; that's what she needs help with. She said she wanted to talk about her boyfriend and the impact of her HIV on the relationship. As she was talking, Tania interrupted her and started to complete her sentences.

I decided it was time to draw on the positive relationship I felt I had developed over the first four meetings, and stopped the group and pointed this out. I tried to make what I call an "empathic demand for work." While confronting Tania, I simultaneously acknowledged what I believed to be her underlying feelings.

I said, "Tania, you know, you haven't let Theresa finish a sentence." I said, "I could be wrong, but I think you get very anxious about these discussions and that talking is a way of dealing with it." She said, "Oh, did I ?" and made as if to zipper her mouth and put her hand over it. I told her I would help her because I thought she had a lot to give, but I thought other people need the chance to get involved as well. Tania accepted this and, for the rest of the evening, actively tried to catch herself when she was jumping in or cutting people off.

Theresa started to talk about her concerns. She said she was eighteen months clean and sober, and so she was in the middle of the second year, which was a "feelings year." She went on to describe that this was the period when she and, she thought, everyone in recovery, started to face all those feelings they had been running from. She said that it was a complex and difficult time, and it was hard to sort things out. She went on to say that her boyfriend had trouble sharing his feelings with her. When she wanted to talk to her boyfriend about issues like her AIDS, he pulled back and told her it was too painful. As a result, she backed off. She knew he had experienced a lot of losses, including the death of his wife from illness fairly recently, and she realized he was still early in recovery, but she had things she wanted to talk to him about. She had a closeness she wanted to achieve. She had some commitments she wanted from him and she was afraid that he couldn't make commitments at this point. He was holding back. I asked the others in the group if they had any advice for Theresa on this issue.

Theresa had spoken with great emotion and I was determined not to do "casework in the group" by responding to her individually and, instead, to wait for members to respond. Kerry, who usually sits quietly at the meetings, and who indicated that he was going to leave as soon as he could, jumped right in.

Kerry said he thought that her boyfriend was having trouble dealing with his losses and it wasn't easy. He described a very close relationship with his partner, Billy, that ended two years ago, when his partner died of AIDS on Christmas day. He said he still didn't think he'd come to grips with all the feelings that he had and the loss that he'd experienced. I said that must make each Christmas even more difficult for him, and he agreed. He went on to talk about how he had been raised by an extremely physically abusive mother and that his grandmother was the only person who provided him with any support and love. He said he didn't think he had gotten over her dying either. He told Theresa that she had to realize that the process takes a long time and that it might not be easy for her boyfriend to discuss it with her, because he knew it wasn't easy for him to discuss his loss with other people.

As Kerry talked, I saw a sensitive and caring side of him that he keeps covered up with his abrasive, grandiose, angry front, with his consistently telling us he doesn't need anybody and, if they don't care about him, "the hell with them."

Theresa acknowledged his comments and thanked Kerry for sharing that with her, as did the other members of the group. Tania came in at that point and reinforced what Kerry had been saying. Jake was shaking his head as if he understood that difficulty as well.

Whenever a group member raises a general problem there is usually a specific, recent example that is creating a sense of urgency. I attempted to help Theresa elaborate on her "first offering" by using a skill I call "reaching from the general to the specific" (Shulman 1999).

I asked Theresa if anything had happened recently to make her feel so strongly about this issue. Theresa described an incident that led to a major fight with her boyfriend. They were in a car together and she was in the backseat. There was another woman in the front seat whom she experienced as coming on to her boyfriend. The woman was asking him when they could get together and how much she'd like to "bump and grind" with him on the dance floor. Every time Theresa described this woman's comments, she did an imitation of her, making it sound flirtatious and seductive. Theresa went on with a great deal of anger, saying that her boyfriend didn't even acknowledge that she was in the backseat and that she was his woman. Therefore, this woman, a friend of his, was going on right in front of her, which she felt was "disrespecting" her. She thought her boyfriend was disrespecting her by not stopping the woman and not being aware of her feelings.

I asked if she had talked to her boyfriend about this, and she said she had, but he had just told her that she was "insecure." Theresa said, "Look, I don't know how to deal with this. I try to use a prayer I know from the twelve-step program. Maybe I can pray he can change. But I don't think he's going to change because, even though he is in a twelve-step program, I don't think he's really committed to it. I think he can talk the talk, but he doesn't walk the walk. He's got all the words, but he doesn't practice any of it. I'm not sure he's going to change at all."

Theresa continued: "I realize for both of us this is our first recovery relationship, and I know I have to be patient because he's not where I am in recovery, but still it's very hard to sit in the car and have him disrespect me in that way." She said that she was absolutely furious at this woman and that maybe she ought to go have a talk with the lady. She had a great deal of anger as she pointed to the fact that she was just recently released from the penitentiary and had there learned how to fight (pointing to her two missing lower teeth). She said, "I can ask this lady nicely first, but, if I don't get anywhere, then it's my boot up her ass."

As Theresa's anger grew, I was aware of her pattern, one mirrored by most group members, of using what Bion (1961) described as "fight or flight" to deal with pain. Substance abuse itself is a form of flight and violence is a form of fight. These maladaptive approaches to coping with the underlying feelings and cognitions have proved to be devastating to these group members. Most have been employing these techniques to cope with the deep pain and emotional damage of persistent exploitation and oppression related to gender, sexual orientation, race, and class. My goal was to help the members to become aware of their maladaptive defensive maneuvers. I made use of the idea from twelve-step programs of the primacy of maintaining control over your recovery.

I asked Theresa if that would solve the problem, since it might get rid of this woman, but, if she doesn't resolve the issues with her boyfriend, wouldn't there just be another one? She agreed and seemed a bit deflated. I said that it seemed to me she had to talk to her boyfriend. Also, her anger was so strong that if she did take physical action against this other woman, she might be risking her own recovery and even her own freedom, and the last thing she wanted to do was to end up back in prison on an assault charge. She nodded her head and said, "I know it would mean I'd be losing control of my recovery and giving it to someone else, but I don't know if I could talk to him or if he'll listen to me without just putting me off."

Tania then spoke with great feeling about what an important and wonderful person Theresa was, that she deserved respect, and, if she respected herself, which Tania thought she did, then she should stand up for herself and not let this guy get away with this. She had to tell him directly that she wanted him to make a commitment to her, to recognize her as his woman. Also, if there were these kinds of issues, she had to deal with them out in the open and couldn't let them just fester where she would get angrier and angrier. She said, "If you continue to get this angry, you're just going to hurt yourself, you're going to get sick and eventually you're going to threaten your recovery." Theresa agreed that this was going to be a problem for her.

While Theresa presented a real and painful problem, she had still not focused on her AIDS, even though she said at the start of the session that she wanted to address it. I was conscious of this as I tried to explore why she had accepted the current situation with her boyfriend. I was making what Schwartz (1961) has described as a "demand for work" and what I have called a facilitative confrontation (Shulman 1999). It was a gentle demand in which I asked Theresa to examine her reasons for not pursuing the issues.

I asked Theresa why she let her boyfriend back off when she asked him to talk about his losses and her AIDS. She said, "Well, he told me it was hard to talk about." I responded, "Well, you could have asked him what made it hard. Why do you give up when he resists conversations with you?" There was a long silence, and then Theresa's face softened and she said, "I guess I really don't want to hear." Everyone in the room nodded their head in agreement. I said, "Good for you, Theresa. Now you're taking some responsibility. What are you afraid you're going to hear?" She went on and said, "I'm afraid I'm going to be rejected."

Jake jumped in at that point, with a lot of emotion, and said, "That's the problem when you've got the virus. People reject you." He went on and talked about his own family and how he'd gotten in trouble with the law over a fight; he was in court and nobody knew him in that court. (At a later meeting Jake told us the fight was with a drug dealer who had murdered his sister and had successfully avoided arrest.) He said he was about to get released without having to do jail time because of the fight. He said, "My own mother was in the court and she hurt me deeply—she really pained me—when she stood up and told the judge that I was HIV. Well, that changed everything. These people got real angry at me, and they didn't want a guy getting into fights who was HIV positive, who had the AIDS bug, and they said: "Go to jail.'" He said, "'I couldn't believe the rejection I felt from my mother. I tried to explain it to her later, and she didn't understand that I didn't want her telling people I was HIV, not in those circumstances." He then turned to Theresa and said, "So, I can understand why you're afraid of that rejection." He said, "I think we're all afraid of what people will do once they know we have the virus."

Tania had been very quiet, although I could tell she wanted to speak. At one point, I said, "I think Tania wants to get in here, and she's been well-behaved this session, we have to give her a chance." She smiled and jumped in, telling Theresa how much she admired her, how much strength she had, and that she hoped she could handle her own recovery in the way Theresa was handling hers. She told Theresa that she just deserved a lot more.

Theresa asked Tania whether she thought she was an attractive person. There was a silence and Tania said, "I think you're a beautiful young woman and you could have any man you want." Theresa went on at some length about how men come onto her and, if she wanted to, she could "bump and grind" with them as well. But she didn't want that. She wanted one relationship. She wanted a serious relationship. She said she was getting older now and she wanted a commitment from someone, and this was just not enough, and that was what the issue was all about.

Jake, our often quiet yet very thoughtful member, has changed the norm and broken the taboo by raising the fear of rejection associated with AIDS. Theresa's question to Tania about her looks was an indirect way of getting at the issue of fear of rejection. I tried in the next excerpt to facilitate her expression by articulating her feelings.

> I said to Theresa, "Is the question really that you're afraid that he might not stay with you, that, if you actually confront him on this issue of the other women, that he might leave you?" She agreed that it was her concern. At this point I wondered out loud if it might help Theresa to figure out what she might say to her boyfriend. Theresa said that would be helpful because she didn't know when and how to say it. Then she laughed and said, "Maybe I should say it in bed." Tania said, "Oh no. Don't say it before sex and don't say it after sex." And I added, "And don't say it during sex." Everyone laughed and Tania did a hilarious imitation of having a conversation with Theresa's boyfriend, while pumping up and down as if she were in bed having sex with him.
>
> After the laughter died down, Tania said, "You have to find a quiet time, not a time when you're in the middle of a fight, and you have to just put out your feelings." I asked Tania if she could show Theresa how she could do that. She started to speak as if she were talking to Theresa's boyfriend. I role-played the boyfriend and said, "Oh, but, Theresa, you're just insecure, aren't you?" Tania did a very good job of not letting me put her off and instead putting the issue right where it was whether or not he was prepared to make a commitment or if he was too insecure.
>
> Theresa listened carefully and then said, "I know I have to talk to him, but, you know, he told me that he's not sure he wants to be tied down, that he likes to have his freedom." Jake nodded his head and said, "Yeah, that's the problem, they want their freedom and they don't want to make a commitment, and you're afraid, if you push him, he'll leave you because you've got the virus." Theresa said she realized she had to sit down and talk to him because it couldn't keep up the same way. She would just get too angry and do something crazy and screw up her recovery. She felt she had to find another way to get through to him and talk to him. Otherwise this thing was just going to continue and it was going to tear her up inside.

The session was approaching the ending phase and I wanted to bring the maintenance of recovery issue front and center. This would normally have been a focus of John, my missing co-leader. In Tania's moving response to Theresa, we can see the dynamic of "resonance" as described by Fidele (1994) in her discussion of women's groups and "relational theory" as a resounding or echoing and a capacity for empathy. While the *resonance* term was coined in the research on women's groups, it has obvious importance for all genders and groups.

I said, if she did confront him, it was going to be very rough for her, especially with the holiday, and I wondered whom she'd have for support, especially if he said he didn't want to continue the relationship. She said she had her sponsor, and Tania said, "You also have me. You can call me anytime you want." Tania said, I didn't realize when I started this group there were people who have lived lives just like me, who had feelings just like me, who had struggles just like me. You—you're a woman—you've really helped me see that I'm not the only one going through this. I'd do anything I could to help you."

Once again, Theresa asked Tania how she looked. Theresa said, "You're a woman. I know, as a woman, you will be honest with me and just tell me what you think. Do you think I look OK?" Tania seemed confused and said, "Well, sure, you look wonderful." I said, "I wonder if Theresa is really asking, 'Am I pretty enough? Am I attractive enough? If my boyfriend leaves me, can I find someone else who could love me even though I have AIDS ?'" She said, "That's it" and started to cry. She said, "I'm so afraid, if I lose him, I won't find anyone else." She said, "I know I could have guys, and I know I could have sex, and I like the sex. I sure missed it during the time I was in prison, but can another guy love me?"

A number of group members tried to reassure Theresa, with Tania summarizing by saying, "Theresa, it's not what you look like on the outside, it's what you're like on the inside, and you, honey, you've really got it where it counts."

As we were coming to an end, I asked them what they thought about the evening. I pointed out that some members had said they thought one hour was too long for a group, and yet we had gone an hour and a half. Theresa said everybody was really very helpful. Tania said, "You know, I didn't want to come, but it's turned out really to be OK." Jake said he really enjoyed tonight and he liked my leading the group. (This was the first session during which Jake did not provide a twelve-step group handout. I believed he had now come to understand that this was a different kind of group and could also be helpful.)

I credited Tania for her ability to contain herself, even though many times she felt like just jumping in and speaking. I told her I thought she had been very helpful and supportive in her comments. I also credited Kerry and Jake for sharing painful but very helpful parts of their lives. Finally, I acknowledged Theresa for taking a big risk and sharing her problem with us.

After the meeting ended, I spent a few minutes chatting with one of the staff members in the lobby. Tania came down to sit in the lobby area. She said, "This was a really good meeting," and held up her hand for me to give her a high-five slap. I left the session feeling we had experienced an important turning point in the group's development. I felt that the group members had made the "second decision" and were now in transition to the middle phase of work.

The Middle Phase of Group Development

At the next meeting, attended by my co-leader and myself, Theresa informed me before it began that she had "relapsed" during the week, a comment that initially shook my growing confidence in my work with this new population. I was concerned that I had not balanced work on strong emotional issues with attention to maintaining the member's recovery. My co-leader John was very active in this session, bringing his experience dealing with threats to recovery as he supported Theresa in her struggle.

> When I arrived, Theresa was waiting in the lobby looking very distressed. She said she had almost used on the weekend (she has been eighteen months in recovery and has been an example to the other members). She said, instead of using drugs, she used a man. Since we were a few minutes early, I suggested we go up to the group room and she could tell me what had happened. Theresa sat in the high-backed armchair that Tania had sat in the week before and said, "I'm in Tania's chair."
>
> She told me that she had broken up with her boyfriend, but she had done it in a way that she wasn't proud of. He had been arrested over the weekend and his mother and daughter were in a car crash, so it was a tough weekend for him too. She had wanted to talk to him about what we had discussed at the last meeting (her anger over his "dissing" her in front of another woman), but he had been reluctant to do so. She said she was still very mad at him because of his disrespect for her and that she realized now her motives were really just to get even with him and to hurt him. When I asked her what she did, she said she slept with another man, Jim, and that when she called her boyfriend she left a message on his machine telling him that they were breaking up and also telling him that she had slept with another man.
>
> She said she knew this was not the way that we had suggested that she handle it—that Tania had specifically said not to do it on the phone—to do it in person—but she'd just ignored the advice. She said she was so distressed by this that the "dope fiend" in her took over, the illness took over, and she thought she had to use. Instead of using drugs, she used a man. I acknowledged what a terrible weekend this was for her and asked her if she thought she could share this with the group because I knew they would be concerned about what had happened since last week. She said she would.

When I realized Theresa had not relapsed with drugs or alcohol I felt a wave of relief. I experienced an initial sense of guilt at the thought that at the first meeting I had handled alone I may have led a member to relapse. This was related to my own concerns about leading a "new" type of group with a population new to me. I've since realized I was not able to help or, for that matter, hurt that much. Theresa's recovery was in her own hands and she was going through an important stage in the process.

At 4:30 Jake and Tania arrived. Tania said to Theresa, "You're sitting in my chair." I told Tania I thought Theresa needed that chair this week. Tania immediately sat down next to her and reached out to her and said, "Was it a really bad week?" Theresa said that it was. My co-leader John suggested that we start with thirty seconds of silence.

In reflecting on my co-leader's comment while writing this paper, I believe my co-leader was both falling back on his sense of structure in the face of a painful moment but also perhaps reasserting his role after missing a session. Since we did not discuss this in our debriefing after the session I cannot say with certainty what he was thinking about with this intervention.

In the excerpts that follow it is interesting to note that this threat to Theresa's recovery brought forth from the group and my co-leader numerous comments from their own recovery experience, which make use of metaphors, philosophy, and sayings from their twelve-step programs. I had grown to respect these methods as powerful tools for providing structure at points of crisis. It has taught me, once again, how much we can learn from our group members and from models of helping that may differ from our own.

Theresa told her story to the group members, her words full of strong emotions. Mostly, she said she felt guilty for the way she had acted out and tried to hurt her boyfriend. She said, "My disturbed feelings, my addiction, my disease—they can tell me all kinds of lies, but in my heart, I know I did this to punish him, and I did it badly, and I'm feeling lousy about it. I'm feeling rotten." She said, "I know I was angry at him and he disrespected me, but I cheated on him." She said she didn't feel that was justified. She continued to say she always felt that she had to be open in communication with other people because "you're as sick as your secrets," but, in this case, she thought her motives were just to hurt him. I said, "Because you felt he had hurt you." She agreed.

She said, I'm really in love with him and now I think I have broken it up for good, and it's really upsetting, especially with Christmas coming." Tania, who had been sitting quietly, asked if she could speak. She turned to Theresa and said, "You were wrong to do it on the phone. It was a bad way to handle it, but you had a right to be angry and, remember, he started it." Theresa said that she felt really guilty and out of control through the whole situation and all she could do now was pray and try to forgive herself. Tania said to Theresa, "You seem to be taking all the responsibility for this. Don't you think he had a part in it as well?" At that point Theresa got angry again and said, "He did disrespect me. He didn't treat me right. He treated me like his ho instead of his woman."

Tania said, "I know it's rough and you didn't handle it well, but the point is, you're standing up for yourself. You're not letting him treat you like his ho. He wasn't ready to make a commitment to you. He kept ducking all the conversations when you tried to have one with him, so maybe it's better you brought it about now." John said, "You've got a lot of mixed emotions right here," and he described her ambivalence.

Theresa said that she had been faithful to her boyfriends even when she was using. She said, "Even when I was on the street tricking—I was with no man even while I was sleeping with a lot of men." She said, "What I am upset about is that this weekend with Jim—I was a dope fiend with this man, I was using him, and that's just as bad as using drugs. She continued, "I don't know what to do. I am at a loss now. I know I started to put my boyfriend before my recovery. All I can do now is put it in the hands of God. I went to a meeting every day since I made that call and I called my sponsor, and she was helpful as well." Theresa said, "I know you can't keep doing the same thing and looking for different results," and said that this is what happens in all her relationships with men.

Tania, with a lot of emotion, told her "using sex is not like using drugs." John said, to Tania, "You're taking it personally and it might be different for Theresa." Tania said, "She is not addicted to sex, so using a man during the weekend was not as dangerous as using drugs, because she is addicted to them." At this point Theresa got up to get a bagel and was standing in the room and laughed and said, "Who says I'm not addicted to sex?" And then she wiggled her hips and said, "I can be a little nymphomaniac if I want to."

I pointed out that Theresa has told us a number of things on one side of the ledger, she had stood up for herself and asked her boyfriend to treat her with respect and not to continue without commitment. On the other side, she had done it badly. On the good side, she hadn't used drugs, and she went to her resources—her sponsor, her meetings—so she took steps to stay in control. On the other side of the ledger, she used a guy, which she felt guilty and badly about. Theresa said, "I am upset and I am guilty, cause sex is like a drug for me."

Relapses are very much a part of the recovery process. The members and the group leaders attempted to help Theresa see that her choice of relapse was one that reduced the possible harm to her and her recovery. In the recovery process the important thing is to learn from your relapse experiences.

Tania said, "Look, Theresa, if you did drugs, you wouldn't be here today." John asked how long she had been seeing this guy Jim, and she said, "Not long at all." John said that it's not unusual to put a guy or a woman on the "layaway plan." "You come on a little, you let him know you're interested, and, when you need him later, you can cash him in."

I reminded everyone that Theresa had told us last week that one of her real fears of losing her boyfriend was that, because she had AIDS, she would not be able to find another man to love her. My co-leader John said, "You know, Theresa, what I am seeing in you is a lot of progress You held on to your eighteen-month recovery. You didn't do the drugs. You were upset. You needed something, but you didn't collapse. You're taking responsibility for the motives about what you did and you're not trying to explain it away."

Theresa said she was just so angry at her boyfriend. I said, "I think you're also very angry at yourself." Tania said, "All I'm seeing right here is that you didn't use." John said, "You picked the lesser of two evils, but you picked the one that you could walk away from." Tania said, "Don't feel guilty about having slept with a guy. Men have been doing this for years. They don't worry about it. They get a lot of macho bullshit when they're sleeping with women, and it doesn't matter whether they care about them or not. Take my word for it, I've been both! I've been a guy and a woman, and I know that's all people care about: sex—sex and money. When I was prostituting—and I'm not proud of that—for over twenty years, I slept with judges, I slept with teachers, I slept with businessmen, I slept with politicians, and all they cared about was getting sex. If you have enough money, you can get sex."

John, my co-leader, said "Let's get back to what happened. Breaking up is really painful. It's one of the really difficult times when you're in recovery because you're going through all that pain and you can't use the drug to make it go away." Theresa said she also lost her sponsee, a fifteen year old that she was working with. She said the sponsee wanted to switch to another one—she felt that Theresa was going through too much right now to help her. I said, "So, you've had a lot of rejection this week."

The meeting continued with members offering Theresa examples from their own life experiences where they had gone through similar rejections and how these had impacted on them. They were reassuring her that her response was understandable and reminding her that she had chosen a less damaging relapse. In Jake's story he described how a woman, to get to his brother, used him and how when he broke up with her he broke up with his brother as well. He went on to describe the way he cuts himself off to protect himself. Jake said:

"So, I've closed my door, shut off my phone, and I stay in my room and cut myself off because I know, if I try to get close, people are going to hurt me again, and then that's going to stop my recovery." I reminded everyone that Jake had said he had stayed home on Thanksgiving Day, cooked his own turkey, and just had his meal in his room. And Jake said, "And I ate the whole thing." The group members all laughed with him.

Jake went on to say that going to school had given him a new direction. He told everyone in the group he had a great day today because the place he is training and working in picked him as employee of the month, and they had even said he was going to be awarded employee of the year. There was a great deal of pride in his face and voice as he described this. The rest of the group members all burst out in applause and said, "At a way to go," "Nice going, Jake." He went on to say, "I wear a suit when I go to work every day," and he pointed to the jacket he was wearing at the meeting, "because I want to dress right and feel good about myself. I've also wanted to stop taking on other people's nonsense."

He turned to Theresa and said, "For most men it's tough not to think about women as just sexual objects and to treat them as if they had no dignity." He said, when he didn't have any self-esteem himself, it was hard to treat women as equals, as persons you could really care about. I pointed out he was now getting a lot of his self-esteem from his work, and he agreed.

At this point I said to the group it seemed to me that there was a struggle going on here. It was all or nothing. You could have relationships with people and experience a lot of pain, a lot of rejection, especially with the AIDS virus, or do nothing, close your door, cut off your phone, don't have sex, just withdraw. The feeling I get is that you've rarely, if ever, had relationships with people who cared about you and didn't exploit you, and so, as far as you're concerned, there's no middle ground.

Tania turned to Jake, who was on the couch, and said, "You know, maybe if I could find a guy like you, Jake, a guy who could talk about his feelings, a guy who could be sensitive, maybe I could have a relationship again, but men aren't like that out there." She went on to talk about her twenty years of prostituting and how sex and money was what it was all about. I pointed out to Tania that she said Jake was different, and, if he could be different, there might be other men out there who could be different as well. And Jake said, "My HIV gave me a perspective. It made me think about life. I know, when you get the rejection, it's devastating, but you can't let that take you over, otherwise you give up your recovery."

Jake had given us out a list at the beginning of the meeting of fifteen things one should think about when one is in trouble to help the recovery keep going. He always made copies of material he received from his recovery group and brought them in to the members. At this point Tania referred to Jake's list and said, "Number 5 is what it's all about. Number 5 really is the story." She went on to quote number 5 on the list, in which the question was "Do you fear the unknown?" Theresa said, "That's what I'm afraid of—the unknown. If I lose my boyfriend, who's going to take his place?"

Theresa went on to say, "But the trust issue has been broken now. It's really been broken. I have to give him telephone numbers now, so he knows where he can reach me any time during the day. That doesn't feel right. I don't think I should be doing that." John said, "I don't think you need to leave numbers for him. The die is cast. The deed is done, and you have to deal with that now, and maybe it's not going to be possible to "remake the relationship." Theresa said, "I feel stuck on stupid" (a recovery expression meaning that one keeps making the same "stupid" mistakes). Tania reminded Theresa that her boyfriend started it with the "bitch." "He dissed you. Now the way you handled it on the telephone—that wasn't very ladylike, but you were too upset to handle it any other way."

After some additional discussion, we went back to Theresa.

Theresa said that she really tried to hurt him and she was still feeling badly about that. John said, "Didn't you really hurt yourself, Theresa?" She was quiet for a moment and then said, "Yes, I did. I know I do some of this stuff. I just want some attention, any kind of attention, even if I have to screw myself. At least someone pays attention."

She continued, "This is really hard to deal with in recovery." Tania said, "You know, you sound like you were a 'scorned woman.'" Theresa recovered her anger at that point and said, "I'm mad. I'm really mad at him because I let him interfere with my recovery. He has not been taking his recovery seriously. He goes to the groups and he talks the talk, but he doesn't walk the walk."

My co-leader asked, "What are you expecting in the relationship? Maybe you're expecting too much. Maybe it's a waste of energy. Maybe you're setting yourself up to fail." Theresa said, "I have to give him time." Tania said, "Look, if it's not going to work out, isn't it better that it happened now instead of after five years? I know it's painful." John agreed with Tania that, if it was going to break up, it was better to do it now rather than later. Theresa said, "I had high expectations," and then she began to cry. "I was getting sober," she said. "I was OK. I was dealing with my problems. I didn't need another man. I was having fun with friends. I had girlfriends, people I could talk to, but I just didn't give time, time." John told Tina that she had a lot of mixed feelings right now—the stress, the anger, a lot of negative energy. He wondered whether she shouldn't be careful in the next few weeks as she tried to make a decision about what to do next.

Theresa said, 'It would be a lot easier if it wasn't the holidays. The holidays make it so much harder." Tania said, "Look, you were honest, you respected yourself. You may not have handled it well, but you were being grown up." Theresa said, "Maybe I didn't give it enough time. Maybe I should have waited a bit, cause he told me he loved me. He told me he was going to buy a ring and that he wanted to marry me." I pointed out that there was at least a possibility that he may have been trying to hurt her back when he said that.

Tania and others in the group agreed. Theresa said, "I felt violated by this guy." John asked what she was going to do over the holiday. She said she was going to go see her baby girl, and she bought her a present, a little bracelet, which she has to get fixed for her (her child had been taken away by the Department of Social Services and was living with a grandmother). Theresa continued to cry and said, "I need some answers. What should I do? What should I do? You have to tell me what to do." My co-leader said, "No one can do that, Theresa. You will have to decide what to do yourself."

I asked Theresa how she was going to get through the next week or so. She said she was going to meetings regularly, and her sponsor had been really helpful. And then she turned to Tania and said, "And I can call you if I need to, can't I?" Tania said, "Anytime, anytime. I feel a lot of love and respect for you, and I would do any-thing I can to help you get through this." Jake said, "You can call me too." Theresa said, "I tried, but I couldn't get through." Jake said he turned his phone off from incoming calls, because sometimes he just wanted to be alone. I said to Jake that, if he did want to connect up with other people, he'd have to turn his phone back on again.

The group meeting came to a close at that point. Theresa seemed more at peace when she left. I continued to feel that the mutual aid was building in the group and that members were learning how to construct nonexploitive and caring relationships.

So what have I learned from this experience? I have learned to have more re-spect for other models of helping and to be prepared to draw upon them when they are appropriate for different populations. I have seen the powerful way in which clients who are different in so many ways can reach out to each other in aid of their mutual recovery and their struggle with a powerful and deadly illness. My belief that social work with groups and the concept of mutual aid is a crucial element in helping this population also has been reinforced. As a profession, we have much to offer the field of substance abuse and AIDS counseling. Our unique contributions and our understanding of mutual aid as a healing process can be integrated into a wide range of approaches. And, most of all, I have learned once again how resilient our most damaged clients can be, the incredi-ble strength and caring they can demonstrate when we provide the medium of a mutual aid support group and help them use it to help each other.

Note

The author acknowledges drawing upon case material used in an earlier presentation, entitled "Crossing Boundaries: A Support Group for Persons with AIDS in Early Sub-stance Abuse Recovery," at the annual meeting of the Association for the Advancement of Social Work with Groups, Quebec City, Quebec, Canada, October 2003.

References

Bennis, W. G. and H. A. Shepard. 1956. A theory of group development. *Human Relations* 9(4): 415–37.
Bion, W. R. 1961. Experience in groups. In W. R. Bion, *Experience in groups and other pa-pers*. London: Tavistock.
Fidele, N. 1994. *Relationship in groups: Connections, resonance, and paradox*. Wellesley, Mass.: Stone Center.
Hardesty, L. and G. L. Greif. 1993. Common themes in a group for female IV drug users who are HIV positive. *Journal of Psychoactive Drugs* 26(3): 289–93.

Matano, R. A. and I. D. Yalom. 1991. Approaches for chemical dependency: Chemical dependency and interactive group therapy, a synthesis. *International Journal of Group Psychotherapy* 41(3): 269–93.

Prochaska, J. O. and C. C. DiClemente. 1986. Toward a comprehensive model of change. In W. R. Miller and N. Heather, eds., *Treating addictive behaviors: Process of change.* New York: Plenum.

Schwartz, W. 1961. *The social worker in the group: The social welfare forum,* pp. 146–77. New York: Columbia University Press.

Shulman, L. 1999. *The skills of helping individuals, families, and groups.* 4th ed. Itasca, Ill.: Peacock.

Chapter 11

Sharing the Secrets
The Power of Women's Groups for Sexual Abuse Survivors

Linda Yael Schiller and Bonnie Zimmer

D URING THE later part of the twentieth century the field of sexual abuse treatment has gained greater depth and authenticity as previously silent and silenced survivors spoke out and the fields of social work and other allied mental health professions responded with research, inquiry, and specialized treatment planning. Prior to that, survivors' accounts of their histories were often disbelieved and denied, their symptoms and suffering misdiagnosed, misunderstood, and mistreated.

Beginning with the feminist inquiry into domestic violence in the 1970s, the veil of silence began to lift as survivors of abuse spoke up. We began to break through our own denial of the darker realities of life inside American families and to admit that in many families children were not safe and that home was far from a haven. Trusted institutions such as youth groups, schools, and even religious organizations have also been exposed as occasionally harboring sexual predators as children and years later adults disclose the abuse that occurred at the hands of some community leaders as well as family members. Consequently, there has been a kind of revolution in the diagnosis, research, and treatment of adult survivors of childhood sexual abuse (Herman 1992).

Current FBI statistics state that one in three girls and one in six boys will be sexually abused or assaulted before they reach the age of eighteen. To the best of our knowledge, 40 to 60 percent of outpatients and 50 to 60 percent of inpatients in psychiatric treatment report childhood histories of physical or sexual abuse or both. Psychiatric emergency room studies report figures as high as 70 percent (Herman 1992:122). Most researchers agree that the best studies still do not reflect the actual prevalence of sexual abuse and assault but only the reported cases. Experts agree that the actual numbers are even higher. With figures this high, we can assume that all social workers, in the course of their careers, will be working with survivors of trauma and sexual abuse. All social workers need specific training to help us provide caring, compassionate, and informed interventions on behalf of survivors of childhood trauma.

Developmental Tasks and Issues

Developmental theorists agree that the primary task of the first stage of life is the achievement of a sense of basic trust, which thrives inside the secure intimate relationship between child and caregiver(s) (Erikson 1963:222–43). When the caregiving relationship is twisted into one of sexual exploitation and coercion, the child's sense of trust is shattered. She learns that the world is not safe, does not contain the necessary resources she needs to thrive and grow, and is therefore frustrating, unsatisfying, and dangerous. In cases where the perpetrator is someone other than the primary caregiver, the child still experiences a sense of being unprotected by her caregivers, which in turn violates the feeling of basic trust. Without resolving this essential basic task, the child enters future developmental stages at a distinct disadvantage.

The next stage of development involves the establishment of a sense of autonomy, primarily experienced by the thrill of learning the word *no*. By implementing this word, the child differentiates herself from her caregivers, discovers her own limits and boundaries, and exercises control over her complex environment. When a child is sexually abused her right to say no is removed. The child experiences herself as impotent, unable to control her environment. The resulting impact is the establishment of an identity shaped by shame and self-doubt and an increasing sense of danger. One group member said, "We were never safe. Even between rages, we were simply waiting for the next time my father would explode. And I could never go to bed at night without wondering if I'd get through the night without his beer-smelling visit. I still don't feel safe, even though he has been dead for ten years now. As for sleeping through the night, well, I think I've tried every sleeping medication there is."

As the young victim/survivor moves on into the later stages of development, the legacies of her earlier losses can follow. Establishing a sense of mastery, the task of the school-age years, is complicated by the child's isolation, lack of trust in self and environment, and the daily exhaustion of maintaining the secret and facing further abuse at home. We need to honor with our clients the enormous energy they used up to maintain family secrets and to simply survive assault in the domestic arena of the family home. For some there was little left over with which to pursue the nonessential tasks of mastery or self-enrichment.

The establishment of healthy, flexible coping mechanisms is one of the most essential tasks of the early years. We all begin our lives with only the most primitive defenses against psychological harm, and as we develop we replace these primitive defenses with more mature, more flexible, more reality-based coping mechanisms. Because of the developmental disorganization that accompanies sexual abuse, survivors come for help with a fixed set of rigid defenses, which include splitting and projective identification. These two defenses make negotiating the world of interpersonal relationships very difficult. The capacity to tolerate ambivalence and the perception of one's self as separate and autonomous are requirements for healthy, happy adult relationships. Because of the impact of abuse, and the freezing of early defenses, relationships can become minefields for many survivors.

With these difficulties in navigating through interpersonal relationships, survivors become further isolated. The sense of shame that accompanies victimization, coupled with the silence and secrecy imposed by the abuser, serve to further encapsulate the growing child in a world of her own. One of our group members referred to this as her "hermetically sealed glass bubble," while another experienced a "roaring sound" that prevented her from hearing the words of others and contributed to her sense of aloneness and despair.

A distorted body image is another developmental impact of early sexual trauma. Survivors describe feeling "out of my body," "existing only from the neck up," or "being at war" with their bodies. Their ability to feel integrated and intact has been severely impaired by the acts of abuse. This can lead to other "out of control" body experiences, including eating and sleep disorders and difficulties with the regulation of mood, arousal, and emotional responses to stimuli. A roller coaster experience of life follows, and the survivor may have serious trouble soothing and regulating her distress.

One of the consequences of repeated trauma is that the victim experiences stuck or frozen places in her development. Both research and anecdotal evidence indicate that there is a correlation between the time the abuse began (age of onset) and the developmental delays in a person's adult life. Sanford calls this phenomenon "developmental disorganization."[1] In other words, if a woman began being abused at the age of four, she will most likely have some parts of her development "frozen," along with the trauma, at the age of four. She might experience difficulties in establishing personal safety, in making sound judgments, and in cognitive areas such as understanding a correlation between events or recognizing options or choices in her life. Using this same four-year-old girl as an example, the adult she has become may truly not know how to protect herself any better now in some situations than she did when she was four. If the choice or option for saying no was taken from her then, leaving her helpless in the face of the abuse, she may still experience this same sense of helplessness as an adult.

One example of developmental disorganization occurred in a group meeting. Sally, a twenty-two-year-old college student, initiated a group discussion.

> SALLY: I was at a party last Saturday night and I met this man there. At first he seemed nice, and he offered to drive me home afterward. I accepted. As the evening wore on he proceeded to get very drunk. I was scared to death when it came time to leave. All the way home I was sure that he would hit someone or something at any moment. I was so relieved to get out of the car at the end.

WORKER: You sure were lucky that you got home safely. Did it occur to you at any point, Sally, that it would have been OK to change your mind and not take the ride from him when you saw he had been drinking too much?

BRIDGET: Yeah, you could have found another ride home.

ANDREA: Or taken a cab.

SALLY: No, I never thought of that. I felt that since I already said yes that I had to go with him.

WORKER: What do others think?

BRIDGET: I think that you—all of us—have the right to change our minds.

CARMEN: And not put yourself in potentially dangerous situations.

SALLY: You know, that never occurred to me. I only thought that since he was expecting me to go with him, that I had to.

WORKER: Does anyone else ever feel like Sally described here—that you forget sometimes that you have options or that it is OK to say no or change your mind?

CARMEN: All the time. I could really relate to what you were saying. Sometimes it's like a part of me shuts down and it's the five-year-old part of me making the decisions, or saying these things, not the adult part of me.

Current research points to trauma theory as the most useful framework in which to work with survivors of sexual abuse (Courtois 1988; Figley 1985; van der Kolk 1987). Briefly, trauma theory holds that the range of symptomatology seen in survivors is not "pathological." Rather, these symptoms are seen as adaptive responses to the horror of abuse. What were once necessary skills for survival have now become barriers to positive and healthy living. Social work theory and practice fits in well with the field of trauma theory. Social workers have long recognized the importance of looking at the whole person and of taking into account both the external environmental factors as well as the internal intrapsychic ones in the evaluation and treatment of clients.

Social work practice stresses an environmental or holistic approach to practice that incorporates the interactive influence of family, social environment, and cultural context. We address with our survivor clients what it was like to grow up in a family where oppression, victimization, and secrecy were the norms of their daily lives, considering how this atmosphere both in their families of origin as well as in the larger societal system has influenced their lives as adults. Understanding the history and context of their current struggles helps to shape our interventions and allows us to engage with clients from a more truly empathic stance.

Another way in which social work and trauma theories interface is in their recognition of the impact of oppression on human development. Sexual abuse is by definition oppressive as it involves the sexual exploitation of a less powerful person by a person who holds greater power. For survivors this oppression comes not only from outside but also from within the supposedly safe haven of the family. Survivors frequently internalize their oppression and their sense that they have no voice into a false sense of responsibility for the abuse. Healing and recovery requires that they reclaim their own voice and inner core of self, that they are finally heard and believed, and that the reality of their personal narrative be accepted as such. Being heard, believed, and supported by others, both in individual and group work, is one of the primary healing sources for survivors.

Having one's private reality validated and supported by other survivors is healing and empowering. As one survivor in a group stated, "Having the guard down between my private sadness and the public expression of it was awesome." Member after member stated that the most powerful aspect of the group experience was being heard by others and listening to others' similar experiences. "Both hearing and telling knocked me out."

Vulnerabilities and Risk Factors and Resilience and Protective Factors

A child is extremely vulnerable to adult exploitation. What may begin as a low-key, noncoercive game or activity often leads to the gradual escalation of physical contact. The perpetrator imposes total secrecy through threats of harm to the child or mother, grandmother, or siblings. Out of fear the child maintains the secret and remains vulnerable and at risk to retraumatization. The child copes by feigning sleep or dissociating from the experience. Unfortunately, too many such situations are never discovered, and the adult/child is left with distorted body, trust, and intimacy issues. If the abuse is accidentally disclosed, such as through the observation of a third party because of a sexually transmitted disease, physical injury, inappropriate sexual activity, or pregnancy, or if the victim directly discloses, the child is further vulnerable to the reaction of family members and public officials. The offender will do everything possible to undermine and destroy the youngster's credibility. The child may be pressured to retract the disclosure. At this moment the child faces the terrible burden of potentially breaking up the family and being abandoned. It takes tremendous courage to sustain the disclosure. And if family members do not believe the youngster or turn against her or him, the child experiences further betrayal and being alone in the world. If public officials are not sensitive and skilled, the youngster suffers from yet another affront.

Finkelhor and Browne (1985) suggest that sexual abuse effects four life domains: traumatized sexuality, betrayal, powerlessness, and stigmatization. Sexually abused children are at risk of having their sexual identity shaped in developmentally inappropriate ways. Sex and manipulation, sex and force, sex and secrecy, sex and fear become intertwined. Consequences include sexual promiscuity, prostitution, sexual aversion, flashbacks, depression, and eating disorders. The sense of betrayal by the adult world creates a lack of trust, a sense of hopelessness, hypervigilence, relationship with violent and manipulative partners, and chronic grief. Repeated violation of a child's body and space leads to a sense of powerlessness and resultant low self-esteem, chronic fear and anxiety, night-mares, phobias, somatic illnesses, compensatory aggressive behaviors, etc. Child sexual abuse also carries a powerful social stigma. The child is made to feel like "damaged goods"—ashamed and guilty. Self-alienation can lead to depression and suicide attempts and to the numbing power of substance abuse.

During abuse, victims experience a violation of personal integrity, an ex-ploitation of their vulnerability, relative weakness, and youth. Sexual abuse is a criminal act and a physical assault, profoundly distorting and blurring the dis-tinction between nurturing and sexual activity. In general, it has profound and long-lasting negative consequences for the victim. The nature of this kind of as-sault encompasses physical, emotional, cognitive, and spiritual elements. Clients state that during and subsequent to the physical acts of violation their emotion-al responses are either in fight or flight mode, thinking shuts down or becomes distorted, and the spirit itself is frequently described as "soul shattered." It is not by coincidence that abuse survivors often feel an affinity with Holocaust survivors.

The most widely accepted diagnosis currently available for adult survivors of sexual abuse is post-traumatic stress disorder (PTSD) (American Psychiatric As-sociation 1995:247–51). The use of this diagnosis, originally developed to under-stand the experiences of combat veterans, has shifted both the diagnostic understanding of and the approach to the treatment of survivors of sexual trau-ma. The diagnosis of PTSD implies that, had the trauma not occurred, we would likely not see the presenting problems and symptoms. This way of thinking is in stark contrast to earlier misdiagnoses, which implied that survivors suffered from personality disorders or from a failure on the part of the individual to de-velop adequate psychic structures. The DSM-IV states that, by definition, the na-ture of the traumatic event(s) "would be markedly distressing to almost anyone." Depathologizing and universalizing the consequent traumatic responses are an important step in helping an adult survivor move from self-blame, guilt, and shame to an ability to contextualize their responses to the abuse and move for-ward to healing their life. One survivor, Eve, sums up in her own words what Gelinas (1983) calls the "persistent negative effects of incest."

So I give you a random selection, in alphabetical order:

amnesia
anxiety
depression
fear of the dark
endless tears
flashbacks
guilt
insomnia

nightmares
panic attacks
rage
self mutilation
sexual dysfunction
shame
suicide attempts
trembling
being a victim
violent relationships
years of therapists' bills.[2]

Recent scientific advances in brain imaging also show us that traumatic memory is laid down differently than nontraumatic memory. Van der Kolk, McFarlane, and Weisaeth (1996) indicate that during a traumatic experience a more primitive part of the brain (the limbic system) takes over some of the usual functions of our thinking brain. Lang (cited in van der Kolk, McFarlane, and Weisaeth 1996:221) states that the emotionally laden images are stored as "associative networks" that can be triggered or reactivated when a person faces situations similar to the original trauma. Memory of traumatic events may be imprinted in other sensory modalities such as smell, sound, or sensation rather than in linguistic and/or visual modes. In addition, because of this differential laying down of memory, the events are not processed as they ordinarily would be; rather the abusive memories and emotions get "stuck," and become recycled over and over without gaining the relief usually experienced by reviewing material. This knowledge supports the use of expressive arts therapies and multimodal work with our survivor clients both individually and in groups so that activities that engage different parts of our brain and our systems can be used to help "unfreeze" or "unstick" these frozen places. It also implies the importance of keeping ourselves educated on current emerging treatment modalities, particularly in the mind/body/energy fields that show real promise in targeting these recycling or stuck emotions and thoughts and allowing our clients to reprocess them and thus to move on.[3]

The earlier the abuse began the more basic and profound are the developmental tasks that were missed. When the abuse is compounded by multiple abusers, other forms of violence or neglect, substance abuse or "prolonged, repeated trauma," we can then see what Herman calls "Complex PTSD" (Herman 1992). This can include symptoms or patterns on all five axes of the DSM IV, which may include a variety of somatic complaints and/or dissociative phenomenon.

While children who are sexually abused are harmed by the abuse, and develop protective defenses that may become obstacles to later development, they often develop remarkable coping skills and competencies in surviving and adapting to the trauma they experience. Many survivors have extraordinary sensitivity to others, excellent "antennae" for sensing danger, profound protective motivation toward children, an impulse toward social action, and a deep sensitivity to injustice. We emphasize these strengths as a way to balance the following discussion of symptoms, as a reminder that survivors can be strong, creative, and resilient. We urge the reader to remember the importance of openly noting the strengths and competencies in our clients even as we help them come to terms with the effects of trauma in their lives.

One of the factors that promote resilience for both children and adults who have been victimized is the presence in their life of other supportive nonabusive individuals. Whether it is a family member, a friend, a teacher, or a counselor, having supportive others who believe and protect the child is one of the best assurances against developing long-standing and serious symptomatology.

Practice and Group Context

The context for our groups is the arena of private practice. After spending many years connected to public agencies, we found that private practice offered a unique framework for doing this work. A number of factors contribute to the differences between running a group within an agency and running one in a private practice setting.

One of the primary factors is the issue of confidentiality. There is usually a blanket of confidentiality that surrounds an agency as a whole, but within the agency workers are free to discuss, process, and share cases. In addition, in a private practice setting clients are less likely to encounter others from their community in the waiting or common areas. Both of these may be factors for survivors, who may carry a great deal of shame around their reason for seeking help and prefer to have both their confidentiality and their privacy kept at a maximum. The lesser the risk of inadvertently running into someone they know coming into or out of their group meeting, the greater the sense of control members have regarding the information that they are a member of a group for survivors of sexual abuse.

Other differences involve the mechanics of running a group. At an agency an administrative staff generally does fee setting and collecting, and the referral base for potential clients is within the agency. In private practice the workers do these tasks themselves, and thus issues around money frequently take on a clinical significance. Decisions must be made around the fee itself, whether or not insurance will be accepted, and how and when the payment will be collected. Some of the ways that clinical issues can be expressed through money are clients who continually "forget" their payments, bounce checks, or continue to look for special exception after policies have been clearly articulated. Sometimes "hush" money or bribes are given to children by their offenders, thus adding another complicating dimension to the issue of money and counseling.

The referral base for a group in private practice may consist of colleagues of the facilitators also in private practice, agencies in the area, and the workers' individual caseloads. Some form of advertising is generally done, through word of mouth, ads, or mailings of written notices. Related to the issue of referral base is the relationship between the client's individual counseling and their group counseling. In this model, a short-term time-limited group (the details of which will be elaborated shortly), one of the criteria for participation is that each member concurrently be involved in individual counseling and that she not change the frequency of her individual work for the duration of the group. This criterion is implemented because the group can often be very provocative and stir up previously unfelt feelings or unremembered memories. Therefore, it is crucial that the survivor have her outside support system intact and constant in order to have a place to go with these thoughts and feelings as they arise.

In evaluating clients from the workers' own caseloads, several issues are considered. First, both the client and the worker each take a look at how they feel about sharing with others, the time they are used to having on an individual basis. If the worker decides to broach the subject of "group" to individuals in her own caseload, a respectful decision-making process takes place. Some clients choose not to participate in their individual worker's group but request a referral to a group with other facilitators. If co-facilitators are screening their own clients the principle of "not only one" is held to wherever possible. (See Gitterman, this volume.) In other words, an effort is made not to have only one member of any subgroup, whether it be based on race, ethnicity, sexual orientation, or the "only" client who has one of the facilitators as an individual worker.

A complex relationship often develops between the individual and group services for group members. Workers must carefully consider the potential impact of this interaction on both the individuals as well as on the group as a whole. The group format can serve to either enhance or call into question the relationship a client has with her individual worker. Our clients commented on the relationship between individual work and group work as follows:

"I feel like work in the group expands on individual counseling."

"Having my worker in the group made incorporating the growth in both situations easier."

"The group turned up the heat under the central question of trust, both within the group and with my worker."

Group workers can also become the bearers of transference, but it is generally more diluted because of the short-term nature of the group and the co-leadership format. The literature on group treatment of survivors of abuse is unanimous in recommending co-leadership (Courtois 1988:262–73). The complex dynamics of a group of this nature necessitate two facilitators to balance the needs of the group as a whole with the frequently diverse needs of the individual members. Great demands are placed on the worker by the intensity of the group process and emotional content. A co-worker model allows for mutual worker support and shared observation and processing of group dynamics and issues.

The criterion of concurrent individual and group counseling specifically requires that a client must be in individual counseling that directly deals with the issues of abuse for a period of at least six months prior to the group's beginning. There are three reasons for this criterion: it ensures some prior basis for this work, it gives members a chance to have developed a relationship and support system specifically regarding the abuse, and it provides some homogeneity for members regarding healing process. Group workers ask prospective clients to sign release of information forms allowing them to make collateral contact with their individual workers at the time of the intake interview. The opinion of the worker as to the client's readiness or suitability for this type of group is taken into account during the screening process.

The groups we have run have been composed of adult women ranging in age from early twenties to late forties. There is no outer age limit, and the youngest age limit is simply postadolescence. In spite of adult life-cycle developmental differences with this range of ages, our experience has shown that the commonality of survivors' experiences surpasses the age differences. Andrea stated, "At first I was really worried about being older. I thought 'what are all these girls doing here?' But after a while the difference of age just melted away."

As mentioned earlier, we try to adhere to the "not only one" principle in determining group membership. We are not always able to achieve this. In one group we screened in one lesbian woman, allowing her to make the choice to participate or not once it became apparent that no other lesbians were referred for this group cycle. She chose to join and later stated, "At first I was heavily guarded, not sure if there were other lesbians in the group or even other feminists. Many of my stereotypes of 'mainstream' women were broken as their courage became clearer to me. I found myself admiring all the women in the group for how they used their courage in committing acts of defiance in their own world."

Group services can be an important part of the healing process for adult survivors. The nature of the group format itself is a powerful antidote to the legacy of secrecy, silence, and shame. Here, as members both share and bear witness to each other, they find comfort in their common histories and struggles. Let us look at the overall goals of healing from the trauma of sexual abuse and at the recovery process itself. Then we can examine where and how group services fit into this process.

The *healing process* as outlined by Herman occurs in three stages: 1. safety, 2. remembrance and mourning, and 3. reconnection. But, first, a word of caution.

We need to remember that human growth and development moves in spirals rather than in a continuum. We often find ourselves struggling through a drama we thought was finished, even though in the present we experience it with a deeper level of understanding. Survivors should not be expected to follow a straight course in their healing. These stages should be conceptualized as an overview, not as a recipe for change (Herman 1992:207).

The first stage involves the establishment of safety on several levels. First of all, the abuse must have stopped. Though it may be difficult to imagine, many survivors who come to therapy are still suffering from overt or subtle forms of abuse by their perpetrators. Perhaps their abusing uncle still fondles them at family gatherings or inappropriately kisses them when saying good-bye. Perhaps the woman feels she still cannot say no to demands placed on her by her perpetrator for obedience or participation in illegal, unsafe activities (like drugs or prostitution). Whatever the circumstances of the original abuse, it is essential that social workers ask carefully phrased questions to ascertain that the abuse itself has, in total, ended. If abuse is ongoing, the worker's primary task is to empower and guide the woman to a place where she can act to end the ongoing victimization in her life.

Once the survivor has established safety from ongoing abuse, she can turn to the task of establishing personal safety on other levels. At this time women must focus on achieving sobriety from substance abuse and other addictions. For women who have developed self-abusive behaviors, achieving safety from themselves is the task at this stage. Women must learn to stop hurting their bodies before they are able to truly move on to subsequent healing stages that follow. Inexperienced workers, eager to obtain full disclosures, may easily err during this stage and fail to help their clients establish adequate safety first. This risks client safety, however. The maxim "do no harm" must be applied here both in regards to the client about herself and for the worker to curb an eagerness that may put her ahead of her client's readiness or abilities.

A frequently asked question is what to do with disclosures or discussions of sexual abuse during the early recovery period in sobriety. While the focus of the work at this time needs to remain on maintaining sobriety, the issues around abuse cannot simply be ignored to be "dealt with later," as has sometimes been the case. Rather, an empathic and respectful acknowledgment of the abuse history, as well as its potential impact and contribution to the problem of substance abuse, needs to be part of the treatment plan, while the main focus remains on recovery skills.

During this stage clients learn self-soothing, self-containing, and grounding skills and enhance their abilities to manage strong emotion. They work to establish a wide and well-balanced system of support. They must also learn to reach out for help in order to keep themselves safe. Once safety is established (and this can be a lengthy process, taking several years for many survivors of chronic long-term abuse), survivors can move to the next stage of remembering and mourning.

In this second stage survivors testify to their experiences of abuse and victimization. For women who have dissociated from their feelings or their memories, it is a time to retrieve their lost histories and to be heard and believed by workers and by their peers. Many survivors report that in telling their stories and being believed by others they come to believe in themselves for the first time. Jordan (1991:288) states, "Healing occurs when a person returns to the pain of the past, and finds that this time she is no longer alone." As the history of abuse becomes clarified for the survivor, she begins to experience, sometimes for the first time, the multiple losses that accompanied the abuse. The loss of safety, of physical integrity, of childhood, of protection, of faith, of life's meaning must all be acknowledged and mourned. Many survivors go through a period of deep, existential grief. Women must be encouraged to proceed through this grief. In order to fully recover from loss and regain hope and faith, we must fully mourn all the losses. A song our group members have used for inspiration, "Baptism of Fire," includes the chorus, "the only way out is through" (Snow 1981.) During this stage survivors need much reassurance about getting through and finding purpose and meaning in their lives beyond the loss.

The final stage articulated by Herman is reconnection. Reconnection occurs on several levels. First of all, the survivor is now free to reconnect with the parts of her that once held the secret of the abuse. This can include reclaiming the part of her that resists, says no, and fights back. The survivor may also discover her "child self" in a new way. She may now be able to reclaim and reintegrate her spontaneity, playfulness, and innocence. For many survivors the experience of reconnecting with self feels overwhelming. Many women say they don't know how to live in an integrated way. They must learn how to envision a future with new skills, new identity, and new dreams.

Reconnection also happens with other people. The isolation of the victim is replaced with connectedness and community as the survivor uses her new skills to build and maintain healthy, nonabusive relationships. During this stage a group becomes the service of choice for many survivors of childhood sexual abuse. In the group members can explore and rework their skills at reaching out, being vulnerable, receiving and giving feedback, maintaining ties through conflict, and ending relationships when appropriate.

During this stage many survivors also embark upon what Herman refers to as a "survivor mission." They find a way to give back to the community and frequently, as they discover new purpose, find a project or career path that gives their life meaning and transforms their pain. They may pursue further education in counseling or law or social work with the hope of using their own experiences to help others. Some survivors pursue social action and political involvement as a way of working toward social change and prevention. Survivors bring a wealth of energy and vision to such work as they find a way to make meaning out of their own personal suffering (Bass and Davis 1992).

Groups for survivors fit well into the healing process described by Herman and others. Groups move through the stages of the healing process in a microcosm, first establishing safety, then "remembering and mourning" together as each woman tells her own story, and, all along, working on the healing of reconnection and finding strength in sharing common experience. A group provides an opportunity to connect with other women who can really understand their experiences and responses. As one survivor states, "No one who hasn't been through this herself can really know what it is like to live every day with the kind of fear and sense of vulnerability in the world that I have. I feel like I am looking over my shoulder all the time. And the rage—I need to be with others who will comprehend the extent of my fury and not be blown away by it or judge me for it." The knowledge of a shared history facilitates the sense of being truly heard. Schwartz states that a group is "an enterprise in mutual aid, an alliance of individuals who need each other to create not one but many helping relationships" (Schwartz 1961). As Schwartz, Shulman, Gitterman, and others describe the mutual aid process, it is members who provide to each other the healing connections of empathy and understanding from the "same boat" as well as sharing insights and resources for recovery. (See Gitterman and Shulman, this volume.)

This general framework of the power of groups beautifully dovetails with the work of feminist theorists at the Stone Center for Research on Women at Wellesley College in Wellesley, Massachusetts (Jordan 1991, Jordan 1997). These writers emphasize the importance of groups for women. In addition, trauma experts such as Herman and Schatzow (1984) and Yassen and Glass (1984) write about the central importance of women's groups for incest survivors. Fedele and Harrington (1990) outline four healing factors in women's groups: validation, empowerment, self-empathy, and mutuality. They stress that women's groups "provide opportunities to work through previous relational wounds within a sustaining relational context. Both the 'then and there' and the 'here and now' relational experiences play key roles. As the woman experiences the juxtaposition of the hurtful past and the affirming present in a relational context, healing proceeds."

Schiller's (1995:1997) relational model of stages of group development is directly applicable to how most groups of this type develop. This model states that trust and connection are necessary prerequisites in group process, before members feel safe and secure enough to proceed, through staying connected in spite of differences and finally to the ability to remain connected in the face of conflict (in contrast to the traditional model, which suggests that the stage of power and control follow the initial stage of preaffiliation ; Garland, Jones, and Kolodny 1976).

Survivors groups generally follow the relational model's group developmental stages of preaffiliation, followed by establishing a relational base, mutuality, and interpersonal empathy, challenge and change, and separation/termination. One can readily see the correlation with Herman's stages of recovery from trauma.

In addition to the relational context that aids survivors in groups, powerful healing elements include naming the abuse—both what and who—breaking silence in a larger context, working through defenses, help with splitting, and working through self-blame through compassion for others. This latter concept corresponds with the concept of self-empathy. Through extending compassion and empathy to others, and by seeing the similarities between themselves and others in the group, the survivor can then move to a place of self-forgiveness. One survivor stated, "I was alternately enraged and saddened by what I was hearing from the other group members about their abuse as children. I was so struck by Sally's innocence and helplessness when I looked at the childhood pictures that she brought in when it was her week to tell her story. And then it suddenly hit me for the first time ever . . . that I too was once a little girl and that if it wasn't Sally's fault that she was abused, then maybe it wasn't mine either. I flashed back to a picture of myself in my green plaid jumper and white blouse with the Peter Pan collar and thought, "My God, I was only five years old then!"

Work and Group Themes

This model of short-term groups for women survivors of sexual abuse draws from the work of Emily Schatzow and Judith Herman of the Women's Mental Health Collective in Somerville, Massachusetts. Their model is of a twelve-week group involving the creation of individual goals for each woman and then a full session's time for each woman to tell her story and receive feedback from the other group members (Herman and Schatzow 1984). Our model takes this format and expands the time frame to cover fifteen or sixteen weeks, depending on the number of women participating in that particular group cycle. Group size ranges from five to eight women, giving each member an adequate chance to be heard and maximizing the potential for the development of group intimacy. Each session is closely structured, and there are four distinct stages. The first stage is the introduction, which includes the development of personal group goals, the second is story/history telling, the third is the enhancement of group themes that have emerged, and the final stage is termination.

Each individual session has a consistent structure as well. A group session is one and a half hours in length. It opens with a check-in time, during which each member has a time to talk, describe any items she may have brought in, raise a group or outside concern, or pass. One half hour is set aside for check-in, and if time remains after each member has spoken, members may use the remaining time for open discussion. The next fifty minutes are filled with the activity planned for that week, and the final minutes are spent in a closing meditation using guided imagery. The purpose of this exercise is to add closure to the work of the group for that day and to allow members to ground and transition.

While this is not specifically an "expressive arts therapy" group, we have found that using a multimodal approach to the work seems to enhance the growth and healing process, as indicated previously. Use of expressive arts, myth, music, guided visualizations, and movement adds a dimension that both addresses the issue of differentially stored traumatic memory as well as that of women less comfortable with verbal expression. While some survivors may have been ordered by their offenders not to speak of the abuse, few have been given an injunction not to draw pictures about it or compose poems about it.

One member, Becky, was dismayed when it came time for her turn to tell her story. She said, "You never told me this was to be a storytelling group. I can't talk about it. I don't even trust the few memories I do have." With support from the workers she agreed to share her story in whatever format she was comfortable, "as long as I don't have to talk I'll do it." She arrived the following week armed with journals, pictures, and impressive clay sculptures she had made. With the help of her art and writing, she revealed a profoundly moving story. All of the members as well as the workers were impressed and moved by her "story without words."

During the initial session the workers introduce themselves and make a statement of purpose to the group. Members are given an opportunity to introduce themselves in two rounds of introduction (one focusing on the abuse and one not). They are asked to identify their perpetrator(s) and how old they were when the abuse took place (if they remember, or as best as they can determine from what they do remember). Thus one level of naming and breaking silence takes place right from the first meeting. Members begin to develop this group culture, which allows and encourages sharing and risk-taking within a safe environment. Group agreements are jointly developed by members and facilitators and placed on charts on the walls of the room, where they remain for the duration of the group cycle.

The next few sessions are spent helping each member develop an individual goal she would like to accomplish before the end of the group. Members and facilitators work together to help each woman develop a personalized goal that can be achieved within the time frame of the group program. This part of the group structure is designed so that each member can complete the group experience with a concrete sense of accomplishment and movement toward healing. The weeks that follow are spent with each member telling her story. Members are encouraged to challenge themselves in this process but not to overstep their own bounds of safety. Members are encouraged to bring whatever props will enhance their telling and/or help them feel comfortable and safe. Members have brought stuffed animals, photos from childhood, works of art, literature or music they have created or that has meaning for them. After telling their story of abuse, members receive feedback, empathy, consolation, and comfort from other members, which aids their development of new perspectives and self-perceptions relative to their abuse. Following this powerful section of the group experience, the workers structure the next few sessions to enhance themes that have arisen thus far in that group cycle. This section varies from group to group. Various activities, which may include writing, psychodrama, drawing, or role playing, become the basis for ongoing discussion and expansion of group themes, such as trust, managing flashbacks, dealing with anger, intimacy, or confrontation.

Trust

Imagine walking into a room filled with strangers with the goal of disclosing your most private, deeply held secret. Imagine that you had been told when you were young that if you ever disclosed this secret terrible things would happen to you or to those you loved. Imagine the deep need you would feel to protect yourself, to "check out" the others in the room, to silently assess whether in this place truth could be told. This is the experience of survivors entering their first group meeting.

Until initial trust is developed, everyone in the room is terrified. The facilitators move swiftly to help members create safety, an essential prerequisite to the development of trust. The theme of trust is a central theme of all groups, but for these groups, whose members had their trust exploited and violated by those closest to them, the issue of trust becomes paramount.

We begin by acknowledging that everyone is feeling afraid and that they all have terrific courage for just walking in the door. We ask each member to introduce herself first by sharing some personal information other than her abuse history (is she an artist, what she does for exercise, what was her favorite vacation ever, or what her worst fantasy was of coming to this group today). Members have to view themselves and one another as more than "just" survivors of sexual abuse. We hope their relationships with one another will be based on broad, deep understanding of each woman's unique self, only a piece of which involves her identity as a survivor. The message given is that the abuse is something that happened to each one of them, but not who they are. We believe it helps build trust for each woman to begin her relationships with the others on this broader "nonabuse" note. From there we move on to the second introduction described earlier, where each woman states the "who" and "when" of her abuse history. By setting clear limits on this first disclosure, we reassure members that we will not move any faster than they are able, and we create an atmosphere of truth telling without "spilling."

In one group the discussion of group agreements unveiled many of the trust issues that were to arise later.

CARMEN: There are so many things I'd need to trust in order to feel safe; it's hard to list them all. I'd like to make an agreement that we not talk on and on without regard for others' need for time. I'm afraid I have the potential to do that myself and need help holding on to my limits. I've also been in groups before where one person dominated and it was really frustrating for me.

BRIDGET: I know what you mean. Maybe we can set a fixed amount of time for each person to talk and monitor ourselves, like five minutes each or something.

JO: Yeah, but there's also the problem of whether you want to be interrupted while you're talking or get feedback during check-in. I feel jumped on when people respond before I'm ready.

CARMEN: What if we ask for feedback or say specifically "I don't want feedback on this" and agree to respect whatever the person says?

(The discussion goes on to include several other agreements that are listed on a poster board on the wall.)

WORKER (*noticing Carmen looking distracted and far away*): Carmen, can I check in with you? You seem to have "left us" suddenly.

CARMEN (*crying and agitated*): Well, I'm looking at this list and I suddenly feel very constrained. With all these rules, how will I ever feel spontaneous enough to say anything?

Carmen eloquently reflects the dual wish of many survivors to have both clear limits and yet have no boundaries on oneself. In order to trust, she feels, she must keep tight constraints to "rein in" her wishes and desires (and those of her fellow members), yet she also longs for uninterrupted attention. By being able to discuss both sides of her ambivalence, she was able to find a balance for her needs for both spontaneity and for regulation.

Another example of trust building in the group was the use of transitional and comfort objects that members brought from home. In the initial meeting Becky told the group that she wore her "booties" and curled up in her blanket to soothe herself. She also introduced the group to her two teddy bears, which she cuddled throughout sessions. The following week facilitators noticed that others were removing their shoes and assuming more relaxed poses. By the third or fourth group meeting, other members brought their own dolls, animals, or comfort clothing and explicitly told others about how these objects had provided much-needed safety and comfort during difficult moments in their healing journeys. Members responded openly, without shaming, and this further extended the circle of trust that was building in the group.

This atmosphere of nonjudgmental sharing was beautifully revealed in the final termination session, which the members themselves designed. Each woman contributed something: cards she had written, tapes of healing songs, poems, and gifts chosen specifically for each woman. Particularly touching was the gift that Jo gave to Becky, the member who had emotionally retreated into her "shell" for many weeks during group sessions. Becky had served as the one who held the group's fear and inability to trust for the longest. Using their own experiences of working through trust issues, members were able to gently guide this woman out of her silence, using her own unique language and honoring her own path. At the termination session Jo gave her a "turtle shell" made from an avocado skin, painted green in a spiraling pattern, which symbolized depth and evolution. In this way Jo was able to honor Becky's need to disappear and not trust as much as she also celebrated her reemergence into the group at group's end. That signified both Becky's growing capacity for trust within intimacy as well as the group's having "earned" this trust.

Relationships/Intimacy

A central theme in survivor groups arises around intimacy and closeness in relationships. Survivors experience profound difficulties in forming and maintaining relationships with others in their lives, as the issues around the theme of trust and boundary maintenance get in the way of healthy and safe intimacy. Group becomes a microcosm for life, as relationships developed and nurtured within the relatively safe confines of group become prototypes for relationships outside group. Pacing is problematic for survivors. They experience either too much intimacy too soon or too little too late to maintain the connection. Through guidance, structure, and modeling, the workers provide a format in which members can try out safe ways of relating and reworking blocks to closeness.

> CARMEN: It's always been difficult for me to really trust people. I know that I hold back when I'm meeting people.
>
> BRIDGET: Me too. I know what you mean. It's like you're not sure if you really want them to know who you are.
>
> JO: I think that if people really knew me—I mean really knew me—they'd run in the opposite direction.
>
> WORKER: How are these feelings being manifested here in this group?
>
> BRIDGET: Well I know that even though we're all here for the same reason, I still worry that you all might judge me or think that I don't really belong here since it was only my brother who abused me, not a parent or anything.
>
> BECKY: I worry about the same thing, but that's because I'm not even clear who it was who abused me. I have all these vague feelings and images, but not any clear memories.
>
> WORKER: So are you both saying that part of the reason that you hold back is that you worry about being judged by others or that somehow you feel not good enough or entitled to belong?
>
> BECKY: Yes, that's it.

WORKER: Well, I'm struck by the fact that even though you have these worries and fears you still had the courage to become members of this group and to take the risk of letting people in. Even the information you've shared today, about your worries about letting in and trust issues, is itself a break in the armor. And it makes sense to take it slowly, a little bit at a time, while you check out others' reactions and see if it feels safe to let out a little bit more of yourself.

CARMEN: That's true. It's comforting to know that I'm not the only one who has these concerns.

JO: Yeah, it seems like I either jump the gun and blow someone away by telling them my whole life story on the first date or I am so worried about what they'll think of me that I get all cold and nervous and can't say anything.

WORKER: This group might be a place to practice finding a middle ground between those two.

This interchange illustrates the notion of "paradox" described by Fidele and others in doing relational group work. This concept addresses the primary issue of connection, and the paradox is that if one speaks of the disconnection one is experiencing, it actually leads to greater connection. (Fedele and Harrington 1990).

One of the group agreements is that members are allowed to have contact with each other outside of group meetings if they choose, but it is considered "group business" and needs to be reported to the group as a whole. In addition to this being common practice in all groups, it is particularly important here for members not to be holding secrets from each other about contact. One member was writing the group agreements on the poster board as the issue of outside contact was raised.

SALLY: Well, what about if we want to call each other or something during the week?

CARMEN: Well, I don't think that I'd call any of you now, but I can imagine that I might want to later on. One of the reasons that I joined a group was so that I could have people around me who could understand what I'm going through.

WORKER: It's OK for members to contact each other outside of group meetings, but while we are meeting as a group, if you do, you need to report that contact back to the group. We want everyone to feel as safe as possible while in the group and don't want people to have to worry about any secret connections while they're here. Secret connections are a part of the reason you're all here today!

JO: Boy, that's sure true. I for one vote that we put that on the poster board too.

Women healing in a relational context were a theme encouraged and supported by the group workers. Workers regularly acknowledged and described the ways in which the members were able to help and support each other. Workers

occasionally dialogued with each other, both as genuine and spontaneous expressions of feeling and as a model of women working together in a supportive
way.

> WORKER 1: I was really moved and impressed by how you all came to Bridget's aid
> a few moments ago. You really validated her feelings and let her know that she
> was not alone.
> WORKER 2: I agree. I think you (worker 1) expressed just about exactly what I'm
> feeling too. (*To the group as a whole*): How wonderful that you're able to pro-
> vide that kind of support to each other.

The worker's role is to help facilitate both personal growths in each member as
well as group process. Women with histories of sexual abuse come to the group
with the shared experience of having been victimized and disempowered by a
person in a position of power and authority. From the outset, we structure our
groups in such a way as to rebalance the power relationships among members
and between members and facilitators. The first and primary task of the group
facilitators is to create an environment safe enough for members to ultimately be
able to explore in relational issues among members and between members and
facilitators.

From the first group meeting, we set out to establish an atmosphere of self-
help, mutual aid, and member empowerment. We do this by having the members establish their own contractual agreements, as was described earlier. Group
members answer the question "what agreements do you need to make with one
another to create an environment of safety in this group?" Members and facilitators alike may then remind themselves and each other about the importance of
abiding by the group agreements. The two facilitators also post a separate chart
listing our own commitments to the group, which include: being responsible for
the setup and maintenance of the meeting space; providing supplies; maintaining consistent boundaries around time, structure, and content of the group;
helping members monitor adherence to group agreements; sharing our knowledge and experience working with other survivors and groups; and checking in
with any member who is in distress (this may include withdrawal in sessions,
threats to sobriety and safety, or seeming potentially suicidal).

As facilitators, we encourage group ownership of problems and dilemmas
and encourage members to solve conflicts and differences themselves. For example, when one member requested a group photo as a commemorative at
group's end, the group embarked on a fruitful conversation about confidentiality and public exposure. The eventual group decision included all members' input
and specified the conditions for sharing the photo with others outside the group.
Facilitators reach for clients' feelings and tune in to the meaning of their struggle by posing such questions as "Does anyone have any fears that come up when

you imagine the photo leaving this room?" or "What do you need to ask from one another in order feel safe when you think about taking this photo home"? We hope to offer our experience and analysis of the common struggles of survivors of sexual abuse without taking over control of the group process or making decisions for members.

Another role we assume in facilitating is to carry group memory, history, and themes. We point out changes in individual participation, elucidate for group members their movement through various stages of group development, and carry and build upon group themes in designing and facilitating group activities or discussion topics. We pay particular attention to the twin dynamics of authority and intimacy and the unique and loaded history each member brings to the group in these areas.

We invite members to participate in activities but also make ourselves open to critique. We remain cognizant of ourselves as role models of women working cooperatively to empower groups of survivors. In doing so, we also challenge sexist misconceptions about women as victims. We include an analysis of oppression as we work with women to unravel the multiple layers of victimization in their lives. Members begin to make connections between the racism, sexism, classism, and heterosexism they have experienced that have further hampered their healing from sexual abuse. Members have given us feedback about the power of seeing two co-workers working together and learning from one another. One member comments, "Seeing how the two workers carefully handled situations where we are victims and where we put ourselves in that role helps me, models for me, how to be gentler with women in general and myself as a female." The members' experience of positive and respectful co-facilitation provides a relational model for safe intimacy and cooperation.

As a group progresses, it becomes common for members to call or see one another outside of group sessions for support, feedback, or advice. The mutual aid system emerges as a theme both in and out of the group. One member described how wonderful it was for her that, on the day she told her story to the group, at group's end they all exchanged phone numbers. She felt a sense of pride for her part in moving people closer.

A common phenomenon in many survivor groups is the "group after the group" that takes place in the parking lot or waiting room after the session has formally ended for the day. Members linger to continue the connections they have been forging during the session itself. As one group reached its final weeks, the workers would frequently find members still clustered around the picnic table in the parking lot forty-five minutes after they had left the building following processing and cleaning up the group room. It is also common for members to hold a separate termination celebration after the last group session that does not include the group workers, as a way for members to continue contacts made after the actual group sessions end. Some groups continue to meet as "self-help" support groups without the workers. The growth and emergence of one member exemplifies the complex process of relational development inside survivor groups.

Becky initially participated freely in group check-ins and activities. Shortly after the group sessions began, however, she began withdrawing in a very noticeable manner. She would pass on check-in, having less and less to say during other members' times as well. Becky described to the group that she felt like she was retreating into her "turtle shell," a pattern she identified as common at other times and places in her life. Members initially allowed her to withdraw and respected her need for distance. However, after some time, they began to experience her withdrawal as withholding. They expressed their sentiments by saying that they "wished to hear more" from her or that "I always get a lot out of what you say" or even "I miss you. Where did you go?" As time went on, Becky continued to speak briefly only of the shell she now lived in. She would say, "I'm not really here. My body is present but that's all." I asked her if she could describe for the group in more depth what it was like for her to be in there in her shell. Becky described feeling shut off from others. I asked if she was open to hearing feedback from others about their experience of her absence. She agreed.

> CARMEN: You know, Becky, I'm really angry with you for not sharing more of yourself here. We all came here for the same reason, and it feels unfair that you aren't willing to take the same risks we do. (Becky had recently said she wasn't sure she could take her turn telling her story in the group as the others had done.)
>
> JO: I wonder what you're thinking when you are so silent, and I worry that you're sitting there in judgment on the rest of us.
>
> WORKER: How do you feel, Becky, and do you want to respond?
>
> BECKY: I don't blame you for being angry. I'd probably be angry with me too. But I'm certainly not judging you. I never thought it would seem like that. I just feel so stuck.
>
> BRIDGET: I will really miss it if you don't tell your story as well. I feel like you're sitting on a lot, and we really need to hear what that is.
>
> CARMEN: I will feel cheated if you don't tell your story. I always learn something from you when you do speak. But I will respect it if you can't.
>
> WORKER: The members truly liked and learned from your participation, Becky, and are experiencing a sense of loss as you are keeping all your pain inside you.

Becky came in the next week and told a moving story of her process of beginning to remember her abuse. She shared many details with the group through her writing, artwork, and dreamlog. She acknowledged how powerful it had been for her that the members and workers had not "given up on her" despite her withdrawal. She told us, "I remember the feeling of being sucked up into the woodwork and being cognizant of the very moment of decision when I could either get lost in the woodwork or open my mouth and be present." Becky also said that it had never occurred to her that the other members would think she was judging them by remaining silent. It gave her a new level of understanding into her roadblocks in other relationships outside group.

The group facilitators and members enthusiastically welcomed her back into the group and Becky remained connected, verbal, and participating for the remainder of our time together. The members, together with the structure of the group and the support of the workers were able to make the demand for work here (which, at week eleven of a fifteen-week group, corresponded with the "challenge and change" stage of the relational model of group development). It included their expectations from each other for pushing through stuck, scary places within the relative safety and connectedness of the group. As members expressed the impact Becky's withdrawal had on them personally, she was able to step outside herself and see more clearly the role she had played in becoming distant and isolated within the group. She also saw how this consequence of her early abuse continued to impact on her present life by interfering with her ability to make and sustain connections.

The workers' role was to encourage connection and sharing as well as to respect individual differences and needs for silence. The co-facilitators continued to gently engage Becky and let her know she was a valuable part of the group in whatever style she was able to participate. They also encouraged other members to use the group experience to practice skills they would like to expand on in their outside lives and to recognize where they now had choices in relationships as adults that they did not have as children.

Anger and Grief

The following conversation opened the group's second session:

ANDREA: I've been really angry ever since last week's group. I'm so sick of being in therapy and having to talk endlessly about this abuse. What if it doesn't help? I swear, I'm going to sue my therapist if I'm not better by the end of therapy!

BECKY: I can really relate to that. I've been in a rage. It feels like some entity inside me. As I named my perpetrators here in this group, I heard myself for the first time. And I thought, "Oh, my God, those animals!"

CARMEN: Well, this may sound strange but I've been really happy since last week. I felt so "given to" by each of you and so good about myself that I was finally "giving myself" the group I've wanted. But this group is so great that my individual therapist isn't measuring up anymore. Actually I've been really angry at her for not being an expert on this like Bonnie and Linda. I feel safe here but I'm furious with her for not having what I need now.

WORKER: It's clear that the group is already having a powerful impact for many of you and that hearing and talking about your abuse is elicits a lot of powerful

feelings. (Notices Sally in silent distress.) Sally, I want to check in with you and
see how you are.

SALLY (*bursts into tears*): I'm so jealous of all of you. I've never gotten angry. I need
to get angry, but I can't! What if I never get angry?

WORKER: Can you name what it is that keeps you from feeling your anger?

SALLY: If I get angry at him, I'll lose my whole family (*more tears*)!

CARMEN: Boy, I understand that one! I feel responsible for annihilating my family.

JO: I'm afraid of losing my family too. I really relate to your fears around that.

SALLY: Yeah. Thanks. That's good to know. As I'm sitting here I realize I can get
angry at one person. I'm really mad at my mother for just standing by. She
should have protected me. I call her "the psycho bitch from hell." (*Murmurs and
heads nodding all around.*)

WORKER: Certainly your anger is justified. You had your rights taken away and you
were left unprotected. You are entitled to feel angry about both those things.
And there are lots of different forms of anger. Some make us feel helpless and
some help us feel powerful. As we move along in this group, I encourage you
each to discover a way to move out of the kind of anger that feels helpless and
impotent (the anger of the victim) into an empowering anger (the anger of the
survivor). This is something we'll undoubtedly come back to again and again.
You have a lot to teach one another from your varied yet similar experiences.

Two common themes of survivor groups are revealed in this vignette. First, the
survivors' fear of the destructive potential of their anger and, second, the displacement of anger at the abuser onto others, such as safer caretaking people like
mothers and workers who are perceived as nonprotective.

When a child is sexually abused, the perpetrator commonly threatens the
child in order to mandate secrecy and silence. He tells her "Your mother will go
crazy if she finds out," or "There's no telling what might explode in this family
if our secret is found out," or, simply, "No one will believe you." This silencing
leads to isolation and fear. The child learns to bury and silence her growing rage
at the injustices being inflicted on her. She learns to find ways to preserve her relationship with the abuser, which she hopes will in turn "preserve" her threatened family security. The child comes to believe that she has the omnipotent
power to preserve or destroy her family. She comes to believe that her rage and
anger (which implore her to tell someone and seek justice and escape from the
abuse) are her enemy. Like Sally and Carmen, she fears that her anger will "annihilate my family" by telling the truth.

In addition to this dynamic specific to sexual abuse, there are other factors
that inhibit women's ability to express and harness their anger in their own defense. Sexist child rearing has taught women that anger is "unfeminine," dangerous, and powerful. Girls are taught to turn their anger inward rather than
express it in outward ways, as boys do. Thus, sexual identity becomes tied in with

the management of anger and aggression. Women who express their anger outwardly often face clear negative social consequences. In our groups women assess the climate created by the other members and the facilitators before revealing their anger. For these reasons facilitators make validating comments about the power and importance of anger as a healing tool in efforts to counteract the powerful social sanctions we all hold against "angry women." For the group to become a healing circle, all feelings, including anger and rage, must come to be accepted.

The second issue is the one of displacement of anger onto "safer" targets. There is legitimate anger harbored by victims toward nonprotective caregivers that does need expression and healing. We distinguish between this healthy anger and the displaced anger that is often referred to as "mother blame." Some survivors are so terrified of their anger at their perpetrators that they cannot even hold them accountable for the abuse. They say, "If my mother had been different he would never have abused me in the first place," or, "Actually, my mother sort of drove him to this." Sally's inability to feel angry with her father and her ease of anger with mother is typical. This overt protection of the abuser and failure to hold him accountable for his actions ultimately does not lead to healing. The survivor must learn to direct her anger at the person/people directly responsible for the abusive behavior. They may also rage and grieve over the nonprotection they experienced, but it is essential to appropriately assign responsibility (Bass and Davis 1992).

Without this appropriate assignment of responsibility, survivors tend to remain locked in self-blame and self-hatred. Mother blame can also become self-blame as the female survivor identifies with mother. It is important for women who have children to know that they can act to protect their children and, if their children are also sexually abused, they do not "cause" the abuse. No matter how neglectful or nonprotective a caretaker is, no one makes another adult sexually abuse a child. It is the perpetrator's choice.

Workers can become good stand-ins for mothers, as women work out their confusion around responsibility for their suffering. Andrea, who threatened to "sue my therapist," later named "suing Mike, the bastard," as her group goal. She may use her relationship with her worker as a trial ground, but, if counseling is to be successful, her rage and desire for justice will need to be redirected onto the appropriate and far more threatening arena of her relationship with her abuser.

The expression of years of repressed anger is frequently followed by a sense of grief. Groups move through a period of group mourning for themselves and one another. This may be openly acknowledged by very verbal members or may simply be reflected in a "depressed" group tone.

The week following the above vignette, two members reported missing work because of their experiences of being flooded with sadness and grief. By group session 7 members were openly acknowledging their grief for one another, with statements like "I'm so sorry that happened to you." Members cried during the telling of other's stories as well as their own. This collective sharing of grief and mourning provides a grieving ritual for members that aids and speeds the healing process.

This group also chose an ending ceremony that further enabled them to move through grief into recovery. They created a "ritual burning" in which members wrote down things they wanted to leave behind in the group room; outmoded defenses or strategies, or people, places, or things they were ready to say good-bye to. They then stepped to the center of the room, lit the paper on fire, and watched it burn. The women burned their fear, shame, the names of their perpetrators, their self-hatred. We played the tape "Baptism of Fire," brought in by a group member, to accompany this ritual. In this way, members willfully let go of outdated defenses but grieved and mourned the loss of these trusted former allies in healing.

CONFRONTATION

Writing about the theme of confronting offenders has been the most difficult part of preparing this chapter. Many survivors say that this is one of the hardest parts of their healing process and, uniformly, one that requires a tremendous act of courage. By the time women are ready to join a group of this type, many are beginning to consider the act of confrontation. Some members have already had a first encounter with their perpetrator, and others are not yet ready for this step in their own lives but are looking forward to hearing from others and being inspired by them at some future date. Confrontation is not a requirement for healing, but many clinicians are beginning to look at how important some form of confrontation is in order to correct the relational imbalance that follows the original trauma (Gelinas 1992). Confrontation can be the "NO" that the child was once unable to voice. It is important to remember that confrontation does not mean to imply a loud, defensive, or abrasive encounter (Schiller 1998). It simply implies that the survivor holds the perpetrator directly responsible for the abuse and the subsequent difficulties in her life, whether this encounter is face to face or at a distance.

Members began dealing with this theme very early in one group. As previously described, one member, Andrea, clearly stated that her personal goal to achieve from the group was "to confront Mike Taylor, the bastard." This announcement helped set the tone for other members to think about the role that confronting their offenders had in their own lives. Interestingly, the two youngest members, both in their early twenties, had already achieved some level of confrontation before starting in the group. The lack of an age barrier was apparent as the youngest member, Sally, described her confrontation with her father.

SALLY: Last year I decided that I couldn't just let him get away with what he had done to me and my sister. I wonder all the time if he molested my brother too. He doesn't say anything, but he has all the signs. So I talked to him.

BRIDGET: You did? What did you say? I would have been so scared.

SALLY: Well, I was nervous, but after talking with my worker I knew that I was safe now and that he couldn't hurt me again. One of the first things my worker had me do was move out of my parents' house. It's unbelievable what a difference that made. I didn't have to look at his mug every day.

WORKER: How long did you work on a plan for the first encounter?

SALLY: Oh, at least a year. We'd talk about it every couple of weeks until I felt really ready and in control.

JO: So, what did you do?

SALLY: I told him that I remembered everything that he had done to me. How he used to come into our bedroom at night and how he'd have us perform oral sex on him. And how he used to touch me underneath a blanket while we watched TV when he thought no one could see him. And I told him how to this day I am terrified by the smell of beer on someone's breath, because he was so often drunk. And that I'm nervous all the time and can't stand to ever have someone come up behind me.

BRIDGET: I can't believe you said all that. It was almost exactly like that for me too, except it was my uncle. My parents are both alcoholics too.

SALLY: My mother is too.

BRIDGET: And I get nauseous if a man tries to kiss me and he has been drinking. I never realized why before but it must be because my uncle drank before he molested us too. You're so brave, Sally. I've wanted to say something for years but have always been afraid that he'd just call me a liar anyway. Did your father admit it or apologize?

SALLY: Well, he didn't exactly admit it, but he didn't deny it either. He did say that maybe things happened when he was drinking that he doesn't remember. But it still felt so good to get it out . . . like coughing up a big brick!!

(Two weeks later Bridget came in and announced that she had confronted her parents about her uncle's abuse and their own alcoholism.)

BRIDGET: Well, I did it. I've been wanting to do it for years. Hearing your story a few weeks ago, Sally, really inspired me. I thought, well, Sally did it and she still seems to be OK. He didn't kill her or anything.

CARMEN: How did it go for you?

BRIDGET: Well, my mother cried, and my father huffed and puffed and neither of them really said or admitted anything. It was his brother who did it, who abused me. Mostly they just made excuses. But I'm really glad I said something anyway. It felt freeing to me, to actually speak up. The next step will be talking to my uncle.

WORKER: You all show tremendous courage when you choose to confront the perpetrators and other family members. Often the result isn't exactly what you
may have hoped for, but just the act of speaking up, as Bridget said, moves you
past a certain barrier, a certain deep-seated fear.

Confrontation isn't something that happens one time and is over with, rather it
is an ongoing process. Each person needs to decide what the meaning of it would
be for her individually and to prepare carefully the time and place. She needs to
plan how she will cope and feel if the response is not a positive one. In other
words, the confronting needs to be for the survivor, as a part of her healing and
empowerment, not to obtain a particular result or response (Schatzow and Herman 1989.

Several weeks later Andrea, whose personal group goal was to confront her offender, came in with a first draft of a letter she had written. Because her offender lives out of state, her process of contacting him will take several stages to
accomplish. The first stage was this letter, filled with venom and hate, demanding that he look at what he had done and requesting restitution in the form of
payment for her many years of therapy. She also reported that after writing the
letter she had a dream where she was flushing a penis down a toilet and felt very
empowered when she awoke. Jo told the group that she too was beginning to
think about confrontation and had had the fantasy of bringing Andrea with her
for moral support when she did so.

The workers' role here was to offer support and respect to members for their
acts of courage and to normalize the accompanying feelings of fear, excitement,
and disappointment. Stressing the need for careful preparation for this act is crucial, so that each member can carefully assess her own safety (both internal and
external) and the reasons she is making this choice. The workers also function
as resources of information, sharing with the group the experiences of other survivors who have taken this step. It is clear that members use their relationships
within the group setting to help them make changes in their outside lives.
Whether or not they choose to confront their perpetrators, they draw courage and
learn options from the experience of others. Sometimes they think about taking
other members with them, either in reality or in their mind's eye.

IN SUMMARY, the experience of participating in a small group for women survivors of sexual abuse can be a powerful and compelling one. The invaluable opportunity for sharing the dark and painful secrets of the history and legacy of
abuse helps members to grow and find strength both from each other and within themselves. The wonderful ability survivors often have to empathize with others can be brought inward with the help of the workers to greater self-forgiveness
and understanding. The particular structure of a time-limited group helps
members concretize parts of their work and achieve a sense of satisfaction in the

accomplishment of carefully delineated goals. Short-term groups limit the level of anxiety a survivor may have around long-term commitment and provide containment for the frequently intense and disorganizing aspects of other parts of the healing process.

Working from the premise that women heal in relationship, members often make significant steps toward healing the relational wounds caused by trauma and abuse through their connections with other group members. A collaborative co-leadership model allows members to witness a positive working relationship that can be used as a model in their own lives, in addition to providing a positive experience of authority that is "power with" not "power over."

While this chapter cannot deal with all the themes that arise in these groups, the ones we have explored in depth are trust, intimacy, anger and grief, and confrontation. Additional themes frequently arising in these groups are empowerment, oppression, recovery of obfuscated memories, recognition and honoring of old defenses while developing healthier coping styles, and gaining a more integrated sense of self.

We continue to learn from our clients and honor them by sharing this knowledge with others. When we informed members of one group that we would be writing this chapter and asked permission to use their words, they were thrilled at the opportunity to contribute to others' healing process. They spoke of feeling special and important. One member states:

> It made me feel wonderful to hear that the awesome power I felt in this group was apparent to you (facilitators) as well. And to be told that we are so powerful that our experience might guide others made me feel proud. We are a group of women who, I am certain, as children did not know we mattered at all, let alone that we were unique and treasured. Being told that, in this struggle, in this work, we are powerful and wonderful made me feel good all over.

Notes

1. Linda T. Sanford, personal communication.
2. Eve Diana, personal communication.
3. Some of the recent advances in the body/mind/energy field include techniques such as EMDR (Eye Movement Desensitization and Reprocessing), developed by Francine Shapiro, TFT (Thought Field Therapy), developed by Roger Callahan, and TAT (Tappas Acupressure Technique), developed by Tappas Flemming. While definitive studies have not yet been completed for these relatively new methods, anecdotally and in practice they show great promise. Some are based on the ancient healing practice of acupuncture. None are meant to substitute for solid clinical practice and the healing power of the therapeutic relationship.

References

American Psychiatric Association. 1995. *Diagnostic and statistical manual of mental disorders*. 4th ed. New York: American Psychiatric Association.

Bass, E. and L. Davis. 1992. *The courage to heal*. New York: Harper and Row.

Courtois, C. 1988. *Healing the incest wound*. New York: Norton.

Erikson, E. 1963. *Childhood and society*. New York: Norton.

Fedele, N. and E. Harrington. 1990. Women's groups: How connections heal. Paper presented at the Stone Center Colloquium at Wellesley College, Wellesley, Mass, June 7, pp. 3–5.

Figley, C. R. 1985. *Trauma and its wake*. New York: Brunner/Mazel.

Finkelhor, D. and A. Browne. 1985. The traumatic impact of child sexual abuse: A conceptualization. *American Journal of Orthopsychiatry* 55(4):530–41.

Garland, J., H. Jones, and R. Kolodny. 1976. A model of stages of group development in social work groups. In S. Bernstein, ed., *Explorations in group work*, pp. 17–71. Boston: Charles River.

Gelinas, D. 1983. The persistent negative effects of incest. *Psychiatry* 46:312–32.

———— 1992. Lecture notes from presentation at Leonard Morse Hospital, Natick, Mass., April 3.

Herman, J. 1992. *Trauma and recovery*. New York: Basic.

Herman, J. and E. Schatzow. 1984. Time-limited group therapy for women with a history of incest. *Journal of Group Psychotherapy* 34(4): 605–16

Jordan, J., 1991. Empathy, mutuality, and therapeutic change: Clinical implications of a relational model. In J. Jordan, A. Kaplan, J. Miller, I. Stiver, and J. Surrey, eds., *Women's Growth and Connection: Writings from the Stone Center,*, pp. 283–89. New York: Guilford.

Jordan, J., ed. 1997. *Women's growth in diversity*. New York: Guilford.

Schatzow, E. and J. Herman. 1989. Breaking secrecy: Adult survivors disclose to their families. *Psychiatric Clinics of North America* 12(2): 337–49.

Schiller, L. Y. 1995. Stages of development in women's groups: A relational model. In R. Kurland and R. Salmon, eds., *Group work practice in a troubled society*, pp. 117–38. New York: Haworth.

———— 1997. Rethinking stages of development in women's groups. *Social Work with Groups* 20(3): 3–19.

———— 1998. Confrontation can be a misnomer. Unpublished monograph.

Schwartz, W. 1961. The social worker in the group. In *New perspectives on services to groups: Theory, organization, and practice*, pp. 7–34. New York: National Association of Social Workers.

Snow, J. 1981. *Baptism of fire*. Recorded by Lui Collins. Philo Records.

van der Kolk, B. 1987. *Psychological trauma*. New York: American Psychiatric.

van der Kolk, B., A. McFarlane, and L. Weisaeth, eds. 1996. *Traumatic stress: The effects of overwhelming experience of mind, body, and society*. New York: Guilford.

Yassen, J. and L. Glass. 1984. Sexual assault survivors groups: A feminist practice perspective. *Social Work* 29: 252–57.

Chapter 12

From Victim to Survivor
Group Work with Men and Women Who Were Sexually Abused

Carolyn Knight

I N   T H E   P R E V I O U S chapter Schiller and Zimmer write about group work with women who have been sexually abused in childhood. In this chapter I focus on a survivor's group for men and women. My first experience working with men and women together grew out of necessity. I tried, unsuccessfully, to find a group for an individual client, a man. It was clear to me that, like my female clients, he would greatly benefit from a group experience. Perhaps more so than the women, he needed the validation and acceptance that would come from being with others who were similarly victimized. As a man, living in a culture that viewed sexual abuse as a female problem perpetrated by male offenders, he felt particularly alone and different.

At the same time that I was searching for a resource for this client I was facilitating a survivors group for women. In one session I casually mentioned this situation to the members. Their response was immediate and intriguing. They asked me if I ever considered facilitating a group for women *and* men. These women recognized, even before I did, that there would be unique benefits associated with being in a group that included men. I brought the members' suggestion back to the individual client, and his reaction also was interesting. He was eager to participate in such a group. In fact, he made it clear that his preference was to be in a group that included women, that it would feel safer to him than a group comprised only of men.

As a result of these informal conversations with clients, I decided to facilitate a mixed group, once the women's group ended. At that point I had no idea what to expect, as there was very little written about facilitating this type of group. Even now, not much exists to guide the worker. A mixed group is not appropriate for all clients because of its intensity and the issues that inevitably surface. For those men and women for whom it is appropriate, however, it offers a powerful opportunity to confront their victimization and, in the process, work on their relationships with one another.

As I contemplated writing this chapter, I spent some time thinking about how I would portray group sessions and members' comments. I wanted to capture the raw and powerful emotion that surfaces in these groups, Yet I was concerned about the impact on the reader. I decided, however, that it was important to describe members' disclosures honestly and accurately. The result is that many of the examples contain graphic language and describe painful, sometimes terrible, victimization. Yet, what I describe *is* what adult survivors of childhood sexual abuse have experienced. I believe that to "clean up" the examples for publication would be to do a disservice to survivors and ultimately to those who chose to work with them.

If a survivors group is going to be helpful to its members, it must be a place where they feel free to talk openly about what happened to them, how they feel about it, and the effects it had on them. In my work I all too often hear from clients that in prior therapeutic relationships they did not feel they had permission to disclose their deepest secrets, that much of what they experienced was taboo and off-limits. Therefore, what was supposed to be helpful ultimately enhanced their sense of being freakish and different. I take the position that, if survivors have the courage to survive and confront their past, the least I can do is to show the same strength by encouraging and allowing them to give voice to the trauma and its consequences.

When facilitating a group for adult survivors, several important considerations should be kept in mind. First, members' stories are disturbing and will evoke powerful responses in the worker. Therefore, it is critical to have the support and assistance of colleagues to process honestly and openly not only what transpires in group but also her or his affective responses to it. Some of the examples I have included will likely evoke in the reader the sorts of reactions—anger, disbelief, disgust, sadness—that surface, in a much more powerful way, in the group. These reactions are *normal* and to be expected.

Second, some of the most important issues members will need to confront are expressed indirectly. Members are likely to collectively avoid the subjects that are most important and central to the work they need to do. It's not just that the sexual abuse itself is taboo, it is all the other all too common consequences and reactions that accompany it, like guilt over having "enjoyed" the abuse and being orgasmic, and rage—and I do mean rage—at perpetrators and those who didn't protect. It is the worker's responsibility to bring these issues out in the open, even if members do not yet feel ready to face them.

Third, the social worker should anticipate that at some point in the group members' anger and resentment may be directed at her or him, as a result of transference phenomena and the worker's demands for work. Whatever its source, the worker has to be prepared to respond in a way that helps members confront and manage their anger over their victimization and resist the understandable urge to respond defensively or diffuse the anger in an attempt to avoid it or "protect" the members.

Fourth, adults who were sexually abused in childhood are incredibly resilient. They are called survivors with good reason, though rarely will they view themselves this way when they embark on their journey toward recovery. The group becomes a powerful way to help members recognize their innate strengths and mobilize the coping strategies they developed to deal with the past to assist them in moving forward in the present and future.

Finally, members need to talk about sex—the abuse, their adult sexuality, and their sexual relationships. The worker must be comfortable engaging in and facilitating this discussion. This means that she or he must be able to accept the use of the everyday slang terms to describe sexual activity and male and female genitalia. From the survivor's perspective he or she was not "forced to perform oral sex" on an offender, she or he had to "suck his cock." This distinction is not just a semantic one. The words convey in a powerful way what the experience was like for survivors. If they are going to be able to deal with what happened to them and move on, survivors have to be able to talk frankly and in an uncensored way about it.

Developmental Issues and Tasks

Much has been written about the effects that sexual abuse has on women, as discussed by Schiller and Zimmer in their chapter. Far less attention has been focused on the effects of sexual abuse on men. For that reason this section will focus on the impact of sexual abuse on men and its differential effects for men and women.

A number of the more common long-term consequences of sexual abuse are experienced by both men and women. These include, among others, low self-esteem, guilt, shame, fear, social isolation, depression, and sexual dysfunction. In addition, a number of the most often identified maladaptive responses and problematic reactions to the victimization, like substance abuse, eating disorders, and PTSD symptoms are exhibited by both male and female survivors (Black and DeBlassie 1993; Browne and Finkelhor 1986; Bruckner and Johnson 1987; Finkelhor 1990; Ratican 1992).

There are also differences in how men and women respond to and experience sexual victimization, and this can be attributed to the nature of the sexual abuse itself as well as to the sociocultural context within which it occurs (Gold et al. 1999; Roesler and McKenzie 1994; Widom, Ireland, and Glynn 1995). Most men have been sexually abused by men. Therefore, they struggle with what they perceive to be the homosexual nature of their abuse. As one group member, John, exclaimed, "I must have given off some message that I was gay. I mean, he [the perpetrator] must have sensed something about me that told him I was gay. Otherwise, why would he have picked me?" John's confusion was compounded by the fact that like many survivors, both male and female, his body responded sexually to the victimization.

Whether abused by a man or a woman, male survivors must reconcile their victimization with what they perceive to be expected of them as men. Another client, Paul, stated, for example, "I'm the man. I'm supposed to be the one who comes in like the knight in shining armor who saves the poor young damsel in distress. I'm not supposed to be the helpless victim." What is particularly poignant about Paul's perspective is how removed it was from the reality of his sexual abuse. He and another boy were invited to attend a weekend "spiritual retreat" at a cabin in the mountains with their parish priest. Over the course of the weekend, he and the friend were systematically sodomized, forced to perform oral sex on each other and on the priest, and photographed in sexually explicit activities. Paul contemplated escaping, but the cabin was in a remote area. Moreover, the priest threatened to harm his family if he resisted or told. Paul was ten years old.

Even when the sexual abuse is perpetrated by a woman, the male survivor is likely to question his sexual adequacy and masculinity, since he may have felt powerless to say no. Adding to the male survivor's confusion is the "myth of nonabuse," a widely held belief that sexual abuse of a boy is not abuse, particularly if it is perpetrated by a woman (Thomas and Nelson 1994). The effects on the male survivor are likely to be especially damaging if the perpetrator was his mother, given the significant boundary violation this represents. Jim's mother began fondling him at age five. By age ten she was having intercourse with him. It never occurred to him that he could say no or resist. She was, after all, his mother. Also, as he saw it, because he was aroused, he must have "liked" it. Describing his relationships with women, Jim commented, "Women scare me. They make me feel like less of a man. Like I have to prove something. And the more I try, the more I fail."

The unique, often lonely, position that male survivors find themselves in was powerfully conveyed to me in an informal conversation I had with several male group members. I casually remarked that I noticed that they congregated outside of the building rather than in the agency's waiting room before group. They informed me that they didn't feel comfortable sitting in the waiting area with other clients. The agency was a "sexual abuse treatment center." Parents brought children in for treatment. The adult clients seeking treatment were typically women.

These men felt acutely the stigma associated with being a male survivor. As one man observed, "I know when they [the other clients] see me, they are thinking I'm one of the ones who did it. Not one of the ones who had it done to them." Another revealed that on at least one occasion a parent had moved her child away from him, assuming, he believed, that he was a perpetrator. I urged the men to discuss their experiences in the group. While they were eager to do so, they worried that the women would not understand or, worse, would react to them as others had. To their surprise, but not to mine, the women were very understanding, and the result was a deepening intimacy between the members. As one woman commented, "You know, until you mentioned this, I never thought about what it would be like to be a guy. I've just assumed it was worse for us [the female members]. I've been so wrapped up in my own shit that I never realized that you suffered too."

Male survivors, then, may experience more extreme feelings of isolation than women. In addition, it appears that men are more likely to struggle with sexual identity issues and possess particularly intense feelings of inadequacy. In response to these feelings, authors note that male survivors may have greater difficulty managing their feelings of anger (Dimock 1988; Hunter 1990; Singer 1989; Thomas and Nelson 1994; Vander-Mey 1988). Most males who were sexually abused in childhood do *not* go on to molest children as adults, despite widely held views to the contrary. Yet, there is limited evidence that male survivors may be at greater risk for offending, perhaps as a way of managing the feelings of inadequacy and anger (Fromuth and Burkhart 1989). At the very least, male survivors must deal with the stigma associated with their victimization, whether they personally struggle with sexual feelings toward children or not.

The experiences of two group members with whom I have worked typify male survivors' difficulties in this regard. Keith was sexually abused for eight years, first by an uncle and then by the uncle and several acquaintances. Keith sought out treatment after he felt compelled to molest his nephew who was the same age he was the first time he was molested. Keith reported being sickened by this urge, but also concerned that he might not be able to control it. George was sodomized by an older brother over a ten-year period. While he did not experience any sexual attraction toward children, nor ever exhibited or even fantasized about sexually aggressive behavior of any sort, he saw himself as a "monster," likening himself to the serial murderer Ted Bundy. With the group's help, George was able to see that his fears reflected his feelings of self-loathing and hatred as well as his accepting the stereotype of a sexual predator.

In a group for adult survivors both men and women face several important challenges. First, they must adopt a more realistic and accurate view of their victimization. One of the most deeply rooted beliefs held by survivors is that they somehow caused their abuse. Whether because of something they did or didn't do, many survivors assume it was their fault they were victimized and not "worthy enough" to be protected. An essential first step in coming to terms with their experience is to understand what sexual abuse is, who does it and why. While it would seem that this realization is inherently therapeutic, in fact, it brings with it powerful feelings as survivors begin to accept that they weren't protected and should have been; that they didn't deserve the abuse and didn't cause it; and that as a result of the victimization they experienced a profound loss of innocence and sense of self.

Therefore, a second challenge to group members is to acknowledge and manage the feelings that result from this realization: rage at the exploitation and injustice and sadness at the loss. In groups that include men and women, these feelings will be particularly apparent. As a result of very different socialization experiences, men typically will have an easier time getting in touch with and acknowledging their anger, while women will more readily express feelings of sadness and grief. In group together they are able to give voice to the full range of affective reactions to the victimization.

Group members also need to recognize the connection between their sexual abuse and behaviors they engaged in or decisions they have made that left them feeling ashamed and embarrassed. In addition to problems with substance abuse, eating disorders, and self-injurious behaviors, survivors often have participated in a variety of sexually risky and acting out behaviors like prostitution, promiscuity, and sadomasochism. A number of the clients with whom I work, both male *and* female, report that as children or adolescents they fondled another child. Many survivors have children who were sexually abused, often by the same perpetrators who offended them.

One of my individual clients was repeatedly raped by a friend of her parents over a six-year period. Later she was molested by an uncle and brutally raped by an acquaintance. Her anguish was far greater, however, when she revealed that as an adolescent she used to go to her bedroom and expose herself at the window, often masturbating as she did so. Another client, also a woman, revealed in group that she could only achieve orgasm if she was being injured or hurt by her partner. She expressed much embarrassment and confusion about this but could not stop it. A man in the same group disclosed that he was embarrassed by his need to take numerous showers each day, although he never felt clean enough.

Behaviors such as these exacerbate survivors' already intense feelings of guilt and low self-esteem. A group affords survivors the opportunity to engage in what more than one of my clients has called "true confessions." They have the chance to talk openly about subjects that are particularly taboo and to discover as Shulman discusses in an earlier chapter and elsewhere (1999) that they are "all-in-the-same-boat," a realization that is exceedingly therapeutic and affirming.

A final task emerges as members work together to confront each of these challenges. Because of their victimization, survivors are extremely mistrustful of others. In a group that includes men and women, this mistrust is likely to be especially apparent and hostile. Women will tend to view male group members through the lens of their victimization at the hands of a male perpetrator. As discussed above, regardless of their perpetrator, male survivors' feelings of inadequacy will color their perceptions of the women in the group. Yet, when the members share their stories, they begin to see their underlying commonality. As they engage in mutual aid, developing a level of intimacy with one another that many will not have experienced before, they begin to let go, at least a little bit, of the mistrust and suspiciousness that is so deeply ingrained. Therefore, as the members work together to come to terms with their victimization, they also are, at the same time, working on their relationships with one another.

Vulnerabilities and Risk Factors and Resilience and Protective Factors

In recent years interest has grown in identifying variables that mitigate or intensify the effects of sexual abuse on its victim, although, in almost all instances, the focus has been on female survivors (Alexander et al. 1989; Boudewyn and Liem 1995; Briere and Conte 1993; Johnson, Pike, and Chard 2001; Valentine and Feinauer 1993; Zlotnick et al. 1994). One line of inquiry has focused on the nature and circumstances of the abuse itself. Results of a variety of studies suggest that when the victimization is more frequent and chronic, occurs at an earlier age, involves penetration, fear, and/or sexual arousal, and is perpetrated by a parental figure, the long-term effects are more negative and are more likely to include symptoms of PTSD and dissociation as well as a heightened risk of subsequent sexual and physical victimization (Johnson, Pike, and Chard 2001; Koverola and Proulx 1996; Messman-Moore and Long 2000).

Attention also has been focused on examining the role the child's family plays in mediating the effects of the sexual abuse (Harter, Alexander, and Neimeyer 1988; Koverola and Proulx 1996; Ray, Jackson, and Townsley 1991). When the abuse itself occurs within the family, this becomes more difficult to determine, and much of the research in this area depends upon retrospective self-reports of adult survivors. However, it appears that survivors who characterize their family of origin as lacking in cohesiveness and support, controlling of members, and engaging in frequent conflict and aggressive behavior display more pathology and experience more distress. In contrast, families in which there is a high level of commitment and cohesiveness among members not only seem to protect members from sexual abuse in the first place but also seem to mitigate the abuse's effects, should it occur.

Circumstances surrounding disclosure of the sexual abuse, particularly in childhood, are presumed to be especially significant determinants of a survivors' long-term adjustment (Arata 1998; Everill and Waller 1994; Kelly, Coenen, and Johnston 1995; Roesler and McKenzie 1994; Testa et al. 1992). When a child discloses the abuse and is believed and supported, and the abuse stops, this tends to moderate the long-term impact of the abuse. However, when disclosure results in anger at and/or blame of the child and the abuse continues, this appears to enhance its harmful effects and may be even more damaging to the survivor than if she or he didn't disclose the victimization at all.

Agency and Group Context

When I facilitated my first group for survivors, I was fortunate enough to do it under the auspices of an agency with a long history of providing group work services to clients. Agency staff had a clear sense of what was required in order to successfully create and facilitate a group and taught me a number of valuable lessons. Over the years, I have adhered to those lessons and refined them, particularly in light of the unique features of a survivors group that includes men and women.

Many of the groups for survivors that are described in the literature operate with a great deal of structure and have an explicit educational focus. These groups can be critically important for many individuals just beginning to confront their past and its effects. As Schiller and Zimmer describe in their chapter, a structured group format provides members with much-needed sense of safety, allowing them, in their own time and in their own way, to recount what happened to them and begin to deal with their feelings about it.

I rely upon a less structured approach that leads to more spontaneous interactions between members. As members come to feel comfortable with and accepted and understood by one another, they will be able to engage in mutual aid in the truest sense of the word. As Shulman discusses (1999), the group will consist of multiple helping relationships, not just one, and members will need each other as much, if not more, than they need me. As they share their stories and their pain, members learn from each other and discover in the process that they truly are not alone. As they reach out to one another to offer solace and support, members realize they have something to offer someone else. And as they do this very important work they are simultaneously working on their relationships with one another in a natural and unselfconscious way.

A group for men and women certainly could operate with more structure if the needs of the members warranted this. However, it is likely that its potential to assist members with their relationships with one another would be diminished.

COMPOSITION

The less structured the group, the more powerful the affect that surfaces and the more intense the interactions are between members. For this reason, an individual's appropriateness for the group is particularly important to determine. Therefore, the worker needs to be sure that she or he has the ability to adequately screen and prepare prospective members.

I have an individual session with any client who is referred or self-referred for the group. I use this session to collect pertinent information about the individual, including the nature of the abuse, previous experiences with therapy, current and previous problems in living, and the like. I also acquaint the client with the type of group I will be facilitating and explain its purpose and what she or he can expect in the first session and in general. Both the content of this session as well as the process are helpful in determining whether the survivor is able to handle the demands of the group, since the client's interactions with me are likely to be indicative of how well she or he will relate to others in the group.

I deliberately ask clients about the more sensitive aspects of their abuse and its aftermath. So, for example, I always ask if the client's "body responded sexually" to the sexual abuse, explaining that this is a common reaction and that the body, if stimulated correctly, will react, regardless of the circumstances. I also will ask about self-injurious and compulsive behaviors and raise openly the possibility of subsequent sexual, physical, and emotional abuse. I may not always get honest and complete answers, but in asking these questions I am conveying that it is acceptable to talk about subjects that are considered to be taboo. I have found that many survivors are quite frank in this initial session and, in fact, experience a sense of relief at being asked questions about subjects that they would have had great difficulty raising on their own.

The point in asking about such sensitive topics is two-fold. First, it provides the worker with valuable information about issues the member may want or need to share in group, despite fears about doing so. I credit clients for having the courage to be honest with me, but also advise them that it will be their job, not mine, to share the information with the group, though I will help them if necessary. Second, the worker is modeling for clients what will be expected of them in the group and that is to engage in an honest and uncensored discussion with others who were similarly victimized.

When considering an individual survivor's appropriateness for a group for men and women, the worker should attend to basic exclusion criteria like active abuse of substances, suicidal ideation, psychotic behaviors, and the like. Many survivors exhibit these symptoms, but a more structured group that deliberately focuses, for example, on the substance abuse *and* the sexual abuse would in most instances be a more appropriate option. Individuals deemed by the worker to be particularly fragile or who are confronting their victimization for the first time also are likely to be poor candidates for a more unstructured group and would be better suited to a group that provides more direct assistance with regulating and managing affect.

I strongly encourage, but don't mandate, members to be in concurrent individual treatment. Others, like Schiller and Zimmer, require this of members, a position that has a great deal of merit since members are likely to need a great deal of assistance dealing with issues generated by the group. Whenever possible, though, I want members to feel empowered to make their own decisions in this regard. What I do find, almost invariably, is that the group can serve as a powerful impetus for members to get into individual therapy if they are not already. The worker may want to determine on an individual basis whether the survivor can meet the demands of the group without the support of and experience with individual therapy.

The worker should anticipate that appropriate candidates are likely to have had a variety of sexual abuse experiences and different reactions to it. They may be young adults, just embarking upon the challenges of adulthood, or individuals in middle, or even late adulthood, that have created families and have children, even grandchildren. The challenge to the worker will be to help members recognize their underlying commonality, despite the differences that appear to exist, and to use the variety of experiences that members present with to enrich the process of mutual aid. Members will have coped differently, reacted differently, and developed different perspectives on their experience. As they share these, they are learning from one another and developing a more realistic perspective on their own victimization.

Like Schiller and Zimmer, I subscribe to Gitterman's "not the only one" principle of not having a single member from any one subgroup. Since my clients come from a fairly small community and there are few options for group treatment, it is often difficult to adhere to this guideline. I have found, like Schilller, that the differences between members are not barriers to their connecting with others in the group, possibly because of the intense sense of urgency survivors feel about being with others like themselves.

The worker also should expect that appropriate candidates will have varying abilities to recall their victimization. While there continues to be much debate about the accuracy and validity of "recovered memories," the reality is that given the age at which many survivors were victimized as well as the protective function that repression serves, many survivors do have incomplete memories of their victimization (Briere and Conte 1993; Feldman-Summers and Pope 1994; Mayer 1995; Williams 1992).

In my individual session with clients in advance of the group, I ask about unexplained sensations, thoughts, or feelings they may have. I also ask if, "in their gut," they believe there is more to the abuse than they have recalled. If survivors reply in the affirmative to one or both of these questions, it is likely that some repression has taken place. The group often serves as a stimulus to memory recall for members. Therefore, it is important for the worker to alert clients to this possibility in advance. Remembering the abuse shouldn't be the reason that someone joins a survivors group, but members' disclosures may ultimately trigger this phenomenon either in the group session itself or outside of it as the following example demonstrates.

In the previous session, members discussed their anger and sadness at having not been protected by a parent, particularly their mother. While none of the members recalled having been molested by their mother, most recalled instances where there mother or another female caregiver knew about what was going on but did nothing. This discussion became quite intense, with several members stating that they were angrier at their mother than they were at the person or persons that had abused them.

In the session that followed this one, I began by summarizing our last session, observing how painful members' disclosures and reactions were and wondered how members felt about what we had talked about. Mark was one of the first to respond. Mark had previously disclosed to the group his recollection of being sodomized by his father. He also revealed that his father used to bring prostitutes into the home and forced him to watch as he (the father) had violent sex with them. He had no recollection of where his mother was during these episodes and had expressed puzzlement over this. In the previous session, Mark expressed a great deal of anger over members' disclosures about their mothers but none towards his own. In the current session, Mark tearfully revealed that two days after the group, "out of the blue" he remembered that his mother had, on several occasions, been raped by his father in his (Mark's) presence. He also reported to the group that he recalled his mother being present when he was raped and beaten by his father and his mother being "too weak" to do anything about it.

The way in which Mark's memory of this abuse came back to him is typical. As disconcerting as the memory was for him, talking about it in the group helped to normalize the experience of spontaneously recalling it and also provided him with much-needed support and understanding. Members were quick to reassure Mark that they had had similar experiences. Further, the anger that members expressed over his mother's inaction gave voice to feelings Mark considered to be taboo, since she, too, was victimized by his father.

GROUP STRUCTURE

While different models have been proposed in the literature, most authors agree that groups for survivors need to be small and membership closed. A growing body of research supports the efficacy of these groups (Alexander et al. 1989; Bagley and Young 1998; Morgan and Cummings 1999; Richter, Snider, and Gorey 1997; Singer 1989). The difficult work that members are there to do will be easier if the group is limited in size and members understand that they are all in it for the duration, that is, that they will be starting and finishing together.

I have worked with as few as six members in a group and as many as nine, which felt too large to me. It's not so much that a larger group limits any one member's ability to "have her or his say"; it's that the amount of information and the array of dynamics that has to be attended to is overwhelming and the sense of intimacy among members is more limited. Therefore, the worker should consider that a group that contains six to no more than eight survivors provides maximum benefits to members.

Most groups for survivors described in the literature are time-limited, though there is considerable variation in the number of sessions. The literature on time-limited groups, generally, supports their efficacy (Budman and Demby 1983; Budman et al. 1985; Burlingame and Fuhriman 1990). I have experimented with groups of different lengths, beginning with groups that were ten sessions in length and ending up with groups that were twenty sessions long. At the completion of each group that I facilitate, I ask members to complete a client satisfaction survey. It was only when I began running twenty session groups that the majority of members indicated that the group length felt "about right." Group sessions are ninety minutes in length.

Admittedly, decisions in this regard are somewhat arbitrary. The worker has to take into consideration her or his own commitments as well as agency mandates and requirements. However, she or he should plan on facilitating a group of at least twelve sessions. While members will connect quickly, at least in a superficial way, they will have to develop a deeper level of trust in and comfort with one another before they are able to tackle the most painful aspects of their abuse and its consequences. This will take time, particularly given survivors' mistrust and suspiciousness of others.

I learned the hard way about the need to pay attention to the physical space. While I had always recognized members' need for privacy, as well as the need to conduct the group in a space that was separate from where members' children were being watched, I had not been as sensitive to considerations associated with open and uncensored displays of anger. In the group session that I described earlier in which Mark discussed his memory regarding his mother's role in his abuse, Mark became very agitated and upset and began pounding his fist on the door to the room, which he was sitting beside. The door splintered. Mark wasn't hurt, as the door was quite flimsy, but I, and the agency, learned how important it was to provide members with *safe* ways to vent their anger. The door was repaired and padding was placed on the inside. Large pillows were added to the room, so that members could use these, both to hit and cuddle, as needed. Of course, plenty of tissues are available.

Group Rules

Rules that are commonly used with groups of all sorts have relevance for a group for survivors. One of the most important is the need for members to come each week and if they consider quitting, to talk it over with the group. As I'll discuss, a common theme in the middle phase is disillusionment with the group. Many members will feel that the group is making things worse, not better. They feel overwhelmingly angry and sad, new memories may have surfaced, flashbacks and nightmares may have occurred. In my view, these reactions suggest that the group is doing precisely the sort of work it should be doing, but one or more members may not see it this way and desire to quit. It is important for the member to discuss her or his intentions with the rest of the group both to develop a more realistic perspective on what she or he is experiencing and to help all achieve a sense of closure, if she or he does, in fact, leave.

> After the sixth session, Carol, who had become increasingly quiet, called me to say that she was thinking of quitting the group because she was trying to cope with the suicide of her son ten months before, and she didn't feel members could help her with this, since the group was for survivors of sexual abuse, not survivors of

suicide. I pointed out to Carol that while she was technically correct, the bottom line was that her feelings of guilt and loss about her son's death were intertwined with her feelings about her sexual abuse, that each reinforced the other. I also questioned whether it was just coincidence that her thoughts about leaving surfaced at a time when the group was beginning to talk honestly and openly about members' pain about their losses. Carol acknowledged that she was finding it harder and harder to attend the sessions because it "hurt so much," but agreed to come the following week and talk about her concerns with the other members.

As I began the next session, I observed that the group had been doing some very difficult work, that members had been able to talk, not only about the loss of childhood and innocence they felt as a result of their victimization, but also about other losses they had experienced. I then informed them that Carol had called me to tell me she thought of quitting and that I thought this was connected to where the group was in its work. I invited Carol to share with the members what was going on for her. Carol talked about her grief at the loss of her son and the loneliness she felt, as she could not talk with her husband about his (the son's) death. She began to cry, as did others, as she stated, "In my whole life, the only thing I thought I did well was raise my children. And now, I realize I didn't even do that right. How could I not have known how depressed Sam [her son] was? Why couldn't I see he was in such pain?" Peter, who was not himself a parent, was the first to respond, "I may not have lost a son, but I think I can appreciate how awful you must feel. I want you to know that you can talk about it here. You need to talk about this, and I hope you feel you can talk to us." Others in the group shared their agreement with Peter's comment.

Ultimately, Carol decided to remain in the group. Her disclosure about her son's suicide and her accompanying feelings of loss served as powerful stimuli to the group and its work. Other members began to talk about their own experiences with loss. Gary disclosed that, "the only thing that ever loved him," his dog, had recently died, leaving him "totally and completely alone." Sally revealed that she had lost a close friend, who was more like a mother to her, to cancer, while Bill questioned, "How can you feel loss, when you never had anybody to lose," referring to his own intense feeling of being utterly alone in the world and unloved by anyone. The bottom line was the group needed Carol, and she needed the group. As Carol talked with the group about her desire to quit, she was expressing feelings that others also had about how hard the work was. Members' reactions to her, however, assisted her in seeing that she truly was not alone, either in her feelings of disillusionment or in her grief, providing her with the courage to continue.

A second important rule in a group for survivors was illustrated in the previous example, and that is, that if members want to talk with the worker outside of group they may do so, but they need to understand that whatever is shared with the worker will be shared with the group. As I've noted, survivors have many "secrets" associated with their sexual abuse and with their behavior as adolescents and adults. Many of these are sexual in nature. While it is understandable that members are reluctant to share these secrets with the group, the full healing potential of the group is only realized when they finally do so. As long as the survivor holds on to the belief that she or he is harboring a "dirty little secret," she or he is in some way cutoff from the help that members have to offer. I assume that when members want to tell me something outside of the group, then at some level they want the group to know and what they are really asking for is my assistance in accomplishing this.

George was a fairly silent member of the group. He was the youngest member, had less experience with therapy, and was socially quite awkward. Although his abuse experiences were similar to others in the group, he often said he felt uncomfortable and different from them. After one session, George asked me if he could talk with me. With great hesitancy and embarrassment, he said he was worried about himself, found himself doing "weird shit" to himself. When pressed, he told me he had been getting angrier and angrier over the last several weeks and that the only thing that was helping him release the anger was to watch pornography that featured anal sex while sodomizing himself with the handle of a large hairbrush. George began crying as he shared this with me, saying he was embarrassed by this but couldn't stop it. I credited George for being able to tell me, acknowledging that it might have been particularly hard because I was a woman. I also reminded him that I saw my job as one of helping him tell the group what he had shared with me, and while he was understandably reluctant to do this, saying, "They'll think I'm really fucked up," he also admitted that he wanted to be able to talk about this, because he didn't like the feeling that somehow he "deserved to be fucked." We then talked about how I could be helpful to him in disclosing his "secret" to the group.

George agreed to come the following week, and I called him before the next session to make sure that he wasn't going to "chicken out." I began the group as I always did, by summarizing my sense of the previous session. I then said that George had talked with me after the last session and had something he really needed to talk with the members about. As George and I had agreed, I began the conversation by saying that I sensed that the group was bringing up a lot of anger for members and that anger was a really difficult emotion for survivors to manage, that survivors often turned it inward against themselves. I also said that my sense was that what George needed to talk about was related to this as well as to the confusion that he and others in the group felt about sex and their sexuality. At that point, George began to talk about his behavior. Members listened intently, nodding their heads in agreement. The first to respond was Sally who said, "I can only get off if the guy is hurting me, like biting me or something." Another man reported, "Things are so bad between me and my girlfriend now that I can't even get it up anymore. My girlfriend wants to have sex and I just can't. But when I go to an S and M bar and get picked up and fucked up the ass I get all excited. I must be sick or something." Another woman revealed that as an adolescent she had posed for a variety of hardcore pornographic photos and still had the photos and "got off" by looking at herself.

At times such as these, it can be difficult for the worker to maintain a clear sense of role and purpose. George's pain and humiliation was acute, and I was tempted to respond as I would if he was my individual client, with a great deal of empathy and support. Yet, this would have diluted the healing power of the group. What George needed more than my support was the understanding of those who could relate to him best, and those were the others in the group. His disclosure was a catalyst for this group's focus on the most taboo of topics. It also provided him with much-needed validation and served to normalize his feelings and reactions. It was only when he felt less crazy and "fucked up" that he could begin to examine the feelings of anger and self-loathing that were at the root of his actions.

A third expectation for a survivors group such as this is the need for the group to maintain confidentiality. This should be self-evident. What is important to emphasize here is the implications that this expectation has for the members and for the worker. In those instances when a member is in individual treatment, I make it clear that unless there's a compelling reason related to the client's well-being, I will discuss her or his progress in group with the individual worker. I, or the group, might suggest that the individual talk about a particular issue with her or his therapist and the group might provide the member with the opportunity to "rehearse" how she or he will go about doing this. But, ultimately, it is the member's responsibility to do this, not mine.

The community from which my clients come is a small one and members often refer others to the group. Members attend AA or NA meetings together, or come from the same family or had the same abuser. A common rule that exists in many groups holds that members should not interact with one another outside of the group. I understand and generally agree with this expectation, but I realized long ago that it wouldn't be feasible with the clients with whom I work. I also felt it would be demeaning to these clients who already felt so powerless in so many relationships to make a "demand" that they avoid each other. In fact, many of the groups for survivors described in the literature specifically encourage members to connect with one another outside of the group, and in their chapter, Schiller and Zimmer describe the advantages of this.

What I suggest to members is that they be respectful of each other's privacy, that what we talk about in the group stays in group, even in their conversations with one another on the "outside." I also remind members that their relationships with one another outside of group will affect their relationships with one another in the group, and that if one becomes a barrier to the other, they need to let me know. In a group that includes both men and women, the worker should be particularly sensitive to members' interactions on the outside, given survivors' tendency to sexualize relationships. In my experience, this has not emerged as a problem, perhaps because of survivors' well-developed ability to split relationships, but given the disruptive influence such relationships could have on the group, the worker must be prepared to deal with them directly in the group. Rather than representing a distraction, discussing *in* group members' relationships with one another *outside* of the group will be an important part of members' work.

Another important expectation that must guide members' interactions with one another and with the worker is the need for honest communication. The reasons for this are self-evident but worth repeating. Sexual abuse is taboo. The feelings that it generates are taboo. The ways in which survivors have coped with their feelings and their reactions may be taboo. Members' shame, embarrassment, and humiliation will only lessen if they feel able to talk openly about their experiences.

In addition, members' unresolved issues with significant others may surface in group as transference phenomena, while the worker inevitably will have affective reactions to members' disclosures. These interactions and reactions may be useful in enhancing members' understanding of themselves and each other, but only if they and the worker can talk openly and directly about them.

Single Versus Co-Leadership

The need for the leader to attend to the complex interplay of process and content issues has led the majority of authors to argue that groups for survivors should be co-led. It is assumed that two leaders are better able to manage group process and handle the intense affect that surfaces in these groups. Authors also point to the advantages of having two individuals serve as models of healthy adult communication. Because most of the groups described in the literature are for women, the co-leaders also are almost always women, sending an important message of empowerment to members.

As I noted at the outset, I began working with men and women together out of necessity. I have always facilitated these groups alone, mostly because a co-leader wasn't available. Based upon members' comments, I would argue that if the group is to be individually led, it should be by a woman. The male survivors with whom I have worked consistently have said that they feel more comfortable working in group with me because I am a woman. Both men and women have told me, often quite emphatically, that they would *not* participate in group if the leader were a man.

A number of authors have noted that women may be ill-served in groups that contain men and women, since the power inequities that exist in their everyday relationships may be recreated in the group. I believe that while this is a possibility, the fact that I am a woman reduces the likelihood that it will happen. Even more important, the expectations that the leader holds for members, regardless of her or his gender, will have a lot to do with how members interact with and view each other.

I often have speculated as to the impact that co-leadership would have on this mixed group. I assume that the advantages noted above would exist. I also suspect that if the group were facilitated by a man and a woman, my preference, the potential for their relationship to serve as a model to members would be particularly powerful as would the emergence of transference phenomena. In any case, it is important for the worker to consider how members' victimization and their subsequent experiences with individuals of both genders will shape their views of and interactions with her or him and each other.

Work and Group Themes

The worker can anticipate that survivors' desire to connect with others who have been similarly victimized will be strong, thus promoting rapid engagement. In a mixed group, however, members' fears about and hostility towards the opposite sex will be readily apparent from the beginning and will influence their earliest dealings with one another.

Beginning Phase

Schiller and Zimmer describe a structured approach to member introductions in the first group session. I rely upon a strategy that is less prescribed, allowing members to disclose as much, or as little, about themselves as is comfortable. In my individual session, I inform prospective group members that I'll ask them to introduce themselves and suggest that they share with others as much as they feel they can about the sexual abuse and the effects it has had on them. I reassure them that everyone in the group will be feeling the same way about starting—hopeful that they will feel accepted and understood by others who have experienced the abuse, but fearful that somehow they are "different" and the "only one." I also tell them that the only way that they will really know that they aren't alone will be to put "something of themselves out there for the rest of the group to see."

Clients are entitled to their defenses. I can't "make" anyone disclose anything she or he isn't ready to disclose. Members' revelations in the first session will be tentative and somewhat superficial relative to what will come later, but it is likely that one or more members will be quite frank and open, as the following example reveals.

Mary was a returning member of the group. While there were two other returning members, the other four were new. During most of the previous group, Mary's memory of her abuse consisted of an incomplete recollection of being raped by a cousin when she was 12 and a growing "sense" that she was molested at a younger age, by an uncle. Mary continued in individual treatment after the previous group ended, so that by the time the new group started she had recalled terrible abuse at the hands of her grandmother and uncle (the grandmother's son).

When it came time for Mary to introduce herself she hesitantly provided her name, age, and marital status. She disclosed the abuse by her cousin and said, "Well, I guess that's it." I was preparing to move to the next member when Mary said, "Wait a minute. I might as well tell the whole story. I mean, I think I'd rather just get this over with now than have it hang over my head." Mary then shared with the group what she had remembered: when she was three years old, her grandmother tied her to a kitchen table spread-eagled. Her grandmother began inserting objects, including the handle of rolling pin, into her vagina, "preparing" her, she said, for her son [Mary's uncle].The uncle then raped her. This began a pattern of rape that continued for a number of years. Mary also revealed her memories of being locked in a basement closet and only being let out when she performed oral sex on the uncle and engaged in other sexual acts with him.

By the time she finished, Mary was crying as were several others. I thanked Mary for her honesty and commented to the group, "Mary's story has had a powerful effect on you all. I know it's upsetting to me. I can only imagine how it is for you. My sense is that what Mary has said may be hard for some of you to hear. Because you don't know what to say, or because it hit too close to home, too close to your own experiences." Joe, a new member of the group, who had already provided a quick introduction of himself, replied with tears in his eyes, "Jesus Christ! What is wrong with these motherfuckers, anyway? How could your uncle do that to you? How could your *grandmother* do that to you? I'm so . . . sorry." Others members echoed Joe's sentiments and as the session progressed, other members were able to reveal equally painful and sensitive aspects of their abuse.

Before the group started, Mary shared with me her nervousness about disclosing her abuse with the members. The previous group had been much easier for her because what she had remembered was, in her view, "normal" sexual abuse. This time around, Mary's abuse made her feel like a "freak," and my reassurances that it was not she who was freakish or crazy, it was those who had done those things to her, provided little comfort. Mary's extreme anxiety is what led her to "tell all," and it was the immediate support and understanding she received from members that began to reduce this anxiety in a way that nothing I said could have done.

I should note that as with any session this intense, particularly a first session, it was important for me to process with members their reactions, asking them how this might impact on their ability and willingness to return the following week. While some expressed misgivings, all reported a sense of relief and assured me that they would return, which they did.

This excerpt reveals the twin themes that will predominate throughout the group: pain at the losses members have experienced and rage at those who exploited and did not protect them. It also demonstrates another important dynamic: it was another member who articulated the anger that Mary was feeling about her abuse.

This example nicely illustrates another significant theme of the earliest phase and that is the dawning awareness among members of their underlying commonality. This is particularly powerful given the hostility, misconceptions, and stereotyped thinking the men and women bring with them about each other. While the worker should assume that members' disclosures will quickly draw them together, she or he also must expect that, at least initially, another theme, tension and antagonism between members, will be high. This was brought home to me quite vividly in the first mixed group that I facilitated.

> Jean was in the women's group in which the idea of a mixed group first surfaced. In fact, she was the first woman in this group to suggest the mixed group format. She decided to join the first mixed group. She expressed an eagerness to work with men and acknowledged she had difficulty getting along with and trusting them. In the first session, I introduced myself and the group and talked about how we would all be learning something from being together in this unique format. I then invited members to introduce themselves. Several members, including two of the three men had provided introductions, and had talked fairly openly about their abuse. Jean had been sexually abused by at least ten men in her extended family, including her father, grandfather, uncles, and cousins. She also had been in three abusive marriages where she had been psychologically, sexually, and physically victimized. She shared this information with the group and became increasingly agitated. I pointed this out to her, and she replied, "I'm trying to keep calm, trying to remember that these guys are like me. I was sorry to hear their stories. But I am really pissed off. When I look that them [the men in the group] all I see is a bunch of snakes and lizards. I feel like I'd like to spit on them or something. Like, who the hell do they think they are coming in here and acting like they're like us [the other women in the group]?"

Jean was clearly confused by her reactions. On the one hand, she was moved by what she had the heard the men reveal about their own experiences, but on the other, their presence in the group brought out in a powerful way her deeply felt and long-held resentment towards men. It was one thing for Jean to know intellectually that she needed to work on her relationships with men. It was quite another to be in their presence. I shared this observation with the group, suggesting that Jean was probably not the only one with such feelings, and several members were able to say they held similar views, including two of the men. Members were not yet able to go beyond a basic acknowledgement of their fears about each other, but the stage was set for the important work that they would do in this regard as the group progressed.

The early phase also is characterized by the "everyone but me" phenomenon. Members assume that everyone else in the group truly is a victim who did not deserve the abuse, who deserved to be protected, and warrants the care and concern of the group. In contrast, the individual member holds onto the belief that somehow she or he is different, that she or he was unlovable or seductive or gay, or in some other way caused what happened to her or him. These feelings protect the survivor from considering the alternative, and that is that she or he was betrayed, a realization that, in turn, generates overwhelming feelings of rage and despair, feelings that are frightening.

In a previous example of a first session, Joe expressed a great deal of anger at Mary's abusers, her grandmother and uncle. As this same session continued, I observed that when Joe had described his own abuse in his introduction (he was sodomized by a family friend beginning when he was ten years old), he seemed to blame himself for the abuse, yet seemed sure that Mary was not responsible for hers. He replied, "Well, yeah, it's just different. I was older. I should have said no. I was a boy. I should have hit him or something." This is typical of members' views of their abuse in the early phase of the group. Even *Mary* questioned why she never told anyone, though others were adamant in reassuring her that she was in no way responsible for what happened to her.

As the group progresses and members share more significant and painful aspects of their abuse, it becomes harder to maintain the view that they were somehow to blame for their victimization. Initially, the worker will have to be the one to point out the discrepancy between members' views of themselves and others in the group. Members should be helped and can be expected to assume this responsibility as they develop greater comfort with one another. For example, in a later session of the first group that I facilitated, members were talking about feeling responsible for their abuse. Jean commented, "I know in my head that it wasn't my fault, that I didn't cause this. But, in my heart, where it counts, I feel like it must have been me, something I did." Andrew responded, "No, you're right. Your uncles, your father, all of them. They were sick. How could you have caused the abuse? You were eight years old for Christ's sake! Eight year olds don't ask to be fucked!" This powerful comment was made even more so because it came from another member who himself struggled with accepting that his parents, particularly his mother, had never been there for him, thus leaving him vulnerable to the abuse he suffered.

MIDDLE PHASE

In many ways the beginning phase can be characterized as a "honeymoon" period. Members may be anxious about meeting and connecting with others who were sexually abused, but they also approach the group with much hope and anticipation. As members develop greater comfort with one another and begin to talk more openly about their abuse and its effects, the work becomes more difficult, and optimism often is replaced by disillusionment, an important and challenging theme in the middle phase.

As mentioned earlier, some members may consider quitting. The sentiment of many will be that the group is harder than they thought it would be, leading to questions about whether it is really helping. On more than one occasion, I have found myself wondering the same thing. It is terribly difficult to observe members' pain and anguish week after week, *and* to realize that the demands I have made on them have brought this about. It also is difficult when members' pain and anger is directed at me. It is in moments such as these that the reassurance, support, and guidance of my colleagues are invaluable.

> In the fifth session, Lucy and June were discussing their feelings about and relationships with their mothers. Both had been abused by male family members, had indirectly told their mothers about the abuse, and had been ignored. June said, "I feel like I've moved beyond anger at anyone about the abuse. What I need to work on now is trusting men and learning how to have normal relationships with them. As far as my mom, I know we'll never be close. She just doesn't seem to want it, and that's okay with me." Lucy responded, "I know what you mean. I've been angry and it didn't get me anywhere. I think it really is better to forgive and forget." Two other women then commented they were envious of Lucy and June, since they seemed to be making so much progress and others voiced their agreement.
>
> I said, "I know that you have dealt with your feelings toward your mothers, but my sense is that you haven't even scratched the surface. This will probably make you angry, and maybe some of the rest of you as well, but I think both of you harbor a lot of rage about what happened, about how your mothers could have ignored your cries for help, and how they didn't care enough to see your pain. June, I know that you, particularly, want a relationship with your mother, that you're lonely and want her to be there for you. But wanting it and having it are two different things. I have the feeling that any relationship with her will be on her terms with you doing all the giving. I think you're afraid to deal with these feelings."
>
> Members' responses to my comments were quick. Fred, whose mother had engaged in many seductive behaviors with him, and who was raped at age 11 and then again at age 15 by two different men, angrily said to me, "There you go again. You're not content unless someone is crying or feeling bad. Isn't it possible that they really have dealt with their feelings about their mothers?" Kevin, mentioned earlier and abused my his uncle and several other adult men, agreed, "Why do you always have to look for problems?" Both Lucy and June both admitted they were angry with me for my comments.
>
> I replied, "Well, it seems like folks are pissed off with me, which I can understand. But I have to say again that my sense is everyone wants, maybe even needs,

to believe that June and Lucy are through with their anger. The problem is, it's just not that simple. I wish it was, I really do, but it just isn't."

There was silence. Kevin was the first to speak. "I don't know why I come here week after week. I leave here feeling disgusted, angry, pissed off. Everything. What the hell's the point?" June replied, "I feel the same way. But I know what the point is, even if I don't want to admit it. We don't get over this shit if we don't talk about. I know my mother is as crazy now as she ever was. Maybe more. But I just want her to be a mother to me. Just once."

This was a difficult moment in this group for everyone, including me. The members were disheartened, questioning the point of the group, and angry with me because I was asking them to directly face their feelings about those who exploited and did not protect them. Lucy's and June's own difficulties confronting their anger provided the group with an opportune way of avoiding this most difficult of discussions. Yet, the group *was* ready, as June's comment revealed.

This exchange actually marked a turning point in the group's work, wherein a second theme, expression of intense affect, became apparent. The difference between how affect is expressed at this point as contrasted with the earlier phase is that members are actually able to *experience* it, not just talk about it. At this stage, the worker needs to be particularly concerned that members are provided with safe ways to vent feelings. Shulman's two-client paradigm also is an important consideration (1999). The worker must be sensitive to the needs of the individual member displaying intense affect, as well as to the needs of the group as a whole. Members are likely to be deeply distraught at a fellow member's distress. However, unless the member is a danger to self or others, the leader is most helpful to all if he or she allows the individual to get out the feelings and then, afterwards, processes the situation with everyone.

Earlier in this chapter, I mentioned that Mark, upon realizing that his mother played a larger role in his abuse than he had so far been able to acknowledge, pounded on the door to the room and, as a result, the door splintered. The problem was *not* Mark's anger; it was that I had not thought through carefully enough what members' needs would be in this area. Even with something as dramatic as a broken door, Mark's and the other members' reactions to this incident were typical of how this theme is manifested. As Mark got angrier and angrier, others sat quietly. Some appeared to be fearful, later acknowledging they were mostly afraid *for* Mark, not *of* him. When we processed this later, all said that they wanted to help Mark but didn't know how. Several said that they "zoned out," suggesting dissociation, addressed later. For example, Mary said that Mark's anger reminded her of her father, whose alcoholic rages led to much violence within her family, and she "couldn't take it." Sarah and Peter both observed that as they watched Mark get angry, they found themselves getting angry, too, first at his mother and father, and then at their own abusers; they also said this anger scared them, and they tuned him out.

I asked Mark how it was for him to have vented so much anger, and what he wanted from the group. As is typical, he said that in the midst of his rage, he didn't need anything, only the reassurance that, if necessary, I would intervene. Mark also said that had I or anyone else in the group attempted to console him or in some other way interrupt his expression of anger, it would have shut it off. This last comment is particularly important and is one I hear repeatedly. It further underscores the need for the worker, like the members, to be able to tolerate the intense expression of affect. What members learn from such encounters is that they can experience honest exploration of feelings and *survive* them, which is immensely empowering.

Assisting members with the expression of affect requires that the worker have a very clear understanding of her or his own reactions to members' disclosures as these are occurring. In some cases, the worker will have to resist the urge to share her or his own feelings with the members, allowing them the opportunity to do this first. In others, it will only be when the worker lets the group know what is going on for her or him that the members will be able to get at their own feelings. In the example just noted, I did have to initiate the discussion, as members were too deeply moved and affected by Mark's reactions to have responded without my assistance.

In other cases, however, members will be perfectly capable of responding to the distress of another and to not allow them to do this is to deny them the opportunity to give and receive mutual aid of a most powerful sort.

> Denise presented herself as aloof and tough, stating to members that, "I'm never going to let anyone fuck with me again." She had been sadistically raped and beaten throughout her childhood and adolescence by her father. Her father also forced her brothers to rape her in his presence. Denise was a very vocal member of the group, and unlike the other women, was quite able to articulate anger at her abusers. In the eighth session, members were focused on sadness and loss, including the death of individuals that had been special to them. I noticed that Denise appeared to be particularly uncomfortable. I commented on this, suggesting that for the first time I thought I saw something other than the anger that she typically exhibited. Denise replied, "I've never talked about this, but I feel the need to do it now." She then told the group that during her adolescence, her boyfriend "was the only one in the whole world" who cared for her and for whom she cared. When she was fifteen and while she was talking with the boyfriend on the phone, he shot himself in the head and killed himself.
>
> Denise's disclosure had a powerful effect on the group, particularly since she had been such a stoic and angry member up to this point. Her comments were met with silence. Some members were teary-eyed, others appeared nervous. Denise herself had tears in her eyes. Finally, Janet, who was sitting next to Denise, tearfully commented, "Oh, Denise, I am so sorry for you. I wish I could say

something to make you feel better. I hurt for you. For me. For all of us." With this, Janet patted Denise on her shoulders and handed her some Kleenex.

It is hard to capture how poignant and dramatic this moment was. The fact that Denise had had the courage to risk such a painful disclosure was significant, but Janet's response was equally compelling. Janet was a sad, lonely woman, who had said on many occasions that she felt as if she was a failure at everything she attempted in life. She cried easily at other members' pain, yet had never been able to reach out to them, fearing that she would be rejected or laughed at, as had so often been the case in her childhood.

I was deeply moved by Denise's disclosure. I wanted to reach out to her, console and comfort her. Yet, I knew it was important to let the group members do this, if they could. Denise benefited from Janet's comforting words and gestures, but *so did Janet*. Had I intervened with my own comments, I would have denied Janet this powerful opportunity to be of assistance to Denise and Denise the experience of being truly accepted and understood by Janet, and, ultimately, by the rest of the group.

During intense moments such as these, the worker can expect that some dissociation, another theme of the middle phase, will occur. Many members simply will be unable to tolerate the intense expression of affect and will need to resort to coping mechanisms that have served them well in the past. I learned about this in a most dramatic and unexpected way. In the session following a particularly dramatic one in which there were many tears and much anger, I began by sharing with members that it took me several days before I could stop thinking about our last session, and that if I was distressed, I could only imagine what it must have been like for them. Members—*everyone one of them*—looked at me with blank stares. They had no idea what I was talking about. As the group members and I processed this, it became clear to all of us that each of them had dissociated, and therefore, had no clear memory of the session. As we talked more about it, some began to recall the session in bits and pieces, but most were unable, even after the discussion, to remember all of what had transpired.

Usually the dissociation is not this dramatic. One or more members will tune out at points where the discussion hits particularly close to home. In my individual session with members and then again in the first session, I let them know that this may occur and explain why. During difficult moments in the group, I pay close attention to individual members' behavior, looking for signs that they have "taken off." Rather than interrupting this dynamic as it unfolds, I have found it more useful and productive to process later, with the individual and the group as a whole, what triggered the dissociation and what, if anything the member, or others in the group, could have done to assist her or him with staying with the discussion. With experience, members typically become better able to monitor their behavior and those of the others in the group and to tolerate more intense interactions and affect.

A fourth theme in the middle phase reflects members' attempts to understand and reconcile behaviors, decisions, and choices they made as adults. It is at this stage that the "true confessions" as mentioned previously are most likely to take place. These disclosures don't just represent an unburdening of long-held secrets. Members begin to understand the reasons why they engaged in behaviors or made decisions that cause them such embarrassment. Many members refer to this process as one of "forgiving" themselves. I personally struggle with the use of this term and tell members that I prefer to view what they are doing as accepting, or coming to terms with, their actions. However it is framed, as members talk about their most taboo actions and are met with understanding, their ability to understand *why* they did what they did and *how* it connects to their victimization is enhanced, thus lessening their guilt and shame.

In an earlier case illustration, this dynamic emerged quite powerfully as the group reacted to George's disclosures about his obsession with pornography and compulsion to sodomize himself with the handle of a hairbrush. Members literally rushed to share their own stories of comparable behaviors. In the course of this discussion, members began pointing out to each other how their actions were connected to their abuse. So, for example, it was another member of the group who pointed out to George that his actions represented his anger at his brother who had abused him, and that he had turned it inward against himself. Another member added, "Maybe the reason you do this to yourself is that you think you need to punish yourself. Because you feel like you are dirty, because of what your brother did. But *he's* the one who's a dirtball. He's the one who should have something shoved up his ass, not you."

As this group progressed, members became better able to put their own behavior in perspective, not just that of others. Denise, who had been a prostitute for many years, was able to say, "The truth of the matter is, I took the money, I solicited sex. No one forced me to. I'm not proud of it but it's a part of my past that I have to accept if I'm going to get past this stuff. I used to think that when I prostituted I was in control, but I realize that I was just letting men control me just like they had for all those years. I just didn't know any different."

Inevitably, the themes that have so far been identified contribute to a final one and that is members' attention to their here and now interactions. Members' increasing comfort with one another will allow them to "show their true colors." Whatever difficulties they experienced in relationships with others, particularly those of the opposite sex, will surface in a real and dramatic way in the group. Classic examples of transference phenomena are likely to abound in this phase and will be apparent in members' relationships with and reactions to one another and the worker.

In a previous example, I mentioned Denise, who for much of the group maintained a "tough as nails" exterior. Even after her disclosure about the suicide of her boyfriend, she remained aloof and angry. In the twelfth session, Denise was again saying that she was never going to get hurt again: "I'm going to live my life as I see fit, fuck everybody else." Bob refused to look at Denise, and played nervously with his hands. One of the other women said, "Come on Bob, you look upset. What's up? Is it Denise?" Bob acknowledged, "As soon as she opens her mouth, I get pissed off at her. I'm sick of her bullshit. This 'I don't care' shit gets on my nerves big time." Such an outburst from Bob was very uncharacteristic. However, he openly struggled with his feelings about his mother, whom he described as cold and uncaring and as never having hugged or touched him. It was another member of the group who was able to point out the transference: "Denise really stirred up something for you, didn't she? Who does she remind you of? Isn't that how you think of your mother, like she's cold and hard?"

This was a particularly mature working group. In many prior sessions, I had pointed out instances in which the "baggage" they brought with them interfered with their ability to connect with each other. The significance of this exchange was that it was the first time that the members, themselves, took on the role of identifying and interpreting such behaviors.

The worker should anticipate that members' difficulties in interpersonal relationships will play out in their relationship with her or him. As I discussed earlier, some resentment of the worker will exist simply because the worker makes demands on the group. But some of the anger will inevitably reflect members' unresolved issues with others, for example parents who didn't protect and therapists who didn't help or who exploited them. Members' anger also may reflect their sense of injustice and the basic unfairness of their victimization. For example, a male group member, in a moment of anger, said to me, "I just don't get it. Why me? Why not you? Am I so bad, so awful that I should have been raised by the perverts who were my parents? Why couldn't it have been you? Are you so much better than me?"

There really is no good answer to this member's question, because it reflects a fundamental, but frightening, reality that survivors have to face, and that is that there is no good reason why they were abused and others weren't. In replying to this particular member, I said this, adding, "It could have been me, but it wasn't. It was you, and that must make you angry as hell."

ENDING PHASE

In a time-limited group like the one I've described, endings tend to be difficult for members. They have developed a level of comfort with one another that is gratifying and, as more than one member has commented, the group has become, for many, a family, providing a sense of connectedness and intimacy that is completely new. Because of this, the worker can anticipate that denial of the group's ending will be a prominent theme in this last phase. In the very first session, I remind members of how many sessions we will have together. Beginning at the halfway point in the group, I inform members in each session how many sessions we have left. Yet, members' typical reaction to my reminders is to disregard them. While I will point this out to the group and allow time in each of the remaining sessions for discussion of members' thoughts and feelings about the prospect of not being together, it rarely makes a difference.

> In the sixteenth session of the twenty-session group, I reminded members that we would only have four more sessions. I observed that members seemed to want to forget that in another month they would no longer be together. Sally replied, "You're right about that. I know we will end, though sometimes I think maybe something will happen and we'll still keep on. I know that sounds silly, but I just don't want to stop. I need this group and these people. I have no one. It's just me and my daughter. I really don't know what will happen to me if I don't have this group. So I just pretend that we'll just keep on meeting." Other members indicated their agreement with Sally's comments.

Sally's comments are typical of members' struggles in this regard and reveal a second theme that characterizes the ending phase, regression to earlier themes. Members are likely to assume all of their progress is due to the group and as a result, feelings of inadequacy are likely to resurface. Members wonder about their ability to go on without the support and understanding of the group. June's comments are illustrative of members' sentiments: "All of a sudden I began to think, I won't be seeing these folks again after two more weeks. That scares me. I wonder about whether I can manage. I realize I still have all these problems in my life and suddenly they seem worse to me."

The reality is that members' problems in living will not have gone away at the close of the group. In fact, as a result of the group, many members may become even more aware of difficulties they need to address. It is important for the worker to encourage members to talk about their fears openly. It is only *after* they have had the chance to talk about these feelings that they will be able to develop a more realistic view of the gains they have made.

In addition to an increase in feelings of inadequacy, expressions of sadness are also likely to resurface. Members may not be able to talk directly about how they feel about ending with one another. But the fact that grief and loss once again become important topics of discussion suggests that, to the extent that they are able, members are beginning to address this painful reality. It is nonetheless important for the worker to point out this dynamic, providing members with the opportunity to deepen their work, if they are able.

I have found, actually, that it is not until the very last session that members are truly willing or able to confront this significant transition in their lives. Even then, it is me who has to initiate the discussion. I start by sharing with members my own feelings about the group's ending, and this includes my observations about how the group members worked together and the issues they tackled together. I also specifically ask about things that I think I could have done differently and invite members to provide me with feedback about my handling of the group. I then address each member individually, sharing with each their contributions, progress, and my suggestions about issues that are likely to still require their attention. This is an incredibly difficult exercise for me, one that usually brings on tears, not just for me but also for others in the group. Yet, as I do this, I am modeling a way for members to achieve closure for themselves.

Once I finish, I ask the members to talk about their experience in the group, what they learned and gained from each other, and what they envision for themselves in the future. It is particularly important for members to express feelings of affection and caring for one another. While those feelings have clearly been there, many members will not have been able to share them, fearing rejection. I find, therefore, that I often have to be persistent in reaching for these feelings, as well as for members' honest assessments of me and my handling of the group, as the following example reveals.

Much of the twenty-session group had been dominated by George's concerns about his termination from individual therapy during the fifth week, due to behavior his therapist labeled as "inappropriate" and "hostile." George understandably felt rejected and "crazier" than before as a result of this and was preoccupied with these feelings and with his therapist's actions. Most of his comments dealt with the ineptness of the agency and the therapist.

Initially members were supportive and understanding of George, but as the group progressed they became frustrated by his inability to move beyond his rather narrow focus on the professionals' incompetence. Two female members continued to support George and expressed anger at the others for not "standing by" him. There were frequent conflicts between members about how best to be helpful to George, discussions that, for the most part, George did not participate in. George's concerns did not inhibit the group's work but as a result, the group spent a good bit of time dealing with anger and managing conflict, as well as feelings of betrayal and worthlessness.

In our last session, I said I sensed that there were still unresolved issues associated with George's situation and how the group responded to it, and how I dealt with both George and the group as a whole. Initially, members were reluctant to say much of anything and there was an awkward silence. Joan, who had supported George throughout the group, said she was angry at the group for not being concerned about George and his problem. One of the men replied, "Of course,

I care. I'm really concerned about George. That's why I get so angry with him. He can't let those assholes at the agency make him feel crazy."

George remained quiet as members continued to debate amongst themselves their reactions to him. When I asked him to share his thoughts, he expressed confusion, anger, and bitterness, claiming, "The group probably will be glad to get rid of me." This comment led to even more discussion as members reacted, alternately, with guilt, understanding, anger, and frustration. I observed, "You know, we all have made some mistakes. I'm not sure that I handled this correctly either. I think we can all learn something from this." At this point, members, including to a limited extent George, were able to engage in a productive discussion of what they and I did right and what we could have done differently.

This particular group was a very challenging one for me, given George's persistent focus on his termination and the resulting conflicts members had with one another over this. I should point out that with the group's and my assistance, George resumed therapy with another, very capable therapist. However, it was a constant struggle balancing George's individual needs against those of the group as a whole. Therefore, I was particularly interested in obtaining members' feedback. I felt I could have handled things differently, and in sharing this with members I was reinforcing the idea that none of us, certainly not me, are perfect. As members shared their observations about me with me, they were able to ease into a discussion of their reactions to and opinions about each other. As a result of this discussion, they developed a keener understanding that disagreements are normal, inevitable aspects of relationships that need not be hurtful and, that, as I ultimately concluded, "We can agree to disagree."

THIS WAS A very difficult chapter for me to write, much more so than I had anticipated. It required me to revisit in a very real and dramatic way the anguish and distress that survivors bring with them to therapy, feelings that I inevitably took on and made my own. Earlier in this chapter I suggested that the worker needed collegial support to process all that goes on in a group for survivors, including the worker's affective reactions to the work. As I finish up this chapter, the importance of this advice is brought home to me even more clearly. I have become acutely aware of how my views about human nature, relationships, and good and evil have been altered by what I have heard over the years.

In order to truly be helpful to clients who have been so traumatized, the worker must open her or himself up to their stories and their pain. In doing so, however, the worker places her or himself at risk. Even with the support of several trusted friends and colleagues, I live with my clients' stories every day. What I have realized as I have written this is that my colleagues and I all do the same work. We hear the same stories. Therefore, we rely upon the same defenses and cope in the same way. A friend and colleague said recently, "I believe anyone is capable of anything." I have said the same thing. Often. This cynicism, I believe, might just come with the territory. It is important for the reader to understand that her or his views and perspectives *will* change, will inevitably be colored by the inhumanity and cruelty that she or he will experience vicariously as a result of clients' sexual abuse.

These words of caution notwithstanding, I wouldn't trade one moment of my work with these wonderful, courageous, and resilient individuals. They have taught me much about myself. We've cried together, grown together, even laughed together. It has been an incredible journey for me, one that I am still on and still relish.

Note

Adapted from Carolyn Knight, *Group therapy for men and women sexually abused in child-hood.* Holmes Beach, Fla: Learning, 1996.

References

Alexander, P. 1993. The differential effects of abuse characteristics and attachment in the prediction of long-term effects of sexual abuse. *Journal of Interpersonal Violence,* 8:346–62.

Alexander, P., R. Neimeyer, V. Follette, M. Moore, and S. Harter. 1989. A comparison of group treatments of women sexually abused as children. *Journal of Consulting and Clinical Psychology* 57:479–83.

Arata, C. 1998. To tell or not to tell: Current functioning of child sexual abuse survivors who disclosed their victimization. *Child Maltreatment* 3:63–71.

Bagley, C. and L. Young. 1998. Long-term evaluation of group counselling for women with a history of child sexual abuse: Focus on depression, self-esteem, suicidal behaviors, and social support. *Social Work with Groups* 21:63–73.

Black, C. and R. DeBlassie. 1993. Sexual abuse in male children and adolescents: Indicators, effects, and treatment. *Adolescence* 28:123–33.

Boudewyn, A. and J. Liem. 1995. Childhood sexual abuse as a precursor to depression and self-destructive behavior in adulthood. *Journal of Traumatic Stress* 8:445–59.

Briere, J. and J. Conte. 1993. Self-reported amnesia for abuse in adults molested as children. *Journal of Traumatic Stress* 6:21–31.

Browne, A. and D. Finkelhor. 1986. Impact of sexual abuse: A review of the research. *Psychological Bulletin* 99:66–77.

Bruckner, D. and P. Johnson. 1987. Treatment for adult male victims of childhood sexual abuse. *Social Casework* 68:81–87.

Budman, S. and A. Demby. 1983. Short-term group psychotherapy. In H. Kaplan and B. Sadock, eds., *Comprehensive group psychotherapy,* pp. 138–44. Baltimore: Williams and Wilkins.

Budman, S., A. Demby, M. Feldstein, and M. Gold, 1985. The effects of time-limited group psychotherapy: A controlled study. *International Journal of Group Psychotherapy* 34:587–603.

Burlingame, G. and A. Fuhriman. 1990. Time-limited group therapy. *Counseling Psychologist* 18:93–118.

Dimock, P. 1988. Adult males sexually abused as children. *Journal of Interpersonal Violence* 3:203–21.

Everill, J. and G. Waller. 1994. Disclosure of sexual abuse and psychological adjustment in female undergraduates. *Child Abuse and Neglect* 19:93–100.

Feldman-Summers, S. and K. Pope. 1994. The experience of "forgetting" childhood abuse: A national survey of psychologists. *Journal of Consulting and Clinical Psychology* 62:636–39.

Finkelhor, D. 1990. Early and long-term effects of child sexual abuse: An update. *Professional Psychology Research and Practice* 21:325–30.

Fromuth, M. and B. Burkhart. 1989. Long-term psychological correlates of childhood sexual abuse. *Child Abuse and Neglect* 13:533–42.

Gold, S., B. Lucenko, J. Elhai, J. Swingle, and A. Sellers. 1999. A comparison of psychological/psychiatric symptomatology of women and men sexually abused as children. *Child Abuse and Neglect* 23:683–92.

Harter, S., P. Alexander, and R. Neimeyer. 1988. Long-term effects of incestuous child abuse in college women: Social adjustment, social cognition, and family characteristics. *Journal of Consulting and Clinical Psychology* 56:5–8.

Harvey, J., T. Orbuch, K. Chwalisz, and G. Garwood. 1991. Coping with sexual assault: The role of account-making and confiding. *Journal of Traumatic Stress* 4:515–31.

Hunter, M. 1990. *The sexually abused male: Prevalence, impact, and treatment.* Vol. 1. Lexington, Mass.: Lexington.

Johnson, D., J. Pike, and K. Chard. 2001. Factors predicting PTSD, depression, and dissociative severity in female treatment-seeking childhood sexual abuse survivors. *Child Abuse and Neglect* 25:179–98.

Kelly, A., M. Coenen, and B. Johnston. 1995. Confidants' feedback and traumatic life events. *Journal of Traumatic Stress* 8:161–69.

Koverola, C. and J. Proulx. 1996. Family functioning as predictors of distress in revictimized sexual abuse survivors. *Journal of Interpersonal Violence* 11:263–80.

Mayer, A. 1995. *Repressed memories of sexual abuse.* Holmes Beach, Fla.: Learning.

Messman-Moore, T. and P. Long. 2000. The revictimization of child sexual abuse survivors: An examination of the adjustment of college women with child sexual abuse, adult sexual assault, and adult physical assault. *Child Maltreatment* 5:18–27.

Morgan, T. and A. Cummings. 1999. Change experienced during group therapy by female survivors of childhood sexual abuse. *Journal of Consulting and Clinical Psychology* 67:28–36.

Ratican, K. 1992. Sexual abuse survivors: Identifying symptoms and special treatment considerations. *Journal of Counseling and Development* 71:33–38.

Ray, K., J. Jackson, and R. Townsley. 1991. Family environments of victims of intrafamilial and extrafamilial child sexual abuse. *Journal of Family Violence* 6:365–74.

Richter, N., E. Snider, K. Gorey. 1997. Group work intervention with female survivors of childhood sexual abuse. *Research on Social Work Practice* 7:53–69.

Roesler, T. and N. McKenzie. 1994. Effects of childhood trauma on psychological functioning in adults sexually abused as children. *Journal of Nervous and Menal Disease* 182:145–50.

Shulman, L. 1999. *The skills of helping individuals, families, groups, and communities.* 4th ed. Itasca, Ill: Peacock.

Singer, K. 1989. Group work with men who experienced incest in childhood. *American Journal of Orthopsychiatry* 59:468–72.

Testa, M., B. Miller, W. Downs, and D. Panek. 1992. The moderating impact of social support following childhood sexual abuse. *Violence and Victims* 7:177–86.

Thomas, M. C. and C. Nelson. 1994. From victims to victors: Group process as the path to recovery for males molested as children. *Journal of Specialists in Group Work* 42:24–33.

Valentine, L. and L. Feinauer. 1993. Resilience factors associated with female survivors of childhood sexual abuse. *American Journal of Family Therapy* 21:216–24.

Vander-Mey, B. 1988. The sexual victimization of male children: A review of previous research. *Child Abuse and Neglect* 12:61–72.

Widom, C., T. Ireland, and P. Glynn. 1995. Alcohol abuse in abused and neglected children followed-up: Are they at increased risk? *Journal of Studies on Alcohol* 56:207–17.

Williams, L. 1992. Adult memories of childhood sexual abuse: Preliminary findings from a longitudinal study. *APSAC Advisor* 5:19–22.

Zlotnick, C., A. Begin, M. Sheat, T. Pearlstein, E. Simpson, and E. Costello. 1994. The relationship between characteristics of sexual abuse and dissociative experiences. *Comprehensive Psychiatry* 35:465–70.

Chapter 13

Uncovering Kindness and Respect
Men Who Have Practiced Violence in Intimate Relationships

Dale Trimble

SINCE 1977 when I began working with men's violence against women partners there have been enormous changes in the field and in society. In the late seventies several articles on the issue of partner assault included reference to the masochism of a victim who would stay in a relationship in which she experienced violence (Martin 1976). Such references would be virtually unheard of today. Even in the early eighties in Canada police intervention frequently included mediation and referral of the man to counseling. This practice reflected the unexamined value that men's violence in the family was somehow not a criminal matter but a psychological one. Increasingly tragic stories in the media have documented how successful, professional men have brutalized and even murdered their partners behind closed doors.

Primarily through active lobbying of the women's movement, men's violence against women partners has been brought to the forefront of our consciousness and changes have been implemented in the criminal justice system. Assault within the family is now generally seen as a crime, at least as serious if not much more so, than violence between strangers. Serious, because we know the implications that violence has for any children present and who may be subjected to physical injury, psychological trauma, and learned patterns of behavior to bring to the next generation. We know that boys who have witnessed their father assaulting their mother are three times as likely to be violent toward their partners as adults (Stark and Flitcraft 1985).

We now see women as having the right to safety, respect, and dignity that supersedes the historical dominance of men over their wives. In numerous communities throughout North America a coordinated response to violence against women has been developed. Community coordination is frequently mandated from a state or provincial level and brings together all societal aspects that bear a responsibility and/or contribution to ending violence against women. Most states in the U.S. and provinces and territories in Canada now have guiding principles for work with men who assault their partners (Austin and Dankwort 1999). This article will focus on our counseling group for men who have assaulted their wives. Assault is a crime for which the offender should be held responsible. At the same time, violent men can be helped to change their behavior.

Before pursuing the specifics of our service, I would like to put it in context. A recent telephone survey in the U.S. suggested that nearly 2 million women are physically assaulted every year (National Institute of Justice/Centers for Disease Control and Prevention 1998). Nearly 30 percent of Canadian women in relationships with male partners were assaulted at some point in their lifetime (Johnson and Sacco 1995). Given the reluctance of victims to report violence, many researchers believe that figures like these could be at least double (Browning 1983).

Developmental Tasks and Issues

What are the life-cycle issues especially pertinent to a group of men who have assaulted their wives? In *The Seasons of a Man's Life* Levinson (1978) described a view of normal male adult development. He divides what he calls the "male life cycle" into eras. The majority of clients in our service fit into Levinson's "Early Adulthood Era" beginning at seventeen or eighteen and ending at about forty-five years of age. Major components with which a man must struggle, although different in each phase, are "occupation" and "marriage and family." A man experiences a "developmental crisis" in Levinson's terms when he has great difficulty with the developmental tasks of the period he is in. "In a severe crisis he experiences a threat to life itself, the danger of chaos and dissolution, the loss of hope for the future." These words reflect the feelings of many of our clients who have lost contact with their wife and children as a result of their violence. Many of the men are separated from their families and do not know whether the separation will be permanent. Some have no way of contacting their spouse and family because their wives will not reveal their whereabouts for fear of threats, harassment, or further violent attacks. They are often prevented from entering the family home by a court order. Some are in our group as a term of probation after a conviction for wife assault. Many men coming to our service have never been in trouble with the law before and are now dealing with having a criminal record. Others are struggling with a withdrawal from alcohol and/or drug abuse and the habit patterns and social circle surrounding substance abuse.

Central to all these crises is a loss of control (chaos and dissolution). This is the reverse of the control the man maintained in his family through his violence, threats of violence, or verbal abuse. It's not unusual for a man to feel desperate and even suicidal, as well as to feel loss of hope for the future. Unfortunately, some men will cope with this crisis of loss of control in the same angry and aggressive way that caused the crisis in the first place.

One stage in the early adulthood era, the "Novice Phase" of development, covers the years from seventeen to thirty-three in Levinson's system. Most of our group is in the twenty-eight to thirty-three-year-old age range. The tasks of this period are the ones with which our clients have the most difficulty. Levinson states that the "primary, overriding task of the novice phase is to make a place for oneself in the adult world and to create a life structure that will be viable in the world and suitable for the self" (58). The ability to have "adult peer relationships with women that involve affection, friendship, collaboration, respect and emotional intimacy" is very difficult for men who are, as Ganley (1981:58) says, "very dependent upon those they abuse."

The characteristics of our clients are diverse; nonetheless, a common dynamic often appears. Some of our clients have a great investment in the "macho ideal" (power, money, and winning the attractive wife), accompanied by strong fears and doubts about their ability to measure up to that ideal. Given that being a "real man" involves not talking about feelings of insecurity, a real pressure cooker situation arises. High expectations produce doubt and insecurity, while at the same time part of the expectation is not to have and especially not to show or talk about insecurity.

To be insecure in a "macho" definition is to be feminine. In a small unpublished study I conducted in 1982, I found that violent men were more homophobic (afraid of homosexuality in themselves and others) than nonviolent men. It seems that one of the most frightening aspects of homosexuality for men is that it is too much like being a woman; in other words, fear of the feminine in oneself. One of the tasks of early adulthood described by Levinson is to live out both masculine and feminine aspects of the self. This description of violent men is not meant to be either predictive or proscriptive. Not all macho men are physically abusive with their wives, although I would say that being macho is psychologically abusive of women in general. In addition, just helping a man to experience and express his feminine side will not stop his violence.

Another theorist of adult development is Erik Erikson (1950). Within his system of the "Eight Ages of Man" the stage of "Intimacy versus Isolation" covers twenty to forty years of age. Erikson (1950) sees a man's task during this period as "the capacity to commit himself to concrete affiliations and partnerships and to develop the ethical strength to abide by such commitments, even though they may call for significant sacrifices and compromises. Body and ego must now be masters . . . in order to face the fear of ego loss in situations which call for self-abandon." Some of the clients I work with experience compromise in a marriage as emasculation, e.g., "I'm not letting a woman run my life." Any giving up of what they want is experienced as a loss of self or identity. Outbursts of domination, violence, and abuse at home may be a way for the passive man to redress a power imbalance that he experiences in other parts of his life. Men who are chronically domineering and aggressive may even feel that agreeing to go to their second choice of a movie or restaurant threatens their sense of self.

Erikson (1950) describes the opposite of intimacy as "distantiation" or "the readiness to isolate and, if necessary, destroy those forces and people whose essence seems dangerous to one's own. . . . The danger of this stage is that intimate, competitive, and combative relations are experienced with and against the self-same people." Certainly all men struggle with the tasks described by both Erikson and Levinson. However, the attitudes and history of violent men keeps them stuck in this struggle. When violent men gain control of their violence, they are able to return to normal developmental tasks with a sense of hope.

Vulnerabilities and Risk Factors and Resiliencies and Protective Factors

As we began the process of brainstorming the possible issues men might have who would attend our group with our consultant Lawrence Shulman, we identified several themes. We believed the men's concerns might include fear of negative judgments from the group leaders, a fear of intimacy yet a tremendous need of it, loneliness due to the loss of their wives and children, and a low self-image, especially as it related to "being a man." A group member confirmed our assumptions about fear of intimacy and male self-image one evening:

> JOE: I remember my girlfriend and I would get into these horrible arguments and I'd reach a point where I couldn't take it anymore and I'd go into the bathroom and cry. Then I'd come out and hit her. . . . I guess I was afraid to let her see me cry. I haven't cried in front of anyone since I was a kid and my dog died.
> FACILITATOR: What was it about her seeing you cry that concerned you?
> JOE: I didn't want to look weak in front of her, to feel like I wasn't a man.
> FACILITATOR: Was that what happened when your dog died and you cried; you didn't feel like a man?
> JOE: Yeah. My dad really put me down for it.
> FACILITATOR: Has your wife ever put you down for crying?
> JOE: No, actually she says she would feel closer to me.
> FACILITATOR: So when you feel like crying, you believe that anyone around will put you down even though they aren't. It's kind of like your dad is still in the room for you.
> JOE: Yeah.

We see how risk is associated with men's fear of intimacy. Don Dutton (Dutton and Gollant 1995) described the relationship between violence and fearful attachment issues. One evening in a later group the same dynamic was illustrated again. Our client Doug was about twenty-eight years old and began working in the oil fields of Alberta as a "roughneck" when he was eighteen:

FACILITATOR: What else might you have been feeling besides anger at your wife when you raised your hand to strike her?

BILL: Don't know. I was just pissed, really mad. It happened so fast I don't remember.

DOUG: I think you were afraid.

BILL: What would I have to be afraid of?

DOUG: I don't know. But I remember when I worked as a roughneck. After work we'd go to the bar. A fight might break out. I'd start to get scared. I was never really a fighter before. When I'd hear the fight beginning I'd feel my neck tingling, my stomach get tense and sick. I'd shake inside. I wanted to run away. But what would my buddies say? I'd really get shit the next day. So I would make my fear into anger. It worked. I got a pretty tough reputation. Guys in my crew looked up to me. I didn't even realize I did the same thing at home till later. My girlfriend would want to leave when we would argue about my drinking and not being home.

FACILITATOR: So you were afraid to lose her but you showed her your anger and your violence? You scared her into staying?

DOUG: Yeah.

Clearly, risk increases, as fear does, particularly fear of not being seen as a "real man," whether by a woman or other men.

My philosophy in working with violent clients in my early work was an outgrowth of my training leading personal growth groups. I assumed that if I showed empathy, worked at developing rapport, and tried to show the men that I judged their violent behavior and not them as people they would stay in counseling, learn how to experience and understand their feelings, and therefore learn to control their violence.

I became disillusioned when men would come to a few group sessions and then stop attending (This was in the early days prior to men attending under court order). When I asked why they had stopped, the answers given included (the implicit message appears after each quote): "We've separated for good so I don't need it anymore." (She provoked the violence; I'm not a violent person). "We had a really good talk after the last group session. We really communicated. I know it won't happen again." (Communication problems cause violence and good communication prevents violence.) "I've stopped drinking. I only hit her when I was drunk so I won't be violent again." (Alcohol caused my violence, not me). Or, "The group sessions that I attended really helped. I can control myself now." (Because I feel better, I won't be violent again).

As workers, we doubted that many of these men had made sufficient progress toward controlling violence in a few sessions. The men's answers mentioned above are common themes and defenses for violent men and sometimes for their wives and the professionals who deal with them. These ideas and others like them prevent men from taking responsibility for their own behavior. In the mid-eighties I formulated these beliefs offered by my clients into a system and eventually incorporated them into a counselor training program entitled "Themes of Defense" (Trimble 1995).

It's easy to become angry and impatient with men's denial of their violence and apparent resistance to taking responsibility. Treatment approaches based on demanding accountability and confronting denial began to predominate in the 1980s (Adams 1988; Pence and Paymar 1993). This made sense, as we compared stories from men and their partners. The men's arguments about injustice seemed insignificant in relation to their partner's stories about their fear, his need for control and his violent behavior. However, I began to feel more like a hostile cop trying to get a confession than a counselor who was working to help a client learn to become respectful. I often left a group feeling that though I might have obtained an admission of guilt, I wasn't sure if I'd been effective in helping the man make a lasting change toward stopping his violence—what really counted for their partner's safety and well-being. How could it be possible to lead men toward relationships based on safety, equality, and respect by criticizing, arguing, and telling them what's wrong with their ways of thinking?

Finally, in the early 1990s, the influence of narrative therapy brought respect for clients and accountability for behavior together. Jenkins (1990) was the first to articulate a respectful approach to working with clients who use violence or sexual offending practices against others. Jenkins assumes that men do not want to be violent, but that their ways of thinking are not helpful. Nor does he find many professional explanations helpful in the treatment process. Men's explanations typically involve blaming the victim, substance abuse, the criminal justice system or a "bad temper." Professional explanations often focus on family of origin trauma, personality disorder, impulse control problems, etc. Jenkins suggests that an explanation is only helpful if it encourages the man to take full responsibility for his violence. He advances what he calls a "theory of restraint" focused on what is stopping the client from accepting responsibility. This approach presumes that the client sometimes has the ability to take responsibility for his behavior and explores what restrains him from doing so more often.

The process of the therapy focuses on three stages of "engagement." First, the counselor "declines invitations" from the client to argue, give advice, confront, etc. Jenkin's view is that the harder the counselor argues for responsibility the less responsibility the client takes. Second, the counselor "offers invitations" to the client to explore his actions through detailed and respectful questions. For example, the counselor may ask, "Can you handle telling me what you did that resulted in the police being called to your home?" In the third stage, not necessarily sequential, the counselor "highlights evidence of responsibility" by pointing out those moments when the man talks about his violence or abuse without blaming. The counselor may also challenge the man further as to whether he can maintain his nonviolence, e.g. "Are you sure you can stand up to your old view that you should be the boss over your wife? Or, "Do you think you can handle your feelings of insecurity or do you need your wife to handle them by being careful of what she says or does so as not to trigger you?"

This process stresses the man's strength and courage and invites the man to explore how continued acts of responsibility will affect both him and his family for the better. Central to Jenkins's approach is respect for the client. He sees the counselor who is "breaking down denial" or "overcoming resistance" as perpetuating the same abuse of power that we hope to help the client cease using. Instead, by taking a respectful stance, the counselor demonstrates the desired outcomes for the client's own life and relationships: equality, respect, and compassion.

In my initial idealism I wanted men to come to our program because they realized they had a problem, had hurt another person physically and psychologically, and through this had harmed themselves. I hoped they would realize they needed to change, even if it would not result in the return of their partner. In reality few of us face our problems unless we have to. As Carl Jung said, "It is from need and distress that new forms of life take their rise and not from mere wishes or from the requirements of our ideals. All creativeness in the realm of the spirit as well as every psychic advance of man arises from a state of mental suffering" (cited in Jorad 1972:9).

It has been my experience that most violent men who come to our group and stay long enough to make a change are there because they have to be, at least initially. That "have to" is usually a court order and their wives saying they won't return unless the men get help. This does not mean that most men want to be violent, but rather that most of them cannot tolerate for long the pain and fear I mentioned earlier. Their inability to tolerate pain, fear, and loneliness forms part of the foundation for both their violence and for the impulsiveness that can carry them out of the group. Because of this, an outside pressure (the authority of a court order) is needed to keep them in the group past their usual tolerance level for self-confrontation.

For these court-mandated clients we serve partly as an arm of the law. We report nonattendance to their probation officer, who may return them to the judge for consequences. If men are absent more than twice during their term, they may be asked to leave the group, start over, or face a charge of breech of probation for not completing one of the conditions of their order. However, it is important for workers not to confuse their role and get caught up in being the authoritarian leader. Jenkins (1996) refers to this stance as the "inner tyrant" of the counselor. This stance may be a reflection of the worker's fear that a man is at increasing risk and resentment at the client for the worker's apparent inability to reach the man. In my experience, the more I increased my role as attendance enforcer, the more I lost my ability to connect with the man.

In the remainder of this discussion I'll explore how the themes explored in group work also work as protective factors.

Agency and Group Context

In 1977 five male workers gathered to develop the first group for violent men in our province. This meeting grew out of a request from women's shelter workers for counseling for the perpetrators of the violence toward women that they were seeing. They had become increasingly frustrated seeing many of the same women return to their partners and then return to the shelter when violence escalated again. Due to the lack of literature to guide us, we were left to our own devices to formulate an approach. For the first four years we worked on a voluntary basis to provide groups or managed to beg a few hours from a supervisor to keep the groups alive.

In the early days of our service, judges became interested in the development of another sentencing option for men found guilty of violence against a partner rather than the alternatives of either prison or probation. With support from the Corrections Branch, we were able to fund a pilot project through the federal and provincial governments. Our service continues now on provincial funding alone, providing for five sixteen-session groups of approximately eight to ten men. Each man is required to complete sixteen weekly sessions. Convicted men who are required to attend the group as a term of their probation are our priority. Referrals from other social agencies or self-referrals are rarely possible, given the demand for this service for court-ordered men.

When our project received funding in 1981 we were the first service of this kind in our province and one of the first in Canada. There are now over fifty programs in the province of British Columbia, a province with a population of 4 million. Health Canada lists over 130 programs for men nationwide.

The criteria for admittance to our group include 1. an ability to converse, read, and write in English; 2. absence of mental illness; 3. participation in an alcohol or drug treatment program concurrent with our program if substance abuse problems are present; and 4. adequate restrictions in place to ensure the safety of his partner, if necessary (such as space in a shelter or a restraining order). It is important that alcohol or drug treatment begin before working on violent behavior. Our service is based upon the assumption that men learn to be violent and can learn other behavior to replace the violence. Learning is not possible in an intoxicated state or in an individual who is still running away from self through alcohol or drugs. Our approach demands that the man face and tolerate some pain: the pain of facing that he has hurt the person he loves, the pain and fear of being alone, and the pain and self-disgust at having driven away his wife and children through repeated cruelty.

Work and Group Themes

One of the ways I have developed for dealing with the men's feeling of loss of control in the situation, whether it's caused by the court order or through their wives' pressure to "get help or I won't come back," is to point out how much control they have.

> LEADER: I'm sure it is possible to follow all these group rules and not change, not open up to facing yourself or the other men here. You can probably get through this group without changing. That's up to you. The judge may order you to be here or your wife may be saying that she won't come back unless you get help. As I said, we require your participation and regular attendance in order for you to stay here, but no one can reach into your mind and heart and order a change. That's where you have complete control.

There are several reasons why we provide this service in a group format rather than individually or through family or couples' sessions initially. Most men feel so embarrassed about what they have done that they hide it even from themselves. Some men say that they "feel like a freak." Many men present a cocky or belligerent attitude about their violence but feel bad beneath that aggressive exterior. By seeing there are others like them, most men experience a sense of relief and begin to talk about the self in ways they never had.

Groups can set up a new peer group and a new peer pressure. In the case of male values, the group can support new values such as not blaming other people for your violence, sharing your feelings and problems, admitting hurt does not make you less of a man, and realizing violence and use of male privilege is a tendency that will always have to be controlled in oneself. When a peer group can hold values like this, it has much more impact than a therapist telling a client about the values that are "good" for him.

VALUES

The first session of a new group is very tense. The men are awkward, silent, and avoid eye contact. One or two may joke with each other, but the attempts at humor generally fall flat. Even as an experienced facilitator I find the first night uncomfortable. A few years ago my co-facilitator and I we were searching for a way to break the ice. We try to help the men feel comfortable while not losing focus on taking responsibility for behavior, ending violence, and developing relationships based on respect. My co-facilitator suggested we start off with a discussion of values. He asked men to brainstorm the following question. "What values are most important to you in your relationship to your partner?" (Dr. Harry Stefanakis, men's group co-facilitator, 1996). Men participated slowly and then became livelier. Words like *communication, trust, loyalty, love, compassion,* and *honesty* went up on the board. Then Harry asked, "If you stick with your values, how do you feel about yourself?"

JIM: I can look at myself in the mirror.

BILL: I feel calmer. Not like I've got to prove myself.

HARRY: I'd like to ask another question. If you think your partner is not living up to some of these values; then what should you do? Do you throw your values out, or is it important to stick to your values even if you think she is being unfair?

ALEX: That's a really hard one. I was sure Sue was seeing some guy at work so I was a jerk whenever she tried to talk to me.

HARRY: So was that sticking to your values (I think you offered the word *respect* to the list)? Or was it turning your back on your values?

GUY: Well, why should he put up with that! Women will walk all over you. Why should he be a nice guy, especially if she's going after someone else?

ALEX: As it turns out, I was the one who really was the jerk. It's a long story, but I found out that she wasn't. Boy, did I feel dumb. Then she was mad at me for not trusting her and "my stupid jealousy again." And I was mad at myself for being a jerk.

DALE: So, if you had lived up to your values and treated her with respect, even when jealousy was trying to tell you she was not being respectful with you, how would that have been different?

ALEX: I wouldn't have made things worse. I wouldn't have pushed her away and made her mad at me for no reason.

DALE: So the value of respect is an important one for you. And the challenge for you may be to remember how important it is even when jealousy is trying to get a grip on you.

ALEX: If I could have remembered *respect,* I would have saved a lot of pain for everyone.

This exercise and line of inquiry highlights our underlying assumption in this work that many men who have practiced violence with their partners still have positive values. Our task as counselors is to assist men in uncovering and reinforcing these values in their lives. While we witness their longing to respect themselves again and feel the respect of others, we at the same time model respect for them as persons. As we do this, we work to discover the restraints and fears that prevent respect and caring. Some of these were expressed above, i.e., "Women will walk all over you" or "If someone hurts you, you've got to hurt them back."

FAIRNESS

Fairness is a strong theme with men who have practiced violence in relationship. Protests about fairness sound like the following:

HANK: Why don't our wives have to come to this group? My wife has been violent too, but when I told the cops that they just shrugged and handcuffed me.

ROB: Boy, that's the truth. This whole system is out to get men. Don't get me wrong. I don't mind coming here, and I'm sure I'll learn something, but women literally get away with murder these days.

SAMMY: A friend of mine did three months in jail just based on his wife lying. (*A few group members are nodding or smirking, and the atmosphere in the group is beginning to heat up. Men are more animated.*)

As group facilitator, one of my standard responses to this used to be: "We're not here to talk about your wives. We're here to talk about you." This received passive cooperation but did not increase participation. Guided by Gardner's (1968) words: "If you have some respect for people as they are, you can be more effective in helping them become better than they are" (45), I now make time for the group to express their views about unfairness. I avoid agreeing or disagreeing, but simply listen and reflect back what I hear. If anyone is silent, I ask if they have any ideas they would like to contribute to the discussion. When I feel everyone has had a chance to be heard, I proceed as follows.

DALE: I would like to ask the group something (*pause*). I would like to know how much time over the rest of the group we should put into talking about the system being unfair. Is this something we should devote more time to?

ANDY: I think it's unfair, but that's not why I'm here. I'd like to learn something. I don't want a bitch session all the time.

CURT: Same here. Let's not waste our time.

I go around the room and check in with others. Now the voice promoting learning has become strong, but it's their voice, not mine as the authority telling them what's OK to feel or talk about. There seems to be a feeling of relief that their complaints were heard and a readiness to get on with the group.

DALE: So is what I'm hearing from the group is that we have decided to focus on what we can learn and stay away from discussions about the unfairness of the system?

GROUP: Heads nod and several say, "That's what I want."

DALE: So we have an agreement as a group, and anyone can remind any one of us if we slip back into complaining and away from learning. Are you sure? Have we actually spent enough time on what's wrong with the system or why she isn't here?

TOM: I thought I'd come here and some guy would just tell me what to think. Boy, was I pissed. (*Turning to me*) You're not doing that. I had planned on just doing my time here. So let's get on with it.

The above process reflects my assumption that men do want to learn and practice alternatives to violence and control. When I support them in voicing a perception of unfairness, I show them they have been heard. When I support their goals, I find a self-existing interest in learning and leaving blame behind, not one that I must enforce from a "superior" position. In short, I believe in the resilience of men's desire to change and learn. Calhoun and McGrath (2000) speak of the "innate worth" of the violent men they counsel, "the belief that everyone is born and remains lovable, worthy, valuable and deserving of respect" (2). I share this view, even though it's not always easy to practice.

RESPONSIBILITY

A major task of our work is to help men take responsibility for their violent and controlling behaviors. This isn't possible when men don't see some of their behaviors as abuse. Often, this is because they grew up in an abusive family and consider some abusiveness as normal or as "not taking any shit." I have struggled with how to confront men while not shaming them as persons. The following exercise reveals that many men are ready to acknowledge their behavior. We begin by saying, "All marriages have some arguments. It's part of life. In your relationship, what did you argue about?" Under the word *Conflicts* on the board we write their ideas: money, work, time with friends, chores, sex, and kids, etc. Then we ask what they felt during and after these arguments. Under the word *Feelings* we record their responses, including *pissed, depressed, frustrated, powerless,* etc. Finally we ask the men: "When you've had arguments about these things and felt this way, what have you done? What have been your "behaviors"? Under *Behaviors* they list terms like *pushed her, slammed the door, broke something, threw something, yelled, called her names,* etc.

Here the men are already volunteering their aggression as a topic of discussion rather than hiding it. They are talking about it, while not yet being completely revealing and not describing the most serious violence. Eventually, when conflict is seen as something everyone experiences and their feelings are seen as common to most human beings, though what they do about those feelings may be unacceptable, it becomes safe for at least some of the men to take responsibility for their violent behavior.

What's missing usually are any of the positive behaviors they've used. When we make a point of asking, we hear things like "went for a walk," "listened to her side," "apologized," etc. These men who have been violent have sometimes used positive solutions—what Epston and White (1992) refer to as "unique outcomes." Our task is also to witness, support, and emphasize these self-generated solutions lying dormant or forgotten.

One of the most difficult but important aspects is getting the men to tell their stories. Most men feel bad about their violence, even if their attitude is one of justifying their actions, blaming their partner, or even defending their right to do as they please in their own homes. Many workers (and, more important, partners and the men themselves) mistake this guilt and/or remorse for an ability to control behavior at times of stress. However, strong feelings of guilt are not tolerated by anyone for long. Eventually a blurring of what happened and a clouding of responsibility set in as a defense against guilt.

CONFRONTATION

Within the first few sessions of a new group we invite the men to tell us more about their behavior that resulted in a charge and order to attend the group.

> LEADER: I'd like each man who has joined the group tonight to tell the rest of the group what brought him here.
>
> PHIL: Well, my wife and I have been having marriage problems for a while. Two weeks ago I got upset 'cause she came home really late. We started yelling at each other and I pushed her around. I've done it before. I came home from work the next day to find that she had left with the kids. I'm here 'cause she said she wouldn't come back until I got some help.
>
> FACILITATOR: So you're primarily here because you want your family back?
>
> PHIL: I don't feel good about what I did. I can't sleep at all since they left.
>
> FACILITATOR: It's tough on you being alone, really lonely. It must be hard to work without sleep.
>
> PHIL: Yeah.
>
> FACILITATOR: What do you mean, "pushed her around"? What exactly did you do?
>
> PHIL (*Goes into a story about her going out with her girlfriends more and more often*): Then I slapped her.
>
> FACILITATOR: Where did you hit her?
>
> PHIL: On her face and back.
>
> FACILITATOR: How often?
>
> PHIL: Three or four times, I guess.
>
> FACILITATOR: You guess. So it might have been five or six times or more?
>
> PHIL: It could have been. I was really hot. I don't remember too well.
>
> FACILITATOR: Did you hit her with your fist or with an open hand?
>
> PHIL: My fist.
>
> FACILITATOR: I know it's hard to face it, to realize you hurt someone you love. Many men feel guilty and don't want to talk. But you can't change a problem that you try and forget. The basic goal here is to help you stop being violent. To do that we start by asking you to tell exactly what you did when you were violent with your wife.
>
> SAM (*looking at Phil*): I was in your position when I walked in here two months ago. I felt like a creep . . . thought everyone would look down on me. But it really helps to get it off your chest. We're all in the same boat here. That's really

helped me. Knowing we're all here 'cause we hit our wives.

PHIL (*who had been looking down, looks at Sam and seems to soften*): Thanks.

As I reflect on the discussion above, I see anger and sarcasm expressed by myself in the statement, "You guess." It's not easy to strike a balance between confrontation and support in this work. It can be especially difficult for a worker not to respond in a mimicking or angry way when faced with the denial and resistance that usually surround violence. I tried to catch myself by coming back with a response reaching for the man's feelings: "it's hard to face" and "many men feel guilty." The feelings are not pursued in depth at this point. However, it is important to help the man both acknowledge his own behavior and experience his feelings in relation to that behavior.

FACING VIOLENT BEHAVIOR

Behavior intervention groups for men need to focus not just on ending physical violence but all forms of abusive and controlling behaviors. The Power and Control Wheel is one way of educating men about other forms of abuse and controlling behaviors (Pence and Paymar 1993). We use a list of violent and abusive behaviors our clients and their partners have shared with us (appendix A). We invite men to complete this inventory in the group. The instructions also ask men to record the kinds of abuse or violence they have experienced from their woman partners. Woman partners are asked to complete a similar inventory. When a man reports much less of his own behavior then his partner does, it is likely that he has some denial about his violence. Frequently men do acknowledge many of their violent behaviors. One evening the following exchange happened in the group after completing the inventory.

FACILITATOR: What did you learn from doing that? Would anyone be prepared to share what that was like, looking at that list and thinking about your behavior and your partner? (*Noticing Carlos is very quiet, seems to have tears in his eyes*). Carlos, this seems to have really gotten to you somehow. Do you mind me asking what's happening right now?

CARLOS (*shaking his head slowly from side to side*): I had no idea (*speaking quietly and gently*). I had no idea. (*He looks up and the tears are filling his eyes.*)

FACILITATOR: No idea? No idea of . . . ?

CARLOS: Seeing all of these together on one piece of paper (*swallowing hard*). I've really put her through a lot.

FACILITATOR: What do you imagine it's been like for her, to be on the receiving end?

CARLOS: That's what I get (*a tear rolls down one cheek*). She's been so hurt. And who wouldn't be? I never saw how much I'd put her through. I always thought it was just the last. I'd forget. I want to never forget.

The whole group is silent. It seems we're sharing Carlos's moment of reflection. After a minute or two:

CARLOS: It's strange.

FACILITATOR: Strange?

CARLOS: I feel terrible and I feel relieved too. Can I keep this (*holding up the paper*)? Can I keep this?

FACILITATOR: Of course. We'd like to look at them and make a copy, but you are free to take it. It's your work.

CARLOS: I want to take this home. I want to show her I understand. I want her to know I see what I did.

FACILITATOR: What's the relief about? You said you felt relieved.

CARLOS: It's terrible to see this; to see what I've done. But it's a relief not to hide from myself. Not to pretend.

FACILITATOR: So as you see the fear you put her through and the pain, as you really face what it's been like for her, you begin to feel . . .

CARLOS: I'm not a coward too. I've hurt her, but I'm not a quitter.

FACILITATOR: So by facing the worst and not blaming her, by seeing what it's really been like, you start to feel some self-respect. By facing your problems you are starting to be the kind of man you want to be.

CARLOS: Finally, yes (*he sits upright and smiles a little through tears*).

After that, Carlos would often talk of the paper in the group. He would pull it out of his hip pocket, saying he carried it with him all the time. It reminded him of who he'd been and how he wanted to be different. However, we do caution men who want to run home and share their insights with their partner. In fact, men may encounter her anger: "Now you want me to feel wonderful about you because you finally get it!" When a man has begun to acknowledge her experience and fear in contrast to blaming her for his behavior, only now may she feel safe enough to express her anger. It's important to remind men that this is, in fact, a sign of trust. Hearing her anger and her pain and really listening will take courage. After six to eight weeks of group, many of the men have made some progress in controlling their anger and aggression.

MANAGING VULNERABILITY IS MANAGING RISK

Some of the early errors in our work resulted from our ignorance of the impact on their partners of men's psychological abuse. Many of the men start to say, "I've been working on my problems. When is she going to get some help?" Or, "When is she going to trust me or forgive me?" Sometimes their partner has left and not indicated when or if she will come back. Or, she may have decided to leave but not told him, because in the past he has threatened her when she mentioned separation. If they are together again, she may still be very cautious and afraid of him even though she can see some changes in his behavior. It's not un-likely that he may have "changed" for brief periods of time in the past and then gradually returned to an abusive and violent response to her. During this time the men often become impatient with their wives' "lack of goodwill."

The key task is to help clients deal with their impatience, helplessness, and fear rather than expecting their wives to relieve it. Growth depends on no longer requiring the constant support, approval, and reassurance of his wife to feel OK about himself. The following process recording shows two men struggling with this issue.

> FACILITATOR: Allen said something valuable earlier. He said, "No matter what hap-pens with my wife (whether or not she returns), I'm going to learn something from this experience. I am going to change me."
>
> ALLEN: One part of me tells me to go find another girlfriend, but if I'm real honest with myself, I'd only be doing that to manipulate another person . . . to try and cover my own hurts. It wouldn't work for me anyway 'cause I wouldn't be look-ing at the problem. The problem (in me) never really went away.

A few minutes later in the group.

> FACILITATOR: Now your wife is saying no (to getting back together). When you were living together and she said no, what did you do?
>
> MITCH: I'd panic. I got mad, angry, totally outraged, sometimes to the point where I'd actually strike her. I'd panic 'cause I'm so afraid of losing her.
>
> FACILITATOR: For a lot of men it's difficult to have a woman say no to them. No to being loved when you want it, no to being taken care of when you feel you need it, or no to having sex.
>
> MITCH: Yes, I guess it is.
>
> FACILITATOR: About the only way a woman can say no in a relationship sometimes is to not be in the relationship at all.
>
> MITCH: I see your point. I imagine my wife feeling that.
>
> FACILITATOR: I imagine your wife didn't feel she had a "no." If she said no, she'd have to pay sooner or later.
>
> MITCH: I wish she could believe she could say no to me now and not hold it all in. Talk about it.
>
> CO-FACILITATOR: Could she?
>
> MITCH: Huh?
>
> CO-FACILITATOR: Could she?
>
> MITCH: Absolutely.
>
> CO-FACILITATOR: Could she say no to you now without your going into a tailspin, panic, freaking out, getting angry?
>
> RALF: You're in a tailspin now.

MITCH: You know this has cost me a lot already. I don't want it to cost me my wife.

FACILITATOR: What would be necessary for you to regard your separation as positive regardless of whether your wife returns, the way Allen was talking earlier this evening? That, regardless, "I've got something I can change in me." Is it possible to be in his shoes, to have that attitude?

MITCH: I don't know how.

CO-FACILITATOR: You are doing it. You just don't want it to hurt so much. It's going to hurt. For you to be with your wife, you need to control your anger but also your panic. Though it hurts like hell. If you got back with her now, you'd hit her again.

MITCH: It started when I went to school. Guys put me down and I'd panic and then I'd talk up. I didn't realize I've been doing that for years until I came here. That's a big plus.

FACILITATOR: The worst thing that could happen to you now would be if your wife called and said, "Let's get back together."

MITCH: You feel that would be the worst thing that would happen? (Mitch appears shocked and sounds incredulous.)

FACILITATOR: You wouldn't have the opportunity really to work with your own panic and trust yourself that you could get through it and handle it. Right now you're looking for Anne to bail you out. If she comes and says, "We'll get back together in six months," she's given you a safety net. You haven't had to deal with it (the panic) yourself.

MITCH: What do I do to deal with it?

RALF: Just live day by day.

FACILITATOR: Just saying to yourself, "I'm not a bad person because I'm afraid, because I'm needy, because I'm hurt." I get the sense that you give yourself that message; that you are a bad person because of all of that.

MITCH: Yes, I really do (spoken with some relief).

FACILITATOR: Dealing with the panic doesn't mean turning it off. It means feeling it and not adding to it that you're a bad person.

BILL: After you have been alone, on your own, for awhile, you start to feel—well, you feel down and low and useless and nobody wants me for so long and afterward you start to build confidence in yourself and it starts to grow and it's really a good feeling. At least that's what I experienced.

The co-facilitator mentioned in this process recording is a woman. We have found a male-female therapy team to be advantageous. The facilitators are able to model a different kind of male-female relationship than most of the men have ever seen or thought possible. They can see a man being intellectually and emotionally equal in relation to a woman and not lose any "masculinity" in the process. In fact, they can observe how much both sexes can gain, without loss to the other, in an equal relationship.

Some men expressed misgivings and awkwardness when we told them that a woman co-facilitator would be joining the group. Many felt that they would be inhibited and not be able to express themselves as easily as they did with all men. I think what sometimes passes as open communication in all-male groups often remains image management. No matter how hard the male facilitators work at catching this, our own male conditioning keeps us unaware to some degree. Other men expressed appreciation that a woman would be present. Many of them looked forward to a chance to hear from a woman about male/female relationships. One evening a man in our group said to our female co-facilitator, "Every time I hear your voice, I feel angry. It's not you personally. I realize now that I always feel that way when I hear a woman's voice." I think that, as these men acknowledge, with safety, "unacceptable" feelings like these, they can increase their ability to control their behavior.

EXPELLING FROM GROUP RESPECTFULLY

Sometimes a man might maintain a hostile attitude toward the counselors, group members, and women in general. I feel a responsibility toward the woman partner and toward the community. Allowing a man to stay in and complete a group while he continues to maintain a stance of blame and anger misrepresents to her and others the meaning of his completion. She may relax her vigilance simply because he is in counselling and even more so because he has "completed" a group. Therefore it often becomes obvious that I must ask a man to leave a group and let his partner know that. But how do I model respect while at the same time making a demand for work? Men who are unreachable and a high risk provoke a feeling of powerlessness in me. Then, due to the position of power I'm in as the leader, I've been tempted to shame or even ridicule a man. In this way I am simply doing to him what his behavior and attitude may do to her; using power to control when I feel powerless to have an influence. This is not what I want to model to other men in the group either. At the same time I carry a responsibility toward other men in group for emotional safety. Men who are hostile toward the group will often put down other men who sincerely want to make use of the program. The following quote is from a group when I did ask a man to leave.

> I regret that we will have to ask you to leave the group tonight. Being in this program is a privilege for men who want to work on changing. I'm worried that we haven't found a way to help you see the pain you've caused others and yourself. I'm also worried because I see you at great risk of hurting others in the future, which will undoubtedly cause suffering for you as well. We've tried hard to find a way to reach you. Perhaps if we were more skillful we could have been effective. But we haven't. So I will have to ask you to leave the group this evening. However, I want you to know that if at any time you feel that you might benefit from attending the program to better your life, I hope you will feel free to call.

The man in question has not called me yet. But other men in the group seemed to breath an audible sigh of relief. Trust seemed to increase as the work went to a deeper level. One man remarked, "I was glad you asked him to leave. I just shut up whenever he looked at me. But it was also good that he was here. He reminded me of how I used to be and what I don't want to go back to ever again."

THESE ARE not all the themes that can be worked with during the course of group work. Other useful topics have included 1. self-respect—how have they lost it and how have they gained it, 2. consequences of violence—what has verbal and physical violence done for them and what has it cost them and those close to them, 3. personal "buttons"—what are the things that another person might say or do that will easily enrage them and how does that relate to their past, and 4. practicing time-outs—getting the men to rehearse leaving a situation in which they feel their anger increasing dangerously.

I look for specific things in the behavior and feelings of a man to feel reasonably safe about him leaving the group. If a man feels that he has "fixed" his problem, that violence is behind him, then I become worried. One group member expressed it in a realistic way. He said, "It's like being an alcoholic. I have to realize that I'm always in danger of being violent again. I always have to watch myself."

Due to funding constrictions, our group is shorter in length than we would prefer. As a partial remedy we have started a follow-up group that meets once a month. This support group is run more by the men, with one facilitator present. We prevent men who have not been in our regular group from attending the follow-up group because of our concern about men using it to convince their wives to return while never attending long enough for real change.

We continue to modify our approach as we learn more about what is most effective in helping men to be nonviolent. The combination of demanding accountability for the man's violence and offering support for the positive changes he makes remains consistent. This work is demanding, and the burden of constant vigilance for signs of aggression or denial can be exhausting. Many women are seriously injured and sometimes killed at the hands of their husbands. Workers need to be aware of that always present danger without becoming hopeless, enraged, or burnt out.

Teamwork and networking are extremely important in this field. Effective networks in the field of wife assault are modeled after some of those that have been developed for dealing with child abuse. It is important to include members from a local women's shelter and from the different components of the criminal justice system. Most important of all is listening ourselves to the message we share with the men in our groups. "We can make a difference. We can change."

Note

The author would like to acknowledge the following agencies and individuals for their contributions. Funding for this service is provided by the Province of British Columbia, Ministry of the Attorney General, Corrections Branch. This service was founded by myself and Dr. Donald Dutton of the Psychology Department, University of British Columbia. The co-facilitators mentioned in the process recordings are Dr. Sue Johnson, who is now at the University of Ottawa, and Dr. Harry Stefanakis. Dr. Jim Browning has contributed to the development and leadership of this service.

References

Adams, D. 1988. A profeminist analysis of treatment models of men who batter. In K. Yllo and M. Bograd, eds., *Feminist perspectives of wife abuse.* Beverly Hills: Sage.

Austin, J. and J. Dankwort. 1999. Standards for batterer programs: A review and analysis. *Journal of Interpersonal Violence* 14:152–68.

Browning. J. 1983. Violence against intimates: Toward a profile of the wife assaulter. Doctoral thesis, University of British Columbia.

Calhoun, A and F. McGrath. 2000. *The genesis group : Narrative therapy with men who use abuse.* Paper presented at the National Conference of Counsellors of Abusive Men: Bridging the Gap Across Canada, October 29.

Downey, J. and J. Howell. 1976. *Wife battering: A review and preliminary enquiry into local incidence, needs and resources.* Vancouver, B.C.: United Way of Greater Vancouver.

Dutton, D. and S. Gollant. 1995. *The batterer: a psychological profile.* New York: HarperCollins.

Epston, D and M. White. 1992. Consulting your consultants: The documentation of alternative knowledges. In D. Epston and M. White, *Experience, contradiction, narrative, and imagination.* Adelaide: Dulwich Centre.

Erikson, E. 1950. *Childhood and society.* New York: Norton.

Ganley, A. 1981. A participant's manual for a workshop to train mental health professionals to counsel court-mandated batterers, p. 31. Washington, D.C.: Center for Women's Policy Studies,

Gardner, J. 1968. *No easy victories.* New York: Harper and Row.

Hughes, H. M., D. Parkinson, and M. Vargo. 1989. Witnessing spouse abuse and experiencing physical abuse: A "double whammy"? *Journal of Family Violence* 4:197–209.

Jenkins, A. 1990. *Invitations to responsibility: The therapeutic engagement of men who are violent and abusive.* Adelaide, Australia: Dulwich Centre.

———— 1996. Moving towards respect: A quest for balance. In C. McLean, M. Carey, and C. White, eds., *Men's ways of being.* Boulder: Westview.

Johnson, H. and V. Sacco. 1995. Researching violence against women: Statistics Canada's national survey. Special issue: Focus on the violence against women survey. *Canadian Journal of Criminology* 37(3): 281–304.

Jorad, B. 1972. *The spiritual odyssey of a modern man,* p. 9. London: Hodderd Stoughton.

Levinson, D. 1978. *The Seasons of a Man's Life.* New York: Ballantine.

Martin, D. 1976. *Battered wives*. San Francisco: Glide.

National Clearinghouse on Family Violence, Family Violence Prevention Division. Health Promotion and Programs Branch, Health Canada. 2002. *Canada's treatment programs for men who abuse their partners 2002*. Ottawa, Ontario: NCFV.

National Institute of Justice/Centers for Disease Control and Prevention. 1998. *Prevalence, incidence, and consequences of violence against women: Findings from the National Violence Against Women Survey*, pp. 1–2. Washington, D.C.: National Institute of Justice.

Pense, E. and M. Paymar. 1993. *Education groups for men who batter: The Duluth Model*. New York: Springer.

Stark, E. and A. Flitcraft. 1985. Woman battering, child abuse, and social heredity: What is the relationship? In N. Johnson, ed., *Marital violence*. London: Routledge.

Straus, M., R. Gelles, and S. Steinmetz. 1980. *Behind closed doors: Violence in the American family*. Garden City, N.Y.: Anchor.

Trimble, D. 1995. *Themes of defense: Understanding men who assault their partners*. Vancouver, B.C.: B.C. Institute Against Family Violence.

Chapter 14

No Place to Go
Homeless Women and Children

Judith A. B. Lee

Far from ushering in a new order marked finally by social and economic justice, the early years of the twenty-first century have been marked by a dramatic increase in poverty and attendant social problems. Outstanding among these problems is the rise in homelessness and the lack of affordable housing. The American tragedy of homelessness continues to escalate ominously for the most vulnerable groups, in particular for single-parent families, headed mostly by women. Devastating attacks on the welfare system and its virtual dismantling parallels this dramatic increase in homelessness (Schmitz, Wagner, and Menke 2001; Lens 2002). The tragic interplay of structural forces, including poverty, oppression, discrimination, and the low-income housing crisis with individual and family biopsychosocial vulnerabilities perpetuates and maintains the unacceptable possibility of institutionalized homelessness in the fabric of American society (Lee 1999; Lee and Nisivoccia 1997; Lindsey 1998). Conditions, factors, programs, policies, and practices that militate against this and promote both communal and individual resilience and empowerment within the context of greater structural equity must be identified and developed. The use of a socioeconomic safety net such as in kind and cash welfare programs are, in fact, a mainstream experience in the United States. The findings of a thirty-year longitudinal study by Rank and Hirschl (2002) show that two out of three of all Americans between ages twenty and sixty-five will at some point fall below the poverty line and turn to a public assistance program in at least five different years during their working years. Here it is important to note the five-year lifetime limit on TANF (Temporary Assistance for Needy Families) use and the particular vulnerability of poor mothers and children. Social work practitioners and the people they work with can be instrumental in seeing inequities accurately and participate in reconstructing the American dream of justice for all, starting with basic human needs such as housing.

In a survey released December 2001 by the U.S. Conference of Mayors 67 percent of the homeless in a twenty-seven city survey were single-parent families, the vast majority of whom are female headed (NLCHP 2002). Many social work, social policy, and mental health professionals warned of the lack of understanding of the complexities and difficulties faced by poor women and single mothers affected by "welfare reform" and its Temporary Assistance for Needy Families program (TANF; *American Journal of Orthopsychiatry* 1996). The program has had a ripple effect, making poor women and children more vulnerable to hunger and homelessness. By 1998 food pantries across the country reported an increase in requests. And in some shelters nearly half the families had recently lost their benefits (Lens 2002).

According to 2002 study on "Life After Welfare Reform" by the Institute for Women's Policy Research, an estimated 3.1 million families lived in poverty after welfare reform, including 1.5 million who subsist on incomes at less than 50 percent of the poverty level. The "welfare reform" legislation of 1996 changed the structure of income support for poor women and singleparent families in the United States by eliminating any entitlement to federal cash assistance and imposing a time limit for federal aid (Peterson, Song, and Jones-DeWeever 2002). What TANF failed to recognize is that there are women, with and without children, who are essentially unable to work because of mental illness (diagnosed or undiagnosed) and other disabilities and circumstances. For those women with children who can work, child care and after-school care was a major problem, and studies show an increase in unsupervised adolescents who are assuming the role of parent to the detriment of their school performance while mothers worked two or more jobs to make ends meet (Lens 2002). While the participation of poor single mothers in the labor market dramatically increased, their earnings and wages remained low and their employment concentrated in low-wage, traditionally female, occupations such as service, clerical, and sales. While incomes increased slightly, they experienced a decline in access to employment-based health insurance. They also continued to earn significantly less than low-income single fathers. While minimum wage issues effect everyone, the need for education and training programs to move women out of lowest income jobs and equal opportunity policies for women in the labor market were highlighted in this important study. The poorest single-parent families, usually female headed, are poorer after welfare reform. African American single mothers are the most vulnerable of this group to increasing poverty while working jobs that have minimum wages, no health or child care benefits, and no future (Peterson, Song, and Jones-DeWeever 2002). The most likely person to become homeless in New York City and Philadelphia is a poor African American child (Bernstein 2001).

Consistent with the national trend, in 2001 homeless shelters in New York filled to highest levels since the 1980s, with the largest increases among women and children over the last few years. Ironically, this is also related to the economy of the 1990s (favorable to the well-to-do), which skyrocketed the price of housing, making low-income housing even more unavailable (Bernstein 2001; *U.S. News* 2000). It is important to note that in no state does a full-time minimum wage job cover the costs of even a one-bedroom unit at fair market rent, and in forty-five states, including the District of Columbia, families would need to earn at least double the minimum wage in order to afford a two-bedroom unit at fair market rent (Salt of the Earth n.d.). Low-income families have no cushion for changes in housing costs. They frequently spend up to 70 percent of their income on rent. They are at risk of homelessness at transition points in their own lives or in the economy (Schmitz, Wagner, and Menke 2001). The lack of affordable housing, low minimum wage, gender, race, and ethnic inequity, and slashed services and government assistance has accelerated the homelessness crisis of the new millennium (NLCHP 2002).

This is a "public issue" relating to the wider issues of social structure and the times in which we live, but for the sufferers it is also an intensely "private trouble." Schwartz argues strongly for a unified conception of social work function that does not separate private troubles from such public issues. He says that such polarization, in which we have the planners and changers on one hand and the direct practitioners, or doers, on the other, "cuts off each from the other and from the reinforcing power of the other. . . . There can be no 'choice' . . . between serving individual needs and dealing with social problems, if we understand that a private trouble is simply a specific example of a public issue, and that a public issue is made up of many private troubles" (Schwartz 1994a:390). This chapter addresses my work at both levels, social work practice with unattached homeless women in small groups and mediation on the larger or more "public" level in New York City as well as group work with homeless single African American mothers and other homeless women in Connecticut.

The following is an example of the private trouble/public issue that speaks to the oneness of the tasks at hand. It also speaks to utilizing an empowerment approach that recognizes and maximizes the strengths of individuals and the inherent power of women coming together in groups to help themselves, particularly women that have experienced homelessness and its multiple difficulties. It is an excerpt from a group meeting of women living in a transitional living facility for homeless women and children in Connecticut where each has a separate apartment but participates in a common empowerment-oriented program. The group meets weekly, and most of the women have been in the group for several months. While the group is open-ended, as individuals may leave and "graduate" to permanent housing, women may stay in the residence up to two years. This forms a strong nucleus of women working together toward self-empowerment and having an impact on policies and programs that effect their lives. The work is often intensely personal, reflecting the various reasons for each woman's homelessness. Such personal themes are often related to domestic violence, health concerns, relationship problems and loneliness, parenting concerns, and drug and alcohol issues. Racism, gender bias, and discrimination in housing, employment, and education, getting along with each other and staff, trying to get ahead, developing skills in work and parenting while living in a residential program, and negotiating difficult systems and environments are frequent areas of discussion. With a skilled worker's help, the work also moves from the personal to the wider, more political level of consciousness-raising and having an impact on the problems that perpetuate and maintain homelessness (Lee 2001).

Twelve women were present for this meeting ranging in age from nineteen to forty-seven. Seven were African American single mothers, two were Jamaican American parents, two were Puerto Rican women, one with adult children who lived in Puerto Rico, and one an Irish American mother. In the last few meetings the worker shared information about the newly passed welfare reform legislation with them. They decided to invite an administrator from the local Aid to Families with Dependent Children (AFDC, soon to become TANF) program to meet with them and discuss what Connecticut's welfare reform would mean to them. Indeed, they anticipated the consequences of the welfare reform legislation.

The administrator, Mr. P., presented the new policy realities, noting that women on AFDC would need to get a job within a twenty-one-month time period. Maria asked in disbelief, "How will my children eat if I don't get a permanent job?" She worked for a temp agency and was supplemented by AFDC. She had already been trying to get a full-time job for a year. Several echoed this. Muriel said that she had found that her skills were not marketable here (crocheting and sewing). Mr. P. told the women about an entrepreneurial program for low-income women at a local college. Muriel said that was a good idea, but wisely asked how you started a business with *no* capital, even if you went to classes on it? Cora said she was always the last to be hired and the first to be fired, as many black women have been throughout the history of this country. This new policy needed to guarantee job opportunity structures to take American history into account. Peg, Brenda, and Keisha agreed strongly. They shared their stories of losing low-paying jobs and becoming homeless. Ivette said she was ready to leave here and take advantage of the rental subsidies now available for Transitional Lives Facility graduates, but she was too scared to go now. "What if I lost my job and had no income out there with three children?" Marta said she had four little ones. Dot asked who would pay for daycare for her toddlers while she worked. She added that the daycare facilities in the area were already full. Mr. P. listened and said, eventually, that he could see the problems the new policies caused for mothers and children. He gave them the names of influential people to contact. The group members decided to devote the next meeting to strategizing, letter writing, and planning to lobby on their own behalf (Lee 1996).

The reality of Schwartz's formulation of social work function once again rings true:

> The general assignment for the social work profession is to mediate the process through which the individual and his society reach out for each other. . . . [This] emerges from the fact that, in a complex and often disordered society, the individual-social symbiosis grows diffuse and obscure in varying degrees . . . to . . . where the symbiotic attachment appears to be all but severed.   (Schwartz 1994b:264)

The very existence of massive homelessness in America and policy divorced from the realities of everyday life for poor women (Saloman 1996) are prime examples of this nearly severed attachment.

Schwartz believed that society was made up of "complex ambivalent systems that are hard to negotiate by all but the most skillful and best organized." He asked, "How can such systems be kept functional?" He suggested, "What they need, and what each tried feebly to provide in some form or other is a force within the system itself that will act as a hedge against the system's own complexity. Its charge is to see that people do not get lost." He argues, "It is this 'mediating' or 'third force' function for which social work was invented and that historically it is the function in which it has done its best work" (Schwartz 1994a:392). This concept of social work function assisted me in entering a municipal shelter for homeless women in New York City on a voluntary basis as a direct practitioner and consultant who would also have a role in "reporting back" to the city administrators on my observations. This mediating role was negotiated openly with the administrators and the clients. Using the mutual aid group would be extremely important in empowering and in building and rebuilding primary ties and human connection for women living in shelter programs.

Developmental Tasks and Issues

While 45 percent of homeless people are men, about 14 percent are unattached women, while single mothers and children, estimated at one-third of the homeless population in 1993, are the most rapidly rising sector of the homeless population (NLCHP 2002; Lee 1999). Extreme poverty, single parenthood, pregnancy, youth, biopsychosocial vulnerabilities such as substance abuse histories, mental illness, health problems, family dissolution, inadequate education and job training, and minority of color status are the highest risk factors for homelessness among women (Lee 1999; NCH 1999). Domestic violence is also a major risk factor, with a 1990 Ford Foundation study finding that 50 percent of homeless women and children were fleeing abuse (Zorza 1991). Living with violence in homes and neighborhoods is a common precursor to homelessness for women and children, who continue to experience violence while homeless

(Bassuk et al. 1997; Fitzpatrick, LaGory, and Ritchey 1999; Schmitz, Wagner, and Menke 2001; NCH 1999;COHHIO 1999). Studies have found significant rates of posttraumatic stress disorder and anxiety disorders among homeless populations as well (North and Smith1994). In a study of 27,638 homeless adults with and without accompanying children who used public shelters in Philadelphia over a three-year period, 65.5 percent were identified as having once had a mental health or substance use problem, treated or untreated. For unaccompanied adults, women had nearly double the treatment rates for mental disorders than men. Among those with children, men had nearly double the rate of substance abuse treatment (Culhane, Avery, and Hadley 1998). Homeless families have higher rates of substance abuse, domestic abuse, child abuse, more mental health problems, and weaker social support networks than their housed counterparts (Robertson 1991: Shinn, Knickman, and Weitzman 1991). Clearly, in addition to the normative needs of homeless women and families, services and treatment for serious disorders are frequently needed.

While homeless women and their children are amazingly resilient, homelessness is a life-threatening, extremely stressful and degrading experience (Banyard and Graham-Bermann 1995, Banyard and Graham-Bermann 1998; Ziesemer, Marcoux, and Marwell 1994; Schmitz, Wagner, and Menke 2001). Posttraumatic stress syndrome, depression, anxiety, and feelings of loss, abandonment, and failure add to the already painful state of affairs. When we reflect on the personal meanings of "home" for each of us, being without a home takes on new meaning.

The dictionary defines home as "the place of one's dwelling or nurturing, with the conditions, circumstances, and feelings which naturally and properly attach to it, and are associated with it" (*Oxford English Dictionary* 1971). Dwelling and nurturing are indeed basic human needs; to be deprived of either takes its toll on humanity and mental health. Home is "not merely 'place' but also the 'state,' and is thus construed like youth, wedlock, health and other norms of state" (*Oxford English Dictionary* 1971). As to be without health is a serious blow to one's state of being, so it is to be without a home. Homelessness compounds the issues faced by families in poverty, adding the loss of friends, belongings, neighborhoods, schools, and a place to be (Schmitz, Wagner, and Menke 2001). Even when housing becomes available, the impact of having been without a home is profound. Add to that the experience of hunger, ill health, fear, living in doorways or cars, of keeping warm on steam pipes, or of constantly riding the trains, or of endless walking with nowhere to go, or of finally finding shelter in a place that gives three meals and a bed but is often as frightening and unsafe as the streets and more humiliating to the spirit. It is a tribute to say that anyone survives the state of homelessness.

Yet people more than survive, they help each other and even grow under these circumstances (Thrasher and Mowbray 1995). The developmental tasks of parenting are particularly difficult under these circumstances. Support is a key factor in helping homeless and other economically stressed mothers to develop secure attachment bonds with their children (Easterbrooks and Graham 1999). Low social support is an important predictor of homelessness, particularly among participants in substance abuse treatment. Interventions to bolster social relations are preventive in assisting people vulnerable to homelessness (Kingree et al. 1999). Promoting mutual aid and helping people to strengthen or find new primary group ties is also critical to ameliorating the effects of homelessness, for home is restored not merely with place but only when a state of belonging somewhere and to someone where some level of nurturing is available.

Having a home is a basic developmental need of all stages of adulthood. Developmentally, homeless women range from eighteen to ninety, from youth to old age. Some are experiencing severe adolescent identity and separation struggles, including those fleeing abuse or emerging from the foster care system unprepared to be self-sustaining. Some are young adults struggling with issues of entering the work force and relationships (intimacy versus isolation). Most are adults striving for a measure of socioeconomic stability, generativity, and productivity. Particularly striking are the older adults, both well and frail, subsisting with or without minimal social security, whose tasks of life review to attain integrity are now weighted heavily in the area of despair (Erikson 1959; Lee 1989). In terms of ego development, homeless people range from well intact, well-functioning people who met with calamity and crisis, including coping with sudden or severe poverty, situations that were objectively and subjectively unmanageable, to the acutely decompensated mentally ill person perhaps with co-occurring mental disorders, and all the shades of functioning between the extremes. For some the level of human (object) relatedness is impaired, and the ties to significant others are weak or nonexistent, making living in the streets or seeking public shelter the only viable alternative. Some were the "different" members in families, and, as family structures weakened, became outcasts or dropouts from family life. Still others lost families because of illness and death or migration and, well able to establish close ties, still found themselves alone and without primary group ties to count on. This is a highly heterogeneous population.

Vulnerabilities and Risk Factors and Resiliencies and Protective Factors

As noted, low social support and factors such as poverty, youth, pregnancy, and single parenthood, the lack of labor market skills, and other biopsychosocial vulnerabilities such as mental illness, substance abuse, family disruptions, trauma, and minority of color status interacting with structural inequities are the highest risk factors among women (Lee 1999; Kingree et al. 1999; Easterbrooks and Graham 1999). Policies and programs that help eradicate poverty, illiteracy, and develop work skills, real job opportunities, and living wage jobs are preventive measures against homelessness. The creation and development of large-scale affordable housing programs is essential to stop rampant homelessness. At the same time, programs that provide a four-tier solution to remedy homelessness are effective and critical. Full-service temporary shelters, transitional housing, and permanent housing with and without social services offer the possibilities of support and skill development needed to end homelessness (Lee 1999). Within these programs group work is an essential tool to motivate, encourage, and sustain people in their struggle to end homelessness and empower themselves and others who are homeless (Lee 2001).

Resiliency is promoted, developed, and cemented by social support. Yet social supports, particularly in friends and families, need to be reciprocal or they may be perceived as draining. Parenting, often seen as a risk factor and drain, is also a source of strength, connection and attachment, and purpose. Hence, it is also a protective factor. Relationships with their children's fathers also may offer challenge as well as potential support. Connections to church and spirituality are often a strong source of support in the lives of low-income mothers. Programs that promote academic attainment and upward mobility for women and their children coincide with their hopes and aspirations (Brodsky 1999). Preparing homeless women to assume new roles and make transitions, for example, to work and permanent housing are protective factors (Gitterman 2002). When obstacles such as substance abuse or mental health problems, including depression, further impede mobility, resilience is promoted by treatment opportunities and housing that provides assistance in challenging these obstacles for homeless women of all ages and backgrounds (Lee and Nisivoccia 1997; Banyard and Graham-Berman 1998). Homeless women demonstrate remarkable strengths in coping and problem solving in the face of extreme adversity. Shoring up these strengths and promoting cognitive, affective, and task-oriented problem solving as well as alliance and connection that lead to personal and political empowerment are key foci of group work with this population.

Agency and Group Context

A critical problem of many shelter systems is that they seek to meet differential needs in one catchall way, through offering a bed and meals and the most minimal social service help to this complex group of people. They thus become simply a revolving door for many clients.

In a shelter for unaccompanied women in New York City, one can identify different groups in need of services designed to fit their special needs. First, there is a large group of young adults who have been disenfranchised from the American dream. Having extreme difficulty in finding work and an affordable place to live, and often serious difficulty in living alone when ejected from families or couples relationships, they have established a new kind of counterculture. While some of these young people come from middle-class and intact families, most are from poverty-level families. Many have been in foster care and other forms of group care. Some have children in foster care. Many have experienced institutionalization for juvenile or other crime, drug addiction, or mental illness. They are the children we have failed with, grown just above the age where society must plan for them. Most are hardened and streetwise. If they entered the shelters without a drug or alcohol problem or propensity for violent behavior, they are soon influenced to become part of the counterculture that boasts these "attributes." They are also introduced, often with some coercion, to a rather tough, sometimes lesbian and alcoholic subculture within the group. And they are faced with an army of men, often from the men's shelters, including pimps and drug dealers, who wait outside for them each day. It is a difficult place for a young adult to find herself. As one young adult shared in a group meeting: "My bed has been next to murderers on one side and prostitutes on the other. I've seen crazy people scream at themselves and women take knives to each other. I've also met some good people, but I'm scared to death here. I can only look within myself and remember who I am." While some of these young adults "hit bottom" and find strength to move on quickly, many others make shelter life a way of survival, moving from one shelter to another. This group needs attention for many reasons. They are young and often open to help, they have and will have children to learn to mother, and, sadly, some also prey upon other shelter residents, even as they are preyed upon themselves.

Then, there is "the vulnerable group," those who are mentally ill of all ages, the elderly, the mentally retarded, and the physically handicapped or medically ill. Shelters have made little provision for meeting the special needs of these people. In one of the smaller public New York City shelters, there were four medical beds, a nurse, and a part-time psychiatrist available, but in the others there were no medical staff. Neither prescribed drugs nor psychotropic drugs can be administered. The "recreation room" may look more like a locked ward in a state mental hospital without the help of medication. Women hallucinate, disrobe, rage, and withdraw. While there is now some day programming in some of the shelters, it is minimal. Clients with a history of mental hospitalization who enter the shelter in a fairly compensated state decompensate quickly under these conditions. Others who may be retarded or elderly with or without organic damage also face the prospect of long empty days filled only with fear and need. The atmosphere and lack of service shock those clients who have none of these problems but have entered the shelter in an economic or family crisis. They feel trapped and betrayed by this system.

Finally, there are within the population substance abusers of all ages. Chronic alcoholics, young adults experimenting with drugs, and hard-core drug abusers are in need of a type of help, including detoxification, unavailable in such a catchall shelter service. In trying to "provide beds for all," with little attempt to group clients in order to serve them best, shelters help few clients. Although New York City has developed some specialty shelters, both public and private, and there are now several model programs for unattached individuals as well as family shelters, the need outstrips the availability. A shelter stay could range in time anywhere from one day to more than a year, with some coming and going in a revolving cycle.

Differential services are needed to meet these differential needs. While intensive individual work is important for many, the need for connection and human relatedness can best be served by providing a variety of group services. The overall strategy I employed in one New York unaccompanied women's shelter was to help restore relatedness and to develop actual primary group ties for the group members as they sought to empower themselves. In a Connecticut shelter for women and children I utilized a variety of empowerment-oriented groups differentially according to member need. The common ground of the need for shelter and the need to belong somewhere made mutual aid groups, both formal and informal, an effective way to help. In the shelter for unaccompanied women, three types of mutual aid, empowerment-oriented groups were used: the small, homogeneous discussion/ counseling group of both a planned (formal) and a spontaneous (informal) nature, the larger, heterogeneous discussion group, and activities groups where both doing and talking were vehicles of helping. This chapter will illustrate work with a smaller discussion group of young unaccompanied adults, with a large activities group, and with one group in a women and children's shelter.

In the New York shelter the homogeneous small discussion group was intended for those able to verbalize coherently, form ties more easily, and benefit from mutual sharing, support, and problem solving. The larger talking group, called "The Rap Group," was somewhat different. Developed by experienced social worker Jean Anmuth, this was an open-ended meeting held on a weekly basis with the intent of helping the women verbalize their concerns, exchange feeling and experiences, make suggestions on improving the shelter service, and begin to work on their concerns. The group was large, often having thirty or more people. There may be a nucleus of ongoing members or many new members each time. Since whoever wanted to could come, each meeting was unique; some meetings were dominated by the participation of the more decompensated mentally ill and some by the more intact. The large size and open-ended nature of their group had both positive and negative effects on its purpose. Women who were afraid of greater intimacy did find a place for themselves at a safe distance in the large group, and it also enabled "case finding" and outreach. But people who wanted and needed closer ties, who were frightened of large groups, or who had trouble talking at all needed the service of small groups and groups where something besides talking was the primary vehicle of service. Activity groups meet needs on multiple levels and are satisfying to the worker and the residents who enjoy creativity and doing together (Middleman 1983) They are particularly useful with vulnerable homeless populations (Racine and Sevigny 2001). In one shelter a "plant group" served this latter function. In addition to involving people who were not able to work well by talking, it symbolically met a need for growing something and caring for it, a strong need for women deprived of such opportunities.

This need to be competent in doing and producing as well as having a nondemanding and safe place to meet other clients with similar interests and struggles was also met by an activity/talking group. The activities were initially suggested by the worker(s) and then determined by the women's interests. More than one activity might take place at a time, leaving room for choice. Activities ranged from knitting and crocheting (a favorite) to painting and drawing, making posters or collages, working in clay, printing T-shirts, and so on. I initially began this group with a recent MSW graduate who had skills in group work and art. The response was strong, and the group was often large (fifteen to thirty-five) and heterogeneous, so co-workers were needed. I worked on forming small subgroups within the larger group and on helping people to connect with each other and talk as they worked. We all worked on helping each one with successful skill mastery, never pressuring to "do it right," which is assaultive to the weakened ego, but in helping each one get "good results" as they themselves defined good results.

The informal groups, those groups naturally formed by friendship or commonality or even proximity in one of the large dormitory rooms, were also powerful helping networks the worker could help promote and strengthen. This chapter will also show the use of the group in the informal system and the development of one particular primary group.

Work and Group Themes

The first group to be discussed is an unaccompanied young adult group formed by using a population approach. This approach to formation is used in a setting where clients are already present. It may be employed on a hospital ward, in a residential or neighborhood center, or in a playground, dormitory, or waiting-room setup. The common ground of being on the service may be enough to form a group. Looking for other homogeneous factors within the population can also increase commonality. In this case I used both age and natural friendship ties to strengthen the common ground.

My first steps were to determine the needs of the overall population with the director. We discussed possible natural clusters of clients such as the angry young people, alcoholics, old people, barely compensated mentally ill and pregnant women. I took a tour of the shelter with a staff member. Together we stopped and engaged people on each floor. We engaged a group of angry and loud young women. There were two leaders, Jean and Iris, and three group members. Iris raged about a woman across the room who hit her with a chair. Jean asked us to listen to several complaints: the TV was busted, the staff was rude, the toilets were stopped up, and so on. The others watched our reactions. Both of us were empathic, and I then introduced myself as a social worker and offered to meet with them later in the day to work on these grievances and to talk about getting themselves together to get out of the shelter. They enthusiastically accepted my invitation.

Getting Started

Present for the meeting were Jean, age thirty-one; Carla, age twenty-five; Ana, twenty-four; Iris, twenty-four; Sheryl, thirty-two; and Dora, thirty-five. All are African American except Ana, who is Hispanic. Jean and Sheryl were waiting for me in the appointed place. Jean called out the window and the others arrived. We put chairs in a circle and began.

I asked their names and ages and told them I was a social worker who worked here voluntarily on a part-time basis because I wanted to help. There were so many people here and not enough help to go around. "You can say that again" and "There's no help" were the replies. I told them the rest of the time I was a teacher at a school of social work, but I felt concerned that women were in such trouble and living under these conditions—maybe I could help them to help each other. This group, if they wanted to become one, would be a place to talk about making this place better and about getting out and back on your feet again. I didn't need to ask what they thought because they were telling me as I spoke by saying, "Yeah" and "Right on." Now Iris angrily and very loudly said she didn't want to meet with me as a go-between; I should send them the director or the big boss above all the shelters. I said I couldn't do that today and I couldn't promise any fast results, but I would act as mediator or go-between until I could arrange that if they wanted to do it later. Iris reluctantly agreed. They all expressed fear that there would be reprisals for coming to this meeting. Staff would "get them" for it. I said I didn't know if that were so or not, but they should tell me if anything happened. I asked for their concerns, and they began. In a steady stream, Iris, Jean, and Carla shared what the problems were. Ana and Dora agreed with all that was said by nodding. Sheryl seemed uncomfortable with the tone and barrage. At various points I turned to her to get her in. A few times she clarified where the others were not aware that the service they wanted did exist in some form. They went on with a list of fifteen grievances. All this was said with much feeling of anger, depression, and desperation, and I related to these feelings with empathy as the process unfolded, naming the feelings when they were particularly strong.

In this beginning excerpt I introduced my role and myself and offered the group service. I began to negotiate the contract on the group's purpose, mutual aid and mediation. I got their feedback and asked for their specific concerns in order to begin the work. When I noted Sheryl's indirect cue that she was uncomfortable with the process, I included her. I also conveyed empathy and put the feelings into words as they strongly emerged, saying, for example, "I can understand why this makes you so angry." I accepted questioning of my authority and clarified my role. At this early stage of the work I allied with their sense of injustice. My own tuning in and observations of the shelter enabled me to do this.

The Lack of Dignity and Respect, Rage and Hopelessness

Later in the meeting, Carla said there is frequent cursing at clients, and hitting of residents has also been observed. "We're all treated like we're crazy or in prison. It's hard enough to be down and out, but to be treated like dirt gets us desperate." Then Jean said, "This place is so tense, it's going to explode." Everyone agreed. Iris said she felt really close to hurting someone and going to jail. I said I understood how angry they were. I asked if Iris really wanted to go to jail; she said no. I asked the group what she could do then. Jean suggested, "Just what we're doing, talk about it here. I'm so glad you came. I don't explode, but I am so depressed." I said I heard her pain and asked how the others felt. Everyone agreed to being very depressed. Carla said, "You need hope, you need to know your options, how you can get out of here or you don't know what you'd do in time." Sheryl said people who felt they were so angry they would hurt someone should get some help. Many would not hurt anyone and didn't want to be hurt. I said that I heard her and understood she didn't feel that way, and it was scary when others did. But everyone here is hurting in her own way. This brought forth more outpouring …

Jean said she'd sum it up for us: "There is a lack of compassion here. Everything is hard and tough, and soon you become hard and tough. You get treated like dirt, so you feel like dirt. To be treated like a criminal is the worst part of the pain. You already hate yourself for messing up and landing here. Where is the compassion?" It was a moving moment. I said I agreed, and everyone nodded solemnly. I said I saw today that they cared about each other, and that's why I brought them together as a group. Jean said, "God bless you for coming here. This is the first time I talked my heart out and felt caring from anyone since I got here." Everyone agreed. I thanked them for giving me a chance to hear them and work with them and share their pain and frustration. I suggested they could become a group here with me and we could worry about taking care of each other. I honestly didn't know how much I could do about the shelter system. I would be pleased to try. But I did know they could care for each other and I could help with that. Jean said, "It's happening right here, right here, right now, I'm so glad I spoke up this morning." Iris started joking and singing about everyone needing a little love.

In this excerpt my interventions were aimed at helping the group members to tell the story of life there and to reach for and show understanding of the pain they were feeling. In particular, I tried to welcome the expression of anger not only because this brought relief but also because I wanted to model an authority who did not punish them for their anger and who could "take it." While their anger was not easy to take, I also let them know what would be hard for me (the demand to change the system overnight) and that I would try. I tried to show myself as a human being that had feelings about them and their plight. I continued to include the member who felt different, recognizing her feelings. The sharing of feelings on both sides brought us to a next, more intimate phase in the meeting. As we shared a close feeling, I also broadened the contract.

GETTING BACK ON YOUR FEET

I took this moment of a little warmth and tension relief to share a bag of candy. This brought further relaxing. I then said I'd like to have the group be about getting back on your feet and out of here, not just changing it here. What did they think about that? There was 100 percent agreement.

They said they want to "get back out there" and "make it in the world." I asked if each one could tell a little about why she was here and what it would take to get back on her feet. Ana suggested we go around the circle. Carla was first. Iris kept cutting in. The group put excellent pressure on her to "let Carla finish" and to quit "acting the fool." Carla said that she's not from New York and she's been here two weeks. She's had no one to tell her where to get welfare or what the housing options were or where to go for job training. I said I would make sure she got hooked up to a caseworker today. She went on that she is scared of the psychiatric cases and wonders why they are here. They need some help. Again, I agreed that she was right and recognized they could be scary. She said she worked as a social work aide at home, and she knows you have to treat psychiatric problems gently. She gave an awful example of someone hallucinating on her knees and an aide telling her "to get up off the damn floor, bitch." Now, if she knew the lady was frightened and needed a gentle talk, why didn't the aide know? Iris cut in. The group told her to let Carla continue. Carla went on to share that she had a daughter who lives with relatives and this breaks her heart. The group members empathized. Jean shared she had a daughter too, and it was hard; she needs public assistance and a place to live. I said separation from loved ones is very hard. Everyone agreed. I asked if any one knew how to get public assistance. Sheryl knew and filled the others in. . . . They then asked about housing options; did I know anything? I told them about two possibilities they had not been told about. . . .

After Iris told a little about herself, Ana said she has her public assistance and food stamps but not enough for an apartment, since she lost her allotment for rent money when her friend "threw her out." She had nowhere to go, so here she is. Her eyes filled up. She said, "I'm only twenty-four years old. I've been here two other times when I got thrown out. I need to learn how to make it on my own. I don't belong here." Jean put her arm around her and said, "You feel like crying, huh?" Ana wiped her tears. I looked around; everyone was feeling with them. I said, I feel like crying too, it hurts me that you're here. I felt like it when I left this morning. This is a painful place to be. Jean choked up as she said, "It's my first time, I'm never coming back here, if I can get out." Iris said, gently this time, "Never say never, here I am and here's Ana." I said it's very painful to try and not make it and come back. But I agreed with Ana, we need to help you learn how to make it on your own. Maybe we can work on that. Everyone agreed except Iris, who began to complain about the staff again. Jean said, "Look, staff is shit, but we got to get out of here. I want to be in this group." Jean said she'd kill herself before coming back here. Iris said she'd kill someone else. I said they felt very depressed and angry. Let's see if we can help with this group. Jean eagerly went on with her story.

In this very moving excerpt we see a sharing of real pain on a personal level. I continued to reach for, name, and show understanding of their feelings. I established common ground between members to deepen the empathy they had for each other. I gave information and helped them to do the same. I shared my own feelings about their struggles and lent some vision of hope. This latter skill is a very important one in working with any of the shelter populations.

I credited all of the sharing and mutual help they did today. I promised to look into their grievances and do what I could. I offered to meet with them again. Iris said, to her "surprise," if we meet next week, she had something to wait for, something was happening. It will help her hold herself "together." We worked out a time to meet. Then spontaneously they began to recite the words of a popular song. I recognized it and finished it with them. They were surprised and delighted that I knew it. We repeated, "Don't push me 'cause I'm close to the edge" a few more times. I said the song told it like it was. Carla said, "It's the fruits of oppression." I said it was, and I heard they were feeling on the edge, but to try to hang in there until we could get it together as a group and see if it helped. We ended on that note. They sang as we went down the stairs.

In ending the meeting, I credited their work, giving them hope of accomplishing the task and also recognizing their strengths. This also reinforced the contract and lent further vision to this enterprise in mutual aid. When we sang together, it was again a moment of sharing difficult feelings. Because the young women were in such a state of crisis, the feeling level of this meeting was deeper than many first meetings could be. It was also important for me to work on the very real grievances and in concrete ways show the meaning of mediation.

My work with this group lasted only a few sessions because half of the group was transferred to another shelter. I did begin the next meeting with follow-up on several specific grievances. The group provided a vehicle for social action and contributed to empowering this relatively powerless population. Jean and Carla remained in the group, but Iris became too drunk to participate. The mood was depressed, although new people joined the group. After a few meetings Jean got into a fight with a security guard that cut her with a bottle. The guard was suspended, but I was able to get Jean and Carla transferred to another shelter where the atmosphere was less chaotic and tense. In the new place I continued to work with them as a dyad and individually. They became my connection to the young adult population. I was able to enter the informal network with them and also to have some formal group meetings. I learned to treat each meeting as a "happening," a unique time together that might only occur once or continue the next week.

The transience of the population is a factor to reckon with. But I still found the group approach helpful on this spontaneous basis. I learned to live flexibly, turning any conversation with two or three into a possible group meeting. Over time I did have a nucleus to work. A popular theme of the mutual aid was job and educational opportunities. They were good at finding and sharing resources in this area. Housing resources were highly limited, but were shared when found. The important developmental work of "making it on your own," separation-individuation, intimacy and identity issues were always pursued. I also attempted family mediation for Carla and Jean but found family doors shut painfully tight.

The tendency for young adults to be pulled into a substance-abusing and violent subculture was strong and was always a factor in the work. The longer the stay, the stronger the pull in this direction. Jean left after two months, but not before she began drinking intermittently. Carla, on the other hand, stuck it out nine months until we could help her get adequate housing. She became part of another group that I worked closely with ("the primary group" to be discussed below).

TALKING AND DOING: AN ACTIVITIES GROUP

The following process excerpt shows the activities group at work. It is the fifth meeting of the group. There is a nucleus of six to nine that have attended all meetings; about twenty-two attended this meeting.

·The room was set up with two tables and several chairs in two or three semicircles. In preparation for the coming holidays, the primary activities were making cards or tree ornaments. There were also several that preferred to knit or crochet. My co-worker began the meeting by welcoming everyone and demonstrating the new skill for today, decorating Styrofoam balls. She also invited group members to talk about being here for the holidays or whatever else they wanted to talk about as we worked. They waited eagerly to begin, so we organized the new activity with the card making at the large table. Others preferred to paint and cast plaster ornaments at the smaller table. Those who worked with wool sat in the semicircles, with a staff member helping. We moved about, mingling in each grouping.

At the smaller table Anna and Clara sat on one side. Anna is a middle-aged, white Catholic woman with a history of mental hospitalization, nicely dressed, soft-spoken, and appropriate in behavior. Clara, her friend, is an older Jewish woman, more lined and hardened, also with a history of hospitalization. On the other three sides there are young adults, all black except one: Kiki, a creative pretty and verbal twenty year old, Donna, a thin, quiet, intent, cautious thirty year old who reaches out nonverbally, and Nina, twenty-eight, obviously slow, with a deformed hand. Also in the group were Cheri, twenty-seven, recently released from a state hospital (she smells of urine and unwashed clothing and is somewhat dazed, sometimes laughing to herself), Tami, a rather agitated, pregnant nineteen year old, and Kara, a heavy, white, twenty-five-year-old drug user. The group is remarkably tolerant of Cheri, except for Tami who holds her nose and attempts to get the others to laugh but receives no response, as the others are absorbed in their work.

I am working with Cheri and Nina on holding the brush and choosing colors. Anna is helping Clara. Kiki makes a point of painting all of her figures black. She comments that Christmas is for black people too, and she is tired of white Santas. Anna said she thought it was for everyone and Santa could be any color. Kara said her baby's father is black, if she is pregnant . . . they need a black and white Santa. I agreed, and asked if she was worried about being pregnant. She poured out her fears. Tami, with concern, told her where to get a checkup and prenatal care. Tami then got up and found some paper and began to draw. Kiki encouraged Kara to get help for her drug problem and told her own story of getting off drugs. Kara was interested in Kiki's program.

Noting the card Clara was making now, I said that there are a few people here who celebrate Chanukah rather than Christmas, introducing Clara to Lorna, an internal group leader who is a forty-five-year-old woman of observant Jewish background. Lorna came over and said she felt left out when we spoke only of Christmas. Clara agreed. Donna said it's "holidays," that's what we should call it. All agreed.

In addition to the sessional contracting skills done verbally, setting up and demonstrating the activity is also necessary. Helping each member to choose and start an activity is important, as is beginning to establish some level of member-to-member interaction. In a heterogeneous group such as this finding common ground is helpful (like ethnicity or a common problem like pregnancy), but the activity itself also provides a meeting place for differences. Additionally, I reached for feelings in a taboo area (race and religion) as a way of helping the group to talk about real issues and to accept differences. This was also a way of giving them access to a different kind of authority, one who encourages the discussion of taboos and of feelings. We also see the beginnings of mutual aid on the nonverbal and verbal levels. Later in the meeting:

> Kiki finished five objects and began to mix another batch for the group. Everyone praised her well-completed work. She said she was keeping them all. Anna said we could put hers on the tree; she couldn't keep them. I asked why not and asked her to show them to the others. They praised her work. She said she doesn't feel like Christmas inside. Cheri looked up and nodded that she agreed. I sensed the sadness all around and said, "It's very hard to spend your holidays here, isn't it?" Tami finished her drawing and held it up. It was a great cartoon of the "Grinch Who Stole Christmas." I got the attention of the whole group and asked Tami to show it. Those who knew what it was laughed heartily. I asked her to tell the rest what it meant. She said it means some of us feel we can't really be happy enough to celebrate Christmas here. Christmas is stolen from us. "Or the holidays," Lorna said. My coworker said that was a very sad feeling. "P.J.," an articulate thirty-five-year-old black woman who did beautiful craft work, said, "But I don't feel so bad today. This is fun, and some of us are beginning to have hope, and none of us are on the street." Several others agreed. I said, "So for some of you it feels OK to be here now, and you can feel hopeful and some holiday happiness, and others are very sad." Tami said, "That's a sorry-looking tree. The least we could do is decorate it." Nina and others got up to put their ornaments on the tree. The others continued working and talking to each other.

The themes of competence, self-esteem, and also deep sadness run through this excerpt. The activity enabled Tami to express her feelings without words, and we used it to help her and the others put words on those feelings of loss. Yet it was done with respect for the fragile defenses of several and with the balance of some laughter and some good feelings. The workers reached for and understood both the sadness and the healing power of at least being here together enjoying something. The group affords the feeling of camaraderie and competence and in that way adds balance to despair.

Another strategy we employed was to help group members reach out to other shelter residents who did not attend the group.

> Lorna then asked me if she could bring some of the craft material down to the old people who couldn't get up to the group. I asked what the others thought of that and if anyone wanted to go with Lorna. All said it was a good idea. I said I thought it was too. Donna and Nina said they would go too, and I worked with them on how to show the crafts to the older people. I later went to see how they were doing and was moved to walk into another group meeting. They were duplicating what they experienced, to the delight of several of the older women.

This multiplying of the mutual aid effect was also seen within the group. For example, Rina and Sally were two middle-aged black women who had exquisite knitting skills. As group members admired their work, we asked if they could become the knitting teachers. They self-consciously assumed the role but soon were sought after and spent much time during and after the groups teaching their skills. This was amazing to Sally, who had been hospitalized for depression and felt she had nothing to offer. Rina, who recently came from the West Indies, felt like "a stranger" here. This helped her find her way in and make some new friends. We introduced people of similar backgrounds to each other. Rina was then particularly helpful to a frightened young girl from her own country. Rina and Sally became friends, and we were able to find rooms in the same newly renovated building for them. When they left, other women had learned enough to assume their teaching/helping role.

Developing a Feeling of "We": The Primary Group

Rina and Sally formed a small primary group quite spontaneously. Others needed help and encouragement to be able to do this. A common problem for most of the women in the shelter was the striking absence of dependable primary group ties. Some had "worn out their welcome" with families and friends for reasons ranging from severe mental illness to substance abuse to family problems and scapegoating. Others never had such ties to wear out, as they were raised in institutions or had been considered odd and outcast for most of their lives. They now found themselves in a setting with a wide range of women who were in the same boat. In addition to finding resources for housing and making the shelters more livable and service oriented, a key goal was to help restore the capacity for human relatedness and to help residents form some level of friendship, to reform and restore primary group ties. For those who are alone, alienated, and isolated, *we* is a wonderful word and a statement on the road to coming back to fuller humanity (Cooley 1963). Our strategy then was to observe and encourage friendship groups and to encourage greater interaction and sharing to promote closer quasi-familylike behavior.

As we look back through this essay with these lenses, we can view the work with Jean and Carla, Rina and Sally, and with Lorna, Donna, and Nina's subgroup in this light. These last three became the nucleus of a group of four that I worked with to form deeper primary group ties. Carla was added later on. I worked with them within the larger activities group, individually, in the triad, and finally in the group of four. Lorna and Donna were also living in the same dormitory-style room. Lorna continued to take on various leadership roles although she actually looked up to Donna for being "very smart." As Donna received, she slowly began to be able to give back a little. Donna, who had had two psychiatric hospitalizations after being severely beaten by a boyfriend, needed help in learning how to give and take in a relationship and in beginning to see how others responded to her aloof, childlike, but sometimes angry quality. This was similar for Nina, who completed the triad. Nina, mildly retarded and with mild physical deformity, constantly sought out Lorna, who enjoyed caring for her. But it was hard for Nina to allow Lorna space to breathe. In time Nina was also able to express her desire to be seen as an adult, someone capable in her own right who in turn could help others. It was hard for the others to allow her to help them. Nina also had to learn what was appropriate to ask of others and what she could indeed do for herself. Donna, on the other hand, had to learn that it was all right to ask something of a friend as well as how to return a favor.

The basic "rules" of relating were unknown, since they had not really had friends in reciprocal relationships before. As Lorna put it, "Before, I was only a burden on others. Now I see I have something to give too." The giving for both Lorna and Donna was easier than the taking. Lorna's family had given up on her as "worthless" when, after the death of her mother and sister ten years ago; she was bereaved and unable to function. They "placed" her with an old woman, and she did not leave the house for ten years, until the woman was placed in a nursing home and she was again alone. She was directed to the shelter, where, ironically, she began to discover that she was capable and worthy of receiving from others. (For Lorna's journey of empowerment and faith after the shelter, see Lee 2001).

This primary group also affected other clients. Networks revolved around both Lorna and Carla. By working with them, I could influence a ripple effect of caring and helping. One of the problems Carla faced, however, was that she was easily pulled into a drinking and fighting subculture in order to further demonstrate her leadership and get what felt like caring to her. At twenty-five, she deeply missed her mother, who had cast her out as "the black sheep of the family" after she had been raped. As Carla and I worked on this one to one, we both thought it might help her to be part of a different subgroup where drinking and violence were not expected. At first Lorna, Donna, and Nina expressed a fear of Carla because of who her friends were. So I encouraged her to attend the activities group and get to know them. She did this, and I began to work with the four together. Their common ground was strengthened because they were all interested in going to the same halfway house. Carla's strengths added to this group because she could deal in the outside world more effectively and teach the others.

Another area of common ground was that each woman felt bereft of family ties and was a family outcast. This held them together as a new primary group. I met with them formally or over dinner or on trips, for it was critical that they get back into the world again. The primary themes were how families have let them down and how they had to "pick themselves up" and "get back on their feet," without their families but with the help of each other. We also worked on how to be friends and how to negotiate the complex systems "on the outside."

After nine months in the shelter (a statement on how scarce resources are) they were finally able to leave it. And they kept in touch, by letter, phone, and visits, actively helping each other. They were able to form primary ties they could count on. Each one noted, "I know I'm not alone anymore." Nina, Lorna, and Donna moved on to a single room occupancy transitional facility for people with mental health problems. It is sad though remarkable to note that within three years Nina was diagnosed with AIDS and was transferred to a government hospital where she lived out her short life. Lorna was her only visitor, remaining her friend until the end.

Engaging the System: Social and Political Action

Mediation between the women and the systems they needed took place on many levels. The group of young adults was a vehicle for making the shelter more responsive. Some of the specific things attained by groups were setting up a suggestion box to which the director was responsive, placing a pay telephone inside the building so clients did not have to go outside, especially at night, decorating several rooms, obtaining arts and crafts materials, establishing an informational bulletin board, forming linkages with a job preparation program, and other helpful changes. Within the groups themselves mediation took place between members having difficulty with each other and in the dormitories and the informal network. Attempts were also made to mediate between clients and their families where any possibility of engaging the families existed. Mediating with welfare, housing, adult homes, foster homes, halfway houses, employment, jobs and job training, and a host of other agencies were at the very heart of the professional job in this setting.

In the areas of larger program and policy change the needs and service gaps are glaring and the bureaucratic response correspondingly slower to achieve. My primary effort in this area was to propose a design for functionally specific shelters characterized by more homogeneous groupings. For example, using age as a general dividing line, a shelter would be set up to serve young adults; using a history of mental illness or current bizarre behavior as a criteria, one for the more vulnerable, including the elderly, would be established as well as one geared to the needs of substance abusers, and so on. There would also be one or two general shelters as currently exist for clients who can't tolerate a more specialized approach. Within the general shelters existing space could be arranged to create homogeneous groupings. This is less desirable but still better than no effort at meeting differential needs as currently exists. In one shelter the director did set aside a floor for the elderly. This was a good start, but the next steps of differentially assigning and training staff to meet the special needs would have to be taken. The proposal took into account needs for supervision and training of staff. It also highlighted several policies that needed to be enforced such as seeing clients within twenty-four hours of arrival. It involved no new expenditure of money.

The pre-initiation and initiation stages of the proposal were handled from two directions (Brager and Holloway 1978; Germain and Gitterman 1996, Lee 2001). I actually worked out the ideas in consultation with the administrative staff and medical social worker in one shelter to sound out reality. We also began to try out some of the notions there. My availability and direct practice "on the front lines" in this shelter was not only helpful to clients but also lent credibility to my thinking. I knew the job of caseworker because I did it. I knew how hard it was and yet, coming from outside, I could also envision how it could be different and what changes were needed to develop services. The proposal was written after several months of direct practice.

I also met with the top city administrators in charge of shelter programs on three occasions: first, on entering the system, defining my interests and mediating role, second, on discussing my proposal for specialized shelters, and, third, on how to implement the proposal in at least one shelter. My interest and ideas were welcomed. It was acknowledged that in the midst of this "housing emergency" social work service had taken bottom priority to providing beds and bathrooms in the new shelters. Everyone was respectful. However, I soon got the point that nothing would move quickly, if at all. In retrospect, it took several years and the work of many people and groups before specialized shelters became part of the NYC shelter system. One cannot fully take on a bureaucratic structure without a sanctioned role in the agency structure. But it was, nonetheless, a fruitful effort at direct service that led to helpful notions of program and policy design and change rooted in the reality of that practice.

GROUPS IN A SHELTER FOR WOMEN AND CHILDREN

In a four-tier program for homeless women and children in Connecticut, many types of groups were used to help the women empower themselves on the personal and political level. These ranged from resident's councils, life skills groups, activity planning groups, in which the women would plan and implement programs for themselves and their children such as cultural events, parties, and outings, and specific empowerment groups where they would share and reflect on their personal experiences and, sometimes, bridge from these into political action (Lee 2001). The following process is excerpted from an empowerment group working on wider/political issues related to homelessness.

In this example the worker helps the group members to connect their experiences to the regulatory issue of cutting an existing program. She discusses what lobbying and testifying at hearings entails, using role-play and rehearsal. Afterward, the women reflect on their actions. Jean Konon is the social worker for this empowerment group and a member of the Advocacy Committee of the Connecticut Coalition to End Homelessness. My consultation work with the coalition included developing similar groups in shelters throughout the state.

Eight African American women, mostly single mothers, twenty-two to thirty-six years old, are present. Jean stated:

"I have to tell you something very important. The state's Security Deposit Program was canceled as of the 15th of January. I went to a legislative training session yesterday that was set up by the coalition. They believe the best people to speak to the legislators would be the people who are living in the shelters. I want to hear what you think about this. There are expected to be further cuts in programs. The RAP (Rental Assistance Program), which most of you want, was only available for a few months. This week there are legislative hearings where you can go and testify about your experiences and how these cuts would affect you." Johnette responded, "I think we should speak up. They only had a few shelters; now they have a lot. And it's going to keep on getting worse, because there are a lot of homeless people out there." The others elaborated with feelings of anger and sadness. I recognized their feelings and said, "Well, we can go talk to the legislators in their office. That's called lobbying. And we can go the legislature and give testimony at hearings that will be held on these cutbacks." The women were eager to go. I suggested rehearsing. I asked, "How would it help you if these programs were now available?" Each one responded. I replied, "These are serious withdrawals of programs that you need!" They agreed. I asked, "How would you say it's been for you being in a shelter if you were testifying? Let's play it out." Sandra said, "Well, I'd tell them that it hasn't been too great. It's crowded here. My children are so confused. Where do they live? Where's home? Where will they live? Will we have to go to Drug Village or Death Row [the nicknames for the nearby housing projects]? They'll have to change schools again! What if those programs are gone forever? Where is the hope?" Erna said, "I've been without my own place for eight months. My relatives got tired of us. Our only hope is a subsidy." Johnette said, "I'd tell them that I'd like some help. It hurts to be in a shelter. I just want to be given a chance for decent housing for my children."

I credited their fine rehearsal and explained who the legislators were and what visiting their offices and testifying publicly would be like. Marla said that she was too scared to talk but she would go for support. Johnette and Verlaine said they would talk. I recognized that it is "nervous-making" to talk in front of an audience but said I thought they could do it. And they could also speak face-to-face with an elected official. There was then more discussion of whether to bring the children to lobby. They thought it was a good idea. Johnette said, "Well I can say I've been helped a lot by different people in the shelter, but I need the security deposit to move on." I said, "That's very well said!" Johnette said, "I think they will listen. I think I can say it."

Taking Action

The women testified at the legislative hearings and went with the worker to lobby an elected official. The Security Deposit Program was reinstated, but the Rent Assistance Program continued to be frozen. Although this made them angry, they experienced a sense of accomplishment in speaking for themselves to legislators and in the positive outcome on the Security Deposit Program. One woman, Johnette, also volunteered to represent the group at the legislative breakfast sponsored by the coalition. The group helped her rehearse what "eating with important people" would be like. She felt able to handle the experience and brought it back to the group. Johnette describes the legislative breakfast experience (Jean records): "They had a homeless breakfast, I call it. It was for the people who make the laws to meet with people who need the laws changed—that's us. I went to represent myself and our shelter. They had some people from other shelters get up and talk about the cuts they had in the programs. I spoke to a white man from the suburbs and to a Puerto Rican woman legislator. I gave her my name and phone number. I told them what my experiences were."

I asked, "How was that experience for you?" Johnette replied, "Well, it was OK. I was nervous first. I sat and waited a while because there were a lot of people there. They had wanted to put my son in the nursery, but I kept him with me because he's homeless too. I talked to the legislators with my baby asleep in my arms. It was good for them to see me with my son because there are a lot of women and children who are homeless. I told them about how the Security Deposit Program helps us and how hard it is without it." Verlaine agreed and added, "Last week we also went up to the state capital and testified." Erna, Johnette, Shandra, and Tashika said they went too. Shandra said, "We sat before microphones. But I wasn't afraid because I was prepared. I told them we can't get out of shelters without RAP." Each told what she said. Johnette concluded, "We did something important." Everyone agreed (Lee 2001:388–90).

WHEN WOMEN are empowered through their own personal and political work to act for themselves, their families, and others in the same boat, it is important. Those who experience homelessness know best what it is like and what is needed to change it. Social workers can be allies in the effort of poor people to create their own revolution against injustice (Baptist, Bricker-Jenkins, and Dillon 1999; Cohen 1994).

It can be said, ironically, that the shelter system itself is often a cause of homelessness. Many clients avoid living in frightening, authoritarian, and chaotic places until they are forced to do so by starvation and bitter cold winters. Unless help is given to turn lives around and to create and maintain adequate housing and other placement resources, clients will remain lodged in the system.

When efforts are made to use the strengths of clients individually and in various kinds of groups, clients are able to move on and even grow from the shelter stay.

Clients are able to reach out to help each other in many ways, including joining together to have an impact on policies and programs that create and maintain homelessness. Helping strategies, which employ consciousness-raising, promoting competence and mastery, mutual aid, human relatedness, empowerment, and systems negotiation and change skills, are particularly effective. The creation and support of primary group ties can have lasting effects in increased relatedness, competence, and actual support networks over time. A key concept is that services to this population, which promote increased relatedness and build actual support networks, can be effective in helping the homeless establish a home in society, with all that can mean.

Simultaneously, the homeless need to be empowered by social work intervention to have an impact on shelter systems, as well as on the broader structural, program, and policy issues that contribute to homelessness, and to take leadership in this effort. They also need advocates and mediators to help create the resources needed to house and support them in permanent independent and semi-independent (for those who need this) living situations. They need social workers who see their jobs as allies that may be a "third force" to make sure the tie is not severed, people do not get lost or cut off from their life support systems, and justice is served.

References

American Journal of Orthopsychiatry. 1996. Special Issue on Welfare Reform and the Real Lives of Poor Women. Vol. 66, no. 4.

Banyard,V. L. and S. A. Graham-Bermann. 1995. Building an empowerment policy paradigm: Self-reported strengths of homeless mothers. *American Journal of Orthopsychiatry* 65(4): 479–91.

———— 1998. Surviving poverty: stress and coping in the lives of housed and homeless mothers. *American Journal of Orthopsychiatry* 68(3): 479–89.

Baptist, W., M. Bricker-Jenkins, and M. Dillon. 1999. Taking the struggle on the road: The new freedom bus—freedom from unemployment, hunger, and homelessness. *Journal of Progressive Human Services* 10:7-29.

Bassuk, E. L., L. F. Weinreb, R. Dawson, J. N. Perloff, and J. C. Buckner. 1997. Determinants of behavior in homeless and low-income housed preschool children. *Pediatrics* 100:92-100.

Bernstein, N. 2001. Homeless shelters in New York fill to highest levels since 80's. *New York Times,* February 7. Retrieved April 23, 2002, from www.nytimes.com.

Brager, G. and S. Holloway. 1978. *Changing human service organization: Politics and practice.* New York: Free Press.

Brodsky, A. F. 1999. Making it: The components and process of resilience among urban, African-American single mothers. *American Journal of Orthopsychiatry* 69(2): 148–60.

Cohen, M. B. 1994. Overcoming obstacles to forming empowerment groups: A consumer advisory board for homeless clients. *Social Work* 39:742–49.

COHHIO. 1999. Homeless Fact Sheet—domestic violence and homelessness. Housing Ohio. Retrieved April, 23, 2002, from www.cohhio.org/dvfactsheet.html.

Cooley, C. H. 1963. *Social organization.* New York: Scribner's.

Culhane, D. P., J. M. Avery, and T. R. Hadley. 1998. Prevalence of treated behavioral disorders among adult shelter users: A longitudinal study. *American Journal of Orthopsychiatry* 68(1): 63–72.

Easterbrooks, M. A. and C. A. Graham. 1999. Security of attachment and parenting: Homeless and low-income housed mothers and infants. *American Journal of Orthopsychiatry* 69(3): 337–46.

Erikson, E. H. 1959. *Identity and the life cycle: Psychological Issues.* Monograph 1. New York: Columbia University Press.

Fitzpatrick, K. M., M. LaGory, and F. J. Ritchey. 1999. Dangerous places: Exposure to violence and its mental health consequences for the homeless. *American Journal of Orthopsychiatry* 69(4): 438–47.

Germain, C. B. and A. Gitterman. 1996. *The life model of social work practice: Advances in theory and practice.* 2d ed. New York: Columbia University Press.

Gitterman, A. 2002. Vulnerability, resilience, and social work with groups. In T. Kelly, T. Berman-Rossi, and S. Palumbo, eds., *Groupwork: Strategies for strengthening resiliency,* pp. 19–34. New York: Haworth.

Kingree, J. B., T. Stephens, T. Braithwaite, and J. Griffin. 1999. Predictors of homelessness among participants in a substance abuse treatment program. *American Journal of Orthopsychiatry* 69(2): 261–66.

Lee, J. A. B. 1989. An ecological view of aging: Luisa's plight. *Journal of Gerontological Social Work* 14:175–190.

———— 1996. The empowerment approach to social work practice. In F. J. Turner, ed., *Social work treatment: Interlocking theoretical approaches,* pp. 218–49. New York: Free Press.

———— 1999. Innovation in practice with homeless populations: Partnership in the struggle for empowerment. In D. E. Biegel and A. Blum, eds., *Innovations in practice and service delivery across the lifespan,* pp.221–46. New York: Oxford University Press.

———— 2001. *The empowerment approach to social work practice: Building the beloved community.* 2d ed. New York: Columbia University Press.

Lee, J. A. B.and D. Nisivoccia. 1997. Substance abuse and homeless mothers: Multiple oppression and empowerment. In E. P. Congress, ed., Multicultural perspectives in working with families, pp. 288–310. New York: Springer.

Lens, V. 2002. TANF: What went wrong and what to do next? *Social Work* 47:279–90.

Lindsey, E. W. 1998. Service providers' perception of factors that help or hinder homeless families. *Families in Society* 79:160–72.

Middleman, R. R., ed. 1983. *Activities and action in groupwork.* New York: Haworth.

NCH. 1999. *Who is homeless?* NCH Fact Sheet no. 3, National Coalition for the Homeless, February 1999. Retrieved April 24, 2002 from www.nationalhomeless.org/who.html.

NLCHP. 2002. *Homelessness and poverty in America; Overview.* National Law Center on Homelessness and Poverty. Retrieved June 26, 2002 from www.nlchp.org/FA-HAPIA.

North, C. S.and E. M. Smith. 1994. Comparison of white and nonwhite homeless men and women. *Social Work* 39:639–47.

Oxford English Dictionary. 1971. New York: Oxford University Press.

Peterson, J., X. Song, and A. Jones-DeWeever. 2002. Life after welfare reform: Low-income single parent families, pre- and post-TANF. Institute for Women's Policy Research. Research-in-Brief. IWPR Publication no. D446, May 22, 2002. Retrieved June 26, 2002, from www.iwpr.org.

Racine, G. and O. Sevigny. 2001. Changing the rules: A board game lets homeless women tell their stories. *Social Work with Groups* 23:25–38.

Rank, M. R. and T. A. Hirschl. 2002. Welfare use as a life course event: Toward a new understanding of the U.S. safety net. *Social Work* 47:237–48.

Robertson, M. 1991. Homeless women with children: The role of alcohol and other drug abuse. *American Psychologist* 46:1198–204.

Saloman, A. 1996. Welfare reform and the real lives of poor women: Introduction. *American Journal of Orthopsychiatry* 66(2): 486–89.

Salt of the Earth. N.d. Stat house-homeless statistics. Retrieved April 23, 2002, from salt.claretianpubs.org/stats/homeless/home.html.

Schmitz, C. L., J. D. Wagner, and E. M. Menke. 2001. The interconnection of childhood poverty and homelessness: Negative impact/points of access. *Families in Society* 82:69–77.

Schwartz, W. 1994a. Private troubles and public issues:One social work job or two? In T. Berman-Rossi, ed., *Social work: The collected writings of William Schwartz,* pp. 377–414. Itasca: Ill.: Peacock.

—— 1994b. The social worker in the group. In T. Berman-Rossi, ed., *Social work: The collected writings of William Schwartz,* pp. 252–76. Itasca, Ill: Peacock.

Shinn, M., J. Knickman, and B. Weitzman. 1991. Social relationships and vulnerability to becoming homeless among poor families. *American Psychologist* 46:1180–87.

Thrasher, S. P. and C. T. Mowbray. 1995. A strengths perspective: An ethnographic study of homeless women with children. *Health and Social Work* 20(2): 93–101

U.S. News. 2000. New York struggles with rise in homeless population. *Social Work* 2:93–101. Cnn.com. *U.S. News.* December 25, 2000. Retrieved April 23, 2002 from www.cnn.com/2000/US/12/25/ny.homeless/.

Ziesemer, C., L. Marcoux, and B. E. Marwell. 1994. Homeless children: Are they different from other low-income children? *Social Work* 39:658–68.

Zorza, J. 1991. Woman battering: A major cause of homelessness. *Clearinghouse Review* 25:34–42.

Chapter 15

Families Journey Toward Equilibrium
Children with Developmental Disabilities

Judith S. Bloch, Joan Weinstein, and Martin Seitz

O NE OF THE most important tasks of adulthood, parenting, has often begun, for most of us, with too little training or preparation. Families that include a child with a developmental disability are usually even less prepared than other families for the impact and changes that will take place in their lives. With rare exceptions, these children are part of families who initially have neither the knowledge, skills, nor support systems to deal with this challenge.

Traditionally, there has been a sharp division between the responsibilities of the home and those of the school. Today there are many who express concern about this gap. The Home/School Collaborative Model (HSCM) that was developed at Variety Child Learning Center (VCLC) reflects an appreciation for both systems: the central role of the family and the "outside" early life experiences of the child in the early care and education system.[1] At VCLC the agency's mission, to promote the development of the child and the competence of the family, created an interactional process between the home and the school (interdisciplinary team) where social workers (often the team leader) carry responsibility for the link to the family. The HSCM approach was based on the conviction that both child development and family resilience and competence would be most effectively promoted through our collaborative efforts (Allen and Petr 1998).

Developmental Tasks and Issues

Families rarely move with tranquillity from one with typical children to one that includes a developmentally disabled child. Planning for parenthood and anticipating the birth of a child or adopting and adding a child are major developmental milestones in family life (Minuchin 1974). With parenthood comes aspirations for the family; dreams of love, security, and achievement. The plan is for a healthy, happy child. The expectation is that the child will be an asset, although the specific form of this fulfillment depends on individual parental needs and fantasies. For many this is a critical way to meet their need for purpose and responsibility (Satir 1967).

The birth of any child changes the marital dyad, but the usual stresses accompanying change can be exacerbated when a child's disability requires a special kind of care. We have seen families in which the relationship between husband and wife becomes tense and without joy. Sometimes, when a mother cannot successfully comfort or control her child's behavior, feelings of impotence, incompetence, and even anger at the child may interfere with the bonding that needs to take place (Dane 1990; Greenfield 1972; Naseef 2001). Sometimes, too, mothers may react to such feelings by withdrawal and depression or become "consumed" by efforts to meet the needs of this child and behave in ways that exclude other family members. Fathers can become angry at their wives and resent their preoccupation with the child. In other families fathers may react to their own hurt and disappointment by disengaging from parenting and focusing all their energies on work and their obligation to meet their financial responsibilities.

Self-esteem and image, parental expectations, and dreams are threatened by the presence of a child's impairment. The pain and disappointment that is generated, especially at the very first phase when parents have a beginning awareness of the possibility of disability, may precipitate a crisis. Reacting to the "real" can be problematic. The internal and natural resistance to this unwelcome change of status evokes a family maelstrom, as primary parental hopes are threatened by a suggestion of impairment (Moses 1987). Many families seem unable to cope. Parental behavior, at this point, is often characterized by anxiety, uncertainty, even anger. The intensity of these initial reactions sometimes prompts clinicians who evaluate the child to question the capacity of such parents to nurture their child.

It is helpful in this connection for clinicians to consider that oftentimes parental reactions to the birth (or later identification) of a child with a disability[2] is similar to reactions described in the American Psychiatric Association's *DSM-III-R*:

> The essential feature of this (Post-Traumatic Stress) disorder is the development of characteristic symptoms following a psychologically distressing event that is outside the range of usual human experience. The stressor producing this syndrome would be markedly distressing to almost anyone, and is usually experienced with intense fear, terror, and helplessness. The most common traumata involve either a serious threat to one's life or physical integrity; a serious threat or harm to one's children, spouse, or other close relatives and friends; sudden destruction of one's home or community.
>
> (309.89)

Parental reactions that professionals observed sometimes led them to unfortunately and mistakenly conclude that these parents were irrational, dysfunctional, or part of the problem.

We have found it is not unusual, perhaps "normal," for parents to react in this "abnormal" fashion to this life crisis. It is understandable that parents who are threatened with the loss of their parental dream may at first deny the presence of the problem or tend to minimize the magnitude of the disaster. It takes time to deal with grief and to come to terms with changed life circumstances. Denial, at this stage, may be necessary for some parents to help them maintain their personal equilibrium, acquire the information needed, and make crucial decisions about services.

Vulnerabilities and Risk Factors and Resiliencies and Protective Factors

No one in the immediate family escapes from the chronic stress and anxiety that a child with special needs generates. Almost always, especially in the early years, family life revolves around, and is planned around, this central concern. The intensity of the despair and turbulence in the household has an impact on the most stable families. Each member, in turn, responds to this ongoing state of distress, overtly or covertly, with reactions and coping mechanisms that are functional and adaptive or limiting and problematic Only in part are these responses shaped by personal and family attributes. "Many vulnerability or protective processes concern key turning points in peoples lives, rather than long-standing attributes or experiences" (Rutter 1987:318).

With many kinds of trauma, it is likely that life offers protective processes to reduce the impact of risk factors on individuals and families. Constitutional endowment, personality and ego-strengths, a loving and supportive immediate family, friends, extended family, and the availability of professional services serve as mediating mechanisms resulting in resiliency and coping. However, the birth and subsequent care of the special needs child represents the kind of trauma where these protective factors, although present, may themselves be compromised. For the wife and mother, the birth of a less than perfect child may represent her personal failure. The baby came out of her body and therefore she is mostly to blame. Even at a time of increased blending of gender roles in our culture, her self-esteem may sustain the hardest blow because of "poor achievement" in motherhood. Some husbands and fathers may cope with the trauma by distancing themselves from the home and put all of their energies into occupational activities. Self-esteem may be sustained by success in business or the professions and underlying unhappiness or depression is less apparent. Even the presence of a "well sibling" in the family as a kind of "balancing" source of pride can impose a burdensome responsibility for achievement on that child (Bloch, Margolis, and Seitz 1994).

Protective processes afforded by friends and extended family may also be compromised in this kind of trauma. Mothers, in particular, may feel embarrassed to have friends know about the special needs child in the belief that they wouldn't understand and would not be empathic. Feelings of envy and the pain created by seeing other better endowed children at play can result in the avoidance of friends and subsequent loneliness. Even grandparents are sometimes viewed as a source of additional stress rather than as sources of support and love. For fear that they will be terribly disappointed, the secret of the "special needs" grandchild is sometimes kept for as long as possible.

In addition, the external resources afforded by the professional community may not always be considered a completely protective factor. Paradoxically, as an array of professionals such as teachers, language therapists, occupational therapists, psychiatrists, and psychologists offer, or, in fact, service the child, the risk factors for parents may actually intensify. The presence of "experts" and even the subsequent improvement of the child may only serve to undermine the confidence and self-esteem of the parents. Such therapists may unintentionally contribute to a parents' perception of impotence, leading to feeling a loss of control and decision-making responsibility for their child. The child's disability and extraordinary need for attention and care, the parental tendency toward isolation, chronic anxiety, and the distress regarding the reduction in personal and parental autonomy all contribute to an increased risk of family disequilibrium (Vigilante 1983).

Reducing the impact of these risk factors is possible through the introduction of mediating mechanisms in a timely and appropriate way. "An 'inoculation' against stress may best be provided by controlled exposure to the stress in circumstances favorable to successful coping or adaptation" (Rutter 1987:326). Germain and Gitterman (1996) suggest that "All people have strengths and resilience, although for some these strengths have been dampened by circumstances. Practitioners must identify, mobilize and build on people's strengths and resiliency" (22).

According to Rutter (1985), protective factors include "influences that modify, ameliorate or alter a person's response to some environmental hazard that predisposes to a maladaptive outcome" (600). Three major strands are thought to characterize resilience: coping strategies; recovery in response to trauma; and "processes that moderate the relationship between stress and risk, on the one hand, and coping or competence on the other" (Smith and Carlson 1997:236). An approach that promotes resiliency recognizes the families' need for a support system, both at home (marital or partnership dyad) and in the larger community that provides opportunities to network with others in similar circumstances. Assistance in the acquisition of "planning skills in making choices" (Gitterman 2001:27), a necessary empowerment skill, is linked to services that increase parental knowledge and personal control.

Agency and Group Context

At VCLC we recognized that the family system did not always function in a way that met the needs of all its members. Maladaptive family patterns repeatedly emerged for reasons that we already described, yet offers to help in the "old traditional" ways were not readily accepted. Parents came seeking intervention or a good preschool education for their child, but most did not perceive of themselves as clients. In fact, even when they were struggling and experiencing problems, parents distanced themselves or were angered and complained that they were demeaned when it was assumed they were "clients" (Dunst, Trivette, and Deal 1994). They were not likely to seek out or utilize counseling for themselves. Indeed, some mental health agencies alienated parents who came asking for help with their child because of the automatic assumption that they too should be clients. An appreciation of the volatility of parental feelings combined with the pressing need to acknowledge and address specific problems in family or child functioning sometimes created internal conflicts and pressures for staff and caused some "outreach" hesitation. Social workers at VCLC saw that, despite the stressful nature of family life, parents did not usually consider themselves clients.

To persist in the idea that a family had to choose client status in order to provide service would have resulted in too few being helped. Direct suggestions recommending counseling (even to the many troubled families we knew) were often disregarded or responded to with distress. Staff needed to remain sensitive both to parental needs and to their right to decide what kind of help they wished. Furthermore, many parents, in fact, did not need to choose client status for something of value to happen.

In order to prevent or reverse dysfunctional family behavior patterns, it was necessary to reorganize the professional service delivery model. This understanding prompted the development of an empowerment perspective. "The heart of the process for enabling and empowering families is the *relationship* established between the help seeker and help giver" (Dunst, Trivette, and Deal 1988:52). Linkages between home and school (Bloch and Seitz 1985) put into practice Bronfenbrenner's (1979) proposals that child development is advanced by frequent interactions with professional providers, goal consensus between settings, and collaboration.

We also found that the likelihood of having a significant effect with this approach is strengthened by a two-year placement that provides enough time for relationship building and collaboration. "Those programs which were particularly effective in producing substantial changes in children's functioning and in parental behavior have worked with parents for a minimum of 18 to 24 months. Long-term consultation that changed in keeping with the increased competence of the parent and the child appeared to be critically important for substantial and sustained changes" (Stevens 1978:60).

What emerged from this new understanding is a system of support different from conventional offerings because it views parents as participants and partners rather than as clients. As Froma Walsh (1998) states, "The same stressors can lead to different outcomes, depending on how a family meets its challenges. A core conviction in a family resilience approach is that there are strong advantages to family members' working collaboratively on finding solutions to shared problems" (25). The significance of relationships and social and professional supports, along with the processes that strengthen family resilience, are incorporated in the agency'sHSCM. The HSCM is based upon the assumption that parents are best able to identify and articulate their own needs and should share responsibility with staff for problem solving (Dunst, Trivette, and Deal 1994). In effect, the agency, as a whole, views itself as a school espousing a group culture based upon democratic values, with the predominant parental role as group member, not client. Opportunities for mutual aid are widespread and take many forms. The design is directed toward enhancing protective factors in families and in creating additional ones.

This new gestalt recognizes

- The primacy of the family
- The presence of a child (or children) with disabilities living at home
- The value of a system of linked and integrated professional and parent services with responsibility carried by both
- The value of an interfamily mutual aid network

The idea of a group culture creates new ways of addressing family needs without alienating parents. It makes available many additional entry points into the family system. In this way more parents are engaged after the assessment process, which includes them. This method is further strengthened by the opportunities parents have to observe their child in the classroom and in therapy without requiring prior appointments or permission. Demonstrated interventions and ways to learn without conferring client status expand the dialogue between the professional staff and the parents. "Exposure" of staff practice recognizes the value of parental input and subtly changes the balance of power.

The mutual aid network created in the parent lounge, hallways, and groups gives parents a chance to make friends, expand their support system, and benefit from the advice that is often unavailable from the usual sources (family, friends, and popular press). This approach creates new sources of support, information, and recreation; supplementing and enriching professional help as the family adapts and parenting practices are modified. Ongoing, unscheduled, and frequent informal contacts through the use of the parent lounge continue to create new entry points into the family system. Often informal exchanges move on to the use of individual counseling, group offerings, parent education and training, and increased utilization of social work department services (Dane 1990).

At the same time, parents are still not assumed to be either interlopers or clients but are rather approached as partners in the education and socialization of their child with a disability.

While increased interaction amongst families and staff provides more opportunities to expand and enhance the nature and quality of supportive exchanges, it also introduces the potential for problematic exchanges. It exposes "fallibility." Flaws or limitations in professional competence or in the service delivery system are more easily observed and more likely to be noted (Fish 2002; Malekoff 2001). A strenuous effort needs to be made not to create any unnecessary conflict between the informalities; the "exposure" of staff practice, the functions of the new structure, and the increased power of parents (Hartman 1997). However, in this group culture differences between consumers and providers are not to be avoided. It is better to create an environment where disagreements are to be expected, accepted, and addressed. What is important is that there is an established structure for conflict resolution.

Work and Group Themes

Families differ greatly in their circumstances, in coping abilities, and their use of salient components of the group culture. It is possible, however, to make some generalizations about the process most parents experience at VCLC.

The first stress point for most of these families is the initial phase of identification and classification of their child's handicapping condition (Bloch 1978), required to access services. There are many uncertainties that attend this process. Characteristically, this stage of first identification and the parental tendency to be secretive keeps others in the family's extended circle in ignorance and may deprive parents of needed emotional and social supports. Most parents are likely to struggle privately, alone, with this newly perceived possibility: Their child may have a handicap. Even as parents arrange for their child's evaluation, there is hope mixed with resistance to the possibility of a confirmation of handicap (Bloch 2000; Gallagher et al. 2002).

At entry to the program, the focus needs to be on immediate concerns. Families want to know how a program operates and what is expected of them. Social workers are particularly suited to carry responsibility for providing this information and for initiating a relationship. At the same time, the agency staff provides a sensitive and responsive reception that encourages parental involvement in their child's program, increases their understanding of the child's special needs, and promotes and strengthens their attachment to key staff as well as collaboration with the interdisciplinary team.

Many different kinds of experiences may be offered, starting with a series of evening orientation meetings for all entering parents that gives them information about the HSCM, their opportunities to participate, and assurances that their children are in competent and caring hands—in a safe place. These orientation sessions can focus on beginnings for both the parent and the child in the program. The child's initial task is to separate from home and adjust to school; the parents' task is to acquire more information about their child's strengths and special needs, the team concept, and the collaborative model.

Shared assessment is a key aspect of the initial phase. At VCLC parents and teachers, separately and independently, observe and rate behaviors of the child in the home and classroom using *The Five P's (Parent/Professional Preschool Performance Profile)*,[3] an assessment tool developed at VCLC. *The Five Ps* integrates data from parent and teacher rating judgments on 458 observed behaviors with clinical tests and observations. Parental input contributes to the establishment of their child's performance baseline and helps set functional learning priorities. The assessment instrument and process provide a method to link the child's baseline to the goals and to develop interventions that involve parents. In this way the stage is set for an ongoing alliance with parents that can help overcome patterns and perceptions of powerlessness. "Knowledge is power." As a tool in parent education *The Five P's* promotes the development of realistic behavioral expectations.

Including parents in the assessment process paves the way for collaboration and empowerment. This approach increases the accuracy of the data collected and is one of the best ways to get a good picture of the child's performance in multiple settings (Bagnato and Neisworth 1991; Bailey and Wolery 1989; Bredekamp and Copple 1997; Meisels and Fenichel 1996).

A note from a parent on *The Five P's:*

Five reasons why I love *The Five P's*

When I first received this questionnaire, I thought, "Oh, how will I, a working mom, have time to fill this in." But, I decided to take a chance and allocate some time for it, in hopes that it might give me some insight and guidance in handling my son, Sammy.

Well, it gave me more than that.

The Five P's:

1. Gave me a specific breakdown and baseline profile of how Sammy was doing in each area of his development with no stone left unturned.

2. Helped direct me as to what new ideas and concepts I should/could introduce to him. I did this and believe that taking these chances helped push him to new amazing levels.

3. Made me realize what I could aspire to and still do.

4. Helped me as I continually review this assessment looking for any way in which to help my son. I make sure to look at it every 2–3 weeks and keep it handy. It helps me to focus on his strengths and areas needing improvement and in demonstrating this to others.

5. Helped me to make Sammy's life better and to understand what is going on with my son.

Thank you *Five P's*. (Mrs. T., March 27, 2002)

This first step provides parents with some relief from their tension and anxiety as they begin to see an agency's potential for remediation and the opportunities for their input and involvement. VCLC's orientation sessions also offer a "group within a group" experience where social workers meet with small groups of parents to discuss "beginnings." This affords parents the opportunity to have a closer encounter with other families as well as a preview of a group experience. In this way, families are familiarized with the school system—the way it works and the concept and value of a home/school partnership.

SOCIAL ISOLATION

A recurring theme for families of children with special needs is their social isolation from the larger community. Development of relationships with other parents and mutual aid are highly significant factors in promoting resilience (Gitterman and Shulman 1986; Silverman 1980). Parent groups whose members are all parents of special needs children provide a secure milieu for revealing their isolation and their need to protect their own fragile selves and, by extension, their children from scrutiny and judgment. The transition from social isolation and loneliness to social integration can be noted in the following process:[4]

> CAREN: Friends don't understand. They want to reassure me that everything is OK. You see, he likes everything in rituals. They are trying to help him accept some changes here, but it's very hard. My friend and I recently went out to dinner. She had not seen him for a long time, but she just did not get it. He's four, but she was comparing him to her two-year-old to normalize his behavior. Probably will be another long time before we have dinner again (*laughter*). Funny story. I had signed him up for nursery school, but when I realized that he would have to go to Variety, I tried to avoid all my friends who would ask me about the community nursery school where all the neighbors' kids were going. However, one day, I couldn't avoid a neighbor and had to tell her. I felt very uncomfortable.
> JOYCE: I give myself a pat on the back for coming to Variety and for getting Eric help. I am so happy to be here. As I said earlier, leaving will be hard for me.
> WORKER: I notice that many of you are in different places. Doesn't it seem that way?
> BARBARA: Yes, we are in different places. I am very comfortable with my child's issues. I don't know why exactly, but I am not embarrassed and don't feel judged about it.

SUSAN: I am not so comfortable. I will go to the next park over to avoid my neighbors. I feel sad for my son, but I don't want to answer questions that people
ask. I don't understand why strangers act so nosy, but I try to avoid that.

YVONNE: Well, if you are not comfortable, it is better to go to another park, because your son will pick up on your discomfort.

BARBARA: We all handle things differently because we are at different stages. If
you prefer, the next park over, then that's OK for you.

WORKER: Is it OK for you, or do you feel undercover?

YVONNE: I am not sure. I don't like the way I feel about it. I'm somewhat ashamed
that I don't stay in the neighborhood.

WORKER: It's a hard thing to acknowledge when one of our own children has a
special need. How many of you have told your families that you come to Variety? Yvonne, have you shared that yet?

YVONNE: Well, with my sister-in-law who is in the special ed field, yes. With the
others, no.

WORKER: God, it's such a hard thing to talk about sometimes, isn't it?

YVONNE: (*Starting to wipe eyes again*) I can't stand the accusatory eyes of others
or to hear others talking about him. They don't know how it feels. I get so
angry.

BARBARA: Some people go through life that way. Yvonne, I think when others are
asking questions, like when they would ask why my daughter, five months,
wore glasses, I didn't see it as malevolent; just curious.

YVONNE: Maybe for some, but not others who have no right to ask so many questions.

CAREN: I have three brothers and all three grew up and ended up having issues.
One had narcolepsy, one got involved with drugs, and the other was just a lazy
whatever. No one knew to get help for them.

YVONNE: I feel proud that I was smart enough to get help for my son when he
needed it. I don't know how he will be in the future. I mean I don't worry as
much as I did, but I still worry plenty.

This excerpt is from a group meeting early in the life of a group. Group members are discussing similar issues characteristic of the initial phase: not trusting
family and friends to understand their pain and anxiety, fear of embarrassment
and rejection, and efforts at coping. The worker facilitates the sharing and validates the different ways that members are coping. In this way the worker promotes the idea of "all in the same boat," but, additionally, introduces the group
value of "acceptance of difference." At some point the worker also helps members move from describing behaviors (theirs and others) to some expression of
their subjective experiences. She notices that one member, Barbara, seems to
hold herself to be less troubled than the others or perhaps may need to avoid a
more personal expression of her feelings (Gitterman and Shulman 1986).

The Family-Friendly Open Agency and Group Culture

Protective processes (and a mutual aid network) are introduced with the VCLC "family-friendly," "open" agency (Spiegle-Mariska and Harper-Whalen 1991); parents are always welcome and no appointment or permission to visit is needed. This "open door" policy is in sharp contrast with a "closed door" position described by Powell (1989) where "community participation is kept to a minimum because the presence of parents would hamper staff in the performance of their duties" (55). One-way mirrors and intercoms facilitate the observation of children in the classroom and at all therapies. A parent lounge, which houses a specialized parent/professional library, provides a place for parents to network and to find respite, information, and comfort. It creates a gathering place where families can meet one another, make new friends, or simply relax. Sunday programs can offer year-round respite to parents and mainstreamed social/recreational/educational opportunities for children and their siblings (Bloch and Seitz 1985).

A group culture is created to promote parental involvement and encourage and welcome visits. As staff practice is "exposed" through one-way observations, a "climate" is created that encourages parents to share information and raise questions. A multitude of role and linkage opportunities becomes available to parents, prompting them to take advantage of the family-friendly open agency, visit frequently, make friends, expand their mutual aid network, and contact and work with staff, both informally and formally. Psychoeducational groups available to parents will increase their understanding of child development, the specific nature of their own child's special needs (e.g., autism, attention deficit/hyperactivity disorder [ADHD]), and specific interventions to enhance learning at home. While these groups have as a primary task, skill development, significant attention needs to be paid to the process of group development and group problem solving.

The group culture and parent networking concepts also shape a "tour guide" mentor program. "Seasoned" parents may be recruited to serve as tour guides for prospective parent visits. These tour mentors participate in a group that encourages reflection and consideration of the concerns of new parents. This experience often serves to hasten the growth process for participants. Additionally, the opportunity for parents to transition from client status to provider of service for the agency often serves to enhance the "acceptance and adaptation" process (Weinstein et al. 2002).

Professionally led groups play an important part in the middle phase process. At this time the overall group culture will have already contributed to feelings of trust. A majority of parents may choose individual or couple counseling and/or join more traditional, psychoeducational discussion groups providing opportunities for support and problem solving. While each family should be assigned to one social worker "for the duration," parents may elect to join groups or seek out other professional staff.

Some of the major tasks for parents are conceptualized as 1. transition from trauma and mourning to acceptance and adaptation as well as 2. transition from family disequilibrium to family balance (Weinstein et al. 2002). In the middle phase parents are moving along the continuum working toward these goals. In the process the families' equilibrium is often challenged by their increased understanding of their child's functioning as they begin to allow themselves to also understand the possible chronicity of their issue. The implications for the long-term impact on the family system, both on the couple relationship and on siblings, may become more evident and worrisome.

A key area of focus is to define the unique set of developmental tasks families are facing in their life cycle. Life cycle events or holidays often precipitate crises where resources are challenged and where, with appropriate and timely social worker intervention, opportunities are created for strength building and enhanced adaptation. The social worker needs to remain mindful and alert to the varied ways in which these opportunities for work become evident and present themselves. Attunement to these critical moments and developmental touch points can transform parental stress and distress into strength and empowerment and family disequilibrium to family balance (Middleman and Wood 1990). The balance between process and content (knowledge and information) requires careful and sensitive consideration (Meyer 1987).

Family equilibrium can be promoted by addressing couples' perspectives around the special needs child, any siblings, and extended family issues. Increased dialogue and collaboration may promote parental confidence and abilities, strengthen parental knowledge, insight, and problem-solving skills as well as help families access community resources.

A many-pronged approach to promote family equilibrium and family adaptation that responds to their diverse learning and coping styles will encourage parents to make choices. These can include membership in formalized groups; training seminars that use a psychoeducational approach, e.g., understanding sibling issues and how to help; programs that use group format but are single group events, e.g., Sibling Day, Grandparent Day; informal social networks forged through participation in the parent organization or in the parent lounge; as well as individual counseling services. In fact, there is a fluid nature among the internal systems. Parents may also be informally "referred" by staff and parents alike to utilize various services. For instance, an issue may arise in group where one member of a couple is a member, and it appears that the couple together, or even the parent and child, may need to do additional work. In these instances a group worker will encourage that work, and often another parent will tell how individual work helped her resolve a struggle and help "refer" the parent as well.

Coping with Realities

The following excerpt from group process highlights parents' struggles as they move toward coping with their realities, with the social worker gently reaching to illuminate the mourning theme omnipresent in groups of parents of special needs children.

> WORKER: I'm feeling very touched by the sharing today. Anyone else having reactions to it?
>
> YVONNE: Yes. It feels so good to talk (*others nodding*).
>
> CAREN: (*Teary now*) I guess we can come here and cry a bit on Tuesdays.
>
> BARBARA: Funny, I am sitting here wondering why I am not so affected like others here. I am not sure why exactly.
>
> WORKER: Everyone reacts differently.
>
> BARBARA: I am trying to reflect on my situation. My daughter has lots of issues. Maybe because my others are older so I feel differently. We were living abroad, and, if I hadn't moved home, she probably wouldn't have gotten all the services that she needed. So I am very appreciative of that.
>
> CAREN: I am very appreciative of the small changes. For example, I can read him a story now. I couldn't before. It has to rhyme, and then he can sit through it. Before, he just pushed me away, went off by himself. That feels so good to me now.
>
> BARBARA: I can't hold her and read to her like I could with the others. I used to rock the others and read to them. I loved that so much. She won't let me. She can't tolerate that.
>
> CAREN: You could try the rhyme books. I can recommend some to you.
>
> WORKER: Caren, that is such a nice suggestion, but I think Barbara is reacting to something more. I think (*to Caren*) maybe it feels like a loss to you?
>
> BARBARA: (*Now starting to cry*) yes, it does feel like a loss.
>
> SUSAN: It is a loss. We have had loss.
>
> BARBARA: What helps me so much is being able to reflect and discuss my daughter with people who understand, like all of you.
>
> WORKER: People who get it (*nodding*)?

The above discussion took place at a meeting that had been ongoing for some time. The group members did much sharing of feelings. Individuals had begun to talk more openly about their sadness and feelings of loss and to obtain some relief from such expression. The group, as a whole, had achieved a state of "intimacy" that enhanced its cohesion and its potential to induce changes in its members. Barbara is particularly influenced by the discussion and is able to lessen her "tight controls." She has begun to allow herself to feel with the other members. Her behavior in previous meetings minimized upset, involved advice giving to others, and generally conveyed "strength"—probably at some emotional cost, since she avoided a connection to any painful feelings. Early in the group's development her role was useful to the group because it provided a balance as other members were feeling overwhelmed and in panic. The present state of the group and its new intimacy provided Barbara with support and encouragement that allowed her to integrate her "other" feelings into her coping efforts.

Spousal Strain

Middle phase issues also include efforts by family members to reestablish good relations and balance in their lives in the face of the disequilibrium often caused by the entry into the family of the child with special needs. Frequently, the child's issues produce strain on the marital relationship. Husbands and fathers are sometimes resented and accused by wives and mothers of not helping, although they themselves may create barriers to their participation. But, there is a reality to the need to anticipate and manage some of the children's behavior at home. Their inordinate demands and volatility require finely honed "expertise" in tandem with the required attention to other family members and general home management tasks. As many mothers may have gained these skills, their wish for paternal involvement can be tempered with their wish to promote home stability—a conflict that can create a barrier to their husbands' participation. In contrast, fathers may view their role with their children in a different way than their wives may have envisioned. They are often willing to take risks with their children that their wives, in the interest of promoting stability and protecting this child, may view as threatening to the child and undermining her role as child expert.

In the following excerpt, most of the meeting was spent talking about husbands/fathers.

SUSAN: My husband worries continuously. He calls me several times a day to find out what is happening. I have to tell him to calm down. He becomes overbearing.

CAREN: Why doesn't he call the teachers directly? Why do you have to do all that?

SUSAN: I wish he would. I just tell him that I can't deal with him this way, and he has to stop or I will hang up. I worry about him. He is taking this harder than I am. My husband is an overachiever, and it worries him already whether Sammy will go to college or not. He seems stuck. He has no outlets. This group and coming here, my social worker—they are my outlets. My social worker helps me understand what is typical for a four-year-old boy and what is different. My husband blames all of Sammy's behavior on the ADHD, but it's not all that. We are older parents, and even though we are in the health field (he's a doctor), we never worked with pediatrics.

CAREN: Do you share the information with him? I mean, you go to the social worker and learn all this; you feel better, and he's still in a panic.

SUSAN: Some, not all. I try to protect him because he seems so disappointed in Sammy. It's very painful to see him feel so negative about Sammy (*tearing*).

CAREN: (*At this point, Caren asks Susan more questions about Susan's marriage. Susan appears sad.*) Do you think he is very different from the other husbands here?

SUSAN: I don't know. I never thought of it. He excessively worries, but he doesn't get involved. He keeps his distance. I don't know.

WORKER: Fathers react differently, just as mothers do. Some excessively worry, keep a distance; that is the way some react.

CAREN: Why don't you go together to see your social worker? You say she is a release for you.

SUSAN: He won't come. He can't take time off from work.

WORKER: We are here on Wednesday nights until 9:00.

SUSAN: Really; I did not know that. I think he will be afraid to come.

LINDA: Could you focus on Sammy and information? He probably worries about being judged, but if it's just informational, and then you can switch the topic once he's there. (*Laughter.*)

SUSAN: I am not sure if he'll come, but maybe if I approach it in that way.

LINDA: My husband is a very hard worker, always at work. I call him "Mr. No Man" because he's prone to saying no for everything. I work really hard to keep him involved. It wasn't easy, but I started that from the beginning of my marriage. I leave notes and share with him how I feel. I have to. It's so painful. He has to be there for me. I don't think he worries much, though. I do that job. He's in denial.

CAREN: (*Again, asking lots of questions of Linda.*)

WORKER: This is a very important topic for you, Caren. Linda's husband deals one way and Susan's husband deals another. What's it like in your family?

CAREN: My husband has a professional side and a family side. He is two different people. His professional self to the world is just terrific; everyone loves him. His side at home sucks. He does not take responsibility in the home. He waits for me to do it all. He shows no initiative. He doesn't help with the kids. I feel bad for all of them because he is not emotionally available to them either.

WORKER: And for yourself? Do you feel bad for yourself?

CAREN: Yes, but I take care of myself. I have the resources to hire people, go to the gym. Mostly I am angry with him. He does not give me the emotional support that I need. I did everything until my daughter came along. The older two were a breeze. I lived a jeweled life abroad. We had lots of parties. It was great. I realize now that I kept it going. I took care of everything. He depended on me. Now, with Sharon, I need to depend on him, and he is not there.

WORKER: You took care of everything; now you want to change things. What is different? How did it change?

CAREN: After Sharon came along, she needed so much. She was very vocal about what she wanted and what she needed. I started to consider what it is I need. Sharon is asking for her needs, but what are mine. I was busy all the time with her. I tried to get him involved, but he just can't. It's his upbringing. His parents are very cold people. It's just not in him. I started to realize that I had needs too. I had not acknowledged that before. I wanted him to do more. I needed him in different ways. Not just physically and financially, but now emotionally—especially emotionally.

SUSAN: You suggested that I meet with my social worker. Have you met with yours for help?

CAREN: No, but he does go to a therapist and is trying to change. He has to, or the marriage won't work. He is so disconnected.

LINDA: My husband would be too, but I don't let him. Do you keep him involved?

CAREN: I try, but he's not interested.

LINDA: Did he go with you to the reviews (she means *The Five P's* meeting)?[5]

CAREN: No.

LINDA: Maybe you can invite him to meet with your social worker or to call the teacher. You can share the reports with him too.

WORKER: Caren, did you invite him to come to *The Five P's* meeting?

CAREN: No.

WORKER: You want him involved, but you did not invite him. Are you protecting him like Susan does? I am confused.

CAREN: I set him up. Pause. I am angry with him, and I think I want to stay angry with him. I am angry that he can't give me more. Don't get me wrong; he is a wonderful man. If you met him, you would think he is so charming. I just wish he could go through this thing with me. I am going through it alone. I celebrate every accomplishment that Sharon makes. Having my daughter has prioritized my life, but he doesn't get it. I don't know what I am going to do.

SUSAN: I can't articulate my needs as well as you can, Caren. You seem clear on what you want. I don't know what I need right now, but I am going to make an appointment with my social worker. I am tired of being in the middle. It's too much work.

WORKER: Sounds like you do know what you don't want, Susan. Remember, we spoke previously that you all are going through a crisis? You liked that analogy. You all agreed it was true. During a crisis people do not make good decisions. It is not a good time to make big decisions. People don't think very clearly in a crisis. This is a very stressful time on a marriage. It won't always be this stressful.

LINDA: I am not leaving my husband. He's not the greatest now, but he will be great to retire with. (*Laughter.*) Really. I tell him that all the time. He loves to sit around looking at the sky. I can see myself on a rocker next to his gazing out. He knows how to relax. I am not able to relax. I wish I could.

>SUSAN: (*Very reflective*) it's true. Now is not the time to assess one's marriage.
>WORKER: Use your social worker to help get your husbands involved. It can make a difference for the family. Just having some quiet time to talk together without the children . . . with your social worker. . . . We are available to you.

In this excerpt from a meeting of a mothers' group, the members express feelings of being overstressed and direct anger at husbands who don't help enough. In addition to the support they receive from unburdening themselves in discussion, the worker helps them to do some reflective thinking. Some members become more empathic to their husbands and even consider that they themselves may create barriers to their husbands' participation. The group discussion moves from venting anger to a consideration of strategies for improving their relationships with their husbands and their situations at home.

An additional guiding construct identified in our work at VCLC is the parental journey from lack of understanding to increased insight, knowledge, and skill (Weinstein et al. 2002). As families move toward the termination of their stay at VCLC, there is an increased focus on future planning for the child. The team anticipates and discusses the transition and the group works on empowerment of the family as an advocate for their child with knowledge of educational systems and legal rights.

FACING CHANGE

All of this takes place as families face change, separating from a place of comfort and trust to embarking on new beginnings. The anticipation prompts a range of responses. For some it is a joyous time coupled with reawakened past anxieties. For others it is a time of reconciling hopes and dreams and working through the disappointment toward greater adaptation to their child's unique abilities and needs.

At a final meeting of a group, amidst refreshments, Carol reads aloud a poem that appeared in a local newspaper.[6]

Welcome to Holland
Emily Perl Kingsley

I am often asked to describe the experience of raising a child with a disability—to try to help people who have not shared that unique experience to understand it, to imagine how it would feel. It's like this . . .

When you're going to have a baby, it's like planning a fabulous vacation trip—to Italy. You buy a bunch of guide books and make your wonderful plans. The Coliseum. The Michelangelo David. The gondolas in Venice. You may learn some handy phrases in Italian. It's all very exciting.

After months of eager anticipation, the day finally arrives. You pack your bags and off you go. Several hours later, the plane lands. The stewardess comes in and says, "Welcome to Holland."

"*Holland*?!?" you say. "What do you mean Holland?? I signed up for Italy! I'm supposed to be in Italy. All my life I've dreamed of going to Italy."

But there's been a change in the flight plan. They've landed in Holland and there you must stay.

The important thing is that they haven't taken you to a horrible, disgusting, filthy place, full of pestilence, famine and disease. It's just a different place.

So you must go out and buy new guide books. And you must learn a whole new language. And you will meet a whole new group of people you would never have met.

It's just a *different* place. It's slower-paced than Italy, less flashy than Italy. But after you've been there for a while and you catch your breath, you look around . . . and you begin to notice that Holland has windmills . . . and Holland has tulips. Holland even has Rembrandts.

But everyone you know is busy coming and going from Italy . . . and they're all bragging about what a wonderful time they had there. And for the rest of your life, you will say, "Yes, that's where I was supposed to go. That's what I had planned."

And the pain of that will never, ever, ever, ever go away . . . because the loss of that dream is a very very significant loss.

But . . . if you spend your life mourning the fact that you didn't get to Italy, you may never be free to enjoy the very special, the very lovely things . . . about Holland.

Carol said she wanted to read the poem to tell how much the group has meant. "After all the discussions and sharing, I can now appreciate Holland."

In yet another group, a mother shares her adaptation regarding her four-year-old son, cognitively delayed and behaviorally disordered, as she is supported by the group:

JULIE: I have changed a lot since I first came here. I am more accepting of how my son is and what I have to be grateful for. Maybe he won't be an astronaut, maybe he's not the sharpest knife in the drawer, but he is very loving and appreciative. If I cook a good dinner, he says, "Mommy, that was so good. Thank you."

Beginnings and new relationships may be stressful, but endings and leave-taking are more difficult. Even though both sides, families and staff, know it is time, some of the old fears may surface again. As the ending time draws near, earlier anxieties often arise as well as sadness for some dreams that remain unrealized and culminate in palpable pain. For many families the agency will have provided a safe holding environment for themselves and held at bay community eyes and judgments.

At this juncture the agency provides brief groups focused on educational rights and advocacy as well as on transition. Some alumni parents are selected and invited to share their experiences as parents consider ways to meet their and their child's needs in a different program. Additionally, parent support groups address termination. These combined efforts serve to give parents opportunities to work through their separation anxieties and network with other parents. Hopefully, as one parent reported, "It is scary, but I am talking myself through it this time, using the skills I learned here. I need to hold on to my confidence."

As MORE SCHOOLS across the country implement a federal policy that requires children with disabilities to be included in regular education classes, social workers with an understanding of the impact the presence of a child with a disability has on family life have an important role to play. Involving parents in their child's education, providing them with information and services that support the family, and recognizing their central influence on the child's development is of value to the school and child. Elizabeth Dane (1990) contends and concludes that the objective of social work is to "empower parents" (150). She states:

> The strength and unswerving commitment of families to seek the best for their children revitalizes the professional social worker, who often is too closely bound by institutional reality. The answer, "It can't be done," must be countered by the question, "Why not?" For those who are listening, it is clear that families of children with disabilities are reinvesting the social work profession with its commitment to innovative service.
>
> (Dane 1985:509)

At VCLC we saw that time alone did not necessarily resolve all adaptation steps or ease the pain the entire family experienced. For some, worry and the extraordinary burdens of child care eroded family strength and resilience (Dane 1990:122). We saw how the plight of one affected the destiny of all. We came to realize that a family empowerment perspective is, indeed, a resilience-based approach. Knowledge, increased skills, mutual support, good communication, shared efforts, and resources helped parents acquire confidence and learn that they could prevail and overcome duress. The social work staff efforts increased family resilience, assisted with immediate crises, and, at the same time, prepared parents to surmount later problems, serving as a prevention measure.

We add one final thought. This design for practice administration must guard against any tendency to elevate professionally led groups (an important service) as the only and best way to accomplish "work issues." Parents may choose any number of pathways as they journey toward increased resiliency and improved coping abilities. It is the *agency* as *group* that is the key construct. The following excerpts from a recent letter describes the process for one family:

Dear Ms. Bloch,

My name is Linda R. and my son has been attending VCLC since September 2001. As it is the end of this chapter and we are about to embark onto a new one, I wanted to relate my experience at the school . . .

When my husband and I first toured the school, it felt warm and inviting and we heard sounds of "happy" children. . . . It did not feel like a "special school," if that makes any sense to you. I was still having a difficult time accepting the idea that my son needed a special program. Looking back now, I realize what a painful emotional state I was in. Today, you cannot stop me from discussing his delays and his progress. My son is special in all the ways that count for me . . .

And then, of course, there is my social worker. She has journeyed with us from the first phone call. She answered our questions. She refrained from giving easy answers but encouraged us to have cautious optimism. She could allow us to talk, cry, and vent. She made Wednesdays (our group meeting) worth canceling any other appointments just to be there. . . . I think what the school did for me was to remind me that I was still Mom, and, in the midst of what the teachers and therapists did, I could parent him as I felt best.

So, here we are, one year later. I cannot believe how quickly the time has passed. With all the progress that I have witnessed, I felt it only appropriate that I pause and take the time to extend these heartfelt words of thanks. Without this program, I wonder if I would be hearing my son saying, "Mommy, I'm sad" when he does not want to do something, or "Good mornin', Mommy; how are you today?" all this from a child who had about ten words last September. I wonder if I would actually be able to watch him "know" how to play with his "Little People" toys for twenty to thirty minutes, rather than move the pieces around for a few minutes with no particular purpose. I wonder if I would see this child approach another and say "Hi, friend" . . .

Thank you for this school, which not only serves the children but the parents. Our children not only learn to master new skills, but upon us is conferred the renewed confidence to be our child's best caregiver and advocate.

Notes

1. Variety Child Learning Center (VCLC), formerly Variety Pre-Schooler's Workshop (VPSW), established in 1966, was in the forefront of program development for young children with learning, language, and behavior problems.
2. "The term 'child with a disability' for a child aged 3 through 9 may, at the discretion of the State and the local educational agency, include a child—experiencing developmental delays, as defined by the State and as measured by appropriate diagnostic instruments and procedures, in one or more of the following areas: physical development, cognitive development, communication development, social or emotional development, or adaptive development." *Individuals with Disabilities Education Act [IDEA] Amendments of 1997,* Sec. 1401, Definitions.

3. *The Five P's* (*Parent/Professional Preschool Performance Profile*), developed by Judith S. Bloch at Variety Pre-Schooler's Workshop (now known as Variety Child Learning Center), is a shared assessment instrument for children six months to five years old with learning, language, or behavior problems. Parents and teachers rate the child on 458 developmental skills and interfering behaviors. *The Five P's* was favorably reviewed by the Buros Institute of Mental Measurements in *The Tenth Mental Measurements Yearbook* (1989) and *The Thirteenth Mental Measurements Yearbook* (1998).

4. The authors would like to acknowledge Vicki Leopold, CSW, a social worker at Variety Child Learning Center, for providing most of the process recording for this paper.

5. *The Five P's* Meeting: Share and Compare: Setting Instructional Objectives. A parent-teacher meeting to discuss a child's progress as well as to set goals.

6. Emily Perl Kingsley, "Welcome to Holland" copyright © 1987 Emily Perl Kingsley. All rights reserved. Reprinted by permission of the author.

References

Allen, R. I. and C. G. Petr. 1998. Rethinking family-centered practice. *American Journal of Orthopsychiatry* 68(1): 4–15.

American Psychiatric Association. 1987. *DSM-III-R/Diagnostic and statistical manual of mental disorders*. 3d ed. Washington, D.C.: American Psychiatric Association.

Bagnato, S. J. and J. T. Neisworth. 1991. *Assessment for early intervention: Best practices for professionals*. New York: Guilford.

Bailey, D. B., Jr. and M. Wolery. 1989. *Assessing infants and preschoolers with handicaps*. Columbus: Merrill.

Bloch, J. S. 1978. Impaired children: Helping families through the critical period of first identification. *Children Today* 7(6): 1–6.

——— 2000. What do I say to parents when I am worried about their child? *Early Childhood News* 12(3): 8–16.

Bloch, J. S. and M. Seitz. 1985. *Empowering parents of disabled children: A family exchange center*. Syosset, N.Y.: Variety Pre-Schooler's Workshop.

Bloch, J. S., J. Margolis, and M. Seitz. 1994. Feelings of shame: Siblings of handicapped children. In A. Gitterman and L. Shulman, eds., *Mutual Aid Groups, Vulnerable Populations, and the Life Cycle*, pp. 97–115. 2d ed. New York: Columbia University Press.

Bredekamp, S. and C. Copple, eds. 1997. *Developmentally appropriate practice in early childhood programs*. Washington, D.C.: National Association for the Education of Young Children.

Bronfenbrenner, U. 1979. *The ecology of human development: Experiments by nature and design*. Cambridge: Harvard University Press.

Dane, E. 1985. Professional and lay advocacy in the education of handicapped children. *Social Work* 30:505–10.

——— 1990. *Painful passages: Working with children with learning disabilities*. Silver Springs: NASW Press.

Dunst, C. J., C. M. Trivette, and A. G. Deal, eds. 1988. *Enabling and empowering families: Principles and guidelines for practice*. Cambridge: Brookline.

——— 1994. *Supporting and strengthening families*. Vol. 1: *Methods, strategies, and practices*. Cambridge: Brookline.

Fish, L. S. 2002. Nightmare in aisle 6. *Psychotherapy Networker* (April-May), pp. 36–37.

Gallagher:A., J. Fialka, C. Rhodes, and C. Arceneaux. 2002. Working with families: Rethinking denial. *Young Exceptional Children* 5(2): 11–17.

Garland, J., H. Jones, and R. Kolodny. 1965. A model for stages of development in social work groups. In S. Bernstein, ed., *Explorations in group work*. Boston: Boston University School of Social Work.

Germain, C. B. and A. Gitterman. 1996. *The life model of social work practice: Advances in knowledge and practice*. New York: Columbia University Press.

Gitterman, A. 2001. Vulnerability, resilience, and social work with groups. In T. Kelly, T. Berman-Rossi, and S. Palombo, eds., *Group work: Strategies for strengthening resiliency*, pp. 19–33. New York: Haworth.

Gitterman, A. and L. Shulman, eds. 1986. *Mutual aid groups and the life cycle*. Itasca, Ill.: Peacock.

Glassman, U. and L. Kates. 1990. *Group work: A humanistic approach*. Beverly Hills: Sage.

Greenfield, J. 1972. *A child called Noah: A family journey*. New York: Holt.

Hartman, A. 1997. Power issues in social work practice. In A. J. Katz, A. Lurie, and C. M. Vidal, eds., *Critical social welfare issues: Tools for social work and health care professionals*, pp. 215–26. New York: Haworth.

Individuals with Disabilities Education Act (IDEA) Amendments of 1997, P.L. 105–17.

Levine, B. 1967. *Fundamentals of group treatment*. Northbrook, Ill.: Whitehall.

Malekoff, A. 2001. From the editor. *HUH?!?* [Quarterly Newsletter of the Long Island Institute for Group Work with Children and Youth], vol. 6, no. 2 (Spring). Roslyn Heights, N.Y.: North Shore Child and Family Guidance Center.

Meisels, S. J., and E. Fenichel, eds. 1996. *New visions for the developmental assessment of infants and young children*. Washington, D.C.: Zero to Three: National Center for Infants, Toddlers, and Families.

Meyer, C. H. 1987. Content and process in social work practice: A new look at old issues. *Social Work* 32(5): 401–4.

Middleman, R. R., and G. G. Wood. 1990. *Skills for direct practice in social work*. New York: Columbia University Press.

Minuchin, S. 1974. *Families and family therapy*. Cambridge Harvard University Press.

Moses, K. 1987. The impact of childhood disability: The parent's struggle. *Ways* (Spring), pp. 7–10.

Naseef, R. A. 2001. *Special children challenged parents: The struggles and rewards of raising a child with a disability*. Baltimore: Brookes.

Powell, D. R. 1989. *Families and early childhood programs*. Research Monograph vol. 3. Washington, D.C.: National Association for the Education of Young Children.

Rutter, M. 1985. Resilience in the face of adversity: Protective factors and resistance to psychiatric disorder. *British Journal of Psychiatry* 147:598–611.

——— 1987. Psychosocial resilience and protective mechanisms. *American Journal of Orthopsychiatry* 57(3): 316–31.

Satir, V. 1967. *Conjoint family therapy*. Rev. ed. Palo Alto: Science and Behavior.

Shulman, L. 1992. *The skills of helping: Individuals, families and groups*. Itasca, Ill.: Peacock.

Silverman:R. 1980. *Mutual help groups: Organization and development*. Beverly Hills: Sage.

Smith, C. and B. E. Carlson. 1997. *Social Service Review* (June), pp. 231–56. Chicago: University of Chicago.

Spiegle-Mariska, J. and S. Harper-Whalen. 1991. *Forging partnerships with families.* Missoula: Montana University, Division of Educational Research and Services.

Stevens, J. H., Jr. 1978. Parent education programs: What determines effectiveness? *Young Children* 33(4): 59–65.

Vigilante, F. W. 1983. Working with families of learning disabled children. *Child Welfare* 62:429–36.

Walsh, F. 1998. *Strengthening family resilience.* New York: Guilford.

Weinstein, J., J. S. Bloch, J. M. Lichter, and M. Seitz. 2002. *Recurring themes in work with families.* Syosset, N.Y.: Variety Child Learning Center.

Chapter 16

Finding Our Way Back
Parenting Skills Group for Addictive Parents

Beatrice R. Plasse

PARENTAL substance abuse has far-reaching consequences in the lives of the children and the extended family of the addicted parent. Parental addiction is the single most frequently cited cause for out-of-home placement of children (Child Welfare League of America 1992). Despite stipulations by the Agency for Children's Services and family court that drug rehabilitation include parent education, many substance abuse agencies do not have groups for parents. The self-help group movement recognized early on the importance of mutual aid systems for alcoholics and drug addicts. During the crack epidemic of the 1980s, for example, there was a growing awareness that the issues of child-rearing practices and drug addiction overlapped, and more parents were offered parent education groups on the premises of substance abuse agencies.

Today the groups offered in most drug treatment agencies focus on HIV prevention, drug abstinence, and the biopsychosocial effects of addiction. The policy of substance abuse treatment agencies for dealing with parents is to refer them to community or family service agencies. The trend in substance abuse treatment is to shorten length of treatment and reduce services. Parents may be reluctant to go to a family or child welfare agency, fearing that it is connected to the foster care system that removed their children. Parents need a safe haven for treatment.

Gender differences affect perceptions about the prevalence of maternal and paternal substance abuse. Although some research has shown that male partners are more often involved in abuse of children, with or without the knowledge of the mother, the stigma of being a drug addict falls most heavily upon women (Frieze and Schafer 1984). The literature on parental addiction therefore focuses more on mothers than on fathers. One reason for this is that women are legally responsible for their children and identify with their roles as parents more openly than do men. Among one group of men in a residential treatment center where the author worked, when asked if they were fathers the men replied no.

Later, when the question was posed as "do you have children?" the same men answered yes, but because they were not involved in the lives of their children they did not think of themselves as fathers.

To focus primarily on eliminating the parent's addiction does not necessarily result in improved parenting behaviors and attitudes. The literature on parenting and child welfare consistently recommends that various services for addicted parents be integrated with services to children (Tracy 1994; Yaffe, Jenson, and Howard 1995; Goldberg 1995; Carten 1996; Finkelstein 1993). Some studies on women in treatment show that one of the chief reasons women enter treatment is because their children have urged them to do so. Ironically, one of the reasons that women do not complete treatment is the conflict in fulfilling their responsibilities to their dependent children while getting treatment for themselves.

Perspectives on the nature of addiction reflect two basic paradigms: addiction as disease and addiction as social deviance. Under the disease perspective, rehabilitation and treatment are emphasized. The disease and treatment perspective can include a range of approaches from zero tolerance and total abstinence to the harm reduction approach in which clients set their own goals for reducing use or tapering off to abstinence.

The response to addiction as social deviance, rather than as disease, has a profoundly different impact. Under the Rockefeller laws of the 1980s and early 1990s, a woman charged with possession or drug sales could face incarceration and removal of her children from the home. In 1988, when the introduction of crack cocaine into urban neighborhoods was at its height, 167 women in 24 states were prosecuted for drug use while pregnant and thousands more had their children removed from their custody. Many women with young children spent time in prison (Beckett 1995).

Today, most often the penalty for drug use among first time and nonviolent users or sellers is mandated treatment rather than prison terms. The current response to parental addiction almost always involves the parent's enrollment in a parent training program as well as treatment for substance abuse.

When an adult with dependent children enters treatment for addiction, it is a critical turning point for the entire family. Someone in the family may expose the parent's addiction as a result of a complaint to a state child abuse registry. Often grandparents or relatives will have taken over the care of children prior to the parent entering substance abuse treatment. Although some families rally around the addicted parent, many other families are bitterly disappointed and distance themselves from the person. Addiction is a condition that is chronic and marked by relapses. Each episode of relapse depletes the family's hope. Young children suffer the loss of the parent as they would the death of that parent. Latency age and teenage children will overhear the denunciation of their parents by others in the family and the community. Children of drug addicted parents are at high risk for mental illness and future drug addiction.

Groups for addicted parents have no standard curricula. Most groups cover such topics as child development, nonviolent discipline, communication skills, and building self-esteem in children. Some groups for parents are more like classes and are primarily educational, while other groups are less structured and function like support groups and therapy groups.

In a study by La Salvia (1993) on parenting groups among parents with severe ego deficits, the format of a psychoeducational group was found to be beneficial. In an analysis of group characteristics that measured more structured versus less structured therapy groups, research has supported better outcomes in programs that had a high degree of structure for nonpsychotic patients. More highly structured groups were found to have produced greater cooperation and harmony between group members.

The parenting skills group described in this chapter was structured as a psychoeducational group. A psychoeducational group combines two methods of helping, the cognitive and the emotional. One definition states that a psychoeducational group is a group whose members are facing a life crisis that requires them to acquire knowledge and skills that will promote growth and personal transformation (Brown 1998). For addicted parents the life crisis may occur when the addict "hits bottom" and seeks treatment voluntarily. More commonly, the crisis occurs when there is legal action taken that results in public exposure of the parent's addiction. Entering a parenting skills group offers the possibility of growth and transformation when the parent leaves behind a lifestyle of drug abuse and returns to the family as a mother or father. A psychoeducational group devotes time and energy to teaching concepts and practicing skills, but the real learning occurs on a deeper level where ideas are synthesized and made personal through the evolution of the mutual aid system in the group.

Garvin (1997) has written about the power of social work groups to take advantage of the environmental opportunities for growth and change. A window of opportunity opens when parents are ordered to seek treatment in parent education programs. Neglectful parents with problems of substance abuse most often come from family systems with no role models to learn from or emulate. Despite the continuing high rates of adolescent pregnancy, classes on parenting and child development in public high schools are a rarity. Only after the maltreatment of children comes to the attention of child welfare may parents be offered instruction in healthy parenting.

The mandated client may present a facade of conformity to appease authorities who represent subtle and sometimes not so subtle forms of racism, sexism, and class discrimination. It is not unusual for parents who have been charged with child abuse or neglect to be treated with contempt by court workers, child welfare workers, and others in social services. Moving beyond superficial compliance to finding one's personal stake is an ongoing challenge that group leaders face in work with addicted parents.

Court-mandated as well as voluntary clients attend a pregroup interview for the PIR (Parenting in Recovery) groups. Parents who are psychotic or seriously cognitively impaired are screened out. All other parents who express an interest can attend the groups. A substantial percentage of the parents who graduated from the PIR groups were actively parenting their children before and during treatment. Most children in foster care returned to their parents some time after the parent completed drug abuse treatment. Nevertheless, not all the parents in the PIR groups were able to succeed in being reunited with their children. Some parents would lose their parental rights through family court proceedings; others had tangential relationships with their children because of psychiatric disorders, chronic illnesses, and HIV.

Developmental Issues and Tasks

Each stage of human development in the life cycle builds upon the stage that preceded it. Whether through disruptions caused by trauma or chronic family dysfunction, the addicted parent enters adulthood with many unmet needs. Addiction can be viewed as a symptom of these larger problems. Lack of positive parenting during childhood and a sense of inferiority, deprivation, and failure characterize the self-image of addicted parents.

In the Ericksonian model of human development, the establishment of trust versus mistrust is a hallmark of development in the first year of life. Mistrust, alienation, and a feeling of being the outsider reflect disturbances in the first year of life. Parents in prescreening interviews reported that they had spent part or all of their childhoods in the care of relatives, grandparents, or in foster homes. Poor infant care occurs among teenage parents, and many of the parents in the PIR groups were the children of teenage parents. Separations, losses, and traumatic events in early childhood punctuated the life histories given by many group members.

The PIR curriculum uses Erikson's model in the session on infancy. During a group discussion about the establishment of basic trust, a mother who had been a heroin user for many years compared the satisfaction of needs that an infant experiences for basic trust to the state induced under the influence of heroin. She added, "I couldn't trust people to make me feel good, but I could always depend on my fix." Psychoanalytic theory posits that the earliest formation of ego boundaries develops through maternal regulation of the infant's states of pain and pleasure (Kernberg 1984). In effect, the narcotics addict, at the cost of losing conscious sense of self, is regulating states of pain and pleasure.

The stage of childhood known as latency is a time when the child needs to experience a sense of industry, mastery, and achievement. Latency is a stage when children want to be stimulated by new ideas and challenges in sports or academics. The school setting should provide these opportunities. Listening to the accounts of addicted parents, one hears of school failure and academic problems. The inner-city schools that group members attended reflect the lack of resources and the social problems of the communities where they are located. The poor writing and reading skills of the parents in the parenting skills groups described here may also be rooted in learning disabilities that went unrecognized and untreated.

Often it is during adolescence that drug and alcohol abuse become problematic. Erickson's model of adolescence is one in which youth face the crisis of carving out an identity that is distinct from the family. Although the importance of the family recedes and the peer group and culture come to the foreground, if the fabric of family has fallen apart, the task of identity formation is made more difficult for the teenage child.

In the adult stage of development Erickson sets forth three central endeavors and concerns: establishment of an intimate relationship, engagement in the world of work, and the drive for generativity. Generativity is the ego-expansive, creative drive to guide and mentor the next generation. The wellsprings that nourish generativity are a belief in one's progeny and the furtherance of the species as a whole. Drug addiction tends to freeze the forward movement in all these arenas of adult functioning. Generativity is the most obviously impaired drive for some addicted parents. Though substance abusers yearn for intimacy, the lifestyle of addiction is based on exploitation, lies, and secrecy. Among women who abuse substances, intimate relationships become entangled in the exchange of drugs for sex, power, or money (Zelvin 1999).

The inwardness and self-absorption of the addict may be a component of a narcissistic personality disorder. However, the physiological aspects of addiction can mask an individual's innate strengths and personality. When addicted parents stop using drugs, many of them demonstrate a strong will to be protective and instructive to their children, particularly around issues of prevention of addiction and criminality.

A reoccurring theme for men in a father's group concerned failure in the world of work. Many of the men had spent time in jail and found it hard to get jobs afterward. They spoke of being excluded by the mothers of their children because they had little money. Without careers or money they felt they had no role to play in their childrens' lives.

Adult developmental theory has been expanded and enriched by feminist theory. Feminist theory proposes that women possess a capacity for relationship, connection, and compassion that parallels the drive for individuation and autonomy during childhood and adolescence (Gilligan1982). This capability can continue to unfold throughout the years and decades of adulthood. Although feminist studies focus mainly on women, work with fathers in parenting skills groups have shown their capacity for connection, attachment, and understanding, if only as a cry from the margins for inclusion in the family. In a follow-up interview a father who had been homeless until coming into treatment said, "I learned from men in the group who were fathers, even if they slept on the subways like some of us. They knew their children. They were lucky. Some of us didn't have anyone at the end of the line. They encouraged me not to give up."

Men in a father's group developed a culture for mutual aid that continued even after the group ended. "I have kept in touch with the men in the group. We took our kids to Ringling Brothers and we are going to Great Adventure. When the children are there everything else changes, we have to share how to be fathers for each other."

Vulnerabilities and Risk Factors and Resiliencies and Protective Factors

Poverty and deteriorated socioeconomic conditions in urban neighborhoods have been identified as predisposing risk factors for child maltreatment, parental stress, and substance abuse (Fraser 1997). Group members of PIR live in poor neighborhoods where the marketplace for drugs thrives and legitimate jobs, especially for the unskilled, are scarce. For both men and women the lack of opportunities in the work sector is matched only by the plentiful opportunities to supplement welfare or low wage earnings with the sale of drugs. Many of the women who participated in the groups became mothers in their teens, did not return to high school, and had no employment histories or vocational skills. The parent who sees so few options for escape from a life of poverty is vulnerable to becoming addicted to the drugs that they may sell to others. Cheap and readily available drugs such as crack cocaine and heroin offer a way to self-medicate against depression and hopelessness.

Intergenerational drug use is another risk factor affecting parents in the PIR groups. A child growing up in a household where alcohol and drug use is part of everyday life will be more likely to adopt a lifestyle of heavy substance use. Group members frequently report that their addictive behaviors began at very young ages. In the methadone maintenance clinic, where a group was conducted, several parents told of being injected with heroin by parents or older relatives when they were in elementary school. More commonly, addiction begins in adolescence. One father told a group that for his sixteenth birthday his father presented him with a package of cocaine. In these ways the legacy of substance abuse is passed from generation to generation.

A major risk factor for substance abuse is trauma. The link between addiction and posttraumatic stress is well documented (Brown, Recupero, and Stout 1995). In a national epidemiological sample of women who received treatment for a substance abuse disorder, more than 80 percent had histories of sexual assault, physical assault, or death of a family member that resulted from a homicide. These have been identified as predisposing factors for individuals who later become addicted (Goldberg 1995). In preliminary interviews a number of group members reported that within the past six months they had had a violent incident with a spouse or had gone through a divorce or separation.

Other factors that place individuals at risk for substance abuse and child maltreatment are poor social skills and deficits of a physiological and cognitive nature. Contwell identifies some characteristics of parents who neglect their children to be low frustration tolerance, lack of judgment, and lack of motivation (Wallace 2002).

The question arises as to why some individuals living in similar situations in the same community are able to avoid addiction. Although resiliency can come from genetics, temperament, and constitutional endowments, other protective factors come from the environment. For the person with an addiction disorder, going back to the "old neighborhood" is not unlike walking through a minefield. But even in neighborhoods saturated with drugs there are protective factors. The graduates of substance abuse programs and survivors of the crack epidemic have become a generation of leaders and mentors in their communities. Alongside the subculture of drug and alcohol abuse, there are growing networks for recovery, prevention, and postrecovery resources. Some substance abuse agencies, including one where the parenting skills groups were conducted, have built low-cost apartment complexes that include childcare and other family-oriented services for the graduates of their programs. It is not unusual to find recreational rooms and playgrounds in many public housing projects that are staffed by residents who have survived addiction and whose agendas are to provide children with alternatives to drugs as recreation.

Religious institutions have increasingly become involved with the social problems of their congregations, viewing drug addiction as a spiritual dilemma. In otherwise deteriorated and economically depressed neighborhoods, churches and mosques have become vibrant centers for families with a background in substance abuse.

On the agency level settlement houses and family service agencies offer family recreational programs whose underlying mission is drug prevention. The most well-known and easy to find recovery resources are twelve-step programs such as Narcotics Anonymous, Alcoholics Anonymous, and Alanon. Some of these self-help groups have developed social programs with activities for children and alcohol-free dances and nightclubs for parents.

The person who returns from treatment to a relationship or a family with one or more supportive adults may overcome the odds of relapse. Parents with young children need affordable and accessible day care in their communities and respite from the demands of child caring from a member of the family. The parent who goes back to a job, to college, or to a job training program also will be less likely to relapse or return to the drug trade.

In one of the final sessions of the PIR groups, group members add their names and addresses to a list of community resources and become part of the network of supportive people they can contact once they leave the group and the treatment agency.

Agency and Group Context

The psychoeducational group known as PIR was conducted in two substance abuse agencies located in the southeast Bronx; the poorest congressional district in the New York metropolitan area. This community tops the list of virtually every social indicator of dysfunction in New York City. It is a community that has seen the deterioration of the institutions that support economic, cultural, and social networks that sustain families. The causes of the devastation of the community are twofold: the epidemic of crack cocaine in the late 1980s and the effects of economic decline on an already marginalized local economy. The most intractable problems are high rates of HIV infection, loss of jobs, and lack of housing.

The agencies where the PIR groups were conducted are large, multiservice community-based substance abuse agencies. They have women's and men's residences, day treatment programs with vocational and GED programs, methadone programs, and HIV clinics. One agency has a nursing home for AIDS clients and is currently constructing a residence for HIV-affected mothers and children. The agencies also have constructed low-cost residential apartments in the surrounding neighborhoods where the substance abuse facilities are located.

The agencies' missions are to provide accessible and comprehensive services. Women with children are a large segment of their client population. The agencies recognize that it is often difficult for women with children to travel to areas outside their neighborhoods in order to attend parenting groups. The need is especially pressing for parents mandated to attend some form of parenting education as part of their treatment for substance abuse.

Work and Group Themes

The author developed PIR as a fifteen-week curriculum that has been used in a variety of mental health clinics and substance abuse agencies over a period of fifteen years. Some of the sessional topics include infant, child and adolescent development, establishment of basic family life routines, attachment needs of children, understanding children's misbehaviors, positive discipline, prevention of sexual abuse, and anger management. The format of each session involves group members reading and discussing assigned weekly journal entries, a brief talk by the group leader on a topic, and an activity such as role-playing, brainstorming, creative writing, and practice of communication skills. The purpose of the early sessions is to enter into a contract for a working alliance with group members based on mutuality of goals. In reality, the work of contracting and keeping to the work goals goes on throughout the life of the group.

To have a working alliance it is necessary to clarify the responsibilities of group members and the group leader (Northern and Kurland 2001). The requirements for attendance, journal writing, and the importance of participation are discussed. Rules and guidelines about sharing time to speak and the limits of confidentiality are reviewed as well.

Group members use journals to do written assignments, and although group members are encouraged to read, no one is required to read unless they are comfortable doing so. One of the first tasks that each member of the group does together is to make a list of their goals, which is written in their journals. Parents' goals have been "to learn how to be more patient," "to show them that I love them," and "to help my children understand why I am in recovery." The first session of the group culminates in the signing of a written contract that sets forth the worker and group members' tasks and expectations.

The worker's responsibilities include preparation of material for each session and returning homework to parents with written comments from the group leader each week. The worker also offers to provide support for group members who might be struggling with the journal work. Whenever a group member does not do the assignment, the group leader needs to explore what this means to the group member and find ways to adapt the homework so that it is relevant to the parent. The group leader may give parents who are visiting children from whom they are separated a report form to fill out. This report asks the parents to describe how the visit went, what they discussed or did with their children, the skills they used, and the nurturing actions taken.

Some group members became self-conscious about writing because of the deficits in their education. There have been several solutions for handling the issue of writing. One solution has been to use a buddy system in which a group member agrees to help another group member or, in the lingo of recovery, "each one, teach one." Another solution is for a parent to bring the assignment to their case manager or counselor. Almost invariably the assignment can reinforce one or another of the treatment goals that the group member is working on in individual counseling. Several parents decided to take assignments to their teenage children for help with spelling and grammar. For these parents turning to their children for help with the homework opened up communication into previously taboo subjects. As one woman told the group, "My daughter used to throw my addiction in my face just like her father and the rest of the family did when I was using. When I showed her my journal I felt like I was finally bringing this up on my own time. She could read about what my recovery means to me as a person and as a mother."

WHETHER TO TRUST

All too often, after extensive planning groups fail to materialize or to continue beyond the first few sessions. Premature termination of treatment and serial relapsing have become accepted as the norm and most substance abuse agencies have come to expect high rates of dropping out. In some ways the high rate of client termination reflects a failure of trust. Early life experience has taught the addict that it is not safe to trust others. Trust is established at the beginning of the group and will need to be strengthened throughout. At the contracting stage the group leader begins to set a climate that in some ways models the qualities of a positive and committed parent. The group leader must be supportive and compassionate but also able to demand work and keep the focus on moving toward the group goals. In the first session much information on the format, structure, and rules is shared. Even with these guidelines, group members may have reservations and ambivalence about the competency of the group leader, the potentiality for being blamed, and the use of authority to compel participation. In this session the issue of trust was raised, as the group was about to sign the formal written contract.

There seemed to be agreement that the curriculum topics were interesting. The group was enjoying putting together their journals with their name labels. Group members had made a list of their goals and I had given them the assignment to choose one goal and write about that one in their journals for the next session. Everyone seemed to understand the assignment and see how the homework would reinforce her goals. It was near the end of the session and I thought the group was ready so I distributed the written contract and read over the work agreement for myself and for group members. Then Gloria, who had not said much up to that point, said she couldn't sign the contract until I answered two questions. Had I been through recovery myself, and did I have any children? The sharp edge in her tone of voice sounded like a challenge, and I felt myself tense up. A brief silence followed as I collected my thoughts. But, before I could speak, another woman in the group said that if I was uncomfortable I didn't have to answer the questions. (I could see that the question had made her, as well as others in the group, uneasy.) I said that I found it interesting that Gloria's questions were put to me just as the contracts were to be signed. "Here I am asking you to make a commitment of time and effort, to sign a contract with me that puts you in this group for fifteen weeks, tells you to write about some pretty difficult topics. Maybe you're wondering if I can keep up my end of the work." I said that although I have not gone through a recovery program myself I have been a part of a generation that used and abused drugs and I had lost friends and seen lives destroyed by drugs. Then I said I am the parent of two teenagers and as a parent I worry about how they'll handle themselves with drugs and alcohol.

Still I wondered if the question that had been asked had also to do with a general concern of the rest of the group about my ability to understand what they are going through. One way for me to understand them was for them to take a risk on trusting me. My training and experience was in leading parenting groups and, with some rules about how to cooperate together, I would try to make it safe for them to trust each other and me.

The structure of journal reading has been a valuable method for helping groups develops mutual aid to overcome mistrust. In this group of mothers there was an initial atmosphere of suspicion and mistrust that came in large part from the disparity in the women's varied life situations. The group was comprised of mothers who were in outpatient programs and living with some support from a family member. They brought their babies in strollers and sat next to each other. There was also a subgroup of four women who were older and lived either in the general residential treatment center or in the primary care residence for HIV-infected mothers. The older women looked careworn, and it was clear they had health problems. They did not have their babies with them. I knew that one of the women, Myrna, had a baby who had been born with low birth weight and was in an intensive care unit at a hospital. There was another woman in her forties. Dolly had just given birth to her fifteenth child, who was in the custody of her mother and Administration for Children's Services. The younger women were visibly shocked. Dolly could have been seen as the deviant member, but, as will be seen the excerpt, she was able to help another group member by offering her sad experience in a cautionary message of caring.

There were times in this group when distractions and activity by the new mothers seemed to keep them from looking at the unresolved discord in their family lives.

I asked the women to share what they remembered of their hopes and fantasies about having a baby when they were pregnant. I said that I hoped that during this session we would make a list and I asked them to brainstorm some ideas about why women who have used drugs might become pregnant. Several young women spoke about the wish to be a mother and have a baby that was all their own. Some of them said that being pregnant was exciting and they anticipated the joy of being mothers. Myrna, who is HIV positive and looked thin and drawn, said in a very low voice that she didn't have any hopes or dreams because she didn't know she was pregnant with either of her two children. She just went into labor and was shocked when she gave birth; both babies were premature but survived. Her baby was still in the hospital and wouldn't be released until the baby was five pounds. I asked if others in the group had actually planned to become pregnant. There was so much activity around the babies that I wasn't sure I was being heard. In a slightly louder voiced I said that perhaps some of them also hadn't known about birth control or realized they were pregnant. The noise continued as some of the younger mothers played peekaboo with one of the babies and passed around some rattles and toys. "I don't think that Myrna is the only one here who wasn't prepared to have her baby." There was a momentary silence followed by more playful handling of the babies. I passed out a list that I had made of reasons for becoming pregnant, which I said I hoped they would read and choose to write on for the next session. Myrna looked at me and said that she wasn't sure she could make the group next week; she had to spend time in the hospital with her baby.

The next session began with reading from the journal homework. I asked who would like to begin. Sally, one of the younger women who had her baby with her, said she would begin. She had chosen to write about how she had gotten pregnant hoping that her boyfriend would stop using heroin and would marry her. They used to do heroin together and during her pregnancy she stopped the intravenous use. "Thank God my baby was born without going through withdrawals." Her boyfriend had been able to help her stay off drugs during her pregnancy, but now he was shooting heroin again. "So my dream of being with him is probably never going to come true." Sally began to cry. Dolly spoke up, telling the group that she understood how Sally must feel. "I've had fifteen babies, and I always think this time it's going to be different. I'm going to keep this man. But, take it from me, you are better off staying away from that man and his needle." Then Myrna turned to Sally and told her that she was lucky that her baby wasn't born with drugs in his body. "You did the right thing by your baby." Myrna said her baby had suffered so much that she would never forgive herself, she cradled her head in her arms on the table and began to cry. Some of the women reached out and stroked her back.

The mutual aid system in a psychoeducational group develops through the focus on group participation in learning new concepts and personal sharing. The tendency in the new mothers group was to avoid facing the stress that accompanied the transition from pregnancy to birth. The joy of having a newborn became the focus, and the group resisted talking about their pain and disappointment. The group leader's demand for work helped Sally talk about her disappointment with the father of her child and made it possible for Myrna to express her anguish and receive comfort. The group's mutual aid can provide the climate in which women come to discover the fantasies and unrealistic motivations that lead them to repeated pregnancies in a destructive cycle that results in poor parenting and substance abuse relapse. These person-to-person exchanges of feelings become the teachable moments that are an essential part of a psychoeducational group.

The Desire to Heal

A continuing theme of the groups is the parent's anxieties over how to heal, comfort, and reassure their children. Parents have very similar values and goals— they want to respond to their children's needs for love and security. At the same time the theme of healing is common ground for the group there is also fear and reluctance about sharing painful emotions. Creative expression through poetry can sometimes be the least threatening and most direct route to uncovering the theme of healing. In one of the early sessions the group writes a poem by having each person finish the line beginning "The first time I held my child." The group leader encourages members to write freely not being overly concerned about rhyming, grammar, spelling, or sentence structure. The framework for the poem helps to bring the group together around one of life's peak experiences—the experience of childbirth. The poem can capture the parent's hopes and dreams and focus the group around the essential values and goals that were expressed earlier by the group. The following is an excerpt from a poem with a range of feelings that brought the group together:

> The first time I held my child
> I knew I was truly blessed.
> My love blossomed all over me.
> I was overjoyed at what I brought into this world.
>
> The first time I held my child
> I was afraid.
> Was I holding her too tight?
> Or not tight enough.
>
> The first time I held my child
> I said, oh God look what all my drugging
> has done to this precious life?
>
> The first time I held my child
> I promised her that I would always be there
> and make her life better than mine.

After the poem was read a young woman in the group said she felt sad and began to cry. She had only written about the happiness of being a mother, but she was crying because others in the group had expressed the feelings that she was afraid to look at in herself. Her baby had been born with drugs in his body. She was grateful to the people in the group who had the courage to put into words some of the pain she had felt. The poem unlocked the group's creative energies and its potential to become a mutual aid system for expression of unspoken but shared emotions.

Dealing with the Addicted Parent's Childhood

The theme of the parents' deprivation and family dysfunction came up frequently, as it did in this session. The session was devoted to practicing communication skills to help parents develop self-esteem in their children. In this excerpt some parents expressed their bitterness in the disparity between the ideal of a positive, nurturing parent that is being taught and the lived experiences that parents had as children.

> JANET: What I want to know is how can you ask me to give them all this praise and encouragement when that is something that I never got myself. It makes me so mad to always hear about these mothers who just drool all over every little drawing their kids do. As far back as I can remember, before my brothers and sisters and I got placed in foster homes, I was taking care of my mother; she wasn't taking care of me. When my father hit her, I'd go to her and ask her if she was OK and I'd try to help her. I remember waiting for her to hug me or tell me she loved me. My mother died last year and I'm still waiting for those hugs and kisses. But it's too late to get them now.
>
> LEADER: You were a loving child and a worthwhile person and deserved to be told. I wonder if others here can identify with what Janet went through? (*Several women nod their heads.*)
>
> GENA: I understand where she's coming from. When I was a teen my mother's drinking got bad, especially after my father left. So my brothers and I would carry her to bed and tuck her in night after night. She was supposed to tuck me into bed and tell me how proud of me she should have been when I was still doing well in school. But we did all that because we loved her, even though we hated her drinking. Janet, you loved your mother too, and if you could do that for her you can give that love to your children.
>
> GROUP LEADER: It makes me very sad but also very much in awe of how you both were able to take care of your mothers when you deserved to be protected and cared for yourselves. You comforted them when they were hurting. I also hear you saying that you don't want your children to show their love for you because you are sick and suffering. I think you want to have them love and respect you because you have overcome hardships and are stronger and healthier.

In this session one group member's feelings of bitterness and anger were supported and understood by another group member. This exchange of mutual support is part of what the group leader will build upon to create a mutual aid system for the whole group as the issues of childhood trauma are shared. Here the group leader transfers the mutual aid from the individual member as client to the group as client. This is an example of how the group leader addresses the issue of survivorship over childhood struggles as a group issue through moving the mutual aid from the individual to the group as a whole.

Conflicts with Foster Care and Concern Over Separation

The following vignette is from a session of a group where attachment theory and separation were discussed. The group discusses the themes around the parent's anxiety over how to talk to children about the separation.

> At the start of the session I presented the classic study done by Bowlby and Anna Freud concerning the separation reactions of institutionalized infants and young children during World War II after the bombing of London. The study was the first to define failure-to-thrive syndrome. I prefaced the discussion with the information that volunteers and nurses on rotating shifts staffed the hospital and were equipped with first-rate medicine and up-to-date amenities for the children. As I described the symptoms of failure to thrive that the children displayed I asked the group what they thought was missing for these children. The women quickly responded, raising their hands and calling out. Someone said that the key missing ingredient was love, another person said consistency of care from the same person, not from different people all the time. I let them know that they were right on all accounts. Then I told the group that this study heralded a sweeping policy change in childcare for infants and young children in America and England. Instead of congregate care of young children in hospital wards or asylums, children who couldn't be with their parents would be placed in foster homes with a consistent nurturing figure.

Many of the parents in the groups have children who were placed in foster homes when the parent came into treatment. The purpose of the session is to offer parents a framework for understanding foster care in the light of attachment theory. This understanding can reduce some of the conflicts that parents have with foster parents or family members who may be caring for their children while they are in treatment.

In a group held at the methadone maintenance program the conflict between the addicted mother and the foster mother is illustrated.

> Darlene, a teenage mother, spoke up. She said that she felt the foster mother looked at her with contempt. Since he was placed away from Darlene, her four year old was throwing temper tantrums and was difficult to control. Maybe part of the problem was that he was becoming confused about who his real mother was. Darlene angrily added that the foster mother was probably only in it for the money. What would stop her from abusing her child? Darlene had heard lots of stories about children being abused in foster care. The group leader told Darlene that she could see how badly she felt for her child and that she seemed to be in a helpless position. The group leader threw the question out to the group, asking to hear what they could do or what they have done for their children in foster care. One mother said she calls the agency and they connect her to the foster

mother and she asks about what goes on there. Darlene replied that she is not allowed to call the foster mother but has to go through a caseworker. To this a woman said that Darlene could insist on a conference with the agency. Another woman said she calls the agency "every day if I need to" to let them know the special needs, the likes and dislikes of her child. "Don't t worry about making a nuisance of yourself." As the discussion wound down, the group leader noted that there were many ways mothers could make sure their children were safe and cared for. They did not have to accept a bad situation, but they would have to stay on top of things and try not to become discouraged. The group leader said she wanted to go back to the concern Darlene had about losing closeness with her child. This brought the group back to the discussion about the importance of keeping visits and of the child's need for secure attachment. Even Darlene agreed that if she could not be with her child he was better off with the foster mother than in an institution.

In this session, the group leader acknowledged the anxiety in the parent and distress of the child. The group leader then made a demand for work by asking the group what they could do to ensure that their children were safe in foster care. The problem-solving process of the group led to suggestions that offered information and plans for action. Women were able to give each other knowledge from lived experiences. The mutual aid of the group empowered the women to be proactive in a system that could make them feel completely helpless. One of the dynamics of the mutual aid that occurs in groups is the sharing of data and the swapping of strategies. More experienced group members can teach the less experienced group member how to get the system to respond to their needs. The mutual aid process is reciprocal, enhancing the esteem and efficacy of those who are able to share their knowledge and helping those who need to learn the skills and strategies. Finally this example shows how the group leader reached for feelings that had been voiced in the session—the sadness over the loss of closeness between parent and child.

The pain of separation from children is a major theme for parents. Group discussion, practice of nurturing behaviors and positive communication skills, and creative writing are some methods used to help parents work through the extremely painful events in the separation crisis. Dramatic enactment or role plays are a powerful tool that gives parents the chance to rehearse pivotal moments of contact with their children. The scenario, which parents with children in foster care go through, is at the moment when the parent must say good-bye to the child at the end of a visit at a foster care agency. The following vignette comes from a videotape of a group with men and women at a day treatment outpatient program.

In this role play Linda played the part of the parent and Ruth played her child.

LINDA: Honey, I've got to go now but I want you to behave with the foster mother and be a good girl. Now give me a hug and kiss.

RUTH: Mommy, please don't go. I miss you so much. I don't want to stay here. Why do you have to leave me here? Is it because I did something wrong?

LINDA: No, you didn't do anything wrong, it was me. I did something and it wasn't good.

RUTH: But why do I feel like it's me that's bad? If you bring me home I'll behave, I promise, I won't t do anything to make you mad. Don't make me stay here.

LINDA: (*Wiping away tears*) no, you didn't do anything bad. If I got angry, it wasn't because you were bad, it was because I was having problems. I need time to get myself together, but you are not here because you did anything wrong. It was me, and I need you to be here now while I'm getting help. I'm working on a plan so we can be together again and have all the good times we used to have—not the bad times. For now I want you to respect the foster mother. She is in charge while I'm not with you.

The role play ended and some group members got up and hugged Linda and Ruth. A woman in the group said how much she admired the women for volunteering to do the role play. Linda said, "This was so hard, but my child does say things just like that to me." The group discussed how much to share with children. They agreed with one person who said that younger children get overwhelmed by too much information while older children needed to be told more specific information. The group felt that Linda handled the child's need for comfort well by telling the child that she was getting help and making a plan for them to be together. I pointed out to Linda that she had done something very important; she had relieved her child of guilt and self-blame by telling her that their being apart was not her fault. Some of the mothers talked about how their children acted up with the people caring for them as if they had to bring on punishment by being bad.

The mutual aid function of the group is illustrated here as the group showed its appreciation to the women who volunteered to do this role play. The two group members doing the role play scene were able to risk themselves and face difficult emotions in the crisis of separation. In the mutual aid process some group members will be able to help others who are more vulnerable or who aren't ready to take the same risks. This role play provided the context that gave all the group members a chance to begin to discuss the problematic behaviors of their children. The discussion that followed concerned the maladaptive ways that children have adjusted to the separation. The climate of compassion and understanding engendered after the role play allowed the group to express greater empathy for child behaviors that could have been labeled simply as bad.

REASSERTING PARENTAL AUTHORITY

One of the themes for parents in the group is that of discipline, management of children, and reasserting parental authority. Parents who had been stripped of their authority or had custody of children transferred to family members struggled to regain not only the respect of their families but also the right to make day-to-day decisions for their children. The parent in treatment often feels too guilty to set limits, and when children get out of hand the parent may feel overwhelmed and inadequate. During recovery, parents tend to overcompensate for past neglectful parenting by overprotecting, overdisciplining and being too controlling over the lives of their children (Mejta and Levin 1996). The tensions inherent in the issue of the parent's authority are illustrated in the group's response to one young mother.

> Susan was the youngest member of the group. She became a parent at age fifteen and had another child by the time she was eighteen years old. Her mother and aunts baby-sat for her children while Susan tried to continue to complete high school. With each pregnancy she became more dependent on her mother. Her casual use of cocaine became more compulsive. During Susan's s addiction to cocaine she would disappear for days on end. When she was with the children she would try to assert her authority but they would ignore her and turned to Susan's mother as the person in authority. In the session we were reading from the journal assignment, which was about how the group members could put positive discipline strategies into practice and the consequences of verbal or physical abuse. Susan wrote that she could not get her kids to listen to her. Whereas she used to hit them and be verbally abusive she was trying not to do this now, but when she was in her mother's house she still felt like the bad child. She told the group that she thought about running away when the children misbehaved. Her mother seemed to be "poisoning" the rest of the family and sending the message to her children that she was a failure. Ann, an older woman with a teenage daughter in an agency group home, angrily said that Susan should be grateful to her mother. Carrie, whose children are also in a nonkinship foster home added with scorn that Susan was being selfish and had to earn the respect of her mother and her children. She had been pampered long enough and had to grow up. I asked the women why it was so hard for them to understand Susan's feelings about being left out of her children's lives and criticized by the family. Didn't they know what that felt like? Susan got up and gathered her things to leave the room. Carrie told Susan that she was sorry she'd gotten angry. Maybe it was because Carrie felt jealous that Susan had her mother in her life. Ann said that if Susan left the group today she would be doing the same thing that made her mother give up on her—just leaving her responsibilities behind. Slowly, Susan walked back and sat down.

In a later session of the group there is an activity in which the women compose a letter to their mothers. The group leader takes dictation from the group and offers clarification about content when needed. Several group members, including Susan, edited the letter and asked Susan to read it to the group at the next session.

Dear Mom,

I want to let you know my feelings about my recovery. I wish you were here to see me getting my life together. I know we've both had a lot of anger and pain and been through ups and downs during my addiction. There are things I never got to tell you when I was growing up because I was too scared or too young to know how important the things were that you told me. Things like when I got my period or my experiences with boys. I never told you that you are a loving grandmother to my children. I'm grateful to you for your love. Since we didn't have much of a talking relationship, I looked for attention and love through drugs, other people and families, and in ways that hurt me. But now I am picking myself up, learning to listen to others, being responsible to myself and to others. Today I have a better outlook and I know where I'm going. My goals are to make a home for the children that's comfortable, drug free, and loving.

I want to give you a second chance to do what you want to do for yourself because time is moving on and you deserve a life too. I want to keep on the right path so that I can give you the peace that you have been waiting for. I am no longer your lost daughter, one of the "walking dead." I am alive. I am not going to waste another day of my life. It's hard to change, but I want to enjoy and make something beautiful to give back to the world. I want to thank you for helping me find what is good and beautiful in me and allowing me to get my life back together.

In a group for mothers that was held at the methadone maintenance program another young mother wrote about the mutual aid process that helped her to overcome her sense of powerlessness with her daughter. She read this to the group.

I always turned to my parents for help, but you have told me that I am the mother and I need to be in control. Your feedback helped me talk this week to my daughter. She opened up to me. You don't know how good it makes me feel. Now I think I will be able to talk to her about the kind of problems I had when I started using, which began just about at my daughter's age.

Concerns About Health

HIV-infected parents and children: a growing proportion of parents coming into the groups are HIV infected and may also have children who are were born with the HIV virus. The difficulties of sustaining the group among this population cannot be underestimated. Disruptions due to medical appointments and ill health make keeping up with attendance in the group quite frustrating for the group leaders. The group leaders need to reach out to group members between sessions in order to work around these scheduling conflicts and to encourage attendance when parents become demoralized. The mutual aid system and empathy of group members who were also HIV positive allowed this mother to talk over her troubles.

> Carmen spoke about her eight-year-old son who was born with HIV. He is prone to getting colds and ear infections, but he doesn't think he is any different from other kids. Carmen said, "He is my last baby, the one that is paying for my addiction. I can't die until I take care of him." Elizabeth, another resident of the HIV nursing home said, "Just hang on, you have to give yourself time to get stronger." She said that Carmen was looking better every day. Carmen expressed her appreciation to Elizabeth for her encouragement but said that she couldn't find any peace since the weekend visit with her sister and her five children. Her sister, who takes care of Carmen s teenage girls, told her that they said they had had sex with some boys at school. As she spoke Carmen's agitation grew. "What can I do? I'm not even a part of their lives." When she was with them, they were "cold as ice." They don't say so, but Carmen felt them blaming her for their younger brother's illness. Carmen put her face in her hands and cried out, "What have I done to them? My daughters could end up like me." The group leader and Elizabeth held her for a moment. Elizabeth said that Carmen could turn all of that around. Like Carmen, Elizabeth's children were angry, but they were also looking for her to be strong. She probably has talked more openly about sex and AIDS, dating and love, than most other mothers of teens. Elizabeth looked closely at Carmen and said, "Carmen, you are still the mother and you are going to be alive for a long time, but you need to use every day to talk to your girls."

DISCIPLINE AND ABUSE

As many as 80 percent of parents who maltreat their children have past or current substance abuse problems. (Fraser 1997). The themes of managing anger and the link between drug use and punitive parenting receive much attention. There is a strong focus on learning nonviolent positive and nurturing ways to discipline children. The group leader's presentation on discipline and punishment draws upon the work of Selma Fraiberg (1959). Fraiberg turns to the root of the Latin word "Disciplere" to correct common misconceptions around the punitive nature of discipline and return it to its ancient and honorable function, that of teaching and learning. The concept of discipline eschews corporal punishment and has as its ultimate goal the achievement of self-discipline.

Taking responsibility for past mistakes is one of the ethics of substance abuse recovery that parallels the norms and culture in the PIR group. In the safe environment within the group, parents begin to take risks and tolerate the discomfort of self-scrutiny. In one group a mother shared her feelings as she recognized the consequences of hitting her child.

> Sasha told the group that during the most recent foster care agency visit her son flinched when she reached over to tie his shoes. She said that she used to flinch that way to avoid being hit by her father and as she got older she became fast enough to outfox him, eventually running away from home at the age of fifteen. "When I saw my son do that thing, well, it just shocked me, and suddenly I saw myself in him because that was exactly what I did when I was a kid. At that moment I realized that my son has learned that he has to be afraid of me."

As social workers we have a responsibility to advocate for the oppressed and vulnerable. Despite the disadvantages of the addicted parent, their children are even more vulnerable. The sessions on discipline can stir up strong feelings for group leaders. As a group leader I often struggle to contain my feelings of anger when parents try to justify what I consider harsh punishment. In one group I conducted a parent described how she made her daughter kneel on rice for ten minutes and ignored the child's tears and protests about being in pain. Several women in the group said that they thought she was being abusive. In a defensive manner the woman replied, "My grandmother did that to my mother and my mother did it to me and it didn't do me any harm." To this a group member mumbled "Yeah, and just look at how you turned out." This comment was ignored as if it were not heard. In reflecting on this interaction, I think that as the group leader I could have explored what this mother actually remembered about how she felt as a child receiving this punishment. She might have expressed some ambivalence if she wasn't feeling attacked by the group. My overlooking this opportunity reveals the anger I felt toward the group member.

Human Rights and Empowerment

The themes of power and powerlessness come up in the later stages of the program. Parents know that soon the group will end and problematic situations will persist. There are some in the group who are full of anger, guilt, and regret over lost possibilities and damage done to the children. Others struggle to pull away from the undertow of despair with an existential affirmation in the resurrection of their self-worth. The interactionist approach of Schwartz is a "stepping stone" to empowerment practice (Lee 1996) and drives the work in the final PIR sessions. Calling upon the mutual aid system that has grown up during the life of the group, the group leader assists in mediating an exchange of the group's energies and benefits to the larger system of the agency and the community outside the group (Shulman 1999).

In one of the final sessions the group draws up a document called the position paper. The paper is like the voice of the group and is meant to be heard by concerned others outside the group. The group leader works with the group to get them to define their beliefs and understandings of the critical issues that parents face in the present and as they move into the future. The group leader must stay true to the ideas, values, and beliefs of the group. The group leader then translates the spoken words of the group into a language borrowed from the traditions of governments and professional bodies to officially document and bear witness. After the group leader writes the first item in this form, group members join in using this language for each subsequent article in the paper.

One position paper was read at a graduation ceremony attended by the district councilwoman. Groups have made their position papers part of the graduation program notes and agency newsletters. Other groups have distributed the paper at meetings attended by clients, staff, and administrators. Here is an example of a position paper that was written by parents in one parenting skills group.

This we believe:

1. Mothers and fathers are the most important people in the world to their children.
2. Parents need to have quality affordable health care for their children.
3. Pregnant women, whether using drugs or not, need access to free prenatal care by nonjudgmental doctors, nurses, and hospital personnel.
4. Fathers are vitally important in the lives of their children.
5. Children deserve to live with parents who do not hit or in any way physically hurt them.
6. Children should be protected from violence between parents.
7. Parents should be protected from violent spouses.
8. Parents with drug problems need and should have prompt access to treatment.
9. Parents in treatment should have help to find child care so that they are able to use all forms of help available to them.
10. Women should not become pregnant until all children who are in kinship or foster care are returned and stabilized with them.
11. Parents, including teenagers, should have access to birth control and knowledge about birth control.
12. Parents with a history of substance abuse should limit the size of their families.
13. Children with special learning problems and other handicaps should be given equal opportunities for quality education in the public schools.

The origins of mutual aid groups are rooted in the self-help movement used in alcohol and substance abuse treatment. Personal sharing in the twelve-step model can be seductive for some group members who may disclose too early or who may adopt a shallow facade of openness. Addicted adults in parenting skills groups face the necessity of learning new concepts and making profound personal changes in their behavior and lifestyle. Often these needed changes are precipitated by crisis. The PIR groups used a psychoeducational model with a formal structure that evolved into viable and effective mutual aid systems. The structures of the psychoeducational model for the PIR groups incorporated educational content, journaling, creative writing, and a focus on sessional topics. The mutual aid functions of the groups promoted the type of learning that could lead to personal growth.

Parents in the PIR group were expected to learn new cognitive frameworks about emotionally charged issues. The educational and therapeutic mix in the PIR groups helped parents pace themselves and find their personal stake in self-disclosure. Cognitive concepts from the literature on nurturance, child development, and positive child-rearing practices were processed through personal reflection and then shared in the groups. Group members discovered they were not alone in having gone through traumatic early life experiences, poor parenting, abuse, and neglect. Despite differences in age, race, and drug history, the groups established a mutuality of goals in the contracting phase and the early stages. The rigor of the requirements, combined with the group leader's compassion and clarity of purpose, created the safety that allowed the group to cross the boundaries of denial and shame. The group leader reduced the isolation of some group members by pointing out the linkages of experience and feelings between members.

Creative writing and narrative methods were widely used in the PIR groups. In the first session the group created a poem about the universal experience of giving birth. The poem helped the group become aware of their power to express a wider range of emotions which most group members have felt at some time in their commonly shared experience of becoming parents. Letters written in the groups and the final position paper gave voice to the individual and collective aspirations of parents.

One of the most difficult tasks for the group leader is to focus the group on work issues rather than flights into denial. In a new mother's group the mutual aid dynamic was illustrated in the early life of the group as the women were able to overcome barriers caused by perceptions of difference between mothers based on age and HIV status.

Initially group members are reluctant to trust that the group will not replicate prior experiences where they have been blamed or harangued. The humanizing culture of the parent groups described here allowed group members to find a level of trust and mutual support. This then allowed parents to become more realistic about their capabilities and limitations. With the support of the group leader and of group members, parents confronted the painful impact of addiction on their children. Themes that came up concerned the effects of separations and losses, the struggle to regain the trust and confidence of their families, the resumption of parental authority and concerns about the health and safety of their children.

The PIR groups have included parents raising their children at home and parents separated from their children, parents living in poverty and parents with psychiatric disorders, parents with legal problems, and parents with HIV and AIDS. Most mothers and fathers who have graduated from the PIR groups have gone on to raise their children before, during, or after treatment. In a survey that included thirteen fathers, at some time during the three months of attending the PIR group, six had made contact with a child they had never seen or had a visit with their children after a period of more than five years. In fifteen years of consulting and training at substance abuse agencies it is not unusual for me to meet former group members who have graduated college and been hired as counselors or case workers.

Getting a group off the ground in a substance abuse agency requires stability, coordination, and long-range commitment. But large urban substance abuse agencies have to deal with contingencies and unpredictable events that can derail even the most carefully planned groups. In a psychoeducational group the group leader has many functions, in addition to the role of mediator, counselor, advocate, agency representative, and social worker there is also the role of teacher. Successful group leaders need to be highly organized during the planning and contracting stages of the groups. They must keep track of attendance and respond sensitively to journal work. They need to be committed to following up when clients miss a session and not become discouraged when group members relapse or disappear.

The rewards for group leaders more than make up for the difficulties and hard work. The group leader has the privilege of being present and witnessing parents, as they become a working mutual aid resource for each other in the group. Here is a journal entry that was written by a mother who was working on reuniting with her family after years of addiction.

> This time I am not running the streets, proving that everyone is right, that the kids are better off being raised by my mother because I am hopeless and worthless. I am not finished yet. I going to be somewhere in their lives because I do have something to give them.

References

Beckett, K. 1995. Fetal rights and "crack moms": Pregnant women in the War on Drugs, Contemporary. *Drug Problems* 22(13): 587–607.

Brown, N. 1998. *Psychoeducational groups*. Philadelphia: Taylor and Francis.

Brown, P., T. Recupero, and R. Stout. 1995. PTSD, substance abuse comorbidity, and treatment utilization. *Addictive Behaviors* 20:251–54

Carten, A. 1996. Mothers in recovery: Rebuilding families in the aftermath of addiction. *Social Work* 41(2): 214–23

Child Welfare League of America. 1992. *Children at the front: A different view of the war on alcohol and drugs*. Washington, D.C.: North American Commission of Chemical Dependency and Child Welfare.

Erickson, E. H. 1950. *Childhood and society*. New York: Norton

Fraiberg, S. 1959. *The magic years*. New York: Scribner's.

Fraser, M. 1997. *Risk and resilience in childhood*. Washington, D.C.: NASW.

Frieze, J. and P. Schafer. 1984. Alcohol use and marital violence: Female and male differences in reaction to alcohol. In S. Wilsmack and L. Beckman, eds., *Alcohol problems in women*, pp. 260–79. New York: Guilford.

Finkelstein, N. 1993. Treatment programming for alcohol and drug-dependent pregnant women. *International Journal of addictions* 29(2): 1275–1309.

Garvin, C. 1997. *Contemporary group work*. Boston: Allyn and Bacon.

Gilligan, C. 1982. *In a different voice*. Cambridge: Harvard University Press.

Goldberg, M. 1995. Substance-abusing women: False stereotypes and real needs. *Social Work* 40:(6): 789–96.

Kernberg, O. 1984. *Object relations theory and clinical psychoanalysis*. New York: Aronson.

La Salvia, T. 1993. Enhancing addiction treatment through psychoeducational groups. *Journal of Substance Abuse* 10:439–44.

Lee, J. 1996. The empowerment approach to social work practice. In F. J. Turner, ed., *Social work treatment*, pp. 218–49. 4th ed. New York: Free Press.

Mejta, C. and R. Levin. 1996. Facilitating healthy parenting among mothers with substance abuse or dependence problems: Some considerations. *Alcoholism Treatment Quarterly* 14(1): 33–45.

Northen, H. and R. Kurland. 2001. *Social work with groups*. 3d ed. New York: Columbia University Press.

Shulman, L. 1999. *The skills of helping individuals, families, groups, and communities*. 4th ed. Itasca, Ill.: Peacock.

Tracy, E. 1994. Maternal substance abuse: Protecting the child, preserving the family. *Social Work* 39(5): 534–40.

Yaffe, Jenson, and M. O. Howard. 1995. Women and substance abuse: Implications for treatment. *Alcoholism Treatment Quarterly* 13(2): 1–15.

Wallace, H. 2002. *Family violence legal, medical, and social perspectives*. Boston: Allyn and Bacon.

Zelvin, E. 1999. Applying relational theory to the treatment of women's addictions. *Affilia* 14(1): 9–23.

Chapter 17

Healing the Hurts
A Short-Term Group for Separated, Widowed, and Divorced Single Parents

Lawrence Shulman

T HIS CHAPTER focuses on the practice issues involved in working with sin-gle parents in groups. Families headed by one parent are no longer the ex-ception. In fact, single-parent families are increasingly the norm as a result. Our understanding of the average family as a working father, a mother at home, and two to three children has become a myth. Jackson points out that "substantial in-creases in rates of divorce and nonmarital births have led to fewer children liv-ing with two parents (Jackson 2001:769). She cites Castro and Bumpass (1989) who estimated that nearly one half of all children will live in a one-parent family before reaching age eighteen.

Gitterman (2001) points to a strong correlation between poverty and family structure. He observes: "Namely, children living in one-parent families are more likely to be poor than those living in two-parent families. Over the last three decades we have witnessed a dramatic change in family structure and living arrangements. Between 1970 and 1996, the number of divorced persons has grown from 4.3 million to 18.3 million (more than quadrupled)" (5).

The definition of a single-parent family used here is drawn from Jackson (2001:769). She classifies families by "(1) whether a child is living with two parents (either a biological parent and a stepparent) and (2) whether a child is living with only one biological parent without a co-residing step parent." She points out that not all scholars agree with this definition. She also indicates that single parents may be divorced, separated, never married, or widowed. The fam-ilies described in this chapter fit Jackson's second classification (one biological parent without a co-residing step parent). There are group members who are separated, divorced and widowed. I use as an example a group that I led in Canada in the late 1970s While the demographics were different at that time, many of the issue and themes continue to be relevant today.

Developmental Tasks and Issues

The parents and children in a single-parent family must face all the normative developmental tasks for their age and stage of life; however, in addition, they must also face the stresses generated by significant transitions in status. For example, one member of the group who is discussed later in this chapter was in his late twenties and had just become a parent. His ability to cope with the transition to the parent role was severely affected by his wife's decision to leave him and the new baby. Thus he had to deal with the change in status from nonparent to parent, a difficult enough transition, while simultaneously coping with the change in status from married partner to single parent.

The teenage children of another group participant were facing the normative developmental challenges associated with adolescence but now found themselves also having to cope with the inevitable stresses associated with the disruption of their family and the departure of their father. The impact of the change in status from being a child from what long has been considered to be a "normal" family to a child from a "broken" family exacerbated the already difficult transitional issues associated with adolescence. The increasing prevalence of single parenting in our society may mean the adolescent does not feel as much stigma. However, some of these feelings will still be present.

Other associated status changes included a sharply decreased family income after the split. Thus both the parent and the children were faced with changes in their economic status from "well-off" and secure to indigent and insecure. As will be illustrated later, the difficulties single women, particularly, may encounter when they try to establish their own credit and the prejudicial responses of the community may mean resources needed to cope with this change (such as credit) are unavailable.

Compounding all these issues faced by single-parent families is the reality that the single parent often has to handle these problems alone. For this reason a mutual aid group, in which parents can share their frustrations and challenges with others who are "in the same boat," can provide an important alternative source of support.

One area of unique concern for the single parent centers on the world of work. Many women and single-parent dads who try to work face serious discrimination in their efforts to obtain jobs. There is the myth that they are "unreliable," that is, they have too many distractions associated with parenting and child-care responsibilities. They often run into inflexible employers. For many of the women, when they do get jobs, they are often poorly paid and find themselves in dead-end jobs facing what has been called the "glass ceiling" preventing promotion. Between low-paying jobs and welfare, two thirds of single mothers try to live on income below the accepted poverty line, a factor that significantly adds to the stress of trying to raise a family alone. The welfare reform act of 1996 has also pressured single parents to find work. The savings in welfare were originally designated to provide increased child-care options. However state decisions on funding have fallen short of the original goals. Even when child care is available, it is often only available during the day. Single parents who work in jobs requiring evening hours have few child-care resources available to them. Whether on welfare or not, being a working-class single parent raises many concerns and issues.

Second, closely related problems relate to finances and housing. Many options are not available to single parents, with the result that they often must pay a higher percentage of their income to obtain any housing at all. If single parents with one income wish to obtain a mortgage for buying a house, they may be refused because of their status and a concern about their financial stability. One female member of the group discussed in this essay was denied a personal loan and was told that her credit rating was attached to her husband, who had recently died. When she inquired as to how she could get a good credit rating, she was told she needed to demonstrate a good credit history. This financial discrimination cuts across all forms of credit, with many single parents facing this catch-22 situation.

While low-income housing purchase programs and rent subsidies have helped somewhat in the area of housing, they are still limited and often restrictive. When low-income single parents do obtain loans they are often at higher interest rates. They can find themselves in a trap of having to pay a significant interest charge without reducing their principle. Easy credit in these situations can be as much of a hardship as no credit at all.

Third is the problem of dealing with friends. Many single parents report changes in attitudes toward them after separation or divorce as former close friends seem to take sides in the marital split. Another problem is sometimes referred to as the Noah's Ark Syndrome, where friends seem to operate under the general belief that people come "two by two." Old friends seem to slip away and new friends seem to be hard to find.

Fourth is the difficulty of trying to balance personal needs against all the responsibilities of raising a family. At the time when the single parent is most vulnerable and most needy, he or she must also deal with school meetings, dental appointments, homework, and all the rest. Finding time for oneself can be extremely difficult.

Fifth is the ongoing relationship with the noncustodial parent, whether or not he or she is still actively in the picture. In those instances in which single parenthood results from separation or divorce, a major problem becomes how to work out a new relationship that can overcome the bitterness and hard feelings associated with the split, so that the children don't feel torn between parents. Often, the ongoing legacy of anger from the marriage and from the way in which the split was handled by overzealous lawyers can remain to haunt all members of the family even when the ex-spouse is no longer around.

Finally, dealing with the children can take its toll. For example, finding child care assistance, either during the evening for a night out or during the day to facilitate working, can be extremely difficult. The makeshift arrangements that are often necessary in such situations can lead to heightened anxiety for the parent and an increased sense of guilt.

Vulnerabilities and Risk Factors and Resiliencies and Protective Factors

In addition to the concrete vulnerability and risk issues related to children, there are the problems of dealing with their emotional needs. These can cause even more difficulty for the single parent whose own emotions may be raw if there has been a separation or divorce. Although children's reactions to parents' divorce and separation differ according to age and according to the specific situation, it is not uncommon for children to go through phases of grieving similar to those associated with death and dying.

First, there is the shock, followed by depression and denial. This may be followed by anger and a lowered sense of self-esteem. Often, there is also a feeling of being responsible for the split in the marriage. These feelings are expressed in different ways, ranging from regression for toddlers to problems in school and with peer group for young teens. The children's anger at the parent thought to be at fault, their struggle with the loyalty problem when parents force them to take sides, their feelings of sadness, depression, anger, and guilt can cut them off from friends and others close to them just at the time they need them the most. Often, one of the most difficult challenges for the single parent is trying to help the child deal with these emotional strains at precisely the same time they are feeling most vulnerable themselves.

Both the parent and child may have a range of protective factors that help to keep them resilient in response to the risks they face. First and foremost is the bond between the single parent and his or her children. While the family has been disrupted by the loss or absence of the other parent, the strength of this bond, developed over a number of years, can provide support to both parent and child. Second is the network of family and friends that the single parent and the child can draw upon as they attempt to cope. Support can be tangible (i.e., babysitting, financial support) or emotional (i.e., a family member who is able to listen and empathize, a friend who makes a point of spending time with the parent or inviting him or her to social events). Third would be a supportive employer for a working single parent who provides flexibility and understanding when the demands of parenting conflict with the demands of work. Finally, the availability of financial support that allows the parent to obtain services such as day care, respite care, vacations, housing, etc. All these can serve to mitigate the risks associated with the status.

I have reviewed some of the major issues facing single parents and their children. I would now like to examine the practice implications for dealing with these concerns using examples as they emerged in a mutual aid group I led for single parents. The practice skills employed to help these parents will also be identified and illustrated.

Agency and Group Context

I was the group leader for a single parents group held in a small, rural, northern town in British Columbia, Canada. The service was offered as part of a university community psychiatry outreach program. The mission of this program included bringing psychiatric services to rural areas of the province that were lacking in resources. While individual services to single parents existed in this small community, local professionals felt that group work could also be helpful in unique ways. Since the local staff felt they lacked the skills required to initiate and conduct such a program, they had requested support from the university.

I was employed on a contract basis to lead a short-term group consisting of an evening followed by a full day. This was the first group of this kind in this community. The session also served to demonstrate the use of the group process and group leadership skills for attending professionals. Thus the group had both service and training purposes. The presence of other professionals was also a condition of my leading the group, since I felt it was important to have back-up resources available to group members after I left town. Thus, the group members would have made direct contacts with sources of support to deal with issues that might emerge in the discussion. While a short-term group can serve as an educational as well as a mutual support experience, it can also lead to the emergence of issues and feeling that require more intensive and continued counseling. As will be seen in the excerpts from the first meeting, this was an important safeguard, since one member did raise the issue of suicide. At my suggestion, one of the local professionals was able to initiate a follow-up contact following the group session.

Thus, in addition to demonstrating the processes in a single parents group, this chapter also illustrates how a social work professional who is not employed full time by an agency can be used to initiate short-term outreach and developmental services in areas that are poor in resources.

The group was advertised as a mutual aid discussion group for single parents, focusing on their unique concerns and what they might be able to do about those concerns. The group met for one evening (three hours) and the following day for seven hours. This can be considered a variation on a "single-session" group. Participants included eight single mothers, three single fathers, and three community professionals who worked with single parents. One of the things they all had in common was that their single-parent status was created by the actions of their partners. There was no screening of participants. Some were referred by counselors and others responded to posters and ads in the local paper. The order in which I will discuss the issues generally follows the order in which they emerged in the group; however, I have grouped some of the excerpts together for ease of explication.

Work and Group Themes

Beginnings

The session began with our contracting work. I hoped to set the stage by using the skills of clarifying purpose and clarifying my role. To help them understand the purpose, I had tuned in to possible themes of concern and included in my opening statement some handles for work by partializing the overall purpose into potential issues for discussion. This was followed by my reaching for feedback from the group members.

> I explained the purpose of the group as an opportunity for single parents to discuss with each other some of the special problems they faced because they were alone. I said that my role was not as an expert who had answers for them, but rather as someone who would try to help them talk to and listen to each other and to provide help to each other from their own experiences. In addition, I would throw in any ideas I had that might be helpful.
>
> At this point I added the fact that I had been a single parent myself raising a son after a separation. I was careful to point out that even though I had been through similar experiences I thought it might be different for each of us. The choice of disclosing this information was a personal one, and I could just as well have not done so. It was my belief that this information could enhance the comfort and the work of group members without compromising my role as leader.
>
> I then offered a few examples of possible concerns (these were similar to those described earlier in this paper).
>
> There was much head nodding in agreement as I spoke. I completed my opening by describing some of the phases that both parents and children go through after a separation. These were based upon the phases associated with loss as identified by Kubler-Ross (1969). I invited the participants to share some of their own experiences, their concerns and problems, and suggested that we could use their issues as an agenda for our two days of discussion. I pointed out that this was a small community and that it would be important for all of us to respect the need for confidentiality.
>
> There was a brief silence, and then Irene asked how long it took to go through the phases. I asked her why she was asking, and she said it was three years since

her separation, and she didn't think she had passed through all of them yet. The group members laughed, acknowledging their understanding of the comment. I said I thought there must have been a great deal of pain and sadness both at the time of the split and since then to cause it still to hurt after three years. I asked Irene if she could speak some more about this.

Although Irene responded in a lighthearted manner, my tuning in prior to the group had prepared me to put into words what I felt would be the hurt they were experiencing. I wanted to be sure to communicate to the members that if they were prepared to discuss even these painful areas, I was ready as well. I felt it was crucial to do this early with a short-term group. I understand the importance of being direct this early in all of my groups regardless of the number of sessions. However, the importance is increased in a short-term group since the members need to know early on that the discussion will be real, not superficial, and that the group leader is prepared to deal with difficult material. The group members still have control over the content and pace of their participation. When this early reaching for real work is missing in a short-term group, one often sees the "illusion of work," with the real issues either never emerging or being raised at the end of the final session ("doorknob therapy"). Irene accepts my invitation and the group members watch closely to determine how I will handle the disclosure.

Irene continued in a more serious tone by describing her ongoing depression. She described days in which she felt she was finally getting over things and picking herself up, followed by days when she felt right back to square one. Others in the group agreed and shared their own experiences when I encouraged them to respond to Irene's comments. I told them it might help just to know that they were "in the same boat" with their feelings.

I then asked if the group members could be more specific about what made the breakup difficult. A number of concerns were raised including dealing with money and finances, problems with the ex-spouse, problems with the kids, and the strain in their relationships with friends and family.

In reponse to this last issue, there was a great deal of emotion expressed as members acknowledged anger at others who "didn't understand" and who related to them in ways that hurt more than they helped. Dick, a young man in his mid-twenties, spoke with great agitation about his wife, who had left him with their six-month-old baby only six weeks before. The group seemed to focus on Dick, as he expressed a strong sense of urgency and was clearly still in a state of shock and crisis.

Dick had arrived early and had carried on a long and animated discussion with another member in the premeeting "chatter," listing all the crises he had to get through in order to get to the session that evening. He was also upset about efforts of friends and family members to assist him. As I listened before the session formally started, I believed that Dick's comments were indirectly addressed toward me as well as the other group members. As is often the case with premeeting chatter, I understood the talk to be an indirect call for help. For Dick the desire to be heard and helped was crucial.

I pointed out to the group that it seemed like Dick was feeling this concern about friends and relatives rather strongly and in fact had had a great deal of difficulty even getting here tonight. I asked if they would like to focus on friends and relatives first, perhaps using Dick's example to get us started. All agreed that would be helpful.

The way this group began was similar to married couples groups I have led. In both types of groups they started by externalizing the problems. That is, the first offerings dealt with others who didn't understand. With the married couples group, it was the spouses or all of the psychiatrists and helping people who had not been helpful. With these single parents it was friends and family who created the problems. In both examples it was important to begin with the clients' sense of urgency and to respect their need for defenses and maintaining control over the process. It was important that I be accepting of their feelings at this stage until I had built up a "fund" of caring upon which I could draw in order to confront. The issue of timing was important, since there would be only an evening and a day for work with the group. I felt I had to move rather quickly to confront the participants with the need to look at their part in their problems; however, it was also important that I take some time to acknowledge how it felt to them.

THE TRANSITION TO THE MIDDLE PHASE OF PRACTICE

In a short-term group like the one described in this chapter the transition from the contracting or beginning phase is likely to start in the first session. This is the time in the group when members must make a "second" decision. The first decision was to come and to begin to share their concerns and issues. As they begin to realize that the group would be a serious one and that they might have to face difficult feelings and even take responsibility for their own part in the problems that brought them to the group in the first place, and they have initially moved past the "authority theme" related to the group leader and the "intimacy theme" related to other members, the second decision launches them into a deeper level of work. The issues associated with authority and intimacy still remain, but at least a start has been made on the working relationship between the group members and the leader as well as between each member and the group.

Dick's sense of urgency helped the group to make the transition to the middle phase of work. While the members began with the theme of friends and family, the supportive nature of the work created the atmosphere where the members felt safe and free to move into other themes as well. In the sections that follow I present the major themes of the work.

Relationship with Friends and Family

During the course of the following discussion I was struck by how the crisis for the single parent was simultaneously a crisis for friends and relatives. It appeared that the single parent was sending mixed messages to "significant others." On the one hand I heard, "I'm hurt, lost, overwhelmed. Help me." The contrary message was, "Don't get too close. I'm afraid of losing my independence."

> After Dick described the details of his separation and his current living situation with his six-month-old child, he went on to describe the problems. He emphasized the difficulty of living in a small town and, in his particular case, being in a personal service occupation that put him in daily contact with many town residents. He said, "Sure I feel lousy, depressed, and alone. But some days I feel I'm getting over things a bit, feeling a little bit up, and everywhere I go people constantly stop me to tell me how terrible things are. If I didn't feel lousy before I went out, I sure do by the time I get home."
>
> Dick added a further complication in that the baby had a serious case of colic and was crying all the time. He told the group that everyone was always criticizing how he handled the baby and even his mother was telling him he wasn't competent and should move back home with her. He continued by saying he was so depressed by this that he had taken to not talking to anyone anymore, avoiding his friends, staying home alone at night, and he was going out of his mind. Others in the group shared similar versions of this experience. I said to Dick, "And that's the dilemma, isn't it? Just at the time you really need help the most, you feel you have to cut yourself off from it to maintain your sense of personal integrity and sanity. You would like some help because the going is rough, but you are not sure you want to have to depend on all of these people and you are not sure you like the costs involved."
>
> Dick nodded, and the other group members agreed. It became clear to the group members and me that Dick was actively sending two apparently conflicting messages and not being really clear about either. It appeared that his ambivalence about the central issue of independence and dependence was the major dynamic in relating to friends and family. The crisis appeared to evoke unresolved conflicts. Dick was feeling that he wanted to give up and let someone else handle things for him. This frightened him and made it difficult for him to take any help at all. All the group members expressed one variation or another on this same theme.
>
> After providing recognition and support for these feelings, I tried to move the group members into an examination of what they could do about the feelings in terms of how they handled their conversations with friends and relatives. I encountered a good deal of resistance to this idea, with Dick balking each time I tried

to get him to look at how he might have handled a conversation differently. He evaded this by jumping quickly to other comments or examples or by saying, "If you only knew my mother/friends, you would realize it is hopeless." When Rose, a member of the group in her early fifties with children close to Dick's age, confronted him from the perspective of his mother, he rejected her comments. I interpreted this as the point at which Dick, and all of the group members, needed to make a second decision. Coming to the group was the first decision to face their problems. Starting to take some personal responsibility for them was the second and more difficult decision. I wanted to integrate, at this moment, empathic support for their struggle with a clear demand for work.

I pointed out what was happening. I said, "It seems to me that when I or a group member suggest that you (Dick) look at your part in the proceedings, you won't take in what we are saying. I only have a day and a half with this group, so I really can't pussyfoot around with you." I wondered if it was tough for Dick, and all of them, to take responsibility for their part in their problems. Dick smiled and admitted that it was hard. He already felt lousy enough. Others joined in on how easy it was to blame everyone else and how hard it was to accept any blame themselves. I agreed that it was tough, but I didn't think I would be of any help to them if I just sat here for a day and a half agreeing about how tough things were for them. The group members laughed, and a number said they didn't want that.

At this point Doris, one of the three workers participating in the group, surprised us all by saying that she had intended to listen and not talk during the session but that listening to Dick's problem made her want to share hers. She said she had come to the group as an observer; however, she was pregnant, unmarried, and was, therefore, about to become a single parent. She thought she was having the same problem in communicating with her mother that Dick was having with his. It was a classic example of a conflict between a mother who is hurt and embarrassed and a daughter who feels rejected at a critical moment in her life. At my suggestion Rose offered to role-play the mother as Doris tried to find a new way to talk to her mother. The group was supportive, but, at the same time, following my example, they confronted each other during the discussion in a healthy way.

Dick listened and participated in the work on Doris's problem, and as is often the case, was able to learn something about his own situation as he watched someone else struggling with the same concerns. When I asked him later if he had taken something from it, he said it had helped him a lot to see how he was holding back his real feelings from friends and his own mother. I pointed out to all the group members what a shock their situation was to their friends and close relatives and how at first contact they could not respond in a way that met their needs. I said, "This does not mean they don't love you. It just means that they have feelings and aren't always able to express them. Your mixed messages also make it difficult."

In longer-term groups the leader has more time to develop the working relationship through empathy and understanding. With the existence of this "fund" of positive feelings, when the worker confronts the group member and the group as a whole, they are more able to hear the confrontation as "facilitative" and coming from someone who understands and accepts their feelings. In a short-term group this process must be speeded up if the group members are to develop a culture for work that supports direct conversation, the expression of real feelings, and the taking of personal responsibility. It is important that the group leader makes the "invitation" with an expectation that the members have come for that purpose. Too often the group leader will say that the members were "not ready" when actually it was the group leader who hesitated.

Cerise, another worker/observer in the group, joined the discussion at this point and described how she had felt when close friends had separated. She realized now that it had taken her a couple of months to get over being so angry at them for ending their marriage because she loved them both. She hadn't been able to reach out to support them. They, however, had not given up on her, and she had been able to work it out. Dick said that hearing that helped a lot. That was what was probably going on with some of his friends.

Carrie, who was both an unmarried parent and a worker in the community, described her own experiences with her mother when she split up. She shared how she had involved her mother in the process, had let her know her feelings, and that she wanted her mother's love and support but felt she had to handle the problems herself. Dick listened closely and said that this was probably what he had not been able to do. We did some role play on how Dick could handle the conversation with his mother and articulate his real feelings. The group was supportive. When I asked the group how they felt about the discussion thus far, Doris said it was helpful because I kept stressing the positive aspect, the reaching out and caring between people. Most of them had been so upset they could only see the negatives.

The discussion turned to the question of how much they needed others to talk to about what they were going through. Near the end of the session, in typical doorknob fashion, Dick revealed that a close male friend of his, in a similar situation with a young child, had told him he was considering committing suicide. He went on to tell us, with tears in his eyes, that the friend had carried through with the threat and had just killed himself. I said, "It must have hit you very hard when that happened, and you must have wondered if you could have done something more to help." Dick agreed that was so, and the group members offered him support. After some time I asked Dick if he was worried about his own situation, since he had many of the same feelings as his friend. He said he was worried, but that he thought he would be strong enough to keep going with the goal in his life to make it for his child. I told him he had shown a lot of strength just coming to the group and working so hard on his problem. Carrie said that he was not alone and that he could call her if he needed someone to talk to as a friend or as a worker. Rose pointed out that there was a single-parent social group at the church, and Dick said he had not realized this. Others in the group also offered support. I asked Dick how he felt now, and he said, "I feel a lot better. I realize now that I'm not so alone." Irene, who had opened the discussion by saying she had not yet gone through all the phases, summarized the evening's work when she said, "I guess we are all struggling to find ways of saying to friends and close relatives please love me now. I need you." The discussion ended, and we agreed to pick up again in the morning.

Relationship to the Children

A central theme that emerged when the group members discussed their problems with their children had to do with their guilt over their feelings of failure as parents. Both the men and the women members expressed feelings of responsibility for the marital split and therefore also felt responsible for their children's reactions. Thus, when indirect cues of the children's negative reactions emerged, they had difficulty in dealing with them. Also, the guilt made it hard for them to make appropriate demands upon their children. For example, in the first part of the discussion that follows, one mother has difficulty in asking for an older child's help in baby-sitting a younger child. When the mother raises the general question, I relied on the crucial skill of moving from the general to the specific to obtain details for our discussion. If I had not asked for the specific incident, our discussion would have remained general and would not be helpful to the member who raised the problem or to the other members who try to help her. As in all mutual aid groups, as they help this mother they are also helping themselves.

There were a few new members in the morning meeting. Some indicated they could not make it the evening before because of child-care issues and others said they had heard from members that the group was very helpful. I took some time to review the contract. The discussion picked up again with Irene raising the problem of dealing with the children. She described how tough it was on her when she asked her eleven-year-old boy to baby-sit his five-year-old brother. I asked if she could describe a specific incident, and she told us about one that had occurred the previous day. Her older son was about to go out to play when she asked him to cover for her, since she needed to take care of some business. His face dropped, but he did not say anything. I asked her if she could tell us how she felt when she saw his face drop. She said, "Miserable!" I asked her what she said to him, and she replied, "Nothing!" I pointed out how Irene had not leveled with her son and how she had avoided a frank discussion about her expectations for him and his feelings about having to carry some of the load. I asked if she had any ideas why it was so tough on her. She said he had not been getting along with his friends for a while after the split and, in fact, was moping around alone. Now that she saw him out and around, she hated to do anything that interfered. John, a new member, revealed that he had been a son in a single-parent family and that he felt the same way her son felt. He resented having to be responsible at such a young age. He said he would have very much appreciated it if his mom had talked directly to him about it and had allowed him to get some of his feelings off his chest.

I said, "I wonder if you parents really want to hear how your kids are feeling. I wonder if your kids' feelings are too close to your own." Gary said there was a lot of guilt in these situations—you feel responsible for your kid's problems because you've split up. He went on to say, "I'm also a little bit like a third-year medical student. Every time I see any sign of trouble with my kid, I'm sure it's going to be something really terrible." As Irene was describing her problem, I kept reaching for her feelings associated with their conversation. Clients often describe an incident without explaining their associated affect. In a sense, I was asking Irene to go back to the moment and try to remember and then share with us how it felt to her. By pointing out the gap between how she felt and what she said, I was trying to help all the group members to see how hard it is to be honest in expression of our feelings. We often expect the other person to "divine" our feelings without accepting the responsibility of letting them know what those feelings are.

In the group situation, I wanted to move further than just understanding, since I wanted to help the group members develop the skills needed to relate differently to those people who were important in their lives. I suggested a quick role play, consciously trying not to make it a major production (for example, "Let's put two chairs in the middle of the circle"). Role play in the group is difficult enough without the complications associated with formal structure. Irene resisted the suggestion. This resistance was important and was in many ways part of the work. Just as Rick's defensiveness in the opening session was a signal of underlying feelings, Irene's hesitation was also sending a signal. I tried to be empathic by exploring the reason for her hesitation while simultaneously making a demand for work. In this case the "process" and the "content" were closely related, since Irene's feelings of how difficult it would be to role-play the conversation was related to how difficult it would be to have the conversation with her child. The group could be a safe place to "try it out," but, as the leader, I could not let Irene off the hook because it was hard. In the end, if Irene insisted that she didn't want to role-play, I would accept her feelings and suggest someone else play her part and she listen.

I asked if a little role play might help here, and, since he was a child in a family like this, maybe John could help by playing Irene's son. There was some hesitation by Irene, who said that was hard to do. When I asked about the hesitation, she said she was afraid she would make mistakes. Carrie pointed out they would be the same mistakes they all make, so she shouldn't worry about it. Irene responded by saying it was hard to role-play. I agreed and then told her that I never said this work would be easy. She agreed to give it a try. The role-play revealed how hard it was for the members to reach for the underlying feelings that they sensed were expressed indirectly by their children.

I introduced the skill of looking for trouble when everything is going your way as an active way of reaching for underlying feelings. I illustrated how they could ask the child for negative feelings even when the child seemed to say everything was fine. There was a general recognition of how immobilized they often felt by their guilt. Irene tried again and this time was direct in opening up the question of mutual responsibility and her son's feelings. John told her that as her son he would be relieved to have it out in the open and would feel good that she respected him and needed him in this way. He still would not like to stay home and baby-sit, but it would sure make it easier. Irene said, "I guess if I get this off my chest, it will be a lot easier for me as well."

As is often the case, when the group members saw how a first offering of a feeling-laden theme is handled, they felt safer about moving into a deeper, more painful area. The difficulties arising from their guilt and their reluctance to make demands on their children were real problems, but, still, only "near problems." That is, each issue exposed just the surface of a much more difficult area of feeling. Maureen, a recently divorced member, raised the issue directly in a way that touched each of the other members. Their first reaction was to avoid the feelings that were just under the surface of her question. Interesting enough, this process in the group replicates the way in which they avoid the feelings under their children's questions. Once again, the group leader's task is to confront the members, but to do it gently and in recognition of the understandable reasons for the denial.

Maureen jumped in and asked how you handle it when your kid says, "Why can't we be a normal family?" This hit the group like a bomb, and they all jumped in with their versions of how they would answer the child's question. Most of the responses were variations of defensive explanations, long analogies or examples, and so on, all designed to provide the "good parent's answer." I intervened and said, "You know, you have jumped in to answer Maureen's child's question, but I wonder if we really know what the question is." I explained that it often takes some time for others to really tell us what they are feeling and that a quick response may not be getting at the real feelings, particularly when a question hits us in our gut and touches our feelings. I asked, "What would happen if you asked your child what he or she meant by the question?" There was a thoughtful silence in the room, and then Rose said, "Then we might really find out, and I'm not sure I want to hear."

I asked if we could get back to Maureen's example, and Maureen said, "Could we go on to someone else's example? I've been in the spotlight too long and people are probably bored with my problem." I asked the group members if this was true. They vigorously shook their heads, indicating they were very interested. I said to Maureen, "Look, they are interested. Why is it you want to get off the spot? Is it very tough to be on the spot?" Maureen replied, "It's hitting too close to home." The group members laughed in acknowledgment. I credited her for being honest and asked what she meant by "hitting close to home." She said, "I want to feel like I'm a good mother." There was silence in the room, and Lenore, another recently divorced mother, finally said, "I know what you mean. I feel I failed in my marriage and now I'm desperate about not wanting to feel I have failed as a mother."

This was followed by a discussion of their sense of guilt, of how harsh they were on themselves, and how their feelings of failure in their marriages and their fears of failure as parents often translated into overconcern and overprotection in relation to their children with a resulting fear of revealing the underlying, painful feelings. We returned to Maureen's example. She role-played a number of ways she might reach for her daughter's real feelings and the meaning of the question "Why can't we be like a normal family?"

Group workers often believe they face a dilemma in having to deal either with the group process or its content. The dilemma is experienced only because the worker believes in the existence of what is really a false dichotomy. In this group the process by which the members attempted to avoid the pain underlying questions raised by other group members was simply an illustration of the same problem they had with their children's questions. Thus the process and the content are synthesized, not dichotomized, and as the group worker deals with process, he or she is simultaneously dealing with content. I tried to use this dynamic by asking the members to reflect briefly on the morning's discussion, as illustrated below. It was important that I be brief, to ensure that the group would not lose its purpose and become lost in a discussion of its process.

Before we broke for lunch, I asked the group members to reflect on what had just happened in our group. I thought in some ways our group was an illustration of some of the problems they faced. I pointed out how Maureen had said she wanted to be off the spot because others were bored. Instead of just accepting that, I reached for other feelings that might be behind her discomfort. It turned out that she was feeling many things and her concerns were very much the concerns of the whole group. I wondered what they thought about my observation. Irene said that she could see what I meant. They had feelings they needed to talk about and they would only get to them if I helped them. The same was probably true for their kids. I said, "Lecture's over, how about lunch?"

RELATIONSHIP TO THE EX-SPOUSE

The work on the difficulty of being direct with one's child led to the subject of the relationship to the ex-spouse. The central theme for this group was related to their deep feelings of rejection. Even when they had initiated the break, it had been in response to their own feelings of rejection by the other partner. It soon became clear that their difficulty in helping the children deal with feelings of rejection related directly to their difficulty in dealing with their own similar feelings.

Ginette, recently separated from her husband with a five-year-old boy and a younger child, initiated this discussion by asking, "Is it always good to be honest?" When I asked why she raised that question, she described a situation in which her husband was rejecting their five-year-old boy while at the same time caring for their youngest child. He had refused to visit or call this son while promising to do so each time she raised it with him. When I asked her to describe her telephone conversations with the ex-spouse, it quickly became clear that she was pushing him, and he was denying that any problem existed. When I asked her how all of this had made her feel, she replied, "I'm really tired of trying to get Dad to be Dad."

I told Ginette I thought this must have put her in an awful bind with the child when, for example, he asked her, "When is Daddy going to visit me?" I wondered how she dealt with it. Ginette described her conversation with her son, which indicated she attempted to cover up the problem with "white lies" and to do whatever she could to avoid dealing with the child's feelings. I pointed this out to the group, acknowledging that I could appreciate the bind she felt. June, a new member who had been listening quietly all morning, began to speak. She spoke with a low, soft voice and began to cry before she could complete her comments: "I have been sitting here listening to Ginette, thinking that she is describing my problem exactly. And now, I think I realize (*crying softly*) that I'm going to have to face my own rejection by my husband who walked out on me before the healing can start and before I can help my kids face their rejection."

When a member expresses strong feelings in a group, it can be uncomfortable both for the individual and the other group members. Our societal taboos make it difficult for us to offer and accept such emotions; however, they are genuine emotions and need to be dealt with in some way. In this instance the group members seemed to turn away from June; however, it was not because they did not care. Actually, it was because they cared too much. These were their own emotions they needed to face, and June was simply expressing them.

As group leader, I tried to help the members reach out to June, to overcome the norms they had brought with them to the group that called for them to pretend they did not notice her pain. As they helped her with her feelings they also helped themselves with their own. We all felt moved by June's words. I could see the group members were upset. Marie was sitting next to June, and I could tell she was very agitated, looking around the room, looking at June, and literally moving in her seat.

I said, "I think June's feelings have hit all of us very hard. I have a feeling you would like to reach out to June, wouldn't you, Marie?" Marie said she really would. When I asked her why she didn't do it, she said, "Well, I'm afraid to." After a slight pause, she reached over and took June's hand, holding it tightly. June responded warmly to the gesture. I reassured her that it was OK to share her feelings with us and that her tears were an important part of how she felt. I told her that I felt she spoke for all of the group members, and they quickly assured her that I was correct.

We returned to Ginette at this point and the issues of being honest with her children and allowing them to express their feelings. She said, "I want my son to share his feelings within certain guidelines." I responded, "You mean, you want him to share the feelings that are not too tough for you." The group members, including Ginette, laughed in recognition. Ginette said, "I realize I have to be straight with him. When I lied and tried to make it sound as if his father loved him, it didn't make any sense, just like it wouldn't make any sense to make it sound like he didn't care at all."

The group members agreed to role-play the conversation so that Ginette could find a helpful way to be honest and to recognize her child's feelings of rejection. After a few difficult starts she finally decided on the following way of handling his questions: "Your Daddy does care about you, but right now he is having a hard time and feeling very upset and bad himself. That is why he hasn't visited you or invited you to stay with him. I know it must be very hard for you to understand why he doesn't spend more time with you if he really cares. It must make you feel very bad as well." As Ginette spoke these words, she was close to tears herself. I suggested that she might share with her child how hard this was for her. Then she and her son could cry together. Ginette said the discussion had helped, and she realized there was no easy way to handle this.

Throughout this conversation, and others as well, I was struck by the pattern in which the group members tried to deal with their own hurt through the medium of the children. I pointed out to the members that their feelings of rejection were strong; however, their sense of vulnerability made it difficult for them to admit their own feelings to the ex-spouse, the children, and even to themselves.

RELATING TO THE WORLD OF FINANCES

Rose, a woman in her early fifties, raised the many financial questions she had to face when her husband had left her. Her problems related to suddenly having to take responsibility for many of the questions that her husband had always handled. One particularly frustrating example was her problem obtaining credit. When she applied for a bank credit card, she was told she would need to establish a positive credit record. She was surprised that the credit record developed over twenty years of marriage was considered to be her husband's and she was judged not to have a credit rating at all. When she inquired how she was to establish a good credit rating, she was told she needed to obtain credit and to handle it well. At this point, feeling trapped, she had just given up.

When I asked Rose how she felt about the whole experience, she replied, "Damned angry!" Carrie told her she had given up too soon. She said that Rose was going to have to assert herself if she wanted to obtain her rights. I asked Carrie how she thought Rose could do this, and she suggested the following plan. She advised Rose to visit the credit bureau and discuss her desire to establish a credit rating. She pointed out that Rose was making monthly payments on a number of bills, for example, rent, telephone, utilities, and that she could use this to impress the credit bureau with her credit worthiness. She should also speak to the bank manager directly and point out that she had been part of the family that had given his bank the family business up to that point and that she would like his cooperation in developing a plan to establish a credit rating on her own.

The group members agreed that this might be her first step. They also felt that, if she ran into difficulty with this approach, she should consider bringing this to the attention of the bank's head office by writing the president. She could also consider contacting the Human Rights Commission, since this actually constituted a form of discrimination. It was obvious that everyone was angry at her situation. Rose agreed she could do more on this than she had thus far. She said, "I guess I began to believe that they were right about me not having earned a credit rating. It never occurred to me to refuse to accept the decision." Carrie said, "The hard part is understanding that you're going to have to fight for your own rights because nobody else is going to do it for you."

While some of the issues facing Rose in the late seventies may not be quite as relevant today, nevertheless the general feeling of financial stress is shared by most single parents. In addition, there are more options open to individuals who feel they have been discriminated against providing some tools for advocating for oneself. Still, the sense of powerlessness and the associated bitterness can still be observed.

Loneliness and the Fear of Risking

As is often the case, the group members seemed to leave the theme that was most difficult to deal with until close to the end of the session. For most of the parents in this group the change to single-parent status, for whatever the reason, had resulted in a state of loneliness. After having experienced years of being integrated, for better or worse, as part of a couple, they were suddenly facing the problem of being differentiated and alone. While many single parents enter into new relationships, the members of this group had not. Perhaps that is why they attended the group. What became even more striking, as the following discussion reveals in a most dramatic fashion, is that the hurt they experienced in their separations created a fear of risking in new relationships. They wanted closeness but were afraid to be vulnerable again to the pain of another separation. The crucial aspect to this work involved the group members' understanding the connections between their feelings and the way they acted. Also, they needed to see that changing their state of loneliness might be up to them.

The conversation about finances, which was discussed in the preceding section, had actually emerged in the midst of another discussion. I would like to go back to the beginning of that segment, when Rose told us she was afraid of being alone when her last child, now fifteen, grew up and moved out. All of her other children had left the home. Even though Rose wanted to deal with this question of loneliness, a part of her wanted to avoid it. It is interesting to note that the group members and the group leader backed off and, in a silent conspiracy, allowed the subject to change to the issue of finances. Perhaps the group members, and the leader, were affected by their own ambivalence about discussing such a painful area. What follows is the start of that discussion.

Maureen said to Rose: "Maybe the problem is you've never been Rose. You've always been somebody's mother or somebody's wife". Louise said that it was almost another form of rejection, being alone. She continued, "My kids aren't moving out, but I find myself feeling the same way just putting them on the school bus in the mornings." I asked Rose if she could be specific about the loneliness: when did she feel it and what did it feel like? She said the worst time was the emptiness in the house in the evenings.

After a few more comments by other group members, I noted that the discussion had shifted to the question of credit. It was at this point that the work in the previous section took place. I decided to make a "demand for work," an intervention that has also been termed a facilitative confrontation.

I intervened at the end of the credit discussion and said, "You know, it seems you have all decided to drop the issue Rose raised at the beginning, that is, how to handle the terrible loneliness of the empty house." They all laughed, recognizing they had silently agreed to drop the hot potato. Brett spoke for the first time and said that when we figured out that answer, to let her know, since she had the same problem. I commented that probably they all did and that was why it was hard to help Rose.

Carrie wanted to know what Rose did about finding friends. I said I thought that was a good start in helping Rose. Rose described how she had been invited to a dance by a group of her friends, all couples, and then spent the whole night sitting there when no one asked her to dance. I said I could imagine how uncomfortable they might all have felt. Lenore said that when she goes to a dance and no one asks her, she asks them. Connie wondered if she couldn't find a female friend to go to dances with. A pattern started to emerge, with Rose saying, "Yes, but . . . " to each suggestion. When I asked her if she had spoken to her friends about her discomfort directly, so they could better appreciate her feelings, it was obvious that she had not. Instead, she had been hurt and angry and had cut herself further off from her closest friends.

As her resistance stiffened, I finally confronted her and said it appeared as though she was not willing to work at maintaining her close relationships. She seemed to be saying that she wanted friends once again to "divine" her feelings, but she was not willing to take the risk and let them know what they were. At the same time she was complaining about being alone. There was a long silence, and then with great feeling she said, "I don't want anyone to ever get close to me again." The group was somewhat stunned at the force of her feelings, since she had been speaking quietly and in control for most of the session. I asked her why she felt this so strongly. Rose went on to tell us that her husband had left her for her best friend. I said, "So you really had two losses. You must have felt betrayed and very bitter." She replied that she still felt that way, hurt and bitter.

This initiated a powerful discussion by all group members of their feelings about intimacy. Their losses made them wonder if they should ever let themselves get close to anyone again. Irene said, "I think that's what I meant last night when I asked when you get over the last phase. I realize I have been depressed because I'm holding back. I'm not risking getting hurt again." The conversation dealt with their feelings about risking with friends of the same sex as well as with members of the opposite sex. Many of them described men who had attempted to date them whom they had liked but whom they had been afraid to get to know. The men in the group remained silent, perhaps reflecting a gender difference in their feelings and the way that they handled this issue. In retrospect, it would have been helpful if I had pointed out this gender difference.

I tried to take us back to Rose by asking what she thought about this conversation. She shrugged her shoulders and said, "Well, maybe in a couple of years it will get better." I said, "And maybe in a couple of years it will get a lot worse." I pointed out how all of them had been concerned that the kids come out of the situation whole, and yet their message to their kids appeared to be that when one gets hurt it's better not to try again. Rose pointed out how much she has done about her life, even learning to drive a car so she could be a bit more independent. I agreed that she had shown a great deal of strength in tackling the strains of being alone and that was why I felt she had the strength to even tackle this one, perhaps the hardest one for all of them. Irene said, "You're right, you know. We complain about being alone, but we are afraid to let ourselves be vulnerable again, afraid to get hurt." I said, "And that's the real dilemma, isn't it? It hurt so much to lose what you've had, you're afraid to risk. And then you find it also hurts to be alone. The important point, right now, is that you are aware of the question of loneliness and what to do about it is really in your hands."

I HAVE TRIED to share some of my observations about working with single-parent families, illustrating them with excerpts from my own group work practice. I have focused on identifying the specific themes of concern and the associated feelings that are somewhat unique to this group of clients, including their ambivalence about independence and dependence in relation to their family and friends, their feelings of guilt in relation to their children, the feeling of rejection that dominated the relationship to the ex-spouse, their anger at the world of finance and business, which often does not recognize them as separate individuals, and, finally, the one that emerged powerfully as a doorknob theme, their fear of risking intimacy and their desperate need for it.

When we evaluated the group in the ending phase, the participants felt it was helpful to see other people with the same problems. They also appreciated my pushing them to be specific about their problems, even to the point of asking them to recount their actual conversations. They liked getting new ideas about what to say and do and didn't feel quite so helpless about some of their concerns. They also felt it was important that I didn't let them off the hook. Finally, they felt I was really listening to them and that I could understand what they were struggling with. I pointed out that these were probably some of the same qualities their children wanted from them.

I thanked them for their honesty and for teaching me a great deal more about the problems of being a single parent. There were exchanges of positive feeling at the end and some discussion about how they might continue to stay in touch. They also shared other sources of support in the community. The workers, who had been invited to attend the group in part to be available to the members for follow-up counseling, offered their telephone numbers and invited group members to contact them if they wanted to talk.

References

Barnes, B. C. 1980. *The single parent experience*. Boston: Resource Communications in cooperation with the Family Service Association of America.

Canada's Families. 1979. Ottawa: Statistics Canada, Demography Division.

Castro, T. and L. Bumpass. 1989. Recent trends in marital disruption. *Demography* 26:37–51.

Gitterman, A. 2001. Social work practice with vulnerable and resilient populations. In A. Gitterman, ed., *Handbook of social work practice with vulnerable and resilient populations*, pp. 1–36. 2d ed. New York: Columbia University Press.

Jackson, A. P. 2001. Single parenthood. In A. Gitterman, ed., *Handbook of social work practice with vulnerable and resilient populations*, pp. 769–787. 2d ed. New York: Columbia University Press.

Kubler-Ross, E. 1969. *On death and dying*. New York: Macmillan.

Rosenthal, K. M. and F. H. Keshet. 1981. *Fathers without partners: A study of fathers and the family after marital separation*. Totowa, N.J.: Roman and Littlefield.

Schlesinger, B., ed. 1979. *One in ten: The single parent family in Canada*. Toronto: Guidance Centre, Faculty of Education, University of Toronto.

Shulman, L. 1998. *The skills of helping individuals and groups*. 4th ed. Pacific Grove, Cal.: Brooks/Cole.

Part 5

Mutual Aid and
Vulnerable and Resilient
Elderly

Chapter 18

Dealing with the Death of a Group Member
Visually Impaired Elderly in the Community

Alberta L. Orr

FOR THE 95 percent of the population over the age of sixty-five in this country who live independently or semi-independently in the community, a community-based facility such as a local senior center can serve as a primary resource. Attending a senior center is synonymous with group involvement, whether the older person actively participates in various group activities or programs or merely attends the center for a hot meal in a congregate setting. Both formally and informally, older people are involved in mutual aid in a senior center. Many may not even perceive their involvement as such, nor may the professionals who plan and implement the service think of it as mutual aid, but indeed it is. The informal groups that naturally form around an activity or topic of mutual interest (these can range from a crafts program to a lobbying effort) informally serve as mutual aid for the members of the group.

In New York City, senior centers are plentiful. Older people who attend represent an extremely diverse group, ranging from the newly retired professional to the physically and/or mentally frail older person, from early sixties to the late nineties. All in one way or another seek to find a network of peers with whom they can share identified common ground, in this case age-related vision loss. Those who attend do so for a broad range of reasons: to find companionship, to use time productively and satisfactorily, to make a contribution, to discover new areas of learning interest or skills, or to rediscover and maximize old ones. In some centers groups are organized for the purpose of helping members deal with a situation of stress or concern. The frequently offered widows and widowers group is organized as a network to enable these older people who have lost their spouses to share their experiences and common life crises and to develop strategies for coping with loss. The English as a second language (ESL) class not only serves to teach the language but also establishes a mutual aid network for those who speak another primary language and share a common culture. The men's group represents another mutual aid support system frequently organized in centers by men who seek the companionship of other males, since they are routinely outnumbered by older women in the center ten to one.

The mutual aid group that is the focus of this chapter is comprised of visually impaired senior citizens, most of whom are experiencing vision loss as a concomitant of aging. Originally, the mutual aid group was formed to provide older people with a forum in which to address the problems and concerns imposed by recent vision loss. While the group was formed to help these older people share their frustrations and fears around this particular loss, the group's process of mutual aid expanded to include more generalized concerns of older persons encompassing a broad range of losses. Members have used the group as a place to bring and share their feelings related to the loss of a spouse or significant other, the loss of physical functioning based on a health problem, and other vulnerabilities.

The focus of the group meeting presented here deals with the death of a group member and the group's struggle to express their feelings about this loss, to reminisce about previous traumatic losses, and to consider and verbalize their fears related to their own impending death. The function, tasks, and skills of the social worker in enabling the group as a whole, as well as individual group members, to express their feelings openly are presented, followed by a set of practice principles to guide the worker through a mutual aid group's attempt to deal with the death of a group member. While this group deals with a special population of older people, those who are visually impaired or blind, much of the content is applicable to any group of older people dealing with the same or similar situation of stress. Hopefully, therefore, the material presented will be helpful to those social workers working with all groups of older people. Special attention is also given to the needs of the hearing impaired older group member—a major service concern to all social workers working with groups of older people, where invariably at least one member if not a substantial percentage of group members experience varying degrees of hearing impairments.

Developmental Tasks and Issues

Life after sixty-five for many is a period of tremendous satisfaction. Those of us who are working in geriatric social work settings, particularly community-based services, witness the degree of activity, productivity, and life satisfaction among older clients daily. We see older people assume new contributing roles, senior citizens involved in political and social action activities, the beginnings of new significant relationships—all of which make working with older people professionally satisfying, rewarding, and invigorating. While many older people still maintain an amazing vitality and zest for life, the future, and its infinite potential, others feel that the best years of their lives are long past. In the midst of tremendous growth for such positive satisfying experiences, we recognize that at this last stage of the life cycle the primary developmental task for all older people is to deal with the preponderance of losses that dramatically impact on their lives. For all older people, no matter what else is occurring at this stage of the life cycle, no matter how successful or productive or how withdrawn or isolated, losses begin to occur in many areas of their lives at a rate never before so dramatically experienced. These older people may have ten, twenty, or thirty more years of their lives to live; yet they live these years experiencing one loss after another. This accumulation of losses may appear quite obvious in some older people and in others not obvious at all because of the differences in individual ability to cope and resources available to motivate the older person to develop coping strategies. These losses are a true test of resilience within the older person.

The task at this stage is to adjust to these losses, to understand them as events of this stage of the life cycle, to incorporate having had and having lost something or someone so significant into one's sense of self and identity in order to be able to continue to experience life as still worth living, as holding the potential for growth and development, and as having a future. The capacity to cope with so many losses and vulnerabilities, and the availability of essential supports to enable such coping are critical factors for the older person to live with satisfaction, dignity, self-confidence, and self-esteem, which are severely shaken by each loss.

The task then, at this stage, is to deal with loss in a psychologically healthy manner in order to be able to invest in other areas of interest or to be able to develop new areas of interest. The need is to be able to "replace," or attempt to replace, the losses with other significant people and activities. This bombardment of losses has been referred to by Stanley Cath (1971) as an "omniconvergence" of losses. The stresses and strains characteristic of the older person are represented by loss of income and financial security, loss of the work role and sense of productivity, loss of spouse and/or significant others, loss of other meaningful interpersonal relationships such as friends and neighbors, loss of close geographic proximity to children, loss of health through physical illness or impairment, loss of physical functioning, such as that experienced by those with severe arthritis or heart disease, or, less commonly thought of, visual impairment, loss of opportunities for self-expression—and the list goes on (Orr 1991, 1998). Loss of these positive elements characteristic of previous stages of the life cycle are or can be replaced by feelings of physical and psychological dependence, social isolation, and loneliness, dramatically reduced self-confidence and self-esteem, hopelessness, helplessness, and uselessness. The result is a state of dependence or perceived dependence. These dependencies are referred to by Blenkner (1969) as the normal dependencies of aging occurring in the areas of economic, physical, mental, and social dependence. As one loss is compounded by each additional loss, the life crisis intensifies.

Understanding the nature and scope of the developmental tasks and needs of older people as well as the developmental life crises and situations of stress is essential for all social workers and human service professionals, including those not working exclusively in geriatric settings. This is the segment of the population expanding at the greatest rate and requiring the broadest range of social services.

The "omniconvergence" of losses places the older person in a state of vulnerability, jeopardy, or potential jeopardy, which may be further compounded by a serious disability such as severe visual impairment or blindness. Older people experience vision loss at a time when they are experiencing losses in other areas of their lives. One of the most devastating and commonly reported combinations of losses occurs when older people lose their vision and begin to depend on their spouses for help with daily living activities and then lose their spouse soon after the onset of severe visual impairment. When this essential link to involvement and activity is pulled out from under the older newly visually impaired person, the results are devastating. Many risk factors become apparent. Independence feels like an impossibility. A mutual aid group for this even more specialized segment of the special population may serve as the critical network to enable these older people to cope with and adjust to this most difficult combination of losses.

According to Lessner (1973), the loss of independent mobility is the most devastating loss for the older visually impaired person. This loss of physical freedom leads to feelings of both physical and psychological dependence, dependence on someone else where often there is no one else. Dependence on something, like a white cane, is frequently psychologically unthinkable; it seems totally out of the question for the older person who is visually impaired to consider carrying this stigmatizing symbol of dependence and defectiveness.

Vulnerabilities and Risk Factors and Resiliencies and Protective Factors

Older people who lose their vision later on in life have lived all their lives as sighted people and bring with them to this stage of the life cycle all they have "learned" about disabled people throughout their lifetime. They enter the myths about blindness and act out societal stereotypes—that all blind people are dependent, that they are not productive, that they are a burden to someone, either their family or society, and that they are out of the mainstream of life. A struggle ensues within older persons who are visually impaired as they attempt to adjust and identify where they are on the independence/dependence continuum.

As they enter this line of thinking, it becomes increasingly difficult to replace the loss of independence with substitutes for renewed independence. If allowed to perpetuate, this state of dependence leads to dramatically lowered self-confidence, self-reliance, self-esteem, and self-worth Thoughts of premature and unnecessary nursing home placements run rampant as a natural consequence. However, vision rehabilitation services can convert feelings of vulnerability to feelings of resilience. Receiving services can serve as a key turning point resulting from being able to plan for the future and make a positive choice for one's self (Rutter 1987).

Getting involved in rehabilitation services is a step toward regaining functioning following the adversity experienced in the onset of vision loss. Auslander and Levin (1987) refer to the consumer's involvement in services as the instrumental type of support (provision of goods and services) among their four types of support. The other types of support include emotional (the provision of empathy and encouragement, informal (provision of advice and feedback), and appraisal (the provision of information relevant to self-evaluation). The worker as the group experiences puts these last three types of support into operation.

As older people lose their vision, very frequently through a gradual deterioration, they perceive themselves as less and less capable of remaining in the mainstream of community life. Many withdraw from the community to their homes or apartments because they are unable to cope with the stresses that accompany remaining actively involved in the community. This withdrawal from neighborhood involvement leads to both physical and social isolation so detrimental to the emotional, psychological, and social well being of any older person.

After a period of time, older people who are visually impaired begin to perceive of themselves as homebound, an extremely vulnerable position, and to describe themselves as homebound to others. This helps to perpetuate the thinking on the part of other people, even service providers to older people, that to be blind is to be homebound.

One blind woman's request for help speaks to just this issue. Mrs. Q. called me indicating that she was blind and homebound, asking for help in locating an appropriate nursing home placement. Since she was visually impaired, she was seeking a nursing home knowledgeable about working with blind people and, therefore, called an agency for the blind for help. Mrs. Q. sounded young, bright, articulate, and healthy, and it was initially incomprehensible to me why she would be seeking a nursing home placement.

Exploration of Mrs. Q.'s living situation revealed a spry woman, sixty-three years of age, who had gradually lost her vision but had no physical or mental health problems to speak of, someone who became a victim of her own environment. Mrs. Q. described that she used to (two years before) travel independently on public vehicles, walk around her neighborhood to stores and community center, but "gave it all up." Like many older people who are visually impaired, Mrs. Q. had been trained to use a cane but was embarrassed to be seen among her sighted neighbors as needing "that white thing" in a community where she was once like everyone else. She was frightened to walk the streets with a cane.

It tells everybody that you are less able to take care of yourself; you're an easy target, especially in a neighborhood where old people get mugged. . . . I used to ride the bus. Sometimes I stood in the wrong place, and the bus would pass me by. If I got the bus, I'd ask the driver to let me know when I got where I was going, but he'd forget and then I was terribly lost in a totally unfamiliar place. So I just don't go anywhere. I'm captive of my apartment. Don't you call that homebound?

And of course, to some extent, she was; but, most important, she need not be. This represents what can happen to any older person experiencing a dramatic change. Involvement with others in similar circumstances can make a significant difference.

The need for group involvement with others experiencing the same or similar circumstances goes without saying. Barber (1976), Galler (1972), and Mummah (1975) have each described the needs of older people who are visually impaired for the social support of other visually impaired older people to be able to adjust to their vision loss. Minkoff (1972), in describing a community-based program to integrate blind elderly people, expressed the need for a separate support group (as a mutual aid network) within that context. Several have called with the need for group therapy to work through the depression and reactions resulting from vision loss (Wilson 1972; Evans and Jauregy 1981). In the program presented here, visually impaired clients' requests for services to this agency serving people who are blind or visually impaired represent a direct call for group services, group support, and mutual aid. Each group member's memories of prior losses reemerge, including their vision loss, and they benefit from working through these losses in a group.

Agency and Group Context

This agency serving people who are blind or visually impaired has an interesting and inspirational history in relation to the development of group services for older people who are visually impaired. The agency began in 1926 as a camp for blind adults offering visually impaired adults of all ages, eighteen to one hundred plus, the opportunity for a vacation in an environment where physical adaptations enabled people who are visually impaired to move about independently. As the need for year-round services became evident, the agency became a year-round social service agency where adults who are visually impaired could receive assistance with individual social service needs related to their visual impairment.

Many older people who are visually impaired and attended the agency's camp discussed with social work staff their need for year-round services, beyond individual social services. The requests for services were represented by a common theme. One client's request is representative of this theme.

I look forward to coming back to camp from the time I board the bus to go home each summer. The two weeks at camp mean so much to older blind people like us, because we have a chance to be reunited with old friends we otherwise rarely get to see. The other fifty weeks of the year we never see each other. There are five of us who literally live within a ten-block area, but it could be ten miles for all we know. We can't get to each other's apartments. We use the telephone—thank God—otherwise we're really very isolated. I used to go to the senior center when I could see, but now I can't go. It's only four blocks from my apartment, but I can't get there. Besides, "they" don't know what to do with blind people if we could get there. Maybe you [the agency] could do something for us, get us out of the house, so we could get together to talk about what it's like being blind. Fifty weeks is a long time. We need something.

The theme of the requests became crystallized: the need to be with other people, no longer to be socially isolated, to get out of the house, to see other blind people who were sharing common concerns and stresses associated with vision loss, and to have access to a once utilized local resource, the senior center, like other older people in the neighborhood. For the majority of older people experiencing recent vision loss, a state of ambivalence exists. Visually impaired older people want two things simultaneously: 1. to have access to a local senior center they once had when they could see and 2. to withdraw from the mainstream of community life to the protected environment of a segregated service for the blind. The underlying psychological stresses remain to be like everyone else, to be accepted within the mainstream of community life, but to recognize one's self as different and in need of specialized services. The outgrowth was a combination of services in one setting in an attempt to close the gap. The agency's community-based programs took place in senior centers in over twenty-five local neighborhoods. The community-based design grows out of a particular value base that views older blind people first as senior citizens and second as older people who happen to be visually impaired. The program is comprised of two components: 1. the mutual aid group for the visually impaired older people and 2. opportunities for older people who are blind or visually impaired to participate in programs and activities in the center with their sighted peers.

The necessity of providing group services to older people who are visually impaired, and equally to all older people, speaks for itself: the need for a group of peers with whom to identify, who are experiencing common life vulnerabilities and stresses, and with whom one can easily identify the common themes of concern. The comfort, support, and strength acquired from peers, as professionals, or with friends or children cannot replicate part of the mutual aid process. Group participation also allows the development of new relationships that can ease the pain just by knowing this life stress is shared by other older people. The multiplicity of helping relationships that develop in a mutual aid group have greater support potential than the singular relationship between client and worker. These relationships contribute to individuals' resilience.

Work and Group Themes

In general, the use of groups in work with older people is essential and is considered the primary service modality among many social workers in the field of gerontology. It lessens the social isolation and loneliness and other risk factors that are so devastating at this stage of the life cycle. The mutual aid group is frequently the primary social and support network, a replacement for lost support, a reconstituted family.

This mutual aid group has been meeting for four years, once a week each Friday morning for an hour. The group serves as each group member's primary and in most cases only source of support. It is the place where members bring and deal with the losses in all areas of their lives. Dealing with the loss of significant others is one of the major crisis events individual members bring to the group. Dealing with the death of a group member, the focus of the work presented here, demonstrates how the mutual aid group enables members to support each other and develop coping strategies that they experience simultaneously as a group.

The mutual aid group is composed of twelve older people who are visually impaired or blind, four of whom are also hearing impaired, one severely. They range in age from sixty-one to ninety-two; nine are women, three are men; nine are Jewish, two Italian Catholic, one Protestant; ten are widowed; ten live alone; six are lower middle class, and six are middle class. Members are dependent on door-to-door transportation to participate in the group and in the center in general. The mutual aid group is the lifeline for many who are otherwise physically and emotionally isolated. For ten of the twelve members, the mutual aid group is their only source of support and the center their only source of socialization and recreation. Many experience the devastating emptiness of the weekend, and, for several, the weekend has become a time of emotional crisis.

Since the mutual aid group is perceived as a lifeline, the death of a member is experienced as a weakening of the support system: a link is now missing. This represents a tremendous threat and is experienced as an individual concern by each member and as a group concern by the group as a whole. Each individual group member's sense of integrity and self-worth is severely threatened. When confronted with the death of a group member, members must deal with past, current, and potential losses, and the ultimate—their own impending death, as all losses come into play simultaneously. The harsh realities of being left behind as others die, of being abandoned by a member of a support system, of dying alone, and of not being remembered because everyone else has died before represent the themes of concern and vulnerability involved in this life-cycle crisis. Members are faced with the fear of their own death. Such a crisis event triggers feelings of vulnerability. For some, little time is left and that time will be spent waiting for death. Life loses its meaning as a member of the support system is lost. Each group member's capacity for resilience is challenged.

The worker's role is to enable the group members to make use of the mutual aid group. The worker's plan throughout is to intervene as little as possible, only to step in where the helping process will either stop or go astray without intervention. Each of the group members takes on a distinct role in facilitating or inhibiting the mutual aid process.

Members of the group arrive at the center, having been informed by the driver of the van that Maddie, a seventy-five year-old woman who had been a member of the group for the past year, died the day before of a massive heart attack. This was the first member of the group to die this year (last year four members died). As the members arrive, one member, Goldie, whispers to the worker that Maddie died the day before. As people settle into their seats with coffee and cake, the worker attempts to tune in to what individual group members are feeling and the dynamics of the group as a whole. The following represents the worker's stream of thoughts as she begins to tune in to her clients.

It really hits hard when a member of the group dies; it hits so close to home. I could be next. So Maddie died; I'll hear about two more people soon, you know how they always happen in threes. It's not just Maddie. Maddie's death reminds me of when my two closest friends died, not so long ago. It makes me go back to when I lost my husband. That was so terribly difficult for me. Whenever someone else dies, I remember how long it took me to get over it. You never get over a death of someone that close to you. Maddie's husband will certainly have a hard time. He was devoted to her. That's how it was with my husband. It makes you feel so empty, like the world's caving in . . . like there is no way of knowing when your time is up.

I remember when my daughter died last spring. Nothing can be worse than losing your only child, your only daughter. Nothing is left. I'd lost everything. It's only been a few weeks that Maddie's been sick. Now she's gone. Everyone liked her so much. She was such a quiet stabilizer. But she's gone now; what can we do? Just stand up in a moment of silence, donate money to the center like we always do, and pretend she was never with us. It hurts too much to talk about it. Talking about it would just make me think too much about all the other people I've lost. I'll try to forget. What else can I do? I hope no one gets upset in the group. Some people show so much emotion. That just makes it harder for me when I'm trying to forget. When you're old, there really is very little to life than watching people die and waiting for your turn, very little else. It makes me want to do nothing, Maddie's death. It takes the meaning out of the day. It makes me feel hollow inside—no, it's not really emptiness. It's a painful sadness down deep in the pit of my stomach. No one else can possibly feel this way. No one else has lost what I've lost over the years. I hope we don't talk about it; I hope no one cries—or I may cry, too.

But I want to talk about it; sometimes talking makes it better. You can remember the things that were positive. I want to talk about it, and I don't want to talk about it. It's hard to know which hurts more. There's enough pain in my life day to day. I never forget for a minute how different my life was when my husband was here, when I could see. He won't be here when I die; no one may be here when I die; God forbid, I should outlive them all. Who will be left to say that I meant anything to them . . . that I made life worthwhile . . . that I made a difference? I'll try to forget about what I've heard today. Maddie hasn't been here for a few weeks. That makes it easier. I'm eighty-eight years old; how much longer can it be? The doctor said Maddie was a fighter, but ultimately there is one fight you lose. Maddie lost. I'll lose. We'll all lose. That's what life's about when you're old. I could just cry. It's just one loss after another. So little time left. I never did everything I wanted to do in my life. Maddie had a hard time being blind these past two years. It was hard for her to adjust. They never got to do the traveling they'd planned because she lost her sight. Life's so cruel. Where's the comfort?

Dealing with the Loss

This group session had no formal beginning as group members arrived and settled in, in the midst of discussion.

TESSIE: I just can't believe Maddie died; I've been calling her house every day to speak to her husband, and no answer. I knew something was wrong (*said softly and with despair*).

Brief silence . . .

ROSE: Are you crying, Tessie?

TESSIE: I don't know whether I'm crying or not (*said with frustration*).

GOLDIE: Don't cry, Tessie; you'll only get all upset.

TESSIE: How can I not cry? Now it's Maddie; every week it's someone else (*begins to cry openly*). Rose leans over, reaches out to find Tessie, and puts her arm around her.

ROSE: But we are upset, Goldie, why shouldn't she cry? Why shouldn't we? I cried this morning when I found out in the van. We're all upset.

HANNAH: (*Who is severely hearing impaired*) who's crying?

GOLDIE: (*Whispers to the worker*) we shouldn't tell Hannah; she lives in the nursing home; she gets upset when people die there. She doesn't have to know. (*then loudly to Hannah*) No, nothing, everything is fine. No one's upset.

WORKER: (*To Goldie*) How do you think Hannah will feel when she finds out?

GOLDIE: (*After a long pause*) she'll be upset.

WORKER: I think Rose is right, that we're all upset. Hannah is part of the group.

GOLDIE: (*Loudly to Hannah*) Maddie died yesterday.

HANNAH: I knew something was wrong. I could feel it. Oh, my . . . that's terrible about Maddie.

The worker's first task is to help the group, primarily Goldie, realize the need to include Hannah in the mutual aid process and to help Goldie tell Hannah about Maddie herself. While the death of a group member is experienced as an individual loss and a group loss, it is a group issue. A basic underlying value in group work in general is "we're all in this together" and, in order to share the experience together, we must all have access to the same information, as painful as that information may be, and as much as one member or all the members may want to exclude one member for whatever reason. Because Goldie realizes that Hannah cannot hear what is going on, the temptation is to try to get away without telling her, to protect Hannah and to protect herself—to avoid saying out loud "Maddie died yesterday." Goldie initially assumes the role of "don't make it hurt more than it has to" on behalf of herself and her friend, or at least so she thinks.

This is neither Goldie's nor the group's usual manner of relating to Hannah. Normally group members repeat significant information loudly to Hannah or remind the worker to tell her individually. While not telling Hannah something so difficult seems like the easiest thing to do at the moment, particularly to Goldie, it would ultimately be the worst choice. Emphasis in work with older people, and in group work with older people in particular, stresses the need to confront real issues directly, to deal with real things representative of life at this stage of the life cycle. Death is probably the most real of these issues.

The worker is really saying to Goldie, "Hannah's your friend; she trusts you, and even though she'll be upset, listen to what Rose is saying, that everyone's upset. And upset is the most natural, most appropriate response right now. Hannah has no way of knowing what the most appropriate response is unless we tell her the issue. She can't even participate in the group today, because we're not letting her; we're denying her information, infantilizing her, denying her the right to participate, the right to respond, to feel, to share, and to be equal . . . because we can get away with it—for a little while."

Rather than the skill of facilitative confrontation, the worker uses the skill referred to by this writer as "posing the ultimate question" to enable Goldie to consider the outcome herself. Goldie is then able to think beyond the moment and inform Hannah about Maddie's death. The following principles should guide the worker working under similar circumstances.

1. Even when the content of the group process is emotionally laden, members should not be viewed as so frail that they are overprotected by the worker or other members of the group and kept uninformed.
2. When the communication process of group members is hampered by hearing loss, every effort must be made on the part of the worker and other group members to ensure the fullest participation possible for these members, so that they feel they are an equal and integral part of the group process.

3. The worker must initially model this behavior on behalf of all members of the group.
4. The worker needs to encourage members to enhance the participation and involvement of members who are hearing impaired and not assume all the responsibility for this.
5. Not only must the worker be critically self-aware of the pitfalls of ageism in herself, but she must also be aware of ageism manifested by young elderly members of a group, where other members may be thirty years their senior. The worker must strive to combat ageism and the biological and cultural determinism that permit a stereotypic view of the old elderly among the young elderly.

An interesting phenomenon occurs in work with the elderly where the group spans thirty years or more, really two generations: ageism. Goldie's inclination to protect Hannah is representative of ageism among the young elderly toward the old elderly. Ageism has been identified in the literature by Blank (1979) as an obstacle among workers with older people. Goldie's view of Hannah is that she is too frail, too much at risk, too vulnerable to burden her with yet another tragedy. Goldie stereotypically believes that Hannah's ninety years, previous losses, limited support, and living situation make her less able to handle this information than those members in their sixties. The reality is more often the reverse. As the older person lives longer and experiences more life stresses and losses, they establish coping strategies that make it easier for them to adjust to loss than for younger older people who are just beginning to experience this preponderance of losses. Loss becomes a given (though a most difficult reality), a part of life, more readily incorporated into the individual's sense of self at ninety than at sixty. At ninety most older people recognize that more than likely they do not have thirty more years to live. At sixty thoughts readily go to "I could die tomorrow, or I could live ten, twenty, or thirty more years, and who knows in what condition?" As a result, it is easy for Goldie or others in her position to project their own fears of what it must be like at ninety onto Hannah or someone in Hannah's situation.

Such ageist thinking operates out of a perception of biological and cultural determinism identified in the worker with older people and, in this instance, among the young older population (Berl 1963). Biological determinism views old age as a time of regression and decline in capacities at all levels. Cultural determinism holds that old age is seen as a decline in personal worth. However, it is only by sharing the information with Hannah that her personal worth and dignity can be permitted, by treating her as equally capable of participating in the group's crisis. The value underlying this knowledge base in work with older people is that to deprive one member of the group of human dignity is to deprive the whole group. What may be viewed, then, as protective intervention by an older group member may actually be a threat to human dignity. Overprotection is one of the primary roadblocks in work with older people and can thwart mutual aid on behalf of every member (Lowy 1967). As each older person is treated equally, every member has the knowledge that they too would be treated with dignity as they grow older. It is the worker's task to ensure that this occurs.

Kastenbaum and Cameron (1969) have pointed to the need for cognitive supports in old age, the need for information often denied older people in the disguise of protection. A reduction of cognitive support has been shown to affect dependency greatly in later life, diminishing self-esteem and intensifying feelings of dependency, and so the cycle goes. Cognitive support for Hannah is essential here and equally essential for everyone to experience.

Perceptual losses, that is, vision and hearing loss, have dramatic effects on social functioning and emotional and psychological well-being. Hearing loss results in even greater social isolation than blindness, as reported by Butler and Lewis (1977), and, because communication is more difficult, a sense of belonging is that much harder to achieve for the hearing impaired member(s) of a group. If self-esteem is enhanced by a feeling of belonging, of giving and receiving within the context of a group, informing Hannah is essential to her self-esteem. As Goldie considers and reconsiders, she is able to share this difficult news with Hannah, to say the difficult words out loud.

It is important to note that Hannah is only blind and hearing impaired. Her mental capacity is not at issue, though a lower level of involvement caused by hearing impairment is sometimes attributed to mental dysfunction in group work with other older people. Had Hannah been mentally frail or shown signs of dementia or sporadic inability to process information, it would have been equally important to inform her, to give her the chance to hear the information and the opportunity to filter out whatever she chose at the time, as each of the other members of the group is doing. Such cognitive reinforcement is ego enhancing to the mentally frail in particular. The group continues.

RUTH: I don't think we should talk about it any more. She's gone now, and I'm sorry, but talking about it won't help her any.

ROSE: We should all stand up for a moment of silence in memory of Maddie.

BELLE: And we can donate ten dollars to the center in Maddie's memory.

RUTH: And then we can stop talking about it. Tessie's upset and Josephine's upset and I'm getting upset too. Talking about it won't help. We can go on to something else. We had something on the agenda.

WORKER: What are we going to do with all that we're feeling, though, if we don't talk about it here, in the group? I'm thinking that it's Friday, and we've done a lot of talking over the past few months about how difficult the weekends alone are for so many of you, and especially when something upsetting has happened. Are we going to take all that sadness and pain and emptiness home with us for the weekend?

ROSE: That's right. I open my door and no one's there. No one says let's talk about it, or what kind of day did you have? I know I'll think about it this weekend.

SARAH: It makes you think about other people who have died, people very close to you that you lost (*said softly, almost in a whisper*).

Silence . . .

WORKER: That's right, Sarah, and that's hard. But you know . . . this is a loss we're all experiencing together. If we let ourselves talk about Maddie's death together and about Maddie, it may make it easier later on.

A brief silence follows.

MARY: She was someone we all really cared about. She meant a great deal to us, and losing her certainly means something to me.

TESSIE: It's that so many people have died the past few months. My two best friends, my friend Sam; he did so much for me . . . the woman upstairs. I just can't stand losing so many people. I just can't stand hearing about anyone else dying (*continues to cry*).

The worker walks over to Tessie, putting her arms around her and around Goldie, who sits next to her, and stands behind them as the discussion continues.

ALLAN: Remember when Sol died last spring? We were upset then. He'd been here since the beginning of the group; it was three years then; now it's four. That was a big loss.

RUTH: That's what happens when you get old, you just keep losing people, one right after the other.

HANNAH: Until it's your turn. I know my turn is coming; it's closer every day.

JOSEPHINE: You know it's your turn when it seems like everyone you ever cared about has died.

ROSE: It's closer every day for all of us, but we have to keep going; I go out every day, I make the best of all of it. But this is an especially hard day.

GOLDIE: Are you OK, Tessie?

TESSIE: No, I'm not OK. It hits so hard and hurts so much. Hannah's right, it just makes you think that you've got to be next.

RUTH: I try not to think about it.

ROSE: But its always there, even if you pretend it isn't, even if you don't talk about it.

According to Burnside (1978a, b), when the death of a group member occurs, workers are faced with two tasks simultaneously: they must deal with their own personal feelings about losing a client and begin to move to help the group deal with the loss. The worker's personal and professional orientation in dealing with death and professional values regarding work with older people around the issue of death converge, intermingling to determine steps that will enable the group to confront what has happened.

As Ruth takes on the role of mutual aid inhibitor and begins to set the tone for putting the issue to rest, and Belle calls for the group's traditional ritual response to acknowledging death, the worker's thoughts race to reach for a way to challenge the group to consider another method of coping.

While we may not often admit it to anyone, even to ourselves, we enter the mutual aid process with a preconceived image of how we would like to see it benefit the group. Based on previous experience with the group and knowledge of individual group members' patterned responses to such crises, the worker fears that the group will not be able to work through the pain to completion. Yet the worker believes in the potential of the mutual aid process, in the members' ability to express their most painful thoughts and feelings, and in her own ability to enable the process to be realized. Ruth's call for moving on to whatever is on the agenda indicates that it is time for the worker to intervene, to present an alternative to this movement in the "wrong" direction.

The worker's statement "What are we going to do with all that we're feeling?" is an attempt to lend the group an opportunity to consider another way of dealing with Maddie's death, not instead of their traditional standing in a moment of silence and donating money to the center to perpetuate Maddie's memory but in addition to this standardized ritual observance. Krupp (1972) states that such ritual ceremonies as this group's standing in a moment of silence serve to channel and legitimize the normal flow of emotions and, as such, can be extremely functional in a crisis. The primary issue here is one of timing. Emotions have not even gotten to the surface for most group members. Many members are still trying not to express their pain openly in order to go on in the group as they have been socialized. But to put these emotions in check by standing in a moment of silence would be to bury them prematurely.

When Ruth, in her role as mutual aid inhibitor, calls for moving on to something else, the worker's fear is that the group will enter into a state of mutual denial rather than mutual aid. According to Weisman (1972), denial is a social act. In a group situation, it may originate in one member, be encouraged by a second member, and develop into a mutual strategy to maintain individual and group integrity. When reality becomes too immense, the natural response is to withdraw and avoid contact with it. While the group viewed standing up in a moment of silence as tackling the loss straight on, it was a structured, familiar, and comfortable way of keeping the pain of one more loss in check. The group was not denying Maddie's death, but some members wanted, and needed, to deny the impact. They wanted to withdraw from the meaning and significance of this death for each of them and for the group as a whole. Such denial can serve as an adaptive response, a strategic defense in the face of a crisis.

Of particular importance is the worker's thinking about the moment of silence as it impacts on blind people in particular. Standing in a moment of silence even further isolates the members of the group from experiencing a shared experience, particularly because communication among blind people is so dependent on verbal communication and physical contact, since the visual cues are inoperative. The lack of interpersonal interaction during the moment of silence is a roadblock to the work of the group and therefore cannot be the only attempt at acknowledging Maddie's death.

The worker poses the ultimate question and reaches for clients' feelings by asking "What are we going to do with all that we're feeling?" She hopes the members will consider the impending weekend, which many will spend alone, start to think, "What am I going to do with all that I'm feeling?" and begin to share their feelings, pain, and fears with each other, to engage in the process of mutual aid.

Rose gets the point. It hits home for her, and Sarah is able to move on to verbalize what she has been thinking during the morning, about old losses. The worker moves quickly to validate Sarah's risk in saying what is really painful and moves to "lend a vision" for their work together and the potential for a positive outcome. By suggesting that the group consider talking about what Maddie meant to them, not solely what her death means to them, members are able to consider her death's impact on their lives. They begin to share the experience of previous losses, fears about their own impending death, and what the time between now and that death holds for them.

Supporting clients in taboo areas is an essential skill in work with groups of older people. The underlying value here is that death should not be a taboo area for discussion in a group of older people where death and losses are part of living, part of the developmental tasks at this stage of the life cycle. The worker also wants to present the group with a choice about how to respond to Maddie's death. Such choices and alternatives are significant elements in moral behavior in work with older people. (Lewis 1972). The worker's role in such work with older people is to assist in a process of growth that does not resemble the kind of development that took place during the preceding stages of the life cycle. Growth at this stage occurs by integration rather than expansion and is concerned with the constant imperative to seek out the meaning of life and affirm its value, even in the face of life's impending termination. Butler and Lewis eloquently state that this is not what it means to be old, but a deep understanding of what it means to be human.

The worker's conscious use of the word *we* in "What are we going to do?" points to the fact that "we" (the worker and the members of the mutual aid group) are all in this together. While there are conflicting points of view about the role of the group worker, about whether the worker is solely leader, never member, or can ever become a member-level participant in the mutual aid process, the worker's perception is that she does not relinquish her role as "worker" by expression and demonstration of the fact that she too has been touched by a member's death, and, indeed, she is part of the "we." While the worker's role remains intellectually apparent during the work, emotional support flows from worker to members and from group member to member. Members demonstrate a tremendous capacity to survive repeated painful experiences, loss after loss. This flow of feelings enhances the worker's ability to keep working as worker and group members experience together the loss of a member.

The worker also contributes facts, data, ideas, values, and information essential in all group work. Particularly in work with older people, where the need for cognitive supports has been identified, an emphasis on supplying information, such as the reminder to the group of "how difficult the weekends alone are for so many of you," demonstrates an information sharing skill that the worker has learned through her work with this group. Here, by such sharing, the worker serves as a catalyst, "lending a direction" to the work, to challenge the traditional patterns of dealing with difficult subject matter, of coping with a crisis, and of giving hope for the future. In this way the worker as confidante, leader, and participant builds future into the life of the group (Lowy 1962). The worker strives to identify, mobilize, and build on members' strengths and resilience (German and Gitterman 1996).

A motivating element in the worker's intervention here is previous knowledge through individual work with many members of the group about how they have experienced previous losses and the tremendous pain and unresolved grief many have been living with for too long. The knowledge of these histories and struggles and patterned responses greatly contributed to the worker's intervention through her understanding of individual needs as well as the group's needs. Had this information not been available, such as in the case of a newly formed group or a worker new to the group, it would have been essential for the worker to pose questions that would provide such understanding of individual and group needs.

It is important to stop for a moment and call special attention to Ruth. In the life of every group there is a member who takes on the role assumed by Ruth, who wants to move in the opposite direction, inhibit the work, and create roadblocks. The worker's experience with Ruth led her to believe that, while loss was extremely painful for her, so painful that her patterned response was to push the pain aside and pretend it was not there, it would be better to let Ruth continue in her pattern and be moved by the momentum of the group rather than the worker's intervention. Ruth makes one comment, "that's what happens when you get old, you just keep losing people," demonstrating that she has begun to enter into the mutual aid process. The worker spent considerable time with Ruth after the group session.

The worker's anticipated outcome to the suggestion for discussion, in addition to the moment of silence, is that people will begin to talk about what they are experiencing in response to Maddie's death, to remember past losses in the group and the value of sharing. The worker also anticipates that members will be able to review past losses in their private lives and begin to reminisce about some of the painful pieces of their lives that Maddie's death revives. These hoped-for outcomes derive from the thinking that, by sharing such experiences, the group will achieve greater closeness, the closeness that grows out of crisis, and is necessary to close the gap in the mutual aid network.

The worker's skill throughout is an active reaching out, an invitation to begin to talk, to demonstrate to the group their own strengths in dealing with loss, and their capacity to survive, and to lend a vision for the future. The worker is expressing to the group that time shared together is not time waiting for death, but rather a time to grow—and grow closer. In this way the worker establishes a precedent for future work together around equally difficult issues and thus builds future into the life of the group.

The following practice principles guided these interventions.

1. The worker must establish a safe space and climate for any group of older people to begin to openly discuss issues previously believed to be taboo areas.
2. Death should not be a taboo topic in group work with older people, since it is a primary element involved in this stage of the life cycle.
3. While group members may have been socialized to think of death as a taboo area, the worker must strive to challenge this thinking and enable members to begin to express thoughts and feelings in response to death.
4. In group work with older people who are visually impaired, verbal communication must be emphasized because of the missing nonverbal and visual cues that are taken for granted as part of the communication process.
5. The worker must model physical contact with group members as a supportive skill on behalf of the group.
6. The worker should enable the group to experience a level of closeness through mutual aid in the common group task of dealing with an emotionally charged issue, such as death and loss.
7. The worker should never remove the group's standard ritual of coping behavior, but rather can supplement the patterned response with an alternative coping strategy, where appropriate or necessary.

The mutual aid process continues:

BELLE: Sadie was the only one with a husband here. It's odd that she should have to die and leave him. It's so hard for a man.

SARAH: I didn't know how I would ever survive when my only daughter died last year. My husband's been dead forty years already. I'm ninety years old, and my only daughter has to die too. I thought there was no one left for me. I even stopped coming to the group last spring (*in tears*).

People continue to talk about how they have experienced other losses over the years.

> HARRY: I think we should stand up for a moment of silence now. (*Silence.*)
> WORKER: Would you like to stand up for a moment of silence?

The group and I stood up; several people said "may she rest in peace," followed by a series of amens. A long, intense silence followed as we sat down.

> WORKER: I guess what's always most difficult for me is when I feel there was no closure, that I didn't have a chance to say good-bye, and a feeling that I've been deprived of having that person here with me longer.
> TESSIE: That's what hurts so much about Maddie, that I tried and tried to call and couldn't get through. They didn't know I was calling. That's what I feel deprived of, making sure that she knew that I cared.
> ALLAN: But you've called so many times while she was sick. She knew you cared.
> RUTH: A lot of us called. At least we can feel good about that. You should feel good that she knew you cared, Tessie.
> GOLDIE: That's how I felt, deprived, when my brother died this fall. Only sixty-eight years old and so many more years to live, and died just like that of a heart attack … still working. I felt he was deprived, and I was deprived, and his wife … and children.
> HARRY: Even though it isn't logical, we feel deprived, even if you know it was better for the one who died, so they didn't have to go through so much pain. You're still deprived of having them any more. That's how it was with my wife.
> BELLE: That's how it happens, Etta, most of the time, just like that.
> JOSEPHINE: Maddie wasn't well, she had a bad heart, but she was always cheerful, didn't talk about how she felt; she really kept us going, and now she's gone.
> TESSIE: It's always good to know someone didn't suffer long, it's just hard not to have Maddie here any more.
> WORKER: We've lost someone very special. Maddie touched each of our lives in a very special way. I think we've all touched each other's lives today. We've shared an awful lot of what we're feeling.

Since it was the worker who tried to delay the moment of silence, and it is now called for again after a long and intense session of sharing, it is important that the worker support this last call for the silence when no one is quite sure how to respond to Harry.

All of us know just how difficult silence can be, as thoughts run to how will it be broken, by whom, and what is less painful—prolonged silence or an attempt to break it. The worker's task is to attempt to reach inside the silence here. It will be difficult to go on. So much has already been said, and there is a need now to begin to pull together in order for the members to be able to go on with their lives.

It is often debated how much and just what the worker should share of herself about personal information or feelings with clients, particularly in a group. The worker's willingness to share her own source of pain during such work with older people is essential to the older person's sense of worth. This worker holds strongly to the theory that, when sharing is done to move the group from where it is stuck or past a difficult moment, the expression of the worker's own feelings is facilitating and serves as a mobilizer. It was extremely difficult for the worker to know what to say at the end of the silence. The silence was probably more difficult for her than for the members, for whom it was probably momentary relief from the steady flow of emotion. Sitting down again was difficult, as though it symbolically said "OK, we've said our farewells." The worker felt, or projected, that the group was probably experiencing something similar. The worker could only think that, while the group stood in silence, members must have been considering how the day impacted on their lives, about what Maddie meant to each of them and to the group as a whole. Tessie had struggled with not having been able to reach Maddie's husband to express her concern. The worker is thinking how closely her thinking matches Tessie's: "I never had the chance to say you've been such a pleasure to know and I've learned so much from the opportunity to work with you. Thank you for that." At this point the worker decides to reach inside the silence, to share her own feelings, and to simultaneously display understanding of clients' feelings.

By saying what was always most difficult for her, the worker anticipated that members might be able to say what was most difficult for them at the moment or what typically presents a serious problem for them. The group carried its own momentum from there. Sharing a piece of self in work with older people is essential, but for more than just to move or accelerate the work. According to Burnside (1978a, b) the worker is expected to share herself. This represents symbolic giving—to replace meaning to the group where meaning is lost. The worker is constantly assessing how much to intervene, how much to share, but in group work with older people sharing the worker's own feelings helps to equalize the relationship where age difference is frequently quite obvious. It does for the worker what reminiscence does for the aged client: it establishes a working equilibrium where both the worker and members of the group feel the comfort of a safe space in which to share. It is important to achieve the right combination of personal and professional elements in the work. The right balance is experienced as genuine and human caring by the elderly.

The worker's role in the last statement is to convey a sense of accomplishment, of succeeding in what was initially unthinkable for some members and essential to others. The worker attempts to convey that everyone has invested in the mutual aid process and achieved a sense of the closeness established through this mutual aid. When the worker says "we've all touched each others' lives today," she is saying we all had something to give each other and we have all benefited from each other's humanity. Practice principles guiding these interventions may be useful for work with all age levels, but are essential in work with groups of older people.

1. The worker should share her own feelings in group work with older people in order to enable members to begin to share.

2. It is not only appropriate but essential that the worker share her own feelings with the group when the group is trying to cope with emotionally charged material in a nonpatterned response to crisis.

3. When the group experiences highly emotionally charged material, it is helpful for the worker to pull together for the group elements of the process and bring the work to closure (unless a member is able to assume this role).

WORK WITH older people around issues of loss and death is emotionally and physically intense for both the older person and the social worker. It requires the ability and willingness to tackle the pain straight on—to say what hurts—to relate the current pain to past pain—and to not only survive but continue to grow through the mutual aid process. The mutual aid process has tremendous potential to build life, vitality, and future into the life of the group. For the worker the ability to tune in to each individual group member's situation of stress and that of the group as a whole is key to successfully facilitating the mutual aid process. For the older person the support of a mutual aid network is a lifeline.

References

Auslander, G and H. Levin. 1987. The parameters of network intervention: A social work application. *Social Service Review* 6:305–18.

Barber, A. 1976. Meeting the needs of older blind adults: A method of accountability. *New Outlook for the Blind* 70(4): 166–67.

Berl, F. 1963. Growing up to be old. *Social Work* 8(1): 85–91.

Blank, M. 1979. Ageism in gerontology-land: *Journal of Gerontological Social Work* 2:5–9.

Blenkner, M. 1969. The normal dependencies of aging. In R. A. Kalish, ed., *The dependence of old people*. Detroit: Institute of Gerontology, Wayne State University.

Burnside, I. M. 1978a. *Principles from Yalom, in working with the elderly: group process and techniques*. North Scituate, Mass.: Duxbury.

———— 1978b. *Principles of the preceptor in working with the elderly: Group process and techniques*, chapter 6. North Scituate, Mass.: Duxbury.

Butler, R .N. and M. L. Lewis. 1977. *Aging and mental health: Positive psychosocial approaches*, p. 111. St. Louis: Mosby.

Cath, S. 1971. Some dynamics of middle and later years. In H. Parad, ed., *Intervention*. New York: Family Service Association of America.

Evans, R. L. and B. M. Jaureguy. 1981. Group therapy by phone: A cognitive behavioral program for visually impaired elderly. *Social Work in Health Care* 7:79–89.

Galler, E. H. 1972. A long-term support group for elderly people with low vision. *Journal of Visual Impairment and Blindness* 75:14–76.

Germain, C. B. and A. Gitterman. 1996. *The life model of social work practice: Advances in knowledge and practice.* New York: Columbia University Press.

Harshbarger, C. 1980. Group work with elderly visually impaired persons. *Journal of Visual Impairment and Blindness* 74:221–24.

Kastenbaum, R. and P. Cameron. 1969. Cognitive and emotional dependency in later life. In R. A. Kalish, ed., *The dependence of old people,* p. 41. Detroit.: Institute of Gerontology, Wayne State University.

Krupp, G. 1972. Maladaptive reactions to the death of a family member. *Social Casework* 53(7): 425.

Lessner, N. 1973. A declaration of independence for geriatric blind persons. *New Outlook for the Blind* 67:181.

Lewis, H. 1972. Morality and the politics of practice. *Social Casework* 53(7): 404–18.

Lowy, L. 1962. The group in social work with the aged. *Social Work* 7(4): 43–50.

—— 1967. Roadblocks in social work practice with older people. *Gerontologist* 7(2): 109–14.

Minkoff, H. 1972. An approach to providing services to aged blind persons. *New Outlook for the Blind* 66(3): 104–9.

Mummah, H. R. 1975. Group work with the aged blind Japanese in the nursing home and in the community. *New Outlook for the Blind* 69(4): 160–67.

Orr, A. L. 1991. Psychosocial aspects of aging and vision. In Nancy Weber, ed., *Vision and Aging: Issues in Social Work Practice.* New York: Haworth.

Orr A. L. 1998. *Issues in aging and vision: A curriculum for university programs and in-service training.* New York: AFB.

Rutter, M. 1987. Psychosocial resilience and protective mechanisms. *American Journal of Orthopsychiatry* 57(3): 316–31.

Weisman, A. D. 1972. *On dying and denying: A psychiatric study of terminality.* New York: Behavioral.

Wilson, E. L. 1972. Programming individual and adjunctive therapeutic services for visually impaired clients in a rehabilitation center. *New Outlook for the Blind* 66:215–20.

Chapter 19

The Group as a Source of Hope
Institutionalized Older Persons

Toby Berman-Rossi

G ROUP ASSOCIATION has always been an important part of the lives of institutionalized residents of long-term care facilities. Fueled with the common human need to be part of the social fabric of their collective lives, older residential inhabitants are naturally drawn to each other. For those who can no longer live in their own homes or in the homes and setting of those to whom they are known, group association has special meaning. This complex relationship between elder persons and their institutional world establishes the need for the mutual aid group in the long-term-care facility. The resulting interplay of needs provides the focus toward which social workers necessarily direct their attention.

Developmental Tasks and Issues

Views of aging have evolved over the last century and continue to do so today. Definitions have shifted between positive and negative poles, moving from older persons as wise, capable, integral members of society to descriptions of aging as a period of physical, emotional, and cognitive dependency, disengagement, loss, and decline. Inquiry has been widespread spanning many disciplines, e.g., medicine, philosophy, psychology, psychiatry, humanism, education, feminism, and social work. Definitions of the needs of older persons and recommendations for aging well emerge from these differing conceptions as do declarations of how society should attend to these needs (Reed and Clarke 1999).

Discussions on the evolution of modern thinking about aging in Western countries frequently begin with the turn of the nineteenth century (Cole 1992: Kontos 1998; Reker 2002). Over time the medical study of aging gained momentum. The examination of aging, in the form of geriatrics and gerontology, assumed legitimacy and ascendance in subsequent decades. The medical examination of aging focused upon biological and physiological aging, the study of the aged body, and organic pathologies (Kontos). Though heralded for demonstrating significant knowledge of how we age physically, in time this model came to be viewed as a deficit model. Its primary focus on the progressive deterioration of the older person's body and its presumptive ignoring of healthy older persons was believed to present a distorted view (Allert, Sponholz, Baitsch 1994).

As these ideas and foci took hold, medicine came to be the leading discipline to study older persons. Ideas shifted and a focus primarily upon negative aspects of aging rang less true. Such negativity was viewed as a form of bias with far reaching ramifications. The concept of "ageism" was a powerful idea and provided an additional basis for examining prejudice against older persons (Butler 1969). The power of this concept lay in its ability to be used as a lens through which to view how older persons were thought of and treated. Butler's (1975) Pulitzer award–winning, scathing attack on societal discrimination of older persons left no doubt that older persons in the United States were suffering from ageism.

Increasingly, criticism was heard from many quarters. The "biomedicalizing" of aging was put forth as ageist and problematic for an understanding of the wholeness of older persons and for the provision of services to them. Estes (1979), Estes and Binney (1989) and Lyman (1989) advanced the idea that the prevailing biomedically based notions of older persons were a "social construction" which neglected social and environmental aspects of aging. As late as 1997, the debate continued as to whether gerontology was based in a negative and problematic view of aging (Atchley and Lawson 1997). The view that focusing upon the negative aspects of aging neglected and negated the strengths of older persons, limited the study of non-problematic aspects of aging, and adversely colored policy and the provision of services, gained strength. The development of a "health promotion view" or "successful aging view" was believed to contribute more to older persons aging well, than the biomedicalizing of aging (Ponzo 1992). Disease prevention and health promotion for older persons, even in the case of dementia (Lyman 1989), represented a departure from traditional medical approaches (Rowe 1991).

Descriptions of "successful aging" are quite varied, and provide different bases from which to define needs and strategies of helping. In time, many disciplines expanded their purview to include how persons age well. The emphasis shifted to strengths and away from deficits. No doubt, older persons are living longer and healthier and definitions of successful aging project that we can age well, limited only by our genetic and physiological identities (Rabbit 1992). Rowe and Kahn (1997; 1998) have offered one of the more prominent definitions of successful aging. As a result of their landmark study, over a 10-year period, they put forth the idea that most persons can age well if they attend to improving their lifestyle behavior, e.g., smoking, poor diet, lack of exercise. Rowe and Kahn (1998) believe that "successful aging" includes avoiding disease and disability, sustaining high cognitive and physical functioning and maintaining high engagement with life and believe that "health and functional status in late life are increasingly seen as under our control" (Rowe 1997:368).

Undoubtedly, Rowe and Kahn's (1997, 1998) work has made us more conscious of factors that can increase our health and well being in later years and they have been instrumental in differentiating illness from "usual aging." Nonetheless their definition has come under significant criticism and is particularly troublesome when applied to older institutionalized persons who are the subject of this chapter. Minkler and Fadem (2002) believe that discussion of successful aging are problematic as they do not sufficiently pay attention to (a) aging over the life course; (b) race, class, and gender inequities; and (c) the realities and importance of losses as well as gains in later life (229). They further believe that Rowe and Kahn's definition stigmatizes persons aging with disabilities, who are already a marginalized population. Should all residents in long-term care facilities categorically consider themselves to have aged unsuccessfully? Gutheil and Congress (2002) echo this view noting that to exclude those with disabilities from inclusion in those considered to have aged successfully is to categorically deny the resilience older persons with disabilities display.

Others too have developed similar positions. Baltes (1994) offers than any single standard for "successful aging" will necessarily be inadequate. Additionally, Torres (2002) offers that singular definitions of "successful aging" are insufficiently attentive of cultural and environmental aspects of aging. She is of the belief that cultural and societal values help to determine conceptions of aging, e.g., notions of dependence and independence, indicators of strength, and a sense of obligation to others. Thus, to offer a singular definition of successful aging denies differences among cultural and societal groups and therefore is essentially ethnocentric.

If the aforementioned denotations of successful aging exclude institutionalized older persons, what alternative conceptions can help guide us in our identification of the strengths and needs of older institutionalized persons? Must this definition necessarily separate older community-dwellers from those living within institutions? Sociological, psychological, and humanist definitions hold greater promise of being more inclusive of the vast ways in which older persons' age, including those living in long-term cares facilities. Ford and colleagues (2000) note that perceived control, life satisfaction, perceived self-efficacy, cognitive functioning "coping with stress and loss . . . positive affective states, a sense of meaning in life, and maintenance of valued activities and relationship" (231) reflect a necessary psychological and sociological emphases.

Writing from an existential view, Reker (2002) concurs. He too believes the experience of successful aging is more strongly attached to having purpose and meaning in life than it is to physical, cognitive, and social well being.

He concludes that

> our focus on existential constructs provides an explanation as to why many older adults continue to age well in the face of difficult life situations. The ability to find meaning and purpose in life and to accept death as a natural part of life offers promising ways of transcending personal and social losses, culminating in heightened feelings of well-being, life satisfaction, and overall adjustment. (61)

Others too have also noted a strong association between a sense of purpose and meaning in life and living well. For example, Sarvimaki and Stenbock-Hult (2000) defined quality of life " . . . as a sense of well being, meaning and value" (1025). Solomon and Peterson (1994) note viewing one's life as meaningful as a critical element of living well. They suggest that a sense of purpose strengthens a person's ability to endure enormous hardship. One of the most poignant descriptions of the connection between the power of purpose and meaning in life, the ability to endure hardship, and the will to live, is Frankl's (1963) description of his experiences, and those of others, while in a concentration camp. There, under the most unimaginable conditions, people found meaning in life and the strength to continue. Of course such motivation did not determine whether people lived or died. But Frankl's observation that finding meaning in life *was* necessary for survival has great importance for social workers working with clients facing great adversity. He writes, "There is much wisdom in the words of Nietzsche: 'He who has a *why* to live for can bear almost any *how*.' I can see in those words a motto that holds true . . . that those who knew there was a task waiting for them to fulfill were most apt to survive" (164–65). Mattering to others provides a strong force strengthening the will to live.

Thus, we ask, what are the tasks of aging; what strengthens the will to live and the development and sustaining of meaning in the lives of older residential inhabitants? What increases life satisfaction and morale, associated with a sense of having lived well (Leonard 1981)? What promotes what Frankl (1963) describes as self-transcendence rather than self-actualization, namely, finding meaningful connections to something greater than oneself? "The *existential* questions about meaning are part of the human quest for a vision within which one's experience makes sense" (Cole 1992:xviii). Ultimately we ask what vision of life in the residential setting residents shall develop. Will life seem meaningful or meaningless? How shall we support older residents as they pursue "the journey of life" and the task of sustaining meaning and purpose in their lives?

Within these larger areas of meaning, purpose, and self-transcendence, what needs do older persons living within the institution have? The needs of these residents emerge from the joining of two powerful life streams: aging and institutionalization. It is the combination of these two aspects of the residents' lives that intertwine and shape their search for a meaningful life. These two streams provide the grounds for our work with older residents within the long-term care facility. This combining of the personal and environmental is a central theme in the lives of older persons living within institutional environments. "It is the adaptation of individual people measured against a specific environment and its demands that determine success (Baltes 1994:197). Thus, successful aging is possible for all persons. Lustbader (1999–2000) provides a very poignant discussion on the "meaning of frailty." Her subtext of "how will I let my caregivers know who I am?" places us closer to understanding the needs of those institutionalized. These needs are imbedded in our identification of life tasks of older institutionalized persons.

Using Schwartz's (1971) definition of tasks as *"a set of needs converted into work . . . "* (7), we suggest these needs give rise to a set of life tasks designed to assist with moving into and sustaining institutional living arrangements, one of the most consequential life transitions possible. These tasks can be grouped as follows:

- Task of establishing personalized relationships with caregivers;
- Task of establishing and sustaining meaningful relationships and connections with others;
- Task of remaining involved in one's life, exercising choice, and sustaining one's preferences;
- Task of using help;
- Task of becoming recognized by others;
- Task of sustaining ones identity and making ones self known to others;
- Task of contributing to others and maintaining meaningful roles;
- Task of living with increased loss, growing uncertainty, and significant role shifts as future time diminishes.

Vulnerabilities and Risk Factors and Resiliencies and Protective Factors

Resiliency is a complex concept. It concerns the ability of an individual, family, group, and community to "bounce back" as part of a response to grappling with significant challenges, crises, and adversities. There is no single component of this idea that accounts for such resilience. Rather, it is the distinctive ways in which risk and vulnerability, and protective factors, mechanisms, and processes come together in the lives of individuals, families, groups, and communities that foster or constrain resiliency (Rutter 1987). What is particularly powerful about this concept is that there are multiple ways to strengthen resiliency, thereby offering social workers and group members many possibilities. Briefly stated, Cowan, Cowan and Schulz 1996 indicate that risk refers to the probability of a negative outcome taking place in a specific population, whereas vulnerability "increases the probability of a specific negative outcome or undesirable outcome in the presence of risk" (10). This means that risk only achieves its potency in the presence of vulnerability factors. How do these ideas apply to our population? Our discussion centers on three questions:

1. What increased risks and vulnerabilities do older persons experience when entering and when living within a long-term care facility; and how can their negative effects be mitigated;
2. What personal, interpersonal, and environmental protective processes, mechanisms, and factors can be brought to bear so that the negatives effects of risk and vulnerability can be offset and the resilience of older institutionalized persons can be strengthened;
3. What part can mutual aid groups play in strengthening the resiliency of older institutionalized persons?

Gitterman (2001a) notes that protective factors include "temperament, family patterns, external supports, and environmental resources" (17). Conversely, each of these components can operate in exactly the opposite fashion. As well, just as the risks and vulnerabilities of a younger life continue and are exacerbated in old age, so too do these follow older persons from the community into the institution. Paradoxically, as significant risks and vulnerabilities increase with admission into a nursing home, potentially so too do the protective factors, mechanisms, and processes. As individuals face new risks and develop new vulnerabilities they also develop new opportunities to strengthen resilience (Cowan, Cowan, and Schulz 1996). It is this mix of potentialities that increase the challenge, and satisfaction, of working with older persons within institutions.

The following list is not intended to be exhaustive; rather it is intended to familiarize the reader with the context in which the mutual aid group, within the long-term care facility achieves its power.

Risk

Generally, institutionalization brings with it an increased risk for morbidity, an increased risk of the deleterious effects from chronic illness and disability, and an increase in abuse, neglect, and death (Berman-Rossi 2001). These risks are particularly acute for women as the disadvantages accrued in a long life are brought with them to, and exacerbated by, life in a total institution. Within these categories, the following risks apply.

- Longer life, particularly for women, becomes a risk when associated with increased morbidity, chronic illness, disability, and institutionalization (Padgett, Burns, Grau 1998; Tauber and Allen 1993);
- The risk of abuse and neglect increases with advanced age, dependence, problematic drinking, self-blame, and extreme loyalty to caregivers (Kosberg 1988).

- The risk of physical, sexual, psychological, financial abuse and neglect, acts of omission are associated with old age and increase with age (Kosberg 1988; Roe 2002)
- The risk of institutionalization rises with advanced age, the need for ambulatory aids, increased mental deterioration, the need for assistance with activities of daily living, and living alone (Branch and Jettte 1982).
- The risk of unmet mental health needs and for inappropriate treatment, particularly for women who comprise the majority of persons in long-term institutions (Padgett, Burns, Grau 1998);
- Risk for women of social devaluation (Padgett, Burns, Grau 1998);
- The risk of increased depression, associated with social isolation (Feldman and Netz 1997; Tauber and Allen 1993);
- Risk of poor medical care as only a small portion of the budget of the National Institutes of Health is spent on women's health (Lamphere-Thorpe and Blendon 1993).
- Risk of an exacerbation of social oppression.
- Increased dependence brings with it a greater risk of decreased control over ones life.
- Ageism increases with institutional life (Feldman and Netz 1997).
- With lessened environmental control there is a risk of increased bodily preoccupation (Bergeman and Wallace 1999).

Taken together these risks point to the complex interplay among personal, interpersonal, and environmental factors which when combined serve as a cumulative disadvantage increasing the overall risk for morbidity, an increased risk of the deleterious effects from chronic illness and disability, and an increase in abuse, neglect, and death.

VULNERABILITY

Negative outcomes include:

- Hopelessness can increase morbidity and death (Engel 1968; Lieberman and Tobin 1983; Neeman 1995)
- Diminished roles and physical decline increase vulnerability to learned helplessness (Foy and Mitchell 1990).
- A perception of low control can increase depression and illness (Bergeman and Wallace 1999).
- Decreased contact with kin increases the risk of institutionalization (Freedman, Berkman, Rapp, and Osfeld 1994).
- Loss of family places one at risk for isolation.
- A depletion of roles contributes to a diminution of status and power and is its necessary accompaniment (Blenkner 1977).
- Loss of identity increases physical and psychological decline (Kaufman 1986).

- Decreasing social contacts fosters depersonalization (Coe 1965).
- Passivity increases vulnerability to environmental stressors (Tobin and Lieberman 1976).
- Dependence upon institutional supports increases as loss of social relationships increases (Blenkner 1977).
- Prolonged cumulative stress weakens body and soul (Gitterman 2001b).
- Diminished physical, emotional, and psychological strength increases dependence upon variable institutional caregivers.

These vulnerabilities alert us to the intricate relation among psychosocial factors and their impact on physical health. What is most striking is the interplay among these vulnerability factors and their reciprocal influence on increasing risk for older institutionalized persons.

Protective Factors

Applied to our population, "resiliency theory's hopefulness emerges, not from a denial of risk or vulnerability, but from a recognition that protective factors and processes can protect against risks inherent in the aging experience, particularly for women and minority older persons" (Berman-Rossi 2001:745).

- Openness to change and flexibility foster a wider repertoire of coping mechanisms (Bergeman and Wallace 1999).
- The more hopeful the individual, the greater the perceived control over a stressor (Neeman 1995).
- Hardiness reduces stress (Bergeman and Wallace 1999).
- A sense of positive well being decreases mortality (Janoff and Ronnie 1982).
- A positive and sustained sense of self, contributes to a sense of well being (Bergeman and Wallace 1999).
- Social support fosters mental and physical health (Bergeman and Wallace 1999).
- Family support promotes a sense of well-being and provides instrumental and expressive assistance (Bergeman and Wallace 1999).
- A sense of giving to family and community strengthens a sense of well being by strengthening the experience of reciprocity (Bergeman and Wallace 1999).
- The pursuit of happiness fosters a sense of contentment and continuous growth (Shmotkin 1998).
- Assertion fosters survival in all areas (Tobin and Lieberman 1976).
- Positive interaction with the environment fosters the development of competence (Germain 1987; Germain and Gitterman 1996).
- Increased control decreases the sense of trauma associated with change (Pastalan 1983).

- Hopefulness and perceived control over a stressor decrease the possibility that negative events will have harmful effects (Neeman 1995).
- Active coping and mastery experiences buffer against adversity and increase resilience (Cowan, Cowan, and Schulz 1996).
- Social relationships increase in importance as roles become fewer with aging (George 1980).
- New opportunities assume greater importance as loss of relationships and support increase with increased age (Blenkner 1977).
- Perceptions of control increase a positive sense of the quality of life (Perlmutter and Eads 1998) and decreases trauma associated with change (Pastalan 1983).
- The opportunity for exercising choice contributes to a strengthened sense of self (Perlmutter and Eads 1998).
- A sense of stability offsets the unpredictability and uncertainty associated with aging.
- Differences in power are mediated by a personal connection between client and worker (Kaufman 1986; Nahemow 1983).

The totality and control characteristic of institutional life and dependence upon institutional caregivers combine with the psychosocial and physical factors older persons bring to institutional life, to increase the probability of increased morbidity, abuse, neglect, and death unless there are sufficient countervailing protective factors, processes, and mechanisms which exert a buffering force. The mutual aid group is one such powerful force that serves to offset the injurious effects of institutionalization upon older persons. The mutual aid group stands at the center of collective empowerment. Its attributes are ideally suited to strengthen the resiliency of older institutionalized persons. There are many generic discussions of mutual aid in the literature (Gitterman 1989; Lee and Swenson 1994; Schwartz 1994 [1961]; Shulman 1999; Steinberg 1997). Inherent within these mutual aid group definitions, are three factors, numerous processes and mechanisms critical to enhancing the lives of our group members. Our first three factors position the older person in a positive place to counter the negative valuations generated by institutional life. As such, these factors have far reaching value essential to the lives of this population. First, is the idea that the group is a system of mutual aid in which members help each other. Such a conception intrinsically conveys the belief that older persons are capable of assisting each other. This belief provides the basis for dispelling what often is a profound sense of devaluation associated with advanced age and life within a nursing home. Second, is the idea that mutual aid as a process is based in support, affirmation, and belief that every group member has strengths that can apply to the tasks at hand (Gitterman 1989). Such a process is especially well suited for older women who exhibit a very high level of unmet mental health needs (Padgett, Burns, and Grau

1998). This idea as well, provides the basis for workers and members to make claims on each other for assistance with essential life tasks. Third, is the idea that in a mutual aid group there is a multiplicity of helping relationships thereby decreasing hierarchical power and increasing egalitarian power. Under such conditions group members are strengthened individually and collectively and are more likely to make demands upon others in their environment.

These three factors and the ten specific characteristics of the mutual aid group identified by Shulman (1999) are at the heart of the protective factors, mechanisms, and processes the mutual aid group provides those living in long-term care residences. Taken together, these elements of the mutual aid group promote "the development of mutual support, reciprocal dependence, shared experiences and feelings" which are "sources of community and cohesion and are the basis for social organization" (Kontos 1998:174). As well, the mutual aid group provides an important antidote to the social oppression in the larger society (Brown and Mistry 1994). Providing a socially supportive environment through the provision of supportive groups strengthens ones sense of purpose in life.

Agency and Group Context

Our setting is a non-profit, long-term care facility. It has a service tradition going back more than 125 years of serving older persons in New York City by providing a wide range of community and institutional services at two locations. It is toward a group of thirty-eight long-term residents, living on the same skilled nursing floor, that our attention is directed. At the outset, it should be noted that the services provided by this long-term care facility, including a large cadre of MSW social workers, far exceeds the norm in nursing home settings. More than 80 percent of the nursing homes in this country are for-profit institutions. Most of these facilities provide only the minimum staffing patterns required for licensure and most do not employ a social work designee with social work training. Under these conditions, accusations of financial mismanagement, neglect, brutality, and fraud are common place (Garner 1995).

The thirty-eight residents under discussion closely fit this description: their average age is eighty-six, 87 percent are single (18.5 percent never married, 68.5 percent widowed), 92 percent (thirty-five) are supported primarily by public funds (Medicaid), and all suffer from a multiplicity of chronic physical illnesses. Signs of emotional stress and changes in cognitive abilities are present in most. This is not to suggest, as Fooken(1982) cautions, that older women generally are illness-stricken and hypochondriacal but rather to characterize those most frequently living in nursing homes. Over the last 40 years, these data have remained reflective of those institutionalized in nursing homes (Gottesman and Hutchinson 1974; Jacelon 1995; and Wesson 1965).

For these residents, this nursing home is their last home. What kind of world is a home for the aged? Toward what does it aspire? A long-term-care facility combines elements of two kinds of institutional settings: a hospital and a residential treatment center, both of which are total institutions. The treatment of illness and the sense of total residence have profound effects on the lives of inhabitants. Goffman (1961) identifies homes for the aged as one kind of "total institution." As a total institution, a home for the aged cuts off residents from the greater society, formally directs and administers maximal aspects of inhabitants' lives, provides a life of incredible sameness for most participants, and dispenses its authority from above through a formal system of rules and regulations. The net result is "a kind of dead sea in which little islands of vivid encapturing activity appear. Such activity can help the individuals withstand the psychological stress usually engendered upon the self." (69).

Uhlenberg (1997) is more scathing. Noting myriad ways the nursing home is unlike a home and the fact that residents receive an average of nine minutes of service per day from a registered nurse, he concludes that "these institutions are costly, inhospitable structures, failing to meet the needs of the persons who must spend their last weeks or years of life in them because better alternatives are not available" (73).

Consequently, institutional environments are sought which will allow, as much as possible, the influence of residents as a mitigating force against institutional totality. A highly valued milieu seeks to strike a better balance between the concentration of power in staff and the consequent loss of decision making on the part of inhabitants. Institutionalization removes older persons from the life situation in which they previously maintained the role of decision maker. It does not change the need of older persons to remain meaningfully involved in thinking about, working on and planning for their lives. The need to be in charge of one's life is a common human need. Institutionalization does not eliminate this need, though the expression of it and opportunities for satisfaction of it might change. It is these aspects of the nursing home as a "total institution" that provide the environment in which needs and tasks for inhabitants are generated.

Into an institutional atmosphere with its elements of totality enter those for whom available community health care services are not sufficient to offset dwindling physical, mental, social, emotional, and economic resources. As with the community aged, experiences of loss and challenge predominate. It is not with a sense of accomplishment that older persons enter nursing homes. Fried (1963), in speaking about the effects of forced relocation, poignantly writes that responses to loss

> are manifest in the feelings of painful loss, the continued longing, the general depressive tone, frequency of psychological or social or somatic distress,

the active work required in adapting to the altered situation, the sense of helplessness, the occasional expressions of both direct and displaced anger, and tendencies to idealize the lost place. At their most extreme, these reactions of grief are intense, deeply felt, and, at times, overwhelming. (151)

There is a rise in disequilibria that continues into admission and begins to characterize the first few months of institutional life. The psychological state is one of lessened hope, more body preoccupation, a view of oneself as powerless and vulnerable, and identification with sick older persons. It is as if the older person searches to understand and integrate the forthcoming role and status. Prior roles do not prepare older persons for institutional life because within their community lives they are among the least regimented, least structured, and least observed members of society (Bennett 1963). This depressive view poses special challenges to the long-term-care facility during the first two months of the older person's institutional life.

Tobin and Lieberman's (1976) study of the effects of institutionalization on those institutionalized, remains one of the most poignant such descriptions in the literature. Noting that total institutions always generate harmful effects on inhabitants, they believe there is no way for older persons to escape 1. identifying with those who are sicker, 2. perceiving their own increasing need for care, 3. being closer to death, 4. possessing a limited and uncontrollable future, 5. participating with others, which sometimes leads to an increase in conflict, and 6. experiencing receding family members. While inescapable, there is a wide range of responses to institutionalization. The major task of the institutionalized aged, as with the community aged, is continuance of a meaningful life in the face of enormous change and an uncertain future. In the first year of placement, a significant percentage of those admitted die or deteriorate mentally and physically. Passive individuals are particularly vulnerable (Tobin and Lieberman 1976). It is in this context that the mutual aid group offsets some of the negative effects of institutionalization and gains its imperative.

The following story will illustrate. Miss Anspacher, a ninety-one-year-old woman, was transferred to the long-term-care facility after a six-month hospitalization following a hip fracture. She was admitted weighing seventy-six pounds, with a barely audible voice and multiple decubiti, and was severely contracted. Her eighty-nine year old sister, with whom she had lived all her life, had recently died, unbeknownst to her. Her only living relative, a seventy-three year-old niece, was stressed from visiting both aunts, closing their apartment containing a lifetime's possessions, and contending with her own aging. While we provided a high level of medical and nursing care, ministering to Miss Anspacher's emotional wounds became harder as time passed. She rarely spoke verbally. As she withdrew further, so did the Home's staff, finding it increasingly more difficult to sustain both sides of the relationship. The technical services offered by medicine and nursing could not counter Miss Anspacher's persistent feeling that "no one special" loved her and therefore life was not worth living. She slipped quietly to her death one evening during sleep, three months after admission. While the institution did not cause her death, it could not prevent it. Unable and not desiring to make demands upon her institutional world, Miss Anspacher became increasingly dependent upon the advances of a team already working hard to attend to the demands of the thirty-seven other more vocal residents. Encouraging her to assert herself on her own behalf became more difficult and less frequent. Assertion is required for survival in institutional life. Passivity, depression, and withdrawal are all more likely to be associated with decline and death. Believing that one's life is over can actually help that life to end.

Acknowledging the hardness of institutional life, we ask several questions of this setting serving older persons:

- To what extent will this "new society" reflect the old? To what extent will it attempt to generate and create new life? Is the institution a place to wait for death, or is it a place to look forward to for the rest of one's life?
- Can the nursing home stop a continuous process of loss of significant persons by helping to supply meaningful others?
- To what extent can the long-term-care facility increase the older person's repertoire of roles and sense of well-being?
- To what extent can the institution help older persons feel that their life matters to others?
- And finally can it help to restore a lessened sense of meaning where life once again will be worth living?

The institution therefore can mirror and collude with the older person's dreaded view of institutional life as a "holding place" prior to death, or it can align itself with the older person's hope that institutional life will indeed be meaningful. To align itself with the positive side of the aged resident's ambivalence would result in acknowledging, but working against, the feared belief that nursing home admission is tantamount to death.

Like the immigrants most of them once were, newly admitted residents again become strangers in a strange land. Entering alone, without status and with a predominance of liabilities, new residents find an uncertain future that requires the tasks of establishing friendships, becoming oriented to surroundings, establishing role identities, and responding to the unequal balance of power between caregivers and care receivers. While the long-term resident must ultimately arrive at some resolution in relation to these tasks, life in this new home never really becomes easy. The unknown always looms ahead for those institutionalized, highlighting the existential nature of their lives. Calm can be abruptly altered by staff reassignments, the death of a friend, the admission of a new roommate, changes in the menu, or countless unknown possibilities. The greater the residents' reliance on the external environment, the greater is the possibility of this environment becoming a significant stressor.

Within the long-term facility, group association is fueled by needs that have always stimulated movement toward collectivity. Taken away from their previous society and denied familiar supports, the sense of insecurity in the older person rises dramatically. The impetus to band together against "the powers that be" is a natural outcome of the need to survive and reflects heightened vulnerability, as well as the potential for strengthened relationships. Interestingly, while group association offers a buffer against institutional life, it also simultaneously provides an organized means for making use of agency service. In fact, it becomes the mode of institutional living. Schwartz (1969) has described this impetus as follows:

> In the individual's struggle to negotiate the various systems of demand and opportunity that his society offers him, he will, whenever it is made possible, enlist the aid of persons with similar systems to manage. The peer group— or the mutual aid system—then becomes a way of helping him negotiate the larger system and getting what it was designed to offer him.   (38)

If allowed and even encouraged, the movement of persons will be toward each other. At the same time, there are significant obstacles to group association. The totality of the institutional environment promotes total dependence upon staff for satisfaction of critical life needs. Under these conditions residents can consider group association hazardous.

Forman (1971) concurs, suggesting that

> the peer group can become the most important and influential environmental factor for a resident, particularly if it is the only social system available to him in whom he can experience an ego-building alternative to the deprecatory image presented to him by the institution.   (48)

Institutionalized residents face the challenge of establishing and living within their new society. Whether this new world will reflect increasing alienation and estrangement from the mainstream of life, or will offer new opportunities for friendship, meaningful activity, and mutuality is critical in determining the quality of life offered those living in long-term-care facilities.

The quality of life offered inhabitants is heavily influenced by the long-term-care facility itself. The facility stands as a microcosm of the larger society, reflecting both positives and negatives. With its hierarchically ordered structure, ministering to an increasingly infirm population within a medical setting, it also becomes subject to the abuses of power.

Understanding the life-giving potential of mutual aid groups, the nursing home assigned social workers to specific floors, and to all the individual residents on that floor. Resident floor groups were established on each unit, based upon the thinking that each floor represented a building, a block, a community of like persons among whom the ties were potentially quite strong. A unit of thirty-eight residents needing skilled nursing care would become like family to each other, and like family would reflect all the advantages and liabilities inherent within that close association.

The resident floor group was a weekly, voluntary group, open-ended group for all 38 residents living on a particular floor within the Home. While membership changed somewhat each week, the group was open only to the finite number of persons who lived with each other on a specific floor. The group had the function of helping residents work on troubles, concerns, and issues which arose out of their being older persons living on the same floor in a long-term-care facility. It had features of both open and close-ended groups. While the group was offered only to members on a particular floor (and thus close-ended), membership often changed from week to week, depending upon who was able to come from the floor (and thus open-ended). Death, illness, and the admission of new residents, also made for changing group membership.

The range of issues would be potentially vast, as vast as the real issues in their lives: aging, illness, loss, service-delivery problems, peer relationships, family, and friendships, and death and dying, to name but a few. The meetings might resemble a small town meeting or a more intimate family gathering, depending upon the issues with which the group was working. The social worker's role would be to help residents do their work, as the group members worked to make their way through issues of importance in their lives. The group would be a living testimony to the reality that older persons, like persons of all ages, could join together in common cause devoted to improving the quality of their lives. As such, the group would allow for the development of positive social roles, would give continued expression for the creative talents of its members, and most importantly would serve to provide a source of hope, countering the potential isolation and estrangement so possible within the institution. Perhaps the most far-reaching benefit of the group would be as the residents own means for protecting their interests. In a potentially large way, the residents could achieve some increased power, thereby decreasing their experience of being totally dependent upon the Home. As such, the group could decrease the resident's experience of being at the mercy of staff. Increasing the means for residents to make strong claims on the Home would go a long way to equalizing the imbalance of power between the residents and the Home. In this way justice, not mercy could be pursued.

Thus, the mutual aid group becomes a source of hope and is illustrated in the following section from a resident floor group meeting.

About fifteen minutes of discussion occurred in which Mr. Posner and Mr. Katz raised for discussion the behavior of a group member, who due to his severe Alzheimer's could no longer distinguish between his property and that of others. Mrs. Brophy, another resident whose husband also was suffering from Alzheimer's, seemed stressed by the discussion. The worker noticed that Mrs. Brophy was getting upset and said that he could see that what was happening had upset her greatly. She said, "Yes, yes, it does. He is obviously very limited and not sure of what he is doing. He's not stealing because he wants to steal. He is stealing because he doesn't know any better and perhaps this should have been brought up privately with him some time." Mr. Marlin quickly came to the man's defense in the same way. "He really doesn't know what he is doing." Most of the group members were shaking their heads, but Mr. Posner and Mr. Katz were still angry.... Mr. Posner said to them, "We trust each other here in the group and this is about the only place we can talk about anything like this. We all understand that Mr. Schwerner is a limited person. We re not going to hurt him or anything like that . . . but we have no other place."[1]

The group provides the opportunity for real work to occur. Unpleasant work, conflictual work, angry work, and tender work—all must have avenues for expression. The resident floor group provides that avenue.

While the group offers continued opportunity for communion, social work efforts are very much influenced by the special meaning of group experience for institutionalized older persons. Five characteristics stand out.

1. Each person is dealing with the complex feelings generated by the aging experience, institutionalization, and by feelings generated by challenge, change, opportunity, loss, and unpredictability. Change can bring feelings of insecurity, and the need for experiences through which the sense of a competent self is continued and strengthened. As well, new situations provide opportunity and challenge. Opening oneself to others is the vehicle for receiving from others.

2. Each person is dealing with the possibility that the group experience may offer him or her something they cannot receive alone. To receive from the group, exposure and giving are necessary. To receive from the group, openness to others is necessary. To receive from the group, openness to connection and new relationships is necessary.

3. Group members are responding to their awareness that the group may be a source of hope through which the possibility of change exists. For many being closer to death than ever before brings with it a special impetus for investment.

4. Members' needs for communication, connection, sustained meaning, and personal, interpersonal, and environmental change have a stronger chance of being met through collective effort than through working alone.

5. The group becomes the primary means for creating the world in which older persons want to live, a world where connections and influence are strengthened

and loneliness and alienation decline. Under such conditions, residents' resiliency is strengthened.

These characteristics of group experience for the institutionalized older persons have serious implications for practice, as we labor to help older persons in their work. They prompt the need for the social work practitioner to

1. Recognize and deal with the feelings, which are a result of the personal, interpersonal, and environmental changes experienced;
2. Understand the very real existential nature of our practice, as work can be cut off at any point by death;
3. Recognize and respond to the tremendous potential of the group experience for the older persons, as well as the ongoing fear that this enterprise may simply be one more failure;
4. And finally, to view the group and the long-term-care facilities as a microcosm of the larger society and through our efforts join with older persons in the creation of their new world.

The existential nature of the lives of older persons is illustrated in the following vignettes.

Many years ago, at the end of my first group meeting with older persons (average age eighty-four), I said to the members that I would see them next week. Mrs. Gross rose slowly, turned, looked at me, and said, "God willing." She slowly continued walking. I was stunned. Could it mean that she did not know from week to week whether she would be alive? What was it like to live with the reality that life might end at any instant? I was only twenty-nine years old and had just given birth to my first daughter. I could hardly grasp the meaning of what had just occurred between us. It would be a while before I understood how this incident would affect our work together, individually, and in the group.

And

A seventy-three-year-old daughter with a ninety-seven-year-old institutionalized mother with Alzheimer's disease said as she was struggling with the pain of their separation, "My mother is lucky to have me. Whom do I have? My husband is dead. I have no family. What happens if I wake up one morning and I cannot manage? Who will care for me? Who will even know? I have no one."

Work and Group Themes

While themes in the resident floor groups are many, environmental themes often predominate. The negotiation of the environmental world remains an overriding concern for institutional inhabitants. Such discussion offers the possibility of exercising some control in their lives. During fifteen years of working with residents in such groups, food-related concerns have been a central part of the content of group meetings. For this reason efforts to deal with food-related issues will be our focus here.

MEALS AND MEALTIMES

Meals and mealtimes were an important part of institutional life. In the main, they were felt to be a constant, something, on which residents could count. Perceived problems in food preparation, meal presentation, and menu selection were experienced harshly by residents. Having had a lifetime of preparing their own meals in their own kitchens, residents approached food with a highly developed sense of how it ought to be. For many, particularly the women, meal preparation was an area of former competence. While they could no longer carry out their own food preparations, they had not lost a sense of how they felt they would, if they had the opportunity. The Dietary Department, in recognition of varied food preferences and the value of choice in activities of daily living, presented a wide assortment of foods from which to choose. Residents who were able made out menus for all meals. Others had their food preferences communicated to the floor dietitian. Dietitians appeared at lunch and dinner, trying to be available for ongoing reactions.

Understanding how strongly residents felt about their food, as well as the complexity of diminishing taste sensations, prevalence of dentures, and various special diets ordered by the medical staff, the Dietary Department agreed to meet regularly with the chief of social service and a committee of Resident Council delegates to work on food-related concerns. This joint committee, which had been in existence for several years, had been successful in bringing about many satisfying changes. It was not unusual for new recipes to be brought to meetings for sampling prior to being served throughout the house. Residents could even have their favorite recipes tested for use. One could conclude that much was being done to make meals satisfying.

NO ONE CARES

Nonetheless; most of the verbal residents on this skilled nursing floor who did complain did so bitterly. They continued to feel that "if the Home cared" about them, things would be better. Over and over they asked, "Why did problems persist?" Explanations of the complexity of feeding 514 persons, three times a day, carried little weight. At the point we pick up the group, I had been meeting weekly with the members for five years. The process here picks up after many group meetings with complaints but no action.

IS CHANGE POSSIBLE?

September 10—Food problems were again raised. Problems enumerated. I said they had brought up these complaints many times. What did they want to do about them? Without too much deliberation, they indicated they wanted to have the director of Dietary attend the meeting. I discussed their request with the director, who agreed to her staff attending the meeting.

September 24—Two weeks later the floor dietitian and the supervising dietitian appeared. Problems were identified. Discussion was fast and furious. My activity centers on the common ground between them. The meeting ended on a hopeful note. In the next few weeks, food problems were overshadowed by discussion of the death of a favorite member and the difficulties of living with a new admission with Alzheimer's. In addition, the residents prided themselves on their sense of fair play and wanted to give Dietary "a chance."

DISCOURAGEMENT AGAIN

October 15—Mrs. Mann once again brought up problems with the food and broke a momentary quiet in the group meeting. She said that things were always the same, nothing ever changed. There was no point in trying, she insisted; they had been trying for years and nothing ever changed. Her comments brought forth a flood of similarly negative comments. Residents spoke about the futility of further efforts. It was at that moment that I sensed something different in the group's life. Discouragement had mounted. Residents were sitting dead center on their feelings. I sensed that my vision as to the possibility of change was being called upon in a way that it had not been before. If the residents were to continue working on a matter of concern to them, I would need both to acknowledge and to help them move beyond their discouragement. Reaching inside the silence was important. Within the quiet were nagging feelings of despair and discouragement. The power of these feelings obscured all hope. Within myself I, too, was not sure how change would occur. Much effort had already being extended on the Home's part; yet change was insufficient for the residents. Although the steps were unclear to me, I firmly believed that through the process of engagement between residents and the Home, change could occur. Perhaps the three-minute eggs would never be perfect, and the toast might never stay warm and soft by the time it reached the floor, but some positive change could occur. And so the work continued. Keeping my faith in the possibility of change would be imperative. Holding to my mediating function was a requirement.

WHAT'S THE USE?

After a barrage of negatives and the elaboration of discouragement, the following occurred: I listened for a while and when there was a lull I said, "I have been listening to you express these complaints for a long time. . . . Even though you just spoke with Dietary staff a few weeks ago in the group meeting, you still feel things are not better?" Similar negatives came forth. "What do you want to do about feelings that things aren't getting better?" Many persons began talking at the same time: "Why bother? What's the use? There's no point." Comments were not new. There was a silence, and I sensed they were waiting for me to speak.

I said I know how discouraged they became, how they hated it when meals were not better for them, or not enough better, and while I didn't know if things would get better, I did think that what they were feeling didn't feel very good. I was concerned that those feelings would just fester and grow if they didn't try and make things better. Once again all the discouragement was expressed. I was struck by the reality that no one in the group was saying anything positive.

Finally someone challenged me and asked if I thought they could make things better. I said I wasn't sure, but I had worked at the Home for a long time and I did think the Dietary Department wanted their meals to be satisfying, but there were real, hard problems on which they were working. The problems raised were not easy to resolve. I quickly mentioned some. I further said that if they withdrew from working with Dietary, that department would be left to figure things out all by themselves, and then what they felt and wanted might not even be known to the kitchen.

They thought for a moment, seemed challenged and asked to whom they should speak. We went through the various possibilities: Floor Dietitian, Supervisor, Assistant Director, Director, and ultimately Administration. They said they had spoken with all those persons. What made it so hard for them to try again, I wondered? A combination of: "There's no point," to "we don't want them to turn us down," came forth. "Are you afraid they won't care?" "Yes, yes," they replied. "If Dietary cared, the problem wouldn't be there to begin with." I was silent for a moment as the force of what they were saying struck me. I said I wasn't sure I agreed with them, though I could understand that it felt that way. I thought institutions were complex places and it wasn't always easy to figure out things. They continued listening. Didn't they sometimes think I didn't do what they wanted me to do? Yet, they pretty much thought I cared. They seemed thoughtful. I waited. The room was hushed. All twenty-four persons seemed to be in thought, though I certainly wasn't sure what they were thinking. I broke the silence and said, "How about one more chance? One more try! Not doing anything leaves you in a lousy spot. I know you are worried about no one listening, but I do think the Home cares, and I would like to help you talk to them one more time."

TAKING A CHANCE

Reluctantly the members agreed. I helped them strategize about whom to contact. They asked me to speak with the director of Dietary for them. I agreed, sensing that to insist they invite her directly would have taxed them beyond their present ability. Further feelings of impotence might have developed. If they could feel they were activating me on their behalf, they might feel more potent. After all, the social service system was not beyond the systems they had to negotiate, but rather was part of them. My role included helping them use me. There was a pause. I told them I thought they were terrific and that I really thought they had a chance by sticking together and joining forces as they were going to do now. The mood in the group had lifted. Some members recalled other things that had gotten better after they had worked on them in the group. Group members left on a more hopeful note.

I found myself working very hard during this meeting. Discouragement was a formidable force. I sensed strongly that this was the time to confront their hopelessness head on. To allow it to go unchallenged would have had consequences beyond their concerns about food. If they could not challenge food issues in their lives, how could they challenge the harder, subtler aspects of living within an institution? Those issues such as resident-staff relationships, family relationships, and diminishing abilities all needed strength to engage. Strength could come from successfully working on more "manageable" aspects of their lives. Though it would have been easy to tell residents that I thought things would definitely get better, an illusion about change would have been destructive. All I could really offer was my belief that the agency cared and that working on troubles would feel better than not. I would credit even the smallest efforts, hoping to encourage their viewing themselves as potent. My contribution was to help in the process, not to guarantee outcomes.

And so a year of concerted work in this area began. Of course, many other issues were also worked on throughout the year but none so consistently offered the opportunity for residents to develop their collective strength, determine what was of importance to them, and think through ways of articulating their needs. I was also beginning to see that if work on food concerns was to continue, it would take discipline, belief in group process, a vision of service, and a focus upon the dialogue between residents' needs and the Home's service. Without worker attentiveness, residents could easily lapse into their discouraged frame of mind.

OUTSIDE THE GROUP

During the next few weeks, at the residents' request, I sent an invitation to the director of Dietary, inviting her to a floor group meeting on November 13. Prior to the meeting, she and I reviewed particular problems residents had cited, some prior sources of discouragement, and my pressing hard for them to move beyond their weariness to agree to invite her. It was most important that both residents and Dietary be tuned in to the issues for discussion, as well as possible obstacles in the process of working together. Feelings would be riding high on both sides. Feelings of discouragement, anger, rejection, disappointment, and some tiny rays of hope might be present. My function would be to attend to the dialogue between residents and Dietary. Despite the pulls, I could not side with either party but would focus attention on the talk between them. To do less would be to lose the other. I recalled a previous discussion with residents where:

BIDS FOR WORKER'S ALLEGIANCE

October 31—In the midst of a heated discussion of their relationship with some nursing staff members, Mrs. Mann said she thought I should go and tell them off, for them. Mrs. Rosen said she didn't agree, because if I did, the staff would never listen to me again. They would think I was on the residents' side. There was a hush, and Mrs. Mann looked at me and said, "Aren't you on our sides? Don't you agree with us?" I said that I thought she was asking an important question. I said that actually I thought I was on neither side, but rather on the side of working out the troubles between them and nursing. To do that, I had to have a special relationship with each, where each knew I was listening to them, while not siding with the other. Mrs. Mann thought and said, "That's pretty tricky." I said I agreed. I thought she had put her finger on what was the hardest part of being a social worker, listening hard to both sides in a conflict, siding with neither, while working in the middle to help with the conflict between them. Mrs. Mann winked at me, smiled, and said, "But you really know we are right." We all laughed. I let the comment go as I recalled staff making a similar bid for my allegiance. We moved on to thinking through next steps in their work with nursing staff.

The question of my allegiance was not one that lent itself to "solving." It was one which would find its meaning as it was re-enacted in actual experience in the forthcoming meeting, each time residents and Dietary pulled apart, vying for my support in their struggle to ultimately remain engaged. Ms James, the Assistant Director, and Ms Hill, the Floor Dietitian, welcomed the opportunity. Lipton and Malter (1971) describe comparable experiences of a group worker making his way into the group life of paraplegic veterans, who were long-term patients in a Veterans Administration hospital. Their total dependence upon staff to care for their most basic needs made them fearful of retaliation for asserting themselves. They could not imagine collectively communicating their need for improved care unless the social worker could "guarantee" that he was on their side. Similarly to our worker at the Home, that worker conveyed his function as working between clients and staff.

November 13—A faint ray of hope appeared amidst the hopelessness. Ms James and Ms Hill were present. Residents were prepared for the meeting by discussions in the previous weeks about the particulars of their complaints. Whether they would speak up or not remained to be seen. After we were all assembled, I turned to Ms James and Ms Hill and said, "I think it is important for you to know that many residents are feeling discouraged about food problems getting better, and I had to urge them to allow me to invite you." Ms James said she could understand discouragement, but she really did want to hear. Her department would continue to work on the problems, and to do that, it was important to hear what the residents had to say. I asked for someone to start us off.

After a bit of sluggishness, the problems began to be mentioned. As each of the problems was mentioned, I repeated them over the loudspeaker for all to hear. Discussion went freely between Ms James, Ms Hill, and residents. Mrs. Esman was hanging her head and speaking her complaints angrily to herself.

I said that I knew Mrs. Esman felt especially bad about the food, and I wondered if she would share some of her feelings. She just kept shaking her head and repeated that it was no good, no good. What in particular? She mentioned, "Why no blintzes? I love them." Then she hung her head and said, "What's the use?" I said, "Your discouragement is very strong." "Yes," she said, "I've given up." "But it's not as if you don't care. You stay mad, and I see you are bothered about the food all the time." "Yes," she answered quietly.

There was a hush in the room. I turned to Ms James and Ms. Hill and said that I thought they were hearing the kind of feeling from Mrs. Esman that many residents feel. Ms James softly said, "I can understand that. Food is important. It's something to which you look forward. I bet you were a good cook, Mrs. Esman, and preparing the table was important to you." "Yes," she said as her mood began to soften. After her stroke she could no longer do it. Again the room was hushed. One sensed that many recalled pleasures no longer possible. I said, "And now that you can no longer prepare the table, you have to take what the Home provides." Mrs. Esman looked up but said nothing. I turned to the group and asked, "Does not being able to do things as you did before make the problem worse?" There was a round of commiseration with how it was different. When they came to a nursing home, they had to be grateful for what they got; they were sick and couldn't do for themselves. Some of the persons said they were glad they no longer had to cook. I returned us to the particulars of food problems. The complaints were exhausted, and residents reaffirmed their desire for the traditional Friday-night supper. Ms James said that she had heard them last month and had made plans for some of their favorite foods to be returned. The menus were just in the middle of being typed. Eyes picked up, smiles returned. I said I thought that was terrific. "See, bringing your issues to Ms James and Ms Hill did result in Dietary changing the menus as you wanted." She also mentioned the return of the blintzes and cautioned that it was hard to cook blintzes for so many persons. I looked at Mrs. Esman and asked her if she wanted them even if they were hard sometimes. She said, "Yes." Ms James said, "OK." I smiled and said, "How about three cheers for the blintzes and the Friday-night dinner return." The mood had lightened considerably, and we all cheered. I said that it seemed to me that their bringing up complaints and problems together did make a difference and that we ought to offer another round of cheers for them and Ms James, Ms Hill, and the Dietary Department. The mood felt hopeful. Tension had lessened.

After the cheers had subsided, I said that I had the feeling that one of the things that made it harder for them was having the feeling that they couldn't talk with Dietary frequently enough. They answered yes. I turned to Ms Hill and said, "I see you running around, and I know that you have four floors to get to during meals. I imagine that it must be a frustration to you not to have enough time to spend with residents at meals." Ms Hill said it was. At my suggestion, we then strategized about the idea of a monthly meeting with Ms Hill, which would lend some stability and regularity to food discussions. All agreed. Mrs. Hill and I agreed to work out the details.

After Ms James and Ms Hill left and we reviewed the problems and the next steps in relation to them, I asked the residents how they felt about the meeting. They were pretty discouraged when we started. How did they feel now? There was quiet and then many positives began to come through: maybe Dietary did listen; maybe change is possible; I'm glad we had the meeting; we voiced our ideas together, and they listen more when it's from a group.

Did they think that was true that it was different when they spoke as a group? Lots of reactions this time . . . strength in numbers; they think complaints are more real; persons don't feel so alone; the group really helps. We had been meeting for over one and a half hours now and persons were getting antsy to leave before the change of shift time. Many would need help with going to the bathroom. I said that I knew persons wanted to leave, but I wanted them to know I was interested in speaking with them further, at some point, about how they thought the Home was able to listen more when they spoke as a group. They said fine. I said I thought they had worked hard today and had done something to help them get what they wanted. The meeting ended on a high note with lots of small talk amongst the residents.

This was an important meeting. A lot was riding on it. It was important that there be an atmosphere in which residents could "level" with Dietary, bringing forth the full extent of their feelings. Dealing with the authority of Dietary would not be easy. Preliminary work with Dietary, in addition to their own sensitivity, helped prepare them somewhat for what was coming. Both sides were tuned in to the problems and the possible obstacles to successful working together. Listening was deeper, responses fuller. Moving from the general to the specific was helpful in this listening process. Vague comments about the food would not help to improve problems. Questioning the particulars of "what" and "when" allowed for detailed, problem-focused attention. Answers would be found in specifics, not generalities.

Eliciting hidden feelings and comments was also important. Mrs. Esman's blood pressure rose sharply whenever she felt victimized. Her heart literally needed her to express what was within. She could not express rage at the fates for her stroke, but she could be helped to express anger at the blintzes. At least that was a beginning. While displacement was apparent, nonetheless the object of displacement was real. Helping residents see the connection between their current feelings about food and their feelings of loss at not being able to prepare as they had allowed them new insights into their reactions. Here was a synthesis of the expressive and instrumental aspects of our work with persons in groups. The concrete, situational issues gave rise to feelings that became an important part of our work together. Not only was it important that we hear Mrs. Esman's actual complaint about the blintzes, but that we also hear her feelings about them. The blintzes problem mirrored Mrs. Esman's feelings toward institutionalization, her stroke, and the resultant loss of control over her body and her life.

I thought it probably would have been sufficient, in the beginning, for residents to "see" that they could meaningfully talk with Dietary. I also hoped we could focus upon some of the obstacles which made that talk hard. Viewing the structural arrangement of contact between residents and Dietary allowed for this opportunity. And finally, it was most important to credit residents' efforts. They had worked hard, had pushed beyond their fears, and had accomplished what they set out to do. Summarizing and determining next steps left us a continuing focus. Although the future remained uncertain, I thought we had made a good start together.

I was exhausted after the meeting. In addition to the work described I also had to attend to many environmental and personal variables: using the loudspeaker so persons could hear, watching for those who had to go to the bathroom, sitting up those who slumped and needed assistance, comforting those who did not understand, and all the time watching the relationship between the group as a whole and the individuals within it.

THE WORK CONTINUES

December 3—Menu and food problems again arose for discussion in group meetings. This time they just wanted Ms. Hill to come to a meeting.

December 10—Ms. Hill was present; problems were once again discussed, information given. Each time residents felt problems were made better, other problems appeared. Some laughed and said at least they weren't falling behind. Residents once again didn't feel too hopeful, but did experience a sense of working on problems. I sensed a difference too.

The work continued into the New Year.

LIFE TRANSITIONAL STRESSORS AMIDST ENVIRONMENTAL CONCERNS

January 1 to February 11—While food remained a concern, other problems came to the fore more strongly during this period: the resignation of a favorite head nurse, the death of a resident, noise in the dining room. It began to appear as if discussion of food was the mainstay content of the group except if another strong issue appeared.

THE WORK BECOMES MORE PERSONAL WITH ANGER VISIBLE

February 18—Most of the meeting concerned itself with Mrs. Lowry's death. They had been concerned about her for a long time. . . . We spoke of their missing her and their relationship with her. . . . The residents pointed to her disinterest in food and wondered whether her death was a result of the food. They angrily told me that if the food were tastier, Mrs. Lowry would have eaten and would not have died. I said I heard their sorrow very clearly. I too would miss Mrs. Lowry; I had known her for eight years. We paused together in recognition of our mutual loss. I said I also heard them questioning whether the Home had contributed to her death by not providing food which was enticing to her. Mrs. Burke said she really didn't think they meant that. They all knew how Mrs. Hill had prepared special malteds and treats each day. They also knew how nursing had encouraged her to eat at meals. I said what they were saying was true, but was there also some lingering thought that we didn't do all we could have to help Mrs. Lowry? Mrs. Cohen said she thought Mrs. Lowry had died from depression. The group began to share their understanding of the sources of pain in Mrs. Lowry's life and moved away from food as a contributor. I said that I thought they showed great understanding of Mrs. Lowry and had been quite sensitive to her during her life. I wanted to reassure them that she had not died from depression, but rather from a serious physical illness, which sometimes showed itself in lack of appetite.

Once again the theme of the institution's power to harm raised its head. It was important to draw that theme out directly, not mincing words, reaching for the strength of the residents' feelings, no matter how "taboo." Lingering thoughts that we had contributed to Mrs. Lowry's death would have been very destructive to residents. In truth, their comments about Mrs. Lowry were another way of speaking about the food, the resolution of which to them seemed entirely within the Home's control: The Home had the power to give or withhold life.

THE GROUP BECOMES STRONGER

February 25⎯When food problems appeared in this meeting, I asked residents how they wanted to work on the issues. Mrs. Mann and Mrs. Burke said that things had been promised to them but they had yet to see results. Others echoed the sentiment. I said I thought they had some very important questions to ask. I too had heard certain commitments, and while I knew, as they did, that the new menus weren't ready yet, perhaps they wanted to ask when they would be. Much self-conscious talk ensued: we don't want to be seen as complainers; why don't other floors say as much as we? I said I understood their self-consciousness, but I hoped they could get beyond it. They were involved in serious work with the Dietary Department and I thought it important that they hold that department and all staff, including myself, accountable for the work we were doing together. They asked me to invite Ms James and Ms Hill to the next meeting.

Each time we spoke, I had the sense of the members and the group as a whole becoming stronger. The quickness with which the members took to the idea of accountability was suggestive of their growing collective strength and their increasing view that they were not only recipients of what was given to them within the Home, but rather a potentially active force in creating the kind of home in which they wanted to live. It was important that I help them hold me accountable for my performance as well as others. Within a relationship of trust it would be easy to neglect negatives. My power within the group was evident. Checks and balances remained essential. Even within a well-meaning relationship abuses of power could develop. I continued to feel that their regressive potential was ever present and that vigilance was required to keep the possibility of improvement before them. I would need to believe change was possible even when their hope dwindled. There was always a next step, even if it was unknown at the moment unknown.

POSITIVES ACKNOWLEDGED

March 4—Ms James and Mrs. Hill were present. Residents felt engaged; alienation lessened.

March 25—Here was quiet in the meeting. Mrs. Mann said the sunny side eggs were good the other day. All eyes were on her. She was the group member most critical about food. I broke into a smile and said, "I don't believe it!" Mrs. Mann grinned and smiled and said, "I know—they were terrific!" We were all quiet for a moment, as if soaking in Mrs. Mann's comments. I touched Mrs. Mann's hand, smiled and turned to the group and said, "Boy, there's no telling what can happen now if Mrs. Mann liked the eggs." Laughter erupted. Others began to share positives about the food. This was an important moment for the group. If the group's most critical member deemed an item as delicate as Sunnyside eggs excellent, then improvement was really possible. The laughter felt terrific. They took my teasing good-naturedly, joining in with their own. My use of humor de-escalated tension and allowed the members to feel pleasure together. Noting positives had become an important part of our work together.

CHALLENGING EACH OTHER: TRUSTING EACH OTHER AND THE GROUP

April 1—During the past two months, Mrs. Burke and Mrs. Mann were critical of Mr. Delato's performance as a Food Committee delegate. For Mr. Delato, a shy, retiring man, unaccustomed to group living, the acceptance of this position reflected increased comfort with group life. Nonetheless, though he wanted to do well, he felt it hard to represent residents' issues. He did not volunteer to resign and residents would not ask him to.

MEMBER TO MEMBER DEMAND FOR WORK

Mrs. Burke asked what they were going to do. She was on another committee and therefore couldn't be on both. I looked around the room and said, "Well, what you think about Mrs. Burke's question?" Various persons were suggested to "assist" Mr. Delato. All refused. I looked at Mrs. Mann and said "What about you?" She reviewed her limitations. With annoyance she said she had refused for months; why did I keep bothering her? I said, "Because I'm not convinced you can't do the job." "But I can't see or hear," she insisted. I said that seeing wasn't necessary and she heard fine in our group. She said our group was different. She sat next to me, and I catered to her hearing problems. She was worried that she wouldn't be able to manage in a strange group. The residents likened the floor group to being with family and spoke of fear of "being with strangers." I said I could speak with the Chief of Social Service and perhaps she could sit next to her. Mrs. Mann said, "O.K., you win, I'll try it one time." The members congratulated Mrs. Mann, who all along cautioned them not to get too excited. I reviewed the terms of our contract: one try, my talking with the chief of social service. We reviewed problems for the food committee meeting next week. . . .

Outside the Group

April 22—More work on food problems. Residents still dependent upon me to urge them to invite Dietary to group meetings. . . . After the meeting I spoke with Ms James. She felt worn by all the criticism. She and her staff really were trying. Some problems are just so hard to correct. Could she share that with them, I wondered? She had leveled with them all along, and I thought her honesty was helpful. Residents felt a part of her department that way. Ms James mentioned the new items on the menu that they would like. She would give Ms Hill the pleasure of sharing the good news. The work is really difficult for Dietary. Ms James's department is one with hard-to-solve problems. Often things were beyond her control as when a tough cut of liver was sent or the distributor was out of something. Perhaps as residents felt less "at the mercy" of the institution, they would be more forgiving. Perhaps forgiveness was a feeling possible only between equals. Perhaps as engagement rose and alienation declined, forgiveness would be more possible.

Pleasure in Positive Gains: Holding the Home Accountable

April 29—Mrs. Hill announced all the new items soon to be on the menu. Mrs. Esman, who said it was too bad that Miss Idel died before these changes were put into effect, broke the merriment. She would have been happy. She ate so little. There was an embarrassed silence. I said, "Yes, it was sad that the changes came too late for Miss Idel, but knowing they did come would have made her happy." Silence. I said, "Something just struck me. Is part of your pushing on food so much because you don't know how long you will be here?" Mrs. Burke looked at me incredulously. "Of course," she answered, "we never know when we will die." We then moved on to a discussion of the seeming difference between institutional time and resident time. I felt we had hit upon a critical underlying dynamic affecting our work together—different temporal clocks. While it was now seven months since our initial group meeting in which residents appeared so discouraged, desired changes were just now being put into the menus. These changes came too late for residents who had died. Institutional time and resident time were clearly disparate. The Home's saying "change takes time" must fill residents with feelings of contradiction; while they intellectually understood that change took time, they felt their remaining time was uncertain.

DEMANDS UPON EACH OTHER

May—During May residents discussed other concerns: whether life was better in the community or in the home, a depressed resident, table arrangements, and whether life was worth living. Mrs. Mann reported on the two Food Committee meetings she had attended, saying the sessions were really hard on her, despite everyone's efforts to be of help to her. She hoped someone else would take the job. She felt the job was worthwhile. We spoke of how it might be better for her. There were no takers, and as if to avoid too much tension, the issue was tabled until June.

CREDITING MEMBER EFFORTS, SUSTAINING DEMAND FOR WORK, TRYING NEW ROLES

June 17—Mrs. Burke said she felt Mr. Delato should resign as Food Committee delegate. She told him she liked him very much but thought that speaking up went again his grain and that he might feel better if he didn't feel obligated to do a job he really didn't want to do. Discussion ensued and Mr. Delato said he felt he should step down. Residents thanked him for trying. I said, "I think being a Food Committee delegate is hard for Mr. Delato, but he should be pleased at his trying something new. He helped the group when no one else was willing to take on that responsibility." He smiled, feeling good about what he had done. He spoke a little of what was hard for him. He didn't expect it to get easier. Mrs. Burke then said, "OK, who will be our next delegate?" Dead silence. Mrs. Mann made it clear she would not continue. After much discussion and encouragement, Mrs. Frank agreed. Her trepidation in her new role was apparent, but she was willing to try.

The assertion with which Mrs. Burke confronted Mr. Delato with his lack of performance was impressive. Her act seemed symbolic of the growing strength of the members. They were more hopeful and were taking their work seriously. Food and residents sharing the work were real issues in their lives. Mrs. Frank's agreement, after a year of refusal, appeared to be part of this growing strength. Interestingly, there was a reciprocal relation between the growing strength of the group as a whole and the growing strength of the individual members: the stronger the group, the stronger the individuals and the stronger the individuals, the stronger the group. Food, as an environmental problem, had given rise to both inter-and intra-group issues. If the members were to continue their dialogue with Dietary, then the members would also have to work simultaneously on internal member-to-member relationships. Members had to make demands upon each other and had to provide support once leaders emerged. Otherwise, there would be no one to carry on the group's mission.

The Work Is Sustained

July—After my return from vacation, work was devoted to nursing concerns and helping to prepare Mrs. Frank for her first Food Committee meeting. I took notes for her because she could no longer write. It had also become my role to keep track of both the issues and the process of working on the issues. With my trusty notebook, I could be counted upon to preserve our collective memory. Many residents could no longer remember from week to week.

August 5—Mrs. Frank gave her Food Committee report. She was articulate and confident. She inspired residents' confidence in her and the Food Committee. I said she sounded as if she enjoyed going. It was not as hard as she had thought. Preparatory discussion last week had helped. I suggested that in the meeting prior to the Food Committee Mrs. Frank chair a discussion on matters residents wished her to take back. I would continue to take notes for her. They agreed and said that discussion would be helpful. The rest of the meeting was taken up with reactions to my announcement that during September I was to be assigned to another floor. We had worked together for six years. . . .

August 12—Additional separation work. Mrs. Frank was seriously ill with congestive heart failure.

The Group Matters

August 12–15—Mrs. Frank continued to be quite ill. At one point when she, her family, and I were visiting together, she said, "When I get back," then hung her head as if feeling too arrogant, "If I get back to the group meeting, I really want to hear those food problems." I said, "Yes, you really were terrific when you presented your report. The residents have great respect for your abilities. They see you as a fighter." Mrs. Frank smiled and said, "I think it's important that we stick together and fight for what we think is right." We all smiled in recognition of what had become so important to her. She began to rest.

August 16—Mrs. Frank died. She was alert and conscious to the end. She died as she had lived, with continued recommendations for how to make the lives of others better.

Mourning and the Group's Work Must Continue

August 19—This was my last group meeting before vacation. In September I would introduce the new worker. Mrs. Schwartz had died in addition to Mrs. Frank. Three residents were transferred to the hospital on an emergency basis. I felt filled with emotion. I imagined residents might be feeling that way also. Life was so uncertain, especially for the residents.

There was silence at the beginning. It had become our tradition that I would make the acknowledgment of a death on the floor. I began the meeting by saying that I imagined this was a hard week for them; they had lost two residents. Both

Mrs. Schwartz and Mrs. Frank had died. Reactions came forth easily. They had been close to each in different ways. Mrs. Frank had been a hard-working group member. Mrs. Schwartz had not attended but had been part of the floor life outside the group. I said I would miss them. Mrs. Tisch said Mrs. Frank had worked hard for them. Yes, I said, I admired her courage. I didn't think it was easy for her to complain to all the different persons to whom she had to bring criticism. Mrs. Burke said they were all afraid of being seen as complainers. I said perhaps in the future I could help them share those feelings and thoughts with their new social worker. They agreed. . . . Toward the end of the meeting I said, "I'd like to take a moment to tell you about a study I read a few years ago." They were interested and I told them about Tobin and Lieberman's findings that assertion, not passivity, was associated with longevity in institutional life. Some said they found that hard to believe. "Imagine, the complainers live longer." After a short discussion about the findings, Mrs. Burke, with tears in her eyes, said, "I want to thank you for what you have just shared with us. You have given me strength to complain. I always was a complainer, but now I know it is the right thing to do." The mood in the group was quite attentive. It was hard for me to speak. I felt as if a year's work culminated in that moment.

Before I could respond, perhaps sensing my emotion, Mrs. Burke said, "Well, life goes on and now we need another Food Committee delegate to take Mrs. Frank's place." There were immediate refusals. Mrs. Burke shouted, "Well, someone has to be a delegate." No takers. I said, "Several residents who might be delegates are not at the meeting. Mrs. Burke, how about speaking to various persons in the next two weeks while I am away and raise the discussion at our next meeting?" Mrs. Burke and the other residents agreed. What a powerful meeting! Acknowledgment of death and the continuance of life side by side!

There are two primary challenges in considering the Floor Group's development. The first is the matter of identifying distinctive *patterns of group development* in the sixth year of a group that had been meeting together with the same worker for the five years prior, without having studied the first five years of the group's development. The starting point for our analysis follows five years of ongoing weekly group meetings. The second is to consider what the literature on stages of group development can offer when that literature has not addressed such a long-term group with members who stayed for years and a social worker who stayed for six. Can our familiar literature apply? If stages are present, will they be similar to stages already defined in the literature or will we see new patterns emerging? How will our knowledge inform our practice?

The eleven-month period from September 10 to August 19 was chosen because it offered a focused look at a group's singular efforts to work on an issue of importance to the members. Though complaints about food were always part of the group's mainstay content, these particular eleven months reflected a concerted effort to make an impact. Thus we have the exciting opportunity to study a group's focused work on a singular environmental stressor and the parallel development of the group as a whole.

The chosen methodology for this analysis of nearly a year's work is similar to that of Kelly and Berman-Rossi (1999). In both instances, content analysis proved a valuable qualitative tool for the analysis of the group's process. Kelly and Berman-Rossi's four categories of analysis proved helpful for the study of this group. They are

1. on what the members were working (the content),
2. how they were working on their valued content (the process)
3. what the social worker did or did not do to help (professional skill), and
4. how the group developed over time (stages of group development (122).

Critical to our analysis is the recognition that the group members all knew each other, lived on the same floor together, and the group was only one part (albeit significant) of their lives together. In addition, the members were familiar and comfortable with the social worker, whose role it was to help with all matters, individual and collective. Third, this was an ongoing, open-ended group. These three distinctions differentiate this group from the close-ended groups discussed by Bennis and Shepard (1956), Garland, Jones, and Kolodny (1965), Lee and Berman-Rossi (1999), and Schiller (1995, 1997). Nonetheless, the authors' discussion of authority and intimacy in groups, and the process of group development alert us to listen for such themes in this open-ended, long-term, ongoing group. Similarly, Galinsky and Schopler's (1985, 1989) work on open-ended groups educates us to the challenges of such groups, to the need to integrate new members, and to ways of strengthening instrumental and instrumental ties among members. Nonetheless, here too the fit is not exact as in the groups they studied, membership was typically time-limited and the patterns of entry and exist of group members was most often permanent. Berman-Rossi and Cohen's (1988) discussion of five years in the life of a Cooking Group for homeless, mentally ill women comes closest to our discussion of this long-term Floor Group. Strikingly, this open-ended Cooking Group grew stronger over time, despite changing student workers each year. And, strikingly, it was only through a long view that the growth of the group as a whole was visible. The group's development was testimony to the women's strength and resilience and to how the Cooking Group provided a vehicle for the women to develop their strengths. Analysis of this group also points to time as a critical factor in strengthening ties and resiliency among the members.

My analysis of the group meetings points to five stages of group development. Stage 1: Approach-Avoidance/Power and Control, Stage 2: Approach, Stage 3: Intimacy, Stage 4: Differentiation, and Stage 5: Collective Strength.

Stage 1: Approach-Avoidance/Power and Control
(September 9 to October 15 [half])

From the first meeting recorded here, the members are familiar with each other and have long moved beyond their initial anxiety about each other and the worker. In this initial stage, of our analysis, the members demonstrate solidarity and are unified in their doubt as to whether change is possible. Cohesion is visible. There is little difference of opinion and little conflict among the members. The Approach-Avoidance pattern is seen in their ambivalence about the work. Their initial sense that no one cares, gives way to their brief flirtation with hopefulness, only to have them become discouraged again. Issues of Power and Control appear differently than they do in the models identified earlier. The testing of the worker comes in the form of their resistance to her plea to have hope "just one more time," rather than in the form of challenging her competence. While the members trust the worker in many intimate parts of their lives, her experience with the Home is not initially sufficient for the members to generate hope, one more time. Their own negative experiences speak more loudly than her encouragement.

Stage 2: Approach (October 15 [half] to December 10)

A shift begins toward the end of the meeting of October 15. Having expressed their deepest feelings that the Home did not care about them, and with the worker's plea to try "one more time," the members reluctantly agreed to pursue their concerns with Dietary. Asking the worker to be a go-between, they moved off their resistance to trying to influence their environment one more time. The potential peril to the members was considerable. The stakes were high. Failure to positively engage Dietary would visibly confirm for all to see that they were indeed at the mercy of the Home's power. Over the next month the members sustained their work on food concerns. Meeting their Floor Dietician and her Supervisor face-to-face provided reassurance of Dietary's investment in making things better and also provided the opportunity for the residents to have direct influence. Ideally, the residents would be able to increasingly make direct demands upon the Home, not having to go through their social worker. The residents' feelings were buoyed with positive results. They saw for themselves that results were more achievable when they spoke as a group. Though fearful that the slowness of change was a harbinger of failure, they remained engaged. Interestingly, as they worked on this environmental problem, they increasingly shared feelings occasioned by their moving into the Home and no longer being able to cook for themselves.

Stage 3: Intimacy (January 1 to March 25)

Over this three months period there were two streams of work in the meetings and with each of them, residents were more expressive. Residents continued their work on food issues, and the talk became more personal. Discussion of loss became more frequent, e.g., the resignation of their favorite nurse and the death of residents. Their riskiest moment discussing a taboo came when some members accused the Home of killing a resident because she would not eat the food. Their ready acceptance of the view that the Home had tried very hard showed their desire not to have conflict in the group and their collective ability to deal with difference. Undoubtedly, the group as a whole was stronger. The strength of the group as a whole was also shown in members open expression of pleasure with the food. They were not afraid to acknowledge gains.

Stage 4: Differentiation (April 1 to August 5):

Garland, Jones, and Kolodny (1965) suggest that the stage of differentiation is characterized as the period in the life of the group when members are freest to express how they feel without fear of rejection by the group. Intimacy is deepened by this freedom. Significantly, this freedom gives strength to members' ability to differ with each other and to pursue difference without fearing rejection or disruption of the group as a whole. All of this (and more) is possible because the group as a whole is strong and the members trust in its strength. Though all members have not been present for all sessions, members trust that in their occasional absence, work will continue. Affectional and instrumental ties are strong. This stage begins powerfully with the members' demand for work from each other and moving beyond their hesitancy to confront each other. Rather than reject the floor delegate for poor performance they adopted a buddy system where another group member would also represent the floor at Home wide Food Committee meetings. Their ultimate direct face-to-face discussion with each other was marked by sensitivity, appreciation, support, and the demand for work. A win-win situation was achieved, something not possible months earlier.

Stage 5: Collective Strength (August 12 to August 19)

The members' strength and the strength of the group as a whole was shown vividly in the final meeting presented, where not even death could deter residents from their collective task of choosing a new Food Committee delegate. Though saddened by Mrs. Frank's death, the collective's demand for work was strong. Perhaps there was no more fitting tribute to Mrs. Frank, than to continue her work and the work of the group. Strikingly, it was a resident who pointed to the work. Without question, residents were able to act in their own behalf. Their collective strength was visible to all. They did not need the worker to prompt the work.

During the year the group members worked hard on food concerns. Initial discouragement was understandable. Only seeing the problems inherent in institutional living and not feeling enough a part of the process of making things better had the effect of alienating residents from the very institution designed to serve them. They had spoken about food many times. I was never sure why they became so discouraged when they did. There were obviously many factors influencing how they felt, some related to Dietary and some not. Their feelings of alienation were striking, especially since the Food Committee was working well. Mr. Delato, as a Food Committee delegate, did not strengthen their sense of productivity. However, he offered when no one else would take the job.

Many residents were hesitant to take additional responsibility within the group. The potential negative consequences of assertion coupled with self-doubt combined to inhibit assuming additional responsibilities on behalf of herself and others. Although a resident for two years, Mrs. Frank felt like a newcomer. Though esteemed by others, she doubted her abilities and found it difficult to take on new group tasks and responsibilities. She accepted the role of alternate delegate, rather than delegate. Only by taking the Food Committee job was she convinced of how well she could do and how highly esteemed she was by others. She, like many women of her generation, did not see herself in a leadership role.

Mrs. Mann, though of high status and comfortable with the floor group (which she considered family), feared failure within the Resident Council. With decreasing physical abilities, she could not imagine a role of increasing responsibility. Her decision to "assist" Mr. Delato represented a gift to the group and to me.

Mr. Delato, in response to a request from his peers and with considerable group support, took responsibility uncharacteristic of him. His venture deeper into group life reflected growing trust and the pull to belong to the "family" of the group members. These residents and many others who shared their thinking and feelings in the group grew closer by sharing their lives together. I was constantly impressed with how hard residents worked and how important a part of their lives the group was.

The floor group contained the fuel with which residents rekindled old abilities and developed new ones. What was most noticeable was that new roles and abilities were developed in relation to real work. Tasks were not fabricated "to make residents feel better" or "less depressed" or "happier." The pressing reality of work to be done, which reflected the reality of residents' lives, provided the urgent impetus for many to move beyond their fears of inadequacy, discouragement, and self-criticism. George (1980) suggests that role changes and transitions pose challenges for all. In this instance, part of the challenge the group members experienced was that of shifting back to the role of competent, assertive adults. In so doing, the residents would create a Home that Shield (1990) describes as a setting where residents assert control, influence, and decision making, rather than an institution guided by a medical model of physician authority care.

This movement took place within an atmosphere of mutual aid where we can readily see Shulman's (1999) ten mutual aid factors at work. As they *shared data* residents saw that they were still capable of giving and receiving help. Their varied life experiences enriched discussion and provided a breadth of ideas for addressing the work at hand. The *dialectical process* served as a protective process by providing an opportunity for dialogue and change to occur. Through a process of *mutual support* residents were able to *discuss taboos and difficult themes*. Their encouragement and their crediting of each other's abilities were crucial components of group life. Seeing that they were *all in the same* boat decreased hopelessness and the stigma attached to institutional living. *Developing a universalist perspective* fostered extruding society's negative valuation of them. To achieve their goals, support and affirmation were not sufficient. Group members needed to establish a clear *demand for work* if gains were to be achieved. Catharsis was insufficient. Expressing a demand for work by attending to obstacles to the work was of particular significance to group members hesitant to assert themselves in their institutional home. *Individual and collective problem solving* provided the means through which the residents attended to the tasks at hand and figured out their place in the group. *Rehearsal* within the group was integral to residents having the courage to confront institutional power. Ultimately, recognizing their *strength-in-numbers* provided the support needed to challenge institutional totality and service delivery problems.

This mutual aid group helped residents feel more in control over their lives through direct engagement with peers and their environment. Increased feelings of self-worth were apparent as their repertoire of social roles expanded. Residents were once again involved in creating the kind of world in which they wanted to live. They exhibited signs of "bouncing back."

My activity was guided by the five professional tasks identified by Schwartz (1994 [1961]) as the tasks required of social workers as they carry out their mediating function within the group. Executed skillfully, these tasks have great potential for assisting in strengthening the resiliency of individual group members and for strengthening the resiliency of the group as a whole.

1. *Searching Out the Common Ground*: Residents' belief that their views were unimportant and unwelcome ran counter to my belief that there was a symbiotic tie between them and the Dietary Department. In my experience, I observed that Dietary did their work better through dialogue with residents. They wanted to hear complaints and suggestions. In fact, they knew that if residents were to feel more satisfied, their ideas and preferences would have to be included. That the common ground between residents and Dietary sometimes appeared obscured seemed unremarkable to me. This muting was a function of the complexity of institutional life and bureaucratic organization. My simultaneous work with residents and Dietary sought to make the common ground visible to both. I knew if I kept this tie in the foreground, it would become increasingly apparent to the residents. In reality, as residents experienced Dietary's concern and saw some visible signs of change, they too came to believe that their voices were not only

accepted, but actually needed for problem resolution. Identifying the common ground between residents and Dietary made evident the basis and arena for work. Believing in the possibility of change became a critical protective factor and the basis for increasing the resiliency of the residents and of the group as a whole.

2. *Detecting and Challenging the Obstacles*: Throughout the year, residents' discouragement was a major obstacle blocking the quality and quantity of their work together. When they placed responsibility outside themselves, they failed to see their contribution to the lack of resolution of problems. While responsibility for improving food lay with the Dietary Department, residents did bear responsibility for their contribution to that effort. When they felt like victims, they acted victimized. If Dietary changed their way of making fish and residents refused to try it, how would Dietary ever know if the new way was preferred? If residents were too angry to help, things would be that much harder for Dietary.

A simultaneous emphasis upon the content of the meeting as well as the process of working on troubles was essential. Residents needed me to help them "own" their discouragement and then to see the connection between discouragement and inactivity. Asking group members to come to grips with the obstacles to their activity and then moving beyond was critical. Initially, residents were better able to acknowledge their discouragement than they were able to do anything about it. Time and time again they needed me to help them move on by saying, "Enough! What are you going to do?" Sometimes they did nothing. They needed my patience in their process of such hard work. Much was at stake. It was easier for residents to find fault than to exercise their hope, one more time, by being active on their own behalf. Detecting and challenging the obstacles to strengthening the symbiotic tie between residents and Dietary was necessary if residents were to experience an increase in hopefulness necessary to sustain the work.

3. *Contributing Data*: Since residents felt so "stuck," contributing my ideas and thinking about the possible ways to proceed became imperative. What was equally critical was not telling them which path to take. I might urge them to act, but when they decided, they had to "own" their decision. This process of owning would help them in the work to come. Contributing data, so that residents could evaluate and problem-solve rather than assume a directive stance, became integral to residents finding and developing their individual and collective strength. As well, conveying, in action, that I believed in their capacity for change and in the power of the group a long way to supporting their ongoing involvement.

4. *Lending a Vision*: This task was most crucial in helping the group work together. The members continuously called upon my belief in the possibility of change. "Is change possible? Will things get better?" These feelings were present in each meeting. I found it necessary to maintain a high energy level in this area. I needed to have "faith" for all of us. Sometimes I found myself impatient. Why did certain things take so long? I doubted my helping strategy. Perhaps residents

should not have complained only to Dietary. Perhaps it was I who was holding them back. These thoughts prompted me to explore alternative strategies with the members. With hindsight I might have "leveled" more with Ms James and Ms Hill, pushing past initial explanations for why things weren't happening sooner. I suppose I felt I was always treading a thin line between resident needs and institutional possibilities. It was important to me not to be seen as over identified with either side. By remaining within my mediating function my viability as a helping person was maintained.

5. *Establishing the Bounds and Limits of Our Working Relationship*: While an overall agreement existed, the particulars of our working agreement—or contract—seemed to be defined during each meeting. Each new problem demanded that the terms of our agreement be determined, in process, in the moment. I would make a recommendation, but I would not tell them what to do. I would do what was too hard for them but only if it really was too hard. I would have faith in the process of working together even when they lost theirs. I would help Dietary and the group work together, but I would not join either side. I would do my work but could not do theirs. If no one would be a Food Committee delegate, then the floor would not be represented. I would do all I could to help the residents generate a delegate, but it was their job to produce the delegate.

GROUP ASSOCIATION remains an inherent part of institutional living. The impetus for collectivity has its origin in two main sources: 1. the natural impetus of people who need each other to join together, and 2. the recognition by institutional inhabitants that groups offer a buffer against institutional stressors as well as a structural means for engagement with the institution. The institution bears special responsibility for furthering the life-giving potential of group association based upon their recognition of the alienating and isolating components of institutional living and the need for a structured means for furthering ongoing dialogue with consumers. Group service offers assistance to both clients and agency. This simultaneous focus upon resident and environment identifies the purview of social workers. Their focus remains upon the dialogue between client need and agency service, seeking to lessen the distance between the two. The social worker's practice in groups with older institutionalized persons is influenced by 1. the experience of institutionalization, 2. the high degree of uncertainty, unpredictability, and loss experienced, coupled with the positives that can emerge from challenge and change, 3. the existential nature of life, and 4. the need to continue a meaningful life in the face of loss and ongoing uncertainty.

Older persons, like persons of all ages, possess the ability to work on issues of importance to them. The mutual aid group represents a significant means for increasing the resiliency of older institutionalized persons and for working on important personal, interpersonal, and environmental issues. It stands as a primary protective factor with specific protective mechanisms and processes which can strengthen the resiliency of the group as a whole. The mutual aid group can strengthen life itself by providing a significant buffer to the negative consequences of institutionalization and by enhancing the strengths of its group members.

Note

1. I am thankful to K. T. for his process recording, which illustrates the group as a source of hope.

References

Allert, G., G. Sponholz, and H. Baitsch. 1994. Chronic disease and the meaning of old age. *Hastings Center Report* 24(5): 11–13.

Atchley, R. C. and M. P. Lawson. 1997. Is gerontology biased toward a negative view of the aging process and old age? In A. L. Scharlach and L. W. Kaye, eds., *Controversial issues in aging*, pp. 185–96. Boston: Allyn and Bacon.

Baltes, M. M. 1994. Aging well and institutional living: A paradox? In R. P. Abels, C. H. Gift, and M. G. Ory, eds., *Aging and quality of life*, pp. 185–201. New York: Springer.

Bennett, R. 1963. The meaning of institutional life. *Gerontologist* 3(3): 17–125.

Bennis, W. B. and H. A. Shepard. 1956. A theory of group development. *Human Relations* 9:415–37.

Bergeman, C. S. and K. A. Wallace. 1999. Resiliency in later life. In T. L. Whitman, T. V. Merluzzi, and R. D. White, eds., *Life-span perspectives on health and illness*, pp. 207–25. Mahwah: N.J.: Erlbaum.

Berman-Rossi, T. 1993. The tasks and skills of the social worker across stages of group development. *Social Work with Groups* 16(1/2): 69–81.

—— 2001. Older persons in need of long-term care. In A. Gitterman, ed., *Handbook of social work practice with vulnerable populations*, pp. 715–68. 2d ed. New York: Columbia University Press.

Berman-Rossi, T. and M. Cohen. 1988. Group development and shared decision making: Working with homeless mentally ill women. In J. A. B. Lee, ed., *Group work with the poor and oppressed*, pp. 63–74. New York: Haworth.

Blenkner, M. 1977. The normal dependencies of aging. In R. A. Kalish, ed., *The later years: Social applications of gerontology*, pp.78–83. Monterey, Cal.: Brooks/Cole.

Branch, L .G. and A. M. Jette. 1982. A prospective study of long-term care institutionalization among the aged. *American Journal of Public Health* 72(12): 1373–79.

Brown, A. and T. Mistry. 1994. Group work with "mixed membership" groups: Issues of race and gender. *Social Work with Groups* 17(3): 5–21.

Butler, R. N. 1969. Ageism: Another form of bigotry. *Gerontologist* 9(4): 243–46.

—— 1975. *Why survive: Being old in America*. New York: Harper and Row.

Coe, R. M. 1965. Self-conceptions and institutionalization. In R. M. Rose and W. A. Peterson, eds., *Older people and their social world*. Philadelphia: Davis.

Cole, T. R. 1992. *The journey of life: A cultural history of aging in America*. Cambridge: Cambridge University Press.

Cowan, P. A., C. P. Cowan, and M. Schulz. 1996. Thinking about risk and resilience in families. In E. M. Hetherington and E. A. Blechman, eds., *Stress, coping, and resiliency in children and families*, pp.1–38. Mahwah, N.J.: Erlbaum.

Engel, G. L. 1968. A life setting conducive to illness: The giving-up complex. *Annals of Internal Medicine* 69:293–300.

Estes, C. L. 1979. *The aging enterprise*. San Francisco: Jossey-Bass.

Estes, C. L. and E. A. Binney. 1989. The biomedicalizing of aging: Dangers and dilemmas. *Gerontologist* 29(5): 587–96.

Feldman, S. and V. Netz. 1997. Beyond menopause: Vulnerability vs. hardiness. In D. E. Steward and G. E. Robinson, *A clinician's guide to menopause*, pp. 203–25. Washington, D.C.: Health Press International.

Fooken, I. 1982. Patterns of health behavior, life satisfaction, and future time perspective in a group of aged women: Data of "survivors" from a longitudinal study in aging. *International Journal of Behavior Development* 5:367–90.

Ford, A. B., M. R. Haug, C. Kurt, A. D. K. Gaines, L. S. Noelker, and P. K. Jones. 2002. Sustained personal autonomy: A measure of successful aging. *Journal of Aging and Health* 12(4): 470–89.

Forman, M. 1971. The alienated resident and the alienating institution: A case for peer group intervention. *Social Work* 16(2): 47–54.

Foy, S. S. and M. M. Mitchell. 1990. Factors contributing to learned helplessness in the institutionalized aged: A literature review. *Physical and Occupational Therapy* 9(2): 1–23.

Frankl, V. E. 1963. *Man's search for meaning*. New York: Washington Square Park.

Freedman, V. A., L. F. Berkman, S. R. Rapp, and A. M. Osfeld. 1994. Family networks: Predictors of nursing home entry. *American Journal of Public Health* 84(5): 843–45.

Fried, M. 1963. Grieving for a lost home. In L. J. Duhl, ed., *The urban condition*, pp. 151–71. New York: Basic.

Galinsky, M. and J. Schopler. 1985. Patterns of entry and exit in open-ended groups. *Social Work with Groups* 8(2): 67–80.

———— 1989. Developmental patterns in open-ended groups. *Social work with groups* 12(2): 99–114.

Garland, J., H. Jones, and R. Kolodny. 1965. A model for stages of group development in social work groups. In S. Bernstein, ed., *Explorations in group work*, pp. 17–71. Boston: Boston University School of Social Work.

Garner, J. D. 1995. Long-term care. In R. L.Edwards, ed., *Encyclopedia of social work*, pp. 1625–34. 19th ed. Washington, D.C.: NASW.

George, L. K. 1980. *Role transitions in later life*. Monterey, Cal.: Brooks/Cole.

Germain, C. B. 1987. Human development in contemporary environments. *Social Service Review* 61(4): 565–80.

Germain, C. B. and A. Gitterman. 1996. *The life model of social work practice*. 2d ed. New York: Columbia University Press.

Gitterman, A. 1989. Building support in groups. *Social Work with Groups* 12(2): 5–21.

———— 2001a. Social work practice with vulnerable and resilient populations. In A. Gitterman, ed., *Handbook of social work practice with vulnerable and resilient populations*, pp. 1–36. 2d ed. New York: Columbia University Press.

———— 2001b. Vulnerability, resilience and social work with groups. In T. Kelly, T.

Berman-Rossi, and S. Palombo, eds., *Group work: Strategies for strengthening resiliency*, pp. 19–33. New York: Haworth.

Goffman, E. 1961. *Asylums*. Garden City, N.Y.: Anchor/Doubleday.

Gottesman L. E. and E. Hutchinson. 1974. Characteristics of institutionalized elderly. In E. M. Brody, ed., *A social work guide for long-term care facilities*, pp. 27–45. Rockville, Md.: U.S. Department of Health, Education, and Welfare.

Gutheil, I. and E. Congress. 2002. Resiliency in older people: A paradigm for practice. In E. Norman, ed., *Resiliency enhancement*, pp. 40–52. New York: Columbia University Press.

Jacelon, J. C. 1995. The effect of living in a nursing home on socialization in elderly people. *Journal of Advanced Nursing* 22:539–46.

Janoff-Bulman, R. 1982. Mortality, well-being and control: A study of a population of institutionalized aged. *Personality and Social Psychology Bulletin* 8(4): 691–98.

Kaufman, S. R. 1986. *The ageless self*. Madison: University of Wisconsin Press.

Kelly, T. and T. Berman-Rossi. 1999. Advancing stages of group development theory: The case of institutionalized older persons. *Social Work with Groups* 22(2/3): 119–38.

Kontos, P. C. 1998. Resisting institutionalization: Constructing old age and negotiating home. *Journal of Aging Studies* 12(2): 167–84.

Kosberg, J. 1988. Preventing elder abuse: Identification of high risk factors prior to placement decisions. *Gerontologist* 28(1): 43–50.

Lamphere-Thorpe, J. A. and R. J. Blendon. 1993. Years gained and appointments lost: Women and healthcare in an aging America. In J. Allen and A. Pifer, eds., *Women on the front lines*, pp. 75–104. Washington, D.C.: Urban Institutional Press.

Lawson, K. A. 1989. Bringing the social back in: A critique of the biomedicalization of dementia. *Gerontologist* 29(5): 595–605.

Lee, J. A. B. 2001. *The empowerment approach to social work practice*. 2d ed.. New York: Columbia University Press

Lee, J. A. B. and T. Berman-Rossi. 1999. Empowering adolescent girls in foster care: A short-term group record. In C. LeCroy, *Case studies in social work practice*, 269–84. 2d ed. Pacific Grove, Cal.: Brooks/Cole.

Lee, J. A. B. and C. Swenson. 1994. The concept of mutual aid. In A. Gitterman and L. Shulman, eds., *Mutual aid groups, vulnerable populations, and the life cycle*, pp. 413–29. 2d ed. New York: Columbia University Press.

Leonard, W. M. II. 1981. Successful aging: An elaboration of social and psychological factors. *International Journal of Aging and Human Development* 14(3): 223–32.

Lieberman, M. A. and S. S. Tobin. 1983. *The experience of old age: Stress, coping, and survival*. New York: Basic.

Lipton, H. and S. Malter. 1971. The social worker as mediator on a hospital ward. In W. Schwartz and S Zalba, eds., *The practice of group work*, pp. 97–121. New York: Columbia University Press.

Lustbader, W. 1999–2000. Thoughts on the meaning of frailty, pp. 21–24. *Generations*.

Lyman, K. A. 1989. Bringing the social back in: A critique of the biomedicalization of dementia. *Gerontologist* 29(5): 597–605.

Minkler, M. and P. Fadem. 2002. Successful aging: A disability perspective. *Journal of Disability and Policy Studies* 12(4): 229–35.

Nahemow, L. 1983. Working with older people: The patient-physician milieu. In G. G. Rowles and R. J. Ohta, eds., *Aging and milieu*, pp. 171–86. New York: Academic.

Neeman, L. 1995. Using the therapeutic relationship to promote an internal locus of control in elderly mental health clients. *Journal of Gerontological Social Work* 23(3/4): 161–76.

Padgett, D. K., B. J. Burns, L. A. Grau. 1998. Risk factors and resiliency: Mental health needs and service use of older women. In P. B. Levin, A. K. Blauch, and A. Jennings, eds., *Women's mental health services*, pp. 390–413. Thousand Oaks, Cal.: Sage.

Pastalan, L. A. 1983. Environmental displacement: A literature reflecting older person-environment transaction. In G. G. Rowles and R. J. Ohta, eds., *Aging and milieu* , pp. 189–203. New York: Academic.

Perlmutter, L. C. and A. S. Eads. 1998. Control: Cognitive and motivational implications. In J. Lomranz, ed., *Handbook of aging and mental health: An integrative approach*, pp. 45–67. New York: Plenum.

Ponzo, A. 1992. Promoting successful aging: Problems, opportunities, and counseling guidelines. *Journal of counseling and development* 71(2): 210–13.

Rabbit, P. 1992. Ageing gracefully. *Lancet* 339(8802): 1157–58.

Reed, J. and C. L. Clarke. 1999. Nursing older people: Constructing need and care. *Nursing Inquiry* 6:208–15.

Reker, G. T. 2002. Prospective predictors of successful aging in community-residing and institutionalized Canadian elderly. *Aging International* 27(1): 42–64.

Roe, B. 2002. Protecting older people from abuse. *Nursing Older People* 14(9): 14–18.

Rowe, J. 1991. Reducing the risk of usual aging. *Generations* 15(1): 25–28.

——— 1997. The new gerontology. *Science* 278(5337): 367–69.

Rowe, J. and R. Kahn. 1997. *Gerontologist* 37:433–40.

——— 1998. *Successful aging*. New York: Random House.

Rutter, M. 1987. Psychosocial resilience and protective mechanisms. *American Journal of Orthopsychiatry* 57(3):316–31.

Sarvimaki, A. and B. Stenbock-Hult. 2000. Quality of life in old age described as a sense of well-being, meaning, and value. *Journal of Advanced Nursing* 32(4): 1025–33.

Schiller, L. 1995. Stages of group development in women's groups: A relational model. In R. Kurland and R. Salmon, eds., *Group work practice in a troubled society*, 117–38. New York: Haworth.

——— 1997. Rethinking stages of development in women's groups: Implications for practice. *Social Work with Groups* 20(3): 3–19.

Schwartz, W. 1969. Private troubles and public issues: One social work job or two? *The Social Welfare Forum*, pp. 22–43. New York: Columbia University Press.

——— 1971. On the use of groups in social work practice. In W. Schwartz and S. Zalba, *The practice of group work*, pp. 3–24. New York: Columbia University Press.

——— 1994 [1961]. The social worker in the group. In T. Berman-Rossi, ed., *Social work: The collected writings of William Schwartz*, pp. 257–76. Itasca, Ill.: Peacock.

Shield, R. R. 1990. Liminality in an American nursing home: The endless transition. In J. Sokolovsky, ed., *The cultural context of aging: Worldwide perspectives*, pp. 331–52. Westport, Conn.: Bergen and Garvey.

Shmotkin, D. 1998. Declarative and differential aspects of subjective well-being and its implications for mental health in later life. In J. Lomranz, ed., *Handbook of aging and mental health: An integrative approach*, pp. 15–43. New York: Plenum.

Shulman, L. 1999. *The skills of helping individuals, families, groups, and communities.* Itasca, Ill.: Peacock.

Solomon, R. and M. Peterson. 1994. Successful aging: How to help your patients cope with change. *Geriatrics* 49(4): 41–49.

Steinberg, D. 1997. *The mutual-aid approach to working with groups.* Northvale, N.J.: Aronson.

Tauber, C. M. and J. Allen. 1993. Women in our aging society: The demographic outlook. In J. Allen and A. Pifer, eds., *Women on the front lines,* pp. 11–45. Washington, D.C.: Urban Institute Press.

Tobin, S. A. and M. A. Lieberman. 1976. *Last home for the aged.* San Francisco: Jossey-Bass.

Torres, S. 2002. Relational values and ideas regarding "successful aging." *Journal of Comparative Family Studies* 33(3): 417–31.

Uhlenberg, P. 1997. Replacing the nursing home. *Public Interest* 128:73–84.

Wesson, A. 1965. Some sociological characteristics of long-term care. In A. M. Rose and W. A. Peterson, eds., *Older people and their social world,* pp. 259–71. Philadelphia: Davis.

Chapter 20

Accumulated Risk
Mutual Aid Groups for Elderly Persons
with a Mental Illness

Timothy B. Kelly

Eleanor was an African American woman born in the Deep South in the 1920s who spent much of her adult life in a state psychiatric hospital. She began hearing voices almost immediately after the birth of her youngest child. Her husband had her committed shortly after the birth of their daughter; she was diagnosed with schizophrenia, and he quickly moved in with another woman he had been "dating" during his wife's pregnancy. Eleanor was forgotten on the back wards of the hospital for years, and she did not meet her daughter until her young baby was a full-grown woman with children of her own. The voices never fully remitted. As an older person she began receiving mental health services that included medication, case management, and group services. She learned to live with her illness, became a "mother" of her church, a respected member of her community, and a real group leader in the day treatment group. She had a lifetime of horrendous experiences and yet as an older person blossomed and lived a happy life.

Stephen was an amiable, gay, white man born in a small southern town in the mid 1920s. He was "high-strung," had borderline intelligence, and would have frequent bouts of anxiety and panic attacks. At the age of fifteen he and the minister's thirteen-year-old son were caught engaged in adolescent sexual exploration. Stephen was committed to the state mental hospital for the next fifteen years. The minister's son went away to a private boarding school. Stephen continued to have panic attacks and depressive episodes into his old age. He was living a very isolated existence when he entered the day treatment group. Though he still struggled with panic attacks and occasional bouts of depression, he became an active member of the group and soon became a mascot for the group. The other members loved to be around Stephen, and his eyes danced with life as he regaled the group with his humorous stories of life as a misfit in a small southern town.

Ella was a Caribbean woman who moved to the United States in her mid-twenties and lived a productive life filled with family and a job in accounting. In her mid-forties she began to have manic episodes and was hospitalized for several years. She never worked again and her family was thereafter wary of her. She continued to have episodic manic bouts into her eighties. She entered the group and quickly became a real leader, always quick to help other members see the reality of their situations. Through her active involvement in the group she learned ways to cope with the stressors in her family relationships and was eventually allowed to baby-sit her grandchildren. She once again felt she was contributing to her family.

John was an African American who managed to keep his family together and fed during the Depression, despite extreme poverty and horrendous racism. He was by all accounts an engaging, entertaining, and well-respected man. In his late fifties he became seriously depressed, was unable to work, and retreated into an impenetrable shell. He moved from being the leader of his family and community to someone who was pitied and taken care of like a child. After years of living this way, he entered the day treatment group and for the first month he would sit quietly in the group, quick to cry. After a few months his mood began to lighten and the group would occasionally see glimpses of the powerful man he had once been. After some time he began to share stories from his life as a poor African American man raising his family on the same farm where his grandparents had been slaves. As he shared the tragedies and the joys, his mood began to lighten, and he became an elder statesman in the group. Though he never regained the full vitality of his previous functioning, he regained a sense of dignity and purpose and died a respected member of his family and our group.

These are a few of the amazing older persons who have struggled and coped with major mental illnesses and issues of aging. These people have an accumulation of risk: the risks associated with aging, mental illness, and, quite often, membership in other oppressed groups. They represent persons with incredible vulnerability, as there are many risk factors associated with the aging experience and also with having a mental illness. However, older persons with mental illness also demonstrate remarkable resiliency—a resiliency that is supported and strengthened through group work. This chapter will briefly describe common characteristics of elderly persons with a mental illness, describe developmental tasks, vulnerabilities and risk factors, resiliency and protective factors, and finally describe the use of mutual aid groups to mitigate risk and increase resiliency for this remarkable group of people.

The aging population is the fastest growing segment of the population (Meeks and Hammond 2001; Raschko 1991; Toseland 1995; Zarit and Zarit 1998). People are living longer, and as they age they bring with them into old age a lifetime of experience, opportunities, and difficulties. For some, a lifetime of mental illness continues into old age. Others must cope with mental illness for the first time as an older person (Kelly 1999). Regardless of the age of onset of the mental illness, there are many commonalities for the older person dealing with a mental illness. At the same time, the age of onset does present unique vulnerabilities. Additionally, each mental illness presents unique challenges. Many of the challenges and vulnerabilities are similar to those faced by younger persons living with a mental illness. However, the experience of aging represents strengths and protective factors as well as additional risks and vulnerabilities.

Older adults experience all the psychiatric disorders that younger adults experience. In fact, Zarit and Zarit (1998) suggest that the psychopathology of aging is the same as the psychopathology of younger adults. There is some debate about the prevalence of mental illness in the elderly population. Solomon (1990), for example, states that older persons are more likely to have a mental illness than persons of any other age group. Sadavoy (1987) suggests that old age makes character pathology worse. Rose, Soares, and Joseph (1993) disagree with the *Diagnostic and Statistical Manual of Mental Disorder's* characterization of personality disorders becoming less obvious with old age. They believe, conversely, that they become exacerbated. Coolidge and colleagues (1992) concur in that they found that some personality disorders become worse with age. Oxman and colleagues (1987) write, "Aging is associated with increases in physiological dysfunction, physical disabilities, overmedication, social losses, and proximity of certain death. It is, thus, not illogical to expect increases in psychiatric symptomatology, particularly depression and anxiety, in elderly patients" (167). Their research, however, showed a decline in symptomatology as people age. Others agree with Oxman and colleagues' point of decreased symptomatology (Coolidge et al. 1992; Padgett, Burns, and Grau 1988). In a review of the literature, Husaini, Moore, and Cain (1994) found rates of prevalence for psychiatric problems among the elderly that varied from 9 percent to 22 percent.

The prevalence of specific mental disorders is also controversial. For example, rates of depression in the elderly population have been reported to be as low as 2.5 percent and as high as 25 percent (Gianturco and Busse 1985; Zarit and Zarit 1998). Rates of dementia are estimated at between 5 percent and 15 percent for people over the age of sixty-five (Gurland 1991; Kennedy 2000; Zarit and Zarit 1998). Most authors do agree that, over the age of eighty-five, prevalence rates approach 50 percent. Rates for schizophrenia are usually at less than 1 percent of the elderly population (Gurland 1991; Kennedy 2000), though Gurland reports 12 percent of nursing home residents have schizophrenia. Regardless of the exact rates of prevalence, the numbers of older persons with a mental illness will increase because of a demographic shift toward an older population in general. It is also clear that the elderly are underrepresented in terms of service utilization (Husaini, Moore, and Cain 1994; Padgett, Burns, and Grau 1988). Elderly persons with mental illness have great vulnerability, risk, and needs. Their vulnerability and risk increase without appropriate mental health services.

Developmental Tasks and Issues

The developmental tasks for older persons with mental illness stem from normal changing life circumstances and extraordinary conditions: aging and mental illness. The usual developmental tasks for older adults apply to mentally ill older persons as well. Psychiatric illnesses, regardless of the age of onset, require adaptive strategies and impact upon developmental tasks at each stage of the life course. The developmental tasks for older persons will be reviewed, followed by a discussion of the impact of a mental illness on those developmental tasks of aging.

DEVELOPMENTAL TASKS ASSOCIATED WITH AGING

Germain and Bloom (1999) remind us that growing old is not a social problem or a disease. Rather it is a lifelong process of biological and psychosocial change. There is great heterogeneity in this process because of the accumulation of a variety of experiences over many decades (Stoller and Gibson 2000). In order to understand the developmental tasks of older persons, one must use a life course framework and understand the sociohistorical context in which they live. This framework has four premises:

1. The aging process is affected by individual's personal attributes, their particular life events, and how they adapt to these events.
2. Sociohistorical times shape opportunity structures differently for individuals with specific personal characteristics, such as being in a subordinate position on a social hierarchy. Thus, people's life events, adaptive resources, and aging experiences differ.
3. Membership in a specific birth cohort . . . shapes the aging experience. Within cohorts, however, the experience of aging differs depending on one's position in systems of inequality based on gender, race, or ethnicity, and class.
4. Sociohistorical periods shape the aging experiences of cohorts. These historical times, however, have different impacts on the experiences of disadvantaged and privileged members of the same cohort (Stoller and Gibson 2000:19).

In addition, when we speak of the elderly we are not speaking of a uniform group. There is great difference between a sixty-five-year-old and an eighty-five-year-old person (Kropf and Pugh 1995). Neugarten (1978) described the young-old (fifty-five to seventy-four) the old-old (seventy-five to eighty-five), and the very old (over eighty-five). Germain and Bloom used Neugarten's categories, though they begin the young-old category at sixty-five, as a fifty-five year old is not really considered "old" in today's current cohort of elderly persons. Each category of older person faces differing developmental tasks and vulnerabilities.

With the above caveats in mind, there are certain developmental tasks associated with aging and found consistently in the literature. However, the research on aging must be read with Berman-Rossi's (2001) caution in that prior research and concepts focused on pathology rather than on resiliency among older adults. This sentiment is echoed by Zarit and Zarit, who describe the two faces of aging: decline and deterioration as well as fulfillment and satisfaction over continued accomplishments.

There are biological, psychological, and social processes that effect development in older persons. There are numerous biological changes as people age, and older adults must adapt to these changes. The changes include decreased strength and stamina, decreased sensory perceptions, changes in physical appearance, decreases in the efficiency of the major systems of the body (immune, cardiovascular, respiratory, reproductive, muscular-skeletal, and neurological systems) (Burnside and Schmidt 1994a; Cavanaugh 1997). For the healthy elderly these changes usually do not interfere with normal activities. However, the changes do require adaptation and may present as an assault to the self-concept. A major developmental task for an older person is the incorporation of these changes into the concept of self.

There is a wealth of research on the psychological changes in aging. Much of the psychological research has focused on intelligence, memory, and personality traits. A great deal of the early research suggested a decline in intelligence and memory as people aged; however, much of this early research had serious methodological flaws and overstated the declines (see Zarit and Zarit for an excellent review of the literature). There are demonstrated declines that occur late in life, but for most healthy persons the changes do not affect performance of familiar activities, and they find ways to adapt (Toseland 1995). Once people reach seventy-five the age effects become more apparent, especially when in stressful or novel situations. Finally, the research on personality changes in older adults is contradictory. There is, however, no universal pattern of deterioration of personality as people age. In fact, core personality traits tend to be stable over the entire life course (Zarit and Zarit 1998).

Many of the developmental tasks for the current cohort of the elderly are the result of social processes. There are numerous social changes that occur for the elderly, and these include role loss, retirement, death of loved ones, decreased economic resources, and possible dependency (Berman-Rossi 1990; Gray and Geron 1995; Toseland 1995; Zarit and Zarit 1998). An older person must adapt to and incorporate into their sense of self these social changes and their resultant changes in lifestyle.

The physical, psychological, and social changes bring about several needs for older adults and represent the major developmental tasks for older adults. Among these needs are the continuation of a meaningful life, sustaining a sense of self, maintaining influence over one's environment, maintaining social connections, preparing a legacy, understanding the changing modern world while maintaining a connection to the past, meeting fundamental survival concerns, feeling useful, and feeling love and affirmation (Berman-Rossi 1990; Blankenship, Molinari, and Kunik 1996; Burnside and Schmidt 1994b; Lowy 1983, 1985; Toseland 1995).

DEVELOPMENTAL TASKS ASSOCIATED WITH LIVING WITH A MENTAL ILLNESS

The literature on risk factors discusses the concept of cumulation of risk (cf. Smith and Carlson 1997). This concept holds that having several risk factors increases the likelihood of having negative outcomes in life. Being an older person and having a mental illness represents such a cumulation of risk factors in that all the associated risks of aging are compounded by the risks associated with mental illness. This cumulative effect impacts the developmental tasks for mentally ill older persons. For example, Lukens (2001) describes how schizophrenia usually strikes a person in early adulthood. This developmental time period is rife with important developmental milestones: assuming adult responsibilities, developing a partnership, possibly beginning a family, beginning a career, and completing an education. The disruption of the life course has a ripple effect throughout the rest of a person's life as they are often pushed to the margins of society (Zarit and Zarit 1998). Once a mentally ill person reaches old age, the developmental tasks elaborated above are still pertinent; however, they must now adapt to the developmental tasks with few resources and greater risk. For those persons who develop a mental illness in later life, the developmental tasks are also more difficult. However, they usually will have more resources or protective factors. We now turn our attention to risk and vulnerability factors.

Vulnerabilities and Risk Factors and Resiliencies and Protective Factors

There is a growing body of literature on risk and protective factors, resilience, and stress and coping (cf. Gitterman 2001a, 2001b; Kelly 1994; Smith and Carlson). The related bodies of literature highlight the ecological nature of difficult life circumstances and conditions. These concepts are contrary to the dominant medical model of understanding people and their problems, and they help to better understand the nature of people and their particular problems. Berman-Rossi (2001), in comparing resiliency theories to the dominant medical model, describes how disability is too often seen as a personal attribute, something intrinsic to the individual, and not seen as a function of society or a poor person:environment fit. This literature is helpful in understanding the experiences of older persons living with mental illness.

A risk factor is something that increases the likelihood that a person will have a negative outcome. These factors can be categorized into characteristics of individuals, families, social contexts, and the interactions between persons and environments (Smith and Carlson 1997). Vulnerability is defined as "capable of being wounded: defenseless against injury" (Merriam-Webster 2002). Berman-Rossi (2001) points out that there is a relationship between risk and vulnerability in that vulnerability only has "viability and potency when risk is present" (732). So for example, the decreased immune functioning of older persons makes them more vulnerable to infection. However, it is only when the presence of the risk factor of pathogens is present that the vulnerability has potency.

Mentally ill persons have numerous vulnerabilities and risk factors. They may be socially isolated, have smaller social networks, have limited power over their environments, possess poor social skills, display bizarre or frightening behaviors, experience strained family relationships, undergo a loss of self-worth and self-esteem, live with a sense of hopelessness and helplessness, lack a sense of purpose in life, and suffer difficulties with independent living (Berman-Rossi and Cohen 1989; Cooper and Pearce 1996; Cutrona, Schutte, Suhr, and Russell 1990; Leszcz 1991; Lukens 2001; Meeks and Hammond 2001; Taylor and Mosher-Ashley 1996; Zarit and Zarit 1998). Also, it must be noted that mental health needs may be defined as resulting from impairments in psychosocial functioning secondary to psychiatric symptoms, but they can also result from a nonadaptive or maladaptive environment (McGrew 1999). In addition to these individual and family risk factors, social risk factors include extreme economic deprivation, limited educational experiences, prejudice and fear, ageism, lack of adequate community supports and treatment.

The aging process exacerbates the risk factors. For example, Meeks and Hammond report that friendships are more important to older adults' psychological well-being than family relationships. Unfortunately, persons with mental illness may not have established friendships. In addition, older adults with mental illness report fewer links, less reciprocity, and less emotional support than younger mentally ill persons. Cutrona and colleagues state that stress reduction is often a part of the treatment or prevention of mental illness in younger populations, but aging brings about stressors such as bereavement, fixed income, and health declines that cannot be eliminated. These and other stressors can trigger psychotic episodes (Segal and Bandervoort 1996). In addition, older persons with mental illness may suffer from neurological side effects from a lifetime of neuroleptic medications.

Despite the overwhelming risk and vulnerability factors, older persons with mental illness have protective and resiliency factors. First and foremost, they possess great strength as evidenced by their shear survival. They have endured enormous hardships and unspeakable horrors, especially those that became ill in the era when there were few treatments for mental illness. They learned to survive in institutions that were often quite oppressive. This demonstrates adaptability. However, as Kelly (1999) points out, adapting to a total institution often entailed an adaptive dependency that may interfere with successful aging and community living. Mentally ill older adults also respond well to reciprocal and emotionally supportive relationships. Social supports and networks can act as a buffer to the risk factors. Lukens suggests that the ability to recognize and use personal strengths can also be a protective factor.

There are protective factors that can be developed or put in place for mentally ill older adults. The provision of social support and the building of a support network can be an important protective factor (Clark and Travis 1994; Cutrona et al. 1990; Martin and Nayowith 1989; Meeks and Hammond 2001; Safford 1995). The development of social support is especially important, as one of the key symptoms in schizophrenia and depression is withdrawal and isolation. In addition, social support links personal resources with environmental resources, thereby increasing resiliency (Hobfoll and Wells 1998). Self-concept has been reported to be an important resiliency factor for older persons (Berman-Rossi 2001; Leczcz 1991) and should be a focus of social work practice with this population. Finally, environmental factors can promote resiliency. Effective treatment, adequate and appropriate housing options, economic supports, Medicare and Medicaid, and coordinated services can promote resiliency.

Agency and Group Context

The agency context of any group service is an important influence on practice (Gitterman and Miller 1989). The group described throughout the rest of this chapter was not an exception. The group was run under the auspices of a countywide community mental health system with centers located throughout the county. The county was located in a metropolitan area and had distinct urban, suburban, and rural parts. The program was started during a time of budget cutbacks and a push from state officials to provide more group services. The county had a successful and profitable day treatment program for mentally ill older adults in the southern part of their catchments area, and it was running at capacity. The mental health system was serving a large number of older adults in the northern part of the community, but they were only receiving individual case management services. Many of the clients would spend their days isolated in drab and unstimulating board and care facilities. Others lived with family or in independent settings. In addition, some clients who lived in the middle section of the county attended the original program, and it was thought they could attend the new program instead. This would allow clients from the southern part of the county who were on the waiting list to attend the southern program.

The agency was located in and served a mostly white middle class neighborhood, and the clients from the middle section of the county were from an impoverished area rich with ethnic and racial diversity. Central administration made a big push to start the new program and wished it to be at full capacity as quickly as possible for financial reasons. In order to be eligible for participation in the program, clients must have met two of three criteria: a diagnosis of a severe mental illness, risk for admission to the psychiatric hospital, or living in one of the county's board and care facilities. Emphasis was placed on those with a chronic mental illness, though, as Gurland and Toner (1990) point out, defining chronicity is often a vague endeavor. Likewise, simply having a diagnosis does not tell one anything about the types of problems or the severity of problems an elderly person may experience, nor will it tell you how he or she behaves or functions (Perkins and Tice 1995; Travis and Clark 1996). As most of the elderly clients receiving services in the county system were diagnosed with a severe mental illness, they were all at risk for hospitalization.

With the agency's push to begin another group service to the elderly clients in the system and the rather broad criteria for participation in the group, the luxury of careful group membership selection was not possible. Many authors describe rather restrictive criteria for group membership for groups of elderly persons. These criteria often suggest excluding disturbed and wandering persons, incontinent persons, persons with active psychosis or psychotic depression, persons with bipolar disorder, deaf persons, hypochondriacal persons, persons with dementia, paranoid persons, persons with bizarre or threatening behaviors, very deviant behavior, persons who are "too frail" (Altholz 1994; Burnside 1994b; Kennedy 2000; Lesser, Lazarus, Frankel, and Havasy 1981; Toseland 1995). If this list of exclusionary criteria was followed, no one would be eligible for the group. Rather than focus on the exclusionary criteria, the group was formed with the purpose to help members cope with the common problems that older persons with mental illness face and to maintain their residence in the least restrictive environment as possible. As Berman-Rossi (1990) points out, groups should be formed around problems in living rather than on diagnoses. In essence, we believed people could come together to find solutions to their common problems (Schwartz 1991 [1961]). Though many of the exclusionary criteria have a sound basis, we viewed them as potential obstacles to mutual aid instead of grounds for exclusion. Certainly they would have clinical import, but should not rule anyone out.

Another important agency influence on the program was the availability of transportation. The literature is rife with descriptions of transportation being a huge obstacle to group participation for elderly clients (cf. Burnside 1994a). However, the agency provided transportation for many clients.

The group was a psychosocial clubhouse model modified to fit the needs of an elderly population. The program ran from 10:00 AM to 2:00 PM, and members would attend from one to five days a week. The day began with coffee and check-in time, exercise for elderly persons, a group activity in the morning, work time, lunch, followed by another group activity. During the designated group times, staff (which included the author and a series of co-workers who rotated on a daily basis) facilitated a wide range of group work modalities offering what Leszcz describes as the therapeutic "buffet" required for work with this population. The modalities included discussion groups, recreation and activity groups, art, poetry, and music groups, education groups, and reminiscence groups. Work time allowed members to choose an area of interest and engage in activities. The areas included lunch preparation, sewing, programmatic paperwork (clients helped with this), and cleanup detail. The milieu became the group consistent with Martin and Harrington's (2001) description of a twenty-four-hour group in residential work.

Work and Group Themes

The literature on group work with elderly persons identifies fairly consistent work themes. These include continuity with the past, understanding the modern world, independence, physical and cognitive impairments, loss of family members and friends, interpersonal stressors, joys and difficulties with children and grandchildren, resources, environmental vulnerability and adjustment, religious conviction and ethnic pride, leisure pursuits, meaning, loss of functions and tasks, loss of self-worth and self-esteem, loneliness and isolation, depression and demoralization, dependency-autonomy conflicts, death and dying, aging, sexuality issues, infantilization, reminiscence, and life transitions (Blankenship, Molinari, and Kunik 1996; Kennedy 2000; Lee 1983; Leszcz 1991; Toseland 1995; Zarit and Zarit 1998). Though most of the themes identified are derived from literature that address the elderly in general rather than mentally ill older persons, they represent the themes that emerged in the group described here. Mentally ill older persons face many of the same stressors and life stage issues as their non-mentally ill counterparts; however, they must face these with the additional vulnerability of a mental illness. In addition to the themes identified above, group members worked on tenuous living arrangements, grieving lost opportunities, coping with psychiatric symptoms, horrible psychiatric treatment in the past, and competence. These themes were part and parcel of the work of the group: namely, coping with effects of having mental illness while also coping with the stressors accompanying the aging process. Several of these themes will now be illustrated.

Tenuous Living Arrangements

Group members lived in a variety of settings. Some lived independently, others with family members, and others lived in personal care homes of varying quality. Regardless of living arrangements, they were all vulnerable to change of living arrangements and they all feared having to move. Those living independently feared having to move in with family or to a board and care facility. Those living with family feared having to move in with strangers. And those living in personal care homes feared moving into a more dreadful place. The fear of nursing home placement loomed large in all their lives. A worsening of psychiatric symptoms, an increase in frailty, or the changing whims of care providers could quickly change living situations. The group workers believed in what Kahn (1975) called the "principle of minimum intervention." Older adults do best in situations that are familiar to them. Unfortunately, those with limited social support are more likely to be placed in restrictive living environments even if the restrictive environment was unneeded (Clark and Travis 1994; Sommers et al. 1988). Hence, great efforts were taken to help group members age in place. The group helped members discuss fears, provide problem solving, and offer concrete suggestions for maintaining as much independence as possible.

One morning during check-in time Amelia began talking about how her sister was threatening to make her move from her apartment into an assisted living facility. Amelia had managed to live on her own for ten years despite psychiatric hospitalizations every sixteen months to two years. She was diagnosed with bipolar disease and would occasionally stop taking her medications. During these periods she would call her sister, her primary caregiver, at all hours of the night and made frequent use of the mental health systems crisis line "just to chat." Despite her limited interpersonal functioning and bizarre behaviors she had been able to maintain herself. Her apartment was always impeccably clean, she cooked for herself, and even managed to keep a balanced checkbook. Despite these strengths, she was always one psychiatric crisis away from a loss of independence. This morning Amelia was terribly upset about her sister's threat to "put her away." Her speech was angry, pressured, and she looked quite tired.

MARTHA: Amelia, why do you think your sister wants you to go to one of those homes?

AMELIA: She's just an old cow and she hates me. She always has. Ever since we were little girls she's always been mean to me. I've never been anything but sweet to her, and look how she treats me now. If our momma was alive now she'd get what's coming to her.

MARTHA: But Amelia, you've lived by yourself for a long time now. Why is she mad at you now? Are you calling all those people at night again?

AMELIA: You're taking her side now too. Everybody hates me. I hate this damned place. I don't even know why I come here.

JENNY: Oh, Amelia, you're talking crazy again. Everybody knows your sister loves you. You're lucky you got a sister who still talks to you. I'm surprised she does talk to you the way you call her all night long.

AMELIA: Shut up, Jenny. You hate me too.

JIM: (Said flirtatiously) Amelia, you could come live with me.

AMELIA: Shut up, Jim. I wouldn't live with you if you had the last house on earth.

WORKER: Wow, Amelia. You sure are wound up and angry today. Jim, Jenny, and

Martha are trying to make you feel better and help, and you are really snapping at them. What's going on?

AMELIA: They hate me too. I just want to live by myself. I don't want to go to no damn home. I wish everyone would just leave me alone.

ELLA: Amelia, did you stop taking your medicine again? You remember what happened to me when I quit taking my medicine. I stayed up all night long playing my music and singing. My daughter was going to put me out. She was so mad with me. You people kept harping on me to take my medicine so I'd sleep at night and not bother my daughter. I ended up in the hospital, and my daughter almost didn't take me back.

AMELIA: (*Crying*) I hate those damn pills.

MARTHA: Oh, honey. I hate mine too, but I do crazy things when I don't take them.

ROBERT: That's what's wrong with these people. You don't do what they want, and they just get tired of you and throw you away. You better do what she says, Amelia, or she'll get tired of you.

The group began discussing how easy it was to get kicked out of their homes and how frightening it was to have so little control over their lives. Amelia sat quietly listening. After a short while the worker reentered the conversation.

WORKER: Everyone knows how afraid Amelia feels about being forced to move. It's happened to most of you here. (*Amelia looks up from her crying.*) Amelia, it sounds like everyone here thinks being forced to move is a bad thing (*she shakes her head*). I think Ella and Robert were trying to give you some advice about making your sister change her mind.

ELLA: Yeah, Amelia. You better take your medicine or you'll end up in the hospital again, and your sister may think you need one of those homes. I hate my medicine too. I get so I can't even go to the bathroom from it. (*Everybody laughs— even Amelia.*)

AMELIA: I don't want to talk about it anymore.

The group continued talking the rest of the morning about the instability of their living arrangements. Later in the day Amelia approached the worker and asked if she could see the doctor about her medicine. She resumed her medication, and a disaster was averted.

GRIEVING LOST OPPORTUNITIES

Another major theme that emerged was grieving lost opportunities. During the natural life review process, older persons look back on their lives and take stock of what they did well and what they did not do so well. They might examine what they had hoped their life would be and compare it to what it had become in reality. This theme was particularly salient for this group, as many of the traditional milestones of the aging process had been altered by the experience of living with a mental illness. For example, those members who had developed a mental illness earlier in life did not reach "expected" milestones for members of their cohort. Many had not had the careers or family that they had expected and would grieve the nonevents. Others who had developed a mental illness later in life would also have to cope with nonevents or a lifestyle they had never dreamt they would experience. These issues would often emerge in reminiscence groups.

During one reminiscence group activity the worker was using music from the big band era. A song would be played and members would reflect on what they were doing when the song was popular.

MARTY: (*Tapping her feet and smiling*) oh, I loved Glen Miller. I met my husband at a dance, and that song always makes me think of the night we met. He was so handsome and he was such a good dancer.

ELLA: Martha, I bet you were a regular dance hall girl, teasing all the boys.

GROUP: (*All laugh.*)

MARTY: Oh, yes. I loved to dance and I had one dress that made all the guys look at me. I was wearing it the night I met my husband. We fell madly in love and married about six months later. I got pregnant pretty quickly after that, and we didn't go out dancing too much after that. (*Everyone laughs.*)

WORKER: Glen Miller really changed your life! Did anyone else meet their husband or wife out dancing like Martha did?

GROUP: Several members discussed meeting people and falling in love, but no one else met their spouse.

ROBERT: I never got to go out dancing. They didn't let us listen to music so much in the hospital. That's why I never got married, locked up all those years.

JIM: Ah, Robert, there were women in Milledgeville (the state hospital). I had all the ladies I wanted. (*Jim started talking in a rather risqué manner.*)

MARTY: Jim, there you go again. You're always talking like that, and it's gross.

JIM: I can't help it if the ladies loved me.

WORKER: Jim, I don't know how we always end up talking about your sex life (*Jim and group laughs*), but I was interested in what Robert said.

ROBERT: I always did want to have me a wife and family, but, being put away for so long, I never did get a chance. I guess no one wanted to marry a crazy man.

AMELIA: Me too, I always wished I got married. I had a boyfriend once in the hospital, but they wouldn't let us see each other. Now look at me, I'm just an old lady that nobody wants. Now I don't even have no damned grandchildren. All I have is my sister, and she hates me.

ELEANOR: Amelia, you ain't alone. You got us.

AMELIA: It's not the same.

ELEANOR: I know it, but it helps.

GROUP: Several members then began to talk about how they missed out on family because of their mental illness and how lonely they had been in their lives.

MARTY: Well, I did have a family and kids, but that doesn't mean I don't get lonely too. Since I got sick my family won't have anything to do with me. I never get to see my grandkids. Sometimes I think that's worse—having family, but they don't want you (*several members nod*).

WORKER: Some of you had families and some of you didn't, but all of you missed out on some pretty important stuff once you got sick.

GROUP: There was lots of nodding, and then they began to talk about how the group helped them feel less lonely and how you just had to keep on going.

COMPETENCE AND INFANTILIZATION

Kelly (1994) discusses the paternalism that many older persons experience, especially if others see them as marginally or totally incompetent. In addition, many older persons will speak about how they are treated condescendingly by younger people. The judgment of incompetence and infantilization may be subtle (e.g., a certain tone of voice usually reserved for infants, being spoken for, or information withheld). Or it may be quite blatant, as when medical decisions are made for the older person, living arrangements are made, or changes without input, etc. The experience of having a mental illness exacerbates the view of incompetence and childlike status that others have of older persons. In addition, the successful adaptation to the mental health system, especially in earlier years, requires a certain dependency and childlike stance in life (Kelly 1999). A "good patient" was a compliant patient. Neeman (1995) suggests that when one's competence is increasingly challenged one's sense of self-esteem and self-concept suffer. For most people previous life experiences and patterns will buffer this negative impact, but for those (like mentally ill older persons) without a rich history of positive experiences the negative effect is synergistic.

The experience of being treated like a child or being seen as incompetent was a frequent theme in groups. For some members the adaptive dependency had become such a part of their sense of self that to ask them to have some control over their lives was an anxiety-producing event. This aspect will be discussed later, as it had implications on group development. Other members consistently railed against being seen as a child, and this is illustrated in the following example, which occurred during a Monday morning group session on health care issues.

DANIELLA: I hate goin to doctors. If'n there's somethin wrong with me I just think of what my granny would do. She always had some remedy to fix up most problems folks had. Everyone used to come see granny when they was sick. Naw, sir, I try never to go to a doctor. They's not tellin what'll they'll do ta you.

JIM: I hate them too. They always give you pills and don't tell you what's wrong, and them blasted pills make you feel worse than before.

ELLA: You just got to ask them and make them tell you. They get mad at me sometimes, but I just keep asking them till they tell me. I don't care if they get mad at me. That's why Medicaid pays them, to tell you what's wrong and make you better.

DANIELLA: That's a lie, Ella. They don't have to tell you nuthin. They just do whatever they want.

WORKER: What do you mean, Daniella?

DANIELLA: They just took my momma's breast off one time. She woke up and it was gone. And me, I had my baby and when I woke up I couldn't have no more babies. They fixed me so I couldn't have no more babies and they didn't even ask me. They just cut me and I wasn't a real woman anymore. And I wanted me a big family too . . . lots of children.

WALTER: Yes, ma'am, that's right. That's what they do. I'm bad sick right now and they won't tell me what's wrong with me. I'm scared and they won't tell me what's wrong. That doctor talked to my wife and son last week and told them what's wrong, but they won't tell me nothing.

WORKER: That's right, Walter, I meant to ask you about your appointment. What happened?

WALTER: Well they stuck me in one of those big machines to look at my head. Said it would help them figure out why I keep falling and walkin funny. There's something wrong with my breath too. They looked at my chest too. I know something bad is wrong with me, but they just keep telling me not too worry. I'll be OK. They treatin me like I'm some kid, but I know something is bad wrong with me.

ELLA: You got to keep asking, Walter.

WALTER: I do keep askin, but they keep telling me it's nothing to worry about, but I know they are lying. They think I'll go all funny if they tell me the truth, but I won't go funny on them. I take my medicine and I'm just fine.

ELLA: (*Looking at worker*) can't you find out what's wrong with Walter?

WORKER: Walter, do you want me to help you find out what the tests said? (*Walter nods yes.*) What do you think is wrong?

WALTER: My daddy had a growth in his head and it killed him and my momma had lung cancer. That's what I think is wrong with me, but they won't tell me. I think I'm dying. I just want to know. I know when I was off my head they couldn't tell me, but I'm not off no more. I just want to know.

JIM: You're not dying. You'll be OK. (*Several other members try to tell Walter he's not dying, but it's hollow. He looks and sounds terrible. Walter looks upset with their false reassurance.*)

WORKER: We are talking like the doctors and Walter's family right now. (*Walter shakes his head yes.*) None of us like to be treated like we are children, and we all have a right to know what is wrong with us.

DANIELLA: (*With tears in her eyes*) Mr. Walter, I hope you ain't dying, but you needs to know. Did you tell them you think you dying?

WALTER: Naw, I haven't said nothing about that neither.

The group helped Walter figure out ways to tell his family he thought he was dying and to ask again about his medical diagnosis. He took the group's advice, but they would not tell him. He quickly became too ill to attend group and died shortly after this group session, never having been told by the family or doctor that he had a brain tumor.

SEXUALITY

Sexuality is often seen as a taboo subject for the elderly (Brecher 1984). Workers may feel uncomfortable speaking about sexual issues with older persons or the elderly persons may feel it is inappropriate to discuss such topics. However, despite ageist beliefs to the contrary, older persons are sexual beings, and many wish to discuss or come to terms with their sexuality as they age. Issues of sexuality were complicated in this group because of the wide range of sexual opportunities and experiences for group members. Those who had spent great periods of time in institutions during their young adulthood through middle age had limited opportunities for sexual relationships. Sexual expression was frowned upon in state hospitals, and residents often had extremely repressive sexual beliefs forced upon them (Kelly 1999). Many still lived in settings where such attitudes and beliefs were still held. Many members held these negative beliefs. Other members who had more positive attitudes about their sexuality had limited opportunities for sexual relationships. In addition, many of the medications group members took greatly reduced libido. When they complained of this to medical staff or family members, their concerns were discounted because of their age. Finally, there were a few members who were hypersexual, and this made other members uncomfortable. Dealing with the myriad attitudes the members had about sexuality as well as the workers' own discomfort with discussing sexual issues with grandparent figures made such topics quite complicated. This is illustrated in a series of psychoeducational group sessions on the normal physical changes brought about by aging. The group worker was presenting how each system in the body changes as people age. As each biological system was reviewed, members would discuss how the physical changes impacted them and how they adapted to the changes. Due to the worker's embarrassed and uncomfortable feelings about the topic, the reproductive system was saved until the end of the series. As the educational material was being presented, there was rapt attention as well as some uncomfortable giggles and wisecracks. Eventually, one of the members, a seventy-year-old man who lived twenty years in a state hospital and who currently lived in a repressive board and care home, asked a question.

ROBERT: Ms. Smith (*his home provider*) says that abusing yourself makes you weak and will give you voices. Is it true?
WORKER: Abusing yourself?

ROBERT: Yeah, she caught me abusing myself and when I fell in the morning she said it was because I abused myself and said if I didn't quit I'd get my voices back.

WORKER: (*Embarrassed for missing the meaning of his question and by the subject*) oh, you mean masturbation. No, it doesn't do those things to you. Some people have some negative beliefs about masturbating, but it is a pretty normal thing to do. A guy named Kinsey did some research, and he says that about 95 percent of men report having masturbated and the other 5 percent lie (*most members laugh*). He also said most women have done it too. Ms. Smith must have made you feel ashamed.

ROBERT: Yeah, I felt bad and was afraid to do it again.

WORKER: (*Stumbling over words*) well, masturbation won't make you weak, go crazy, or cause you to go blind. Many people do it, especially if they don't have a partner.

ELLA: Look at Tim. He's beet red again! Remember how red he got when Daniella was flirting with him? These young people don't have any strength! (*she laughs*).

GROUP: (*Members start laughing and teasing worker.*)

WORKER: (*Laughing*) Ella, you always catch me don't you? I do get embarrassed talking about sex with you folks; my red face always gives me away (*members laugh*). In fact, I waited until the end to talk about this topic. Remember how we've talked about vision, hearing, muscles, bones, circulation, and everything else in the body (*members laugh again*)? But I think it is an important topic, and I know you folks do too. Many of you bring it up quite a bit.

JIM: I love to talk about it.

ZACH: Me too, but I don't need to masturbate because the ladies love me.

MARTY: There you two go again (*everyone laughs*).

WORKER: I know that just because you are old doesn't mean you aren't interested in sex. But many of you are made to feel badly about your sexual feelings.

ZACH: I don't feel bad about sex, but Mrs. Thomas kicked me out of the house cause me and Sara were having sex. We're grown people and should be able to do whatever we want.

SAM: My daughter wouldn't let me live with her anymore cause I had a girlfriend.

ELLA: My daughter won't let me have a boyfriend either. I have to live with her so I don't, but I sure miss a man. I can't even talk about it with her. She tells me to act my age.

GROUP: Several members had a long discussion about missing sex and wishing people didn't tell them to act their age. Finally, one of the group members (a seventy-four-year old who is actively psychotic) who has a boyfriend asks a question.

JACKIE: (*Looking worried*) can you get AIDS if you are old?

WORKER: Yes Jackie. It doesn't matter how old you are. Anyone can get AIDS if they have unsafe sex.

JACKIE: I'm afraid I might get it. My boyfriend uses drugs but he don't use no rubber. I tell him I won't have sex without a rubber, but I always give in.

Several members are shocked that a group member is talking about AIDS and condoms.

> JENNY: Lordy, Jackie. You are carrying on like a young girl. You just need to act your age.
> DANIELLA: No, Jenny. I'm glad Jackie has a boyfriend. I wish I had me one. But back when I had a boyfriend we didn't have to worry about no diseases like AIDS.
> MARTY: I agree. I miss my boyfriend since he moved up with his kids, but we never thought about AIDS. Jackie, you can't give in. Back when I was married I just said no to my husband. I didn't want to have any more children.
> ELLA: Men are trouble. My husband used to bug me and bug me. Sometimes I'm glad I don't have that bother no more.
> JENNY: Amen to that, Ella.
> WORKER: Sounds like some of you both miss having someone special in your life and also are glad not to have the bother. But Jackie does have someone and she's worried about AIDS. Her boyfriend does use IV drugs and that's one of the risk behaviors for AIDS. Now she's at risk for AIDS too. What can we do to help Jackie with her worry?

The group gave Jackie a great deal of feedback, suggesting everything from leaving her boyfriend to not having sex with him unless he used a condom. Jackie was ambivalent about all the suggestions, but decided she would try to get him to use a condom. Over the next couple of months she struggled with the issue and was able to get him to use a condom, though not consistently. Her boyfriend was arrested a few months later.

This process is an example of mentally ill older persons' ability to openly and directly discuss sexual subjects (sometimes despite the worker's embarrassment). Other times, however, the discussions are more veiled, and the worker must reach for the indirect cues. Once opened, the discussions can be quite frank.

There is a large body of literature that describes common themes as groups develop over time. The work of Bennis and Shepard (1956), Bion (1959), and Garland, Jones, and Kolodny (1965) set the stage for this understanding. Though each model was different, all pointed out how members were preoccupied with relationships between members and worker as well as between members. Issues of ambivalence, authority, and intimacy must be dealt with sufficiently to allow the group to develop. These themes have become part and parcel of our writings and ways of thinking about stages of group development (see, for example, Berman-Rossi 1990; Germain and Gitterman 1996; Glassman and Kates 1983; Schwartz 1971; Seitz 1985.) Since this original work, other authors began to discuss the absence of a universal sequence of group development. Development may look different based on such things as gender, structure, vulnerability, and age (Galinksy and Schopler 1985, 1989; Kelly and Berman-Rossi 1999; Lee and Berman-Rossi 1999; Schiller 1995, 1997).

In groups for elderly persons with mental illness, the "group as a whole" themes are similar to themes from groups comprised of other people from other vulnerable populations. Namely, there are issues of ambivalence, authority, and intimacy; however, the ways and pace in which they address these themes are qualitatively different from other groups. In addition, member characteristics may influence how the worker recognizes and responds to the obstacles of the development of mutual aid. The impact of age, mental illness, and vulnerability is great.

AMBIVALENCE

The ambivalence seen in the approach-avoidance of early group development may be heightened in groups for elderly persons with mental illness. As discussed earlier, there is great diversity in life experience and personal attributes for elderly persons. Additionally, there is a diversity of experience with mental illness (e.g., onset as a young adult versus onset as an elderly person, mild to severe symptomatology, and minimal to extreme functional impairment). This diversity makes it easy for new members to think and say, "I'm not like *these* people," and it probably explains much of the thought on group composition for groups of elderly persons that suggests not having great heterogeneity in group members. In many settings it is not possible to have homogeneous groups based on diagnosis or functional level. Even if there were homogeneity based on functional level and diagnosis, the diversity of life experience will be great. For example, in this group there were people with graduate educations and people with less than an eighth-grade education. Additionally, there were middle-class and extremely poor members who all shared the same diagnosis. It is important for workers to tune in and respond to the particular struggles that will likely give rise to approach-avoidance issues. Additionally, key practice principles include pointing out commonalities in difficulties with life transitions and finding ways for all members to contribute and participate in the group regardless of their functional level.

The approach-avoidance in this group was expressed first around issues of class, age, and functional level. The initial group members had diagnoses of major depression, bipolar disease, schizophrenia, mild dementia, and personality disorders. Some members had extreme extrapyramidal symptoms and others had less problematic side effects from medication. Others were from middle-class backgrounds and others lived their entire lives in extreme poverty. In addition, there was ethnic and racial diversity. Finally, some members were in their early sixties and others were in their early nineties. Few members lived independently, with most living in varying levels of supported living. All members, however, had problems in living associated with mental illness and age.

In an early group session members that were higher functioning and from middle-class backgrounds ignored the other members, made disparaging comments about them, expressed unwillingness to come back to the group, or made attempts to side with the worker at the expense of relationships with other members. Such attitudes and statements were major obstacles to the development of mutual aid. One morning before some of the lower-functioning clients arrived the following discussion occurred between some of the members.

MARTY: I'm glad the van isn't here yet.

SAM: Me too. We can have our coffee in peace.

AMELIA: Those coloreds have come and are ruining everything. I don't think I want to be here anymore.

MARTY: I know. They scare me. They are so old and different. It was better when it was just us.

WORKER: (*Walking over to group after overhearing their conversation*) I guess starting this new group has been a bit hard on you folks.

AMELIA: Yes it has. I liked it better when I had you to myself. I mean when we had you to ourselves. They are ruining everything. Why do they have to be here? (*The others nod in agreement.*)

WORKER: Well, Amelia, I like to work with you too. Remember how you didn't like it when I started working with Martha and Sam either, but we still get to do things (*said just a little defensively. The worker spent a great many hours working individually with this member prior to the start of the group and the intensive case management continued*). The reason we are all here is because, despite some of the differences, everyone has similar difficulties. Before coming to the group people are very lonely and isolated and are having some problems where they live. We started the group to help people not be so lonely and to help people stay out of the hospital or living someplace they don't want to. You have problems with your sister and Ella has similar problems with her daughter. Sam here just lost his wife and James just lost his wife too. So really you have many things in common and we think you'll be able to help each other with your problems.

AMELIA: (*Unconvinced*) well, I don't know about that. I'm not like them at all.

MARTY: I did notice that some of the problems people talk about are the same, but they still scare me.

WORKER: How do they scare you?

MARTY: Well sometimes I see Jenny when she gets confused and I wonder if I'll get like that. Or there's Maritza. She has manic-depression like me, but I was never as bad as her. Sometimes I'm afraid I'll get like her too. I like coming here, but I get scared too, and sometimes I don't want to come.

WORKER: Yeah, sometimes seeing people who have similar problems only worse than ours can be scary. Sounds like a part of you sees how being a part of the group is good for you and part of you wants to run away.

SAM: Yes, sir, that's the nail on the head. If I stay home all I do is miss my wife and cry. I don't cry when I'm here, but I do get nervous sometimes.

WORKER: That's the catch, isn't it? This helps you but it scares you too. Even though you feel unsure about coming to the group, I think it can help you. I know each of you has already been a big help to some of the other members. That's what this group is all about—each of us helping each other. No one says you have come to the group, and you can stop anytime you like, but we would miss you if you didn't come.

MARTY: I don't really want to quit coming. At least not yet.

Later that day one of the "new" members started complaining about how she had no privacy where she lived and little control over her life. Knowing that Marty, Sam, and Amelia had similar problems in their living situations, the worker winked at the three of them and pointed out the similarities. The group began to discuss together ways they had tried to gain privacy and control over their lives. This became a point of connection. Helping members connect around common difficulties was a major task of the worker, and eventually comments about difference were rarely heard. The group as a whole had become strong enough to tolerate the vast differences among members.

When a new member would enter the group, he or she would sometimes voice concerns about difference and become ambivalent about group participation, but the group members became clear about the connections and would most often point those out. For example, after about six months Mary joined the group. She was in her late eighties, had done volunteer work at Hull House (an experience she did not enjoy), and had even met Jane Addams. Mary lived alone, was becoming frail, and had recently began to suffer with depression with psychotic features. The members who had lived with mental illness their entire lives frightened her. She said that coming to the group reminded her of all those "dirty Italians" at Hull House. Martha told Mary that she had felt the same way when she first started coming to the group, but that she really got a lot out of the group. She described some of the similarities between various members and how they had all helped one another. In words very reminiscent of our discussion six month earlier, Martha said, "That's what this group is all about. We all help each other. You don't have to come to the group and you can stop anytime, but you should give it a try. I bet it will help you like it helps me. You won't stay afraid— besides, we would miss you if you didn't come." Mary did stay in the group, but she never fully integrated with all the group members, choosing to be with Martha and those members more "like her." Still, she was able to participate and contribute to the group until she had a stroke and died eight or nine months later.

AUTHORITY

The authority theme is well documented in the literature (Bennis and Shepard 1956; Garland, Jones, and Kolodny 1965; Glassman and Kates 1983; Kelly 1999; Kelly and Berman-Rossi 1999; Shulman 1999). Berman-Rossi (1993) suggests that the group work tenet that members are a part of their own solutions as well as instrumental in contributing to the solutions of group members has bearing on the authority theme. A basic tenet in the group work tradition is that we are a profession of doing *with* rather than doing *to*. The worker is seen as a member of the group, albeit a member with a unique function and set of skills, but a member nonetheless. Having this kind of role definition does not remove the authority theme as an issue; rather it influences how the authority issue will be handled.

The authority theme emerges in groups for elderly persons with mental illness. Yet that which evokes authority issues and how they surface can be quite different from other groups. Common wisdom suggests that a group cannot become a fully functioning group until authority struggles are sufficiently resolved. However, the predominant way in which the authority theme emerged in working with mentally ill older persons did not involve a challenge at all. Rather, the clients would prefer the worker to make all the decisions for them and tell them what to do. It was as if authority were a nonissue. The members were very dependent on the worker and there were constant plays to the worker's authority. The nonexistence of challenges to authority can lull the worker into thinking that the authority issue has been properly dealt with by the group. In addition, the constant stroking of one's position and esteem is quite rewarding and may interfere with the worker's ability to see, or willingness to engage, latent authority issues.

This passivity can be explained through cohort differences and adaptation to the role of "patient." Many older persons were socialized in an era where one was expected to give those in roles of authority their due respect. They would view the worker as a teacher and passively do what was expected. Others who spent great portions of their lives in mental institutions were used to being treated as marginally competent at best. In order to survive in an institution one had to be compliant and dependent.

The workers held the belief that we should be doing with rather than doing to. Hence, we sought to "undo" the nonissue. Berman-Rossi (1993) lists the skills necessary for helping groups work through the authority-laden power and control stage of group development, and the workers made great use of the skills including encouraging the expression of difficult and taboo feelings and issues, particularly negatives toward the worker, offering direct support of expression; uncoding coded messages, and reaching inside the silence to encourage exploration of difficult material. In addition, it was important to take a long view of encouraging independence, continually clarify the worker's purpose and role as well as the group's purpose and role, progressively give members more control over the group, and invite discussions of authority.

As the group grew and developed, members increasingly began to respond to the constant invitation to take an active role in the control of the group, though not without some anxiety on their parts. This was an extended process, and after six to eight months they slowly began to take on the worker. For example, they began to request certain activities, changes in programming, and would question worker wisdom in certain decisions. After approximately a year they began to openly confront the worker, but after confrontation some members were afraid the worker was mad at them, for being a good patient was equated to being compliant, being told what to do, and not making decisions for oneself. As the group began to take on more control of their lives in group a growing closeness developed. They were able to tolerate differences and they developed well-defined roles and structure for work.

An example of this shift from dependency to control of the group involves the preparation for lunch, which was part of the daily group activities. Initially, members would not participate in menu planning, shopping, preparation, or cleanup. Through constant invitation, members began to slowly participate. However, they were quite dependent on the worker for instructions in the minutest details. Members who were excellent cooks and had much more cooking experience than the worker would ask how to do the simplest tasks. The worker would always ask the members to make the decisions, and thankfully only once or twice was the meal ruined! By the time the worker left the group the members were planning the meals, preparing a shopping list, helping with the shopping, cooking the entire lunch, and doing the cleanup. Each member found a way to contribute to the meal. Several members helped with the grocery shopping and would lecture the worker on how to select good produce. Another client with obsessive compulsive disorder supervised cleanliness in the kitchen, and she became comfortable enough to chastise the worker if he forgot to wash his hands. A woman with mild to moderate dementia would make biscuits, though sometimes she would check the dishwasher to see if they were done. Others with limited cooking skills or less stamina would set the table, supervise the buffet line, or help with cleanup. Members eventually controlled the entire meal process, began to own certain jobs, and took great pride in their contributions.

Meal preparation was used as a programmed group work activity, and it often helped to surface group issues and themes including authority themes. For example, when asked about how to cook or what to prepare, the worker would use it as an opportunity to clarify worker role and group purpose. A simple statement such as "What do you think? I may be the worker, but I don't make all the decisions. This is your group too," would clarify roles and give control to members.

As the group strengthened, open challenges to worker authority began to occur. For example, after about a year the worker began an evaluation group. Members were asked what they liked about the group, what they disliked about the group, and what needed to be changed. Simply asking these questions begins to address the authority theme; however, the worker was not prepared for the revolt that occurred when the topic moved to what needed to change.

WORKER: It's good to hear that you are getting so much out of the group. I too think that we have a great group here and I love coming to work each morning to be with y'all. I was a little surprised to hear that the only things you didn't like were the boring menus and too much bingo. I was hoping to find out more things that you didn't like so we could make this an even better group. It sounds like we need to all plan more varied menus for lunch and cut out on the bingo games. But what else is there about coming here that needs to be changed so we have a better group?

JENNY: Well, I don't know why nobody brought this up. I hear everyone bitching and complaining about it everyday on the way here. We hate that damn van driver and the way he picks us up.

JIM: That's right. We hate that ride (*lots of people in agreement*).

WORKER: Well, what about it don't you like?

ELLA: It takes so long and he won't listen to us about how to pick us up. Poor Leanne gets picked up first thing in the morning and has to sit on that van forever. And she's the last one dropped off in the afternoon. I know cause I'm next.

WORKER: You've spoken to John (the van driver) about this?

JENNY: You damn right we did, and he just told us to mind our own business. He was the driver and he was in charge.

ROBERT: He's just as bad as Ms. Smith (his home provider). Always bossin us around and doing like he pleases. I hate these know-it-alls. We're grown people. I got my union card and he can't treat me that way. People always treat us bad.

WORKER: (*Missing the authority issues*) well, you all do live all spread out. Someone will always be the last to be dropped off, and Leanne does live the farthest away.

ROBERT: I knew you would take his side. We don't have to come, you know. We are grown people and we don't have to be treated like babies. (*Robert gets up and begins to storm outside to the smoking area.*)

WORKER: Wait, Robert. I blew that one. I'm sorry (*Robert continues outside and slams the door. Group looks stunned—as does worker.*) Oops. Looks like I really blew that one. I'll have to apologize to Robert when he calms down just a bit. Anyone else sore with me?

JENNY: Well, you did sound just like John (the van driver). Like we don't know who lives where. We know you are the boss here, but we got ideas too (*several nods of agreement*).

WORKER: I do apologize, Jenny. I didn't mean to sound like a boss or make it seem like I wasn't listening to you. I guess it's just that I don't see how to make the van ride any better and figured that John knew how to do it.

ELLA: Aren't you listening to us? John don't know the best way, mon. We tried telling him about shortcuts and different ways to pick us up, and he just won't listen. Some of us are on there for over an hour, and now he won't even let us bring food on the van.

The group expressed anger at John and at the worker for not listening. After a while the worker apologized again for not hearing them earlier and asked for their suggestions. They suggested several different routes, changing the routes so that the same people didn't always have the long drive, and the possibility for contracting with another transportation company. After several different options had been explored, it was agreed that the worker would do two things: speak with John about alternating routes so that the burden of the long ride was shared more equally and investigate using a private transport company for those eligible for Medicaid transport. By this time Robert had returned from his cigarette break and calmed down.

> WORKER: Hi, Robert. I'm glad you came back in. I was going to come out and apologize when we got done here. While you were out we came up with a plan to try and make the ride better.
> ROBERT: I'm sorry I got so mad and yelled. Are you mad at me?
> WORKER: That's OK, Robert. I deserved it. I didn't really listen to how upset you were and ignored your concerns. I know how many bosses y'all have and how frustrating it is. I'd get angry too. At least when you get mad now you don't throw a chair or punch anything (*said with a grin*).
> ROBERT: Yeah, I'm glad I don't punch no trees no more when I get mad (*people laugh*). You're really not mad at me for yelling?
> WORKER: No, Robert. It's OK to get mad with me, especially if I deserve it. I really do know how frustrating it is for you when you are always bossed around and people don't listen.
> ELLA: People do treat us like we are kids and don't know what's best.

Many people were shaking their heads and began to talk about all the authority figures in their lives that treated them badly. This was a painful issue for members, and by being willing to address issues of authority as often as possible, members began to discuss the abuses of authority and also looked for ways to increase the independence in their lives.

INTIMACY

Quite often the literature describes an intimacy stage that occurs after a struggle with authority. Schiller (1995, 1997), however, holds that intimacy in women's groups precedes power and control. Kelly and Berman-Rossi found that intimacy may develop in groups of institutionalized elderly persons prior to struggles with authority. Their findings suggest that, for some groups, members must develop a sense of safety and intimacy before they feel strong enough to take on issues of authority. When members feel vulnerable they are less likely to challenge. In addition, Kelly (1999) notes that when intimacy-starved older persons experience the closeness of the group they may be less likely to risk losing affectional ties. Both reasons for not disturbing the status quo are likely explanations for the development of a cohesive and intimate group prior to dealing with authority issues for the group described in this chapter.

Berman-Rossi (1993) describes intimacy in groups as a climate of trust where members take greater risks and increase self-revelation. Groups for elderly persons with mental illness are able to develop such a climate of trust. In groups with a well-developed sense of intimacy the work of the group is readily apparent and taboo subjects are more likely to be discussed. Work themes described earlier in the chapter, including the taboo subject of sexuality, are examples of the risks and self-revelation that occur in an intimate group. Other such taboo topics include death, dying, and aging.

A beautiful example of the level of discussion of death that demonstrates intimacy in this group was described by Kelly (1999). The process recording centers on a seventy-five-year-old man with a long history of bipolar disease and alcoholism. Zach had been a vibrant and active member of the group, but he began to have less energy and his physical health was declining. One day the following process occurred:

MARTHA: How are you doing, Zach?

ZACH: Not so good. I feel awful, and I think I'm dying

WORKER: What makes you think you're dying, Zach?

ZACH: I can just feel it. I'm tired.

MARTHA: Are you ready to go?

ZACH: Yes, I've had a hard life but I tried. I've done some bad things, but I've done good too. I know the universe will take me to the light. I'll be with my son. I'm ready.

JULIA: Do you really think you're dying? My sister knew when it was her time.

ZACH: Yes, I'm ready to go. I wonder if my family will even know I've gone.

WORKER: It is sad to think of your family not noticing your death. But, Zach, when you do die I will miss you terribly. You've meant a good deal to me and the group.

ZACH: Thank you. You are kind of like a son to me. I'll miss you and the group too.

GROUP: Zach, we'll miss you too (Kelly 1999).

After this brief discussion, the group began to discuss what it meant to die, how they were not afraid of death but worried about dying, and how much the group meant to them. Discussions like these were always quite powerful for the worker, and he was touched by their ability to candidly speak of death and how the group gave them a sense of dignity as they approached their own deaths.

OBSTACLES TO MUTUAL AID

All groups have potential obstacles to mutual aid. Shulman (1999) identifies several of these potential blocks including apparently divergent interests of group members, disruptive group roles and rules, and barriers to open communication. These potential obstacles exist in groups for elderly persons with mental

illness. However, as with other group dynamics and themes addressed previously, the obstacles to mutual aid for this population will be qualitatively different.
For example, it can be difficult for members to identify the common threads and
common needs because of such divergence in the experience of aging and mental illness. In addition, there are many forces inherent in the aging process and
the nature of certain mental illness that can prevent open communication. For
example, the current cohort of elderly persons may not feel as comfortable sharing in group settings. Earlier generations do not have the same comfort with
group work as today's younger generations. Moreover, some topics such as sexuality are more taboo for the elderly than younger groups. Coupled with these
aging issues, certain mental illnesses make open communication difficult.
Those members with paranoia, for example, may be less likely to share and fully
participate in the group. Others with active psychosis may be distracted by internal stimuli, and those with depression may not have the energy to focus outward.
Despite these potential obstacles, mutual aid can flourish in these groups. In
fact, these potential obstacles help to define the worker's purpose (Shulman
1999). However, in well-functioning groups, the worker is not alone in removing the obstacles.

For example, in one group session the members were drawing pictures of
their childhood homes. The use of such programming is useful in incorporating
the more nonverbal members into group activities (Lesser et al. 1981). After
members finished drawing, they would share their pictures with the group and
begin to tell stories of their youth. Barbara, one of the more withdrawn members, seemed to be especially struggling with her voices this day. During the time
when people were drawing their pictures she took a light yellow marker and, in
a very distracted manner, made a few light marks on her paper. The worker made
several attempts to connect with Barbara and help her complete the tasks. Eventually, he decided that it was enough that she was able to tolerate sitting around
the table with everyone else and left her alone. Everyone but Barbara finished
their drawings, and members began to share their pictures. Jenny, as usual, had
drawn her picture with sparse details and very little color, but described how as
a child she had to feed the chickens and was afraid of the rooster. The group was
thoroughly enjoying her description and teased Jenny playfully. Barbara had quit
making marks on her paper, was looking away from the group with a bizarre
smile on her face, and was mumbling under her breath. Eleanor was a group
member who heard constant voices that medication could not touch, but she had
learned to live with the voices. She noticed Barbara and said in a loud but kind
voice, "Barbara, you leave those people alone. They are not here right now and
we are. You leave them alone and talk to us." Amazingly, Barbara turned to
Eleanor and said, "OK." She even asked Jenny a question about the chickens and
then withdrew again. However, this time she seemed to be actively listening to
the group. Barbara never became very verbal in the group, but, with frequent

demands for work from other members, she began responding to internal stimuli less frequently and increased her interaction with group members.

Shulman (1999) identified how groups may distribute roles to members such as a gatekeeper, deviant member, or the scapegoat. Dealing with these problematic roles can be even more difficult in groups for elderly persons with a mental illness because of their vulnerability. Scapegoating is a prime example of the difficulties dealing with disruptive roles. The word *scapegoating* is derived from the ancient Hebrew ritual in which, on the Day of Atonement, the chief priest would symbolically lay the sins of the people on the head of a goat. As Shulman (1967) points out, the innocence of the scapegoat in this historical sense is not always found in the scapegoat in the group work context. The scapegoat may be the member with the most bizarre behavior or visible illness, and in fact may provoke the other group members. The scapegoat role is a dynamic and interactional role in that the members project their own self-fears and loathing on the scapegoat. In addition, the member or members who attack the scapegoat do the attacking with the implicit permission of the scapegoat, members, and worker. To effectively help the group stop the scapegoating process, the worker must be with the scapegoat *and* be involved with the group to help them understand that their projections are a result of their own painful responses to how others see and treat them. The scapegoat in the group may simply be a more extreme "version" of themselves. However, in groups for elderly persons with mental illness, the group worker may be more inclined to rescue the scapegoat than in other client groups because of the overwhelming vulnerability of the member.

In this group the scapegoat was a very timid, quiet, woman with an extreme disfigurement of the neck. She had many ritualistic behaviors and a difficult time with prolonged social interaction. She always came to group, but she rarely participated in group activities or discussions. She would spend hours looking at herself in a mirror, and would use the mirror to view the world. Betty frequently caught the anger of the group by spending long periods of time in the bathroom, sitting in the group room self-absorbed and in the way.

ELLA: Betty . . . we are late. Hurry up. You are so slow. Get out of the bathroom now.
BETTY: Uh . . . . .just a minute
ELLA: Hurry up, or we will leave you.
BETTY: OK . . . I am here (*she shuffles out into the group room*).
ELLA: Betty, you are so stubborn. Why do you have to be so stupid?
ANNIE: Yeah, we wish you wouldn't even come. We are sick of you.
WORKER: Folks. Take it easy on Betty. You know how hard it is for her to be here. You wouldn't like other people to talk to you like this now, would you?
GROUP: No, it's just she's so stupid.
WORKER: Come on, folks. Let's give her a break.
GROUP: Quiet resignation. They go back to getting ready for the ride home.

The worker's feelings of protectiveness of this extremely vulnerable woman got in the way of his ability to stay true to the mediating role of the worker. In retrospect, the worker should have validated the scapegoat's pain and helped her to see how her behavior was invoking the wrath of the group. In addition, the worker should have helped the members see how they were projecting their pain on to the scapegoat. A simple intervention was needed: "You are all getting so angry at Betty, but isn't this the way other people treat you? You have all been hurt by people not understanding mental illness, not being fair with you, not giving you a chance." A question like this would have opened up communication, rather than shutting it down, and given the group a chance to examine the scapegoating process and do some meaningful work on their feelings of being stigmatized by others.

SOCIAL WORK'S mission is one of service to the vulnerable and oppressed, but we must not forget that even the most vulnerable among us have incredible strengths and resiliency. Just the shear survival of vulnerable persons is a testament to the resiliency people possess. However, Gitterman (2001b) reminds us that resiliency is not simply an inherent characteristic of people. It is an ecological concept. There are psychological components to resiliency, but there are environmental components to resiliency as well. It is in the interaction between people and their environments that resiliency either blossoms or withers. By creating supportive physical and social environments individuals, families, groups, and communities can become resilient. The more vulnerable a group of people is, the more environmental supports are required. Elderly persons with a mental illness have extreme vulnerability and risk. They face the stigma of advanced age and mental illness and have the cumulative risks associated with both. Advanced age and mental illness interact synergistically and seriously threaten one's resilient nature. Group work is a powerful medium for increasing resiliency and mitigating risk for mentally ill elderly persons.

Unfortunately, there is a dearth of services for this special population. Most helping professionals would rather work with younger populations, which are seen as being more readily able to change, grow, and benefit from help. In addition, the chronically mentally ill are seen as a group with little hope for psychological growth and change. It is true that when working with elderly persons with a mental illness one does not often see the incredible changes in people's lives that can be seen when working with substance abusers, children enduring stressful life transitions, or young women coping with sexual abuse. Emery and Emery (1987) state that "elderly schizophrenics" are the most difficult populations they ever worked with. It is also true that at times workers must be impressed with even minimal member gains (Sulman, Fletcher, Gayler, and Sokolsky 1997). However, work with this population is critical and meaningful. The group functioned much like other groups, though at a somewhat slower pace, and the unique characteristics of members altered the ways in which issues and dynamics emerged. There were recognizable stages of group development and common group dynamics. Most important, an abundance of mutual aid developed. As the group strengthened, work occurred on the environmental, interpersonal, and intrapersonal levels. By particularizing generic knowledge of group work theory and practice to the special needs and characteristics of elderly persons with a mental illness, the group became a powerful dynamic for increasing resiliency.

In the early stages of group development, the members would share surface information about themselves, but it was obvious there were big areas of their lives that they would withhold. But after they began to trust and risk, the nature of the communication changed. They began to share the pain of their lives and work on an existential level. Many of the clients were struggling with issues of meaning. Having often lived impoverished and institutionalized lives, they got to the end of their lives and asked "why." What does all this mean? They would spend time trying to make sense of all the twists and turns in their lives. Others spent their lives working and raising families only to reach the autumn years in despair. Again they would ask why, what does it all mean? How can I make sense of this thing that has become my life I want to have mattered? One of the things I will always be grateful for is that while walking part of their journey with them I was able to share in their spark of life. No matter how grim their lives were, most had a spark of life that kept them going. In addition, they worked toward developing a sense of personal dignity. There can be no more meaningful work than helping such vulnerable and marginalized people reach the end of their lives with a sense of dignity. The group members taught me much both about being a social worker and a human being.

References

Altholz, J. A. S. 1994. Group psychotherapy. In I. Burnside and M. Schmidt, eds., *Working with older adults: Group process and technique*, pp. 214–24. 3d ed. Boston: Jones and Bartlett.

Bennis, W. and H. Shepard. 1956. A theory of group development. *Human Relations* 9:415–37

Berman-Rossi, T. 1990. Group work and older persons. In A. Monk, ed., *Handbook of gerontological services*, pp. 141–67. 2d ed. New York: Columbia University Press.

——— 1993. The tasks and skills of the social worker across stages of group development. *Social Work with Groups* 16(1/2): 69–81.

——— 2001. Older persons in need of long-term care. In A. Gitterman, ed., *Handbook of social work practice with vulnerable and resilient populations*, pp. 715–68. 2d ed. New York: Columbia University Press.

Berman-Rossi, T. and M. B. Cohen. 1989. Group decision making working with homeless mentally ill women. *Social Work with Groups* 11(4): 63–78.

Bion, W. R. 1959. *Experiences in groups.* New York: Ballantine.

Blankenship, L. M., V. Molinari, and M. Kunik. 1996. The effect of a life review group on the reminiscence functions of geropsychiatric inpatients. *Clinical Gerontologist* 16(4): 3–18.

Brecher, E. M. 1984. *Love, sex, and aging.* Boston: Little, Brown.

Burnside, I. 1994a. History and overview of group work. In I. Burnside and M. G. Schmidt, eds., *Working with older adults: Group process and technique,* pp. 24–38. 3d ed. Boston: Jones and Bartlett.

———— 1994b. Membership selection and criteria. In I. Burnside and M. G. Schmidt, eds., *Working with older adults: Group process and technique,* pp. 82–91. 3d ed. Boston: Jones and Bartlett.

Burnside, I. and M. G. Schmidt, eds. 1994a. *Working with older adults: Group process and technique.* 3d ed. Boston: Jones and Bartlett.

———— 1994b. Demographic and psychosocial aspects of aging. In I. Burnside and M. G. Schmidt, eds., *Working with older adults: Group process and technique,* pp. 8–23. Boston: Jones and Bartlett.

Cavanaugh, J. C. 1997. *Adult development and aging.* 3d ed.. Pacific Grove, Cal.: Brooks/Cole.

Clark, W. G. and S. S. Travis. 1994. Elderly admissions to a state psychiatric hospital: Cohort characteristics, after-care needs, and discharge destinations. *Journal of Gerontological Social Work* 12(3/4): 101–15.

Cohler, B. J., S. A. Pickett, and J. A. Cook. 1990. The psychiatric patient grows older: Issues in family care. In E. Light and B. D. Lebowitz, eds, *The elderly with chronic mental illness,* pp. 82–110. New York: Springer.

Coolidge, F. L., E. M. Burns, J. H. Nathan, and C. E. Mull. 1992. Personality disorders in the elderly. *Clinical Gerontologist* 12(1): 41–55.

Cooper, B. K. and A. A. Pearce. 1996. The short-term effect of relocation on continuing-care clients with a psychiatric disability. *Research on Social Work Practice* 6(2): 179–92.

Cutrona, C. E., K. Schutte, J. A. Suhr, and D. Russell. 1990. Social support and chronic mental illness among the elderly. In E. Light and B. D. Lebowitz, eds., *The elderly with chronic mental illness,* pp. 65–81. New York: Springer.

Emery, O. B. and P. E. Emery. 1987. Resocialization of the elderly schizophrenic. *Clinical Gerontologist* 7(1): 72–75.

Galinsky, M. and J. Schopler. 1985. Patterns of entry and exit in open-ended groups. *Social Work with Groups* 8(2): 67–80.

———— 1989. Developmental patterns in open-ended groups. *Social work with groups* 12(2): 99–114.

Garland, J., H. Jones, and R. Kolodny. 1965. A model for stages of development in social work groups. In S. Bernstein, ed., *Explorations in group work: Essays in theory and practice,* pp. 12–53. Boston: Boston University School of Social Work.

Germain, C. B. and M. Bloom. 1999. *Human behavior in the social environment: An ecological view.* 2d ed. New York: Columbia University Press.

Germain, C. B. and A. Gitterman. 1996. *The life model of social work practice: Advances in theory and practice.* New York: Columbia University Press.

Gianturco, D. T., E. W. Busse. 1985. Psychiatric problems in later life. In E. Palmore and E. W. Busse, eds., *Normal aging iii: Reports from the Duke longitudinal studies, 1975–1984,* pp. 91–105. Durham: Duke University Press.

Gitterman, A., ed. 2001a. *Handbook of social work practice with vulnerable and resilient populations.* 2d ed. New York: Columbia University Press.

——— 2001b. Vulnerability, resilience, and social work with groups. In T. Kelly, T. Berman-Rossi, and S. Palombo, eds., *Group work: Strategies for strengthening resiliency.* New York: Haworth.

Gitterman, A. and I. Miller. 1989. The influence of the organization on clinical practice. *Clinical Social Work Journal* 17(2): 151–64.

Glassman, U. and L. Kates. 1983. Authority themes and worker-group transactions: Additional dimensions to the stages of group development. *Social Work with Groups* 6(2): 33–52.

Gray, C. A. and S. M. Geron. 1995. The other sorrow of divorce: The effects on grandparents when their adult children divorce. *Journal of Gerontological Social Work* 23(3/4): 139–59.

Gurland, B. 1991. Epidemiology of psychiatric disorders. In J Sadavoy, L. W. Lazarus, and L. F. Jarvik, eds., *Comprehensive review of geriatric psychiatry,* pp. 225–40. Washington, D.C.: American Psychiatric.

Gurland, B. and J. A. Toner. 1990. The chronically mentally ill elderly: Epidemiological perspectives on the nature of the population. In E. Light and B. D. Lebowitz, eds., *The elderly with chronic mental illness,* pp. 3–15. New York: Springer.

Hobfoll, S. E. and J. A. Wells. 1998. Conservation of resources, stress, and aging: Why do some slide and some spring? In J. Lomranz, ed., *Handbook of aging and mental health: An integrative approach,* pp. 121–43. New York: Plenum.

Husaini, B. A., S. T. Moore, and V. A. Cain. 1994. Psychiatric symptoms and help-seeking behavior among the elderly: An analysis of racial and gender differences. *Journal of gerontological social work* 21(3/4): 177–95.

Kahn, R. L. 1975. The mental health system and the future aged. *Gerontologist* 15(1, pt. 2): 24–31.

Kelly, T. B. 1994. Paternalism and the marginally competent: An ethical dilemma, no easy answers. *Journal of Gerontological Social Work* 23(1/2): 67–84.

——— 1999. Mutual aid groups with mentally ill older adults. *Social Work with Groups* 21(4): 63–80.

Kelly, T. B. and T. Berman-Rossi. 1999. Advancing stages of group development theory: The case of institutionalized older persons. *Social Work with Groups* 22(2/3): 119–38.

Kennedy, G. J. 2000. *Geriatric mental health care.* New York: Guilford.

Kropf, N. P. and K. L. Pugh. 1995. Beyond life expectancy: Social work with centenarians. *Journal of Gerontological Social Work* 23(2/3): 121–37.

Lee, J. A. B. 1983. The group: A chance at connection for the mentally impaired older person. In S. Saul, ed., *Group work with the frail elderly,* pp. 43–55. New York: Haworth.

Lee, J. A. B. and T. Berman-Rossi. 1999. Empowering adolescent girls in foster care: A short-term group record. In C. W. Lecroy, ed., *Case studies in social work practice,* pp. 264–84. 2d ed. Pacific Grove, Cal.: Brooks/Cole.

Lesser, J., L. W. Lazarus, R. Frankel, and S. Havasy. 1981. Reminiscence group therapy with psychotic geriatric inpatients. *Gerontologist* 21(3): 291–96.

Leszcz, M. 1991. Group therapy. In J. Sadavoy, L. W. Lazarus, and L. F. Jarvik, eds., *Comprehensive review of geriatric psychiatry,* pp. 527–64. Washington, D.C.: American Psychiatric.

Lowy, L.1983. Social group work with vulnerable older persons: A theoretical perspective. In S. Saul, ed., *Group work with the frail elderly*, pp. 21–32. New York: Haworth.

—— 1985. *Social work with the aging: The challenge and promise of the later years*. 2d ed. Prospect Heights, Ill.: Waveland.

Lukens, E. 2001. Schizophrenia. In A. Gitterman, ed., *Handbook of social work practice with vulnerable and resilient populations*, pp. 275–302. 2d ed. New York: Columbia University Press.

McGrew, K. B. 1999. Residents with severe mental illness: how nursing homes respond. *Journal of Gerontological Social Work* 31(3/4): 149–68.

Martin, R. and M. Harrington. 2001. The twenty-four-hour group. In T. Kelly, T. Berman-Rossi, and S. Palombo, eds., *Group work: Strategies for strengthening resiliency*. New York: Haworth.

Martin, M. A. and S. A. Nayowith. 1989. Creating community: Groupwork to develop social support networks with homeless mentally ill. *Group work with the poor and oppressed*. New York: Haworth.

Meeks, S. and C. T. Hammond. 2001. Social network characteristics among older outpatients with a long-term mental illness. *Journal of Mental Health and Aging* 7(4): 445–64.

Merriam-Webster. 2002. Merriam-Webster online dictionary. Retrieved August 25, 2002, from http://www.merriam-webster.com/.

Mosher-Ashley, P. M. and M. J. Allard. 1993. Problems facing chronically mentally ill elders receiving community-based psychiatric service: Need for residential services. *Adult Residential Care Journal* 17(1): 23–30.

Neeman, L. 1995. Using the therapeutic relationship to promote an internal locus of control in elderly mental health clients. *Journal of Gerontological Social Work* 23(3/4): 161–76.

Neugarten, B. 1978. The future and the young-old. In L. F. Jarvik, ed., *Aging into the twenty-first century*, pp. 137–53. New York: Gardener.

Orten, J. D., M. Allen, and J. Cook. 1989. Reminiscence groups with confused nursing home residents: An experimental study. *Social Work in Health Care* 14(1): 73–86.

Oxman, T. E., J. E. Barrett, J. Barrett, and P. Gerber. 1987. Psychiatric symptoms in the elderly in a primary care practice. *General Hospital Psychiatry* 9:167–73.

Padgett, D. K., B. J. Burns, and L. A. Grau. 1988. Risk factors and resilience. In B. L. Levin, A. K. Blanch, and A. Jennings, eds., *Women's mental health services*, pp. 390–413. Thousand Oaks, Cal.: Sage.

Perkins, K. and C. Tice. 1995. A strengths perspective in practice: Older people and mental health challenges. *Journal of Gerontological Social Work* 23(3/4): 83–97.

Raschko, R. 1991. Spokane community mental health center elderly services. In E. Light and B. D. Lebowitz, eds., *The elderly with chronic mental illness*, pp. 232–44. New York: Springer.

Rose, M. K., H. H. Soares, and C. Joseph. 1993. Frail elderly clients with personality disorders: A challenge for social work. *Journal of gerontological social work* 19(3/4): 153–65.

Sadavoy, J. 1987. Character disorders in the elderly: An overview. In J. Sadavoy and M. Leszca, eds., *Treating the elderly with psychotherapy: The scope for change in later life*. Madison: International Universities Press.

Safford, F. 1995. Aging stressors for Holocaust survivors and their families. *Journal of Gerontological Social Work* 24(1/2): 131–53.

Schiller, L. Y. 1995. Stages of development in women's groups: A relational model. In R. Kurland and R. Salmon, eds., *Group work practice in a troubled society: Problems and opportunities*, pp. 117–38. New York: Haworth.

——— 1997. Rethinking stages of group development in women's groups: Implications for practice. *Social Work with Groups* 20(3): 3–19.

Schwartz, W. 1971. On the use of groups in social work practice. In W. Schwartz and S. Zalba, eds., *The practice of group work*, pp. 3–24. New York: Columbia University Press.

Schwartz, W. 1991 [1961]. The social worker in the group. In T. Berman-Rossi, ed., *Social work: The collected writings of William Schwartz*, pp. 257–76. Itasca, Ill.: Peacock.

Segal, S. P and D. J. Bandervoort. 1996. Differences in daily hassle patterns among California's seriously mentally ill sheltered care residents. *Adult Residential Care Journal* 10(1): 54–65.

Seitz, M. 1985. A group's history: From mutual aid to helping others. *Social Work with Groups* 8(1): 41–54.

Shulman. L. 1967. Scapegoats, group workers and preemptive intervention. *Social Work* 12:37–43.

——— 1999. *The skills of helping individuals, families, groups, and communities*. Itasca, Ill.: Peacock.

Smith, C. and B. E. Carlson. 1997. Stress, coping, and resilience in children and youth. *Social Service Review* 71(2): 231–56.

Solomon, K. 1990. Mental health and the elderly. In A. Monk, ed., *Handbook of gerontological services*, pp. 228–67. 2d ed. New York: Columbia University Press.

Sommers, I., D. Baskin, D. Specht, and M. Shively. 1988. Deinstitutionalization of the elderly mentally ill: Factors affecting discharge to alternative living arrangements. *Gerontologist* 28(5): 653–58.

Stoller, E. P. and R. C. Gibson. 2000. *Worlds of difference: Inequality in the aging experience*. Thousand Oaks, Cal.: Pine Forge.

Sulman, J., J. Fletcher, C. Gayler, A. Sokolsky. 1997. A collectivity of impaired elderly in an acute care hospital: Practice and research. In N. Lang, ed., *Collectivity in social group work*, pp. 45–58. New York: Haworth.

Taylor, D. M. and P. M. Mosher-Ashley. 1996. Community-based residential care for mentally-medically ill elders. *Adult Residential Care Journal* 10(2): 88–101.

Toseland, R. W. 1995. *Group work with the elderly*. New York: Springer.

Travis, S. S. and W. G. Clark. 1996. Metropolitan/nonmetropolitan gero-psychiatric patients: A comparison of levels of functioning, family support, and care migration patterns. *Journal of Gerontological Social Work* 25(3/4): 107–20.

Zarit, S. H. and J. M. Zarit. 1998. *Mental disorders in older adults: Fundamentals of assessment and treatment*. New York: Guilford.

Part 6

Historical and Contemporary
Themes

Chapter 21

Mutual Aid
A Buffer Against Risk

Judith A. B. Lee and Carol R. Swenson

S OCIAL WORK VISIONARY William Schwartz said, "Professions have a way of moving periodically through eras of rediscovery in which an old truth comes alive with the vigor and freshness of a new idea" (Schwartz 1974). His own discovery and rediscovery of concepts basic to the heart of social group work and to the theoretical development of social work contain just such relevance and excitement. They resonate in us on the level of the "ah ha!" experience that characterizes discovery: "Yes, that is what I have been doing all along!" or "That is exactly what is important!" It is also exciting to connect these concepts, particularly mutual aid, to currently useful ecological concepts such as resilience, protective mechanisms and processes, buffers, and mediating structures. Such structures and processes militate against vulnerability and risk inherent in people and in the relationship between people and environments in the twenty-first century. If anything brought feelings of hope and reassurance after the September 11 attack in New York City, it was the indelibly etched images of people helping each other to survive in the face of terror and mass tragedy. That level of human courage, compassion, resilience, and faith translated into millions of acts of mutual aid brings new veracity to the ideas discussed here.

Schwartz's development of the concept of mediation and his emphases on generic social work, on the primacy of skill, on process, on the importance of affect (both worker's and client's), on reciprocity, and on the group as "an enterprise in mutual aid" are concepts that are now familiar in social work vernacular. Yet original meanings are important in harnessing the power of these concepts. In tracing the evolution of concepts within a profession, it is difficult to delineate moments of exciting rediscovery from moments of originality or discovery. If, however, bringing focus and clarity to previously diffuse ideas can vitalize them, it was Schwartz's contribution to bring these concepts to life. His teaching and writings raised some of the basic but half hidden truths that social workers have always known, or even used without "knowing," to the level of a coherent theoretical approach that can guide practice.

It is difficult to separate the interrelated concepts of the interactionist approach. Like a group, this theoretical approach is more than the sum of its parts and becomes a whole in a unique way. The concept of mediation, for example, is central to this approach, for it clarifies the social work function itself, forming the base from which all else follows. It moves social work thinking forward dramatically, by overcoming dichotomies such as the individual and society, the one and the many, the individual and the group, change of individuals and social reform, and even the so-called intrapsychic and interpersonal. This concept of the social work function, mediating the "process by which the individual and his society reach out for each other through a mutual need for self fulfillment," places us in a new arena of practice (Schwartz 1974). We are "at the point where the two forces meet"—in the interactional /transactional arena. This does not allow us to choose "either-or" but requires "both," thus giving new clarity to the term *psychosocial*.

It is Schwartz's concept of the "mutual need for self-fulfillment" of people and their systems that gives further meaning to his emphasis on mutual aid. People need each other and the social groupings of which they are a part; there is no wholeness or real existence in isolation. Yet Schwartz did not romanticize systems or see them as particularly benign. He recognized that systems could be nearly dysfunctional and in need of mobilization in order to be relevant to people who need them for life-sustaining survival. He believed that social progress could only occur by strengthening, not destroying, the connection between people and their institutions. The mediating function of the social worker was conceptualized both within the group of people who came together around common tasks and between that group and the difficult systems they needed to negotiate. The group was seen as a multiplicity of helping relationships characterized by shared power and control, egalitarian relationships, and collective strengths (Berman-Rossi 1994). According to Shulman, Schwartz's view of the individual-social interaction is a statement of interdependence that is fundamental to our belief in social responsibility for the welfare of each individual (Shulman 1999). Gitterman (1979) defines the mutual aid system in the group as one in

> which people share relevant concerns and ideas, and begin to experience others in the same "boat," moving through "the rocky waters of life." As they confide, share and move into taboo areas, they feel less singled-out, their concerns/problems become less unique, less unusual, and often less pathological. By its very nature the group mutual aid system universalizes people's problems, reducing isolation and stigma. . . . This unleashes a group's inherent potential for "multiplicity of helping relationships"; with all members invested and participating in the helping process.   (15)

The concept of mutual aid does not belong to social work alone, but it is inherent in most of the early group work formulations. It was clearly Schwartz, however, who gave primacy to the concept. In one salient passage he stated:

First, the group is an enterprise in mutual aid, an alliance of individuals who need each other, in varying degrees, to work on common problems. The important fact is that this is a helping system in which the clients need each other as well as the worker. This need to use each other, to create not one but many helping relationships, is a vital ingredient of the group process, and constitutes a common need over and above the specific task for which the group was formed.   (Schwartz 1974)

The primacy of mutual aid relates to Schwartz's thinking about the nature of the helping process as well. He was clear that change resides in the client, not in the helper.

The uneasy attempt to take over the language and the sequence-of-treatment concept of the medical profession has confused and retarded our own attempts to find terms and concepts that would truly describe the helping process in social work. For the helping relationship as we know it is one in which the client possesses the only real and lasting means to his own ends. The worker is but one resource in a life situation that encompasses many significant relationships (Schwartz 1974:214).

The tasks of the worker in helping the client to work follow from this premise. This view of the client as the source of help and this division of labor in the helping relationship differentiate interactionist and later related approaches like Germain and Gitterman's life model approach and Lee's empowerment approach from "medical model" approaches where the helper studies, diagnoses, treats, and prescribes (Germain and Gitterman 1980, 1996; Lee 1994, 2001). The emphasis on the need and potential of people for mutual aid also bespeaks a faith in the ability of the client not only to help himself/herself but also to help others. It moves us beyond the self-centeredness of our age to a social centeredness that emphasizes the relationship between the one and the many. It is also an important underpinning of a social justice and community-centered focus in social work practice (Lee 2001; Swenson 1994, 1998). In offering the concept of mutual aid and in transcending the dichotomy between the individual and his social groupings, Schwartz captures the essence of group work history and, we think, the primary contribution of group work to social work.

A practice example illuminates our understanding of the powerful nature of the mutual aid process and its relationship to resilience. It is drawn from a group of homeless women who resided in a temporary public shelter (described in chapter 14). The group members are four women ranging in age from twenty-six to forty-five. Nina, who speaks first, is a black, mildly retarded twenty-eight year-old who ran away from a physically abusive, alcoholic mother and found herself in the shelter. Carla is a bright, heavy, twenty-six-year-old, middle-class black woman who was cast out of her family after she was raped. Lorna is a forty-five-year-old observant Jewish woman who became depressed and agoraphobic, and eventually homeless, after the death of her parents. Donna is a bright and artistically creative thirty-year-old black woman who had two psychiatric hospitalizations after being beaten by her boyfriend. The common ground on which these women met was that they all found themselves alone and homeless, and they shared several months together in the women's shelter. The worker formed the group to promote friendship and a mutual aid system, which would help them leave the shelter and support them once they were on their own. This meeting marked a new step in the intimacy and mutual aid they were developing. The group members had spent a lot of time sharing how difficult life was in the shelter and how they tried to cope.

Nina then said that she was not afraid to express her depressed feelings, because when they hurt, they hurt. The way she was treated here hurt a lot, but the way she was treated at home hurt more. And the workers here kept telling her to go home; they didn't want to know why she couldn't do that. In a lengthy and somewhat vague way she alluded to handcuffs, ropes, and a big dog at home. The others very patiently listened as Nina tried to find words for what happened to her. They kept saying supportive things like "yeah, it sounds hard." I did the same, encouraging her to tell her story, which I knew already, to the others. Donna then said, "It sounds like you had a very hard life, and you did have good reason to leave home, but could you try to tell us about it a little more clearly?" In response to this support and demand for work, Nina struggled on. "My mother was nice sometimes and then suddenly she was mean. . . . She would tie me up . . . to the hot radiator . . . all alone . . . and make the dog guard me. I had no food, either."

Lorna held Nina's hand. They were all outraged for her and let her know that.

Carla said, "I know just how you feel. I was in the same boat. My father beat me bad, too. I ran away first when I was thirteen. My mother would give me candy to smooth it over, but I never forgot the pain, never." Donna said, "I know, too. People put their hands on you and try to control your life, but they can't get your soul. You leave and run away, you can't let them get you, and then your family blames you for it." Carla said, "Exactly. They didn't cause me being here, but they add to my pain by blaming me for it." Lorna added, "Yes, when I was well, I was a sister. I cooked for them, and baby-sat for them. Now I bring them shame, and I'm not a sister any more." Carla said, "Right, I have parents and six brothers and sisters, but I'm all alone."

Donna said, "Well, maybe not all alone," and smiled shyly at the others. It was a close moment. Nina said, "I don't know if I will have you all forever, but I can say I have you to talk to now." Carla said that without us she'd have no one. She said we brought her hope. She said she loved me for helping them. I said that I was very moved by their caring for each other and the help they gave today. I loved them all, too, and I knew they had what it takes to make it. Carla then cracked a joke about the mayor of the city trying to live in a shelter, and "how would he fare?"

This moving excerpt exemplifies exactly what Schwartz, Gitterman, Shulman, and others in this book describe as the mutual aid process. At that moment the group was theirs. They were the helpers: reaching each other, sharing pain, healing old and present wounds, and mobilizing coping abilities and hope as the process unfolded. Their mutual aid system itself formed a buffer against the assaults of homelessness and living in an overburdened city shelter. Both the worker and the group members provided a familylike protective mechanism in the provision of caring relationships where confiding was valued and coping was facilitated and encouraged (Rutter 1987). Collective action was also facilitated. As noted by Lee (chapter14) such experiences of homelessness are once again on the increase in New York City and nationwide. This is due to the increase in poverty and the lack of affordable housing.

Now more than ever Schwartz's words ring true: our times have "compelled social workers to look again at the forces of mutual aid and peer group association " (Schwartz and Zalba 1971). This chapter will examine these forces through tracing the concept of mutual aid and related concepts in the writings and programs of the helping professions. In so doing we hope to reaffirm mutual aid as a critical concept for social work practice and promoting resilience at the current time.

Mutual Aid in Social Work

HISTORICAL PRECURSORS

Before the industrialization of England and America the family and clan were self-sufficient units of mutual aid that assured survival (Spencer 1975). As time passed, other formal and informal means of protecting people from pauperism evolved, some taking the form of mutual aid. We know more, however, about the historic provision of economic aid than of social or emotional support. The English Poor Law emerged in early seventeenth-century England to take care of the exceptional cases where the family could not meet its obligations. Under the Poor Law the "truly indigent and helpless," such as orphaned children, were differentiated from the "idle, able-bodied, and unworthy" poor. The former were provided for, while the latter were considered a threat to the community and were treated harshly.

> In colonial America "the early deprivations were so extreme that sheer survival was dependent upon mutual aid." Records from Plymouth and other early colonies indicate individual and institutional responses to need in the form of mutual aid obligations to family and kin, to other members of the community, and even to "all accessible people in trouble, whether they be kin, neighbors, or strangers."
>
> (Pumphrey and Pumphrey 1961)

Mutual aid, then, flowed side by side with organized efforts to deal with need and its assumed causes and effects.

As early as the seventeenth century, Friendly Societies existed, which "as well as meeting a threefold desire for security in sickness, a lump sum to spend at a future date, and avoidance of a pauper funeral—were social clubs for members" (Woodroofe 1962). Since people were providing for themselves through mutual aid, such attempts at self-help were viewed as posing no threat to the social order, in fact they were seen as desirable. These societies were important forerunners of more organized group work efforts such as the YMCAs, Sunday schools, and other youth movements in nineteenth-century England and America. In America, in addition, the Jewish youth movement was also the forerunner of the Jewish center movement. All provided group-oriented solutions to the problems of a rapidly changing social scene dominated by the effects of the Industrial Revolution (Wilson and Ryland 1949).

Simultaneously, organized private charities were attempting to deal with the same social changes. This resulted in a proliferation of diverse and uncoordinated efforts that many felt pauperized the poor and proved an expense to the rich. The Charity Organization Society sprang out of this chaos to bring "scientific order" to the giving of charity. Both social casework and community organization can trace their roots to this common source, though the former located the problem more in the individual and the latter more in society, emphasizing social processes, social control, and social reform (Spencer 1975). Group work shared the passion for social reform with community organization and the concern for the individual with casework. It also shared a history of religious motivation, philanthropy, and an emphasis on morality. Many of the early ancestors of group work were dedicated to "character building."

THE THREE MAJOR INFLUENCES ON SOCIAL GROUP WORK

The origins of social group work are most clearly to be found, however, in nineteenth-century England, when the impetus to social work first arose in the awakening of social conscience. Changes in political thought occurred, as people began to recognize laissez-faire as an inadequate basis for social reform. Philanthropy was the first motive behind social group work, while the second was even older, the motive of mutual aid. Mutual self-help developed spontaneously and indigenously within communities to mitigate against the proliferating effects of industrialization. This heritage became part of social group work and may well represent its most important legacy (Germain and Gitterman 1980).

Group work in its modern American form emerged during the 1920s with its roots in the settlement, recreation, and progressive education movements. As Germain and Gitterman (1980:353–54) stated, "From the settlements, the group work method derived its institutional base. . . . From the recreation movement, social group work gained its interest in the value of play and activities. . . .

[And] from the progressive education movement group work acquired a philo-sophic base." John Dewey, who was a frequent visitor to settlements, influenced them in the direction of democratic group life. The group, whether in the class-room or the settlement house or in informal living, represented the microcosm of a democratic society. To Dewey the group was an experience in practicing the ideals of democracy. It was the organized recreation movement, however, that promoted leisure time group activity as a step toward personal development and the acquisition of desired social skills. Nonetheless, the settlement movement was the most prominent ancestor of social group work.

THE SETTLEMENT MOVEMENT

Placing emphasis on the economic and social conditions of the day as more problematic than individual weakness, the settlement movement added two im-portant and unique dimensions to social work. These were the provision of ser-vice to the competent as well as those in need and an incorporation of mutual aid into formalized social welfare efforts. In using mutual aid, we can say that the settlements formed a bridge between informal and formal social welfare organi-zations. The American version of the settlement sovement also added an em-phasis on the small group as the "building block of democracy" and had "a fierce passion for social reform" (Lindeman 1980). Such leaders as Jane Addams, Flo-rence Kelley, Lillian D. Wald, and others brought about changes in local condi-tions and remedial legislation in areas of female and child labor, education, sanitation, recreation, housing, industrial relations, and discrimination against immigrants (Woodroofe 1962). The emphasis on reform and mutual aid differed sharply from the philosophy of individual causation of the Charity Organization Society, and the two movements were often antagonistic around the turn of the century. Some interests merged, however, and Jane Addams was elected to the presidency of the National Conference of Charities and Corrections in 1909 (Alissi 1980). In serving individuals in small groups with an emphasis on mu-tual aid, in all areas from child care to clubs for the aged, and in organizing for social reform, the settlements themselves formed an early context for the practi-cal and conceptual healing of this split.

The settlements also left a profound mark on our understanding of the nature of the helping process in social work through including the client-worker rela-tionship as a mutual aid relationship. Reciprocity occurred not only between clients working together but in the worker-client relationship as well. Woodroofe (1962) observed that "settlements were designed, not only to bring culture and light into the hard, hopeless lives of the East End, but also to deepen the Uni-versity men's understanding of the poor and their problems" (68). Canon Samuel Barnett, who founded Toynbee Hall in 1884, emphasized that the resi-dents (workers) should take up civic duties that would "bring them into contact with others and put them in a position both to learn and to teach" (Woodroofe

1962:69). While "teaching" was a clear goal of all early social workers, learning from the poor was a rather unique notion involving reciprocity. Indeed, many American settlements provided the locations for leading thinkers such as John Dewey and his cohorts to meet with neighborhood residents for open sharing and mutual discourse (Addams 1961:299; Lee 1994:104–12). The purpose was not only for the more well-to-do to give to the poor but also to foster "a solemn sense of relationship," as Octavia Hill has said (Woodroofe 1962:65). This concept of relationship emphasizes reciprocity. While some of the founders of the first settlements had a sense of noblesse oblige and most had no conception of the massive economic and sociopolitical shifts necessary really to bridge the gaps, they must be given credit for a vision of reciprocity, mutual aid, and social unity that crossed class barriers. Jane Addams even hoped that this reciprocity and collective action would help level the "over-accumulation at one end of society and the destitution at the other." Addams (1961:98) said of her workers that they "must be content to live quietly side by side with their neighbors, until they grow into a sense of relationship and mutual interests. And Canon Barnett said of Toynbee Hall:

> We have too . . . the opportunity of building up a new system of relationships side by side with our old . . . forming around the Hall a new world of student-friends and guest friends, acting and reacting on one another, by whose means refinement and knowledge may pass electrically as from friend to friend, and not professionally as from tutor to pupil.
>
> (Woodroofe 1962:73)

This vision of a new world, which had mutual aid as its underpinning and reciprocity as its hallmark, was the unique contribution of the settlements to social group work and to social work's philosophy of helping (Schwartz 1959).

COMMUNITY

Further, settlements and other group work agencies reaffirmed for society and our profession the importance of belonging, of community, of collective action for the collective good. Woodroofe (1962) noted that the existence of group work agencies was

> based on the realization that, faced with demoralizing hugeness of the modern industrial state, men and women often labored under a sense of disability, for they felt that, having lost social control, they stood alone and unprotected. Groups, consciously organized around selected interests, could compensate for this sense of loss . . . they could recreate that sense of intimate purpose, which had once belonged to the village of an earlier age.
>
> (73–74)

From the nineteenth century to the present day, group work agencies and group workers have been aware of this compensatory and healing power of the group.

Innovative social caseworkers were convinced of this as well. Bertha Reynolds (1970), for example, pioneered service delivery arrangements based organizationally and theoretically in a context of mutual aid. She recognized the importance of groups, saying, "We have taken our clients aside for individual treatment, not knowing their usual group relationships, or those through which they might find better solutions than are possible for them to work out alone" (22). She was very concerned about diminishing stigma and offering services in the ordinary life space of people—in her case in the labor union. Reynolds touched on many issues, such as the nature of reciprocity, the conditions of altruistic helping, the power of the helper's role and its potential abuse, and the context of social relationships in which helping occurs. Reynolds (1975) said:

> Outside of social work . . . people seem to look upon taking and giving help as they do any other activity of life. . . . Among friends, the repayment may not be immediate nor to the same person, even, but the possibility and the will to do as much must be felt. . . . It is not hard to take help in a circle in which one feels sure of belonging. . . . It hurts to be helped when one is thereby relegated to the status of a child.   (10)

In 1943 Reynolds (1970) called for a generic base for social work and suggested that group work and community work should be the cutting edge of our professional growth.

As group work developed and drew from the emerging science of small group dynamics, the mutual aid concept continued to be important, though it was often couched in other language, such as morale and cohesion, group problem solving, efficiency and productivity, and group integration (Cooley 1909; Lindeman 1924;Heap 1977; Homans 1950). The acknowledgment of people as beings whose essence was quintessentially social, that is to say, reciprocally interactive, was fundamental. The recognition gradually emerged that the relationships between the members in a group were the primary resource in accomplishing the aims of the group and its members.

In the 1930s Grace Coyle (1979) stated that

> human beings . . . cannot live without social contacts and without the expression of common interests. The decline of the neighborhood as a significant unity has meant inevitably the growth of organizations, which provide psychological neighborhoods of a specialized sort.   (11)

Coyle and others represented what Papell and Rothman (1980) later called the "social goals model" of group work, with its objectives described by Germain and Gitterman (1980) as the development of personality to its greatest capacity; the fostering of creative self-expression; the building of character and the improvement of interpersonal skills. For them group work functions also included the development of cultural and ethnic contributions; the teaching of democratic values; the support of active and mature participation in community life; the mobilizing of neighborhoods for social reform; and the preservation of ethical values.

(354)

Also in the 1930s Samuel R. Slavson (1937) used the metaphor of a family, with its implied interdependence and intimacy, to describe the helping qualities of the planned group. He said, "The general plan in the conduct of a therapy group is to simulate as closely as possible family relationships with the members as siblings and the worker as a substitute parent" (369). While he suggested this as a compensatory measure for children and youth with serious emotional difficulties, he also recognized that all groups go through a stage of high levels of mutual aid, intimacy, and interdependence. Studies of the stages of group development also show that achieving a high level of mutual aid and intimacy precedes growing into more separated, but still interdependent, individuals (Garland, Jones, and Kolodny 1968; Whittaker 1980).

Throughout social work history it was recognized that a variety of groups were the building blocks of communities and that communities had the potential to strengthen individuals and to promote social change. The history of community organization can be divided into three early periods: from the turn of the twentieth century through the 1930s, when the thrust was for effective leadership in planning for voluntary social services; the 1940s through the 1950s, when professional expertise in social planning was emphasized even though massive problems were developing; and the ferment of the 1960s, when a vast array of social programs and several new models of community organizing based on full citizen participation emerged . These included grassroots organizing, the use of community development models, and the use of power analysis to promote power and access to resources within indigent communities. Community organizing texts reflecting his period devoted significant attention to group work and group processes. Promoting a sense of belonging and attachment to the group was felt to be primary in building vigorous community action groups and organizations (Brager and Specht 1973). Some important current streams in social work thinking also emphasize the importance of community building as both the process and goal of social justice–oriented social work practice. This current thinking builds on the belief that people, particularly poor people, can work together to develop organizations and movements that can end poverty and socioeconomic injustice (Baptist, Bricker-Jenkins, and Dillon 1994; Lee 2001; Swenson 1994).

Related Conceptualizations

Social Support

When mutual aid is given attention by the mental health professions, it is often conceptualized as informal social support. "Informal" support is distinguished from help offered through formal community institutions or by professional helpers. Social support has been variously defined. Caplan, one of the prime developers of the concept, defined support as follows:

> a) the significant others help the individual mobilize his psychological resources and master emotional burdens; (b) they share his tasks; and (c) they provide him with extra supplies of money, materials, tools, skills, and cognitive guidance to improve his handling of his situation.   (Caplan 1974)

Tolsdorf (1975) has described support as having both instrumental and emotional dimensions. He said, "Instrumental support refers to the provision of tangible resources such as advice, money, the loan of equipment, or the provision of a job. Nurturant support, on the other hand, describes warmth, understanding, empathy, or encouragement" (3). Cobb (1976) took a unique position in arguing that social support is information only. He excluded goods and services on the grounds that they may foster dependency, whereas information encourages independence. In this view, "social support is information leading the subject to believe that he is cared for and loved, esteemed, and a member of a network of mutual obligations" (300).

Interest in social support has been greatly influenced by research on crisis, stress, and coping. Social support was identified early on as one of the variables that facilitates a return to precrisis functioning. Social support was also identified as an intervening variable between stressful life events and adverse health consequences. It appears that support is particularly important in influencing outcomes under conditions of high stress and makes less difference when the stress is lower (Cobb 1976; Kaplan, Cassell, and Gore 1977; Leavy 1983).

The "Helper Therapy" Principle

Riessman (1965) drew the attention of helping professionals to the notion that it could be helpful to be a helper. He observed that there was a distinct lack of research in this area, but that many self-help groups (Alcoholics Anonymous, Recovery, Inc., Synanon) operated effectively on this principle. He pointed out that deriving positive effects from helping is consistent with the behavioral principle that action in support of something is more reinforcing than passively taking it in.

About ten years later, Skovholt (1974) energetically developed the same theme, noting that changes occur in nonprofessional helpers that are like changes associated with successful counseling. He referred to data from foster grandparents, drug-dependent youth, correctional settings, and so on. Skovholt explained that helping enhances the helper's sense of effectance and competence and being able to give as well as receive enhances maturity. The helper principle also affirms reciprocity and mutual aid as an effective way to live. The helper has a sense of social balance between doing for others and receiving from them. The helper also learns about talking personally, as is being modeled by the helped.

Orlando (1974), who was concerned about the dehumanizing aspects of many institutions, particularly mental hospitals, and the "pathological" quality of the relationships among the patients, sought to alter patient-to-patient relationships. She taught basic nondirective counseling skills, such as attending visually, communicating empathy, and reflecting feelings. The connection to the "helper therapy" principle is clearest in Orlando's decision to focus on evaluating the helper's changes. Orlando reported impressionistic findings that the subjects improved in their ability to relate. She felt that subjects showed more self-integration, a greater sense of personal significance, and increased awareness of themselves as compassionate and caring persons.

Ho and Norlin (1974) reported a second, even more direct application of the helper principle. They used the helper principle in a children's residential center. They observed,

> Since meaningful living and encounter require the reciprocal processes of giving and receiving, the helper role provides [residents] . . . the opportunity to reverse their customary role . . . unless they are afforded the opportunity to give, further efforts to help them tend to become futile and dehumanizing. (111)

This concept is operationalized in a pairing system where older residents are assigned as orientors and guides to new residents, and as co-therapists in family treatment and aftercare. The principle is also extended beyond the residents. Parents are involved as helpers in multifamily therapy. Staff is involved in defining criteria for new staff and in screening new applicants. The authors stated that the helper principle evokes responsiveness because it actively engages clients and coworkers and convinces them that they are worthy of acceptance, trust, and esteem.

The Self-Help Concept

In some literature, self-help and mutual aid seem virtually synonymous—an equation of "people helping themselves" with "people helping each other." Nevertheless, beginning in the 1960s self-help began to acquire the meaning of more or less formalized associations of people sharing common statuses, conditions, or predicaments. Self-help groups explicitly use such concepts as mutual aid and helper therapy in an ideology that emphasizes people's need for each other. Katz and Bender (1976) provided this description of self-help groups:

Self-help groups are voluntary, small group structures for mutual aid and the accomplishment of a special purpose. They are usually formed by peers who have come together for mutual assistance in satisfying a common need, overcoming a common handicap or life-disrupting problem, and bringing about desired social and/or personal change. The initiators and members of such groups perceive that their needs are not, or cannot be, met by or through existing social institutions. Self-help groups emphasize face-to-face social interactions and the assumption of personal responsibility by members. They often provide material assistance, as well as emotional support; they are frequently "cause" oriented, and promulgate an ideology or values through which members may attain an enhanced sense of personal identity   (9)

Historically, notes Kropotkin (1902), self-help groups probably go back to the earliest stirrings of civilization (51). Currently, there appears to be a self-help group for every conceivable type of need or interest. Levy has organized self-help groups into four types: those dealing with some form of conduct reorganization or enhancement of self-control (Alcoholics Anonymous), those offering mutual support to ameliorate the stress of a common stress or predicament (Parents Without Partners, muscular dystrophy associations), those enhancing the well-being of people whose life style or subculture is generally discriminated against (ethnically based organizations, gay organizations, women's groups), and groups with a personal growth focus (integrity groups). Groups vary widely in their interest in social as well as personal change (Levy 1973).

Implicit in the self-help concept is a reevaluation of professional helping. This may be expressed in positive form, emphasizing those positive qualities of self-help that arise from egalitarian relationships, from the common ground of shared predicaments, from experiential knowledge, and from the power of collective action. The reevaluation may also be expressed in negative form. According to Katz and Bender (1976:9) the "initiators and members of such groups perceive that their needs are not, or cannot be, met through existing institutions." At its sharpest, the critique would maintain that professionals are actively involved in maintaining the misery or devalued status of the self-help group members. The conflicts between some homosexual and some feminist groups and mental health professionals and between some welfare rights groups and social welfare agencies are examples. The stance of the worker in the interactionist approach, however, may well be compatible with the aims of self-help groups, for the worker's job is not to define or take over the tasks of clients but to help the group achieve its own ends.

Ideas about why self-help is effective have varied. Of course, all of the ideas about helper therapy would apply. Katz (1965) has suggested that self-help makes it easier to communicate feelings, to accept one's problems, to want to change, and to relearn or resume social roles and competencies as well. Today we would say that such groups also potentially help their members to empower themselves. Many of these groups eventually take on a social action function. We note these as the very assumptions that social group workers have made about the social group work process and mutual aid groups that include a social worker. Professional responses to self-help have varied greatly, ranging from hostility, to disinterest, to co-optation, to excessive enthusiasm. Nonetheless, there are many professionals who are optimistically, if cautiously, supportive of self-help. They are seeking respectful and mutually satisfactory relationships with self-help groups.

Risk, Mediating Structures, Protective Mechanisms, Buffers and Resilience

Current literature describes mutual aid groups as critically important in developing people and environments that promote resilience (Kelly, Berman-Rossi and Palombo 2001). Each chapter in this volume demonstrates how the worker and group members develop a system of attachment and mutual aid that forms a buffer against the onslaughts of contemporary life throughout the life course of individuals. The first chapter by Gitterman and Shulman discusses the concepts of mutual aid, vulnerability, and resilience and shows how social work practice with mutual aid groups can respond to difficulties in life transitions, including crises, maladaptive interpersonal processes, and environmental stressors. These concepts, including resilience, are also a part of the ecological perspective introduced to social work by Carel Germain (1976, 1979) in the 1970s and further refined in the life model of social work practice (Germain 1987; Germain and Gitterman 1980).

Germain advanced the idea that in an ecological perspective attributes such as competence, autonomy, relatedness, identity/self-esteem, and resilience are developed in the transactions between people and environments. Adaptation, stress, and coping are also products of such transactions. These attributes and skills in negotiating the world are not innate to the personality. Environments, including families, caretakers, neighborhoods, communities, jobs, and schools must be good enough to provide nutrients for the development of these attributes throughout the life course. Hence the profession of social work seeks to enact a dual commitment to help people and change environments and to improve the transactions between the two. The ecological perspective is concerned with relationships among living entities and the properties of their environments that support or fail to support human potentialities (Germain 1979).

Resilience is a concept that entered the literature in studies of "at-risk" children who were hardy and "stress-resistant" in extreme adversity. It was initially thought to be a personality trait. However, the concept is now evolving from a static concept fixed within personality to a concept anchored in the transactional arena as the fields of psychiatry, psychology, and social work appreciate and utilize an ecological perspective in viewing and intervening in human phenomena (Waller 1997). Germain (1987) discussed the extensive longitudinal studies of children conducted by Chess and Thomas and Thomas and reported in 1977 and 1981 respectively. She noted that they found "amazing resiliency and dramatic improvement in later functioning" when there was a positive change in care and overall environment. Further, she challenged stage development theories that grant all-important status to early development as they "do a disservice to human potentiality and resilience and to the significance of the developmental context across the life course." The environment can provide protective mechanisms and processes, buffers and mediating structures that help people withstand the onslaughts of living from birth through old age. Rutter (1987) noted in his study of institutionally reared women that harmonious marriage, support, and having someone to confide in were protective effects with respect to the quality of parenting. In the comparison group of women not raised in institutions a good marriage was less critical in good parenting. He concluded that protective factors are more critical in high-risk groups. He noted that protective processes include those that "promote self-esteem and self-efficacy through the availability of secure and supportive personal relationships or successful task accomplishment, and those that open up opportunities."

Mutual aid groups, as amply demonstrated in this volume, can indeed offer secure and supportive relationships as well as opportunities for successful task accomplishment and the opening up of opportunities. From children experiencing fear, trauma and loss, to those living in and attending school in inner cities, to adults facing violence, homelessness, illness, stigma, poverty and loneliness, groups of peers struggling together buffer life's blows and can even turn adversity into opportunity.

Hirayama and Hirayama (2001), deftly extrapolating from resiliency theory and vignettes of resilient children and adults who experienced the most severe trauma, including Kasumi Hirayama's own nearly unspeakable experience as a thirteen-year-old girl facing uncertain survival after the bombing of Nagasaki, identify a range of protective mechanisms in children, families, and communities. They suggest that social workers form groups with these factors explicitly in mind. They feel that group work in community-based normative settings such as settlements, boys and girls clubs and Y's can best promote resiliency. Gitterman (2001) suggests that protective factors include temperament, instrumental support, family patterns, external supports, and environmental resources. External supports are material, emotional, and appraisal supports. Using an example from a teenage boys group, Gitterman shows how he suggested a format that enhanced planning and decision making, which members also internalized as they worked on life's challenges.

Lee (2001) suggests that family, culture, subculture, small and larger groups, empowerment groups, social agencies, and communities are mediating structures between people and their potentialities and the noxious, unjust, often oppressive qualities of environments. A critical professional task, then, is to aid in strengthening these mediating structures so that they are effective in mediating, challenging injustice and oppression, buffering, protecting and promoting resilience. Facilitating mutual aid and empowerment groups so that members take ownership of the group and promoting programs that increase protective and buffering processes helps to shore up mediating structures so that they can do their jobs in promoting member and group empowerment and resilience.

Professionally Planned Programs

There are many programs that are explicitly or implicitly based on mutual aid and reciprocal help. Sometimes the literature on such programs is simply descriptive; sometimes the program is linked to a theoretical rationale; and sometimes research or evaluation is also reported. It would be impossible to review these programs exhaustively, but we will note a few such endeavors. In view of the focus of this volume, we have organized this discussion around the life course.

1. Programs particularly for children and adolescents: Numerous programs include mutual aid groups for children and adolescents. Lee reported the use of groups with mentally retarded adolescents and, with Park, with depressed adolescent girls in foster care (Lee 1977; Lee and Park 1978). Nisivoccia and Lynn (1999) describe group work in an inner-city school with girls who have experienced violence and trauma. Antle (2001) discusses the Leading the Way Program, which focuses on group work with children and youth who are affected by HIV and AIDS. Chardarelle (1975) reported a group for children whose parents had died. Through sharing their common experiences and feelings, they gave and received help. This concept of forming groups around shared experiences can, of course, be applied in any setting, with any population sharing a common situation. Another example is Lipton's (1978) work with dying children and their families. Moving flexibly between modalities and age groups, he capitalized upon the healing potential of peers for the ill children, their well siblings, and for the parents. The potential for mutual aid within the family unit was also mobilized. Again, it would seem that most practitioners could include elements of such work in their existing positions.

On a more comprehensive scale, the Unitas program has been developed, implicitly using mutual aid concepts, for the children of a "burned-out" area of the South Bronx. It has expanded to the point that almost a hundred children are involved at any one time. Teenagers are taught to be helpers for the younger children, and the theoretical base is concepts of helping and sharing, though the language is that of the therapeutic community and open systems. The "catalysts" are social workers, but the children identify the older children as their helpers. Unitas includes some children who are growing up relatively smoothly, some that are having difficulty, and some that are seriously troubled or even psychotic (Eismann 1975).

2. Programs particularly for adults: The Companion Program is one of the most creative programs developed for young adults. It was designed to offer a peer relationship to college students, such as foreign students, handicapped students, and others, who are known to be at high risk of dropping out and other problems. The at-risk student was invited to request a companion, who then developed whatever relationship the two found mutually satisfying. The only guideline was that the companion attend regular group discussions and remains willing to discuss the relationship (Boylin 1973). Other programs for adults are organized around developmental tasks such as parenting or transitions such as widowhood. Increasingly, health problems, whether chronic or acute, are the focus of support groups. In addition, most self-help groups orient themselves primarily toward adults.

There has been considerable application of mutual aid concepts in programs for psychiatric patients. Early work grew from the concept of the therapeutic community, moving "outside" into halfway houses and so forth. More recently, efforts have been directed to helping ex-patients construct a community support network for themselves and each other. In his research Gordon (1979) found that, among patients with less than four months' hospitalization, the "network" group had about half as many rehospitalizations, and only a quarter as many days of rehospitalization, as a control group. Rubin (2001) shows how mutual aid and empowerment principles are utilized in group work in psychosocial rehabilitation agencies.

3. Programs particularly for elders: Programs for elders may be oriented toward the elders themselves, and, as the number of impaired elders grows, toward their caretakers as well. Becker and Zarit (1978) reported training older people successfully as "peer counselors," using measures of unconditional regard, empathy, and genuineness as their indicators of change. The Benton Hill project employed community workers to organize small social groups in neighborhoods. Participants in these groups showed more friendships, visiting, helping, and community involvement than the group that received conventional social services (Ehrlich 1979). An example of an extensive mutual aid group program with the elderly, the Elmhurst General Hospital Senior Program, was also described and analyzed by Lee (Lee 1982). Orr, Kelly, and Berman-Rossi in this volume show the power of mutual aid groups in work with the frail elderly.

The Foster Grandparents Program provides a nice link between children and elders. This program, still going strong across the nation, was found to have positive effects upon the well-being of the volunteer "grandparents" and on the development of institutionalized, handicapped children as increasing attention is being given to the caretakers of frail or impaired elderly, especially the family. One such program is the Natural Supports Program (1981). This emphasizes group programs for the caretakers, built on mutual aid concepts. The professionals go to great lengths not to supplant the natural helpers but rather to supplement their efforts.

4. Programs organized within ecological units: There are many programs emphasizing mutual aid concepts that are oriented to ecological units such as a school, the workplace, a hospital ward, or a neighborhood. All these programs use the existing web of relationships and seek to enhance its supportive qualities.

Lela Costin (1975), for example, has conceptualized social work in the school in a systemic fashion, seeking to exploit the potentials in relationships among students, between students and teachers, and among teachers. Elliott Studt (1968) has applied similar concepts in a correctional setting. Studt has helped inmates discover that they can make things better for themselves through group action and that they can actually benefit by helping one another. Walter (1998) illustrates the use of a community-building orientation with an AIDS organization that produced an AIDS walk.

Joan Shapiro (1971) has applied mutual aid concepts in relation to another difficult setting—the socially and physically impoverished environment of the single room occupancy hotel. Careful study of naturally occurring relationships indicated the existence of natural leaders, processes of caring for the most damaged members, and cooperative efforts at negotiating the "outside world." Shapiro described processes of entry, observation, and intervention based on profound respect for the existing social arrangements and their positive aspects.

Weiner, Akabas, and Somer (1973) have reported the application of mutual aid concepts in the world of work. They conceptualized a program based on maximizing job functioning, which is a common ground for employees, union, and employer. They were thus able to engage supportive help from many directions to prevent a worker's problems from intensifying and to enhance the operation of the work unit. Weiner and his associates emphasized the delicate processes of gaining entry and legitimization in such organizations. Intervention strategies included training union stewards in case finding and referral, consultation to key union and management personnel, and mediating with workers and coworkers around interpersonal obstacles right at the job site. Members of the organization were seen as the most effective resources for helping, and the professional's role was to facilitate their efforts.

At the level of the neighborhood, Lee and Swenson (1978) have described a small social service agency that attempted to apply interactionist and ecological concepts in a large housing project. This community was plagued by all the problems of discrimination, joblessness, and despair of the urban ghetto. Nonetheless, sources of hope and mutual aid were to be found, and residents proved highly responsive to helping based upon promoting reciprocity and competence.

Schwartz and Zalba (1971) have reported a number of programs that use mutual aid concepts and show the mediating function of the social worker in a variety of settings. These include further examples from schools, prisons, hotels, single room occupancies (SROs), and neighborhoods as well as hospital, foster care, residential treatment, and trade union settings. Many of the interventions described can be undertaken by the creative social worker in any setting; they do not require elaborate programmatic supports.

To this point we have considered several streams of thought, which converge on the concept of mutual aid. We have offered a conceptualization of mutual aid and briefly examined altruism and reciprocity as these concepts have been studied in psychology and sociology. We have discussed a series of related concepts such as social support, helper therapy, self-help, mediating structures, protective factors, and resilience. Finally, planned programs using processes of reciprocity and mutual aid have been discussed.

Several researchers have begun to delineate empirically what mutual aid consists of. They have attempted to develop classifications of "natural" helping processes, just as others have worked on developing classifications of professional helping processes (Abrahams 1976; Colten and Kulka 1979; Gottlieb 1978; Patterson et al 1972). This knowledge is important if helping professionals are to continue to develop practice strategies based upon processes of mutual aid and natural helping. Swenson's (1983) work is seminal in this area. In this study natural helpers were found to help with needs ranging from practical matters, to relationships with organizations and with other people, to developmental tasks, to feelings about the self. Skills used included sustaining emotionally, helping with problem solving, mediating with organizations and individuals, providing tangible services, sharing material resources.

Clearly, people need each other and helping is a moral, social, psychological, and spiritual "good." Moreover, people have helped each other throughout human history and in every corner of the earth. Mutual aid can help people empower themselves and their communities and promote resilience in the most adverse circumstances. It appears, however, that helping is not effortless. ,People seem to need norms or beliefs, modeling, teaching, or encouragement or the awareness of some benefit to themselves to engage in helping. The mediating role and skills of the social worker in developing the mutual aid group, and in challenging obstacles to its growth, are critical (Germain and Gitterman 1996, Shulman 1999). However, the worker's faith in the helping and healing potential of the group itself, through the process of mutual aid, is the most essential ingredient. It is his faith in the process that is the heart of Schwartz's interactionist approach.

Groups as Counterbalances, Buffers, and Shock Absorbers

Schwartz (1959) saw the rise of group work agencies and the mutual aid group as a balance to the countervailing forces of industrialization, to the "mobility and rootlessness, the stultifying non-creative work, the rising rates of delinquency and crime, the patterns of neighborhood segregation, and pervading all, the inability of transient and disorganized populations to pool their interests and take action in their own behalf." He felt that one of the outstanding contributions of group work was the "shared belief in the salutary social and personal effects of group association" (114–15).

It is interesting to note that Alvin Toffler (1971), a prominent twentieth-century author, identifies similar social problems as a result of industrialization and comes to similar conclusions about how to cope with these. He wrote,

> To create an environment, in which change enlivens and enriches the individual but does not overwhelm him, we must employ not merely personal tactics but social strategies. If we are to carry people through the accelerative period, we must begin now to build "future shock absorbers" into the very fabric of superindustrial society.
>
> (383)

Toffler suggests that "situational groupings" of people going through similar life experiences/transitions "may well become one of the key social services of the future." While he is quite right that this idea "has never been systematically exploited," he fails to note that the use of the group as just such a shock absorber has been around for a very long time, doing what he suggests. Schwartz's method of forming mutual aid groups around commonalities serves exactly that function. Toffler explains that "members might hear from others who are more advanced in the transition than they are. In short, they are given the opportunity to pool their personal experiences and ideas before the moment of change is upon them" (385). He is speaking of the mutual aid group, which, as we have shown, is not new in day-to-day experience or recorded social thought and had been especially developed in the profession of social work. Toffler says that the "suggestion that we systematically honeycomb the society with such 'coping classrooms'" is new. From the group worker's point of view, group work agencies have been doing this for a long time, though it may well be time to revitalize that effort. Such "coping classrooms" may be empowering and also offer protective factors that strengthen resilience. This is especially important in our troubled times of terrorism and war that overshadow increasing poverty and strong conservative pulls toward voluntarism and abdication of governmental responsibility for social welfare.

Schwartz (1959) saw the handwriting on the wall:

> The call for a new individualism is an attempt to find a solution to the loss of human dignity; but in its plea for a new assertion of self, it proposes the one against the many and seeks the sources of freedom in man's liberation from his fellows rather than in the combined efforts of men to control their environment
>
> (27)

It will certainly take the combined efforts of people and nations to bring peace and justice in our times. Schwartz further suggested that group workers have made a special contribution to social work and society:

> Having developed their outlook on life in an age which had clearly identified the common interest of man and men, group workers built their practice on this insight and were certain, even in bad times, that worthwhile ends could be achieved if men trusted the process by which, together, they could find the means. (127)

Schwartz's faith in this process and in mutual aid shaped his approach to social work practice. The interactionist approach is old and it is new, as are related and allied approaches that build on and utilize it with variations. It is firmly based in social work history and in human history, and it is also able to invigorate and focus social work practice during these present difficult times.

References

Abrahams, R. 1976. Mutual helping: Styles of caregiving in a mutual aid program. In G. Caplan and M. Killilea, eds., *Support systems and mutual help*, pp. 245–59. New York: Grune and Stratton.

Addams, J. 1961. *Twenty years at Hull House*. New York: Signet.

Alissi, A. S. 1980. Social group work: Commitment and perspectives. In A. S. Alissi, ed., *Perspectives on social group work practice*, pp. 1–15. New York: Free Press.

Andrews, E. and D. Norton. 1979. *Summary of preliminary natural helper interviews: Neighborhood self-help project*. Chicago: University of Chicago, School of Social Service Administration.

Antle, B. J. 2001. No longer invisible:Group work with children and youth affected by HIV and AIDS. In T. Kelly, T. Berman-Rossi, and S. Palombo, eds., *Group work: Strategies for strengthening resiliency*, pp. 101–18. New York: Haworth.

Baptist, W., M. Bricker-Jenkins, and M. Dillon. 1994.Taking the struggle on the road:The new freedom bus—freedom from hunger, and homelessness. *Journal of Progressive Human Services* 10(2): 7–29.

Becker, F. and S. H. Zarit. 1978. Training older adults as peer counselors. *Educational Gerontology* 3(July-September): 241–50.

Berman-Rossi, T. 1994. Overview. In T. Berman-Rossi, ed., *Social work: The collected writings of William Schwartz*, pp. xv–xxiii. Itasca, Ill: Peacock.

Boylin, E. R. 1973. The companion program: Students as helpers. *Psychotherapy* 10(Fall): 242–44.

Brager, G. and H. Specht. 1973. *Community organizing*. New York: Columbia University Press.

Caplan, G. 1974. *Support systems and community mental health*. New York: Behavioral.

Chardarelle, J. A. 1975. A group for children with deceased parents. *Social Work*. 20(July): 328–30.

Cobb, C. 1976. Social support as a moderator of life stress. *Psychosomatic Medicine* 38 (September/October): 300.

Colten, M. E. and R. Kulka. 1979. The nature and perceived helpfulness of formal and informal support. Paper presented at a meeting of the American Psychological Association, New York, September.

Cooley, C. C. 1909. *Social organization*. New York: Scribner's.

Costin, L. 1975. School social work practice: A new model. *Social Work* 20(March): 135–39.

Cowen, E. L., et al. 1979. Hairdressers as caregivers. *American Journal of Community Psychology* 7(December): 633–48.

Coyle, G. L. 1979. *Social processes in organized groups*. Hebron, Conn.: Practitioner's.

Ehrlich, P. 1979. *Mutual help for community elderly*. Carbondale, Ill.: Southern Illinois University Rehabilitation Institute.

Eismann, E. 1975. *Children's views of therapeutic gains and therapeutic change agents in an open-system therapeutic community*. Bronx, N.Y.: Lincoln Community Mental Health Center.

Garland, J., H. Jones, and R. Kolodny. 1968. A model of stages of development in social work groups. In S. Bernstein, ed., *Explorations in group work*, pp. 12–53. Boston: Boston University School of Social Work.

Germain, C. B. 1976. Time, an ecological variable in social work practice. *Social Casework* 57(7): 419–26.

——— 1987. *Human development in contemporary environments*. Social Service Review. 61(December): 565–80.

Germain, C. B., ed. 1979. *Social work practice: People and environments*. New York: Columbia University Press.

Germain, C. B. and A. Gitterman. 1980. *The life model of social work practice*. New York: Columbia University Press.

——— 1996. *The life model of social work practice: Advances in theory and practice*. 2d ed. New York: Columbia University Press.

Gitterman, A. 1979. Development of group services. *Social work with groups in maternal and child health*, pp. 15–21. Conference proceedings, New York, Columbia University School of Social Work and Roosevelt Hospital Department of Social Work, June 14–15.

——— 2001. Vulnerability, resilience, and social work with groups. In T. Kelly, T. Berman-Rossi, and S. Palombo, eds., *Group work: Strategies for strengthening resiliency*, pp. 19–33. New York: Haworth.

Gordon, R. et al. 1979. *Utilizing peer management and support to reduce rehospitalization of mental patients*. Tampa: Human Resources Institute, University of South Florida.

Gottlieb, B. H. 1978. The development and application of a classification scheme of informal helping. *Canadian Journal of Behavioral Science* 10:105–15.

Heap, K. 1977. *Group theory for social workers*. Oxford: Pergamon.

Hirayama, H and K. K. Hirayama. 2001. Fostering resiliency in children through group work: Instilling hope, courage, and life skills. In T. Kelly, T. Berman-Rossi, and S. Palombo, eds., *Group work: Strategies for strengthening resiliency*, pp. 71–83. New York: Haworth.

Ho, M. K. and J. Norlin. 1974. The helper principle and the creation of a therapeutic milieu. *Child Care Quarterly* 3(Summer): 109–18.

Homans, G. C. 1950. *The human group*. New York: Harcourt Brace Jovanovich.

Kaplan, B. H., J. C. Cassell, and S. Gore. 1977. Social support and health. *Medical Care* 15(May): 47–58.

Katz, A. J. 1965. Applications of self-help concepts in current social welfare. *Social Work* 10(July): 68–74.

Katz, A. J. and E. I. Bender. 1976. *The strength in us: Self-help in the modern world.* New York: Franklin Watts.

Kelly, T. B., T. Berman-Rossi, and S. Palombo. 2001. *Group work: Strategies for strengthening resiliency.* New York: Haworth.

Kropotkin, P. 1902. *Mutual did: A factor in evolution.* Boston: Extending Horizons.

Leavy, R. L. 1983. Social support and psychological disorder: A review. *Journal of Community Psychology* 11(January): 3–21.

Lee, J. A. B. 1977. Group work with mentally retarded foster adolescents. *Social Casework* 58(March): 164–73.

———— 1982. The group: A chance at human connection for the mentally impaired older person. *Social Work with Groups* 5(Summer): 43–55.

———— 1994. *The empowerment approach to social work practice.* New York: Columbia University Press.

———— 2001. *The empowerment approach to social work practice: Building the beloved community.* 2d ed. New York: Columbia University Press.

Lee, J. A. B. and D. N. Park. 1978. A group approach to the depressed adolescent girl in foster care. *American Journal of Orthopsychiatry* 48 (July): 516–27.

Lee, J. A. B. and C. R. Swenson. 1978. Theory in action: A community social service agency. *Social Casework* 59 (June): 359–70.

Levy, L. H. 1973. *Self-help groups as mental health resources.* Bloomington: Indiana University Press.

Lindeman, E. C. 1924. *Social discovery.* New York: Republic.

———— 1980. Group work and democracy—a philosophical note. In A. S. Alissi, ed., *Perspectives on social group work practice,* pp. 77–82. New York: Free Press.

Lipton, H. 1978. The dying child and the family. In Q. J. Sahler, ed., *The child and death,* pp. 52–71. St. Louis: Mosby.

Natural Supports Program. 1981. *Strengthening informal supports for the aging.* New York: Community Service Society.

Nisivoccia, D. and M. Lynn. 1999. Helping forgotten victims: Using activity groups with children in crisis. In N. Webb, ed., *Social work with children,* pp. 176–98. New York: Guilford.

Orlando, N. J. 1974. The mental patient as therapeutic change agent. *Psychotherapy* 11(Spring): 58–62.

Papell, C. P. and B. Rothman. 1980. Social group work models: Possession and heritage. In A. S. Alissi, ed., *Perspectives on social group work practice,* pp. 77–82. New York: Free Press.

Patterson, S. L. et al. 1972. *Utilization of human resources for mental health.* Lawrence: University of Kansas, School of Social Welfare.

Pumphrey, R. E. and M. W. Pumphrey. 1961. *The heritage of American social work.* New York: Columbia University Press.

Riessman, F. 1965. The "helper" therapy principle. *Social Work* 10(April): 27–32.

Reynolds, B. 1970. *Learning and teaching in the practice of social work.* New York: Russell and Russell.

———— 1975. *Social work and social living.* Washington, D.C.: NASW.

Rubin, M. 2001. Knowledge and skills needed by managers and supervisors of social group work practice in agencies serving persons with severe mental illness. In T. Kelly, T. Berman-Rossi, and S. Palombo, eds., *Group work: Strategies for strengthening resiliency,* pp. 135–58. New York: Haworth.

Rutter, M. 1987. Psychosocial resilience and protective mechanisms. *American Journal of Orthopsychiatry* 57(3): 316–31.

Schwartz, W. 1959. Group work and the social scene. Iin A. J. Kahn ed., *Issues in American social work,* pp.110–37. New York: Columbia University Press.

———— 1974. The social worker in the group. In R. W. Klenk and R. M. Ryan, eds., *The practice of social work,* pp. 208–20. 2d ed. Belmont, Cal: Wadsworth.

Schwartz, W. and S. Zalba, eds. 1971. *The practice of group work.* New York: Columbia University Press.

Shapiro, J. 1971. *Communities of the alone.* New York: Association.

Shulman, L. 1999. *The skills of helping individuals and groups.* 4th ed. Pacific Grove, Cal.: Brooks/Cole.

Skovholt, T. J. 1974. The client as helper: A means to promote psychological growth. *Counseling Psychologist* 4:58.

Slavson, S. R. 1937. *Creative group education.* New York: Association.

Spencer, J. 1975. Historical development. In P. Kuenstler, ed., *Social group work in Great Britain,* pp. 29–48. London: Faber and Faber.

Studt, E. 1968. Social work theory and implications for the practice of methods. *Social Work Education Reporter* 16(June): 22–24.

Swenson, C. R. 1983. Natural helping processes. Ph.D. dissertation, New York, Columbia University School of Social Work.

———— 1994. Clinical practice and the decline of community. *Journal of Teaching in Social Work* 11(2): 195–212.

———— 1998. Clinical social work's contribution to a social justice perspective. *Social Work* 43(6): 527–37.

Toffler, A. 1971. *Future shock.* New York: Bantam

Tolsdorf, T. 1975. Social networks, support, and psychopathology. Paper presented at a meeting of the American Psychological Association, Chicago, Illinois, September 1.

Waller, M. A. 1997. Resilience in ecosystemic context: Evolution of the concept. *American Journal Of Orthopsychiatry* 71(3): 290–97.

Walter, C. L. 1998. Community building practice: A conceptual framework. In M. Minkler, ed., *Community organizing and community building for health,* pp. 68–83. New Brunswick, N.J.: Rutgers University Press.

Weiner, H. J., S. Akabas, and J. Somer. 1973. *Mental health in the world of work.* New York: Association.

Whittaker, J. K. 1980. Models of group development: Implications for social group work practice. In A. S. Alissi, ed., *Perspectives on social group work practice,* pp. 133–53. New York: Free Press.

Wilson, G. and G. Ryland. 1949. *Social group work practice.* Boston: Houghton Mifflin.

Woodroofe, K. 1962. *From charity to social work.* London: Routledge and Kegan Paul.

Chapter 22

Contemporary Group Work Practice

Varsha Pandya

THE PURPOSE of this chapter is to highlight contemporary group work trends and demands as reflected in the published literature since 1990. Such a literature review indicated that the client populations, their characteristics, and issues are rapidly changing and becoming multidimensional and complex. Traditionally the social group workers served children, adolescents, and adults with behavior disorders, issues of survival, addictions, health and mental health issues, and effects of poverty. Besides continuing to work with these clients and their challenges, the contemporary group workers would increasingly work with individuals with alternative sexual orientations, persons affected by HIV/AIDS, older elderly (75-plus years), family as well as paid caregivers and persons affected by war, terror, and ethnic strife (Beigel, Sales, and Schulz 1991; Berman-Rossi 1994; Bertcher, Kurtz, and Lamont 1999; Capuzzi, Gross, and Friel 1990; DeCrescenzo 1994; Getzel 1996; Kelly, Berman-Rossi, and Palombo 2001; Mistry and Brown 2001; Stempler, Glass, and Savinelli 1996).

Contemporary group workers would increasingly use empowerment and community asset building approaches to improve the environment for the above-mentioned at-risk populations (Bender and Ewashen 2000; Francis-Spence 1997; Lee 1994). Interventions at small group level would become most common for social change and community rebuilding where clients with sociobehavioral and health mental health problems could attain long-term maintenance of personal changes acquired (Berchter, Kurtz, and Lamont 1999; Mistry and Brown 2001).

This chapter discusses the above-mentioned topics within the context of paradigmatic shifts that have taken place over the last three decades from medical and psychodynamic models to strengths-based, social justice–oriented, ecosystems, empowerment, and resiliency models of mutual aid through group work (Edleson and Tolman 1992; Ewashen 1997;Gitterman 2001; Kelly, Berman-Rossi, and Palombo 2001; Malekoff 2001; Mistry and Brown 1997; Rhodes and

Johnson 1996, Shulman 1996). The following discussion highlights the growing eclecticism in the group work practice as well (Capuzzi, Gross, and Friel 1990, Edleson and Tolman 1992; Peters 1997). The chapter concludes with the discussion on the future of small groups research and the education for the development of competent and effective social group workers.

Contemporary Client Populations and Issues

Persons with HIV/AIDS

When HIV infection and its subsequent development into AIDS was discovered initially in gay communities, support groups models for gay men and family members of these men (Antle 2001; Getzel 1996) were quickly developed. Since then the mutual aid approach has been found to be effective with HIV-infected individuals who commonly experience social isolation, stigma, and anxiety related to the progression of the disease as well as loss, death, and grief issues. However, the faces of HIV infected individuals are quickly changing. Women, adolescents, and children are rapidly being added to the list of HIV-infected individuals (Antle 2001; Edell 1998; Getzel 1996). The group facilitators serving this population must recognize the commonalities and differences between the needs of these subgroups of HIV-infected persons.

Edell (1998) identifies that, besides social isolation and anxiety, women who generally acquire HIV infection through heterosexual activities have other issues to deal with because of their reproductive abilities. They face additional social alienation and stigma for their potential for the vertical transmission of the disease to their children. And if they already have children who may not be infected, they face issues related to functional abilities as mothers. Edell observes that an open, long-term support group for HIV positive mothers in a clinical setting was effective in combating their sense of isolation, building a renewed sense of community, and establishing surrogate family ties when the connections with their own families were seriously compromised because of the nature of the illness. Edell further discusses other helpful themes for such a women's group, for example, 1. empowerment of these women through raising questions about the society's perception of them as vectors of transmission of the virus to men and children, 2. learning negotiating skills to portray themselves as being victims of transmission of the virus from their sexual partners to the society at large, 3. disclosure of their illness to their children, 4. disclosure to or confrontation of their partner/s as relevant, 5. how to resolve emotional conflicts and dilemmas related to parenting issues, and 6. celebration of mother's day.

Antle (2001) outlines specific issues faced by teenagers who are HIV positive. These young persons generally fear attending the support groups because it would identify their family as living with HIV/AIDS. They also fear hearing the traumatic experiences of others when overwhelmed themselves with their situation and whether other group members would maintain confidentiality. Besides these fears, the teenagers have specific issues related to schoolwork, self-esteem, and entertaining thoughts of committing nonrational acts. Antle recommends use of a cofacilitation model so that one facilitator can give individual attention to a member during the group session if needed.

Another emerging population that contemporary group workers in this field would increasingly face is the HIV negative or serodiscordant partners of persons with AIDS (Land and Harangody 1990; Saporito 2001). Saporito (2001) observes that the HIV negative partners of HIV positive persons increasingly prefer to continue their relationship with the same partner. However, emotional upheaval associated with this preference can best be addressed in the supportive, mutual aid environment of a group of persons sharing a similar situation. Fear of transmission, prevention of transmission, dealing with loss of normal sexual activities and reproduction, as well as other ways of meeting the sexual needs of each other are issues that group facilitators are called upon to deal with.

Contemporary group workers in this field would need to keep up with the new knowledge about the disease and its treatments, acquaint themselves with the special needs of diverse group members affected by the disease, and develop skills to use the cofacilitation model effectively (Antle 2001; Getzel 1996; Saporito 2001).

Persons with Alternative Sexual Orientation

With the gay and lesbian rights movement growing stronger, establishments attempting to diversify their consumers as well as employees through proactive recruitment efforts, and the increasing availability of adult role models among these populations, many teenagers and young adults are now "coming out" to acknowledge their alternative sexual orientation (DeCrescenzo 1994). Homophobia and negative attitudes against these populations are widely prevalent in society. Therefore Jackson and Sullivan (1994) contend that those coming out need mutual support and the ability to be resilient under the hostile situations they may encounter during the process. Gays and lesbians are not yet protected under antidiscrimination legislation in our society.

Travers (1996) posits that group work intervention is most appropriate for people coming out as it can be nontherapeutic in nature or, in other words, it can be devoid of being pathogenic. At the same time, a small group can provide powerful support and guidance during this process of major identity shift from the previously held social status. When such a small group engages in critically exploring social construction of gender, sex roles, and sexuality, it can be empowering and serve as a protective factor boosting members' self-esteem.

Peters (1997) recounts issues presented by gays and lesbians that require therapeutic intervention: the high risk of suicide, substance abuse, and HIV infection. Peters claims that these issues are generally rooted in emotional isolation that the person coming out may face from family, friends, and neighborhood. Contemporary group workers must acquire adequate knowledge about the experiences of these populations, their needs for healthy ways of separating from homophobic elements in their lives, and the high-risk issues listed above.

Cranston (1992) suggests that the contemporary group workers must acquire adequate knowledge about the experiences of these populations in a majority "straight" society. Group workers must acquire skills to help members build self-esteem in the face of emotional isolation and to build productive peer relationship with both types of individuals: straight and those with alternative sexual orientation. Travers (1996) emphasizes that group workers validate experiences of the group members through the use of reality checking and confronting high-risk behaviors. I would go a step further and recommend that we learn from the success of cofacilitation in domestic violence groups (Edleson and Tolman 1992; Pandya 2001),and attempt the same with a "straight" person and one with and alternative sexual orientation as cofacilitators when working with groups of gays, lesbians, and bisexual persons. This would further the professional goal of integration of persons with alternative sexual orientation in mainstream society.

Older Elderly

This population generally has chronic and acute health problems that require serial hospitalization or long-term health care in their own homes or in a residential facility (Moffat and Kay 1996). These patients and their family caregivers, often elderly themselves, require medical education, supervision, and social support on an ongoing basis. Moffat and Kay observe that the young elderly have increasing responsibility for their older elderly patients. This creates a new, highly vulnerable group of caregivers contrasted with the common image of female, middle-aged adult caregivers of yesteryear. This situation has created a need for social workers to liaison with the hospital as well as community resources and support for ongoing care required after their discharge from the hospital. Moffat and Kay recommend that social workers engage parallel groups of the older elderly and their caregivers as well as the multidisciplinary team contributing to the recovery and continuing care of the older elderly and their younger elderly caregivers.

Groups for the older elderly patients provide an opportunity for restoring and maintaining meaningful social interaction with persons other than their family caregivers, developing new ways of coping, and resolving ego integrity issues of previous life stages (Moffat and Kay 1996; Thomas and Martin 1992). Similarly, groups for the elderly caregivers provide opportunities to increase their knowledge about community resources available for the patient and themselves, express their feelings related to caregiving, improve coping skills, and get support from other group members.

Thomas and Martin (1992) identify four types of groups for the elderly that the facilitators may choose depending on their assessment of the needs of the elderly. Other authors (e.g., Capuzzi, Gross, and Friel 1990; Myers, Poidevant, and Dean 1991) support the use of these groups as well. Reality orientation groups help the older elderly to deal with the disorientation as to time and place and help prevent further deterioration. Remotivation groups help less impaired older elderly to gain renewed interest in their surroundings and encourage activities. Psychotherapy groups help members to work through emotional issues. Reminiscing groups enhance the sense of belonging and renew their sense of continuity. More functional elderly benefit from the last two types of groups. All four types can be useful for patients as well as their elderly caregivers. These groups require group facilitators to be competent in knowledge of group dynamics and gerontology. The facilitator must possess skills to assess the functional abilities of the potential group members (Capuzzi, Gross, and Friel 1990; Thomas and Martin 1992) so that they can appropriately choose the modality of the group, group structure, frequency and length of the sessions, and the physical setting that would most effectively contribute to the success of the group.

CAREGIVERS

Though the previous two subsections addressed the issues related to family caregivers of HIV-infected persons and older elderly, a separate subsection addressing the tasks and vulnerabilities of family as well as paid caregivers is appropriate and much needed. Traditionally caregiving was considered a natural task of the females in the family or as paid caregivers. It was considered to be like any other routine task carried out by women, such as cooking or cleaning. In recent years men taking up the caregiving task have been increasing (Ford et al. 1997). Stress, grief, and loss issues experienced by the caregivers of the chronically ill and dying have received considerable attention in the past decade (Biegel, Sales, and Schulz 1991; Lachs and Boyer 1998; Richardson and Sistler 1999; Turner and Street 1999). The caregiving of persons with chronic illnesses like Alzheimer's disease, dementia, heart disease, stroke victims, and AIDS can cause depression, decrease in the level of happiness, anxiety, anticipated grief, anger, guilt and shame, fear, financial burden, emotional trauma, social isolation, and physical illness. The support group approach, psychoeducation group approach, task-centered group approach, and combined approaches have been found to be effective in helping caregivers cope with the multitude of emotions and conditions brought on by caregiving tasks (Biegel, Sales, and Schulz 1991; Ford et al. 1997; Pomeroy, Rubin, and Walker 1995; Wright, et al. 2001).

The methodologically rigorous quasi-experimental effectiveness study by Pomeroy, Rubin, and Walker (1995) of psychoeducation and task-centered group for the family member caregivers of AIDS patients establishes the effectiveness of mutual aid and bringing forth protective factors in caregivers for daily problem solving as most effective method in reduction of feeling of stigma attached to AIDS, anxiety, and depression. The study found improvement in the quality of health and daily living as well as social support. The psychoeducation part of the group provided the support and education about the disease while the task-centered part helped the group members learn the problem-solving skills for daily living. The authors recommend that group practitioners educate themselves about the needs, concerns, and affective responses of family caregivers of persons with AIDS. Their rationale is that in the environment of diminished resources, with hospital / residential care being paid for through Medicare/Medicaid dollars, the group workers can play pivotal roles in enabling family members to function better as caregivers and thereby reduce the number of days in residential care for the patients.

The contemporary group facilitators are likely to work with multifamily groups where families have one or more children with mental health and behavioral problems. Similar to the caregivers of adults, the family caregivers of the children are likely to experience blame for the patient's condition, have inadequate information about their disorder, and interference with other family roles and relationships. Goldberg-Arnold and Fristad (1999) studied the outcomes of psychoeducation groups of families with children diagnosed with mood disorders. Besides covering the traditional topics of psychoeducation groups (like information about the disorder, treatment options for the disorder, mutual support for emotional experience), this group includes learning of communication and problem-solving skills, and general review of family issues arising out of caregiving demands. Another unique feature of the group was joint meeting of the child and family at the beginning and end of each session. The findings of the study revealed that the members demonstrated improved information and enhanced social support immediately after the group ended, whereas they showed a change in attitude toward the child with the disorder and how they perceived themselves in its context after some time had elapsed since the group ended. The description of the group and the preliminary outcomes of this type of group appear promising. Contemporary group workers have a challenging task to document the intervention models and evaluate their outcomes and effectiveness to develop an evidence-based group practice with multiple families experiencing myriads of social problems.

Turner and Street (1999) identified commonalities and differences in training group needs between family and paid caregivers. Information about the patient's disease and resources available was one of the common needs. Learning skills to deal with the difficult behavior of the patients as well as coping with one's own stress and emotions related to caregiving were also found to be common needs of both these groups of caregivers. However, the family members needed more intense training in the latter area than the paid caregivers. Paid caregivers identified need to learn how to not get caught up in the volume of caregiving work, not to take their work home with them, and to find time for themselves to do the things that they enjoy. Meier (1997) discusses online stress management support groups that technologically competent and connected caregivers may use and benefit from.

PERSONS AFFECTED BY WAR, TERROR, AND ETHNIC STRIFE

Group work practice needs to advance knowledge, skills, and values to address the unique issues presented by the emerging and increasing client population affected by war, terror, and other kinds of person-made disasters. During contemporary times, the form of wars have changed from just between countries to within nations as well as across country borders by groups with extremist political ideology and agenda. Civilians frightened by war as well as groups with different political ideologies than those in power flee their home country and seek asylum as refugees in other countries. The conditions in refugee camps are generally subhuman, posing high risk to the health, mental health, and socioeconomic well-being of people living there. These also cause stress on the resources of the country in which refugee camps are set up. Resettlement or repatriation is a difficult decision faced by refugees and asylum-giving governments alike (Brenton 1999; Minhas 1997; Patel 1997).

Brenton (1999) points out that the refugees face many losses: loved ones, identity, ties with their roots, home, work, and so on. They experience cultural dissonance in a strange country, social isolation, and sometimes the challenge of having to learn a new language. Patel (1997) adds the variable of dissonance in gender-based role expectations in the home country and adopted country that refugee women experience. Brenton (1999) explains that refugee group members may be grieving and feeling alienated, resulting in difficulty in engaging in the group process, and perceive worker-defined goals as disempowering. This may slow down their adaptation and integration in the new place. Contrarily, Patel (1997) advises that the women refugees from cultures that assign submissive roles to their gender may initially benefit from the worker-defined goals. Brenton (1999) recommends a structural approach to group practice with refugees. This approach is user centered and takes on the task of identifying and understanding the societal structures and the barriers therein to service utilization and initiatives toward assimilation. Gender sensitivity, recommended by Patel (1997), could be integrated in this approach to promote the participation of members in finding solutions that would work for them. Besides refugees, war veterans pose similar challenges to work through but have additional issues to deal with as well. Killing in a war situation is legitimate and not murder. This may leave emotional and traumatic scars on the killer warrior, loved ones of the killed, and the witnesses and survivors of such carnage. These populations experience emotions like guilt, remorse, anger, pain, grief, and so on. The war and terror attacks cause righteousness as a defense in order that the individual may kill or survive at any cost. Blind obedience and strict discipline required for fighting a war cause patterns of behaviors that are not suitable to civil life. When working with veteran groups, the facilitator would require special skills to create an environment where emotions and political views may be expressed safely. Learning of social skills for civil society must be at the core of any group interventions with veterans and other war survivors. Structural approach used with refugees may also be suited to groups of veterans where members may express their identification with the politics that sanctioned war or dissent with that ideology without any consequences. The processing of one's beliefs, suppressed by the demands of war time, is central to regaining one's civil identity, which in turn would prepare the members for relearning social and civilian skills.

This section on contemporary clients and issues has raised challenges likely to be faced by the contemporary group facilitators. It highlighted specialized competencies for contemporary group workers. The next section introduces the way in which the promotion of mutual aid may be used for empowering clients and engaging them in the community-building process through initiating and/or participating in the process of environmental change.

Mutual Aid Groups for Social Change and Community Rebuilding: A Mission Not Forgotten

Contemporary social group workers have been engaging their clients in therapeutic groups to reach a level of resiliency and empowerment so that they may become active members of consumers' groups, coalitions, or movements leading to asset building in their communities and social change favoring their development and that of those like them (Bender and Ewashen 2000; Bertcher, Kurtz, and Lamont 1999; Cohen and Muellender 1999; Ewashen 1997; Francis-Spence 1997; Gutierrez and Lewis 1999; Lee et al 1997; Minhas 1997; Rhodes and Johnson 1996). Feminist social workers have dominated the scene by using small groups to empower women in different social situations and facing multitude of social problems (e.g., Bender and Ewashen 2000; Cohen and Muellender 1999; Francis-Spence 1997; Henderson 1998; Pollio, McDonald, and North 1996).

The most common empowering technique used by contemporary group work facilitators is to pointedly discuss when the group members bring their outside, lived world to the group for issues relating to power, equality, and justice (Bender and Ewashen 2000; Gutierrez and Lewis 1999). Ewashen (1997) finds that when one member shares such issues, invariably other members identify with the issues as affecting their lives, creating collective consciousness about environmental factors negatively influencing their lives and actions. Building on the phenomenal works of Paulo Freire on using education to cause critical consciousness, Gutierrez and Lewis (1999) demonstrate how appreciation of strengths, analysis of power structures, and understanding of varied standpoints of group members and the facilitator are essential elements in empowering the clients of small groups. The authors recommend education, participatory study of issues at hand, and capacity/asset building as successful methods available to the empowering group facilitators. Other authors (e.g., Cohen and Muellender 1999; Naparstek 1999; Poole 1999) add use of techniques like acknowledgment of client rights, democratic decision making, conflict management, and dynamic circle exercise that can be used to empower clients and engage them in the process of social change for social justice. Hofmeyr (1999) shares use of marathon groups where the members come together for intensive interaction during long duration group meetings, often residential, that can produce decisions that affect the social course of an issue, organization, or a community.

Mutual Aid and Technology

Technology in designing contemporary group interventions has become vital for two main reasons. First, for the hard-to-reach clients who for physical or mental limitations as well as lack of transportation cannot attend all group meetings. Second, for social services providers and administrators whose workload is high, whose time is metered, but where leadership in building the interagency networking and collaboration is important to serve the clients holistically. The literature identifies two main types of technology-aided groups: Telephone groups (which are often interchangeably referred to as teleconference groups in literature) and computer groups (e.g., Bowman and Bowman 1998; Heckman et al 1999; Meier 1997; Nunamaker et al 1991; Schopler, Galinsky, and Abell 1997; Zook and Luken 2001).

Telephone groups are used to reach out to people with limited mobility or lack of transportation. Generally such groups are used with the elderly, disabled, or those who have been diagnosed as HIV positive, and those with AIDS or other terminal illnesses. The advantages of telephone groups are several. Such groups provide much needed social support to isolated clients in rural areas, clients who are lonely because of the stigmatic condition they may have, and those who may be overly concerned about confidentiality (Heckman et al. 1999; Kaslyn 1999; Weiner 1998). Telephone groups increase accessibility to mutual aid and social support, sharing of information about available resources, convenience, while simultaneously ensuring confidentiality as only voice may be used as a factor for identifying a member (Kaslyn 1999). The disadvantage of telephone groups would be delay in group development due to lack of personal contact, loss of nonverbal cues, and limited participation because a desire to communicate cannot be expressed to the group beforehand when someone is talking (Kaslyn 1999; Rounds, Galinsky, and Stevens 1991; Weiner 1998). Kaslyn (1999) informs the telephone group facilitators to set a rule whereby each member identifies herself or himself before speaking, be sensitive to persons with hearing difficulties, show understanding for the distractions in the environment of the members, and develop sharp listening skills because other senses like observation or touch cannot be used for communication and participation. However, the authors resonate a positive note of valuable contributions of telephone groups despite the listed disadvantages. Rittner and Hammons (1992), Rounds, Galinsky, and Stevens (1991), and Weiner (1998) site examples of HIV and AIDS affected individuals, families, and caregivers who meet all the three conditions of being isolated, afraid of the stigma of being known to the society as having HIV infection, and therefore overly concerned about confidentiality benefiting from telephone groups.

Computers are growing preference for the contemporary social group workers for meeting a variety of purposes. Computer-aided groups are used for task-centered, therapeutic, and planning purposes. Zook and Luken (2001) have interestingly used computers to develop support groups for brain injury patients in recovery. The authors found these specifically useful to those individuals living in rural areas for whom the socially isolating effects of brain injury is increased because of their residential location. Even though the injuries themselves often proved to be barriers in learning to use the computers and participate actively, initial support by the case managers and peers helped develop the confidence in clients to participate in such support groups. The software developers came forward to modify software to make it user friendly for individuals with brain injuries. The success of the group was documented through a focus group discussion with the participants in such computer-aided support groups. Zook and Luken report that members' showed enhanced self-confidence, initiative in seeking vocational rehabilitation, linkage with available resources, and meeting and interacting with able persons for various recreational activities like bowling. Overall several support groups organized of brain injury patients reported success in reducing members' social isolation and promoting their integration in the community.

Work of Nunamaker et al. (1991) at the University of Arizona around the use of Electronic Meeting System (EMS) for administration is indeed very interesting. The system was used in several combinations (e.g., same place same time, different place same time) to facilitate strategic planning. It allows all participants to see all comments without knowing who wrote which comments. This helps avoidance of partisan political decision making as the participants can build on each other's ideas independent of who contributed them. Thus the ideas get evaluated on their own merits. Nunamaker and colleagues describe the components of EMS in detail and how each works to collectively facilitate a mutually aided task group to accomplish its purpose. I recommend that interested readers access the article for more information.

Bowman and Bowman (1998) document six main methods of group work using computer technology: 1. Bulletin board systems, where the public can exchange information, personal experiences, and so on related to predetermined topics. For an example one can find such a bulletin for family members of patients diagnosed with multiplesclerosis. 2. Chat rooms where members can simultaneously view the sending and receiving of messages during a predetermined time. 3. Computer conferencing, which operates much like the chat rooms but where the facilitator may have more editorial control. 4. Listservs that allow easy distribution of e-mail to large groups of persons, who in turn can choose to interact with all or a select few members of the listserv. 5. News groups for posting messages that can be read later by the members. 6. Home pages or Web sites that provide information and serve as referral points to other resources. For example a Web-based course may allow the students enrolled in the course access to relevant information available on the Web as well as an opportunity to interact with each other facilitating mutual learning. Some of these methods may be used more for mutual aid and therapeutic groups while some may be used to meet the developmental and advocacy tasks mandated by the social work profession.

Computer-aided groups have some of the same advantages and disadvantages as telephone groups. Bowman and Bowman (1998) raise an important dilemma that group workers face when using technology as a primary medium for service delivery. The dilemma is to achieve a balance between appropriate integration of high tech with interpersonal touch. Though the use of technology allows group members to access information and resources, find support, and create a new sense of belonging to a larger global community, it can serve both as strength and challenge. The technology can help members find support, which may not be available locally; at the same time, the anonymity provided by the medium may pose risks that are not fully known to date.

The authors share a list of ethical and legal issues for the consideration of professionals using computer groups. Major concerns relate to confidentiality risks, interpretation of written texts, adequate dealing with diversity issues, technical problems, and enrolling a member who may not be suited for the group. These issues are complex and are not addressed in the standards for social work practice with groups published by Association for the Advancement of Social Work with Groups (AASWG) in 1998. As the use of technology in group practice increases, a need for establishing standards for its design, monitoring, and ethical compliance can no longer be ignored.

Small Groups Research

In these times of accountability and diminishing resources for behavioral and social services, showing that group practitioners are effectively using mutual aid and resiliency models for mezzo- and macropractices and for technology-based group work practice is important. The quantitative or qualitative research studies evaluating varied group work practice commonly use individuals as units of analysis of data (e.g., Ford et al. 1997; Ho and Weitzman 2000; Meier 1997; Pandya and Gingerich 2002). Even when researchers study variables related to the group situation like group environment or level of support in the group, their effect is studied on individual members. It has been indeed difficult to find a study that uses group as a unit of analysis and follows the progress of the group toward its goals. Cain (1997) studied group dynamics in Alcoholic Anonymous (AA) and used group as a unit of analysis. The data analysis conducted at a group level showed how AA uses its desired membership characteristics to powerfully make the new member buy into their expectations of attaining sobriety and abandoning drinking forever. It exerts peer pressure for positive behavior and a member not accepting and adhering to the norms is coerced out of the group membership. More such studies are needed that examine the use of group processes like mutual aid and fostering resiliency with client groups at different stages in the life cycle facing varied psychosocial challenges.

Both quantitative and qualitative methods are available for the researchers' use to conduct the study of groups, but social work researchers are primarily trained and exposed to methodology that uses individuals as units of analysis. I think it is pertinent here to also raise an ethical issue concerning the principle of informed consent. How can a researcher resolve the ethical dilemma presented when all the members of a group do not agree to participate in the study? Pandya (2001) had to agree to record observation of only those members who agreed to participate in the research study to comply with the stipulations of the federal regulations and the institutional review board. This situation probably has been largely limiting group work researchers to restrict data analysis to individual units.

The measurements commonly used in quantitative studies of group work practice so far have been traditional behavior or mental state–related inventories or scales. Valuable measurements related to mutual aid and resiliency are developed and rigorously tested (e.g., Macgowan 2000 [engagement for group work]; Jew, Green, and Kroger 1999 [resiliency]), and I strongly recommend that contemporary group practice researchers use these so that we can generate knowledge that is not only rooted in practice wisdom but also in rigorously tested relevant empirical evidences.

Besides practice research, some interesting studies have been reported on group work education in social work programs. Of note is the exploratory evaluation by Abell and Galinsky (2002) of content introduction on computer-based group work practice in the masters curriculum. Abell and Galinsky describe the group-facilitating software used, how students were prepared for its use, and the structure of the computer group simulation in the course. The authors did pretest-posttest surveys of the students to evaluate the knowledge gained about and comfort level in using computer groups. The authors found a statistically significant level of increase in knowledge and comfort in use of computers for group work as a result of exposure to the content described.

The advances and the challenges of contemporary group work discussed so far raise a need for the development of quality continuing education program and group work curriculum in social work programs to develop competent group work practitioners, educators, and researchers.

Organization of Group Workers

As the needs of the clients, issues related to social justice, and administration of social services change, the practitioners need to acquire the relevant knowledge and skills derived from demonstration projects and scientific inquiry. Scholars from the academy and the field need to engage in continuous identification of training needs of professionals and students of social work. The AASWG is an international organization that continues to provide leadership and initiative in development of group practice curriculum in social work programs at baccalaureate and masters levels through collaboration with the Council on Social Work Education (CSWE).

An interesting survey of 212 faculties in BSW and MSW programs by Birnbaum and Wayne (2000) demonstrated the connections between AASWG and CSWE in curriculum development for group work practice. The survey showed that curricular revisions were needed to strengthen content on group norms, group conflict, contracting, planning process for group formation, mutual aid, and group as a social system, in addition to a few other areas. The authors also identified a need to strengthen group work assignments in field education. To this list technology and group work and research methods for group practice need to be added.

Besides organizing annual symposium at CSWE on group work practice and education, AASWG also organizes its own annual conference where group practitioners, educators, and researchers come together to exchange ideas and benefit from continuing education in areas like curriculum development, group practice models, and group work research. An AASWG newsletter provides information about existing resources, the activities of its chapters, and links to the other relevant conferences. It compiles a list of new books, other publications, and Internet resources for its members' use. It can do more to encourage group work research by developing periodic research priorities and funding opportunities for the same.

CONTEMPORARY GROUP WORK demonstrates advances in application of mutual aid, resiliency, and life cycle principles and theories for newly emerged at-risk client populations affected by HIV/AIDS, war, terror, and ethnic strife, longer lifespan, care-giving burdens, and coming out with an alternative sexual identity.

At the same time, the contemporary group work faces challenges like developing skilled and competent group facilitators to work with these populations. Contemporary group workers face the challenge of mastering the use of technology-based groups in order to reach out to client populations that face great difficulties in accessing their services.

Last but not the least important are the needs for developing a revised and restructured research agenda to evaluate contemporary group work practice as well as encourage group researchers through provision of increased funding. It is necessary that AASWG reflect on its own structure and priorities and modify these to continue providing leadership amidst the changed environment of contemporary group work practice in the twenty-first century.

References

Abell, M. L. and M. J. Galinsky. 2002. Introducing students to computer-based group work practice. *Journal of Social Work Education* 38(1): 39–54.

Antle, B. J. 2001. No longer invisible: Group work with children and youth affected by HIV and AIDS. In T. Kelly, T. Bermann-Rossi, and S. Palombo, eds., *Group work: Strategies for strengthening resiliency*, pp. 19–33. New York: Haworth.

Beigel, D. E., E. Sales, and R. Schulz. 1991. *Family caregiving in chronic illness: Alzheimer's disease, cancer, heart disease, mental illness, and stroke.* Newbury Park, Cal.: Sage.

Bender, A. and C. J. Ewashen. 2000. Group work is political work: A feminist perspective of interpersonal group psychotherapy. *Issues in Mental Health Nursing* 21:297–308.

Berman-Rossi, T. 1994. The fight against hopelessness and despair: Institutionalized aged. In A. Gitterman and L. Shulman, eds., *Mutual aid groups, vulnerable populations, and the life cycle*, pp. 385–412. 2d ed. New York: Columbia University Press.

Bertcher, H., L. F. Kurtz, and A. Lamont, eds. 1999. *Rebuilding communities: Challenges for group work.* New York: Haworth.

Birnbaum, M. L. and J. Wayne. 2000. Group work in foundation generalist education: The necessity for curriculum change. *Journal of Social Work Education* 36(2): 347–56.

Brenton, M. 1999. The relevance of the structural approach to group work with immigrant and refugee women. *Social work with groups* 22(2/3): 11–30.

Bowman, R. L. and V. E. Bowman. 1998. Life on the electronic frontier: The application of technology to group work. *Journal for Specialists in Group Work* 23(4): 428–25.

Cain, C. 1997. Personal stories: Identity acquisition and self-understanding in Alcoholic Anonymous. *Ethos* 19(2): 210–53.

Capuzzi, D., D. Gross, and S. E. Friel. 1990. Recent trends in group work with elders. *Generations: Journal of the American Society on Aging* 14:43–48.

Cohen, M. B. and A. Muellender. 1999. The personal in the political: Exploring the group work continuum from individual to social. *Social Work with Groups* 22:13–19.

Cranston, K. 1992. HIV education for gay, lesbian, and bisexual youth: Personal risk, personal power, and the community of conscience. *Journal of Homosexuality* 22(4): 247–59.

DeCrescenzo, T., ed. 1994. *Helping gay and lesbian youth: New policies, new programs, new practice.* New York: Haworth.

Edell, M. 1998. Replacing community: Establishing linkages for women living with HIV/AIDS—a group work approach. *Social Work with Groups* 21(3): 49–62.

Edleson, J. L. and R. M. Tolman. 1992. *Intervention for men who batter: An ecological approach.* Newbury Park, Cal.: Sage.

Ewashen, C. J. 1997. Devaluation dynamics and gender bias in women's groups. *Issues in Mental Health Nursing* 18:73–84.

Ford, G. R., K. T. Goode, J. J. Barrett, L. E. Harell, and W. E. Haley. 1997. Gender roles and caregiving stress: An examination of subjective appraisals of specific primary stressors in Alzheimer's caregivers. *Aging and Mental Health* 1(2): 158–65.

Francis-Spence, M. 1997. Groupwork and black women viewing networks as groups: Black women meeting together for affirmation and empowerment. In T. Mistry and A. Brown, eds., *Race and groupwork.* London: Whiting and Birch.

Getzel, G. S. 1996. AIDS and group work: Looking into the second decade of the pandemic. In B. L. Stempler, M. S. Glass, and C. M. Savinelli, eds., *Social group work today and tomorrow: Moving from theory to advanced practice*, pp. 33–44. New York: Haworth.

Gitterman, A. 2001. Vulnerability, resilience, and social work with groups. In T. Kelly, T. Bermann-Rossi, and S. Palombo, eds., *Group work: Strategies for strengthening resiliency*, pp. 19–33. New York: Haworth.

Goldberg-Arnold, J. S. and M. A. Fristad. 1999. Family psychoeducation: Giving caregivers what they want and need. *Family Relations* 48(4): 411–17.

Gutierrez, L. and E. A. Lewis. 1999. Strengthening communities through groups: A multicultural perspective. In H. Bertcher, L. F. Kurtz, and A. Lamont., eds., *Building communities: Challenges for group work*, pp. 5–16. New York: Haworth.

Heckman, T. G., S. C. Kalichman, R. R. Roffman, K. J. Sikkema, B. D. Heckman, A. M. Somlai, and J. Walker. 1999. A telephone-delivered coping improvement intervention for persons living with HIV/AIDS in rural areas. *Social Work with Groups* 21(4): 49–61.

Henderson, A. 1998. Preparing feminist facilitators: Assisting abused women in transitional or support-group settings. *Journal of Psychosocial Nursing* 36 (3): 25–33.

Ho, C. J. and P. F. Weitzman. 2000. Stress and service use among minority caregivers to elders with dementia. *Journal of Gerontological Social Work* 33(1): 67–89.

Hofmeyr, L. 1999. Rebuilding a divided community through the use of marathon groups. In H. Bertcher, L. F. Kurtz, and A. Lamont., eds., *Building communities: Challenges for group work*, pp. 107–24. New York: Haworth.

Jackson, D and R. Sullivan. 1994. Developmental implications of homophobia for lesbian and gay adolescents: Implications for policy and practice. In T. DeCrescenzo, ed. *Helping gay and lesbian youth: New policies, new programs, new practice.* New York: Haworth.

Jew, C. L., K. E. Green, and J. Kroger. 1999. Development and validation of a measure of resiliency. *Measurement and Evaluation in Counseling and Development* 32(2): 75–90.

Kaslyn, M. 1999. Telephone group work: Challenges for practice. *Social Work with Groups* 22(1): 63–77.

Kelly, T. B., T. Berman-Rossi, S. Palombo, eds. 2001. *Group work: Strategies for strengthening resiliency.* New York: Haworth.

Lachs, M. S. and P. Boyer. 1998. Caring for mom and dad. *Prevention* 50(9): 168–71.

Land, H. and G. Harangody. 1990. A support group for partners of persons with AIDS. *Families in Society* 71(8): 471–82.

Lee, J. A. B. 1994. *The empowerment approach to social work practice.* New York: Columbia University Press.

Lee, J. B., R. R. Martin, J. A. Beaumont, R. Moore-Beckham, G. Bourdon, C. King, J. Konon, E. Thorpe. 1997. Reflections on empowerment groupwork across racial lines: My sister's place. In T. Mistry and A. Brown, eds., *Race and groupwork.* London: Whiting and Birch.

Macgowan, M. J. 2000. Evaluation of a measure of engagement for group work. *Research on Social Work Practice* 10(3): 348–61.

Malekoff, A. 2001. The power of group work with kids: A practitioner's reflection on strengths-based practice. *Families in Society* 82 (3): 243–50.

Meier, A. 1997. Inventing new models of social support groups: A feasibility study of an online stress management support group for social workers. *Social Work with Groups* 20(4): 35–54.

Minhas, B. K. 1997. A community-based approach to the development of Asian women's groups. In T. Mistry and A. Brown, eds., *Race and groupwork.* London: Whiting and Birch.

Mistry, T. and A. Brown, eds. 2001. *Race and groupwork.* London: Whiting and Birch.

Moffat, P. and N. Kay. 1996. The new patient mix: Group work and chronic disorders in an acute care hospital. In B. L. Stempler, M. Glass, and C. M. Savinelli., eds., *Social group work today and tomorrow.* New York: Haworth.

Myers, J. E., J. M. Poidevant, and L.A. Dean. 1991. Groups for older persons and their careivers: A review of literature. *Journal for Specialists in Group Work* 16:197–205.

Naparstek, A. J. 1999. Community building and social group: A new practice paradigm for American cities. In H. Bertcher, L. F. Kurtz, and A. Lamont., eds., *Building communities: Challenges for group work,* pp. 17–34. New York: Haworth.

Nunamaker, J. F., A. R. Valacich, J. S. Vogel, D. R. George, and F. Joey. 1991. Electronic meeting systems to support group work. *Communications of the Association for Computing Machinery* 34(7): 40–61.

Pandya, V. 2001. Learning to be nonviolent: A qualitative study of change processes in domestically violent men in group therapy. UMI Dissertation Services (UMI no. 3001117).

Pandya, V. and W. Gingerich. 2002. Group therapy intervention for male batterers: A microethnographic study. *Health and Social Work* 27(1): 47–55.

Patel, G. 1997. Communities in struggle: Bengali and refugee group work in London. In T. Mistry and A. Brown, eds., *Race and groupwork.* Concord, Mass.: Paul.

Peters, A. J. 1997. Themes in group work with lesbian and gay adolescents. *Social Work with Groups* 22(2): 51–69.

Pollio, D. E., S. M. McDonald, and C. S. North. 1996. Combining a strengths-based approach and feminist theory in group work with persons "on the streets." *Social Work with Groups* 19(3/4): 5–20.

Pomeroy, E. C., A. Rubin, and R. J. Walker. 1995. Effectiveness of a psychoeducational and task-centered group intervention for family members of people with AIDS. *Social Work Research* 19(3): 142–52.

Poole, J. 1999. Toward a community of care: The development of the family caregivers' support network. In H. Bertcher, L. F. Kurtz, and A. Lamont., eds., *Building communities: Challenges for group work,* pp. 17–34. New York: Haworth.

Rhodes, R. and A. Johnson. 1996. Social group work with recovering women: An empowerment model. In B. J. Stempler, M. Glass, and C. M. Savinelli, eds., *Social group work today and tomorrow*, pp. 87–102. New York: Haworth.

Richardson, R. C. and A. B. Sistler. 1999. The well-being of elderly black caregivers and noncaregivers: A preliminary study. *Journal of Gerontological Social Work* 31:109–18.

Rittner, B. and K. Hammons. 1992. Telephone group work with people with end stage AIDS. *Social Work with Groups* 15:59–72.

Rounds, K. A., M. J. Galinsky, and L. S. Stevens. 1991. Linking people with AIDS in rural communities: The telephone group. *Social Work* 36:13–18.

Saporito, J. W. 2001. Group work for heterosexual couples of mixed HIV status. In T. B. Kelly, T. Berman-Rossi, and S. Palombo, eds. *Group work: Strategies for strengthening resiliency*, pp. 181–202. New York: Haworth.

Schopler, J. H., M. J. Galinsky, and M. Abell. 1997. Creating community through telephone and computer groups: Theoretical and practice perspectives. *Social Work with Groups* 20(4): 19–34.

Shulman, L. 1996. Social work with groups: Paradigm shifts for the 1990s. In B. L. Stempler, M. Glass, and C. M. Savinelli, eds., *Social group work today and tomorrow: Moving from theory to advanced training and practice*, pp. 1–18. New York: Haworth.

Stempler, B. L., M. Glass, and C. M. Savinelli, eds. 1996. *Social group work today and tomorrow: Moving from theory to advanced training and practice*. New York: Haworth.

Thomas, M. C. and V. Martin. 1992. Training counselors to facilitate the transitions of aging through group work. *Counselor Education and Supervision* 32(1): 51–66.

Travers, A. 1996. Redefining adult identity: A coming out group for lesbians. In B. L. Stempler, M. Glass, and C. M. Savinelli, eds., *Social group work today and tomorrow: Moving from theory to advanced training and practice*, pp. 103–18. New York: Haworth.

Turner, S. A. and H. P. Street. 1999. Assessing carers' training needs: A pilot inquiry. *Aging and Mental Health* 3(2): 173–79.

Weiner, L. S. 1998. Telephone support groups for HIV-positive mothers whose children have died with AIDS. *Social Work* 43:279–85.

Wright, L. K., M. Litaker, M. T. Laraia, S. DeAndrade. 2001. Continuum of care for Alzheimer's disease: A nurse education and counseling program. *Issues in Mental Health Nursing* 22(3): 231–53.

Zook, B and K. Luken. 2001. Building technology bridges for brain injury support groups. *Parks and Recreation* 36(5): 82–88.